Conceived in Liberty

CONCEIVED IN LIBERTY

VOLUME I

A New Land, A New People
The American Colonies in
the Seventeenth Century

MURRAY N. ROTHBARD

with the assistance of Leonard P. Liggio

ARLINGTON HOUSE·PUBLISHERS
NEW ROCHELLE, N. Y.

Library of Congress Cataloging in Publication Data

Rothbard, Murray Newton, 1926–
  A new land, a new people.

  (Their Conceived in liberty ; v. 1)
  Bibliography: p.
  1. United States—History—Colonial period,
ca. 1600–1775. I. Liggio, Leonard P., joint
author. II. Title.
E178.R8 vol. 1 ₍E188₎ 973s ₍973.2₎ 74–20960
ISBN 0-87000-262-7

Whenever the legislators endeavour to take away and destroy the property of the people, or to reduce them to slavery under arbitrary power, they put themselves into a state of war with the people, who are thereupon absolved from any farther obedience, and are left to the common refuge which God hath provided for all men against force and violence.

John Locke

Contents

Preface

What! Another American history book? The reader may be pardoned for wondering about the point of another addition to the seemingly inexhaustible flow of books and texts on American history. One problem, as pointed out in the bibliographical essay at the end of this volume, is that the survey studies of American history have squeezed out the actual stuff of history, the narrative facts of the important events of the past. With the true data of history squeezed out, what we have left are compressed summaries and the historian's interpretations and judgments of the data. There is nothing wrong with the historian's having such judgments; indeed, without them, history would be a meaningless and giant almanac listing dates and events with no causal links. But, without the narrative facts, the reader is deprived of the data from which he can himself judge the historian's interpretations and evolve interpretations of his own. A major point of this and succeeding volumes is to put back the historical narrative into American history.

Facts, of course, must be selected and ordered in accordance with judgments of importance, and such judgments are necessarily tied into the historian's basic world outlook. My own basic perspective on the history of man, and *a fortiori* on the history of the United States, is to place central importance on the great conflict which is eternally waged between Liberty and Power, a conflict, by the way, which was seen with crystal clarity by the American revolutionaries of the eighteenth century. I see the liberty of the individual not only as a great moral good in itself (or, with Lord Acton, as the highest political good), but also as the necessary condition for the flowering of all the other goods that mankind cherishes: moral virtue, civilization, the arts and sciences, economic prosperity. Out of liberty, then, stem the glories of civilized life. But liberty has always been threatened by the encroachments of power, power which seeks to suppress, control, cripple, tax, and exploit the fruits of liberty and production. Power, then, the enemy of liberty, is consequently the enemy of all the other goods and fruits of civilization that mankind holds dear. And power is almost always centered in and focused on that central repository of power and violence: the state. With Albert Jay Nock, the twentieth-century American political philosopher, I see history as centrally a race and conflict between "social power"—the productive consequence of voluntary interactions among men—and state power. In those eras of history when liberty—social power—has managed to race ahead of state power and control, the country and even mankind have flourished. In those eras when state power has managed to catch up with or surpass social power, mankind suffers and declines.

For decades, American historians have quarreled about "conflict" or "consensus" as the guiding *leitmotif* of the American past. Clearly, I belong in the "conflict" rather than the "consensus" camp, with the proviso that I see the central conflict as not between classes, (social or economic), or between ideologies, but between Power and Liberty, State and Society. The social or ideological conflicts have been ancillary to the central one, which concerns: Who will control the state, and what power will the state exercise over the citizenry? To take a common example from American history, there are in my view no inherent conflicts between merchants and farmers in the free market. On the contrary, in the market, the sphere of liberty, the interests of merchants and farmers are harmonious, with each buying and selling the products of the other. Conflicts arise only through the attempts of various groups of merchants or farmers to seize control over the machinery of government and to use it to privilege themselves at the expense of the others. It is only through and by state action that "class" conflicts can ever arise.

This volume is the story of the seventeenth century—the first century of the English colonies in North America. It was the century when all but one (Georgia) of the original thirteen colonies were founded, in all their disparity and diversity. Remarkably enough, this critical period is only brusquely treated in the current history textbooks. While the motives of the early colonists varied greatly, and their fortunes changed in a shifting and fluctuating kaleidoscope of liberty and power, all the colonists soon began to take on an air of freedom unknown in the mother country. Remote from central control, pioneering in a land of relatively few people spread over a space far vaster than any other they had ever known, the contentious colonists proved to be people who would not suffer power gladly. Attempts at imposing feudalism on, or rather transferring it to, the American colonies had all failed. By the end of the century, the British forging of royal colonies, all with similar political structures, could occur only with the fearsome knowledge that the colonists could and would rebel against unwanted power at the drop of a tax or a quitrent. If the late seventeenth-century Virginia rebel Nathaniel Bacon was not exactly the "Torchbearer of the Revolution," then this term might apply to the other feisty and rambunctious Americans throughout the colonies.

My intellectual debts for this volume are simply too numerous to mention, especially since an historian must bring to bear not only his own discipline but also his knowledge of economics, of political philosophy, and of mankind in general. Here I would just like to mention, for his methodology of history, Ludwig von Mises, especially his much neglected volume, *Theory and History*; and Lord Acton, for his emphasis on the grievously overlooked moral dimension. For his political philosophy and general outlook on American history, Albert Jay Nock, particularly his *Our Enemy the State*.

As for my personal debts, I am happy to be more specific. This volume would never have been attempted, much less seen the light of day, without the inspiration, encouragement, and support provided by Kenneth S. Templeton, Jr., now of the Institute for Humane Studies, Menlo Park, California. I hope that he won't be overly disappointed with this and later volumes. I am grateful to the Foundation for Foreign Affairs, Chicago, for enabling me to work full time on the volumes, and to Dr. David S. Collier of the Foundation for his help and efficient administration. Others who have helped with ideas and aid in various stages of the manuscript are Charles G. Koch and George Pearson of Wichita, Kansas, and Robert D. Kephart of *Human Events*, Washington, D.C.

Historians Robert E. Brown of Michigan State University and Forrest McDonald of Wayne State University were kind enough to read the entire manuscript and offer helpful suggestions even though it soon became clear to them and to myself that our fundamental disagreements tended to outweigh our agreements.

To my first mentor in the field of American history, Joseph Dorfman, now Professor Emeritus at Columbia University, I owe in particular the rigorous training that is typical of that keen and thorough scholar.

But my greatest debt is to Leonard P. Liggio, of City College, CUNY, whose truly phenomenal breadth of knowledge and insight into numerous fields and areas of history are an inspiration to all who know him. Liggio's help was indispensable in the writing of this volume, in particular his knowledge of the European background.

Over the years in which this manuscript took shape, I was fortunate in having several congenial typists—in particular, Willette Murphey Klausner of Los Angeles, and the now distinguished intellectual historian and social philosopher, Dr. Ronald Hamowy of the University of Alberta. I would particularly like to thank Mrs. Phyllis Wampler of

Wichita, Kansas, for her heroic service of typing the entire manuscript in its final form.

The responsibility for the final product is, of course, wholly my own.

MURRAY N. ROTHBARD

December 1973

PART I

Europe, England, and the New World

1

Europe at the Dawn
of the Modern Era

Until the close of the Middle Ages at the end of the fifteenth century, the Americas remained outside the ken of Western civilization. The Americas had been "discovered" and settled as many as ten thousand years before, by tribes crossing over from Asia on what was then a land bridge across the Bering Strait. By the late fifteenth century, one million of these "American Indians" lived north of Mexico alone, in diverse cultures and tribes scattered throughout the continent. As recently as the end of the tenth century, Norsemen, the great seamen of Scandinavia, spread across the North Atlantic and planted a settlement in Greenland. From there, the Viking Leif Ericson explored and settled "Vinland"—somewhere on the northeast coast of North America—about the year A.D. 1000. Norse objects dating from the mid-fourteenth century have been found in North Central America. But these sporadic contacts made no imprint on history, for the New World had not yet been brought into any continuing economic or social relation with the Western world: hence, its existence was not even known beyond the narrow circle of those few who, like the Norsemen, had actually been there. The same holds true for the possibility that French fishermen were already making use of the abundantly stocked waters off Newfoundland by the late fifteenth century. In neither case was Europe really made cognizant of the new lands.

Western Europe, during the early Middle Ages, was a stagnant and war-torn region, burdened by feudalism, a hierarchical rule based on assumed and conquered land titles, and on the virtual enslavement of the peasantry, who worked as serfs in support of the ruling castes. A great revival during the eleventh century, inaugurating the High Middle Ages, was based upon the rise of trade between Italian towns that had remained relatively free of feudal restrictions, and the commercial centers of the eastern Mediterranean. The revival of industry and trade and the concomitant growth in living standards provided the necessary economic base for a flowering of learning and culture. The emerging commercial capitalism and growing civilization soon developed most intensively in the city-states of northern Italy, the centers of the vital Mediterranean trade with the East.

It was this "international trade" that began to break up the isolated, local self-sufficiency at subsistence levels that had characterized feudal Western Europe. The local feudal manor could no longer be a stagnant, self-sufficient, agricultural, and "domestic-industry" unit if it wished to purchase the products of the Middle East and especially of the Orient. The Orient furnished luxury goods of all kinds—silks, damasks, jewels, dyes, tropical fruits—but its great contribution was spices, the preeminent commodity in Mediterranean trade. Spices not only enhanced the taste of food, but also preserved it. For in those days, before refrigeration, spices were the only way to preserve food for any length of time.

The Oriental commodities were produced in China, India, Ceylon, or the East Indies, and transported by Muslim merchants—Indian and Arab—to the ports of the Middle East and the shores of the Eastern Mediterranean, where northern Italian merchants took over to transport the goods to Western Europe. Sales were then made, often by German merchants, at such places as the great "fairs," notably the fairs of Champagne in northeastern France. Thus, pepper, by far the most important of the spices, was largely grown on the Malabar Coast of India, and from there taken to the eastern Mediterranean and thence to Europe. In exchange for these products from the East, Western Europe exported timber, metals, and especially woolen textiles, which had become its major commodity for export. From the late eleventh century, England became the major European supplier of raw wool, because of its advantages of soil and climate, as well as the advanced scientific management of its monastic sheep ranches. The English wool was then exported to Flanders for weaving into cloth. The cloth was exchanged for spices at the great fairs of Champagne, and then carried by the Italian merchants to sell in the Middle East.

Three main routes connected the West with the Orient. One was a virtually all-sea route from China, India, Malaya, and the rest of the Orient to the Red Sea, and thence up to Cairo and Alexandria. A second went up the Persian Gulf to Baghdad, and thence overland to Antioch or to various cities of the eastern Mediterranean. The third, a northerly route, traveled overland by caravan from North China westward to the Caspian and Black seas. This last route was made possible in the thirteenth century by the establishment of Mongol rule over this vast trading area. In all of this trade, the northern Italians, as we have indicated, were predominant in Europe; they were the great merchants, shippers, and bankers of the Western world.

In the mid-fourteenth century, a severe blow was struck at this vital pattern of European trade with the Orient. This blow was the general collapse of Mongol rule in Asia. The end of Mongol rule in Persia destroyed the freedom of Italian—especially Genoese—traders in that critical terminus of the overland route. And the liquidation of Mongol rule in China ended Mongol friendliness to Western trade, which had permitted both commerce and cultural contact with the West; thereafter, traditional Chinese suspicion of foreigners reasserted itself. The consequent forced closing of the overland route doubled the price of silks in Europe.

Ordinarily one would have expected the Mongol collapse and the closing of the overland route to spur a search by northern Italians—especially the Genoese—for an all-sea route to the Orient. Indeed, Genoese captains by the late thirteenth and early fourteenth centuries had already sailed through the Strait of Gibraltar and south along the western coast of Africa in search of new spice routes, and had already discovered the Canary and Madeira islands. But a cataclysmic set of changes at the turn of the fourteenth century was to divert attention from such sea exploration and drastically alter the pattern of European production and trade.

The expansion of medieval production and trade and the concomitant cultural progress of Europe came to an abrupt halt at the beginning of the fourteenth century. As wealth and capital continued to accumulate in Western Europe from the eleventh century on, this growing wealth provided great temptations to Power to seize and divert that wealth for its own nonproductive, indeed antiproductive, purposes. This power loomed in the emerging nation-states of Western Europe, particularly in France and England, which set about to confiscate and drain off the wealth of society for the needs and demands of the emerging state. Internally, the state siphoned off the wealth to nurture an increasingly elaborate and expensive state apparatus; externally, the state used the wealth in expensive wars to advance its dynastic power and plunder. Furthermore, the states increasingly regulated and intervened in, as well as taxed, the market economy of Europe. The several nascent states of the modern era ruptured the harmonious and cosmopolitan social and economic relations of medieval Europe. A unity in free-market relations was sundered and ravaged by the imposed violence and plunder of the governments of the new nation-states.

Specifically, the new policy of statism of England and France at the beginning of the fourteenth century involved first the immediate expulsion and confiscation of the wealth of Jewish merchants, Italian bankers, and vital independent financial institutions, such as the crucial fairs of Champagne. For the longer run, the monies necessary to support

17

the state apparatus and army were derived from privileges and monopolies granted by governments to associations of merchants and craftsmen who aided in the collection of taxes, in return for the assurance of profits by excluding native and foreign competitors. The consumer was completely sacrificed to that producer who proved the best help in the collection of taxes, and incentives for initiative, inexpensiveness of product, and technical progress were destroyed. Detailed regulations and controls were established by government-privileged guilds to assure the collection of taxes and to prevent competition from more efficient producers within and without the guild monopoly. As a result of the growth and development of warfare, the state apparatus, monopoly, and taxation, the fourteenth and fifteenth centuries in Europe were marked by stagnation, depression, and even retrogression.

Not only were there no further expansion in the scope of international trade and no increase in the volume of commerce, but this trade was forced to take far different directions. The commercial centers of Italy—the northern cities—remained relatively free of restrictions of monopoly and the state apparatus, and Italian capitalists now sought a commerce free from control by the regulations and taxation of governments. The crucial problem of the capitalists was the loss of their overland trade route to northern France, brought about by the destruction of the great fairs of Champagne, by the taxation and controls of the French king. The Italian merchants therefore had to find an efficient route to Flanders, the source of European cloth. The only alternative for the carrying of large quantities of goods was the sea, and it was natural for Venice and Genoa to turn to the sea as the best means of transportation from the Mediterranean to Flanders. The first Atlantic convoys of ships to Flanders were sent from Venice and Genoa about 1314; they sailed through the Strait of Gibraltar and along the Atlantic coast of Europe to the English Channel port of Southampton, in England, then on to Bruges, in Flanders.

Bruges now became the great center of northern European commerce; it served as the northern depot of Italian trade, even as it had been the western terminus of North Sea and Baltic trade, a trade which now received a great impetus for growth. During the Middle Ages cities were founded along the coast of the Baltic Sea as the German people colonized eastward. These German cities engaged in trade along the North or German Sea, as well as the East or Baltic Sea. For the mutual defense of their trade they formed a confederation of cities called the Hanseatic League. From the Hanseatic western depots, Bruges and the Steelyard in London, the trade of the League extended through the German and Scandinavian countries to the Slavic countries of the eastern Baltic, terminating in the great northern Russian commercial center, the independent Republic of Great Novgorod. The trade of the Hansards, or Easterlings (from which the English measure of silver, the pound sterling, is derived), as the Hanseatic merchants were called, was largely in raw materials and agricultural products. The foundation of Hanseatic commerce was its dominance of the Baltic trade in dried and salted fish, a necessary part of the European diet because of the scarcity of meat and the needs of religious observance. Search for the salt necessary for curing the fish had led the Hanseatic traders to Bordeaux on the Atlantic coast of France, the major source of salt. Bordeaux wine also accompanied the salt to northern Europe. The Bordeaux trade increased the importance of England in European commerce, as Bordeaux and the province of Gascony had been English possessions since the middle of the twelfth century. For the spices and manufactured goods that the Hansards carried to the Baltic from Bruges, they supplied the industrial centers of Western Europe with the dried and salted fish of the Baltic, the grain of Prussia and Poland, the timber of Scandinavia, and the furs, wax, and honey of the Russian forests. The closest to a luxury product for the Hansards was the important fur trade. Fur, because of its rarity and beauty, had become a symbol of social and political importance. The only form of fur sufficiently inexpensive to be available to the masses was hats processed from beaver—the most popular form of headwear. The Russian Republic of Great Novgorod built its greatness by controlling the fur trade with the Finnish peoples who inhabited the forests of northern Russia, and the Hanseatic League controlled the distribution of furs across Europe from Novgorod to the Steelyard in London.

Wool, the principal product of English agriculture, entered Hanseatic and Italian trade mainly through the cloth woven in Flanders. Poundage, the tariff on the export of wool and the import of cloth, was the principal tax imposed by the English government in the process of state formation. Poundage was permanently established by the fourteenth century, even though it was contrary to the provisions of Magna Carta. The newly burgeoning state apparatus was maintained by this tax on wool exports, and the rates increased as England's financial crisis of the fourteenth and fifteenth centuries continued to intensify. This continuing crisis was brought about by the English government's persistent interventions in overseas wars. To ensure collection of taxes on wool exports, the English government granted a monopoly of the export of wool to a group of merchants, drawn from the importing and exporting centers. In return for the monopoly profits gained from this privilege, the merchants would enforce and collect the tariffs and ensure their payment to the government. "The mayor, constables, and fellowship of the merchants of the staple of England" received the monopoly of wool export to the Continent in the mid-fourteenth century, after a succession of ill-starred attempts to grant the monopoly to smaller groups of merchants. It was the first lasting organization of English foreign trade monopoly.

The Merchants of the Staple proceeded to use their monopoly privilege in the time-honored manner of monopoly: by moving to jack up their selling prices and to lower their buying prices. Such procedure ensured their profit, but also eventually crippled the great English wool trade by reducing the demand for wool and by discouraging the production of wool at home. But the free market also has a time-honored way of fighting back against restrictions: by evading them. Despite the restrictions, the free trade in wool persisted in the form of smuggling, which the government policy had forced upon the merchants. From the late Middle Ages through the eighteenth century, England was not so much a nation of seafarers and shopkeepers as a nation of smugglers.

Since Flanders was being carefully watched by the Merchants of the Staple, the Dutch Netherlands became the center of the free trade—the nontaxed trade in smuggled wool, and the Dutch ship captains became the leading carriers and traders in tax-free goods, shipped into and out of small harbors along the coasts of England. When the constitutional procedures of the common law were applied, there could be few convictions for smuggling by juries of ordinary people, who shared in the common interest as sufferers from taxes and monopoly, and hence in the common enthusiasm for smuggling. To circumvent the constitutional courts of common law, the prerogative High Court of Admiralty was established to absorb the jurisdictions of the maritime courts of the seaports, which had administered the traditional sea law and law merchant. A tariff on the importation of wines, called tunnage (the measure of a tun of wine), was imposed with the excuse that it would finance the policing of the seas. The creation of the offices of Lord High Admiral and the High Court of Admiralty increased the burdens on commerce, while their activities were used by the government to advance the claim of an English monopoly over the English Channel and other neighboring seas.

Thus, during the fourteenth and fifteenth centuries, in place of a universal economic system based on international trade, common commercial laws, and efficient economic relationships, unnatural economies were created on a foundation of violence and political power. The purposes were to supply a constantly increasing financial means of support for the civil and military apparatus of the state, and to grant special privileges for groups of merchants favored by, and sharing in control of, the state at the expense of the economy and the rest of the population. This mercantilist system, having its origins in the rise of sustained warfare and the development of the state apparatus, also introduced a permanent hostility between countries by its destruction of the universal European economy.

While Western Europe stagnated under the weight of the mercantilism imposed by the apparatuses of the emerging states, the regions of relative freedom—Italy and the areas of the Baltic producing raw material—continued to develop and progress economically. The Italian cities were preeminent not only by reason of their merchants, shippers, and bankers, but also for their advances in the arts and sciences of navigation—in technological inventions and the sciences of astronomy, cartography, and geography. In the Middle Ages, the development of geography in Europe had centered in Sicily, where a Latin culture had been enriched by classical and Byzantine knowledge, directly by Greek and indirectly by Arab scholars. To classical geographical knowledge, summarized in Ptolemy's second-century *Geography*, was added knowledge of Africa and India from Arab sources, and of East Asia from Italian travelers. A leading Italian traveler was Marco Polo, a late thirteenth-century Venetian merchant who had settled as an official in the Mongol capital of Peking, and had written the most important book on Asia of the late Middle Ages. This new geographic knowledge was incorporated into the scientific charts and maps developed by the cartographers of the northern Italian cities. The most advanced of which was a 1351 map of Laurentian Portolano of Florence. The Arab and Jewish scholarship in Spain led, in the latter half of the fourteenth century, to the development of the important Jewish school of geographers on the island of Majorca, which produced the most accurate medieval map, the Catalan Atlas of 1375. This atlas had a significant influence on future exploration both of Africa and of Asia. Ptolemy's *Geography* had indicated a short circumference of the earth, making Asia three times nearer Europe than it actually was, and had depicted the African continent as short and connected directly to East Asia, making the Indian Ocean an inland sea, In 1410, however, Cardinal Pierre d'Ailly wrote *Imago Mundi*; he indicated that Africa was long and surrounded by water, thus making the Indian Ocean approachable by sea. These works were all to have a profound influence on the explorations seeking the routes to Asia around Africa and across the Atlantic.

But before the advanced geographical concepts could guide exploration, the necessary ship designs, navigational science, and experience of oceanic sailing needed to be developed. The northern Italian merchants had been forced to inaugurate the long Mediterranean-Atlantic oceanic route in the early fourteenth century, and thus had added oceanic experience to their overall stature as the great seamen of Europe. When, thereafter, the major Atlantic countries—England, France, Spain, and Portugal—decided to create governmental navies, they naturally turned to contract with Italian captains to develop, staff, and command these navies. The great northern Italian cities of Genoa, Venice, Pisa, and Florence were particularly abundant sources of those having experience with the sea. Thus, in 1317, Emanuel Pesagno of Genoa contracted to command the Portuguese navy as Lord High Admiral and to keep it supplied with twenty experienced Genoese navigators; these arrangements were continued as hereditary contracts with the Pesagno family for two centuries.

In addition to the role that Italian navigators and sailors, astronomers and instrument makers, geographers and map makers played in the maritime history of Atlantic Europe, Italians made important contributions as ship designers and shipbuilders. The Hanseatic cogs, built in the Baltic, were efficient ships for carrying bulky cargoes in the Hanseatic trade. Italian ship designers maintained this efficiency, but revolutionized the ships' maneuverability and speed; as a result, during the fifteenth century ships became available that could travel long distances at a suitable speed on rough oceans. They had large carrying capacities but needed only small crews, so that they could remain for a long while at sea without stopping regularly to take on provisions. However, as timber supplies in the Mediterranean became increasingly scarce, greater reliance was placed upon such ships built and even manned in the Atlantic European countries.

At the same time that the sailors of the Atlantic countries were gaining knowledge and experience from oceanic voyages, increasingly higher prices of spices in Western Europe encouraged the Atlantic countries to find the gold with which to pay for the spices, or to discover better alternative routes to the Oriental sources of these commodities. Routes were also sought that could bypass the Italian middlemen. Hence, when Portuguese explorers began to be sent southward along the African coast, their immediate and primary objective was to discover the sources of the gold of West Africa with which the North African Arabs were plentifully supplied.

From 1419 until his death in 1460, most of the exploration of the fifteenth century was organized by Prince Henry the Navigator, governor of the southern district of Portugal. Henry accomplished his exploration with the aid of a court functioning as a veritable maritime college, including Genoese captains, Venetian navigators, and Italian and Jewish geographers. The Madeira Islands were discovered definitely by 1420 by a Portuguese expedition, and one of the first officials sent there by Prince Henry was Bartholomew Perestrella, an Italian and future father-in-law of Christopher Columbus. Sugar cane from Sicily was introduced into Madeira and into the Canary Islands being settled by Spaniards, and these islands soon became an important source of sugar for Europe until the establishment of sugar culture in Brazil by the Portuguese in the sixteenth century. These "Western Islands" also became an important center of the cultivation of sweet wines.

During the following generation, numerous expeditions made slow progress down the coast of Western Sahara, while others discovered and settled the Azores in the North Atlantic. In 1441, a few Negro slaves were brought back to Portugal, thus beginning the extensive and barbarous slave trade. After tropical Africa, 1,500 miles from the Strait of Gibraltar, was reached in 1445, large numbers of slaves were purchased from the native chiefs of the coastal districts, and slave stations were constructed by the Portuguese along the West African coast. Although the Cape Verde Islands were discovered in 1445 by a Venetian, Captain Cadamosto, the world of Portuguese exploration largely turned to concentration upon commerce in gold and local West African pepper, as well as to the slave trade for supplying the large feudal estates of southern Portugal, which had been granted by the Portuguese government after taking that region from the Moors.

During the 1470s, explorations under private auspices covered another two thousand miles along the coast of the Gulf of Guinea. The Spanish, based on the Canaries, began to compete with the Portuguese in the Guinea trade, and the warfare resulting from this rivalry was settled by treaty in 1480. By this treaty, Spain recognized Portugal's prior rights to Africa and the South Atlantic, and Portugal accepted Spanish rights to the Canary Islands and the "western seas" beyond the Azores. Thereupon, and being hurried by the rumor of an English expedition to West Africa, Portugal in 1482 commissioned voyages to create a strong fort at Elmina in West Africa to defend the trade in gold, pepper, and slaves. Captains for these voyages included Bartholomew Diaz and the Genoese Christopher Columbus.

A large colony of Genoese captains, pilots, and mapmakers had settled in Lisbon during the late fifteenth century, and by 1477 Christopher Columbus (1451-1506) was established in Lisbon as a mapmaker with his brother Bartholomew. After engaging in the sugar trade from Madeira and in the African trade for Genoese firms, Columbus had gained sufficient experience in oceanic navigation to propose a plan for a westward voyage to the Orient. Columbus had concluded that China and the Orient could easily be reached by sailing westward, if Asia were really three thousand miles west of Europe, as the geographers had indicated. (Contrary to popular myth, the idea that the earth was round was well known to the educated Europeans of the day.) The geographical concept of a feasible westward voyage to the Orient received even wider currency in Europe when printed editions appeared of Ptolemy in the 1470s, D'Ailly's *Imago Mundi* in 1483, Marco Polo's *Travels* in 1485, and Aeneas Sylvius' (Pope Pius II's) *Historia Rerum* in 1477. Columbus was also encouraged in his project by his correspondence with the Florentine scientist Paolo dal Pozzo Toscanelli.

The Portuguese had meanwhile resumed exploration of Africa south of the equator under the command of Diogo Cao, who discovered the Congo River in 1483. Upon Cao's return in 1484, the Portuguese prepared for more vigorous exploratory activity, the Crown appointing a Junta dos Mathematicos, composed of Bishop Diogo Ortiz and two Jewish physicians, to decide questions of navigation and exploration. Late in 1484, Columbus presented his plans to the Junta for a westward voyage to China and Japan; however, as Cao was to begin his second expedition, it was hoped that he would discover the route to the Indies around Africa, so the Junta decided to await Cao's return before accepting Columbus' project. Cao promptly extended Portuguese exploration by 1,500 miles, reaching Cape Cross in 1486; he also explored the Congo River and established diplomatic relations with the ruler of the lower Congo. In the summer of 1487, an expedition under Bartholomew Diaz was sent to discover the sea route to

India; Diaz sailed around the Cape of Good Hope in early 1488, making it clear that an ocean passage to the Indies would soon be found.

Balked by Portugal, Columbus had gone to Spain to seek aid for his projected voyage; and although he was well received, Spain too made no decision on extending its support. Columbus then renewed his negotiations with the Portuguese, and returned to Lisbon in late 1488. But when Diaz returned to Portugal in December of 1488 with news of his exciting discovery, Portugal lost interest in Columbus' plan. Columbus then returned to Spain, meanwhile sending his brother Bartholomew to London to present his plan to Henry VII of England. After receiving no encouragement in England, Bartholomew Columbus went to the French court in 1490, where he received better treatment and remained as a mapmaker. When the Spanish court rejected his proposal in 1491, Christopher prepared to join Bartholomew in France; but Columbus was recalled to the Spanish court, partly because its conquest of the Moorish kingdom of Granada was completed in January 1492.

The agreements between Columbus and the Spanish Crown were completed in April 1492; they provided for Spanish financing of the bulk of expenses of the voyage, as well as for naming Columbus "Admiral of the Ocean Sea" and governor of any lands that he might discover enroute. On August 3, Columbus departed from Palos in three ships. Sailing to the Canaries and then westward, Columbus discovered the Bahama Islands on October 12, 1492, and explored the Greater Antilles—Cuba and Hispaniola. Columbus was convinced that he had discovered the shores of Asia, and so christened the natives he found there "Indians." But despite his error, the New World was now to be opened to the ambit of European society.

Columbus left America in early January 1493, arrived in the Azores in February, and reached Lisbon early in March. Even though Diaz was busy supervising construction of the ships necessary for the voyage around Africa to India, the Portuguese king had the gall to claim the new lands as an extension of the Azores. When Columbus presented his report to the Spanish court in mid-March 1493, it sought to protect its claim from Portuguese encroachment. On the basis of the discovery and of the treaty of 1480, Spain appealed to the pope for a determination of its rights.

As a neutral third power, the papacy made a diplomatic award, affirming Spain's claim to monopoly possession of Columbus' discovery. The respective discoveries claimed by Portugal in Africa and Spain in the West were protected by drawing a boundary between Spain and Portugal west of the Portuguese Azores. The respective routes to the Indies were recognized by limiting the Spanish to the western and southern route, and the Portuguese to their eastern and southern route around Africa. The Portuguese considered the papal opinions a useful base for negotiation, but refused to be bound by them. To gain Portuguese recognition for its claims, the Spanish government was obliged to make concessions to

Portugal, and in June of 1494 the Treaty of Tordesillas extended the boundary 270 leagues further westward than in the papal mediation, which had the unintended effect of allowing Portugal to control the yet undiscovered coast of Brazil. As the dispute was strictly between Spain and Portugal, the treaty and boundary related only to the area that they had explored, and thus did not receive international recognition by the other powers until confirmed by effective occupation of the respective claims. Since the Spanish territorial claim was limited to the west and south of Columbus' discovery, that is, the West Indies and Central and South America, it did not exclude other states from North America, as witness the English, Portuguese, and French explorations; there was conflict only when they approached the West Indies.

Meanwhile, in September 1493 Columbus had sailed again to the West Indies with 1,500 colonists on board in seventeen ships fitted out by his friend, the Florentine merchant of Seville, Gianneto Berardi. After exploring the Lesser Antilles, a colony was established in Hispaniola to be an agriculturally self-supporting mining town that would supply Spain with the much needed gold believed to abound there. After further explorations, Columbus departed for Spain in March 1496, leaving his brother Bartholomew as governor.

In March 1496 Henry VII of England granted a patent to John Cabot, a Genoese captain and merchant lately settled in Bristol, England, who had sailed for Venice and Portugal to explore to the west or north, thereby indicating that England would not intervene in Spanish or Portuguese colonies. Cabot was granted a monopoly of trade to any lands he might discover and claim for the Crown, in the profits of which the government would share; and Bristol was made a monopoly or "staple" port for all voyages to or from the newly explored regions. In May 1497 Cabot and his son Sebastian sailed west from Bristol to Asia; they reached Cape Breton Island and sailed down the Atlantic coast to perhaps the site of Maine. In the spring of 1498 Cabot went to Lisbon and Seville to hire sailors who had sailed with Cao, Diaz, or Columbus, and set sail for Japan and the Spice Islands in May 1498; he succeeded in exploring the coast of North America down to the Delaware Bay or the Chesapeake Bay. Joao Fernandes, called Labrador, a Portuguese who had advised Cabot, received a Portuguese patent for northern and western discoveries and explored Greenland. From 1501 on, a group of Bristol and Portuguese merchants, including Fernandes, explored North America under English patents, while several Portuguese, such as the Corte Real brothers, sailed to Newfoundland in the early sixteenth century.

The Portuguese, however, were concentrating on the voyage to India around Africa for which Diaz had spent almost a decade preparing a fleet. In July 1497 the fleet departed, commanded by Vasco da Gama, and arrived at the Malabar coast of India in May 1498; it returned to Lisbon in September 1499 with a cargo of pepper and cinnamon. The Portuguese had finally found their eastern sea route to India. Early in 1500 a second expedition under Pedro Cabral was dispatched to India; blown off course, Cabral discovered and claimed Brazil for Portugal. In 1501, the Portuguese spices reached Antwerp, which promptly became the major center of spices from Portugal, even as it was then the financial center of Europe.

The Italian merchants were not immediately disturbed at the development of the new spice route, for they considered their competitive position assured by their capital, their commercial ability, and the security of their established routes. Lacking gold or specialized products, the Portuguese were not able to undersell the Arab and Venetian merchants. A major Portuguese voyage of 1505 was, in fact, financed by Genoese, Florentine, and South German bankers, although the complications of bureaucracy led them to provide capital indirectly through investment in "future" cargoes. Similarly, Italian merchants and bankers in Spain provided the venture capital for exploration and discovery. In 1495, on the death of Gianneto Berardi, who had contracted to fit out twelve ships, Amerigo Vespucci, a Florentine who was manager of the Medici bank at Seville, assumed the contract. In succeeding years, Vespucci sailed in Spanish expeditions, and then from 1501 on sailed in Portuguese voyages to explore Cabral's discovery, Brazil. Vespucci wrote accounts of his voyages; they were immediately printed and received wide circulation. As a result, the mapmakers irrevocably attached Amerigo's name to the newly discovered continents.

The succession of the Hapsburgs to the Spanish throne in the early sixteenth century promptly occasioned investments by South German banking houses in Spanish mines and then in American mines. The Fuggers leased mines in Hispaniola and Mexico, while the Welsers leased Venezuela for twenty years. However, the Italians, expecially the Genoese merchants of Seville, dominated Spain's American trade during the sixteenth century, importing gold and tropical products into Europe and exporting manufactured goods as well as slaves under contracts, or Asientos, to America.

In 1498–1500 and 1502–04, Columbus made two further voyages to America, which he still believed to be part of the East Indies. He finally reached the American mainland in 1498. Explorations of the interior of the mainland were begun in 1513, when Ponce de Leon explored Florida, and Vasco de Balboa crossed the Isthmus of Panama to discover the Pacific Ocean, which he believed could be easily crossed to reach the Spice Islands and the Orient.

Portuguese entrance into the spice trade had led to mutual hostility with the Arab and Indian merchants, for these Muslim traders feared the competition afforded by the new sea route. The new route was expected to avoid the heavy expense and taxation that had greatly increased the cost of the route through the Levant. At the same time, the Portuguese feared that they could not compete in the spice trade for lack of capital, gold, or specialized products. In 1509, the Portuguese defeated a fleet of Arab and Indian Muslims, and, under Alfonso de Albuquerque, established trading centers at Goa on the Malabar Coast and at Malacca in Malaya. By 1513, Portuguese trade had extended to the East Indian Spice Islands and to Canton in China. Albuquerque's attacks on Muslim shipping and markets caused a shortage of spices in Alexandria, while the conquest of Egypt in 1517 by the Ottoman Turks temporarily cut off spice supplies to Venice. During the second decade of the sixteenth century, most of the spices for Europe arrived in Portuguese vessels by way of the Cape of Good Hope, and the Venetian merchants were forced to purchase spices in Lisbon to supply their customers, Soon, however, Venice reached a trade agreement with the Turks, the spice trade of the Levant returned to normal, and the Levantine trade in spices and Mediterranean goods remained larger and more important during the sixteenth century than oceanic commerce. The Venetians bought goods of better quality, while the expenses of long voyages, shipwrecks, and military forces for Portugal, and lack of goods for trading raised prices in the Portuguese trade.

The Spanish finally reached the East Indies in a voyage under the command of Ferdinand Magellan, a Portuguese mariner who had lived in the East Indies. Proposing to follow a westward route around South America, Magellan, with a fleet equipped by capital provided by the Fuggers, sailed from Seville in the summer of 1519. He passed through the Strait of Magellan, separating South America from Tierra del Fuego, the following summer and arrived at the Philippine Islands, where he was killed in a native war in April 1521. In September 1522 one ship, commanded by Sebastian del Cano, returned to Spain by way of the Cape of Good Hope, and thus became the first to circumnavigate the world. Meanwhile, in 1519 Hernando Cortez crossed from Cuba to Mexico, and by 1521 had conquered the Aztec empire and begun a search for ports for trade with the East Indies. In 1532, Francisco Pizarro led an expedition to Peru, where, after a number of years, the Inca empire was conquered. In 1527, Sebastian Cabot was to lead an expedition over Magellan's route to the East Indies, but instead explored for gold on the Rio de la Plata in South America. During the early 1540s the Spanish explored the southern part of North America. In 1539 Hernando de Soto landed in Florida from Cuba and traveled along the Gulf Coast and lower Mississippi River, which he discovered in 1541. At the same time, Francisco Vasquez de Coronado traversed the southwestern part of North America up to Kansas, while expeditions sailed along the Pacific Coast of California to Oregon in 1542–43.

France too undertook active explorations in the New World. In 1524 the Florentine captain Giovanni da Verrazano explored virtually the entire east coast of North America. A decade later Jacques Cartier sailed to Newfoundland (1534). A second voyage found him exploring the Gulf of St. Lawrence and the St. Lawrence River (1535–36), which he thought would lead to China. A dubious tradition says he named the falls at Montreal, La Chine, a bitter gesture indicative of his failure to reach China. A colony was established temporarily by Cartier near Quebec in 1541–42, but the Spaniards were the only ones to establish important settlements in the New World in the first half of the sixteenth century.

The pattern of Spanish colonization was based upon conditions in Spain in the late Middle Ages. In contrast to Europe generally, where aggressions against non-European territories had been checked by the growth of Turkish power, the Spanish and the English could still pursue the conquest of lands and peoples against the Spanish Arabs of Granada and the Celts of Ireland. Thus, the two major land-conquering and colonizing powers, Spain and England, preceded their respective transatlantic conquests by the conquest of neighboring peoples—the Moors of Granada by Spain in the late fifteenth century, and the Irish by the English, particularly during the sixteenth century. In these aggressions both the Spanish and the English not only acquired the skills and appetites for further violence, but also established the attitudes and policies to be applied to alien peoples through conquest, extermination, or enslavement.

Due to geographical and political conditions, Spain retained the military spirit of feudalism for a longer time than other European countries. The arid climate and the frontier wars with the Muslims caused the Spanish ruling class to remain essentially horsemen, who in place of agriculture emphasized sheep and cattle farming, occupations in which horsemen could be utilized and trained for war. This style of life had a profound influence on Spanish colonization. The Christian and Muslim farmers conquered by the Spanish nobles were kept in feudal serfdom to provide foodstuffs for the ruling class, to whom their villages had been granted. This feudal system, which had been imposed on the conquered lands of Granada and the Canary Islands, was then applied to the larger islands of the West Indies and later to Mexico, Venezuela, and Peru. The native villages were granted to Spanish conquistadores, who were to govern them so as to live upon the work of the natives. The hapless natives were compelled to provide food, cotton, and forced labor for building the great cities where the Spanish lived and from which they governed, and to work for large mining operations of the Spaniards. Alongside the agriculture of the Indians, the conquistadores developed the raising of sheep, cattle, horses, and mules to provide profits for themselves as well as work and plentiful meat for their keepers. Generally the Spanish colonists did not pursue productive work; instead they entered government and privileged occupations, in which to live from the work of the natives whom they enslaved.

The right to conquer, coercively convert, govern, and enslave the natives of the New World was subjected to intense criticism in a series of lectures in 1539 at the University of Salamanca by the great Dominican scholastic philosopher Francisco de Vitoria. In international law based upon the natural law, insisted Vitoria, the native peoples as well as European peoples have full equality of rights. No right of conquest by Europeans could result from crimes or errors of the natives, whether they be tyranny, murder, religious differences, or rejection of Christianity. Having grave doubts of the right of the Spaniards to any government of the natives, Vitoria advocated peaceful trade, in justice and in practice, as against conquest, enslavement, and political power, whether or not the last mentioned were aimed at individual profit, tax revenue, or conversion to Christianity. Although the Spanish government prohibited further discussion of these questions, the Vitoria lectures influenced the New Laws of 1542, which gave greater legal protection to the natives in America.

Nevertheless, there were defenders of imperialism in Spain who rejected international law and scholastic individualism and returned to the slave theories of the classical authors. Based on the theory of natural servitude—that the majority of mankind is inferior and must be subdued to government by the ruling class, of course in the interest of that majority—these imperial apologists proposed that the natives be taught better morals, be converted, and be introduced to the blessings of economic development by being divided among the conquistadores, for whom they must labor.

The serfdom of the Indians was most strongly and zealously opposed by the Dominican missionary Bishop Bartolome de Las Casas. Tireless in working to influence European public opinion against the practices of Spanish officials in America, Las Casas argued that all men must have freedom so that reason, which naturally inclines men to live together in peace, justice, and cooperation, can remain free and unhampered. Therefore, concluded Las Casas, even pursuit of the great objective of conversion to Christianity cannot be used to violate these rights. Not only was all slavery evil, but the natives had a right to live independently of European government. The papacy, in 1537, condemned as heretical the concept that natives were not rational men or were naturally inferior persons. These progressive views were also reflected in the abolition of conquistador feudalism in the New Laws of 1542; however, this abolition was revoked by the Spanish Crown three years later.

Political control of the Spanish colonies was first exercised by a committee of the Council of Castile, and then from 1524 by the Council of the Indies. In the New World, provincial governments were created, with the two most important, Mexico and Peru, raised to status of viceroyalties. Economic control of the colonies was vested in the Casa de Contratacion, instituted in 1503 to license, supervise, and tax merchants, goods, and ships engaged in trade in the New World. In 1508 a Bureau of Pilots was established under the Casa which advised the Government on maritime matters and supervised navigation and navigators; its first chief pilot was Amerigo Vespucci. Sebastian Cabot held that office for about thirty years, after transferring from English to Spanish service, as England's maritime interests had shifted from exploration to the development of a governmental navy.

The shift of English interests from exploration to naval construction was reflected in 1510, when the English government began to build a shipyard for making vessels for a navy. In 1512 the controller of the navy organized an association of pilots that would provide experienced navigators for the navy in return for privileges in control of English shipping, privileges similar to those granted to the Spanish Bureau of Pilots. With the controller of the navy as its first master, that association was chartered as "the master, wardens and assistants of the guild of the Trinity." The Trinity House Corporation advised the government on maritime affairs and controlled navigation and seamen.

Just as Spain had made Seville the staple port to and from which all colonial commerce was compulsorily channeled, so Bristol was made the staple port for monopolizing English commerce with the New World. Bristol's experience in colonial trade had begun with the grant of Dublin as a colony to the merchants of Bristol when England initiated its occupation of Ireland; that experience was enlarged when Bristol's oceanic trade to the Iberian countries was extended during the fifteenth century to the sugar colonies of Madeira and the Canaries.

By artifically depressing the price of wool in England and raising it abroad from the mid-fourteenth century on, the Merchant Staplers not only had greatly injured the growth and export of English wool but had also unintentionally spurred the establishment of wool and textile manufacturers in England. For woolen manufacturers could now buy wool at significantly lower prices than could their competitors abroad. This rising cloth industry was organized in country districts and villages, where it could be free of the restrictions and the excessively high prices and wage rates imposed by the privileged monopolies of the urban guilds. Furthermore, the merchants of Bristol were now able to bring to England the finer Spanish wool that formed the raw material for the developing manufacture of "new drapery," a lighter and less expensive cloth than that woven from the heavier English wool. Since the technique of manufacture of the new drapery was new, it did not come under the controls and monopolies of the urban guilds, which manufactured the traditional heavy cloth. The period of peace from the mid-fifteenth century on witnessed a rapid increase in population, but the rigid cartel restrictions of the urban guilds condemned large numbers to unemployment. Hence the expansion to the countryside of both the new-drapery and the traditional heavycloth industries of England. Unburdened of guild regulations on production, prices, and labor, the new rural woolen cloth industry was sufficiently elastic to respond to the demands of large-scale export markets for cheap plain cloth, by developing a large-scale organization of production forbidden by the guilds.

From the middle of the fifteenth century, indeed, there had begun to occur a great transformation of the entire economy of Western Europe. Stagnation and depression proceeded to give way to economic progress, as the state-ridden system of protection and regulation broke apart, and capital was accumulated and invested outside the controls that had encompassed the economy. In the Netherlands, in particular, a development occurred similar to England's: the rapid emergence of a rural cloth industry, free of urban guild and municipal regulations and taxation. Furthermore, the controls and high taxation of commerce in Bruges drove trade to Antwerp, where, free of hampering legislation, privileges, and taxes, business was able to organize itself on the basis of a new spirit of capitalist progress and economic growth. For a century, Antwerp now became the commercial capital of Europe, drawing by its freedom not only the traditional trades of English wool and cloth, Baltic grain and timber, and luxury goods of the Mediterranean, but also the growing trade in spices and sugars of the Indies—East and West. Antwerp became the main center of importation not only of English wool, but also of English woolen cloth; for woven cloth would be sent to Antwerp for dyeing and finishing. As Henri Pirenne has noted: "Never has any other port, at any period, enjoyed such worldwide importance, because none has ever been so open to all commerce, and, in the full sense of the word, so cosmopolitan. Antwerp remained faithful to the liberty which had made her fairs so successful in the fifteenth century. She attracted and welcomed capitalists from all parts of Europe, and as their numbers increased so did their opportunities of making a fortune. . . . There was no supervision, no control: foreigners did business with other foreigners freely as with the burgesses and natives of the country at their daily meetings. Buyers and sellers sought one another and came to terms without intermediaries."*

The rise of Antwerp as the great center of European commerce was complemented by the growth of the Dutch merchant marine; for the free-trading Dutch were the major carriers of goods to and from the unrestricted and progressive port of Antwerp, and were as motivated by the spirit of liberty and capitalism as was Antwerp. During the fifteenth century, the herring, upon which the Hanseatic trade had been founded, migrated from the Baltic to the North Sea and became a cornerstone of Dutch commercial development. Holland and Zeeland became the major herring fisheries of Europe; they improved the techniques of curing the herring and transporting it to all the ports of Europe, while simultaneously refining the methods of shipbuilding and fishing. Hence the Dutch were able to compete successfully with the Hanseatic traders in the Baltic, the North Sea, and the Atlantic, to Bordeaux and Lisbon.

Too many historians have fallen under the spell of the interpretation of the late nineteenth-century German economic historians (for example, Schmoller, Bucher, Ehrenberg): that the development of a strong central-

*Henri Pirenne, *A History of Europe* (New York: University Books, 1955), pp. 524-25.

ized nation-state was requisite to the development of capitalism in the early modern period. Not only is this thesis refuted by the flourishing of commercial capitalism in the Middle Ages in the local and noncentralized cities of northern Italy, the Hanseatic League, and the fairs of Champagne—not to mention the disastrous economic retrogression imposed by the burgeoning statism of the fourteenth century. It is also refuted by the outstanding growth of capitalist economy in free, localized Antwerp and Holland in the sixteenth and seventeenth centuries. Thus the Dutch came to outstrip the rest of Europe while retaining medieval local autonomy and eschewing state-building, mercantilism, government participation in enterprise—and aggressive war.*

Despite the rise of rival Dutch shipping, the continued importance of the Hanseatic League in the economic life of England was indicated by the Treaty of Utrecht (1474), which confirmed the trading privileges of the Hansards in England, including the payment of lower duties than the English merchants paid. But the accession of the Tudor dynasty to the English throne in 1485 marked the beginning of a steady growth of the power of the English government. Medieval forms were transformed by the Tudors into a more efficient and complete machinery for repression, especially in regulating those economic activities that had achieved prosperity by freely evading the government's regulations, controls, and taxation. Monopoly rights were granted in 1486 to the Fellowship of the Merchant Adventurers of England in all trade to the Netherlands except in wool; especially important was the export of cloth to the finishing and dyeing centers of the Netherlands. Furthermore, navigation acts restricted to English ships the importations of wines, in the vain expectation of thus increasing the number of English sailors and ships sufficiently to develop a strong governmental naval force. In 1496 the English government negotiated with the government of the Netherlands the Great Commercial Treaty (Intercursus Magnus), which provided favorable commercial conditions for English merchants at Antwerp. The important contribution of the Intercursus Magnus to international law was to recognize the freedom of English and Dutch fishermen on the high seas, especially on the North Sea, which had become the major European fishing area. The fishermen were to be free to fish anywhere and to use the ports of either country in an emergency. For a century and a half, the Intercursus Magnus remained the foundation of Anglo-Dutch commercial and maritime relations. However, by an act of 1497 the English government implemented its treaty power to monopolize and control trade to other countries; specifically, the act excluded English competitors of the Merchant Adventurers from the Netherlands trade by granting that company a monopoly in the trade with Antwerp. The cloth trade to the Netherlands now became the privileged monopoly of a limited number of

*See Jelle C. Riemersma, "Economic Enterprise and Political Powers After the Reformation," *Economic Development and Cultural Change* (July 1955), pp. 297–308.

London merchants, who came more and more to have the closest fiscal relationships with the state through loans at favorable terms to the government.

For more effective enforcement of government power under the Tudors, executive power was exercised by a specially selected group of government advisers that, because it met in secret, was called the Privy Council. The Privy Council acted by means of fiat proclamations rather than by legislation of Parliament. Judicial power was granted to the Court of Star Chamber, a prerogative court that tried the violations of the proclamations by the mere force and whim of government rather than by the traditional common law, which guaranteed the rights of the people. Defending the government from the criticisms of the people (called libels), from conspiracy and riots (that is, any gathering protesting the oppressions of the government), and from infractions of its coinage, the Star Chamber was notorious for the imposition of ruinous fines, cruel imprisonment, whippings, brandings, and mutilations of those who came under its aegis. To aid its work, the Tudor Government had set aside the common-law prohibition of the use of torture.

The Tudors also introduced the first permanent state military force in England, as they had established the foundation for a governmental navy. Military force was most generally used to subject the Irish to English rule. Poynings' Law (1495), which established the model for the control of colonies by the English government, extended to Ireland the repressive and absolutist measures current in England, and required all legislation in the Irish Parliament to receive *prior* approval from the Privy Council in England. When, a century and more later, England acquired transatlantic territories and Englishmen fled there to escape the economic effects of mercantilism or the repressions of the Privy Council, the Star Chamber, or prerogative will, it was the English subjugation and domination of Ireland that furnished the earliest precedents and models for attempted imperial control of the peoples in America.

During the sixteenth century a principal office developed in the Tudor government that would later have the greatest importance for the English colonies in America. This was the secretary of state, a title of Spanish origin, indicating some of the strong political and cultural influence derived from England's commercial and diplomatic relations with Spain. By 1540, there were two secretaries of state, each of whom had full authority to act on a wide range of matters dealing with the king and his officials and the king and foreign governments. The secretaries of state became responsible for the expanding areas that the Privy Council took under its jurisdiction: judicial matters, internal government, taxation and economic controls, leadership of the houses of Parliament, military and naval affairs, foreign affairs, and, finally, colonial affairs, when England acquired and governed colonies.

During the first half of the sixteenth century, while the English government was neglecting the New World for state-building and navy-building, English fishermen quietly but regularly began to enjoy the abundant fishing in the waters off Newfoundland. Fishing ships put out from west country ports, such as Bristol and Plymouth, and then sold the fish in Spain, Portugal, and Italy. On their return, these ships carried the goods of the Mediterranean to northern Europe; for with the decline, and cessation in 1532, of the Venetian-Flanders fleets that had been calling in Southampton, English merchants imitated the Dutch and themselves carried the trade of Italy, Spain, and Portugal to Antwerp. The Venetian fleets could no longer compete in the spice and Atlantic trade because of a growing shortage of and therefore a high price for timber in the Adriatic, and because Portuguese aggression against Venice's Arab allies at the ports of the Persian Gulf cut off its spice routes. Such oceanic voyages, however, were not at this time of interest to the English government, which was pushing for the building of large ships and the maintenance of fishing fleets in the nearby North Sea, where the sailors could be regularly and immediately available to be pressed into the navy for military adventures in Europe, in alliance with Spain. To this end a navigation act was introduced in 1540 requiring the use of the larger, more expensive, and less efficient ships of the English shipowners and captains instead of the smaller, less expensive Dutch ships. However, privileged merchants, such as the Merchant Adventurers, in trade with Spain or its possessions (for example, Spain and the Netherlands), were exempted and could by employing Dutch shipping, gain a competitive advantage over independent English merchants. Decreased English participation in the North Sea herring fishery, caused by the greater efficiency of the Dutch as well as by the Reformation, which greatly reduced the religiously based demand for fish in England, greatly alarmed the English government. To maintain the traditional source of impressment of men into the government's navy, a statute of 1549 imposed upon the English a political abstinence from meat under penalty of fine, in place of the previous purely religious abstinence.

This intensification of mercantilist policy was accelerated by the intervention of England into the dynastic wars on the Continent in the 1540s. To support its military activity, the English government initiated a series of great debasements of the currency as a hidden form of taxation of the people. The depreciation of the currency made England's goods cheaper to foreigners, who were able to purchase more English goods for the same amount of money. This taxation by inflation thus called forth an unnatural expansion in the production of the export commodities of wool and cloth, dislocating the economy both in agriculture and in industry. By 1550 the great increase in the costs of production, brought about by the inflation, caught up with the fall of the foreign exchange rate, thus ending the artificial comparative advantage causing the increased export of cloth. The inevitable end to the overexpansion of export industry, stimulated by the government's debasement in the 1540s, resulted in a severe depression, prolonged during the 1550s by further restrictive and monopolizing economic intervention by the government. Thus Parliament passed laws to protect the guild industry and to bring the free rural industry under the control of the traditional patterns of regulation and taxation; at the same time, the Merchant Adventurers, who were becoming the major tax collectors and lenders of money to the government, received a more complete monopoly of the export of cloths to Europe.

The accession of Queen Elizabeth (1558–1603) was followed by the transformation of piecemeal, unsystematic government interventions, into a comprehensive program of restrictions, privileges, and taxes. Elizabeth's reign brought to culmination the trend to absolutist government, especially noticeable in the exercise of power by the prerogative courts. By the Statute of Labourers and Apprentices of 1563, Parliament extended to the whole nation the restrictions that had formerly been limited to the urban guilds. In order to check and control the free capitalist textile industry based on rural labor, the government bound rural workers to agricultural labor and extended restrictive seven-year apprenticeship requirements and maximum-wage rates to the rural cloth industry. In this way, by crippling the free cloth industry, the government moved to confer special privilege on two powerful groups: the backward urban guilds, who were being outcompeted by the free and progressive rural cloth makers; and the quasi-feudal landlords, who had been losing workers to the higher paying cloth industry. To overcome the protections afforded defendants in common-law trials, the punishment for violating New Laws was placed by the Privy Council into the hands of the prerogative courts, where prisoners could be tortured and were deprived of the benefits of trial by jury. The Court of Star Chamber also developed censorship to control the reading of the people, and the laws of seditious and slanderous libel to protect the government from criticism.

Under the pressure of the financial crisis and of the control of markets by monopoly trading companies, the only possible avenue for the export of cloth appeared to be the opening of new areas of trade. As a result there was a resumption of English maritime exploration by the merchants seeking markets for cloth and sources of raw material. The most successful of these attempts began in December of 1551 with the formation of "The Mystery and Company of the Merchant Adventurers for discovery of Regions, Dominions, Islands, and Places Unknown." To it Sebastian Cabot, the partner and son of John Cabot and chief pilot of Spain for thirty years, was appointed as governor for life. After consideration by the Trinity House Corporation, which was empowered to review petitions for charters of exploration and trade, the company received its charter. Organized according to Italian practice as a joint stock company, it was named the Russia or Muscovy Company. The company received a grant of monopoly in 1553 for all trade with Russia, Central Asia, and Persia through the White Sea port of Archangel. An expedition to Archangel and Moscow returned in 1554 with permission to sell English cloth and purchase Russian furs plus the spices transported along the Volga River from central Asia and Persia. The descendants and relatives of the founders of the Muscovy Company were important in later explorations, most of which were conducted under the auspices of the company.

The English also looked to Spanish America as a market for the export of cloth and the purchase of raw materials. Although Spain maintained a system of monopoly trade to the New World, it could not supply large quantities of goods at low prices due to the regulations, taxes, and privileges of the mercantilist system. By the mid-sixteenth century, the silver mines of Mexico and Peru were not only contributing greatly to a monetary inflation in Europe, but also making the Spanish commerce with America the most valuable part of transoceanic trade. While Europe had difficulty in selling goods in Asia in exchange for spices, and therefore had to reexport American silver for spices, it could not supply enough manufactured goods to Spain for purchasing the silver, hampered as it was by the restrictions, monopoly, and taxation imposed by the Spanish government. These restrictions and inefficiencies of the Spanish monopoly greatly encouraged smuggling by ships from other European countries.

Large amounts of manufactured goods were reexported to the Spanish colonies from the Portuguese colony of Brazil, which around the middle of the sixteenth century became, by virtue of the absence of restrictions and heavy taxes, the major sugar-producing area in the world. Just as the bullion from America in payment for manufactured goods, and loans on the slave trade from West Africa (through which goods were smuggled to the West Indies) by the Genoese, now made Antwerp the banking capital of Europe, so the sugar trade from Brazil to Portugal by Jewish merchants, and from Lisbon to Antwerp by Dutchmen and Portuguese Jews living in the Netherlands, made Antwerp the center of the finest and cheapest sugar-refining industry in sixteenth-century Europe. The English, like the Portuguese, were able to engage in the illegal trade to the West Indies at reduced risks, because of close diplomatic relations between England and Spain. In 1562, Sir John Hawkins of Plymouth, after acquiring 300 slaves in West Africa, received permission to sell them in slave-hungry Hispaniola and to purchase a valuable cargo of sugar. Hawkins made a second voyage in 1564 to sell English cloth. In return for a license to trade in the West Indies and promises as to his peaceful trade, Hawkins offered to aid the Spanish in destroying the colony established in Florida by the French, who were also the leading pirates in the West Indies.

The Spaniards, however, decided to do this job themselves. In 1564 a group of French Huguenots under René de Laudonnière settled at the mouth of the St. Johns River on the east coast of Florida, and there constructed Fort Caroline. The Spaniards, worried about their bullion convoys and the threat of buccaneers, and anxious to enforce their claims of monopoly power over Florida, sent Pedro Menéndez de Avilés from Spain to crush the French. In

1565 Menéndez founded the great base of St. Augustine, the first permanent city in the Western Hemisphere, and fifty miles south of the French settlement. After a French fleet moving against the Spaniards was wrecked in a storm, Menéndez, heavily outnumbering the French, then marched overland and butchered over two-thirds of the settlement, especially including prisoners, save for a hundred colonists who managed to escape to some French vessels in the harbor. Philip II, king of Spain, rejoiced at the news: "Say to him [Menéndez] that as for those he has killed, he has done well; and as for those he has spared, they should be sent to the galley [i.e., into slavery]."

In retaliation, a French nobleman, Dominique de Gourgues, outfitted an expedition at his own expense, landed in early 1568 near the fort (now renamed San Mateo), and mobilized many Indians who were happy to take revenge on the hated Menéndez. Gourgues now swept down on the Spanish garrison, taking it completely by surprise and conquering it easily. The entire Spanish force, prisoners again included, was now in turn put to the sword. Although Menéndez himself escaped punishment by being absent in Spain, Gourgues was able to enforce poetic justice. Menéndez had hanged several prisoners, publicly posting the notice that they were hanging as Protestants, not as Frenchmen. Now Gourgues hanged a score of his prisoners on the same trees, and posted the sign: "Not as Spaniards, but as liars and murderers."

Due to English intervention into the constitutional and religious struggle of the Netherlands against Spain, English activity in the West Indies tended more and more toward piracy against Spanish shipping. The English freebooters were encouraged in their piratic attacks by the Crown, which participated in the profits of the plundering voyages. Sir John Hawkins and his cousin Francis Drake were defeated at Vera Cruz in 1568, but in 1571 and 1573 Drake plundered the Spanish silver depots at Panama. In 1577–80 Drake dared to circumnavigate the globe; he was the first Englishman to challenge the concept of the Pacific Ocean as a vast Spanish lake. Along the way, Drake plundered Chile and Peru, and purchased tons of spices in the East Indies. In 1585 Drake returned to the West Indies; on this voyage his fleet plundered Santo Domingo, Cartagena, and St. Augustine. In 1587, he attacked Lisbon and Cadiz, and in 1588 participated in the defeat of the Spanish Armada, which had attempted to retaliate against English attacks. This was a victory that brought to England domination of the seas.

Although the distraction of Spanish bullion would continue to complicate English colonial activities in the future, the actual settlement of North America was founded on the search for trade by the Muscovy Company and the extension of land conquest and speculation from Ireland to America. A staunch defender of monopoly, special privilege, and the royal prerogative, Sir Humphrey Gilbert, after serving as an officer in the war of extermination against the Irish (1566), had proposed to establish English colonies on the confiscated Irish lands and was appointed governor of southern Ireland in 1569. Gilbert emerged as the great leader of the futile quest for a northwest passage around North America to the Orient. He published in 1576 his tract in behalf of this search, *Discourse of a Discovery for a New Passage to Cataia* (i.e., to China). The Muscovy Company, holding a monopoly privilege for exploration and trade in the Atlantic Ocean north of London, desired to find a northwest passage, as well as stations for its whaling fleets for the whale oil used in the manufacture of soap. The Muscovy Company thereupon licensed Martin Frobisher, a nephew of one of the founders of the company, to explore Greenland and Labrador in search of a passage. Frobisher made three fruitless voyages, in 1576, 1577, and 1578.

Meanwhile, Gilbert perceived corollary possibilities of power and personal profit by the colonization of Newfoundland—both in the conquest of its fishing grounds and as a base for search for a northwest passage. Preparing to petition Queen Elizabeth for a monopoly patent of exploration and colonization of North America, Gilbert sought the advice of "Dr." John Dee, mathematician, magician, astrologer, and mystic adviser to the queen. Dee was much consulted in matters of exploration. To support the petition, Dee submitted reports extending previous historical fantasies that the English Crown possessed the God-given right to North America and to sole ownership of all remotely adjacent seas and to all the fish therein. Gilbert received the patent for exploration and colonization in North America in 1578. Humphrey Gilbert made several preparatory voyages to Newfoundland as did his brother Adrian, his half-brother and freebooter Walter Raleigh, and his associate John Davis. After further engaging in conquest and colonization in Ireland, Gilbert prepared, during 1582–83, another voyage for "western planting" in Newfoundland to establish a fishing colony. He was lost at sea in 1583. In February 1584 Adrian Gilbert and Walter Raleigh were granted a patent for northwest exploration under which John Davis made three voyages (1585–88) in a vain quest for a northwest passage, while in the following months of 1584, Humphrey Gilbert's monopoly patent for North American colonization was renewed in favor of Walter Raleigh.

Sir Walter Raleigh had been inspired by the Reverend Richard Hakluyt concerning colonization of the New World. Hakluyt, a friend of his and Gilbert's, had written paeans to the idea of English colonization. Indeed, Raleigh commissioned Hakluyt to write *Discourse of Western Planting* (1584), to be submitted to Queen Elizabeth in order to induce her to invest money in their colonization schemes. In this work, Hakluyt promised virtually every boon to the English establishment—especially to the merchants and the Crown—markets for its products (especially woolens), raw materials for its purchases, furs, timber, and naval stores; outlets for her surplus population, and bases from which to loot Spanish shipping. Sir George Peckham, an associate of Gilbert and Raleigh, wrote in 1583—in support of Gilbert's project—that a Newfoundland colony would provide a port to increase England's fishing fleet, a supply of valuable furs, and a northwest passage. But all of Hakluyt's and Peckham's propaganda could not induce the queen to loosen her pursestrings.

The products that Peckham and Hakluyt expected America to produce and the trade with foreign countries that they expected American trade to replace—these expectations were not arrived at accidentally. Their program was founded on the experience of the Muscovy Company, which had established trading posts on the inhospitable coasts and in the forests of Russia. But the project was not described merely to indicate the close comparisons between America and Russia, from whose forests had come furs, timber, and naval stores, and over whose routes came the spices and luxuries of the Orient. Rather, the plan was offered as an alternative to the Russian trade that was desperately needed by the London merchants. For England's Baltic trade had been crippled by conflicts with the Hanseatic League, and the English government had granted to the newly chartered Eastland Company a monopoly of exports to the Baltic areas.

The conflict between the Dutch and the Spanish in the Netherlands had brought upon Antwerp a series of calamities that ruined it as the great European center of commerce. Moreover, when the king of Spain acceded to the Portuguese throne in 1580, the Dutch were eliminated from the vital trade in spices from Lisbon, causing a rise in prices. Most important, in the 1580s the Muscovy Company's trade with Russia suffered crippling blows when the Cossacks disrupted the Volga route, by which England had received spices from Persia and central Asia, and when Russia lost its Baltic coast, including the port of Narva, to Sweden. To regain the spice trade, a group of leading merchants of the Muscovy Company formed the Turkey Company and the Venice Company in 1581 for direct trade with the Levant in spices and Mediterranean goods. Because of wars in the Levant, these companies sent English merchants overland to India to establish a direct trade in spices. When these merchants returned, the Turkey and Venice companies were merged into the Levant Company (1592), with a charter to trade with India through the Levant and Persia.

Having secured his monopoly grant of colonization, Sir Walter Raleigh "planted" in 1585 the first English colony in what would later be the United States, on Roanoke Island off the coast of present-day North Carolina. The area had been first explored by Ralph Lane and Richard Grenville under Raleigh's direction the previous year, and was named Virginia in honor of England's virgin queen. The new colony had few dedicated settlers, however, and the people returned to England two years later. In 1587 still another Raleigh expedition, headed by the painter John White, tried to effect a permanent settlement of Roanoke Island. Indeed, the first English child born in America, Virginia Dare, granddaughter of John White, was born that summer at Roanoke Colony. But English interest in and communication with the tiny colony was cut off during the battle with the Spanish Armada, and White, stranded in England, could not return to Roanoke until 1591. He could then find no trace of any of the colonists. The first attempt at English colonization of America had totally failed.

If Raleigh and Gilbert had received their inspiration for colonizing from such men as Hakluyt, their practical experience had been picked up in the course of subduing and enslaving Ireland. After serving in the army attempting to impose English rule on Ireland, Gilbert had proposed, in the late 1560s, to plant Englishmen in Ulster, as the Irish were forcibly driven out. A few years later, Gilbert became governor of Munster in Southern Ireland; in the course of "pacifying" the Irish, he drove out Irish peasants and replaced them with West Country English. Even as late as 1580, Gilbert and Raleigh fought together to suppress the Irish in Munster, and were rewarded with sizable grants of land. After the American colonizing failures, Raleigh turned his attention back to Ireland. There he planted English colonists to grow tobacco on the forty thousand acres of land he had been granted in Munster. In 1589 Raleigh, having expended forty thousand pounds on the American failure and not succeeding in persuading the queen to supply more, was happy to sell his patent for North American colonization to a group of associates and London merchants, largely connected with the Muscovy Company and including John White, the Reverend Richard Hakluyt, and Sir Thomas Smith. Raleigh, however, reserved to himself the right of dominion over the prospective colony.

Leading circles in and around the Muscovy Company had thus resumed the monopoly of rights to exploration and colonization of North America, which monopoly they had briefly held a decade earlier. But now they had a far greater incentive to pursue their grant to try to find compensation for the upheavals of the spice and Baltic trade, and of Antwerp, during the 1580s. Consideration was therefore given to establishing a sea trade direct to the East Indies by English and Dutch merchants. Thomas Cavendish, who had served on the Raleigh voyage to America in 1585, had sailed around the world during 1585–88 and had returned with a cargo of spices. The war with Spain now completely cut England off from the Levant spice trade, and in 1589 the London merchants received permission from the Privy Council to send three ships to the East Indies, carrying silver out of the country to pay for spices. Cavendish and John Davis, another old associate of Raleigh, made an unsuccessful attempt to circumnavigate the world. James Lancaster, who had been a merchant in Lisbon, was in 1591 dispatched with three ships to India; he returned in 1594 with one ship and a cargo of spices. In 1593 the Muscovy and Levant companies moved to the fore, sending George Weymouth to search for a northwest passage to India along the coast of North America.

The Dutch began in 1594 to form companies for distant voyages around Africa to India. Their first fleet returned in 1597, thereby giving a new impetus to the activity of English merchants. In 1598 alone, Dutch companies sent five fleets, totaling twenty-two ships, to the Indies; John Davis was the chief pilot of the Zeeland fleet. By 1601 over a dozen Dutch fleets of almost seventy ships had sailed for the East Indies. Because of renewed English voyages and conflicts with the Portuguese, the Dutch merchants forming the companies that had sent the ships to the East Indies began to amalgamate them, and in March 1602 all the Dutch companies merged into the United East India Company.

In September 1599, London merchants belonging to various trading companies, especially the Levant Company, formed an association on the model of the successful Dutch companies and petitioned the government to charter a company of London merchants having a monopoly of trade by sea to the East Indies. The charter to the East India Company was granted on December 31, 1600, under the title of the "The Governor, and Company of Merchants of London Trading into the East Indies"; the Levant Company was granted a new charter to distinguish the monopoly areas of the two companies. The governor named in the charter of the East India Company was Sir Thomas Smith (or Smythe). Smith's grandfather, Andrew Judd, had been a principal founder of the Muscovy Company. His father had preceded him as a leading tax collector, and had been a key royal official in erecting the edifice of royal absolutism, high taxation, and economic restrictionism during the Elizabethan era. Smith was governor also of the Muscovy Company and the Levant Company, of which he was a founder, and was also the principal member of the group of London merchants to whom Raleigh had in 1589 assigned his patent for American colonization. Indeed, Smith was the governor of every one of England's privileged companies then interested in foreign commerce and colonization. Smith has been referred to as the greatest "merchant-prince" of his era, but it is clear that his status and wealth arose not from private trade, but from the governmental privileges of tax-farming and grants of monopoly.

The first voyage of the East India Company went out under the direction of James Lancaster and John Davis in 1601, and was followed the next year by George Weymouth's second voyage along the coast of North America, sponsored by the East India and Muscovy companies. Meanwhile, Sir Walter Raleigh resumed his interest in the New World in 1602, sending out another futile expedition to search for survivors of the Roanoke Colony. But in the following year, Raleigh's colonizing activities were unceremoniously cut short by the accession of King James I to the throne of England. One of James' first acts was to consign Raleigh to an indefinite imprisonment in the Tower and abruptly to vacate his dominion over Virginia. Among the king's motives was the desire to give Spain a tangible token of the new king's wish to conclude peace between the two warring countries. For Raleigh was now perhaps the most ardent warmonger and plunderer against Spanish shipping and whose colonizing activities sought bases for aggression against Spain; his incarceration was therefore a particularly apt token of peace between the two nations. Indeed, peace was concluded the next year, in August 1604, after which King James cracked down on the formerly lionized captains of piracy and freebooting.

The Treaty of London of 1604 provided for freedom of commerce between England and Spain as it had existed prior to the war. Since England had had the right to sail to Spain and Portugal, England now claimed that its ships could sail to the East and West Indies as well. Spanish America was the source of tobacco, and its use in England increased greatly once trade was reestablished on a regular basis, even though James disapproved of its use as a poisonous weed. Although the London merchants hoped to monopolize the renewed trade with Spain, the protests of the merchants of the West Country ports, especially Bristol and Plymouth, forced the government to backtrack. First it tried to include the west country merchants in the monopoly, and then it decreed for all English merchants freedom of trade to Portugal, Spain, and the Western Mediterranean, a policy that was later to apply to American merchants. At the same time, the privileged merchants of the Levant and Muscovy companies were suffering further losses because of local difficulties, especially foreign invasions of Russia.

While economic pressure was turning the attention of English merchants once again to possible markets and supplies of raw materials in North America, and peace renewed attention to the New World that had been diverted by the war against Spain, the peace treaty also terminated the previously permanent employment of many military and naval officers engaged in the war. In 1605 Weymouth again explored the coast of New England, this time in behalf of a group of soldier-courtiers, including Sir Ferdinando Gorges, the Earl of Southampton, and the latter's brother-in-law, Sir Thomas Arundel. Weymouth's return in July 1605 led to several projects for trade and colonization in America, and in September of that year, petitions were presented to the Privy Council for the formation of companies to engage in these activities. Although the Privy Council was then considering a project to plant English colonists in the lands taken from the Irish in Ulster, the value of North American colonies to English shipowners and to the English navy led the Trinity House Corporation and the Privy Council to approve the petitions. Finally, in April 1606 Raleigh's old dominion over Virginia was granted to two sets of powerful merchants, which included the merchants to whom Raleigh had sold his rights of trade.

The new patent divided the monopoly powers of government over Virginia between two joint stock companies of merchants. The South Virginia Company was to have claim over the land between the thirty-fourth and thirty-eighth parallels, roughly from Cape Fear north to the Potomac River; the North Virginia Company was to rule between the forty-first and forty-fifth parallels, roughly from Long Island to Maine. To stimulate competition and to provide incentive for colonizing, the zone in between was thrown open to settlement by either company, with the stipulation that one could not settle within one hundred miles of the other. Since the South Virginia

Company was headed by leading merchants of London, it soon became known as the London Company; while the North Virginia Company, centered around merchants of Plymouth, came to be called the Plymouth Company. Each company was granted powers to allocate its land in any way it wished; the king reserved the then customary royalty of five percent of whatever gold or silver might be mined from the new land. Insisting upon overall royal control and dominion unique to monopoly charters of that era, the king vested supervisory control of the two companies in a Royal Council of Virginia, which was appointed by the king and which in turn was to appoint resident local councils to govern each of the two colonies. The settlers and their descendants were supposed to enjoy all the "liberties, franchises, and immunities" of Englishmen at home—a clause immediately contradicted by the absence of any provision for elections or home rule.

The Plymouth Company for North Virginia was composed of west country merchants, gentry, and soldiers, and was headed by the governor of Plymouth, Sir Ferdinando Gorges, who desired to establish a fishing and fur-trading colony independent of the London merchant-financiers. Also included in the group were Raleigh Gilbert, a son of Sir Humphrey, and Sir John Popham, chief justice of the King's Bench; Sir John had played a leading role in procuring the charter. The Plymouth Company dispatched an exploratory expedition in October 1606, and sent colonists to America in May 1607 under Raleigh Gilbert and George Popham, a relative of Sir John. A settlement was established on the Kennebec River in what is now Maine, but because of a severe winter and poor crops, and the death of the two Pophams, the colony was abandoned in September 1608. Thereafter the Plymouth Company did not attempt further colonization, but concentrated on the Newfoundland fisheries and some fur trade.

The London Company for South Virginia was composed of members of leading political families. The leading member was the ubiquitous Sir Thomas Smith, the leader of the group that had purchased trade rights from Raleigh, and the governor of the East India, Muscovy, and Levant companies. Other leading members were: the Reverend Richard Hakluyt; Robert Rich, Earl of Warwick, a leader in the monopoly-chartered East India, Burma, and Guinea companies; and the leading London merchants involved in the Muscovy, Levant, and East India companies. And just as the Levant Company had been founded by members of the Muscovy Company, and a quarter of the stockholders in the East India Company were members of the Levant Company, so over one hundred members of the East India Company were now investors in the London Virginia Company, a main purpose of which was to provide a source of raw materials, such as tropical products, spices, and furs. Another prominent member in the London Company was Sir Edwin Sandys, a prominent Puritan and friend of a royal favorite, the Earl of Southampton.

The London Virginia Company sent forth its first settlers in December 1606; they were carried then as in succeeding years on ships provided by the Muscovy Company, which long remained the major operator in the Virginia trade. With them the colonists took the king's instructions to the company, which included the requirement of a public oath of obedience by the colonists and a death penalty for all manner of crimes, including tumults, sedition, conspiracy, and adultery. The president and the council of the company were empowered to make laws for the colonists, consistent with the laws of England, subject to revision by the Royal Council.

The ships landed at Chesapeake Bay the following May 6. A settlement was founded thirty miles inland on the James River, called Jamestown, in honor of the king. This was the first sucessful English settlement in North America. The colony of Virginia had begun.

The new English colonial grants were placed between the French exploration and settlement to the north, and the Spanish occupation to the south. Through trading and missionary posts, Spain had been effectively occupying the coast of what was later to become South Carolina, Georgia, and Florida. The French had been continually exploring and trading on the St. Lawrence for some years; already they had established a trade in furs, which would become the most valuable French export from North America. In 1602 the patent for monopoly of the fur trade to France from North America had been granted to the Company of New France, which sent Samuel de Champlain to explore the St. Lawrence in 1603. The following years, Champlain established a fur post at Acadia (now Nova Scotia) and explored the coast of New England.

In 1607 the Muscovy Company commissioned Henry Hudson, a descendant of the founder of the company, to explore the Arctic regions around Greenland. Two years later Holland and Spain concluded a trade, which the Dutch claimed gave them rights, similar to those accorded to the English, to sail to the New World. Promptly the Dutch sent Henry Hudson, under auspices of the Dutch East India Company, to explore the Arctic regions. Saliing along the North American coast from Newfoundland to the Carolinas, Hudson returned by way of Delaware Bay (South River) and the Hudson River (North River), which he explored up to Albany; he claimed the fur regions for the Dutch. In 1610 Hudson set forth under an English company headed by Sir Thomas Smith, and discovered Hudson's Bay before being abandoned by his mutinous crew. Several of the companies of which Smith was governor were subject to reorganization in the spring of 1609, because of the new Dutch competition in North American waters resulting from the Dutch peace treaty with Spain. New charters were granted in May 1609 to the English East India Company and the closely linked London Virginia Company. The East India Company was granted a perpetual monopoly charter, and in the following year established its first trading posts in India. Analogous to the East India Company charter, the new charter granted to the "Treasurer and Company of the Adventurers and Planters of the City of London for the First Colony in Virginia" a corporate body politic, with Sir Thomas Smith filling the key, royally appointed post of treasurer. The charter was completely distinct from the old joint charter of the unsuccessful Plymouth Company.

The rechartering of an independent London Virginia Company for American colonization was complemented by the chartering of a new company for planting English and Scottish colonists in the lands recently conquered in Northern Ireland. In the spring of 1610 a group of London and Bristol merchants, interested in founding a colony in proximity to the fishing banks off Newfoundland, was chartered as the "Treasurer and Company of Adventurers and Planters of Cities of London and Bristol for the Colony or Plantation of Newfoundland." Under the direction of Sir Ferdinando Gorges, the company prepared to send exploratory voyages along the New England Coast. To improve the financial condition of the London Virgina Company, a new charter was issued in 1612 to Smith as the "Treasurer and Company of Virginia." The boundaries included the islands within three hundred leagues of the continent, specifically the rediscovered Bermudas or Somers Islands, which in 1615 were placed under the "Somers Islands Company" of which Smith was also the governor. Along with the 1612 Virginia Company charter, Smith received a charter as the "Governor and Company of the Merchants of London, Discovers of the North-West Passage" to follow up Henry Hudson's last voyage. In addition, Smith's Muscovy Company was rechartered in 1613; this enlarged the Muscovy Company's privileges in exploring Greenland, Hudson Bay, Newfoundland, and North America, and included a monopoly of the whale and seal fishing, which had become the company's major interest because of the troubles in Russia. As this was an attempt to exclude Dutch as well as independent English whalers, the States-General of the United provinces of the Netherlands granted charters in 1614 to a company for the Greenland whale fishery and, in formal recognition of the exploratory work of Henry Hudson, granted to the New Netherland Company the power to colonize and trade in the area about the South (Delaware) and the North (Hudson) rivers.

2

New World, New Land

The Englishmen and other Europeans of the sixteenth and seventeenth centuries faced westward to the New World in awe and in hope. For here was a vast virgin continent, and its most striking feature was the millions of square miles of new and potentially highly productive land. To a Europe beset by the incubus of feudalism and statism, of absolute monarchy, of state-controlled churches, of state restrictions on human labor and human enterprise; to a Europe with scarce land, which was engrossed by feudal and quasi-feudal landlords whose vast government-granted estates drained in rents the surplus over subsistence earned by the peasantry—to this Europe the new and vast land area appeared as potential manna from Heaven. At home the mass of Europeans—middle class and peasants alike—faced centuries of weary struggle against the frozen cake of status restrictions, a network of taxes, feudal dues and rents, and controls and shackles by states and state-fostered guilds. This was a relatively stagnant Old World, whose population pressed heavily upon the means of subsistence; this was a Europe but recently emerged from the secular depression into which the growth of statism had plunged it at the beginning of the fourteenth century. But abroad they saw a quite different vision: new, productive, and virtually unoccupied land (with the important exception of the rather thinly populated Indians), a land relatively unencumbered with the feudalism and restrictions that humbled them at home. In short, here at last was the opportunity for the individual to leave his unsatisfactory conditions at home to try to carve out of the wilderness a better life for himself and his family—a life offering him the freedom and opportunity to make his own way, stand on his own feet, and keep what he himself had earned. It is not the privilege of many generations of men to experience a revolution—a breeze of fresh air upon the stagnant social structure—and an opportunity to break loose from the old mold and strike out afresh on one's own. Through the discovery of the New World, the men of the seventeenth century experienced at least the potential of such a revolution. For the escape hatch to the untapped storehouse of the New World lay always at hand.

New land, then, confronted the Old World, and this vast stretch of land furnished the most striking fact about the virgin American continent. But how was the ownership of this great new land mass to be allocated? Basically, new and previously unowned land can come into ownership in two different ways: either the settler—the pioneer who, in the later phrase of John Locke, "mixes his labor with the soil" and brings the previously unused and fallow natural resources into productive use—is conceded ownership of the land he has in this way "created"; or he is not.*

If he is not challenged, the pioneer settler of new land will naturally and automatically become its owner. There are two types of threats to this basic principle of first ownership to first user: either existing settler-owners can be subjected to the arbitrarily imposed ownership of some overlord, or else new land can be parceled out to some person or persons *before* any settlement has taken place. In both cases, the arbitrary parceling is performed by the state—that institution that asserts its claim to a monopoly of legalized coercion in a given territorial area. The former is one of the chief methods of feudalism: the parceling out of peasant-owned land to the ownership of overlords favored by the state. But this method requires previously existing settlers. Clearly in the case of a new and untapped continent, the second method would be the major threat to settler-ownership of what the settlers would create. And this is precisely what happened in the case of North America.

It is the propensity of the state to parcel out arbitrary subsidies, in disregard of the individual's natural right to own what he has produced. This propensity is here aggravated by the fact that the state always assumes sovereign ownership over new and unused land—it's self-proclaimed "public domain." It hereby assumes the right to dispose of this domain in any way it sees fit. Unless forced by the pressure of public opinion to do otherwise, the state will naturally tend to dispose of such land in a way best calculated to maximize either its own revenue or the revenue of its priv-

*If it be objected that the pioneer has not really created the land, it is also true that no producer "creates" matter. The builder of a factory has not in the ultimate sense "created" the matter in the factory; he has rather transformed by the use of his labor the previously nature-given matter. He has shifted this original matter into other forms more useful to himself and to his fellow men: this shifting is the meaning of "production." And this is precisely what the pioneer has done in transforming the land.

47

ileged favorites. The crucial question then becomes: Will the land pass after a time into the hands of the settlers, or will it remain permanently in the hands of privileged overlords dominating the settlers?

England, the major sovereign over the lands of North America, had been subjected to feudalism since at least the Norman Conquest of the eleventh century. After the conquest of England in 1066, the conquerors parceled out large tracts of land to the ownership of their leading warlords, and this newly created nobility became the liege lords of the subdued peasantry. Since the overwhelming mass of Englishmen were still engaged in agriculture, feudalism became the crucial fact about English—as well as other European—society. The major attributes of the feudal system were: the granting of huge estates to landowning warlords, the coerced binding of the peasants (serfs) to their land plots, and hence to the rule of their lords, and the further bolstering by the state of feudal status through compulsory primogeniture (the passing on of the estate to the oldest son only) and entail (prohibiting the landowner from alienating—selling, breaking up, etc.—his land). This process froze landlordship in the existing noble families, and prevented any natural market or genealogical forces from breaking up the vast estates.

But after the late fourteenth century, the serfdom aspect of feudalism began a steady decline in England, as compulsory labor service imposed on the peasants began to be commuted permanently into money rents ("quit-rents," which quit or freed one of the onerous obligations of feudal—including military—service). By the early seventeenth century, however, feudal military service had not been abolished, and the two other aspects of feudalism—primogeniture and entail—remained intact.

An important specific spur to imposing feudalism on the colonies of the New World was England's experience in subjugating Ireland. In the process of conquering Ireland during the sixteenth century, the English concluded that the "wild Irish" were no better than "Savages" and "unreasonable beasts" and hence could be treated as such—a significant preview of English treatment of the American Indian. As a result, the English decided that, as in Ireland, a colony had to be "Planted" under direction of a central monopoly organization run along military lines; they also decided to favor imposing on a colony a system of feudal land tenure. It was no coincidence that the leaders in the early English colonizing projects in America had almost all been deeply connected with the planting of Englishmen (largely a supposed surplus of poor) and feudal landownership in Ireland. Indeed, many of the active incorporators of the Virginia Company had substantial interests in Irish plantations.*

As recently as 1603, in fact, a crushing defeat of the Irish had spurred renewed colonization in Ulster by the English government. The hapless Irish peasants were declared to have no rights in owning land; instead, their

*See the penetrating discussion in Howard Mumford Jones, *O Strange New World* (New York: Viking Press, 1964), pp. 162-79.

48

lands were handed over by the Crown in large grants to privileged courtiers and monopoly companies, all enjoying feudal powers over the new domain.

The Irish were deliberately exterminated or driven off their land, and the vacant lands compulsorily planted with an alleged surplus of English poor, who were now little better than serfs. The treatment of the Irish and Ireland provided a directly illuminating model for the gentlemen colonizing in Virginia.

That the first English settlements in the New World were organized not directly by the Crown, but by private monopoly companies, meant that the proprietary company would be interested in subdividing its granted land as quickly as possible to the individual settlers, in order to reap a rapid gain for its shareholders. The situation was of course *not* that of the free market; if it were, the British government would: (a) have refrained from claiming sovereignty over the unused American domain, or especially (b) have granted ownership of the land titles to the actual settlers rather than to the company. The privileges to the chartered companies, however, did not prove disastrous in the long run: the companies were eager to induce settlers to come to their granted land and then dispose of the land to them at a profit. The cleansing acid of profit was to dissolve incipient feudalism and land monopoly. It is true that the fact of the land grant to the company engrossed the land for a time, and raised its price to the settlers, thus restricting settlement from what it would have been under freedom; but the quantitative effects were not very grave.*

---

*Defenders of presettler land speculation have claimed that speculators (such as the first charter companies) *spurred* settlement in the hope of profit. This is true, but it does not offset the net restriction on settlement by virtue of the land grants and the consequent raising of the price of otherwise free land to the settlers. In a free market the same companies could simply have loaned settlement money to the colonists, and this productive credit could then have spurred settlement and earned them a profit without the arbitrary restrictions imposed by the land grants.

PART II

The Southern Colonies in the Seventeenth Century

3

The Virginia Company

The Virginia colony did not enter existence as a new entity in a new world devoid of the shackles of tradition. The two key areas of policy—land and commerce—were already clearly established before the Virginia Company was planned and before the Virginia colony was established. In the period immediately preceding the formation of the Virginia Company and colony, a policy toward colonial land, commerce, government, natives and colonists became well established. A primary purpose for colonization was the belief that England was highly overpopulated and that colonies were a suitable outlet for the surplus poor of England. In 1603, the government issued an order for the forcible transportation of sturdy beggars, vagrants, and other troublesome persons to the English plantations across the sea in Ireland. During the preceding decade Ireland had suffered the ravages of the English army battling against a movement of national liberation seeking self-government, freedom of religion, and abandonment of the plantation of English colonists on Irish lands. The defeat of the Irish in 1603 by the studied English policy of destruction of crops, cattle, homes, and people, opened Ireland to renewed colonization by the English government. The Irish had no land rights; they were mere tenants at the will of their lords.

The system of plantations in Ireland provided the pattern for establishing plantations in America. Grants of land were made to courtiers, privileged companies, and purchasers of feudal domains with feudal powers. Like the American Indians, the Irish were subjected to raids whose purpose was to destroy their subsistence and shelter, and to drive them out of the proposed area of plantation. These new feudal domains were settled by the poor of England who were subjected to feudal disabilities. In consequence, these poor not only did not own their lands; they barely owned themselves. The colonial government of Ireland remained the despotism that was established by the Tudors.

Since the English government was deeply engaged in the development of a program for Irish colonization when the Virginia Company was being organized, there were complaints that the proposals for American colonies would interfere with the plantation of Ulster: "It was absurd folly to run over the world in the search of colonies in Virginia or Guiana, whilst Ireland was lying desolate." However, colonies in Virginia or Guiana would not only contribute to the decrease of the burden of overpopulation; they would also be a source of important tropical or semitropical products that were objectives of the privileged trading companies of London. The London financiers purchased from the government the right to retain general customs as well as tobacco duties, since tobacco was becoming a significant imported commodity. Spanish America, especially the lands and islands about the Caribbean, was the source of tobacco, and its use in England grew rapidly once trade was established with Spain in 1604. However, the use of tobacco was much disliked by James I, because it not only was a drain of money from England to Spain, but also was considered poisonous and a sign of intemperance and vice, by which Englishmen allowed themselves to be debased by the barbaric practices of the Indians. But the habit became widespread and an important source of tax revenue.

In 1604 the English government initiated new increases in the customs duties, making the farming of the duties* even more profitable. At the same time, the increases in tariffs made smuggling such a profitable business that it became organized on a professional basis. The smuggling business was a well-organized system of purchase, transportation, delivery, and distribution in which the free trader was not only sailor and merchant, but also policeman, to protect his property from attacks by government officials. Tobacco became one of the most important of the basic items for smuggling. Besides increasing direct taxation, the government, in effect, encouraged smuggling through indirect taxes via sale of monopoly privileges.

James I's first Parliament in 1604 established the tone for the future Parliaments of the seventeenth century: opposition to the government. The Parliament of 1604 strongly stated the grievances felt against the government, and among the fiscal reforms demanded by the House of Commons was the abolition of the foreign trading companies having monopolies. A committee, under the chairmanship of Sir Edwin Sandys, presented a bill "for all merchants to have free liberty of trade, into all countries, as is used in all other nations." Sandys said: "All free subjects are born inheritable as to their land, as also to the free exercise of their industry, in those trades whereto they apply themselves and whereby they are to live."

The Parliament of 1605 continued to state the grievances of the people against the monopolies of London financiers: after the closing of Parliament,

*"Tax farming" was the sale by government of the right to tax.

54

the government sought to quiet opposition by coopting provincial capitalists into the monopoly privileges. However, the desire for the advantages of freedom of trade outweighed the advantages of monopoly privileges, and the attempt to force the investors of the West Country ports, such as Plymouth and Bristol, into the London monopolies proved unsatisfactory. Thus the colonization activities of the West Country promoters had to be separated from those of the London colonial promoters. This resulted in the creation of two Virginia companies and charters (September 1605 and April 1606). In 1606 the Parliament declared void the charters of the monopoly companies trading with southern Europe, which action freed and opened that trade to all English merchants. In response the government refused to call Parliament for almost three years, hoping to raise money by prerogative power—by increasing the duties on imports and exports without Parliamentary consent and by the creation or extension of monopolies. The Parliament of 1610 protested the imposition of increased taxes and deprivation of civil liberties by the prerogative courts, and refused to vote any taxes.

The government continued to gain its income by prerogative power, granting increased privileges in 1612 to such companies as the Virginia Company and the East India Company. Despite the financial manipulations of the government, its debt more than doubled and it sought to gain taxes by controlling elections to the House of Commons. But a House opposed to the government was elected, and by a unanimous vote it criticized the imposition of taxes by the government. Sir Edwin Sandys said of the monopolies and taxes imposed by the government, that what in the past had been done only temporarily and in emergencies was now being claimed by right. The Parliament refused to pass any legislation or approve any taxation until the grievances of the people were redressed by the government. The government dissolved the Parliament, and over a dozen members were punished by the government by imprisonment or house arrest, including Sir Edwin Sandys.

Although the government continued to create and enlarge its inspections, regulations, controls, and monopolies, the rationalization of government power was further undermined in 1614 by common-law court decisions against monopolies. During the constitutional struggle of the seventeenth century, the common law was often used against the government's positive laws. An important aspect of the struggle was the provision of Magna Carta guaranteeing complete freedom of trade as part of the protection of liberty and property. Any interference in economic activity by the government or by any group privileged by the government constituted restraint of trade contrary to the principles of common law. It became evident that there could not be any restraint of trade without government action, and the common-law courts refused to enforce the monopolies whenever the government did not interfere with the freedom of the courts.

Among the bills failing passage in 1614 was one for a navigation act. Following the peace of April 1609 between Spain and the Netherlands, the Dutch were able to compete favorably with English shipowners in the fishing, coastal, and distant trades because of cheaper costs due to more efficient construction. The English government occasionally harassed Dutch shipping, at the insistence of English shippers, by intermittently enforcing old laws and collecting fines. Although in 1602 the English government had insisted to Denmark that "the law of Nations alloweth of fishing in the seas everywhere," the increased competitive ability of the Dutch caused the English government to issue a contrasting proclamation in May 1609. This proclamation claimed that the English government had dominance and political authority over those high seas in which England possessed exclusive fishing rights; therefore, the Dutch should withdraw from these seas or pay taxes to the English government. To the Dutch the fishing industry was highly important, and thus the English sought to strike at the basis of Dutch prosperity.

After thirty years the fantasies of the magician Dr. John Dee had become the program of the English government, a program for which Englishmen would be forced to sacrifice their lives. In place of that spirit of freedom and mutual advantage of the Intercursus Magnus, which had guided English maritime policy for over one hundred years and would remain the letter of the law for another several decades, there was entering into the policy of the English government a spirit of increased restriction and belligerency. This spirit was reflected in the expansion of the mercantilist system during the seventeenth century, aimed especially at the Dutch. In opposition to the claims of exclusive control of the high seas by England in the North Sea and the North Atlantic and by Spain and Portugal in the East and West Indies, the Dutchman Hugo Grotius contended for the freedom of the seas in his work *Mare Liberum* (1609). That the seas were to be open to all and free from government control was an idea that Grotius, the founder of international law, derived from Spanish philosophical thought, especially from the work of Francisco Suárez. Suárez had established the basis for international law by deducing from the variety of peoples and states that the unity of the human race can only be represented by a general rational international law, and not by a general political organization or domination, whether over the lands or over the seas.

In 1613 a Dutch diplomatic delegation, including Hugo Grotius, came to London to negotiate for improved commercial relations, and one of the matters raised was the possibility of greater cooperation between the Dutch and English East India companies, which had traded together in the Indies in amity. There was heavy Dutch investment in England because of the higher interest rates there, and the English East India Company was one of the businesses in which the Dutch had invested heavily. Because of the adoption of a permanent joint stock similar to that of the more advanced Dutch business organization, and the common concern of defense against Portuguese fleets, there was increased Dutch interest in the English East India Company. A merger of the companies was proposed that would have maintained the autonomy of the English body. Although the English would have benefited from the superior Dutch capacity, trading experience in the Indies, and technical competence, the English East India directors rejected this proposal and engaged in armed conflict with the merchants and ships of the Dutch East India Company. Apparently the English preferred the returns of hostile conflict to the profits of peaceful cooperation. This hostility would have been increased and generalized by the proposed navigation act of 1614 that would have imposed upon English merchants the requirement to ship English goods on English ships.

The English shipowners had maintained that English regulations forced them to use uneconomical ships. The regulations required that ships be built so they could be transformed into auxiliary warships—built for speed and maneuverability rather than for carrying cargoes at low operational costs. The English shippers desired compensation in the form of a navigation act forcing English merchants to use the uneconomical English ships rather than the more efficient Dutch ships. In reply to the shipowners and the monopoly companies, the merchants said that navigation acts were "poison" that would destroy the competitive position of the English merchants in foreign trade and reduce the standard of living of the English public as consumers of imports and producers of exports. To use English ships with their much larger crews and smaller capacities, the merchants insisted, would greatly raise their costs and thus reduce English competitive ability in the world market.

The monopoly companies headed by Sir Thomas Smith became the focus of increasing popular criticism leveled against the government's attempt to expand further the system of privileges. Representative of the literate attacks on monopoly and the navigation acts in the Commons was *The Trades Increase* (1615), which centered its attack upon the power nucleus of the London financiers headed by Thomas Smith and the East India Company. The pamphlet declared that monopoly privileges were contrary to the freedom of Englishmen and that no one shoud be barred from carrying on trade equally in all parts of the world. The East India Company directors considered the pamphlet particularly dangerous, even treasonable, and commissioned the writing of an answer: *The Defense of Trade. The Trades Increase* favored the establishment of colonies in America, but charged that the growth of colonies there had been stunted by the grants of monopoly privileges that discouraged settlement.

In fact, the Virginia colony was not doing very well in drawing off England's surplus poor. Besides transporting vagrants and criminals to Virginia, the London Company and the City of London agreed to transport poor children from London to Virginia. However, the poorest refused the proffered boon and the company moved to obtain warrants to force the children to migrate. It seemed, indeed, that the Virginia colony, failing also to return profits to the company investors, was becoming a failure on every count.

The survival of the Virginia colony hung, in fact, for years by a hairbreadth. The colonists were not accustomed to the labor required of a pioneer, and malaria decimated the settlers. Of the 104 colonists who reached Virginia in May 1607, only thirty were still alive by that fall, and a similar death rate prevailed among new arrivals for many years. As late as 1616, only 350 colonists remained of a grand total of over 1,600 immigrants.

One major reason for the survival of this distressed colony was the changes that the company agreed to make in its social structure. The bulk of the colonists had been under "indenture" contracts, and were in servitude to the company for seven years in exchange for passage money and maintenance during the period, and sometimes for the prospect of a little land at the end of their term of service. The contract was called an indenture because it was originally written in duplicate on a large sheet—the two halves separated by a jagged line called an "indent." While it is true that the original contract was generally voluntary, it is also true that a free society does not enforce even temporary voluntary slave contracts, since it must allow for a person to be able to change his mind, and for the inalienability of a person's control over his will and his body. While a man's property is alienable and may be transferred from one person to another, a person's *will* is not; the creditor in a free society may enforce the collection of payment for money he may have advanced (in this case, passage and maintenance money), but he may not continue to enforce slave labor, however temporary it may be. Furthermore, many of the indentures were compulsory and not voluntary—for example, those involving political prisoners, imprisoned debtors, and kidnapped children of the English lower classes. The children were kidnapped by professional "spirits" or "crimps" and sold to the colonists.

In the concrete conditions of the colony, slavery, as always, robbed the individual of his incentive to work and save, and thereby endangered the survival of the settlement. The new charter granted in 1609 by the Crown to the company (now called the Virginia Company) added to the incentives of the individual colonists by providing that every settler above the age of ten be given one share of stock in the company. At the end of seven years, each person was promised a grant of 100 acres of land, and a share of assets of the company in proportion to the shares of stock held. The new charter also granted the company more independence, and more responsibility to its stockholders, by providing that all vacancies in the governing Royal Council be filled by the company, which would thus eventually assume control. The charter of 1609 also stored up trouble for the future by adding wildly to the grant of land to the Virginia Company. The original charter had sensibly confined the grant to the coastal area (to 100 miles inland)—the extent of English sovereignty on the continent. But the 1609 charter grandiosely extended the Virginia Company "from sea to sea," that is, westward to the Pacific. Furthermore, its wording was so vague as to make it unclear whether the extension was westward or northwestward—not an academic point, but a prolific source of conflict later on. The charter of 1612 added the island of Bermuda to the vast Virginia domain, but this was soon farmed out to a subsidiary corporation.

The incentives provided by the charter of 1609, however, were still only future promises. The colony was still being run on "communist" principles—each person contributed the fruit of his labor according to his ability to a common storehouse run by the company, and from this common store each received produce according to his need. And this was a communism not voluntarily contracted by the colonists themselves, but imposed upon them by their master, the Virginia Company, the receiver of the arbitrary land grant for the territory.

The result of this communism was what we might expect: each individual gained only a negligible amount of goods from his own exertions—since the fruit of all these went into the common store—and hence had little incentive to work, or to exercise initiative or ingenuity under the difficult conditions in Virginia. And this lack of incentive was doubly reinforced by the fact that the colonist was assured, regardless of how much or how well he worked, of an equal share of goods from the common store. Under such conditions, with the motor of incentive gone from each individual, even the menace of death and starvation for the group as a whole—and even a veritable reign of terror by the governors—could not provide the necessary spur for each particular man.

The communism was only an aspect of the harshness of the laws and the government suffered by the colony. Absolute power of life and death over the colonists was often held by one or two councillors of the company. Thus, Captain John Smith, the only surviving Royal Council member in the winter of 1609, read his absolute powers to the colonists once a week. "There are no more Councils to protect or curb my endeavors," he thundered, and every violator of his decrees could "assuredly expect his due punishment." Sir Thomas Gates, appointed governor of Virginia in 1609, was instructed by the company to "proceed by martial law . . . as of most dispatch and tenor and fittest for this government [of Virginia]." Accordingly, Gates established a code of military discipline over the colony in May 1610. The code ordered strict religious observance, among other things. Some twenty "crimes" were punishable by death, including such practices as trading with Indians without a license, killing cattle and poultry without a license, escape from the colony, and persistent refusal to attend church. One of the most heinous acts was apparently running away from this virtual prison to the supposedly savage Indian natives; captured runaway colonists were executed by hanging, shooting, burning, or being broken on the wheel. It is no wonder that Gates' instructions took the precaution of providing him with a bodyguard to protect him from the wrath of his subjects; for, as the succeeding governor wrote in the following year, the colony was "full of mutiny and treasonable inhabitants."

The directors of the Virginia Company decided, unfortunately, that the cure for the grave ailments of the colony was not less but even more discipline. Accordingly, they sent Sir Thomas Dale to be governor and ruler of the colony. Dale increased the severity of the laws in June 1611. Dale's Laws— "the Laws Divine, Moral and Martial"—became justly notorious: They provided, for example, that every man and woman in the colony be forced to attend divine service (Anglican) twice a day or be severely punished. For the first absence, the culprit was to go without food; for the second, to be publicly whipped; and for the third, to be forced to work in the galleys for six months. This was not all. Every person was compelled to satisfy the Anglican minister of his religious soundness, and to place himself under the minister's instructions; neglect of this duty was punished by public whipping *each day* of the neglect. No other offense was more criminal than any criticism of the Thirty-nine Articles of the Church of England: torture and death were the lot of any who persisted in open criticism. This stringent repression reflected the growing movement in England, of Puritans and other Dissenters, to reform, or to win acceptance alongside, the established Church of England. Dale's Laws also provided:

> That no man speak impiously . . . against the holy and blessed Trinity . . . or against the known Articles of the Christian faith, upon pain of death. . . .
> That no man shall use any traitorous words against His Majesty's person, or royal authority, upon pain of death. . . .
> No man . . . shall dare to detract, slander, calumniate or utter unseemly speeches, either against Council or against Committees, Assistants . . . etc. First offense to be whipped three times; second offense to be sent to galleys; third offense— death.

Offenses such as obtaining food from the Indians, stealing food, and attempting to return to England were punishable by death and torture. Lesser offenses were punished by whipping or by slavery in irons for a number of years. Governor Dale's major constructive act was to begin slightly the process of dissolution of communism in the Virginia colony; to stimulate individual self-interest, he granted three acres of land, and the fruits thereof, to each of the old settlers.

Dale's successor, Captain Samuel Argall, a relative of Sir Thomas Smith, arrived in 1617, and found such increased laxity during the interim administration of Captain George Yeardley that he did not hesitate to reimpose Dale's Laws. Argall ordered every person to go to church Sundays and holidays or suffer torture and "be a slave the week following." He also imposed forced labor more severely.

Fortunately, for the success of the Virginia colony, the Virginia Company came into the hands of the Puritans in London. Sir Thomas Smith was ousted in 1619 and his post as treasurer of the company was assumed by Sir Edwin Sandys, a Puritan leader in the House of Commons who had prepared the draft of the amended charter of 1609. Sandys, one of the great leaders of the liberal dissent in Parliament, had helped to draw up the remonstrance against the conduct of James I in relation to the king's first Parliament. Sir Edwin had urged that all prisoners have benefit of counsel; had advocated freedom of trade and opposed monopolies and feudalism; had favored religious toleration; and generally had espoused the grievances of the people against the Crown. For Virginia, Sandys wanted to abandon the single company plantation and to encourage private plantations, the ready acquisition of land, and speedy settlement.

The relatively liberal Puritans removed and attempted to arrest Argall, and sent Sir George Yeardley to Virginia as governor. Yeardley at once proceeded to reform the despotic laws of the colony. He substituted a much milder code in November 1618 (called by the colonists "The Great Charter"): everyone was still forced to attend Church of England services, but only twice each Sunday, and the penalty for absence was now reduced to the relatively innocuous three shillings for each offense. Yeardley also increased to fifty acres the allotment of land to each settler, thereby speeding the dissolution of communism, and also beginning the process of transferring land from the company to the individual settler who had occupied and worked it. Furthermore, land that had been promised to the settlers after a seven-year term was now allotted to them immediately.

The colonists themselves testified to the splendid effects of the Yeardley reforms, in a declaration of 1624. The reforms

> gave such encouragement to every person here that all of them followed their particular labors with singular alacrity and industry, so that . . . within the space of three years, our country flourished with many new erected Plantations. . . .
> The plenty of these times likewise was such that all men generally were sufficiently furnished with corn, and many also had plenty of cattle, swine, poultry, and other good provisions to nourish them.

In his Great Charter, Yeardley also brought to the colonists the first representative institution in America. The governor established a General Assembly, which consisted of six councillors appointed by the company, and burgesses elected by the freemen of the colony. Two burgesses were to be elected from each of eleven "plantations": four "general plantations," denoting subsettlements that had been made in Virginia; and seven private or "particular" plantations, also known as "hundreds." The four general plantations, or subsettlements, each governed locally by its key town or "city," were the City of Henrico, Charles City, James City (the capital), and the Borough of Kecoughtan, soon renamed Elizabeth City. The Assembly was to meet at least annually, make laws, and serve as the highest court of justice. The governor, however, had veto power over the Assembly, and the company's edicts continued to be binding on the colony.

The first Assembly met at Jamestown on July 30, 1619, and it was this Assembly that ratified the repeal of Dale's Laws and substituted the milder set. The introduction of representation thus went hand in hand with the new policy of liberalizing the laws; it was part and parcel of the relaxation of the previous company tyranny.

The other major factor in the survival of the colony was the discovery by

John Rolfe, about 1612, that Virginia tobacco could be grown in such a way as to make it acceptable to European tastes. Previously, Virginia tobacco had been regarded as inferior to the product that had been introduced to the Old World by the Spanish colonies in America. By 1614 Rolfe was able to ship a cargo of tobacco to London and meet a successful market. Very rapidly, Virginia possessed a staple and an important economic base; tobacco could be readily exported to Europe and exchanged for other goods needed by the colonists. By 1617 tobacco was being planted even in the streets of Jamestown. An index to the extremely rapid rate of growth of the tobacco production is the quantity of Virginia tobacco imported by England: 2.5 thousand pounds in 1616; 50,000 pounds in 1618; 119,000 pounds in 1620; and 203,000 pounds in 1624.

Even though tobacco was truly the lifeblood of the little colony, the government—of Britain and of Virginia—could not keep from trying to cripple its growth. King James was aesthetically offended by the spread of the fashion for that "idle vanity," smoking, and so placed a heavy duty on tobacco to limit its import. In that way, presumably, Englishmen would only smoke "with moderation, to preserve their health." Sir Thomas Dale, alarmed at the prospects of monoculture, decreed it a crime for a planter not to raise an additional two acres of corn for himself and each servant—presumably no person was to be trusted with the far more efficient procedure of raising tobacco, and with the proceeds buying his own corn from whomever he desired. Even the patron saint of Virginia tobacco, John Rolfe, was appalled at its rapid spread, thus showing a far skimpier knowledge of economics than of the technology of tobacco. Even the liberal Sir Edwin Sandys took this position and deplored the spread of tobacco and the deemphasis on corn. Only Captain John Smith showed economic sense by pointing out the reason for the colonists' seemingly peculiar emphasis on tobacco over corn: a man's labor in tobacco could earn six times as much as in grain.

The first General Assembly added to the regulations on tobacco: every settler was forced to plant, each year, a certain quota of other plants and crops; the price of tobacco was fixed by law, and any tobacco judged "inferior" by an official government committee was ordered burned. The latter regulation was the first of continuing attempts by tobacco planters to restrict the supply of tobacco (in this case, low-priced, "inferior," leaf) in order to raise the price received from the buyers and ultimately from the consumers.

If tobacco was partly responsible for the survival of the colony, it was also indirectly responsible for the introduction into America of grievous and devastating problems. For one thing, the natural process of transferring the land from a ruling company to the individual settler, roughly to the extent to which he brought the land into use, was sharply altered and blocked. Tobacco farming required much larger estates than truck or other individual farms. Hence, the wealthier tobacco planters sought and obtained very large land grants from the company.

One method of obtaining land was distributing to the colonists by "head-right"—that is, each immigrant received fifty acres, and anyone who paid for an immigrant's passage received fifty acres of land per immigrant from the company. As a result, the wealthier planters could acquire vast tracts by accumulating numerous headrights.

Furthermore, large grants of land were made to leading stockholders of the company. For one thing, each individual planter received a grant of 100 acres for each share of stock he held in the company. To raise cash for its hard-pressed finances, the company also sold "bills of adventure," entitling the holders not to stock, but specifically to 100 acres of Virginia land per "bill." Each bill was the same denomination as a company share (£12 10s). Often, billholders joined together to take up allotments of lands to be held for speculation. As a result of these practices, several "particular plantations" emerged as settlements in large land grants, presided over by the private government of the grantee. The largest particular plantation was Berkeley's Hundred, 4,500 acres on the north side of the upper James River, granted as a first dividend to five prominent stockholders headed by the Berkeleys and settled in 1619. Other plantations were Smith's Hundred, Martin's Hundred, Bennett's Plantation, and Martin's Brandon.

Arbitrary land allocations were also made by the governor and the assembly. Thus 3,000 acres in the capital and three other general plantations were reserved to the company, with the settlers being confined to tenants. The proceeds were to go toward the expenses of government. Land was also reserved for support of the local officials and ministers, and as a subsidy for local artisans. A substantial grant was given to Governor Yeardley, and 10,000 acres were reserved for a proposed university at Henrico.

The crucial point, however, is that the planters would not have been able to cultivate these large tobacco plantations—and therefore would not have been moved to acquire and *keep* so much land—if they had had to rely on free and independent labor. So scarce was such labor in relation to land resources that the hiring of free labor would not have been economically feasible. But the planters then turned to the use of forced labor to render their large plantations profitable: specifically, the labor of the indentured servants and of the even more thoroughly coerced Negro slaves. In slavery, the laborer is coerced not only for a term of years, or for life, but for the lives of himself and all his descendants. It was an ironic commentary on the later history of America that 1619, the very year of the Yeardley reforms, saw the first slave vessel arrive at Jamestown with twenty Negroes aboard, to be sold as slaves to the tobacco planters. Until the mid-seventeenth century, the planters preferred to rely on indentured serf labor. These white servants, once their term had expired, could obtain their land, generally fifty acres each, on the western fringe of the settlement, and become independent settlers. But Negro slavery, unlike indentured service, had no means of dissolving into the general society; once introduced, it became the backbone of the Virginian (and other Southern) labor system. It could only remain as a continual canker on the American body social.

The tiny colony was apparently not too young to have "foreign affairs"; and, indeed, it learned all too quickly the ways of interstate relations. French settlers had the temerity to found a colony of their own at Mount Desert (in what was later to be Maine) and on the banks of the Bay of Fundy (in what was later to become Nova Scotia). This "trespassed" upon the land that King James had arbitrarily granted to the Plymouth Company, which had not yet made any settlement in North America. It also trespassed on the greater glory of England. And so, Southern Virginia did the honors: Captain Samuel Argall, disguising his ship as a fishing vessel, sailed from the colony up to Mount Desert in 1613, eradicated the French settlement, and kidnapped fifteen French settlers, including two Jesuit priests. Hauled to Virginia, the prisoners were badly treated. Over a dozen of the hapless French settlers were turned loose by Argall on the Atlantic in an open boat, but they had the good fortune to be rescued by fishing vessels. Later in the year, Argall returned north and expanded his work of destruction, putting to the torch the settlements of St. Croix and Port Royal, the latter in Nova Scotia, and driving the settlers into the woods. A few years later, Captain Argall, now governor of Virginia, continued the tradition by participating in piratical activities against Spanish shipping. He sailed under the aegis of the king's favorite among the company stockholders, the Earl of Warwick.

4

From Company to Royal Colony

King James I encountered growing troubles with the Puritans at home, and grew increasingly restive about the Puritan Virginia Company. For one thing, the king had ousted Sandys from his post as treasurer, only to find him replaced by Sandys' liberal ally, the Earl of Southampton; the disgruntled and influential Sir Thomas Smith persisted in advising the king to confiscate the company. Finally, King James managed, in 1624, to obtain from a court under his domination, the annulment of the charter of the Virginia Company.*

The abrupt change in government, though unwelcome to the Virginia settlers, scarcely altered the social structure of the Virginia colony—for, surprisingly, the king did not disturb the land titles and land privileges that had been allocated to individuals and groups by the company. For many years, indeed, the colony continued to grant land in exchange for the company's shares. These allotments continued to be made in large tracts, and generally the best tracts—in contrast to the small frontier settlements of the indentured servants—along the navigable rivers. One result of this pattern of land allocation, and of the heavy reliance on forced labor, was that Virginia—in contrast, as we shall see, to the New England system—was thinly settled over an extended area with few towns or villages.

*One of King James' maneuvers against the company was to have the Privy Council suspend, in 1622, the use of the lottery as a fund-raising device, although it had been authorized in the amended charter of 1612. This turnabout contributed greatly to the financial difficulties of the Company and its going into receivership in 1623. Lotteries had accounted for £8,000 of the total Virginia Company budget of less than £18,000 in fiscal year 1621. Pressures against the company's right to finance itself by lottery came also from the ousted Smith group, and from capitalists who feared the competition for funds of the lottery device.

The tobacco planters prospered, and increased their reliance on indentured service and, after midcentury, on Negro slavery.

The London Company, after granting land to the individual settlers, had reserved to itself the feudal quitrent, in this case, of two shillings per 100 acres. Since the quitrent was not payable for seven years, until 1625, the Crown upon seizure of the assets of the London Company took over the proprietary privilege and collected the first quitrents from the settlers. However, the British government did not bother to enforce collection of the dues.

At first the governor, now appointed by the king; his council, chosen by the king from among the wealthiest and most prominent of Virginians nominated by the governor; and the representative burgesses continued to sit together. But soon they were divided into two houses: the Council, and the House of Burgesses. The Council also functioned as the supreme judicial body of the colony when sitting as the General Court. Thus the legislative and judicial powers were combined. Before this court came all the major criminal and civil cases. The local county courts had direct jurisdiction over minor cases with appeals permitted to the General Court. The councillors held office indefinitely; they were usually reappointed whenever a new governor arrived. The increase in the number of settlers and settlements, as well as a decline of the importance of the particular plantations, brought about in 1634 a change in the political divisions of the colony. Hence a change occurred in the composition of the House of Burgesses. Instead of the system of general and particular plantations, eight counties were created, counties that followed settlement westward along the rivers of Virginia. The eight original counties were: on the James River, Elizabeth City, Wanasqueoc (later Isle of Wight), Warwick River (later Warwick), James City, Charles City, and Henrico; on the Charles (New York) River, Charles River County; and encompassing the Eastern Shore, Accomack County. Two burgesses were now chosen from each county, and one from each of the leading towns, by qualified property holders.

Thus emerged an English Parliament in miniature. The governor, however, as the king's proconsul in the colony, was the dominant governing influence. He commanded the army and navy, directed religious affairs, appointed justices of the peace and other court officials, and called together or dissolved the Assembly at will; he could also veto any law that the Assembly might pass. He presided over the Council, which consented to the judicial appointments, and, as we have seen, effectively controlled its membership. He was the major ruler of the colony.

Local officials were all appointed directly by the governor and his Council. The major local officials were the justices of the peace, who performed both the judicial and the executive functions for their areas.

5

The Social Structure of Virginia:
Planters and Farmers

But if the royal governor was the leading governing power, *de facto* he shared the rule over Virginia society with an oligarchy of very large tobacco planters, who, as we have seen, were granted large tracts of choice river land, and who were able to command and exploit the labor of slaves and indentured servants for their plantations. This ruling class of large planters permeated the officers of colonial government: they constituted the entire Council—the upper house of the Assembly and supreme judicial body—and a majority of the House of Burgesses. In addition, they were the major county officers—judges, colonels of the militia, and revenue officers. The large planters also made up the vestry that governed each parish, the smallest political unit. The next larger unit, the county, was ruled by several justices of the peace, appointed by the governor from among the planters. The justices of the peace held county court, administered roads and police, and assessed taxes. Orders of the county court were executed by the sheriff and the county lieutenant, commander of the local militia; both were appointed by the governor, with the advice of the county court.

The great bulk of the free populace were not large planters, but small farmers with holdings of fifty to a few hundred acres. These were independent yeomen who had acquired titles to the land they were to settle by headright grant, or at the end of their indentured term of service. A few small farmers had one or two indentured servants, but most had none, the labor being performed by the farmer and his family. Despite the rule of the royal governor and the preemption of choice land and the use of slaves by the large planters, the yeomen enjoyed a far freer, more mobile society than they had ever known. They were free, above all, from the hopelessness of the rigid feudalism and caste structure that they had left behind in England. Here they were, at last, owners of their own land and products. They were pioneers, hewing out their living from a new and untapped continent.

The bulk of Virginians in the colonial era made their living from the soil, and so the society and the economy were almost wholly agrarian. Even the few town dwellers were close to agrarian life and traded agrarian produce. Scattered thinly over a wide area, the agricultural population used the rivers as the primary method of transportation: roads by land were poor and travel difficult. Even merchants were scarce, and the planters depended on English ships for their merchandise. Far-off London and Bristol were virtually their nearest market towns; there they maintained factors as agents in trade. The poorer farmers were often served by neighboring planters, who would thus function intermittently as middlemen in lieu of specialized merchants nearby. The wealthy planters were able to trade in quantity, and to "break bulk" for the smaller farmers.

While the great export staple was tobacco, each of the large plantations functioned like the feudal manor: each was a nearly self-sufficient economic entity, producing its own food, clothing, and shelter, and importing large equipment and luxury items of consumption for the planters.

Tobacco production continued to grow spectacularly: American tobacco imported by England amounted to 203,000 pounds in 1624, reached over 17.5 million pounds by 1672, and 28 million pounds in 1688.* As tobacco production grew, its price naturally fell: from sixpence to a penny or less a pound. As a result, the lot of the small tobacco farmers became increasingly difficult, and they found it harder and harder to compete with the larger plantations, which were staffed with slave and bondservant labor. An increased use of slave labor after 1670 widened the gulf between the planters and the small farmers.

The ruling planters, naturally enough, aspired to the life of the English country nobility. As their prosperity improved, so did their culture and learning. In the colonial period there was little of that aura of "magnolia and roses," or of the pampered idleness, often attributed to the Virginia aristocracy. As we have seen, they were often deep in trade, and the Virginia planters had none of the traditional aristocratic contempt for hard work or for trading. They were not securely wealthy enough to afford shirking the unremitting task of managing their estates.

They were, in short, not yet established enough in privilege to assume a European aristocratic attitude toward business. Even the large planters could not relax from their task of trying to make profits and avoid losses. Despite their privileges, a life of idle dandyism would have led to

---

*The last two figures include imports from Maryland, a colony carved out of the original Virginia Company land grant, but the point is still made.

rapid bankruptcy. Neither did the pseudoheroics of song and story abound, and dueling was virtually unknown anywhere in the colonies.*

Increasingly, the planters cultivated learning: they amassed home libraries of the best knowledge of the time and they sent their sons to good schools in England. Culturally, spiritually, and economically, they felt themselves to be outposts of Europe rather than adjuncts to the wild interior of the American continent. Typical of the great Virginia planters was William Byrd II. Toward the end of the seventeenth century Byrd was sent by his father to school in England. There he had a legal training and later studied business methods in Holland, and then was apprenticed to a firm of merchants in London. While in London, he became a friend of such leading writers as William Congreve; Byrd himself wrote literary and scientific papers. Back in Virginia, he corresponded with various English noblemen, and amassed one of the best libraries in the colonies— over 3,600 volumes—and a handsome collection of paintings by English artists. Books in Byrd's and other libraries included works of law, science, history, philosophy, the classics, theology, sermons, agriculture—indeed, virtually every branch of learning of the time. In addition to the Byrds, some of the other ruling planter families by the end of the seventeenth century were the Carters, the Fitzhughs, the Beverleys, the Lees, the Masons, and the Harrisons.

For those who could not afford schooling in England, the scattered peopling of Virginia made education difficult to come by. The planter would try to hire a tutor for his children, and often several neighboring planters would jointly hire tutors. Often the teachers were indentured servants *bought* from other masters for the purpose.

Early in the colony's history, King James and the Virginia Company tried to found a school, but their efforts came to naught. The first successful school in Virginia was founded by the planter Benjamin Symmes, who in 1635 left 200 acres and eight cows for the education of children from Elizabeth City and Kecoughtan parishes. This school was soon established as the Symmes Free School. The Eaton Free School was established in 1659, in Elizabeth City, by Thomas Eaton, with a gift of 500 acres of land. These schools began a pattern of many private "free schools" founded by wealthy planters of Virginia (generally in their wills). The schools collected tuition from parents able to pay, and admitted poor children and orphans free. The schools generally taught the three Rs and a little Latin. Children on farms remote from the schools were taught, if at all, by their parents or by the local parson.

---

*Dueling was not a venerable tradition in America, but had to wait until the early nineteenth century: "That refinement of chivalry had to wait until our ancestors had steeped themselves in the tales of Sir Walter Scott" (Louis B. Wright, *The Cultural Life of the American Colonies: 1607–1763* [New York: Harper & Row, Torchbooks, 1962], p. 6).

6

The Social Structure of Virginia: Bondservants and Slaves

Until the 1670s, the bulk of forced labor in Virginia was indentured service (largely white, but some Negro); Negro slavery was negligible. In 1683 there were 12,000 indentured servants in Virginia and only 3,000 slaves of a total population of 44,000. Masters generally preferred bondservants for two reasons. First, they could exploit the bondservants more ruthlessly because they did not *own* them permanently, as they did their slaves; on the other hand, the slaves were completely their owners' capital and hence the masters were economically compelled to try to preserve the capital value of their human tools of production. Second, the bondservants, looking forward to their freedom, could be more productive laborers than the slaves, who were deprived of all hope for the future.

As the colony grew, the number of bondservants grew also, although as servants were repeatedly set free, their proportion to the population of Virginia declined. Since the service was temporary, a large new supply had to be continually furnished. There were seven sources of bondservice, two voluntary (initially) and five compulsory. The former consisted partly of "redemptioners" who bound themselves for four to seven years, in return for their passage money to America. It is estimated that seventy percent of all immigration in the colonies throughout the colonial era consisted of redemptioners. The other voluntary category consisted of apprentices, children of the English poor, who were bound out until the age of twenty-one. In the compulsory category were: (a) impoverished and orphaned English children shipped to the colonies by the English government; (b) colonists bound to service in lieu of imprisonment for debt (the universal punishment for all nonpayment in that period); (c) colonial criminals who were simply farmed out by the authorities to the mastership of private employers; (d) poor English children or adults kidnapped by professional "crimps"—one of whom boasted of seizing 500 children annually for a dozen years; and (e) British convicts choosing servitude in America for seven to fourteen years in lieu of all prison terms in England. The last were usually petty thieves or political prisoners—and Virginia absorbed a large portion of the transported criminals.

As an example of the grounds for deporting political prisoners into bondage, an English law in force in the mid-1660s banished to the colonies anyone convicted three times of attempting an unlawful meeting—a law aimed mostly at the Quakers. Hundreds of Scottish nationalist rebels, particularly after the Scottish uprising of 1679, were shipped to the colonies as political criminals. An act of 1670 banished to the colonies anyone with knowledge of illegal religious or political activity, who refused to turn informer for the government.

During his term of bondage, the indentured servant received no monetary payment. His hours and conditions of work were set absolutely by the will of his master who punished the servant at his own discretion. Flight from the master's service was punishable by beating, or by doubling or tripling the term of indenture. The bondservants were frequently beaten, branded, chained to their work, and tortured. The frequent maltreatment of bondservants is so indicated in a corrective Virginia act of 1662: "The barbarous usage of some servants by cruel masters being so much scandal and infamy to the country . . . that people who would willingly adventure themselves hither, are through fears thereof diverted"—thus diminishing the needed supply of indentured servants.

Many of the oppressed servants were moved to the length of open resistance. The major form of resistance was flight, either individually or in groups; this spurred their employers to search for them by various means, including newspaper advertisements. Work stoppages were also employed as a method of struggle. But more vigorous rebellions also occurred especially in Virginia in 1659, 1661, 1663, and 1681. Rebellions of servants were particularly pressing in the 1660s because of the particularly large number of political prisoners taken in England during that decade. Independent and rebellious by nature, these men had been shipped to the colonies as bondservants. Stringent laws were passed in the 1660s against runaway servants striving to gain their freedom.

In all cases, the servant revolts for freedom were totally crushed and the leaders executed. Demands of the rebelling servants ranged from improved conditions and better food to outright freedom. The leading example was the servant uprising of 1661 in York County, Virginia, led by Isaac Friend and William Clutton. Friend had exhorted the other servants that "he would be the first and lead them and cry as they went along *who would be for liberty and freed from bondage* and that there would be enough come to them, and they would go through the country and kill those who made any

71

opposition and that they would either be free or die for it."* The rebels were treated with surprising leniency by the county court, but this unwonted spirit quickly evaporated with another servant uprising in 1663.

This servant rebellion in York, Middlesex, and Gloucester counties was betrayed by a servant named Birkenhead, who was rewarded for his renegacy by the House of Burgesses with his freedom and 5,000 pounds of tobacco. The rebel leaders, however,—former soldiers under Cromwell—were ruthlessly treated; nine were indicted for high treason and four actually executed. In 1672 a servant plot to gain freedom was uncovered and a Katherine Nugent suffered thirty lashes for complicity. A law was passed forbidding servants from leaving home without special permits and meetings of servants were further repressed.

One of the first servant rebellions occurred in the neighboring Chesapeake tobacco colony of Maryland. In 1644 Edward Robinson and two brothers were convicted for armed rebellion for the purpose of liberating bondservants. Thirteen years later Robert Chessick, a recaptured runaway servant in Maryland, persuaded several servants of various masters to run away to the Swedish settlements on the Delaware River. Chessick and a dozen other servants seized a master's boat, as well as arms for self-defense in case of attempted capture. But the men were captured and Chessick was given thirty lashes. As a special refinement, one of Chessick's friends and abettors in the escape, John Beale, was forced to perform the whipping.

In 1663 the bondservants of Richard Preston of Maryland went on strike and refused to work in protest against the lack of meat. The Maryland court sentenced the six disobedient servants to thirty lashes each, with two of the most moderate rebels compelled to perform the whipping. Facing *force majeure*, all the servants abased themselves and begged forgiveness from their master and from the court, which suspended the sentence on good behavior.

In Virginia a servant rebellion against a master, Captain Sisbey, occurred as early as 1638; the lower Norfolk court ordered the enormous total of one hundred lashes on each rebel. In 1640 six servants of Captain William Pierce tried to escape to the Dutch settlements. The runaways were apprehended and brutally punished, lest this set "a dangerous precedent for the future time." The prisoners were sentenced to be whipped and branded, to work in shackles, and to have their terms of bondage extended.

By the late seventeenth century the supply of bondservants began to dry up. While the opening of new colonies and wider settlements increased the *demand* for bondservants, the *supply* dwindled greatly as the English government finally cracked down on the organized practice of kidnapping and on the shipping of convicts to the colonies. And so the planters turned to the import and purchase of Negro slaves. In Virginia there had been 50

*Abbot E. Smith, *Colonists in Bondage*.

Negroes, the bulk of them slaves, out of a total population of 2,500 in 1630; 950 Negroes out of 27,000 in 1660; and 3,000 Negroes out of 44,000 in 1680—a steadily rising proportion, but still limited to less than seven percent of the population. But in ten years, by 1690, the proportion of Negroes had jumped to over 9,000 out of 53,000, approximately seventeen percent. And by 1700, the number was 16,000 out of a population of 58,000, approximately twenty-eight percent. And of the total *labor force*—the working population—this undoubtedly reflected a considerably higher proportion of Negroes.

How the Negro slaves were treated may be gauged by the diary of the aforementioned William Byrd II, who felt himself to be a kindly master and often inveighed against "brutes who mistreat their slaves." Typical examples of this kindly treatment were entered in his diary:

2-8-09:	Jenny and Eugene were whipped.
5-13-09:	Mrs. Byrd whips the nurse.
6-10-09:	Eugene (a child) was whipped for running away and had the bit put on him.
11-30-09:	Jenny and Eugene were whipped.
12-16-09:	Eugene was whipped for doing nothing yesterday.
4-17-10:	Byrd helped to investigate slaves tried for "High Treason"; two were hanged.
7-1-10:	The Negro woman ran away again with the bit in her mouth.
7-15-10:	My wife, against my will, caused little Jenny to be burned with a hot iron.
8-22-10:	I had a severe quarrel with little Jenny and beat her too much for which I was sorry.
1-22-11:	A slave "pretends to be sick." I put a branding iron on the place he claimed of and put the bit on him.

It is pointless to criticize such passages as only selected instances of cruel treatment, counterbalanced by acts of kindness by Byrd and other planters toward their slaves. For the point is not only that the slave system was one where such acts *could* take place; the point is that *threats* of brutality underlay the whole relationship. For the essence of slavery is that human beings, with their inherent freedom of will, with individual desires and convictions and purposes, are used as *capital*, as tools for the benefit of their master. The slave is therefore habitually forced into types and degrees of work that he would not have freely undertaken; by necessity, therefore, the bit and the lash become the motor of the slave system. The myth of the kindly master camouflages the inherent brutality and savagery of the slave system.

One historical myth holds that since the slaves were their masters' *capital*, the masters' economic self-interest dictated kindly treatment of their property. But again, the masters always had to make sure that the property was really *theirs*, and for this, systematic brutality was needed to turn labor from natural into coerced channels for the benefit of the master. And, second, what of property that had outlived its usefulness? Of capital that no longer promised a return to the master? Of slaves too old or too ill to continue earning their masters a return? What sort of treatment did the economic self-interest of the master dictate for slaves who could no longer repay the costs of their subsistence?

Slaves resisted their plight in many ways, ranging from such nonviolent methods as work slowdowns, feigning illness, and flight, to sabotage, arson, and outright insurrection. Insurrections were always doomed to failure, outnumbered as the slaves were in the population. And yet the slave revolts appeared and reappeared. There were considerable slave plots in Virginia in 1687, 1709–10, 1722–23, and 1730. A joint conspiracy of great numbers of Negro and Indian slaves in Surry and Isle of Wight counties was suppressed in 1709, and another Negro slave conspiracy crushed in Surry County the following year. The slave who betrayed his fellows was granted his freedom by the grateful master. The 1730 uprising occurred in five counties of Virginia, and centered on the town of Williamsburg. A few weeks before the insurrection, several suspected slaves were arrested and whipped. An insurrection was then planned for the future, but was betrayed and the leaders executed.

Joint flight by slaves and servants was also common during the seventeenth century, as well as joint participation in plots and uprisings. In 1663 Negro slaves and white indentured servants in Virginia plotted an extensive revolt, and a number of the rebels were executed. The colonists appointed the day as one of prayer and thanksgiving for being spared the revolt. Neither slave nor indentured servant was permitted to marry without the master's consent; yet there is record of frequent cohabitation, despite prohibitory laws.

It has been maintained in mitigation of the brutality of the American slave system that the Negroes were *purchased* from African chieftains, who had enslaved them there. It is true that the slaves were also slaves in Africa, but it is also true that African slavery never envisioned the vast scope, the massive dragooning of forced labor that marked American plantation slavery. Furthermore, the existence of a ready white market for slaves greatly expanded the extent of slavery in Africa, as well as the intensity of the intertribal wars through which slavery came about. As is usually the case on the market, demand stimulated supply. Moreover, African slavery did not include transportation under such monstrous conditions that a large percentage could not survive, or the brutal "seasoning" process in a West Indies way station to make sure that only those fit for slave conditions survived, or the continual deliberate breaking up of slave families that prevailed in the colonies.

From the earliest opening of the New World, African slaves were imported as forced labor to make possible the working of large plantations, which, as we have seen, would have been uneconomic if they had had to rely, as did other producers, on free and voluntary labor. In Latin America, from the sixteenth century on, Negro slavery was used for large sugar plantations concentrated in the West Indies and on the north coast of South America. It has been estimated that a total of 900,000 Negro slaves were imported into the New World in the sixteenth century, and two and three-quarter million in the seventeenth century.*

Negroes came into use as slaves instead of the indigenous American Indians because: (a) the Negroes proved more adaptable to the onerous working conditions of slavery—enslaved Indians tended, as in the Caribbean, to die out; (b) it was easier to buy existing slaves from African chieftains than to enslave a race anew; and (c) of the great moral and spiritual influence of Father Bartolome de Las Casas in Spanish America, who in the mid-sixteenth century inveighed against the enslavement of the American Indians. Spanish consciences were never agitated over Negro slavery as they were over Indian; even Las Casas himself owned several Negro slaves for many years. Indeed, early in his career, Las Casas advocated the introduction of Negro slaves to relieve the pressure on the Indians, but he eventually came to repudiate the slavery of both races. In the seventeenth century two Spanish Jesuits, Alonzo de Sandoval and Pedro Claver, were conspicuous in trying to help the Negro slaves, but neither attacked the institution of Negro slavery as un-Christian. Undoubtedly one reason for the different treatment of the two races was the general conviction among Europeans of the inherent inferiority of the Negro race. Thus, the same Montesquieu who had scoffed at those Spaniards who called the American Indians barbarians, suggested that the African Negro was the embodiment of Aristotle's "natural slave." And even the environmental determinist David Hume suspected "the Negroes to be naturally inferior to the whites. There scarcely ever was a civilized nation of that complexion, nor even an individual, eminent either in action or speculation. No ingenious manufacturers amongst them, no arts, no sciences. On the other hand, the most rude and barbarian of the whites . . . have still something eminent about them. . . . Such a uniform and constant difference could not happen, in so many countries and ages, if nature had not made an original distinction between these breeds of men."

Contrary to the views of those writers who maintain that Negroes and whites enjoyed equal rights as indentured servants in Virginia until the 1660s, after which the Negroes were gradually enslaved, evidence seems clear that from the beginning many Negroes were slaves and were treated far more harshly than were white indentured servants.** No white man,

*Over the seventeenth and eighteenth centuries, only about one-fifteenth of the total Negro imports into the New World arrived in the territory of what is now the United States. That the slaves fared even worse in the Latin American colonies is seen by the far higher death rate there than in North America.

**Cf. Winthrop D. Jordan, "Modern Tensions and the Origins of American Slavery," *Journal of Southern History* (February 1962), pp. 17-30.

for example, was ever enslaved unto perpetuity—lifetime service for the slave and for his descendants—in any English colony. The fact that there were no slave statutes in Virginia until the 1660s simply reflected the small number of Negroes in the colony before that date.* From a very early date, owned Negroes were worked as field hands, whereas white bondservants were spared this onerous labor. And also from an early date, Negroes, in particular, were denied any right to bear arms. An especially striking illustration of this racism pervading Virginia from the earliest days was the harsh prohibition against any sexual union of the races. As early as 1630 a Virginia court ordered "Hugh Davis to be soundly whipped, before an assembly of Negroes and others for abusing himself to the dishonor of God and shame of Christians by defiling his body in lying with a Negro." By the early 1660s the colonial government outlawed miscegenation and interracial fornication. When Virginia prohibited all interracial unions in 1691, the Assembly bitterly denounced miscegenation as "that abominable mixture and spurious issue."**

Other regulations dating from this period and a little later included one that forbade any slave from leaving a plantation without a pass from his master; another decreed that conversion to Christianity would not set a slave free, a fact which violated a European tradition that only heathens, not Christians, might be reduced to slavery.

By the end of the seventeenth century, the growing Virginia colony had emerged from its tiny and precarious beginnings with a definite social structure. This society may be termed partly feudal. On the one hand, Virginia, with its abundance of new land, was spared the complete feudal mold of the English homeland. The Virginia Company was interested in promoting settlement, and most grantees (such as individual settlers and former indentured servants) were interested in settling the land for themselves. As a result, there developed a multitude of independent yeomen settlers, particularly in the less choice up-country lands. Also, the feudal quitrent system never took hold in Virginia. The settlers were charged quitrents by the colony or by the large grantees who, instead of allowing settlers to own the land or selling the land to them, insisted on charging and trying to collect annual quitrents as overlords of the land area. But while Virginia was able to avoid many crucial features of feudalism, it introduced an important feudal feature into its method of distributing land, especially the granting of large tracts of choice tidewater river land to favorite and wealthy planters. These large land grants would have early dissolved into ownership by the individual settlers were it not for the regime of forced labor, which made the large tobacco plantations profitable. Fur-

---

*Ibid. Jordan cites many evidences of Negro slavery—including court sentences, records of Negroes, executions of wills, comparative sale prices of Negro and white servants—dating from 1640, before which time the number of Negroes in Virginia was negligible.

**"Spurious" in colonial legislation meant not simply illegitimate, but specifically the children of interracial unions.

thermore, the original "settlers," those who brought the new land into use, were in this case the slaves and bondservants themselves, so it might well be said that the planters were in an arbitrary quasi-feudal relation to their land even apart from the large grants.

Temporary indentured service, both "voluntary" and compulsory, and the more permanent Negro slavery formed the base of exploited labor upon which was erected a structure of oligarchic rule by the large tobacco planters. The continuance of the large land tracts was also buttressed by the totally feudal laws of entail and primogeniture, which obtained, at least formally, in Virginia and most of the other colonies. Primogeniture compelled the undivided passing-on of land to the eldest son, and entail prevented the land from being alienated (even voluntarily) from the family domain. However, primogeniture did not exert its fully restrictive effect, for the planters generally managed to elude it and to divide their estate among their younger children as well. Hence, Virginia land partly dissolved into its natural division as the population grew. Primogeniture and entail never really took hold in Virginia, because the abundance of cheap land made *labor*—and hence the coerced supply of slaves—the key factor in production. More land could always be acquired; hence there was no need to restrict inheritance to the eldest son. Furthermore, the rapid exhaustion of tobacco land by the current methods of cultivation required the planters to be mobile, and to be ready to strike out after new plantations. The need for such mobility militated against the fixity of landed estates that marked the rigid feudal system of land inheritance prevailing in England. Overall, the wealth and status of Virginia's large planters was far more precarious and less entrenched that were those of their landowning counterparts in England.

7

Religion in Virginia

Religion played an extremely significant role in the life of the man of the seventeenth century—a century of great religious wars, schisms, and revolutions ensuing from the Protestant Reformation of the sixteenth century. England suffered not only under feudalism, but under its corollary, the established state church. Indeed, one of the causes of the Reformation, expecially in England, was the desire of the rising absolutism of the Crown to bring the church in Great Britain under its domination.* The Church of England, appointed and controlled by the Crown, fulfilled this ambition.

The original founders naturally believed that Virginia would be as rigorously Anglican as the old country itself. King James I—that scholarly enthusiast for his own divine right—enjoined the Virginia colonists in the first charter of 1606 to propagate the true religion: "We, greatly commending . . . the desires for the furtherance of so noble a work, which may hereafter tend to the glory of his Divine Majesty, in propagating of Christian religion to such people, as yet live in darkness and miserable ignorance of the true knowledge and worship of God and man in time bring the infidels and savages, living in those parts, to human civility, and to a settled and quiet government. . . ."

Much of the motivation, at least as officially proclaimed, for the founding of the colony was the desire to establish a Protestant bulwark against Catholic Spain. Many leading Anglican ministers, including John Donne, dean of St. Paul's, propagandized for the Virginia Company's settlement

---

*As always, a corollary to power was loot, and one of the attractions of the Reformation to England was the opportunity it afforded Henry VIII to confiscate the property of the monasteries and to distribute and sell the seized assets to favorites of the Crown.

on these grounds. One of the preachers in the earliest settlement, the Reverend Alexander Whitaker, wrote a tract, *Good News from Virginia*, which was published by the Virginia Company in 1613 and which proclaimed that to doubt the future of the Virginia colony was to doubt the promises of God.

From the first settlement at Jamestown, the Anglican religion was the established church of the colony. The Virginia General Assembly periodically enacted laws to compel conformity, but the lure of profits led the landowners—eager for new settlers and servants—to relax *de facto* religious pressures on the immigrants, and such laws as compulsory church attendance were rarely enforced.

The new conditions faced in America—the great distance from home, the new lands, the freer social structure—caused Virginia's Anglican church to develop very differently from the mother church. From the beginning, control by the bishop of London was loose, and each church came to be controlled by its own vestry—elected by vote of its parishioners, but in practice by the leading planters of the parish—rather than by the central government of the Church of England. Whereas the governor of Virginia had the right to induct ministers for life, the vestries called ministers for a year or a term of years, and rarely offered ministers for induction. Thus Virginia developed a decentralized—almost a congregational—government in its dominant Anglican church.

Although the church was decentralized, Virginia was nonetheless theocratic. The affairs of the smallest political unit, the parish, were governed by the church vestry, which had the power to levy local taxes. While theoretically elected by the parishioners, the vestrymen actually filled their own vacancies and so became a self-perpetuating oligarchy.

Informality and decentralization were also fostered by the thin, extensive settlement of the land; hence the scattering of churches over the Virginia countryside. Time and again the high-church hierarchy in England deplored the disorder, the neglect of ritual, the informality of prevailing low-church Virginia practice. One of Virginia's leading planters, Robert Carter, expressed a typical sentiment when in 1720 he wrote:

> I am of the Church of England way. . . . But the high-flown, up-top notions and great stress that is laid on ceremonies, any further than decency and conformity, are what I cannot come into reason of. Practical godliness is the substance—these are but the shell.

Liberalism in religion, however, proceeded but part way, and the hand of theocracy was often evident. Virginia, alarmed at Roman Catholicism in the neighboring colony of Maryland, passed an act "Concerning Popish Recusants." The act levied the very heavy fine of twenty pounds per month for any failure to attend Anglican services. It also imposed life imprisonment and the confiscation of property on anyone who refused to take the Oath of Allegiance of 1605. This loyalty oath had been decreed by King

James I in 1605 as a method of cracking down on Catholics, following the abortive Gunpowder Plot. From the granting of the first charter, King James had imposed a loyalty oath of allegiance and supremacy on all Virginia colonists; refusal was supposed to incur the death penalty. Indeed, the laxity of the London Company in enforcing the loyalty oath, caused by its desire to encourage settlement, was one of King James' major charges against the company that led to its dissolution.

As a further persecution of the few Roman Catholics—they were virtually nonexistent in the colony—the mass and the sacraments were prohibited, tutoring one's children in the Catholic religion was outlawed, and life imprisonment and confiscation of property were decreed for anyone sending their children to English-speaking Catholic schools in France or Spain. This extreme legislation remained in force until 1662, the Restoration period, when the act was quietly allowed to lapse. In 1643 a law was passed forbidding Catholics from holding office and outlawing all priests in the colony. After the Restoration, apart from the imposing of oaths of loyalty to the state church for public officials, the theocratic rule relaxed somewhat, although the heavy fine for nonattendance at Anglican services continued. Again, a partially mitigating factor was that these harsh laws were not always rigorously enforced. Thus, the leading—and virtually the only—Catholic family in the colony, headed by planter George Brent, a relative of the Maryland Carrolls, was allowed to move to Virginia about 1650 and to remain there relatively undisturbed. In Brent's case, laxity was encouraged by the thinness of the population in Virginia, the virtual nonexistence of Catholics in the colony, and the prominence and pronounced royalist sympathies of this tobacco planter.

8

The Royal Government
of Virginia

From their earliest days, Virginians engaged in conflicts with their government. The first open rebellion while Virginia was under royal rule occurred in 1635. This arose from a territorial dispute with the new neighboring colony of Maryland (see below). William Claiborne, a leader of the Virginia colony and secretary of its Council, had obtained a royal license to establish a fur-trading post on Kent Island, between Maryland and Virginia, which he had purchased from the Indians. The Virginia House of Burgesses—which included a representative from Kent Island—backed Claiborne in his refusal to recognize the overlordship of the Maryland feudal proprietor, Lord Baltimore. Egged on by a competing Virginia fur trader's accusation that Claiborne was inciting the Indians to attack the Marylanders, Lord Baltimore ordered the seizure of Claiborne and the confiscation of his property. Maryland's ships attacked and seized a vessel of Claiborne's, and not only killed several Kent Islanders in the process, but also hanged one as a "pirate" after the battle. Governor John Harvey of Virginia angered the Virginians by taking the side of Lord Baltimore, removing Claiborne from his office as secretary, and jailing an official who sided with Claiborne. Harvey here showed his ability to judge the winning side, as the Crown also ruled against Claiborne in 1638. This and other tyrannical actions by Governor Harvey brought about an open revolt by the Council led by Samuel Mathews, a former indentured servant, at the head of several hundred armed men.

Aside from high-handed personal actions, Harvey was accused of making unauthorized expenditures, levying export taxes on tobacco and fees on each immigrant, and requisitioning ammunition from ships entering the colony. However, among the rash of legitimate complaints against Harvey was the charge that he had made a dangerous peace with the Indians without the Council's consent. It must be remembered that the settlers not only protested against despotic actions of the government, but were also hell-bent for grabbing as much land as possible from the Indians; accordingly, peace with the natives was the last thing that the settlers desired.

Thus the Council was driven to meeting and it "thrust out" Harvey from the colony in 1635. Harvey was shipped back to England and Captain John West appointed in his place until the king's wishes could be known. As soon as he arrived in England, Harvey again showed his character by having arrested the two negotiators whom the Council had sent to England to plead its case. One of them, Francis Pott, was still languishing in prison a year later, and under harsh conditions.

Harvey was reappointed by the Crown and returned to Virginia in 1637, thirsting for vengeance against the rebellious colonists. First, Harvey, backed by Lord Baltimore, had his chief enemies arrested for treason and hauled to England to appear before the Court of Star Chamber. Those arrested included Captain John West, Samuel Mathews, and George Menefie, as well as William Claiborne. True to his personal vow that he would not leave Captain Mathews with assets "worth a cow's tail," Harvey confiscated his enemies' property in Virginia. The Crown, however, forced Harvey to disgorge the seized property. Harvey also concluded that humor was dangerous to the state, and he consequently arrested the Reverend Anthony Panton, rector for some of the leading rebels. Panton's crime was apparently calling the man who Harvey had appointed secretary of the colony instead of Claiborne, a "jackanapes." The "trial" of Panton was conducted by none other than Richard Kemp himself—the new secretary in question—who acted as both prosecutor and judge. Sentence was meted out by Kemp with appropriate severity: the seizure of Panton's possessions, his expulsion from his parish, and exile from Virginia—with the penalty of death should he return to the colony. Harvey also moved to impose a tithing tax on the corn of Panton's parishioners, presumably a special punishment for their lack of wisdom in having Panton as their rector.

This monstrous procedure was too much for even the rather callous sensibilities of the day. The Crown suspended the sentence and finally removed Harvey in 1639. The decision against Panton was reversed and his property and parish restored. The imprisoned Council leaders were released and restored to their positions. The "mutiny" of the Virginia leaders against Governor Harvey's despotic rule had finally succeeded. It was Harvey's successor, Governor Francis Wyatt, who was instructed to convene periodic meetings of the Virginia Assembly, thereby making Virginia's representative body a permanent one.

One lasting consequence of Claiborne's colony was the settlement in 1645 of the Northern Neck of Virginia (the peninsula between the Rappahannock and the Potomac rivers) by refugees from Kent Island.

The most prominent figure in the government of Virginia in the seventeenth century was the governor Sir William Berkeley, whose term of office began in 1642 and continued, with interruption, until 1677. In contrast to the later years of his term, Berkeley's first years found him a liberal reformer. The entire poll tax, both the tax paid to the governor and the general tax, was repealed; peace was made with the Indians; taxes on estates were lowered; impoverished debtors in prison were given relief; and such relics of Virginia Company oppression as condemnations were abolished. In addition, a law was reenacted to prevent the governor and the Council from levying any taxes or appropriating any new money except by authority of the Assembly. Berkeley also ended some of the land abuses in Virginia by removing arbitrary James River Valley particular-plantation grants that had never been settled, and allowing settlers to enter these lands and gain title to them.

Soon after Berkeley took office, the Virginia colony found itself confronted with a revolution in Great Britain. Staunchly royalist in that era, Virginia stood firm for the Crown. Virginia's devotion to the royal cause was shaped by its own particular experience. For one thing, Charles I's rule in Virginia had been relatively moderate, far different indeed from the tyranny he was imposing on England. Virginians had been permitted to enjoy more freedom and local rule than Englishmen had ever enjoyed before. The oppressive Navigation Acts had not yet been imposed. The king had removed the hated John Harvey. Governor Berkeley's reforms had been welcomed. Moreover, Anglican-Puritan relations were not nearly as exacerbated as in the home country. As we have seen, Virginia's own Anglicanism was decidedly low church; the Pilgrim fathers had been invited to Virginia in 1620 and an influential moderate Puritan group settled, during the 1640s, in southside Virginia. (This is not to say that religious liberty prevailed: Puritans were sporadically persecuted and dissenting ministers driven from the colony.) Finally, to the Virginians, the rule of the old Virginia Company had been far worse than royal rule: petitioning against any reimposition of the company, the Assembly exclaimed that the colonists, if under the scepter of the company, would be subject to arbitrary rule, their property rights would be taken from them, and their freedom of trade—"the blood and life of a commonwealth"—would be sacrificed to the monopoly of the company.

While attached to the Crown, many Virginians protested immediately when in 1648 the governor and the Council claimed authority to conscript (impress) soldiers without the concurrence of the House of Burgesses, and when they proceeded to conscript a ten-man bodyguard for the governor. The Assembly gave as one excuse for agreeing to this conscription the existence of a "schismatical party" (the Puritans and Dissenters) disaffected from the government.

In 1649, when Parliament had executed Charles I, Virginia stood stubbornly by the Old Order and proclaimed its continued allegiance to the House of Stuart. Indeed, the Virginia Assembly denounced the King's execution bitterly, defied the proclaimed authority of Parliament, and proceeded to uphold this view savagely by decreeing it a crime carrying the death penalty for anyone even to defend the execution. In fact, anyone making so bold as to question the right of succession of Charles II, or to propose any change in the existing government of Virginia, was to be charged with high treason. Even speaking any evil of the king was to be punished at the arbitrary discretion of governor and Council. Virginia also offered refuge to prominent emigrés—the Cavaliers, for example, faithful supporters of the Crown. The Cavaliers, largely of wealthy merchant and landed families, took their accustomed place among the leading planting families in Virginia, including the prominent Lees, Carters, Randolphs, and Masons, and, indeed, the bulk of the men who remained as the dominant planters of Virginia.*

In retaliation, Parliament in 1650 passed the embryo of the first Navigation Act, which forbade Virginia from trading with foreign countries or with any foreign ships lacking a special license—thus hitting at England's efficient Dutch competitors. It is instructive that this first important measure of restrictive mercantilism was specifically proclaimed to be a punishment to a rebellious colony. Parliament concluded by denouncing the Virginians as rebels and traitors.

When news of Parliament's punitive action reached Virginia in early 1651, the reaction of the Virginia rulers was both perceptive and heroically defiant. Comparing the situation in Virginia with that in England, Governor Berkeley told the Assembly: "Consider yourselves how happy you are, and have been, how the gates of wealth and honor are shut on no man, and that there is not an arbitrary hand, that dares to touch the substance either poor or rich." What can be hoped from submission to parliamentary dictates? Now, Berkeley went on, the Virginians enjoyed freedom from oppression, peace, and the opportunity to gain wealth, and "the security to enjoy this wealth when gotten. . . . We can only fear the Londoners, who would fain to bring us to the same poverty, wherein the Dutch found and relieved us, would take away the liberty of our consciences, and tongues, and our right of giving and selling our goods to whom we please." The governor and the members of the Assembly then unanimously adopted a "Vindication" for their actions. The Vindication perceptively concluded that Parliament was punishing the trade of Virginia in order to appease the "avarice of a few interested persons [the big London merchants], who endeavor to rob us of all we sweat and labor for."

In 1652 Parliament sent a fleet with four commissioners to Virginia to bring the recalcitrant colony to heel. Fortunately, the commissioners were moderates and the instructions liberal. Furthermore, the Virginians, after

*See Richard L. Morton, *Colonial Virginia* (Chapel Hill: University of North Carolina Press, 1960), 1:166–68. For a rather different account of this immigration, cf. Bernard Bailyn, "Politics and Social Structure in Virginia," in *Seventeenth-Century America*, ed. James M. Smith (Chapel Hill: University of North Carolina Press, 1959), pp. 98–100.

raising an army of over a thousand men, wisely decided that discretion was the better part of warfare, and submitted to the commissioners' force. In return, the rule of the parliamentary commissioners turned out to be liberating rather than vindictively repressive. Not only was the royalist Berkeley deposed and Commissioner Richard Bennett substituted as governor with the agreement of the Burgesses, but executive and judicial powers were shorn from the governor and the governing power placed in the House of Burgesses, the colony's elected house and miniature Parliament. The supreme legislative, executive, and judicial power was now vested in the House of Burgesses, where at least the Virginians themselves could exercise *some* check on state power. Virginia was declared "free from all taxes, customs and impositions," and it was affirmed that none could be levied without consent of the Assembly, and that no garrisons could be maintained there without the same consent. Virginian trade was no longer to be singled out for discriminatory treatment. Berkeley himself was permitted to retire undisturbed to his Virginia estate.

Again, as in other matters, liberalism went only so far, and all inhabitants who refused to swear an oath of allegiance to Parliament were ordered exiled from the colony. On the other hand, the majority of the people of any parish was permitted to keep using the Anglican Book of Common Prayer.

Partially in fidelity to its revolutionary principles, partially from preoccupation with pressing affairs at home, Parliament left Virginia pretty much alone during the decade of the republic. In one sense, too much alone—for Bennett and the new secretary of the colony, William Claiborne, the veteran anti-Marylander, determined to take up the cause of the Virginia irredenta and forcibly bring Maryland back under the Virginia motherland. However, the new lord protector, Oliver Cromwell, soon scotched these efforts and in a few years Virginia and Lord Baltimore finally settled peacefully the Virginia-Maryland boundary.

The leading home-rule problem within Virginia, in those years, was the grievance of Northampton County on the Eastern Shore. Northampton protested in May 1652 against paying poll taxes of forty pounds of tobacco when it had not been represented in the Virginia Assembly for five years; in short, a cry against taxation without representation.

There were some difficulties between Governor Samuel Mathews, Jr. and the Burgesses during the late 1650s over unauthorized actions of the governor as well as his attempt to dissolve the Assembly in a dispute, but the disagreements were amicably resolved and the Burgesses left in unchallenged control.

With the collapse of the republican Protectorate in 1659, and the virtually coincidental death of Governor Samuel Mathews, the Virginia House of Burgesses proclaimed its "supreme power" until England should reassert a legitimate authority. The Burgesses then voluntarily elected the royalist Berkeley governor once more. Achieving total, if temporary, independence from Britain, however, did not improve the civil-libertarian attitude of the Assembly. For it decreed that anyone who should "say or act anything in derogation of the present government" would be punished as an enemy of the peace. The election of Berkeley in March 1660 preceded the restoration of the monarchy in England by two months, and the new king, Charles II, quickly extended the official commission to Berkeley. Granting the extreme royalism motivating Virginia's action and its purely temporary character, the fact remains that Virginia had the boldness to battle England, and even to declare a short-lived independence from the motherland. Surely, whatever the motives, here was an unwitting training ground in revolution, a testing of Virginia's willingness to stand on its own feet and defy the mighty imperial country to which all the colonists had sworn allegiance.

9

British Mercantilism
over Virginia

Rule in the European governments of the seventeenth century was exercised, not only by the great landowners—through feudalism—but also by groups of merchants and capitalists specially privileged and subsidized by the state, in the system that later came to be known as "mercantilism." The essence of mercantilism was the granting or selling of monopolistic privilege and subsidy by the state to favored groups of businessmen. Thus, Crown, feudal nobility, and privileged capitalists exercised rule over the exploited remainder of the populace—which included the bulk of merchants and capitalists who sought profit by voluntary service in the marketplace rather than by obtaining privileges from the coercive power of the state.

From the beginning, government meddling—especially by the English government—fastened the mercantile system on the American colonies. As early as 1619, the Crown imposed a duty of one shilling per pound of tobacco imported by the Virginia Company and in 1622 prohibited any tobacco from being grown in England or Ireland. The motivation for the latter act was not to benefit Virginia, but to increase the revenue seized by the Crown: domestic tobacco producers, after all, paid no customs duty. In 1621 the Crown indeed delivered a grave blow to the company and to Virginia by prohibiting the colonists from exporting tobacco (or any other commodity) to any foreign country without first landing in England and paying customs duty there. It was in vain that the company protested that other English subjects and companies were allowed to sell their goods in the best markets, that the edict would cripple the tobacco-cattle trade with Ireland, that many Virginia products were not salable in England.

The sweetener for the company in this network of restriction was the granting, in 1622, to the Virginia Company of the monopoly privilege of importing tobacco into England and Ireland. The supposedly liberal Sir Edwin Sandys had led the intracompany fight to accept the monopoly, and he and his faction were appointed to manage the monopoly, at extravagant salaries.

In the period of the republic, Parliament—as we have seen hardly reluctant to impose mercantile restrictions for the benefit of merchant groups—began the famous series of Navigation Acts. In 1650 it outlawed foreign ships from trading in the colonies without a license, thus striking a blow at efficient Dutch shipping. The following year, it decreed that no goods from Asia, Africa, or America could be imported into England or its colonies except when the owner and most of the crew were English or English-American. It also prohibited imports of foreign goods in *entrepôt* trade—from countries where the product did not originate, prohibited the importation of fish by aliens, and outlawed all participation of foreign ships in the English coastal trade.

These were blows to the efficiency and prosperity of interregional trade, and to the property, actual and potential, of the colonies, all for the special privileges accorded to inefficient shipowners. To enforce these sweeping prohibitions required a bureaucratic apparatus mighty for the time and place, including a network of paid government informers. So strict was the enforcement that not enough English vessels existed to replace the outlawed Dutch shipping, and grave complaints of shortages spread throughout the English colonies in the Americas—including the West Indies. The rebellious Virginia Assembly asserted in 1655 that freedom of trade would be maintained, and demanded that sea captains pay bond not to molest Dutch or other foreign shipping.

England, however, continued to tighten its mercantile restrictions, especially after monarchical rule had been restored. Thus, the Navigation Act of 1660 provided that no goods whatever could be imported into or exported from any English colony except in English-owned ships (of which at least three-fourths of the crew must be English), and compelled certain important enumerated colonial products (including tobacco) to be shipped only to England—thus outlawing colonial export trade in these goods to any other country. All ships leaving the colonies were required to give bond that they would not ship the goods elsewhere. The Navigation Act of 1662 extended these privileges: all future ships not built in English shipyards were now to be excluded from this colonial trade.

The mercantilist structure of the Navigation Acts was completed in 1662 with the exclusion of all European goods (except for a few commodities) from the colonial market except as shipped from English ports and in English-built ships. Colonial governors were charged with the responsibility of enforcement of the navigation laws, but in practice the power was delegated to a naval officer appointed in England.

The navigation laws continued to be tightened still further. The Navigation Act of 1673 moved against the attempt of the planters to maintain some of their tobacco trade by selling to other colonies. The act placed a prohibitive tax of one penny on each pound of tobacco shipped from one colony to another, and appointed customs commissioners to collect the duty. This act crippled the flourishing tobacco trade with New England. More sweeping was the Navigation Act of 1696, which confined *all* colonial trade to English-built ships, enlarged the powers of the colonial naval officers, and gave the provincial custom officers the right of forcible entry, which they already enjoyed in England. The act led to the establishment of vice admiralty courts in the colonies to enforce the regulations. Operating under Roman law, a vice admiralty court could try and convict without having to submit the cases to colonial juries, which were almost unanimous in their sympathy with any arraigned smugglers.

We have mentioned the drastic fall in the prices of tobacco in the seventeenth century. Much of this drop was due not to the great expansion of the Virginia tobacco crop, but to the Navigation Acts and their smashing of the export market for tobacco in Holland and other countries in Europe. Before the Navigation Acts, the Dutch had paid three pence per pound for Virginia tobacco; after the acts, the tobacco price had fallen to half a penny per pound by 1667. The fall was aggravated by the heavy losses of the English tobacco fleet in the wars with Holland (the Dutch wars of 1664–67 and 1672–73). To offset the crisis, Virginia turned to domestic mercantilism: compulsory cartels to raise tobacco prices. But since such an increase could only be accomplished by coerced restrictions on tobacco acreage, this meant that tobacco markets were not being widened, and prosperity could not be restored to the colony as a whole. In a compulsory tobacco cartel, some tobacco producers could only benefit at the expense of others, and of the rest of the colony's population. In brief, quotas based on existing production must privilege the inefficient grower and the large grower about to fall behind in the competitive race, and discriminate against the efficient, and the new up-and-coming planters. In the "Plant-Cutting Riots" of 1682, the planters benefiting from the quotas organized bands of vandals to go from plantation to plantation destroying the tobacco crop.

The protection from foreign competition accorded by the Navigation Acts to British shippers not only ruined the Virginians' tobacco market (and that of neighboring Maryland's planters as well); it also raised the prices of the gamut of imported goods now confined to British ships. Thus, Virginians suffered doubly from the imperial restrictions.

English enforcement of the Navigation Acts was unfortunately rigorous, especially in the Southern colonies. Three wars of aggression against the Dutch between 1652 and 1675 drove the Dutch—the more efficient of England's competitors—out of the Chesapeake trade. The very geography of the Chesapeake Bay area made enforcement easy: the English navy needed only to control the narrow entrance of the bay to keep foreign ships from buying or selling to the Virginia or Maryland plantations.

Thus, the English orientation of Virginia trade and finance was compelled by the Navigation Acts, which gravely injured Virginians and retarded Virginia development. Furthermore, the canker of slavery was also due partly to the Navigation Acts. The economic pressure of the acts on the planters led them to look to slavery as a way to cut costs by exploiting forced labor. Moreover, the English government forbade Virginia from restricting the infamous slave trade, the monopoly of which had by the wars against the Dutch been assured to British traders.

John Bland, a London merchant who had traded with the Dutch in Virginia tobacco, presented the excellent case of the Chesapeake planters against the Navigation Acts—but, unfortunately, to no avail.

Added to the devastation caused by the Navigation Acts was the burden of increased taxes. In addition to the crippling penny a pound on all coastal tobacco trade imposed in 1673, the hated poll tax was reimposed, In his first years of rule, Governor Berkeley had abolished the poll tax, which, being levied equally on all, particularly burdened the poorer strata of the population. In 1674, however, when Berkeley reintroduced the poll tax, a number of farmers assembled with their arms in Kent County to prevent collection of the new taxes, by force if necessary. This incipient tax rebellion was dispersed upon Berkeley's proclamation that tax rebels would be accounted guilty of treason and punished accordingly.

Greatly adding to the grievances of most Virginians was the steady accumulation, ever since his reappointment, of absolute rule in the hands of Governor Berkeley and his clique of allies in the great planter oligarchy. No sooner was he reappointed governor than Berkeley seized control of the House of Burgesses: he filled the seats with his own henchmen and repudiated the Virginia tradition of frequent elections. In fact, he refused to call any election for the House of Burgesses from 1661 on, and only called meetings of the Assembly at his pleasure. Any recalcitrant burgesses were bribed with public offices, all of which were appointed by the governor. Berkeley's absolute control of the Council—always dominated by the governor—was assured by the fact that the bulk of the councillors were allowed to die without being replaced, were not called together, or were out of reach. Now Berkeley was in full control of both houses of the Assembly. In 1670 Berkeley and the Assembly further tightened oligarchic control by taking the franchise away from nonlandowners. Berkeley also assumed supreme judicial power as president of the General Court of the colony. Oligarchic control by the leading planters over local government was further tightened; the vestries, for example, became self-perpetuating local governing bodies. County courts, made up of the great planters, met in secret to impose the county levy, which more and more placed tax burdens on the poor. Exorbitant fees were paid to sheriffs, clerks, and other local officials out of these taxes, and there was considerable graft involved in the heavy expenditures needed to construct forts westward on the rivers.

Power is always used to acquire wealth, and here was no exception. Berkeley and his allies granted themselves the best lands, most of the public offices, and a monopoly of the lucrative fur trade with the Indians. Another of Berkeley's tyrannical actions was to have the Assembly re-establish the Anglican church, and also to bring pressure for a governmental college that would include Anglican teaching of the youth.

Whenever anyone in the American colonies in the seventeenth century decided to embark on a policy of tyranny and religious persecution, the first group to bear the brunt was usually the hapless Quakers—of all sects the least devoted to idolatry of church or state. Upon embarking on the dictatorial rule of his second term, Governor Berkeley did not hesitate to revive the old laws against Dissenters, and naturally concentrated on the handful of Quakers. An English Quaker, George Wilson, upon arriving at Jamestown in 1661, was thrust into a dungeon, scourged, and kept in irons until death. While dying, he wrote, in a truly saintly manner: "For all their cruelty I can truly say, Father, forgive them, they know not what they do." The previous year 1660, the Assembly had passed an act outlawing "an unreasonable and turbulent sort of people commonly called Quakers . . . [who are] endeavoring . . . to destroy religion, laws, communities and all bonds of civil society." Apparently these "bonds of civil society" were to rest, not on voluntary consent, but on the dungeon and the torture rack.

In 1662 Berkeley decreed heavy fines on any Nonconformists who refused to have their children baptized, and threatened to exile any ship masters who brought any Dissenters into the colony. The next year two Quaker women entered Virginia, spreading the message in the colony. The two, Mary Tomkins and Alice Ambrose, were imprisoned and inflicted with thirty-two lashes from a whip of nine cords. After this their property was seized and they were expelled from Virginia.

It stands to reason that a man with this sort of attitude toward religious liberty and search for truth should be vehemently hostile toward education, freedom of inquiry, and individual and collective search for the truth. We are fortunate to have on record, however, a classic statement by Berkeley, revealing the despot's fury toward learning and free inquiry. When asked in 1671 by the Crown what he had been doing to instruct the people in the Christian religion, Berkeley, in the course of his answer, declared: "I thank God, *there are no free schools* nor *printing* and I hope we shall not have these hundred years; for *learning* has brought disobedience, and heresy and sects into the world, and *printing* has divulged them, and libels against the best government. God keep us from both!" Learning and culture apparently were to be reserved to the safe hands of the ruling class, and were not to be permitted the ruled, who might learn enough to want to cast off their chains.

The inherent conflicts within Virginia's society, as well as between Virginia and England, were further aggravated by an enormous land grant made by Charles II to Lord Hopton and a group of his friends, including Berkeley's brother, Sir John, in 1649. This was a grant of over five million acres, constituting the partially settled Northern Neck of Virginia between the Potomac and Rappahannock rivers. The Hopton grant was assigned to Lord Culpeper in 1689. Even more startling was the joint proprietary grant of *all* Virginia in 1673 to two royal favorites, Lords Arlington and Culpeper, for a term of thirty-one years. The latter grant generated fierce opposition in Virginia because, for one thing, the Crown had been collecting the quitrents on Virginia lands in haphazard fashion, whereas Lords Culpeper and Arlington could be expected to make the best out of their feudal grant. The new proprietors were given the power to establish churches and schools, to appoint ministers and teachers. And they were given the power to appoint the sheriffs and other officers to grant lands and to create towns and counties.

Suddenly the Virginians were now confronted with the specter of absolute proprietary feudal rule, as well as the deprivation of all their liberties and their considerable measure of home rule. Indeed, no guarantees for the rights of Virginians were included in the Arlington-Culpeper grant.

The alarmed Assembly met the following year (1674) and protested that the grants would threaten the rights of the people, impose upon them new rents and dues, new grants and levies, and deprive them of the present protection of their rights and properties. The Virginians insisted that they wanted no privileged proprietors, whether individuals or chartered company, standing between them and the Crown and exploiting them still more. At heavy expense the Assembly sent commissioners to London to ask for removal of the grant. The negotiators eventually persuaded Lords Arlington and Culpeper to abandon all claims on the colony except quitrents and escheats (revenue from intestate estates). Pressures by the indignant Virginians had ended the threat of proprietary government over the Virginia colony.

In the course of the negotiations, the commissioners and the two proprietors agreed that Virginia should buy back the vast Northern Neck grant for £400 to each proprietor, and that the quitrents on the remaining lands should continue to be paid to the Crown, thus ending feudal quitrents in the colony. The proprietary grant of 1673 was to be revoked and no further grants made without consulting the Virginia Council.

A new liberal charter in preparation would have provided that the governor and the members of the Council of Virginia must be residents of the colony and that no taxes could be imposed on Virginia without consent of the House of Burgesses. The charter drawn up by the king's solicitor-general declared that the taxation provision "contains that which we humbly conceive to be the right of Virginians, as well as all other English-men, which is, *not to be taxed but by their consent, expressed by their representatives.*" Unfortunately this new charter was blocked upon the outbreak of rebellion in Virginia in 1676.

Neither did the losses suffered by Berkeley's administration in the Dutch War, during 1673, endear the government to the people of Virginia. One of the principal motives of the aggressive English war against the Dutch, beginning in 1672, was to drive the Dutch out of the Virginia trade. The Dutch attacked Virginia and succeeded in sinking eleven Virginia merchantmen laden with tobacco. Neither the war nor the losses were calculated to gain the support of the populace; indeed, many Virginians oppressed by English rule welcomed the Dutch invasion and the prospective shift of sovereignty to the Netherlands.

If we consider then the situation in Virginia in the mid-1670s we can see the accumulation of grievances and the aggravation of conflicts: the sudden feudal proprietary grant of all Virginia to Lords Arlington and Culpeper in 1673; the exclusive landed property franchise in 1670; the reimposition of the poll tax in 1674, and the general increase in taxation; and the establishment of tight rule by the Berkeley clique. To these we might add Berkeley's persecution of the Dissenters, virtually driving them out of the colony.

Hints of revolt and mutiny against Berkeley began to emerge in the 1670s. On December 12, 1673, fourteen people met at Lawnes Creek Parish Church in Surry County to protest against excessive taxation and to insist that they would thereafter refuse to pay their taxes. Here was one of the first tax rebellions, or organized refusals to pay taxes, in America. On January 3, the very day that Berkeley's judges issued a writ to haul the fourteen into court for "sedition," the group met again in a field and one of their leaders, Roger Delke, declared that "we will burn all before one shall suffer." Berkeley lost no time in hauling the rebels into court where Delke explained that they had met "by reason their taxes were so unjust, and they would not pay it." Very heavy fines were levied on the protesters, especially on the main leader of the Surry tax protest, Matthew Swan, who continued to insist that the taxes were unjust. Proceedings against Swan lasted longer than against the others, and in April 1674 Swan was brought before the Council and General Court of Virginia for his "dangerous contempt and unlawful project and his wicked persisting in the same." Berkeley was forced, however, by popular resentment at the treatment accorded the tax rebels, to remit all the fines some months later.

Many of the tax strikers were prominent landowners of the county. Matthew Swan was possibly related to Colonel Thomas Swann, a member of the Council; Delke's father had been a member of the House of Burgesses. Several other protesters were related to former burgesses, and one was a relative of one of the judges issuing a writ for their arrest. Furthermore, a near uprising was called off in 1674 and two mutinies occurred in the following year. All in all, the stage was set for one of the most important American armed rebellions against English authority in the colonial era: Bacon's Rebellion of 1676.

10

Relations with the Indians

The spark that set off the great rebellion of 1676 came from the tinderbox of Indian relations. To explain them we must first go back to chart the history of Indian-white relations in seventeenth-century Virginia.

First, we may ask, how did the colonists go about the task urged upon them by King James, of bringing "the infidels and savages living in those parts [the native American Indians] to human civility"? Generally we may say that the native American Indians regarded the newcomers with a mixture of brotherly kindness and eagerness to make contact with the world outside; this, however, was countered by hostility based on the well-founded fear that the colonists were out to seize their lands. The whites generally regarded the Indians as possessors of land ripe for expropriation. This attitude of the whites was partially justified, as Indian land was typically owned not by the individual, but by the collective tribal unit, and furthermore was inalienable under tribal law. This was particularly true of the land itself as contrasted to its annual use. Furthermore, tribal law often decreed land ownership over large tracts of even unused acreage. Still, however, this land inequity provided no excuse for the physical dispersion of individual Indians from their homes and from land actually used, let alone the plundering of their crops and the slaughtering of the Indian people.

Relations with the Indians were therefore a combination of hostility and friendship, underlain by the relentless white urge to push westward. Thus, from the very beginning of the Virginia colony, the Indians first attacked the whites, only to save the starving infant colony a few months later by coming to its rescue with abundant gifts of bread, meat, fish, and corn. A few years of conflict was followed by the peace of 1614, which was effectively wrecked two years later by Governor Yeardley's seizure of corn from the Chickahominy Indians—an ironic contrast to the Indians' supplying needed corn to the infant colony. From that point on, relations with the Indians began to deteriorate. Captain Argall, upon assuming his duties as governor, decided that the colonists were too friendly with the Indians, and took harsh steps to rectify this error. He outlawed all private trading with the Indians, and prohibited the hiring of Indian hunters for the shooting of game. Worse still, Argall decreed the death penalty both for anyone teaching an Indian the use of a gun and for the Indian eager to learn. Thus, Argall moved to cripple the economy of the whites and Indians alike; but perhaps trade and education were not considered part of the "civilizing process." (Guns, of course, as in the case of most weapons, can be used for offense or defense, for highly productive economic—hunting—as well as for martial purposes.)

When the Virginia Assembly first convened in 1619, a part of its liberal reforms forbade any injury to the Indians that might disturb the peace. The brief period of peaceful coexistence, however, was shattered in 1622, when Opechancanough, head of the Powhatan confederacy, led an all-out surprise attack against the colonists. The colony survived but the massacre of over 350 colonists—almost one-fourth of the colony—embittered the whites from that point on, even though the colonists were very quick to wreak vengeance on the Indians, destroying as many crops, homes, and Indians as they could.* During the crisis every settled community was placed under absolute martial rule, and any communication with an Indian was outlawed except by consent of the commander.

Perhaps the most unfortunate aspect of the affair, for its long-run consequence in poisoning Indian-white relations in Virginia, was the white aggression later in 1622 against the friendly Potomac Indians. The powerful Potomac tribe had refused to join the Powhatan confederacy plot to massacre the whites, and indeed had helped to save the colony from destruction by warning the colonists of Opechancanough's plot. While on an expedition to the Potomacs to obtain corn, Captain Isaac Madison allowed himself to believe, without proof, the false tale of an exiled Potomac chief and of a renegade Polish interpreter, Robert Poole, that the Potomacs were planning to massacre the expedition. Madison then kidnapped the Potomac king and suddenly attacked and massacred any Potomac Indian he could lay his hands on.

From then on, savage treachery marked the actions of both sides, and relations were permanently embittered. Most vicious was the colonists' invitation to the Indians in 1623 for a peace parley, at which the whites poisoned two hundred Indian leaders and shot fifty others, taking home the scalps of many Indians with them. Doubtless worst of all, the colonists

*The massacre was also seized as one of the Crown's excuses for dispossessing the Virginia Company.

adopted the barbaric policy of deliberately seeking out and destroying all Indian plantings of corn. Total war by any means was now the watchword, and no peace was even contemplated. When the Virginia Company leaders expressed shock at this despicable method of making war by breaking treaties, poisoning peace negotiators, etc., the Virginians replied: "Whereas we are advised by you to observe rules of justice . . . we hold nothing injust that may tend to their ruin. . .with these [enemies] neither fair war nor quarter is ever to be held."

For years after the massacre, the attitude of the whites was continued aggression against the Indians, who were simply considered "unreconcilable enemies." Laws were passed prohibiting any trading with the Indians. Peace for a time was unthinkable; as we have seen, one of the main charges against Governor Harvey was making peace with the Indians. Finally, however, the advantages of peaceful and mutually beneficial trade with the natives began to become evident and the law to be ignored by enterprising individuals in the colony. During the first Berkeley administration, a treaty of "peace and friendship" was made with the Indians in 1642 and the laws against trading with the natives were repealed.

Unfortunately, the fair prospects for genuine peace were once again ruptured by the old chief Opechancanough, the very man responsible for the tragic massacre twenty-two years earlier. Opechancanough was a hard-liner who would settle for nothing less than total victory over the whites, whom he regarded as invaders of the land. He certainly had a point: the whites were indeed adept at land grabbing; but the point was not good enough. A genuine climate of peaceful coexistence could have permitted voluntary purchase of Indian lands and white settlement on lands which the Indians, while grandiosely claiming them, were not really using. But Opechancanough, hearing of civil war in England, decided that "now was his time or never, to root out all the English" and drive them into the sea. Again, in April 1644, Opechancanough organized a surprise massacre that killed 500 settlers—a greater number than earlier but, of course, a vastly smaller proportion of the colony.

One of the problems of a hard line is that it begets hard-lining by the other side, and this massacre came at a time when genuine peace seemed at hand. The English quickly counterattacked, burning Indian villages and destroying their corn. Opechancanough was taken prisoner and shot in the back by one of the Virginia soldiers.

The Indians then sued for peace, but unfortunately the peace treaty of 1646, instead of providing for peaceful trade and other contacts between the two peoples, forced the Indians to cede territory and drew arbitrary boundaries beyond which the Indians were forbidden to come. Moreover, neither the Virginians nor the Indians were permitted to go into each other's territory on pain of very heavy punishment, and trading could only be conducted at certain specified—and therefore monopolized—forts.

This type of quasi-peace greatly restricted white exploration and settlement of Virginia west of the fall line, as well as fruitful trade with the Indian people.

Since a few military forts were given the monopoly privilege of all trade with the Indians, the commander of each fort now occupied a highly lucrative and privileged position in the colony. The Virginia government not only built the forts, but granted them and their surrounding land to their commanders. Typical was Captain Abraham Wood, a former indentured servant of Samuel Mathews, who was placed in command of the most important of these forts, Fort Henry, at the Appomattox falls. Settling there for thirty years, Wood exploited his position as sole authorized trader for the area; often he had to guard his pack trains against the use of force by rival traders understandably resentful at Wood's compulsory monopoly of the Indian trade. The town at the fort took the name of Wood, and Wood acquired over 6,000 acres of plantation land in the neighborhood. He was also for many years a councillor of the colony.

Yet the inexorable march of settlement westward could not be halted, and once again the English came to settle near the Indians. The arbitrary peace terms of the 1646 treaty clearly needed revision. Happily, after 1656 an Indian found without a badge in white territory was no longer liable to be shot and all freemen were allowed to trade with the Indians. Other provisions of the new law constituted a rather limited advance: for example, Indian children kidnapped as hostages were not to be treated simply as slaves, but to be trained as Christians and taught a trade. Other policies were so arbitrary as to deal unjustly not only with the Indians, but also with the white settlers. Thus, in 1653, as supposed compensation to the Indians, lands in York County were set aside and reserved for them, even though this meant that already existing white settlers had to be forcibly removed.

However, peace and justice to the Indian, as always, went only so far. In 1656 several hundred Indians settled near the falls of the James River, which the whites had decided was to be barred from any Indians—even peaceful settlers. The Assembly sent Colonel Edward Hill with an armed force to drive out the Indians; though joined by Indian allies, the attacking force was smashed by Indian defenders near the present site of Richmond. Hill met not with sympathy for his defeat, but with an angry Assembly that tried him and unanimously found him guilty of crimes and weaknesses and suspended him from his posts.

The relatively sound peace of 1656 with the Indians was shattered by the onset of the second Berkeley administration. It is not surprising that Berkeley's onslaught on the liberties and rights of Virginians should have extended to Indian relations. His first step, in 1661, was the suppression of free trade with the Indians and the reviving of trading monopoly. The Assembly decreed that henceforth no one might trade with the Indians without a commission from the governor, who, of course, would license only "persons of known integrity" rather than the "diverse ill-minded, idle, and unskillful people" currently engaged in the trade. The Assembly followed this with a decree outlawing all trade by Marylanders and Indians north of Virginia with the Virginia Indians, thus further tightening the trading monopoly. Ironically, the old trade monopolist Abraham Wood, now a Colonel, was charged with the enforcement of this prohibition.

The next year, Captain Giles Brent, one of the leading planters of the Northern Neck, hauled the chief of the Potomac Indians, Wahanganoche, into court on the false charges of high treason and murder. And even though Wahanganoche was acquitted and his false accusers forced to pay him an indemnity for the wrongs suffered, the Assembly arrogantly proceeded to require the Potomac and other northern tribes to furnish as hostages a number of Indian children, to be enslaved and brought up by whites.

It is no wonder that under this treatment the Indians of Virginia began to get a bit restive, a restiveness due also, as the Assembly admitted, to "violent intrusions of diverse English" into Indian lands. But this was only the beginning of white aggression. In 1665–66 the Assembly set further arbitrary bounds to Indian settlement, pushing back the Indians once more. It also prohibited any white sales of guns and ammunition to the Indians, and decreed that the governor select the chieftains for the Indian tribes. Militarism was imposed on the white settlers by ordering them to go armed to all public meetings, including church services. Even collective guilt was imposed on the Indians, it being provided that if an Indian murdered a white man, all the people of the neighboring Indian town would be "answerable for it with their lives or liberties." But this law taxed even the often elastic consciences of the Virginians of the day, and was soon repealed.

During the same year 1666, Governor Berkeley declared war on the Doeg and Potomac tribes, as an even more massive form of collective guilt and punishment for various crimes committed over the years by individual Indians against individual whites. But since this act of slaughter was called "war," even its far greater magnitude did not evoke the reproofs of conscience following upon the collective punishment of the previous year. By the end of the sixties, the Indians had been so effectively cowed and suppressed that the administration believed the situation well in hand. In the words of Berkeley, "The Indians . . . are absolutely subjected, so that there is no fear of them."

But Governor Berkeley was soon to learn that the use of terror and subjection does not always quiet fears. Particularly aggrieved was the Doeg tribe, which had been attacked and expelled from its lands by the Berkeley adminstration. The Doegs found new compatriots in the Susquehannocks, a powerful tribe that had been expelled from its lands at the head of the Chesapeake Bay by the Seneca nation, and had then settled on inadequate lands on the Potomac River in Maryland. In July 1675 the Doegs, who had also settled across the Potomac, found that a wealthy Virginia planter, Thomas Mathew, refused to pay them a debt, which they were not allowed to collect in the Virginia courts. They decided therefore to collect the debt themselves, and a party of Doegs crossed the river and took some hogs from Mathew. The Virginians immediately pursued the Indians upriver, and not only recovered the hogs, but killed the Indians. Again, the Indians had no recourse against this murder in the Virginia courts, and so they decided to exact punishment themselves. They raided and devastated the Mathew plantation—rough if inexact justice—in the course of which one of Mathew's herdsmen was killed.

Arrant self-righteousness and a flagrant double standard of morality are often characteristic of the side with the superior weapons in any dispute, for its one-sided version of morality can be supported by force of arms if not by force of logic. Such was the case with the white Virginians: murdering a group of Indians whose only crime was the theft of a few hogs (and this justified as the only available means of collecting a debt) was, well, just one of those things; whereas retaliatory retribution against the one white largely responsible for the whole affair was apparently considered so monstrous that *any* method of vengeance against the Indians was justified. When the razing of the Mathew plantation became known, Major George Brent and Colonel George Mason—leading persecutors of Chief Wahanganoche a decade before—gathered an armed force and invaded Maryland. Upon finding the Indians, Brent asked for a peace parley, at which he seized and then shot the Doeg chief (thus continuing a white tradition of treachery in dealing with Indians). Brent followed this up by shooting ten other Indians who had then tried to escape. Mason's party shot fourteen other fleeing Indians, many of whom were Susquehannocks, up to now wholly friendly to the whites, and who had not participated in Doeg actions. The Susquehannocks were now naturally embittered.

The treachery at the peace parley and the murdering of twenty-four Indians only began the massive white retaliation. Berkeley completely ignored the protest of the Maryland governor against the Virginian invasion of its territory and the killing of innocent Indians. Instead, on August 31, 1675, Berkeley called together the militia officers of the Northern Neck counties, led by Colonel John Washington, and armed them with powers to organize the militia and to "demand satisfaction" or take any other course necessary against the Indians. This could include "attack and such executions upon the Indians as shall be found necessary and just." The officers duly organized the militia and secured aid from the Maryland government. A full-fledged war of aggression against the Indians was then unleashed by Virginia and Maryland. On September 26, the joint Virginia-Maryland force besieged the main fort of the Susquehannocks on the Maryland side of the Potomac, and sought to starve the Indians into submission. An army of 1,000 whites surrounded 100 Indian braves and their women and children. On the invitation of Major Thomas Truman, head of the Maryland force, five of the Susquehannock chiefs came out to parley and seek peace. When the chiefs asked what the army was doing there, Major Truman declared that they were retaliating for various outrages, and he proceeded to murder them on the spot. Even a silver medal held up by one chief, a token of a supposedly permanent pledge of protection by a former governor of Maryland, was of no avail in saving his life. The starving mass of Indians finally escaped their tormentors by rushing out at night in a surprise breakout, and fled into Virginia, where during January they retaliated against many of the frontier plantations. One of the plantations raided was that of Nathaniel Bacon, Jr., a leading planter and one of the councillors of the colony.*

Ready to send out an even larger armed force against the Indian party, Berkeley received word from the Indians that, having killed ten whites for each of their chiefs murdered at the peace parley, they were ready to make peace and ask for compensation for damages. Grateful for a chance to stop the spiraling bloodshed, Berkeley disbanded his new army. But when Berkeley categorically rejected the peace offer as violating honor and self-interest, the Indian raids continued. Instead of peace, Berkeley and his Assembly decided on an uneasy compromise: a declaration of war not only against all Indians guilty of injuring white persons or property, but also against those who had refused to aid and assist the whites in uncovering and destroying the guilty Indians. However, Berkeley also decided to fight a defensive rather than an offensive war by constructing at great expense ten forts facing the enemy at the heads of the principal rivers, and by not attacking the Indians unless they were attacked themselves. The large force needed to garrison these forts was financed by burdensome new taxes, which aggravated Virginia's grievances against the Berkeley regime.

It is another common rule that militarization of a society ostensibly to bring *force majeure* against an enemy often succeeds also (or even only) in bringing that force against the very society being militarized. Thus, soldiers, conscripted into the garrisons, were to be subject to highly rigorous articles of war: any blasphemy, for example, when "either drunk or sober" was punished by forcing the soldier to run the terrible gantlet. Public prayers were to be read in the field or garrison twice a day, and any soldier refusing or neglecting to attend the prayers or the preaching or to show proper diligence in reading homilies and sermons was to be punished at the whim of the commander. A great many Virginians, driven forward by war hysteria, by ingrained hatred of the Indians, and by the desire to grab Indian lands, began to accuse Berkeley of being soft on the Indians. The softness was supposed to be motivated by economic interest, as Berkeley's monopoly of the fur trade was supposed to give him a vested interest in the

---

*Some writers attribute to this incident Bacon's hostility to the Indians. But already the previous fall, Bacon had seized some friendly Appomattox Indians, charging them falsely with stealing corn even though the corn in question was neither his nor his neighbors'.

existence of Indians with whom to trade. The common expression of the day was that "no bullet would pierce beaver skins." The charge, if charge it be, was probably partially correct, at least insofar as trade between peoples generally functions as a solvent of hatreds and of agitations for war. At any rate, in deference to these charges, the Assembly took the Indian trade from Berkeley and his licensees and transferred the authority for licenses to the county justices of the peace.

The middle-of-the-road policy of defensive war, however, was probably the most unpolitic course that Berkeley could have taken. If he had concluded peace, he would have ended the Indian raids and thus removed the constant sparkplug for war hysteria among the whites. As it was, the expensive policy of constructing mighty defensive forts prolonged the war, and hence the irritant, and did nothing to end it. The only result, so far as the Virginians were concerned, was a highly expensive network of forts and higher taxes imposed to pay for them. Furthermore, Berkeley reportedly reacted in his usual tyrannical fashion against several petitions for an armed troop against the Indians, by outlawing all such petitions under threat of heavy penalty.

With peace still not concluded, the frontier Virginians found themselves suffering Indian raids and yet being refused a governmental armed force by Berkeley. They finally determined in April to raise their own army and fight the Indians themselves. While three leaders of this effort were frontier planters on the James and Appomattox rivers, they were hardly small farmers; on the contrary, they were among the leading large planters in Virginia. The chief leader was the eloquent, twenty-eight-year-old Nathaniel Bacon, Jr., descendant of Francis Bacon, a cousin of Lady Berkeley and a member of the select Council of Virginia. The other leaders were William Byrd, founder of the Byrd planter dynasty, and Captain James Crews, another large planter and neighbor of Bacon. The effort quickly emerged, however, not as a new armed force, but as a mutiny against the Virginia government. When the three founders and their friends went to visit a nearby force of militiamen at Jordan's Point in Charles City County, the soldiers decided to mutiny and follow "Bacon! Bacon! Bacon!" and swore "damnation to their souls to be true to him." The mighty Bacon's Rebellion had begun.

11

Bacon's Rebellion

Why? Why revolution? This question is asked in fascination by contemporary observers and historians of every revolution in history. What were the reasons, the "true" motives, behind any given revolution? The tendency of historians of every revolution, Bacon's Rebellion included, has been to present a simplistic and black-and-white version of the drives behind the revolutionary forces. Thus, the "orthodox" version holds Nathaniel Bacon to have been a conscious "torchbearer" of the later American Revolution, battling for liberty and against English oppression; the version of "revisionist" history marks down Bacon as an unprincipled and Indian-hating demagogue rebelling against the wise statesman Berkeley. Neither version can be accepted as such.*

The very search by observers and historians for purity and unmixed motives in a revolution betrays an unrealistic naïveté. Revolutions are mighty upheavals made by a mass of people, people who are willing to rupture the settled habits of a lifetime, including especially the habit of obedience to an existing government. They are made by people willing to turn from the narrow pursuits of their daily lives to battle vigorously and even violently together in a more general cause. Because a revolution is a sudden upheaval by masses of men, one cannot treat the motives of every participant as identical, nor can one treat a revolution as somehow planned and ordered in advance. On the contrary, one of the major characteristics of a rev-

*For the leading expressions of the two points of view, see Thomas Jefferson Wertenbaker, *Torchbearer of the Revolution* (Princeton, N.J.: Princeton University Press, 1940,) for the orthodox interpretation; and Wilcomb Washburn, *The Governor and the Rebel* (Chapel Hill: University of North Carolina Press, 1957), for the revisionist.

olution is its dynamism, its rapid and accelerating movement in one of several competing directions. Indeed, the enormous sense of exhilaration (or of fear, depending on one's personal values and one's place in the social structure) generated by a revolution is precisely due to its unfreezing of the political and social order, its smashing of the old order, of the fixed and relatively stagnant political structure, its transvaluation of values, its replacement of a reigning fixity with a sense of openness and dynamism. Hope, especially among those submerged by the existing system, replaces hopelessness and despair.

The counterpart of this sudden advent of unlimited social horizons is uncertainty. For if the massive gates of the political structure are at last temporarily opened, what path will the people now take? Indeed, the ever-changing and -developing revolution will take paths and entail consequences perhaps only dimly, if at all, seen by its original leaders. A revolution, therefore, cannot be gauged simply by the motivations of its initiators. The paths taken by the revolution will be determined not merely by these motives, but by the resultant of the motives and values of the contending sides—as they begin *and* as they change in the course of the struggle—clashing with and interacting upon the given social and political structure. In short, by the interaction of the various subjective values and the objective institutional conditions of the day.

For masses of men to turn from their daily lives to hurl themselves against existing habits and the extant might of a ruling government requires an accumulation of significant grievances and tensions. No revolution begins in a day and on arbitrary whim. The grievances of important numbers of people against the state pile up, accumulate, form an extremely dry forest waiting for a spark to ignite the conflagration. That spark is the "crisis situation," which may be intrinsically minor or only distantly related to the basic grievances; but it provides the catalyst, the emotional impetus for the revolution to begin.

This analysis of revolution sheds light on two common but misleading historical notions about the genesis of revolutions in colonial America. Conservative historians have stressed that revolution in America was unique; in contrast to radical European revolutions, American rebellion came only in reaction to new acts of oppression by the government. American revolutions were, therefore, uniquely "conservative," reacting against the disruption of the status quo by new acts of tyranny by the state. But this thesis misconceives the very nature of revolution. Revolutions, as we have indicated, do not spring up suddenly and *in vacuo;* almost all revolutions— European or American—are ignited by new acts of oppression by the government. Revolutions in America—and certainly this was true of Bacon's Rebellion—were not more "conservative" than any other, and since revolution is the polar archetype of an anticonservative act, this means not conservative at all.

Neither, incidentally, can we credit the myth engendered by neo-Marxian historians that revolutions like Bacon's Rebellion were "class struggles" of the poor against the rich, of the small farmers against the wealthy oligarchs. The revolution *was* directed against a ruling oligarchy, to be sure; but an oligarchy not of *the* wealthy but of *certain* wealthy, who had gained control of the privileges to be obtained from government. As we have pointed out, the Bacons and Byrds were large planters and the revolution was a rebellion of virtually all the people—wealthy and poor, of all occupations—who were not part of the privileged clique. This was a rebellion not against a Marxian "ruling class" but against what might be called a "ruling caste."*

No common purity of doctrine or motive can be found among the Bacon rebels, or, for that matter, in the succeeding rebellions of the late seventeenth century in the other American colonies. But the bulk of their grievances were certainly libertarian: a protest of the rights and liberties of the people against the tyranny of the English government and of its Virginia agency. We have seen the accumulation of grievances: against English mercantilist restrictions on Virginian trade and property rights, increasing taxation, monopolizing of trade by political privilege, repeated attempts to impose feudal landholdings, tightening rule by the governor and his allied oligarchs, infringements of home rule and local liberties, and, to a far lesser extent, persecution of religious minorities. On the other hand, there is no denying that some of the grievances and motives of the rebels were the reverse of libertarian: hatred of the Indians and a desire for land grabbing, or, as in the allied and later rebellions in neighboring Maryland, hatred of Roman Catholicism.** But even though the spark of Bacon's Rebellion came from an anti-libertarian motif—pursuit of more rigorous war against the Indians, and Bacon's motives were originally limited to this—it is also true that as the rebellion developed and the dynamics of a revolutionary situation progressed, the other basic grievances came to the fore and found expression, even in the case of Bacon himself.

It should also be recognized that any revolt against a tyrannical state, other things being equal, is *ipso facto* a libertarian move. This is all the more true because even a revolution that fails, as did Bacon's, gives the people a training ground and a tradition of revolution that may later develop into a revolution more extensively and clearly founded on libertarian motives. If cherished in later tradition, a revolution will decrease the awe in which the constituted authority is held by the populace, and in that way will increase the chance of a later revolt against tyranny.

Overall, therefore, Bacon's Rebellion may be judged as a step forward to liberty, and even a microcosm of the American Revolution, but *despite*, rather than because of, the motives of Bacon himself and of the original

*See below for further discussion of class and caste.
**Another motive in later rebellion was a desire for a compulsory cartel, in unsound and desperate attempts to force a rise in tobacco prices.

leaders. Nathaniel Bacon was scarcely a heroic and conscious torchbearer of liberty; and yet the dynamics of the revolutionary movement that he brought into being forged such a torch out of his rebellion.

After the start of the mutiny at Jordan's Point, Berkeley, having tried to stop the movement, denounced Bacon and his followers as rebels and mutineers and proceeded west against them. He missed Bacon, however, who had gone north to New Kent County to gather men who were also "ripe for rebellion." Meanwhile, masses of Virginians began to join Bacon—on the most hysterical and bigoted grounds. Berkeley's unfortunate act of war of March 1676 had declared war not only against enemy Indians, but just as roundly against neutrals. The peaceful and neutral Pamunkey Indians, fearful and unhappy at this prospect and terrorized by the Baconians, fled to the wilderness of Dragon Swamp on the Gloucester peninsula. To many Virginians, it was incomprehensible that Berkeley should proclaim men as traitors whose only crime seemed to be hard-line pursuit of victory against all Indians; at the same time, Berkeley was clearly soft on the Pamunkeys. The protests poured in: how can anyone tell "friendly" Indians from enemy Indians? "Are not the Indians all of a color?" Thus, racism and war hysteria formed a potent combination to sweep away reason, as a time-honored phrase of the racists, "You can't tell one from another," became logically transmuted into: "The only good Indian is a dead Indian." Or, as the Baconian rebels put it: "Away with these distinctions . . . we will have war with all Indians which come not in with their arms, and give hostages for their fidelity and to aid against all others; we will spare none. If we must be hanged for rebels for killing those that will destroy us, let them hang us. . . ."

Alarmed, Berkeley rushed back to the capital and to appease the people called an election—at long last—for the House of Burgesses. The election was called in mid-May for a session to begin in early June. This was the first election since the beginning of Berkeley's second reign. This in itself was a victory against tyranny. Meanwhile, Bacon and his band of Indian fighters proceeded against the Susquehannocks, but soon veered their attention, as usual, to the friendly but far less powerful Occaneechees, whom Bacon had even persuaded to attack the Susquehannocks. The Occaneechees had given Bacon's exhausted and depleted band food and shelter, and had attacked the Susquehannocks themselves in Bacon's behalf. The Occaneechees presented their prisoners to Bacon and the prisoners were duly tortured and killed.

A dispute, however, arose over the plunder from the raid and especially over a half-dozen friendly Manikin and Annaleckton Indians who had been prisoners of the Susquehannocks and had helped the Occaneechees destroy the Susquehannock camp. The Occaneechees naturally wanted to keep the plunder from the Susquehannock raid, and to free the friendly Indians they had liberated. But Bacon demanded the plunder for himself and insisted that the Manikins and Annalecktons be turned over to him as slaves. Bacon fell into a dispute with the Occaneechee chief, who balked at selling food to his men, whereupon Bacon launched a surprise attack on the Indians, burning and slaughtering over a hundred Indian men, women, and children, and kidnapping others. To Bacon went the plunder and, in addition, an Occaneechee stock of valuable beaver fur. Some contemporary accounts assert the fur was Bacon's major aim in the surprise attack. In any case, Bacon returned from this irrelevant act of butchery as the leader of a band of heroes in the eyes of the bulk of the Virginia people, and insisted more than ever that all Indians were enemies: "this I have always said and do maintain." Undaunted by Berkeley's denunciation of Bacon for treason and rebellion and his expulsion of Bacon from the Council, the freemen of Henrico County unanimously elected Bacon and his associate James Crews as burgesses. Joining the inner councils of Bacon's Rebellion were two wealthy and influential Virginians: William Drummond, tobacco planter and former governor of Albemarle colony, and the intellectual Richard Lawrence, who had lost land through legal plunder to a favorite of Berkeley's.

Ignoring the election results, Berkeley sent an armed force to capture Bacon and bring him back to Jamestown. Here ensued a patently spurious reconciliation scene, with Bacon in open assembly confessing his guilt and Berkeley, out of character, granting him forgiveness. Clearly an uneasy truce had resulted from the glowering confrontation of armed force and the threat of full-fledged civil war. For Berkeley knew that two thousand men were armed and ready to come to Bacon's rescue. Berkeley also restored Bacon to his seat in the Council, perhaps to retire him to what at this point was a less important seat.

With Bacon quieted, the House of Burgesses, largely supporters of Bacon and certainly anti-Berkeley, did very little. A few feeble essays in reform were quickly stifled by the domineering governor. Except for acts restricting trade with the Indians, and imposing dictates on avowedly friendly Indians by forbidding them to hunt with guns even on their own reservations, the Assembly did little and certainly nothing against Berkeley. Indeed, they saw fit to eulogize Berkeley's rule. Bacon, warned of a plot on his life and seeing how reconciliation had only succeeded in dangerously weakening the revolutionary movement, calming the people, and taming the Assembly, escaped from Jamestown. He still lacked official sanction to fight Indians.

Returning home, Bacon raised an armed troop and on June 23 invaded Jamestown, where, under bayonet, he forced Berkeley and the Assembly to grant him the commission to fight the Indians—the original point of the rebellion. But now the Baconian Assembly, emboldened by the Bacon victory, pushed through in a few days a series of reform measures that became known as "Bacon's Laws."

Several of these measures were invasive of liberty: the inevitable laws for more stringent war and regulation against the Indians, prohibition on the export of corn, restrictions on the sale of liquor. But the bulk of the laws were in a libertarian direction: requiring annual rotation of the powerful office of sheriff; prohibiting anyone from holding two local offices at the same time; penalizing excessive charges levied by public officials; providing for triennial elections for the local vestry boards by the freemen of the parish (thus ending the closed oligarchical control of the vestries). Moreover the Assembly ended the absolute control of the appointed justices of the peace, meeting in secret conclave, over county taxes and expenditures. Annual election by all the freemen was provided, for choosing an equal number of representatives to sit with the judges imposing the county levies and expenditures. Furthermore, the law of 1670 taking the voting for burgesses away from nonlandholding freemen was repealed. Thus, a true revolution had developed from a mere movement to crush Indians more efficiently. Indeed, some leading conservatives hinted darkly of anarchy and menace to private property; one leading Berkeleyan sneered that Bacon's followers were too poor to pay taxes and therefore wanted none levied at all. In the meanwhile, Bacon protested that revolution was farthest from his mind, as perhaps it was; that all he wanted was to fight the Indians. Armed with his coveted commission he proceeded west to do so.

Governor Berkeley, however, was not content with this relatively peaceful resolution of the problem, and he determined on civil war. Berkeley once more cried treason and rebellion against Bacon and proceeded into Gloucester County to raise a counterrevolutionary armed force. Hearing of this treachery, Bacon and his men marched eastward, where the militia of Gloucester County mutinied and to the governor's face chanted, "Bacon! Bacon! Bacon!" Berkeley, in disgrace and opposed by the bulk of the people, fled to obscure Accomack County on the Eastern Shore, where he lamented: "How miserable that man is that governs a people. . . . "

Bacon was now impelled by the logic of events to a radical and revolutionary position. For, despite his wishes, he was now irrevocably a rebel against Governor Berkeley; and since Berkeley was the agent of the king, a rebel against the king of England as well. The logic of events now compelled Bacon to favor total independence from England; for him it was now independence or death. So swiftly had the dynamic of revolution pushed events forward that the man who, just three months before, had had no thoughts of rebellion, who only a few weeks before had only wished to crush Indians more effectively, was now forced to fight for the independence of Virginia from the Crown.

Grievances were abounding in neighboring Maryland and Albemarle. Bacon began to envisage a mighty all-Chesapeake uprising—Maryland, Virginia, North Carolina—to gain freedom from subjection to England. The neighboring colonies were indeed ripe for rebellion, and William Drummond, a leading Baconian and former governor of North Carolina, helped stir up a rebel movement there led by John Culpeper, who visited Jamestown during the turbulent rebellion of 1676. But Bacon had a critical problem: if the choice was only independence or death for *him*, that choice did not face the rest of the Virginians. Thus, one of Bacon's followers, on hearing him talk of plans to fight English troops, exclaimed: "Sir, you speak as though you designed a total defection from His Majesty and our country!" "Why, have not many princes lost their dominions so?" Bacon calmly replied. Less chary of a radical policy was Sarah, wife of William Drummond, who, breaking a stick in two, exclaimed, "I care no more for the power of England than for this broken straw."

Bacon now faced a twofold chore: the cementing of the Virginia people behind the new, difficult, and radical task; and the smashing of the Berkeley forces before they could rally. Unfortunately, it is not surprising that a man dedicated to a hard-line against the Indians would not hesitate in a hard-line against his own people. Bacon began to wield the weapon of the compulsory public loyalty oath. From his headquarters at the Middle Plantation (later Williamsburg), Bacon issued a call for a convention of the leading men of the colony. Once at the convention, Bacon issued a manifesto, grandiosely entitled the "Declaration of the People," demanding surrender of Berkeley and nineteen of his closest cohorts in four days. Refusal to surrender would mean arrest for treason and confiscation of property. In the Declaration, several accusations were leveled against Berkeley: (1) that "upon spacious pretense of public works [he] raised great unjust taxes upon the commonality;" (2) advancing favorites to high public offices; (3) monopolizing the beaver trade with the Indians; (4) being pro-Indian.

Bacon now assumed dictatorial authority over the colony. He forced the convention to subscribe to an oath of allegiance. The first clause caused no trouble—a pledge not to join Berkeley's forces. The second part caused a great deal of trouble—a pledge to oppose any English forces sent to aid Berkeley. The Virginians balked at open revolution against the Crown. Bacon, however, locked the doors and forced the assembled men to take the entire oath. Bacon now proceeded to terrorize the mass of Virginians to take the same oath, and arrested any who refused. Terror is a poor way to persuade someone to be loyal, and from this moment Bacon's formerly great popularity in the colony began to ebb.

At this juncture, when smashing Berkeley's forces was the order of the day, Bacon permitted himself to be diverted to the old sport of killing Indians. Instead of pursuing the Indian war against the tribes actually fighting, Bacon again found it convenient to attack the hapless and neutral Pamunkey Indians, who had fled to the swamps and wilderness of Gloucester County to be left alone. After wasting many days trying to find the Pamunkeys in the swamps and, of course, plundering as they went, Bacon's forces found the Pamunkeys' camp and plundered, captured, and slaughtered the unresisting Indians. Bacon was a hero once more.

While Bacon was off to raid the Pamunkeys, Berkeley had seized the opportunity to win control of the fleet, Jamestown, and the principal river areas. In contrast to Bacon's reliance upon volunteers for his army, Berkeley raised his counterrevolutionary force by the promise of plunder from the estates of those who had taken Bacon's oath, and the promise of subsidy and exemption from virtually all taxes. Each party was soon promising liberty to the servants of the opposing side.

Marching on Jamestown again, Bacon now drove Berkeley out of the capital. In the course of the battle, Bacon used a new stratagem: he kidnapped some of the wives of the Berkeley leaders and threatened to place them in the front line if the Berkeley forces fired upon their fortifications.

Power corrupts, and the repeated use of aggressive violence spirals inevitably upward and outward. So with Nathaniel Bacon, Jr. Beginning with the Indians, Bacon increasingly extended despotism and violence against Virginian citizens. After capturing Jamestown, Bacon burned it totally to the ground, on the flimsy excuse of hypothetical military necessity. The forces of Giles Brent, now a Colonel, in the northern counties, which had shifted from Bacon's to Berkeley's cause, were marching south, but Brent's men deserted him completely when they heard of Bacon's victory at Jamestown. After driving Berkeley's forces back to the Eastern Shore, Bacon enforced his loyalty oath on more masses of people, seized provisions for his army from the populace, and punished several citizens by martial law. Even his cousin, Nathaniel Bacon, Sr., was not spared the plunder meted out to the leading opponents of the rebellion, even though the elder Bacon had previously warned his cousin of an attempt on his life. The elder Bacon's property was looted to the loss of £1,000.

Just as Bacon made ready to proceed against Berkeley and the Eastern Shore, this leader of revolution fell ill and died on October 26, 1676. In a few short months he had brought Virginia and perhaps the neighboring colonies to the brink of revolutionary independence from Great Britain. Who knows what might have happened had Bacon lived? Without the inspiration provided by their leader, the rebellion fell apart and Berkeley's forces conquered the disorganized rebel units. One of the last of the rebel bands to yield was a group of 400 Negro slaves and white servants, fighting for their freedom in Bacon's army. Captain Thomas Grantham of the Berkeley forces persuaded them to disarm by promising them their freedom, after which he delivered them back to their masters.

Governor Berkeley was not a forgiving soul, and he now instituted a veritable reign of terror in Virginia. As he defeated each of the rebel units, he courtmartialed and hanged the leaders. Neither was Berkeley very discriminating in his court-martialing and hanging parties; in one of them he included Thomas Hall, clerk of New Kent County, who had never taken up arms in the rebellion but who had angered Berkeley in other matters. It was enough, however, that Hall, "by divers writings under his own hand. . . a most notorious actor, aided and assisted in the rebellion. . . ." One of the hanged rebels protested, no doubt truthfully, that he had always been a loyal subject of the Crown and only meant to take up arms against Indians. As in the case of many rebels, he was hanged in a cause the rapid progress of which had traveled far beyond his understanding. When the eminent William Drummond, who had incurred the dislike of Berkeley even before the year's events, was captured in the swamps and dragged in before the governor, Berkeley gloated: "Mister Drummond! You are very welcome. I am more glad to see you than any man in Virginia; Mister Drummond you shall be hanged in half an hour." To which Drummond steadfastly replied: "I expect no mercy from you. I have followed the lead of my conscience, and done what I might to free my country from oppression." Allowing for a few hours missed, the promise was indeed carried out, and Drummond's ring confiscated by Berkeley for good measure.

Most defiant of the captured rebels was Anthony Arnold, who delivered a trenchant attack on the rights of kings: "They have no rights but what they got by conquest and the sword, and he that can by force of the sword deprive them of it has as good and just a title to it as the king himself. If the king should deny to do me right I would make no more to sheath my sword in his heart or bowels than of my mortal enemies." The court hung "the horrible resolved rebel and traitor" Arnold in chains, openly regretting that it could not draw and quarter him as well. Berkeley also proceeded to confiscate the estates of one rebel after another, thus recouping his own personal fortunes.

Unfortunately for Berkeley's uninterrupted pleasure, the king's commissioners arrived in January with a general pardon for all rebels. What is more, the commissioners promised that they would redress the grievances of the people. The king further ordered Berkeley back to England. But Berkeley, defying the commissioners, continued imposing his own loyalty oaths, seizing more property for his own use, and delaying publication of the king's pardon. He finally published the pardon, but exempted eighteen nameless people—an excellent way of cowing the Virginians so as to keep them from bearing their grievances to the commissioners. Civil trials for treason proceeded apace, and several more were hanged.

Furthermore, the subservient Assembly now met and quickly repealed all of the bold acts of liberal reform of Bacon's Assembly of June 1676. Under Berkeley's direction, the Assembly proceeded to hang many more rebels by acts of attainder, and to fine, imprison, banish, and expropriate still more. Some rebels were ordered to pay heavy fines and appear before the Assembly with halters around their necks, kneeling to repent of their guilt and beg for their lives. If freed by the Assembly, they were forced to repeat the same ordeal before the county court. All leading supporters of the rebellion were barred thereafter from holding public office. Even the hapless indentured servants who followed Bacon were sentenced to imprisonment whenever their terms of service should expire. Anyone who had written or spoken anything favoring the rebellion, or even criticizing anyone in authority, received heavy fines, the pillory, flogging, or branding on the forehead. Yet the jails were not filled, being kept clear by banishments and executions.

Some hapless Virginians were caught in the middle in the civil war. Thus Otto Thorpe. Wishing not to sign Bacon's compulsory loyalty oath, Thorpe

111

finally did so when his wife was threatened. Later in the rebellion, Thorpe refused to aid Bacon further and had his property confiscated by the rebels as a consequence. Then, when Berkeley returned to power, he sent Thorpe to jail for swearing to the Baconian oath and confiscated his property once more.

The commissioners sadly concluded that no peace could come to the colony, either internally or with the Indians, until Berkeley had been completely removed from his post and the general pardon carried out. The only real supporters of Berkeley in his fanatic campaign of vengeance were twenty friends of his among the oligarchy, known as the Green Spring faction. The commissioners reported that the Green Spring group was continually pleading for the punishment of the guilty, who were "little less than the whole country." The commissioners, indeed, estimated that of all the people in Virginia (who now numbered about 40,000) only 500 had never supported the rebellion. Finally, the Assembly, under pressure of the commissioners, forced the reluctant Berkeley to stop the hangings. As one assemblyman stated, if not for this interference, "the governor would have hanged half the country." Under pressure of the commissioners, the Assembly of February 1677 also reenacted a few of the most innocuous of the reform laws of the previous year.

Despite the intimidation and terror, a large number of grievances were sent to the Assembly and the commissioners by the people of Virginia. The most common grievance concerned the levying of heavy and unjust taxes by officials, taxes that were used for expenditures over which the people had no control. Typical was a petition from Surry County, which prayed the authorities "to ease us His Majesty's poor subjects of our great burdens and taxes." The petition asked:

> *Whereas* there yearly came a great public levy from James City we never knew for what to the great grief and dissatisfaction of the poor upon whose shoulders the levy chiefly lay, *we most humbly pray* that for the future the collectors of the levy (who instead of satisfaction were wont to give churlish answers) may be obliged to give an account in writing what the levy is for to any who shall desire it.

The Surry county petition also humbly asked for a free election for every Assembly so that they could find redress for their grievances.

Not surprisingly, this humble petition received its typical answer: severe punishment for the petitioners by the Assembly, for the high crime of "speaking or writing disrespectfully of those in authority." Other grievances mentioned in petitions were favoritism, illegal fees charged by local officials, restriction of the right to vote, monopoly of the Indian trade, and the arbitrary seizing of property by the government.

While the commissioners were hardly zealous in defending the people against Berkeley's oppression, they at least arranged a peace with the Indians, and the great Indian war was happily ended. Finally, the commissioners decided to carry the king's order into effect, and they ousted Berkeley. Leaving for England, Berkeley made his exit in characteristic fashion, kicking and snarling all the way, and bitterly denouncing the ambition, incompetence, and ignorance of the appointed lieutenant governor left in charge. At long last, on May 5, 1677, Berkeley embarked for England, dying soon after his arrival. Perhaps Berkeley's most appropriate epitaph was the reported comment on the Virginia affair by King Charles II: "That old fool has hanged more men in that naked country than I did here for the murder of my father."

The shadow of Berkeley still fell over the unhappy colony, however, as Virginia, not knowing of his death, still believed that Berkeley would soon engineer his return. The colony was still in the hands of Berkeley's henchmen, the Green Spring oligarchs who had been reestablished in their lucrative and powerful offices. Leading members of this faction were Colonel Philip Ludwell, Colonel Thomas Ballard, Colonel Edward Hill, and Major Robert Beverley. It also included Colonel John Washington and Richard Lee. Green Spring's control was especially strong after the commissioners had returned to England in July. The Green Spring faction ran the council, and engineered corrupt elections to the House of Burgesses. They continued to drag rebels into court to seize their property and they levied another large poll tax on the colony, again laying the heaviest burden on the poorest citizens. Petitions from the counties to redress grievances continued to be punished in the by now traditional manner: severe punishment for statements highly scandalous and injurious to authority.

Finally, in October, news of Berkeley's death arrived in Virginia, and the king was finally able to get his complete and general pardon published. The Baconian remnants, still hiding in the woods, were able to emerge and resume their normal lives. But if Berkeley was at last truly dead, his system was not; Berkeleyism and the Green Spring faction continued to rule the colony. In fact, the next governor, Thomas Lord Culpeper, was a relative of Lady Berkeley. The revolution had failed, but it continued to live on in the hearts of Americans who cherished the memory of its near victory—a beacon light for future rebellions against tyranny.

12

Maryland

Virginia, as we have seen, was England's first chartered colony and the first royal colony in America. The remaining type of English colony was the proprietary, and the first proprietary colony was founded in the early seventeenth century, just north of the Virginia border.

A proprietary grant was a far more feudalistic device than the chartered company. For a company, being a joint venture of capitalists, was bent on parceling out land to its shareholders, on earning rapid profits rather than acting as a long-time or permanent feudal landlord. But the gift of a huge tract of land to a single proprietor was a more enticing invitation to feudalism to come to American shores.

The first American proprietary was a grant of land in 1632 by King Charles I to Cecilius Calvert, the second Lord Baltimore. The grant was carved out of Virginia territory and extended from the Potomac River north to the fortieth parallel, including (but rather larger than) the present boundaries of Maryland. The king reserved for himself but one-fifth of the gold and silver that might be mined each year in the province. Otherwise, Lord Baltimore was as free to govern in his vast domain as the king was in England. The king even expressly granted the power to levy any taxes on Maryland, so named in honor of the English queen Henrietta Maria. The charter granted to Lord Baltimore ownership of all the land, minerals, rivers, and fisheries in the area as well as the right to confer titles, incorporate cities and towns, levy taxes, erect churches and feudal manors, and constitute courts. This was a veritable feudal government—a "Palatinate" as existed in Europe, specifically like the Palatinate of Durham in England. One important limitation on Calvert's absolute rule, as in the case of the king himself, was that he could levy taxes only with the consent of an Assembly representing the freemen, or landholders, of the province.

The first settlement in Maryland was made in 1634 by two small ships, the *Ark* and the *Dove*, carrying about 220 people and landing at St. Marys, near the mouth of the Potomac. From the first, Roman Catholicism was a uniquely important issue in this colony. For Calvert's father, George, the first Lord Baltimore and a leader of the monarchial party in England, had turned Catholic after receiving a promise of the grant. From the first, Cecilius wanted to make Maryland a haven from persecution for Catholics in England. But, eager to encourage settlement (for without settlers there would be no profit from his feudal domain), Calvert made no religious test for settling in the colony. As a result, Protestants outnumbered Catholics among the settlers by nearly ten to one from the beginning—with the Protestant faith predominating among the poorer classes and Catholicism among the gentlemen. Both Protestants and Catholics enjoyed full religious liberty and there was no established church in the colony.

Early relations with the Indians were peaceful, with the land acquired from them by voluntary purchase rather than by force. This peaceful coexistence was assured by Calvert's simple expedient of instructing his men to deal fairly with the Indians. Indeed, the largest wigwam in St. Marys was after purchase consecrated as a church by the two Jesuit priests of the first expedition.*

The land system, however, in keeping with the vast feudal powers given to Calvert, was established on the most rigidly feudal lines in America. Calvert early advertised that every settler who would finance the transport of five other settlers to the colony would receive a grant as "Lord of the Manor" of 2,000 acres of land—not outright, however, or in fee simple, but as a feudal tenancy with a quitrent of 400 pounds of good wheat per year to the proprietor. The manor lords, most of them Catholic, in turn rented their land to smaller planters in exchange for rent in produce. This restrictive method of allocating land or landownership decidedly hampered the growth of the entire colony during the seventeenth century. Furthermore, Calvert gave vast estates as manors to his friends and relatives.

The first governor of the colony was Calvert's brother, Leonard, and Calvert appointed a Council to advise his brother. While the Calverts tried to keep representative government to a minimum, an Assembly soon developed, after persistent pressure from below on the proprietors. The proprietor and the Assembly soon quarreled over the extent of their relative powers, the proprietor claiming the sole right to initiate legislation, which the Assembly could then reject. The Assembly, with the power to hold up the enactment of laws, refused to consent to any imposition of a code by Calvert and thus won the fight to initiate legislation.

*In a few years, however, Calvert became dissatisfied with the Jesuit missionaries in Maryland and "their very extravagant" demands for privileges, and took measures to prevent any increased supply of Jesuits to the colony.

At first, all the landowners sat in the Assembly, but soon the representative principle was adopted. In 1650, the Assembly turned into the familiar two-house type: the Council sitting as the upper house and the elected members as the lower. The governor and the proprietor, who appointed the governor, had veto power over all legislation and the governor could also dissolve the Assembly at will. However, the Assembly assured its continuing existence by refusing to grant taxes for more than a year at a time. The supreme judicial power, as in Virginia, was vested in the governor and the Council, although eventually this provincial court set up subsidiary county courts for minor cases and judges, appointed and removable by the governor, were appointed as higher courts.

We have already alluded to the conflict between Lord Baltimore and William Claiborne, a Virginian who had established a trading post on Kent Island in Chesapeake Bay. This quarrel was embittered by Claiborne's virulent anti-Catholicism, which had spurred him to play a leading role in ousting Calvert from Virginia, before the founding of the Maryland colony. With Claiborne refusing to recognize Calvert's overlordship of Kent Island, Calvert moved to assert his dominion over Claiborne, wielding his land grant as his claim. The conflict was punctuated by a naval battle between the ships of Lord Baltimore and of Claiborne. Finally, the king decided the issue by ruling in Lord Baltimore's favor.

In the mid-1640s, as the Puritan Revolution arose in England, Lord Baltimore sided with the king, and Leonard Calvert received privileges (or "letters of marque") from the king to capture vessels belonging to Parliament. On the other hand, the Protestant tobacco trader, Capt. Richard Ingle, a friend of Claiborne's, received a similar commission from Parliament. The governor ordered Ingle's arrest for high treason in denouncing the king, whereupon Ingle escaped and in 1645 mounted a successful attack on Maryland. Captain Ingle took the opportunity, "for conscience'" sake, to plunder and pillage "papists and malignants," seizing property and jailing his enemies. The venerable Father Andrew White, a Jesuit missionary who had arrived on the first ships to land in Maryland, was sent to England in irons to be tried for treason. Happily, the old missionary was acquitted.

In the meanwhile, Claiborne took the opportunity to retrieve Kent Island from Maryland's seizure. Under Ingle's attack, Leonard Calvert escaped to Virginia, from where Berkeley helped him to recapture Maryland and Kent Island.

Returning to England, Ingle almost succeeded in revoking Maryland's charter, but Calvert retained it by taking pains to placate Parliament. Calvert, for example, encouraged a group of Dissenters exiled from Virginia to settle in Maryland, a little further up the Chesapeake Bay from St. Marys, in what is now Annapolis. Furthermore, after Leonard Calvert died in 1648, Lord Baltimore appointed the Protestant William Stone as governor. He required the governor to take an oath not to violate the free exercise of religion by any Christians, specifically including Roman Catholics. Subsequently, in April 1649, the Maryland Assembly passed the famous Toleration Act, which guaranteed all Christians the free exercise of their religion. However, tolerance and religious liberty went only so far and the death penalty was levied against all non-Christians, including Jews and Unitarians. Neither did toleration extend to freedom of speech, for any use of such religious epithets as "heretic" and "popish priest" was outlawed. Also prohibited on the Sabbath were swearing, drinking, unnecessary work, and disorderly recreation. Actually, the much vaunted Toleration Act was a *retreat* from the religious liberty that had previously prevailed in Catholic-ruled Maryland, and was a compromise with the growing spirit of Puritan intolerance.

Charles II, still in exile, embittered by what he regarded as acts of treachery by Lord Baltimore, deposed him and appointed instead Sir William Davenant as royal governor, for Baltimore "did visibly adhere to the rebels in England, and admit all kinds of sectaries and schismatics and ill-affected persons into the plantation." Davenant sailed from France to try to seize Maryland but was himself captured by the English.

Walking the tightrope of religious liberty between the demands of Parliament and those of the Crown was a difficult feat, and in 1651 the rulers of Maryland fell off. The Catholic royalist deputy governor, Thomas Greene, foolishly decided to recognize Charles II in the same year as the legitimate ruler of England. This proclamation naturally angered Parliament and precipated severe reaction. The following year Parliament sent to the Chesapeake colonies commissioners, of whom the angry Claiborne was one, to subdue the recalcitrants. After settling matters in Virginia, the commissioners proceeded to Maryland, where they removed the governor and ousted the proprietary. Governor Stone was reinstated, but he, in turn, persisted in trying to reinstate the authority of the proprietor. He compounded his difficulties by insisting on imposing an oath of allegiance on Lord Baltimore. The oath offended Puritans. Stone then denounced the Puritans and the commissioners as fomenters of sedition. The result was the capture of St. Marys by the commissioners in 1654, and their appointment of a Puritan Council and of Capt. William Fuller as governor. Catholics were now excluded from voting and from the Assembly, and the Toleration Act as well as the rule of the proprietor were canceled. A law of 1654 declared that "none who professed and exercised the popish religion could be protected in this province." The law disfranchised not only Catholics, but also Anglicans. The Puritans made it clear that freedom of worship would now be extended only to Protestants free of either "popery or prelacy."

Former governor Stone now raised his insurrectionary army loyal to the proprietary, and in 1655 attacked Providence, the principal Puritan settlement in Maryland. The erstwhile governor was crushed by a force of Puritan planters, Stone was imprisoned, and several of his followers executed, even though they had been promised their lives before surrender. Calvert, however, proved extremely agile and managed to convice Cromwell and

Parliament that religious toleration and hence his own rule should be re-established. Calvert was permitted to appoint a new governor in 1656 and this governor, Josiah Fendall, joined with the Puritans in agreeing to establish religious toleration, including toleration for Catholics.

With the death of Cromwell, Fendall tried to seize the opportunity to liberalize the colony further by casting off proprietary rule and submitting himself to appointment by the Maryland Assembly. The restoration of Charles II, however, ended such hopes for the remainder of the century, and Baltimore moved swiftly to crush this move for independence, appointing Philip Calvert as governor.

After the Restoration, tensions and grievances accumulated in Maryland somewhat as they did in Virginia. Falling tobacco prices, the crippling effect of the English Navigation Acts, the raising of the quitrents—each conduced to this effect. In Maryland, too, suffrage was restricted to freeholders in 1670; furthermore, proprietary rule aggravated the problem of quasi-feudal landholdings. Moreover, anti-Catholic sentiment grew among the Protestant masses and focused both against the proprietor and against religious toleration. Another important grievance: the Calverts had tampered with the election to the burgesses in 1670 and after that, in imitation of Berkeley, suspended elections until 1676. The ambivalence of religious toleration in Maryland may be seen in its treatment of the Quakers. Quakers were people who had no priests, declined to swear oaths, and refused determinedly to fight or bear arms. They were, accordingly, highly unpopular wherever adoration of the state ran high. They proclaimed, indeed, that they were "governed by God's laws and the light within and not by man's laws." In Maryland the Quakers were steadily persecuted; forty were publicly whipped within one year. Finally the Quakers were branded as "rebels and traitors," and in a law of 1659 Maryland ordered their expulsion from the colony. The law decreed that "any of the vagabonds or idle persons known by the name of Quakers, who should again enter the province, should be whipped from constable to constable out of it." The proprietary, however, soon ceased to enforce the law, and before long many Quakers were reestablished in the colony. When the founder of the Quakers, George Fox, visited Maryland in 1672, he welcomed the full religious liberty in the province and rejoiced in the number of public officials who had been converts.

Maryland's economy and social structure developed in a way similar to neighboring Virginia's. After a brief period of growing subsistence crops of maize, pork, and vegetables, the colony turned to specialization in tobacco. A large tobacco plantation society and economy, in short, prevailed in the whole Chesapeake Bay area, Maryland as well as Virginia. The plantations were located in the fertile river plains of the coastal tidewater region, and trade was oriented to London and Bristol. Again, quasi-feudal land allocation led to large plantations, although small up-country farms growing subsistence crops and tobacco were more numerous but not dominant in the colony. Once more, the land was extensively settled and thinly populated. The labor base for the plantations was indentured service and Negro slavery.

Perhaps the major economic and social difference between Maryland and Virginia was Maryland's far more feudal structure. The land was kept in a hierarchy of overlordships and tenancies, with the Calverts owning all the land and collecting a quitrent from all the landholders, while the manor lords of the vast estates given to them by the overlords leased the land to smaller planters. The small yeoman farmers of the back country could not therefore gain their land outright, but could only stay as tenants paying quitrents to the proprietary overlord. Large stretches of tidewater land were held by a few large planters.

Although beginning as a rigidly feudal structure, **even** the Maryland land system could not survive the liberating conditions of America: in particular, the enormous abundance of new land and the need to stimulate settlement upon it. By the late seventeenth century, the land was being increasingly transferred to the settlers; through purchases, the feudal land structure was dissolved into its component parts, and ownership progressively devolved upon the actual users of the land. Feudal landholdings, in short, began to dissolve into the market economy.

One of the most important single manifestations of feudal landholdings, especially in a proprietary colony, was the quitrent, exacted from all landowners as tenants of the proprietary. Originally Cecilius Calvert had fixed a quitrent of ten pounds of wheat for each fifty acres, and then of one shilling per fifty acres, to be paid in kind. In 1648 Calvert attempted a drastic increase in quitrents, ranging now from one shilling per fifty acres up to twenty shillings per fifty acres, or ten pounds per manor of 2,000 acres after a term of years. Pressure of the settlers and the need to encourage settlement forced abandonment of this plan, and the Maryland Assembly felt the need in 1654 to pass a law upholding the rights in the land of the settlers as well as of the proprietary. After the Restoration in England, the cocky Lord Baltimore doubled the quitrent to four shillings per 100 acres, which began to be enforced in 1669. In addition, in an attempt to block the quiet dissolution into the market of feudal tenure, the proprietors imposed in 1660 a fine on any alienation of landed property. Happily the fine was never thoroughly enforced. The proprietors also imposed on the settlers a purchase price (known as "caution money"), which considerably restricted the growth of the colony. First levied in 1683 at 200 pounds of tobacco per 100 acres, the purchase price was increased the next year to 240 pounds, and by 1717 had reached the sum of 40 shillings per 100 acres.

As in Virginia, the chief money was tobacco, and so quitrents were paid in that commodity. As the price of tobacco fell drastically, the Assembly began to fix the exchange rate in order to try to keep the tobacco prices above the market rate. Such minimum price control could only create unsold surpluses of tobacco and aggravate conditions further for many tobacco planters, as well as for tobacco consumers. However, an incidental boon was to relieve the burden of quitrents on the inhabitants. Thus, in 1662 and again in 1671, the Assembly fixed the tobacco price at twopence per pound while the market price was a penny a pound, thus reducing the quitrent burden by letting it be paid in arbitrarily overvalued tobacco. The quitrents, furthermore, were enforced by forfeit of land for nonpayment, and by making every debt due to Lord Baltimore a prior lien on the land. Where there were no goods to seize, the delinquent tenant was imprisoned.

The relative growth of Maryland may be gauged by comparing its population with Virginia's: less than 600 as compared with Virginia's more than 10,000 in 1640, Maryland's population rose to 4,500 in 1650, 8,400 in 1660, and almost 18,000 in 1680, compared with Virginia's 44,000. The Negro (almost all-slave) population of Maryland was proportionately greater in 1680 (over 1,200 compared with Virginia's 2,000), but then fell behind because of an enormous spurt in Virginia's slave population. By 1700 there were 3,200 slaves in Maryland, while over 16,000 in Virginia. Slave revolts broke out in Maryland in the early 1680s, in 1688, 1705, 1738, and 1739.

A Negro slave in Maryland had the distinction of staging perhaps the first demonstration of nonviolent resistance in America. In 1656 Tony, a slave of one Symon Overzee, ran away and was captured with the aid of bloodhounds. When he ran away and was captured a second time, Tony sat down and refused to rise and work as a slave. Mr. Overzee bound and beat him repeatedly, but Tony still refused to act as a slave. Enraged because "his property" was refusing to function as property, Overzee poured hot lard over Tony and killed him. A court acquitted Overzee of the murder because, after all, Tony had proved to be "incorrigible."

13

The Carolinas

In the mid-seventeenth century, many settlers from Virginia, disgruntled by the domination of society by the planter aristocracy or by the Anglican church, moved down to the southern part of the Virginia grant, on the north of Albemarle Sound (in what is now North Carolina). The leader of the first settlement was the Presbyterian Roger Green. Many of these settlers were Quakers. At first part of Virginia, this settlement, which was also largely devoted to raising tobacco, was relatively independent. Soon, however, it was to feel the heavy hand of a feudal proprietary grant. For the large territory south of Virginia and down to the border of Spanish Florida was still up for seizure. In 1663 the newly installed Charles II granted a feudal proprietary gift of the territory between the thirty-first and thirty-sixth parallels—from what is now slightly north of the Florida-Georgia border to the northern boundary of North Carolina—to a proprietorship comprising eight of his favorite courtiers and supporters. This grant whittled away the southern portion of the Virginia grant, which had been bounded by the thirty-fourth parallel. The eight proprietors were Sir Anthony Ashley Cooper, the chancellor of the Exchequer (later first Earl of Shaftesbury); the governor of Virginia, Sir William Berkeley; his brother John Lord Berkeley, a high-ranking naval officer; the Earl of Clarendon, chief minister to the king; Gen. George Mack, the new Duke of Albemarle; Sir George Carteret; the wealthy Earl of Craven; and Sir John Colleton, a wealthy Barbadian planter and slave trader. As in the Virginia grant, the territory grandiosely extended west to the "south seas." The idea of the grant originated with those proprietors already interested in the Americas: Colleton, William Berkeley, Ashley Cooper (also a Barbadian landholder), and Clarendon, a land-

121

owner in Jamaica. John Berkeley acted as agent of the others to persuade the king to make the grant. The grant was known as "Carolina," after a previous land grant to the area.*

Two years later, the eight Carolina proprietors received a new charter extending their grant to 36° 30' in the north and down to 29° in the south—the latter, however, being academic, as it covered the Spanish settlements of Florida.

A party of settlers under the new grant established a settlement at Charles Town (now Charleston), at the mouth of the Ashley and Cooper rivers, in 1670. From the beginning, the proprietors had to govern two distinct and separate settlements, unruly Albemarle in the north, and Charles Town in the south, far more under its control. Moreover, the two settlements were, from the beginning, administered by different governors, though under the same proprietary. Albemarle was under the general aegis of Virginia's Governor Berkeley, one of the proprietors who appointed the governor of the district. From 1691 on, Albemarle settlement was known as North Carolina, and the Charleston area as South Carolina, separately administered though for some years under a single proprietary rule.

The proprietors were given a grant with feudal powers virtually as sweeping as the Maryland gift of privilege—a veritable palatinate. The proprietors were empowered to work their will, with the very important exception that an Assembly of the freemen of the colony, or their representatives, had to approve of the laws. Thus, as in the other colonies, the popularly elected Assembly originated less as a sovereign branch of government than as a check on the despotic rule of the executive. Even before Charleston was settled, the proprietors in 1665 drew up for the government of the chartered area, the "Concessions and Agreements," a relatively liberal document granting freedom of conscience, liberal land distribution subject to the inevitable but small quitrent, as well as an Assembly elected by the freemen of the colony. But in 1669 the proprietors, spurred by the ambitious Ashley Cooper, decided to embark on the fantastic project of fastening a feudal rule on the colony that could not be supplanted or dissolved by market processes. For not only were there to be proprietors as feudal lords, but there was to be a fully ordered feudal hierarchy of various degrees of subinfeudation. This scheme, to be imposed on the entire Carolinas, was drawn up for the supposedly "liberal" Shaftesbury by his hired theo-

*In 1629 King Charles I made his first land grant of the area between the thirty-first and thirty-sixth parallels to Sir Robert Heath, and called it New Carolina. Heath transferred his grant in 1630 to Samuel Vassal and others, but they failed to settle the virgin territory. In 1632 Heath conveyed his rights to Henry Lord Maltraven, who also failed to settle the area. The Duke of Norfolk, heir of Maltraven, Samuel Vassal, and the Cape Fear Company of London and New England merchants (who had settled on the Cape Fear River of North Carolina in 1662 but quickly abandoned the settlement) all now tried to invalidate the Carolina charter, but the Crown voided their patents in 1665. And yet, as late as 1768, the Crown granted the Coxe family of New Jersey (to whom had been transferred the Heath title in 1696) 100,000 acres of land in New York as a payment for their tenuous and dubious claim.

retician, John Locke, and promulgated as the *Fundamental Constitutions* of the Carolinas.*

The Cooper-Locke scheme envisioned a hereditary feudal nobility that was to preempt two-fifths of the land of the Carolinas, to be sold to it by the proprietary. Each of these nobles was to have his own seignory of 12,000 acres in each county; underneath the nobles were the landgraves, each of whom was to have four baronies totaling 48,000 acres; next to them, the caciques, with two baronies totaling 24,000 acres; underneath them, the lords of the manor, each with 3,000 to 12,000 acres; and finally, the freeholders, with a 500-acre minimum requirement for voting. The unfree—slaves and indentured servants—of course did not count enough to be worthy of mention in the hierarchical structure. The eight proprietors were to constitute a supreme Palatine Court, with each proprietor also operating a court of his own. The Palatine Court was to appoint the governor and exert sovereign rule over the colony. The Assembly was to be limited to the governor, the hereditary nobility, and the deputies—the last restricted to holders of 500-acre freeholds. All fishing and mineral rights were to be retained in the ownership of the proprietors.

Religious freedom was to be guaranteed—a long-standing conviction of Locke's—even for Quakers, Jews, and slaves, but the Church of England was to be established by the government, with churches to be built and the ministers paid by the state. But although Locke did not agree with the establishment of the Church of England, he was perhaps partially compensated for this disappointment by receiving the title of landgrave. It was, however, also decreed that no non-theist could hold public office or even have the protection of the law. Another libertarian provision was the guarantee of trial by jury.

Fortunately for the Carolinas, the proprietors were never able to persuade the Assembly to accept this scheme. As a consequence, the gravest threat of permanent feudalism in English America was nipped in the bud. Twenty-six landgraves and thirteen caciques were created, but they mostly expired with the original holder and did not become hereditary. Furthermore, no manor was ever created and no large seignory or barony was established.

*The contradiction has often been noted between the archfeudalism of Locke's *Fundamental Constitutions* and the individualist, laissez-faire liberalism of his *Civil Government*— a liberalism destined to have great intellectual impact on eighteenth-century America. The latter was written not much more than a decade later. This is largely true. However, we must also point out that a staunch defense of private-property rights will mean laissez-faire liberalism in a new country largely unsaddled by the yoke of feudal land tenure, while an equivalent defense in a country already hagridden by feudalism will be, at least in part, an apologia for feudal rather than justly private property and a free society. In short, the crucial issue is the justice of the private-property titles that are being defended. Glossing over this question means that the same set of principles may lead to a libertarian society in a nonfeudal America, where land titles devolved fairly rapidly upon the actual settlers, but to retention of quasi-feudalism in an England where land titles had been largely feudal. A conservative bulwark for feudalism, when transplanted, can prove to be a radically libertarian call for a free society.

We have seen that by the mid-1670s, the Southern colonies were becoming ripe for revolution: accumulated grievances in Virginia and Maryland included English restrictions on tobacco, aggravated dictatorial rule by the governor in Virginia as well as growing Indian troubles, and also attempts to impose feudalism and Protestant anti-Catholicism in Maryland. But the Carolinas, small though they yet were, did not need a lengthy incubation for serious rebellion. Indeed, with the attempt to impose an elaborate feudal structure upon the Carolinas, the new colony was ripe for rebellion almost immediately. This was particularly true of North Carolina, where an unusually independent group of small farmers exercised religious toleration, even for Quakers. Unburdened by feudal planters or a theocratic church, they were suddenly confronted with an attempt by a new English ruler to fasten upon them the very conditions for which they had left the Virginia settlement. North Carolina, which had a population of about 1,000 in 1660, grew rapidly, its free atmosphere and complete religious freedom attracting religious sects and great admixtures of ethnic groups: Germans, French, Swiss, Scots, and Moravians. By the 1670s, its population totaled about 4,000, while new South Carolina was still well under 1,000. The English navigation laws and restrictions on tobacco occasioned additional grievances among the tobacco-growing North Carolinian settlers.

The free spirit of the North Carolina settlers was further reinforced by the failure of land grants for large plantations to take root there. This was a colony of small farmers who had largely settled there to assure their independence. It had no large town or city (the largest town was Edenton) that could serve as a convenient seat for governmental rule. The earliest arrivals either settled freely on the land or purchased it from Indian chiefs. The proprietary, anxious to make money by encouraging rapid settlement, adopted the equivalent of the Virginia headright system, first granting 100 acres to each settler, plus fifty acres of land for each person the settler brought over to the colony. By the 1680s the headright was sixty acres for each settler and sixty for each servant brought over. Each servant was also to receive 100 acres of land on expiration of his term of service. This system, while subject to grave abuses through accumulation of headrights resulting in arbitrarily large land grants, at least assured a wide distribution of land in the colony. The land, from the first, was subject to restrictive conditions and charges, including a quitrent of half a penny per acre to the proprietor; but at least no initial purchase price was required to the grantee. Unfortunately, one-eleventh of each division of land was to be reserved to the proprietors.

In the early eighteenth century, the Virginia planter William Byrd was to write of the North Carolinians that they "treat [their governors] with all the excesses of freedom and familiarity. They are of the opinion that rulers would be apt to grow insolent if they grow rich, and for that reason take care to keep them poorer." Another shock to visitors was the absence of churches—apparently the North Carolinians preferred to practice their religion in private. The great English founder of the Quakers, George Fox, visiting Albemarle in 1672, discovered to his chagrin that he could find no place of worship in all the colony. And some years later William Byrd was again stunned to find that "this is the only metropolis in the Christian or Mohammedan world where there is neither church, chapel, mosque, synagogue, or any other place of public worship of any sect or religion whatsoever."

14

The Aftermath of Bacon's Rebellion in the Other Southern Colonies

As Bacon's Rebellion entered its radical phase, Bacon tried to spread the revolutionary movement to the neighboring colonies, each of which had severe and often similar grievances against its government and the Crown. At the height of Bacon's Rebellion, in September 1676, sixty persons, led by William Davyes and John Pate, assembled in Calvert County, Maryland, to declare their opposition to crushing taxation and to Lord Baltimore's disfranchisement of the freemen. They also declared their refusal to swear to a new loyalty oath proposed by the proprietor. They refused to obey the governor's order to disband on promise to consider their grievances in the next Assembly, pointing out that the manipulated Assembly no longer represented the people. But the death of Bacon caused the quick collapse of the embryo Davyes-Pate rebellion, and Davyes and Pate were hanged after being denounced as traitors. The governor observed with satisfaction that the people were now suitably "terrified." The threat was over, but the governor wrote in warning to Lord Baltimore that never had a people been "more replete with malignancy and frenzy." Apparently, the Maryland regime had had a close call. The result increased the bitterness in the colony against the proprietor.

However, the struggle against the oppression of the feudal proprietary in Maryland had not been crushed. The veteran rebel Josiah Fendall of Charles County, elected to the Assembly but barred from his seat for his rebellious activities in 1660, now took up the libertarian torch. In particular, Fendall led a movement against high taxes and quitrents imposed by the proprietor. Fendall also championed freedom of speech — a rarity in that era. Philip Calvert denounced Fendall for "telling the people they were fools to pay taxes" and for allegedly saying that "now nothing was treason . . . a man might say anything." Assisting Fendall were Thomas Gerrard, a veteran rebel and a Catholic, and John Coode, an ex-Catholic and ex-clergyman, in a welcome display of religious amity. In 1681 Lord Baltimore had a law passed forbidding the dissemination of "false" news—that is, news aiming to stir up unrest and rebellion—in an attempt to hamper the Fendall movement. Finally, in the same year, a Fendall-Coode plan for rebellion was betrayed and the leaders imprisoned. The jury, drawn necessarily from the populace, favored the defendants, whereas the judges, being appointees of the proprietor, were hostile. Fendall was convicted, fined heavily, and exiled forever from the province. Coode, an Assemblyman, won acquittal. Lord Baltimore denounced Fendall and Coode as "rank Baconists" and wrote afterwards to a friend that had these leaders not "been secured in time, you would have heard of another Bacon."

North Carolina (Albemarle) was also in a rebellious frame of mind in the mid-1670s. Most grievous was the Navigation Act of 1673, which placed a prohibitory tax of one penny per pound on all intercolonial trading of tobacco. The tobacco farmers of North Carolina, growing over one million pounds of tobacco a year, were heavily dependent on New England shipping for exporting their tobacco, and in turn for importing other products needed by the Carolinians. The tax crippled Carolinian trade, and the result was continual evasion, and sporadic attempts by the government to crack down on the now illegal trade. Another important grievance was the feudal quitrent that the proprietary tried to extract from the North Carolinian landholders. At first, land grants were made there at a relatively small quitrent of two shillings per 100 acres, the usual quitrent rate in Virginia. Then, in the 1660s the proprietary tried to double the imposed quitrent to one-half penny per acre, payable in specie. After vigorous protests, the proprietary in the Great Deed of 1668 retained the quitrent at the former rate. However, the proprietary tried again to raise the quitrent, this time to quadruple the rate to one penny per acre. Rumors, indeed, circulated about an eventual sixpence per acre levy. Attempts (eventually abandoned) to enforce the quadrupled quitrents fanned the flames of rebellion.

To encourage settlement, the Assembly of 1669 limited land grants to 660 acres, but this limitation did not apply to land given out by the proprietors directly. Land was to be subject to forfeit if not worked by the grantees within six months. Trouble began to come to a head in Albemarle upon the passage of the crippling Navigation Act of 1673. With the colonists determined to avoid payment of the tax, Governor Peter Carteret resigned and fled the colony and John Jenkins remained as acting governor. Jenkins, a precharter settler of Albemarle, belonged to the poplar opposition to the proprietary rule, opposition led by wealthy tobacco planter George Durant, one of the founders of the original settlement. Upon his assumption of office, Jenkins heroically determined not to enforce the Navigation Act upon the colony—in short, to occupy the post of ruler in order to diminish the extent of his rule. Jenkins simply ignored the order of the king to appoint collectors of customs with the duty of enforcing the hated levy. Finally, in two years, in 1675, the king appointed a collector for the colony. Until the arrival of the collector, Governor Jenkins could appoint a temporary collector, and so he chose his closest associate, Valentine Byrd, who again simply failed to enforce the law.

The Durant-Jenkins forces, though backed strongly by the bulk of the Albemarle people, were opposed by a faction led by the Speaker of the Assembly, Thomas Eastchurch, and by Thomas Miller. When Eastchurch and Miller moved to appeal to England for enforcement of the Navigation Act, Jenkins moved swiftly to crush the counterrevolution by jailing Miller for "treasonable utterances" and dissolving the Eastchurch-controlled Assembly. The Assembly, however, deposed and summarily imprisoned Jenkins, and Eastchurch went to England to induce the proprietary to crack down on the rebellious and independent colony. There he was joined by Miller, freed by the intervention of Sir William Berkeley.

Thus, when Bacon's Rebellion broke out in 1676, Albemarle was fortunate enough to be without a governor and the hated Navigation Act was still not being enforced. This happy state was not to last for long, however, for the proprietors proceeded to select the two leaders of the pro–Navigation Act clique as the new rulers of the colony: Eastchurch as governor, and Miller as secretary and collector of the customs. On the way to America in 1677, the two men stopped in the West Indies. Eastchurch decided to stay for a while to get married, and sent Miller on to North Carolina to act as governor in his stead.

Miller quickly proceeded to use his double power with predictable ruthlessness. He zealously tried to suppress the illegal tobacco trade, and also to enforce the higher quitrents. In addition, Miller interfered with elections and arbitrarily set a price on the head of many prominent leaders of the province. On the always convenient pretext of "defense against the Indians," Miller organized a military guard that terrorized Albemarle and imposed a heavy debt on the struggling colony.

With Miller now added to the provocation of the Navigation Act and other grievances, North Carolina was truly ripe for rebellion. George Durant had fearlessly threatened the proprietors with revolt upon hearing of Eastchurch's appointment. The revolutionary ferment was stirred further by the example of Bacon's Rebellion in neighboring Virginia, by the influx of rebellious Baconian refugees from that colony, and by the influence in Albemarle of former governor William Drummond, one of the Baconian leaders. Furthermore, the popular opposition had another dynamic leader in John Culpeper, surveyor-general of Carolina, who had years ago been arrested in South Carolina for sedition and rebellion, and had escaped north to avoid the hangman. Arriving in Albemarle, he joined Durant and the opposition, and called upon the people to resist the enforcement of the Navigation Act. The revolution, in short, needed but a spark to be ignited into flame. It found its spark in December 1677, when a New England merchantman arrived at Albemarle with a cargo of supplies. Miller arrested the skipper, who promised to leave at once and not return. When the North Carolinians tried to persuade the master of the cargo to stay, Miller arrested the eminent George Durant on the charge of treason. This tyrannical act touched off the rebellion and Culpeper, Valentine Byrd, and their men arrested the governor and his Council and called free elections for a new Assembly. The elections revealed the overwhelming popular support for the rebellion, and the newly elected Assembly appointed a Council and chose John Culpeper as governor and collector of the customs. The Assembly proceeded to indict Miller, appoint new justices in the colony, and warn Eastchurch, hurrying to the American mainland, to stay out of Albemarle.

Culpeper and his allies governed Albemarle for a period of two years. Culpeper justified his actions in a manifesto charging Miller with tyranny and corruption. The new governor was clearly in a difficult spot. With Virginia again tightly under the rule of the Berkeleyan oligarchy, and with the rebellion in Maryland a failure, Culpeper's tiny colony could hardly hold out in independence indefinitely against the might of England. Culpeper could hardly take the route of ultimate independence, which Bacon had begun to envision before his death. An immediate threat from Virginia loomed when Governor Eastchurch arrived and prepared to lead a military force against the colony. Eastchurch's death, however, ended that menace. Culpeper felt that he had to move quickly. Going to England, he pleaded his case there in conflict with Miller, who had escaped from prison in Albemarle. Culpeper convinced the proprietors of the rightness of his case, but the Crown, more sensitive to rebellion, arrested Culpeper for treason. Culpeper was defended by the leading Carolina proprietor, the Earl of Shaftesbury (Lord Ashley Cooper), and was acquitted, but he had been permanently deposed from power.

Miller was deposed and Durant freed by the proprietors, but the whole system against which the rebellion had protested—including the attempt to levy a quitrent of a penny an acre—remained intact. For a few years, affairs proceeded smoothly, as the newly appointed governor, Seth Sothel, who had bought the Earl of Clarendon's one-eighth share of Carolina, was captured on his way to America by pirates and held captive for three years. In the interim, the Durant party remained in control with Jenkins selected by the Council as acting governor, but now meekly enforcing the British regulations. Attempts by Miller and his associates to stir up counterrevolution met with no success. In 1683, however, the supposedly moderate Sothel was released from captivity, and the North Carolinians were soon to find that if they had been chastised with whips they were now to be chastised with scorpions. For Sothel proceeded to terrorize and plunder the colony without mercy. One of his favorite devices was to seize any property that he fancied, and then to imprison any owner who had the temerity to object. A typical incident: when two ships arrived from the West Indies, Sothel seized their perfectly legitimate captains as "pirates" and confiscated their property. One of the captains died in prison from maltreatment. Before death, the captain made a will naming as executor of his estate one of the leading men of the Albemarle colony, Thomas Pollock. Governor Sothel, however, refused to probate the will and seized the dead man's property hinself. When Pollock threatened to tell the story to England, Sothel imprisoned Pollock as well. The chain of imprisonments continued to lengthen: when George Durant protested against such proceedings as unlawful, Sothel immediately jailed Durant and confiscated his entire estate. Sothel withheld and pocketed the salaries of subordinate officials and accepted bribes from criminals. To make the cup of the Carolinians still more bitter, Virginia passed a law in 1679 prohibiting any importation of Carolina tobacco. The motives for the law were twofold: to stifle the competition of Albemarle tobacco and to assert an irredentist Virginia territorial claim to sovereignty over Albemarle. This crippled Albemarle's tobacco still further and left it even more dependent on the illegal smuggling to New England. Moreover, the Virginians incited border Indians to make war upon the Albemarle settlers.

15

The Glorious Revolution
and its Aftermath

Maryland

Sixteen eighty-eight was the year of the Glorious Revolution in England, the year when Great Britain experienced the last of its great political upheavals of the turbulent seventeenth century. The Stuart king, the Catholic James II, was deposed in that year and the monarchy secured to the impeccably Protestant William and Mary of Orange. This year of upheaval signaled the troubled and oppressed colonies to seize the opportunity of Britain's distraction at home to try to secure their own freedom.

By ironic coincidence, Lord Baltimore sent William Joseph as deputy governor to run the Maryland colony in late 1688, and Joseph opened the Assembly only nine days after James II had been deposed by William and Mary. In his opening address—delivered considerably before news of the Glorious Revolution reached America—Joseph proved himself to be an extreme advocate of divine and feudal right to rule. He declared: "The power by which we are assembled here is undoubtedly derived from God, to the King, and from the King to his Excellency the Lord Proprietary, and from his said Lordship to us."

When news came of the change of regimes in England, people angrily remembered that Joseph had, in the fall of 1688, insisted on the colony's giving thanks for the birth of a Catholic heir to the throne. Agitation also arose in the colony because Lord Baltimore's courier, coming to order the colony to proclaim allegiance to William and Mary, died en route and left Maryland in unresolved ferment. All the latent anti-Catholicism of the Protestant masses in the colony rose to the surface, aided by the fact that the proprietor was Catholic and the privileged oligarchy in Maryland largely so—the appointed Council, for example, had a Catholic majority. Was a Catholic plot under way? Would the proprietary refuse to acknowledge William and Mary and join James II in his plans for war against his successor? James soon landed in Ireland with French troops, and the colonists well remembered that James' proconsul in Ireland was Richard Talbot, Duke of Tyrconnel, a relative and close friend of Lord Baltimore. Rumors swept all the American colonies, not only Maryland: the French colonies were about to march on the English colonies in alliance with James; Catholic subversives were planning to help them; and Catholics and Indians were conspiring together to massacre Protestants. It is understandable that the agitation would be most severe in Maryland, where the proprietor was Catholic and the bulk of the people Protestant.

In April 1689 there was formed "an Association in arms for the defense of the Protestant Religion, and for asserting the right of King William and Queen Mary to the Province of Maryland and all the English Dominions." Leading the association was John Coode, the old revolutionary who had been freed for his part in the Fendall revolt of 1681. Coode had married a daughter of his old confrere, Thomas Gerrard. Other leaders included many eminent men in the colony: Nehemiah Blakiston, collector of the customs; another son-in-law of Gerrard, Kenelm Chesseldine, Speaker of the House of Burgesses; and Colonel Henry Fowles of the militia. When rumors spread that the Catholics were arming themselves in the statehouse at St. Marys, Coode, at the head of several hundred armed men, marched on the capital. On August 1, Joseph and the Council surrendered to the Coode rebels. Coode and the Assembly petitioned William and Mary to end the proprietary regime and finally, in 1691, the new king agreed.

Coode and his followers engaged in violent anti-Catholic propaganda in the course of their revolutionary agitation. However, Coode's close association with Catholics and his ancient opposition to the proprietary lead to the conclusion that, at least on Coode's part, the anti-Catholic agitation was but a convenient *point d'appui* for his aim of ridding Maryland of the tyrannical and feudal proprietary. In Coode's own history of the rebellion, he stressed the "injustice and tyranny under which we groan . . . the absolute authority exercised over us in the seizure of their persons, forfeiture and loss of their goods."

While the Coode rebellion succeeded in overturning the proprietary, the success was only temporary. Aside from the fact that the structure of land tenure remained the same, the proprietor was only displaced for a short period of years. When the third Lord Baltimore died in 1715, the Crown granted the proprietorship once again to the Baltimore family, which had converted from Catholic to Protestant. In the meanwhile, the Crown continued to turn over part of the collected quitrents to the proprietary.

What did change was the religious complexion of the government and society in Maryland. The old tradition of religious toleration in Maryland was abandoned, taxes immediately began to be levied in 1692 for the establishment of the Anglican church, and any further immigration of Catholics into the colony was prohibited under severe penalties. Furthermore, the public celebration of the mass was outlawed. The capital city was summarily shifted from St. Marys, the center of Catholicism in the colony, to Protestant Providence, now renamed Annapolis. (So much was St. Marys strictly a governmental city that it now rapidly diminished to the virtual status of a ghost town.)

Only a small minority of the colony were Anglicans. The Puritans, leaders in the rebellion against the proprietary, were naturally chagrined to be confronted with an established church, but they were appeased when assured in 1702 of freedom of worship, which extended even to Quakers. This limited toleration was established despite the strenuous efforts of the head of the Anglican church in Maryland, Dr. Thomas Bray. Bray had persuaded the Assembly to pass a bill outlawing all forms of worship but the Anglican form in the colony, but fortunately this extreme provision was disallowed by the Crown. Also irritating was the fact that the Anglican ministers were paid by a new poll tax, which was most heavy on the poor. The spirit of Crown toleration, however, did not spread to the Catholics, against whom William pursued his long-time vendetta. The spirit of the government of the time may be seen from a 1704 incident, in which two Catholic priests were arrested for saying mass. They were refused the benefit of counsel; the chapel of St. Marys, venerated by Catholics as the first church in Maryland, was closed down as "scandalous and offensive to the government"; and Governor John Seymour delivered to the priests the following diatribe:

It is the unhappy temper of you and all your tribe to grow insolent upon civility and never know how to use it . . . if the necessary laws that are made were let loose, they are sufficient to crush you, and which (if your arrogant principles have not blinded you) you must need to dread. You might, methinks, be content to live quietly as you may, and let the exercise of your superstitious vanities be confined to yourselves, without proclaiming them at public times and in public places, unless you expect by your gaudy shows and serpentine policy to amuse the multitude and beguile the unthinking weakest part of them—an act of deceit well known to be amongst you. . . . In plain and few words, if you intend to live here, let me hear no more of these things; for if I do . . . be assured I'll chastise you. . . . I'll remove the evil by sending you where you will be dealt with as you deserve. . . . Pray take notice I am an English Protestant gentleman and can never equivocate.

The House of Delegates was so pleased by this tirade that they formally commended the governor for protecting "Her Majesty's Protestant subjects here against the insolence and growth of Popery. . . . "

Anti-Catholic hysteria surged through England and the colonies, in the course of a lengthy war waged by England against Catholic France, and of attempts by the Stuart pretender to return to the throne. The crackdown on Catholics was pursued zealously in Maryland. No Catholic was permitted to buy real estate or to practice as a lawyer. Loyalty oaths were to be forced upon all Catholics, and any who refused would be incapable of inheriting land or holding office. The oaths were deliberately worded in such a way that no conscientious Catholic could swear to them. The Test Oath, as required by an Act of 1699, compelled the oath-taker to swear: "I do believe that in the Sacrament of the Lord's Supper there is not any transubstantiation. . . . And that the invocation or adoration of the Virgin Mary or any other saints, and the sacrifice of the Mass as they are now used in the Church of Rome, are superstitious and idolatrous." If a Catholic widow had married a Protestant, her children could be forcibly seized by the state and placed under Protestant guardians. Catholics were also assessed at rates for emergency tax levies double those of everyone else. A special duty was also levied on all Irish "papist" servants coming into the colony: the duty was doubled in 1717. Catholic priests were in 1698 even prevented by proclamation of the governor (as urged by the House of Delegates) from visiting the sick and dying during a plague. The proclamation ranted:

> Several Popish priests and zealous Papists make it their constant business (under pretense of visiting the sick . . .) to seduce, delude, and persuade divers of His Majesty's good Protestant subjects to the Romish faith, by which means sundry . . . have been withdrawn from the Protestant religion, by law established, and from the due and natural obedience they owe to his said Majesty and laws, whereby the party, so reconciled and withdrawn, as well as their procurers and counsellors, have justly incurred the penalty and forfeitures of high treason.

Not only were the priests and their possible dying converts subject to severe penalty, but also anyone who knew of such offenses and did not inform the authorities.

In 1704 a truly comprehensive act was passed for the persecution of Catholics. Catholics were prohibited from practicing their religion, and priests from exercising their office. A reward of 100 pounds was offered to any informer giving evidence against a priest saying mass, and the penalty for a convicted priest was life imprisonment. It was life imprisonment as well for any Catholic found guilty of running a school or educating a child. Children were encouraged to inform on their parents "to the end that the Protestant children of Popish parents may not . . . want of fitting maintenence. . . . Be it enacted . . . that if any such parent in order to the compelling such . . . Protestant child to change . . . religion, shall refuse to allow such child a fitting maintenance suitable to the degree and ability of such parent . . . then upon complaint thereof . . . it shall be lawful . . . to make such order. . . . "

Fortunately, however, Queen Anne, less intolerant than her Anglican minions in Maryland, decided to *allow* private family practice of the Catholic religion. As a result, Catholic services remained partially underground by being held in family chapels on planters' estates, with other Catholic families of the area invited as "guests."

Benedict Calvert, the fourth Lord Baltimore, had taken the precaution of converting to the Protestant faith, and so when his father and he both died in 1715, the Calverts were handed back the proprietary title, which now went to Charles Calvert, fifth Lord Baltimore. The resumption of the now Protestant proprietary by no means slackened the pace of persecution. The Anglicans were worried about continuing conversions from their faith and Governor John Hart ordered the surveillance of Catholic priests; any suspected of visiting the homes of dying persons were forced to take the Test Oath. Refusal to swear to the Test Oath meant imprisonment. In 1716 a law decreed that any officeholder caught in any "Popish assembly" and participating in the celebration of the mass would forfeit his office. And finally, in 1718 the Catholics of Maryland were disfranchised through making the Test Oath a requirement for voting.

One amusing byproduct of the anti-Catholic hysteria among the Maryland Anglicans was the apparent existence of a plot by Governor Hart and some leading Anglican clergymen to spread the rumor that young Lord Baltimore and his guardian Lord Guilford were secret Catholics. They thereby hoped to persuade the Crown to turn the proprietary over to Hart himself. The man who reported the plot to the bishop of London was himself a leading Anglican minister in the colony, the Reverend Jacob Henderson. Henderson in turn was accused of being soft on Catholics, an accusation he indignantly denied.

The oppressive poll tax for support of the newly established Anglican church was made payable in a fixed rate in tobacco, which was then the medium of exchange in Maryland. Gresham's law operated here as in currency, and since the law did not specify the quality of tobacco, payment was always made in the very poorest and most unmarketable grades. As a result, Maryland's established clergymen were continually impoverished and only the poorest quality of them settled in the colony.

The Carolinas

The North Carolinians, inspired by the Glorious Revolution, seized the opportunity to rid themselves, once and for all, of the tyranny of Seth Sothel. An uprising in 1689, led by Thomas Pollock and other leading colonists, resulted in the arrest of Sothel and his banishment from the province for a year. Sothel was removed permanently from the governorship. He then hied himself to the sister colony of South Carolina, where he was also one-eighth proprietor. The proprietary appointed Colonel Philip Ludwell the new governor of Albemarle, now called North Carolina. Ludwell, Virginia's leading Berkeleyan, was instructed to redress the grievances of the colonists arising from the Sothel regime. Captain John Gibbs, who had apparently been chosen by the Council as governor to succeed Sothel, tried to maintain the revolutionary impetus, and in 1690 launched an armed rebellion against Ludwell. But the conciliatory policy had done its work and Gibbs' rebellion lacked popular support. Gibbs and his band were defeated and fled to Virginia. Gibbs and Ludwell both went to London to put their cases before the proprietary and Gibbs, as might have been expected, was repudiated.

Though growing rapidly, South Carolina had a population of something over 3,100 in 1690, still by far the smallest of the Southern colonies. This colony too was racked by strife and accumulated grievances. Like its fellow colony Albemarle, Charleston colony suffered from the crippling restrictions on its tobacco and intercoastal trade inflicted by the Navigation Acts. It also bitterly resisted repeated attempts by the proprietors—if anything more determined than in Albemarle, for less settler resistance was expected farther south—to impose Shaftesbury's grandiose feudal proposals on the colony. In addition, South Carolina suffered from the demand that quitrents be paid at the far higher rate in coin instead of in commodities. In 1682, the proprietary suddenly decreed that all quitrents must be paid in English money, thus eliminating the option to pay in commodities, and it tightened enforcement of the levy. The aroused Assembly protested that the people had been "extremely hard dealt with," but the proprietors retorted that their regulations had been designed to counteract those who "instilled fancies" into the heads of the people in order to avoid payment of quitrents.

Further problems were caused by the practice of kidnapping Indians to use for slaves and thus make economically viable the tobacco plantations, a procedure that naturally stimulated retaliatory attacks by the Indians. Conflicts unique to this colony arose from the unwillingness of the English settlers to allow the substantial number of new Huguenot immigrants to vote, and from a fear of a Spanish invasion into what the Spaniards regarded as their imperial territory. The Huguenots were French Protestant refugees from the revocation of the Edict of Nantes in 1685.

James Colleton, a brother of one of the proprietors and given 48,000 acres in the colony, arrived in South Carolina to become governor in 1687. He immediately alienated the colonists by preventing them from sailing on an expedition of war against the Spanish headquarters at St. Augustine, Florida. Colleton came to the colony determined to impose his will, and particularly to stop the widespread evasion of the hated Navigation Laws and quitrents. He insisted on enforcing these edicts to the hilt, and even on attempting to collect arrears of quitrents. Particularly bitter for the colonists was Colleton's expulsion, upon arriving at the colony, of all the menbers of the Assembly who opposed the restrictive laws and taxes. All this incurred the growing rage and resentment of the colony and especially of the Assembly. Finally, in 1689 the alarmed proprietors instructed Colleton to suspend all further sessions of the legislature. This tyrannical act further fanned the flames of incipient rebellion, spurred by the fact that the South Carolinian laws had to be renewed every two years to remain in effect, and that a biennial term was now expiring. The final straw occurred in the spring of 1690, when Colleton imposed the despotism of martial law upon the colony. This embraced such actions as imposing a very heavy fine on a minister for delivering a sermon displeasing to the government. In addition, Colleton used his powers of martial law to grant himself a privileged monopoly of trade with the Indians.

Revolution, as we have pointed out, is a time of rapid change, and this often means sharp changes in a person's values and his views of institutions. Seth Sothel, the former governor of North Carolina who was deposed the year before, had arrived in South Carolina to see a similar revolutionary process brewing against the tyranny of the governor in Charleston. Sothel had apparently learned his lesson; his views changed, and he became the leader of the people's opposition to Colleton. When Colleton inflicted the final act of repression in imposing martial law, Sothel led a revolutionary coup against the governor. Declaring himself governor, Sothel reconvened the suppressed Assembly and banished Colleton from the colony. Sothel's action was ignited by a petition signed by over four hundred of the leading citizens. The petition detailed the grievances of the people of the colony, including: the attempts to impose several variants of proposals found in Locke's *Fundamental Constitutions;* the imposition of martial law; the governor's monopolization of the Indian trade; arbitrary arrests; expulsion for any excess of freedom of speech, even by a councillor; and attempts to enforce higher quitrents.

Sothel was allowed to continue his rule for only one year. In the fall of 1691, the proprietors ousted Sothel from office and charged him with high treason. Although Sothel was a one-eighth proprietor of the colony, it was also true that he had organized a revolution against the authority appointed by the proprietary as a whole. Sothel fled back to Albemarle, where his term of banishment was over, and where he soon died in poverty and obscurity. Especially notable in Sothel's brief term in office was his stimulating the Assembly to pass significantly liberalizing laws. In particular, the French, Swiss, and other non-English immigrants were granted rights equal to those of the English settlers, and severe punishment was decreed for anyone who killed a slave. Other new laws, on the other hand, were repressive: requiring licenses of all retailers of liquor, regulating ship's pilots, and regulating the Indian trade. The proprietors, on removing Sothel, unfortunately also nullified the laws of his administration.

The ultimate failure of the revolution did not, of course, end the grievances underlying the unrest in the Carolinas. Grudgingly, the proprietary finally issued a general amnesty. For a while the proprietary tried the unsuccessful experiment of uniting the two Carolinas, appointing

Philip Ludwell as governor of both colonies. The proprietors tried to force the North Carolinian colonists to send their representatives to the distant Charleston Assembly. This plan was quickly abandoned, and each of the Carolinas was governed by a deputy governor of its own, with the main governor stationed in South Carolina. Each colony also retained its own Assembly, and therefore essentially its own separate government. As in other liberalizing moves, the proprietors promised to abandon their attempts to impose the dicta contained in the Shaftesbury-Locke *Fundamental Constitutions;* it was now acknowledged that the Carolinas were to be governed by the original charter. In addition, the proprietary removed all obstacles to freedom of trade with the Indians. It also vetoed an act of the Ludwell administration that harassed the rural Huguenots by requiring a uniform hour for all Sunday church services in the colony. Another constructive measure during the Ludwell term was that permitting quitrents to be paid in commodities.

John Archdale, an English Quaker who had become one of the eight proprietors by purchasing the share of Sir John Berkeley, became governor of the Carolinas in 1695. He assumed office with the intent of allaying the grievances of the colonies. His term lasted for only one year, but that year saw a significant liberalization in the Carolina colonies. In the South, peace was made with the Indians; in particular, the practice of whites kidnapping and enslaving the natives was ended. Furthermore, the quitrent burden was significantly lightened, including cessation of the attempt to collect the arrears. From the 1690s on, the main grievance concerning the quitrent had been the threat hanging over the colonists from the huge arrears of uncollected claims. Also, quitrents were made payable in commodities as well as in money. From that point on, the quitrent of one penny per acre was scarcely enforced in the proprietary colony, and the expected revenue accruing to the proprietary dwindled to a negligible sum, not nearly enough to pay the expenses of the local officials. Furthermore, Archdale reshuffled the South Carolina Council to give the Dissenters the majority, and also decreed that with rare exceptions the proprietors could not annul laws without the Assembly's consent. The liberal reforms continued the following year, during the administration of Archdale's successor, the Dissenter Joseph Blake, also a one-eighth proprietor. Blake's Act of 1697 admitted into full civil rights the important Huguenot population of South Carolina as well as other aliens, and guaranteed religious liberty to all Christians except Catholics. This was an important reform in a colony where the large majority of people were Dissenters of one hue or another from the Church of England. Not until 1704, however, were the alien-born permitted to vote in South Carolina.

The Archdale and Blake reforms hardly eliminated the basic conflicts in the colony. Thus, in 1698 the proprietary reneged on its promise—given in the wake of the Sothel rebellion against Colleton—to forget about the

Fundamental Constitutions and a new variant of this thoroughly disliked proposal was introduced again and continued to be introduced until 1705.

In 1699, indeed, the South Carolina Assembly saw fit to address a list of grievances to the proprietary. The list included violations of the requirement of consent to all laws by the Assembly, and the accumulation of vast landed estates in the hands of a few privileged persons. The Assembly asked that no land tract be granted over the size of 1,000 acres. Even the king's collector of customs, the Tory Edward Randolph, warned the Crown in 1699 that "there are but few settled inhabitants in this province, the Lords [proprietors] having taken up vast tracts for their own use . . . where the land is most commodious for settlement, which prevents peopling the place. . . . " The Assembly also objected strongly to the English tariff on South Carolina rice and naval stores (turpentine, pitch, tar)—but, as in the case of the other grievances, to no effect.

A major grievance soon became Randolph himself, who had arrived in 1699 to enforce vigorously the neglected Navigation Laws and the suppression of popular but illegal trade. Randolph wrote to the Crown of his horror at the pervasive commerce, including trade with the Dutch, all with simply "no regard to the acts of trade." The institution of royal admiralty courts appointed by the Crown for vigorous enforcement also angered the colonists greatly. Indeed, the South Carolina Assembly, under severe pressure by the people, tried to pass laws in 1700 and 1701—all of course vetoed—to restrict the activities of the royal customs officials.

In North Carolina, the Archdale reforms also lowered the quitrents. Ludwell had attempted to do so, but had for his efforts been angrily removed from office by the proprietary. Soon attempts to collect a penny per acre were abandoned and the rate came to be set generally at two shillings per hundred acres, with payment accepted in commodities. For some land the quitrents were far less. Quitrents continued to be collected, at least partially, for the remainder of the proprietary term. Enforcement, however, was often evaded, and the quitrents were generally absorbed in salaries to local officials, so that the return to the proprietors was small.

From their beginning in the mid-seventeenth century, the Carolina counties had been conspicuous and notable havens of religious liberty. Here they contrasted to other American colonies, including their Spanish neighbors to the south. North Carolina, indeed, had been founded by independent settlers escaping religious and political discrimination in Virginia. The proprietary had announced from the first its intention to establish the Church of England in the Carolinas, but driven by desire to profit by encouraging settlers in the colony, had never put this plan into effect. Into this relatively free haven, then, came numerous dissenting groups, including the much persecuted Quakers and Huguenots, and the Anglicans were in a considerable minority. In fact, even the Anglicans in South Carolina believed strongly in self-government on a congregational level and insisted eventually on appointing their own ministers. In this, they were influenced by the decentralizing spirit of the Presbyterian majority of the colony. And as for North Carolina with its preponderance of Quakers, there had not even been a single Anglican church or priest in the colony, so little was there of an Anglican establishment in the Carolinas.

But this happy condition—this approach to separation of church and state—was not destined to last. Instead, at the turn of the eighteenth century, the Anglican Old Guard moved purposefully and aggressively to fasten a state church upon the only Southern colonies that had yet escaped this incubus. This was a particularly bitter pill for the dissenting majority that had enjoyed religious freedom.

The Anglican aggression was ignited by events in England where, about 1700, a renewed wave of Anglican repression under Queen Anne's regime was launched against the Dissenters. The peace accord with the Dissenters that had emerged from the Glorious Revolution and been embodied in the Toleration Act of 1689 was now rudely shattered. One of the leaders of a campaign dedicated to the extermination of the Dissenters within one generation was Lord Granville, who also happened to be the palatine of Carolina—that proprietor entrusted with colonial affairs. In 1704, Lord Granville instructed the new governor of South Carolina, Sir Nathaniel Johnson, a veteran supporter of the Stuarts and the Colleton regime, to secure the establishment of the church in the Carolinas.

Johnson was confronted, in South Carolina, with an Assembly majority of Dissenters. To drive through an establishment bill, therefore, he had to resort to trickery and fraud. First, very early in the 1704 session when many members were absent, Johnson rushed through an act excluding all non-Anglicans from the Assembly. This measure was at least temporarily needed, in order to drive through an establishment bill without fear of the Dissenter majority; and the latter was accomplished by the fall of 1704. The bill established the Anglican church and imposed taxation on the public for its support. Many Anglicans opposed this tyrannical seizure; one, the Reverend Edward Marston, was deprived of his salary, deposed from his office, and almost arrested by the new Assembly.

The understandably bitter dissenting colonists appealed the tyrannical law to the proprietor, who of course rejected the appeal. But the Crown and the Board of Trade were persuaded to nullify the two laws. The Crown did not want an establishment so severe on the rights of Dissenters that the growth and the commerce of the colony with England would be repressed. Even the bishop of London, whose diocese included the Carolinas, sided with the protesting colonists. The act of establishment, however, was disallowed because it was too liberal: it allowed the laymen of a parish to remove a minister, thus striking at the principle of hierarchical control of the church by the state.

If both edicts of the Crown had been immediately obeyed, the Assembly, now including a dissenting majority, would have never passed a new act establishing the Anglican church. Hence, Governor Johnson's new Assembly of 1706, completely excluding Dissenters, rushed through a new establishment act without the provision for lay removal of ministers. Lay members, however, were permitted to select their ministers. Tax funds were appropriated for churches and ministerial salaries; and church repairs were to be paid from assessments on all the inhabitants of the parish. The dissenting Assemblymen were only readmitted after the establishment bill was safely passed.

The Dissenters were naturally angry at their treatment. Though they were no longer excluded from the Assembly, any repeal of the state church would be blocked by the governor's veto. The Dissenters rioted at length during 1707, the riots being led by a political club headed by prominent Dissenters. Included in these rebellious protests was a new phenomenon: a *woman's* political club.

The Dissenters were also embittered because one of their great leaders, Landgrave Thomas Smith, was being persecuted by the Johnson regime. For criticizing the Assembly in a private letter, Smith was ordered arrested; when he escaped, the Assembly sought to disqualify Smith from public office for life. But, in this affair at least, the Dissenters had their revenge. Now Speaker of a Dissenter-controlled Assembly, Smith had the satisfaction of arresting former Speaker Colonel Risbee, the reputed author of the exclusion act, for disrespectful words spoken in private against the new Assembly. Finally, the Dissenters also gained the temporary satisfaction of forcing the proprietors to remove the hated Johnson from office in 1708.

The drive for a state church occurred at the same time in North Carolina, which was at least formally ruled by the South Carolina governor. The northern colony, true to its tradition, was even more dissenting and rebellious than its southern neighbor. North Carolina's troubles began with the appointment of Henderson Walker, a zealous Anglican, as deputy governor in 1699. Walker, deeply disturbed that North Carolina had successfully gone forty years "without priests or altar," maneuvered through the Assembly the Vestry Act of 1701, which imposed a state church on North Carolina, including a poll tax on the colonists for support of the Anglican clergymen. The act was disallowed by the proprietary for not going far enough in paying the clergy—but the fight had just begun.

Lord Granville's instructions to the governor of South Carolina, Sir Nathaniel Johnson, to secure whatever legislation was necessary to impose a state church on the Carolinas, led Johnson to replace Walker as deputy governor of North Carolina with Colonel Robert Daniel. Daniel could not hope to drive the establishment through the North Carolina Assembly, however, as it had a comfortable Quaker majority. The zealous Daniel therefore decided to attain his goal by expelling the Quakers from the Assembly, and used as his weapon a dubious legal application of the new Test Oath of allegiance to Queen Anne, required of all public officials in England. This oath excluded Quakers, who by their religion could only "affirm" and could not swear to oaths. The expulsion of the Quaker assemblymen left the high-church party with a small majority and this party now drove through the new Vestry Act—establishing the church—as well as an act imposing the Test Oath for all public officials (including assemblymen) in the future. The embittered Quakers were able to pressure Governor Johnson to remove Daniel in 1705, but the damage had been done. Despite the establishment, however, Anglican zeal was so weak in freewheeling North Carolina that not until 1732 did the colony see a regular Anglican minister.

The new deputy governor, welcomed by the Quakers for his supposedly liberal views, was Thomas Cary, a Charleston merchant and son-in-law of the great Archdale. But Cary betrayed his supporters by repressing the Quakers even more ardently than had his predecessors. Cary not only expelled the Quakers from the Assembly, but also levied a heavy fine on anyone presuming to enter office without taking the Test Oath. Furthermore, Cary further weakened the Assembly by having an act passed fining anyone daring to promote actively his own election to any office.

The numerous body of North Carolina Quakers finally sent John Porter (a non-Quaker) to England in 1707 to plead their case with the lord proprietors. Two of the proprietors, John Archdale and John Danson, were Quakers, and they persuaded the others of the justice of the Quaker case. The proprietors abolished the Test Oath, deposed Cary, suspended Governor Johnson's authority over North Carolina, and authorized the Council of North Carolina to select its own president, who would assume the full duties as governor.

The Council then selected as president William Glover, who governed North Carolina in Cary's stead, but the Anglican Glover betrayed the Quakers in his turn by still insisting on enforcement of the Test Oath. John Porter and the infuriated Quakers now formed an alliance with the double-turncoat Cary to try to oust Glover from his rule. The election to the Assembly of 1708 was won by the Cary-Porter forces, who disregarded Glover's insistence on the Test Oath, declared Cary governor, voided all the laws of the Glover regime, and appointed many Quakers to office. Leader of the Cary forces in the Assembly was the Speaker, the powerful Edward Moseley, a wealthy planter and devout Anglican, who nevertheless steadfastly supported religious freedom and opposed any establishment. Glover, however, refused to recognize the legality of this democratic upheaval and fled to Virginia still claiming the governorship.

The relatively liberal Cary-Porter rule lasted until 1711, when the proprietary decided to stamp out the seditious popular regime, and sent Edward Hyde, a cousin of Queen Anne, to be the new governor of North Carolina, now permanently separated from South Carolina. Hyde immediately instituted a regime of repression, allying himself completely with the Gloverite faction. All the liberal laws, as well as the court proceedings of Cary's second administration, were nullified, and the Test Oath was reimposed on all public officials on pain of a heavy 100-pound fine for all refusals to take it. The Quaker Assemblymen were once again expelled. In addition, a law was passed to punish severely all "seditious words" or "scurrilous libels" against the government, the government itself, of course, being the judge of what was seditious or scurrilous against itself. Moreover, Cary and Porter were indicted for various crimes and misdemeanors.

To counter this repression, Thomas Cary organized an armed rebellion against the Hyde regime. In the midst of the fighting, Governor Alexander Spottswood of Virginia sent a force of royal marines to aid Hyde, which counterrevolutionary intervention dispersed the rebellion. Cary and other leaders fled to Virginia. There he was arrested, however, and sent to England to stand trial for treason, but was released for lack of evidence. Thus the rebellion failed and the Test Oath remained in force in North Carolina.

These struggles in the Carolinas weakened the authority of the proprietary and helped make them ripe for the abolition of proprietary rule in South Carolina in 1719 and in North Carolina in 1729. By 1730, then, the Carolinas and Virginia were both royal colonies, leaving Maryland with its restored proprietary as the only proprietary colony in the South.

While these conflicts were going on, North Carolina was experiencing a rapid growth. A heavy influx of people came from Virginia, seeking more religious freedom or cheaper land free of arbitrary landed monopolies. North Carolina's status as a refuge is shown by Virginia's repeated accusations that it was harboring runaway slaves. Finally, the first town was laid out in North Carolina: Bath, in 1704, which promptly became the capital. Many of the immigrants were European refugees including French Protestant Huguenots and German and Swiss palatines.

Treatment of the Indians, however, grew increasingly brutal. The white settlers had participated in the Indian fur trade, they had learned from the Indians techniques of clearing the unfamiliar land, of cultivating the soil, and of growing such new crops as corn, tobacco, and potatoes. Now the whites repaid the Indians by embarking on a campaign of decimation. Proclamations stated that the Indians would be exterminated "like vermin," and the legislature of North Carolina granted bounties for Indian scalps. Indian prisoners of war, including many children, were sold into slavery by their captors.

16

Virginia After Bacon's Rebellion

The crushing of Bacon's Rebellion had left Virginia itself in the control of the despotic Governor Berkeley and his Green Spring clique. Even after Berkeley was recalled at the urging of the king's commissioners, the Green Spring oligarchy continued to rule the colony until news arrived in the fall of 1677 of Berkeley's death. At that point, news came of the appointment of Thomas Lord Culpeper as governor; until his arrival, Colonel Herbert Jeffreys, one of the king's commissioners, was to continue as lieutenant governor. But Jeffreys soon fell ill; and the Council, dominated by the Green Spring faction, effectively continued its oppressive rule of the colony.

Jeffreys died at the end of 1678 and was succeeded by Sir Henry Chicherley, who at last held a fair election for the Assembly the following year. The new Assembly began to institute reforms: for example, reenacting Bacon's laws, authorizing the freemen and housekeepers of each parish to select two men to sit with the judges in the county courts. But Chicherley, too, was old and sick and reforms were therefore not pressed forward. Finally the king forced the reluctant Lord Culpeper to sail personally for Virginia or give up his governorship, and Culpeper arrived in the spring of 1680. One of his first acts was to urge the Assembly—at the king's instigation—to provide a "permanent" revenue for the support of the government, but the Assembly refused to turn over the crucial power of the purse into the hands of the royal governor. The Assembly, however, finally passed the bill after considerable bullying and threats by Culpeper. The governor also tried to force a fantastically uneconomic plan on agricultural Virginia: compelling every county to construct a town and warehouse near water, and coercively restricting all trade in the county to that town. Fortunately, while the Assembly passed the law, the Crown realized the impracticality of such hothouse plans and vetoed the bill.

Culpeper also faced the perennial tobacco problem. Tobacco had been suffering grievously from twofold government interference: a fall in prices due to trade restrictions imposed by the Navigation Acts, and the restrictions of compulsory cartels. The restrictions raised tobacco prices, but at the expense of the more efficient farmers and planters, of reducing trade for all, and of greatly injuring American and European consumers. Moreover, the bulk of the price fall had been because of increased tobacco production. The fact that annual tobacco output in Virginia and Maryland in the 1680s reached twenty-eight million pounds shows that, for all the complaining, tobacco was still the most profitable line of investment. The repeated attempts at compulsory cartels cannot be excused on pleas of poverty. The fact that Virginia governors repeatedly tried to force the reduction of tobacco planting without success demonstrates that the profitability of tobacco was enough to overcome even government prohibition and trade restrictions. Thus, in 1640 the planter-dominated government had passed a law compelling the burning of half the colony's tobacco crop, fixing the price of tobacco, and relieving debtors from paying one-third of their debts for three years. In 1662, Berkeley and the leading Chesapeake planters petitioned the king to outlaw all planting and shipping of tobacco during the following year. In response, King Charles II, following the tradition of James and Charles I in wanting to compel a shift from tobacco planting, ordered the restriction of planting. Commissioners from Virginia and Maryland met in May 1663 and resolved to limit tobacco planting jointly; but though the Virginia Assembly obediently agreed, the Maryland Assembly refused. Undaunted, the Virginia planters managed to arrange a conference of commissioners from the three tobacco colonies—Virginia, Maryland, North Carolina—in the summer of 1666, and they agreed to outlaw all tobacco planting for the year of 1667. All three Assemblies then approved this plan for injuring the consumers in order to raise tobacco prices, but the colonies were saved at the last minute by the veto of Lord Baltimore for Maryland.

Now, in 1680, with tobacco crops even more bountiful, Culpeper resumed the old pressure by urging the king to prohibit all tobacco planting in Virginia, Maryland, and North Carolina during the following year. The plan for total prohibition, incidentally, would have particularly benefited tobacco speculators who had purchased the crop; their accumulated stocks would benefit most from the temporary price rise. Most gravely injured would be the most efficient, lowest-cost planters—as well as the consumers. When the king did not agree to total prohibition, the big planters put on pressure for a session of the Assembly to outlaw a year's tobacco planting in Virginia alone. Crowds in each county, led by the prominent local planters, sent petitions and held meetings clamoring for an Assembly session. Under this pressure, the infirm Sir Henry Chicherley, again acting governor after Culpeper had returned to England, called a special Assembly session for April

1682. But Culpeper, at the last minute, vetoed the session, forcing it to wait until November, when he would be back in the colony.

Deprived suddenly of their Assembly session, the planters rose in the "plant cutters rebellion." Beginning in Gloucester County on May 1, gangs of tobacco planters and their retinues engaged in an orgy of destroying tobacco plants, obviously the plants of those efficient and free-spirited planters who were willing to trust their fortunes to the marketplace. Despite arrests and patrols by the militia, the orgy of destruction spread to New Kent, Middlesex, and other counties. Lord Baltimore was moved to place armed guards along the Potomac to keep the frenzy from spreading to Maryland. The opponents of the plant cutting gained control of the Council and charged that the leader of the uprising was Major Robert Beverley, clerk of the Assembly and a leader of the Green Spring clique. They charged also—and with reason—that Chicherley was under Beverley's influence. Chicherley agreed to imprison Beverley, but otherwise issued a general pardon to the criminals, with one exception: for his punishment, one tobacco saboteur was ordered to build a bridge—a bridge conveniently near Chicherley's own plantation.

Returning to Virginia in December, Culpeper, understandably enraged at the soft treatment of the plant cutters, went overboard and declared that tobacco destruction was treason and thereupon hanged two of the leaders as an example to the people. Culpeper showed good economic sense in keeping secret and thus suppressing the king's authorization to end tobacco planting; he realized that if the planting of tobacco were really excessive the inefficient producers would soon shift to other industries.

Lord Culpeper's troubles with Virginia were aggravated by his unpopularity, for Culpeper, along with Lord Arlington, had received in 1673 the proprietary grant of thirty-one years of quitrents and escheats in Virginia. He had not received the right to govern, but his gaining of the governorship had been an attempt to enforce his feudalistic, proprietary claims. In 1681 Culpeper bought out Lord Arlington's share, but on being ousted by the king in mid-1683, he was happy in 1684 to sell his proprietary rights back to the Crown in return for a royal pension of 600 pounds a year for twenty-one years.

But Culpeper's removal by no means meant the end of conflict in the colony. On the contrary, the appointment of the despotic Francis Lord Howard began a four-year struggle in Virginia. Howard promptly launched a determined drive to exalt the royal prerogative over the Assembly and over the liberties of Virginians. Howard demanded a law to authorize the governor and Council to levy a high poll tax, up to the sum of twenty pounds of tobacco. Such a bill would eliminate the need to keep returning to the Assembly for annual appropriations. The burgesses, however, turned down the plan. Howard also wanted to revive the compulsory town-building plan and disclosed the king's instructions to eliminate the cherished custom of allowing judicial appeals from the (royally appointed) General Court to the General Assembly. The change meant that the administration of justice was now completely under control of the governor and his appointed officials, including the Council. Furthermore, Howard, under royal instructions, demanded that the Assembly repeal all permission granted to county courts and parish officials to make local laws, and to replace it by insisting that all local laws receive approval of the central government. But the burgesses failed to act on this proposal.

The lower house, the House of Burgesses, was understandably disturbed at this comprehensive assault on their and Virginia's liberties, and a general struggle ensued between governor and burgesses. Howard also refused to disclose his instructions, and thus to end rule by secrecy.

When the Catholic James II succeeded to the throne in February 1685, a new issue arose to exacerbate relations between Lord Howard and the people of Virginia. For Howard was a Catholic and he promptly proceeded to fire several officials of the colony and replace them with Catholics. To suppress the ground swell of criticism, Howard forbade all seditious discourses, and Colonel Charles Scarborough, a member of the House of Burgesses, was forcibly deprived of all his public offices. In addition, Howard persistently vetoed laws passed by the Assembly, persecuted its leaders, tried to bully it into meeting his demands. In all of this the majority of the governor's creatures, the Council, supported his actions. Another disturbing threat facing the House of Burgesses was use of the royal veto to impose laws, in effect, by vetoing their repeal. The burgesses sent a vigorous protest to the king against this practice, but the king countered by ordering Robert Beverley's removal as clerk of the House of Burgesses in late 1686, transforming the position into one appointed by the governor.

Now that the main threat to Virginian liberties had become the Crown and the royal prerogative, the displaced Green Spring clique, out of favor, shifted to take the lead of Virginians opposed to royal encroachments. The clique was now led by Robert Beverley and Philip Ludwell, and Ludwell assumed the leadership of the liberal popular opposition to royal tyranny in the Council. Ludwell was expelled from the Council by Howard in 1687, the year of Beverley's ouster. Howard also dismissed two other leading burgesses from all public offices.

Lord Howard raised fierce opposition by imposing a large fee of 200 pounds of tobacco for stamping official papers, and by shifting payment of quitrents from tobacco to the higher-valued sterling. Furthermore, Howard quarreled with the burgesses over the military. Howard naturally advocated a bigger militia whereas the burgesses wanted to relieve the colonists of the oppressive tax-and-resource burdens of the armed forces, and urged disbandment of the troops of the colony. Howard also struck a grievous blow at local rights and Assembly powers by personally decreeing repeal of permission given local courts and officials to make their own bylaws.

After dissolving in disgust the Assembly at the end of 1686, Lord Howard determined to continue his rule while the Assembly met in session as little as possible. In early 1688 royal orders compelled Howard to call the Assembly in the spring to pass a law prohibiting the export of bulk tobacco. Since tobacco was exported either in bulk or in hogshead, the scheme was clearly an attempt to grant special privileges to the tobacco merchants who packed their tobacco in hogsheads by outlawing their competition. The Assembly was also asked to aid New York in its projected war against the French. But the Assembly courageously and defiantly refused such aid, since New York—it saw perceptively—was in no real danger, and since it steadfastly refused to levy still higher taxes upon Virginia. The Burgesses persisted in their refusal to bow to the royal demands. The House of Burgesses also rejected the king's bill to outlaw bulk tobacco exports, pointing out acidly and correctly that the bill was originated by London tobacco merchants, and not even by Virginia planters.

During the Howard administration, the burgesses and the Virginians had lost the right to receive judicial appeals, to appoint their clerk, and to control certain revenues and fees. But the fierce struggle also helped retain many liberties for Virginians and the House of Burgesses—especially the general taxing power. Furthermore, a host of oppressive laws were spurned by the independent-minded Assembly.

The battle between Lord Howard and the bulk of Virginians came rudely to an end with the Glorious Revolution of 1688. Howard happened to be in England when the news came of James II's overthrow and the president of the Council became acting governor.

The Glorious Revolution had an unusually mild impact upon Virginia as compared with its effect on the other colonies, south and north. Rumors fed by anti-Catholic hysteria led the people of the Northern Neck, already disgruntled from opposing the Culpeper proprietary, to take up arms in their "defense." The new climate meant the Crown would grant a much friendlier hearing to Virginia's numerous grievances, and to Virginia's agent in England, Philip Ludwell. Howard made a determined attempt to stay in office, but Ludwell finally prevailed, and the Crown ordered the end of the hated fee of 200 pounds of tobacco for the official stamping of documents. Howard kept the nominal title of governor, but Capt. Francis Nicholson, lately lieutenant governor of New York, was sent to Virginia to rule as lieutenant governor. During the Nicholson administration of 1690–92, the governor managed to harmonize with and reconcile the opposition, although no fundamental reforms were passed.

Increasingly coming to the fore was one of Virginia's most bitter grievances—the problem of land monopoly in the Northern Neck. In 1649 Charles II had arbitrarily granted the enormous tract of land between the Rappahannock and Potomac rivers to Lord Hopton and a group of his friends, including Sir John Berkeley. Hopton's circle now had proprietary control of revenues from the area, but not of political power. In 1669, however, a renewed grant gave control of the local governmental policies at Northern Neck to

148

the proprietors. The proprietary menace to the Northern Neck could well have been ended when Lord Culpeper sold his proprietary claim to Virginia in 1684. But not only did the king refuse to buy the Northern Neck claim, he transformed the thirty-one-year grant into a permanent charter.

Philip Ludwell was not destined to remain long in his new role as champion of the liberties of the people. Ludwell joined the employ of Lord Culpeper as agent for managing the Neck, and soon Ludwell began to appoint government officials in the Neck area.

In early 1692, Lord Howard resigned from his nominal post as governor of Virginia and was succeeded by Sir Edmund Andros, formerly head of the Dominion of New England who now came to Virginia to assume the reins of power. Andros was an arch-Tory, fond of the royal prerogative, and so he resumed all the oppressions and conflicts of the Howard era. Andros insisted on a forced town-and-port creation program, but this and another revived bill to prohibit the export of bulk tobacco failed to pass the House of Burgesses. The burgesses also refused once more to send aid to New York, pointing out incisively that New York was not Virginia's first line of defense and indeed that the Iroquois—staunch allies of New York—were a most severe threat to Virginia. Finally, however, in 1695 the burgesses gave in to Andros' pressure and sent military aid to New York, paying for it by a temporary liquor tax.

Andros also introduced a frightening new note into his struggle with the colonists: continued hints that Virginia land titles were really invalid. Nothing could have been better calculated to inflame the opposition of the landowners.

One of the most important men in Virginia beginning in the 1690s was the Reverend James Blair, a young Scottish Anglican who had been appointed in 1689 as representative, or "commissary," in Virginia of the bishop of London. This was the first such appointment in America. Blair was instrumental in inducing the Assembly in 1691 to create a free governmental college, the College of William and Mary, rooted in the Anglican faith. Money for construction was raised from the Crown and the bulk of the governing trustees were selected by the Assembly, which also paid its operating support. Reverend Blair received a life appointment as president from the Assembly and was so confirmed by the bishop of London.

Blair combined political, ministerial, and educational activities, assuming a seat in the Council in 1694. He soon broke with Andros, who was apparently not theocratic enough for the young minister. Blair agitated for increased support for the established church, and King William and Queen Mary responded by asking the Assembly to pay the clergy in money or in tobacco valued at current prices. The House of Burgesses replied tartly that the ministers were well enough paid; whereupon, in mid-1696, the Anglican clergymen of the colony petitioned the Assembly for greater salaries and subsidies. The legislature yielded to the pressure, and increased subsidies for the ministers.

Blair's pressure finally resulted in Andros' removal in the spring of 1698, and his replacement as governor by Francis Nicholson, now returning to Virginia as full-fledged governor, rather than as Culpeper's deputy.

Nicholson effected a few badly needed reforms: on royal instructions, he had the great powers of the Council over the colony reduced; no longer could councillors be customs collectors, naval officers, and auditors all in one—thus reducing the practice of councillors' sitting in judgment on their own actions.

Nicholson also tried to institute land reforms. During the 1680s and 1690s, land engrossing through large arbitrary land grants had grown apace. Governor Andros, in particular, had granted large tracts to individuals, by selling to individual engrossers "rights" to land. The old headright system of granting fifty acres of land for each person settled in or brought to Virginia was hardly ideal; but selling rights to fifty-acre plots at one to five shillings per "right," completely cut the natural link between land settlement and ownership, and added to the monopolizing of unused land by speculators.

Typical of land abuses in Virginia was the case of a large planter, William Byrd II. The law required a land grantee to establish at least one settler to every 100 acres of his grant within ten years of the date of issue. Now this was hardly a satisfactory safeguard against land abuses, since the grantee rather than the settlers themselves was considered the property owner. The settlers either were forced into a quasi-feudal subservience to the privileged grantee, or else had to buy the land at prices far higher than the zero price that would have obtained without the engrossment by the government and its pet grantees. Of course, the settlers still had to spend money immigrating, clearing the land, etc., but at least no arbitrary cost would have been imposed on top of these expenses. Yet, despite these grave weaknesses, the law at least tried to establish *some* connection between landownership and settlement, and grantees like Byrd proceeded to evade even this vague limitation.

Thus, in 1688 William Byrd obtained a grant from the government of over 3,000 acres. He failed to get the land settled within the ten years, but being head of the Virginia land office he managed to delay forfeiting the land until 1701. At that point, Byrd got the same tract regranted to his close friend Nathaniel Harrison, who soon had the land regranted to Byrd for another ten years' chance. An additional tract of 6,000 acres was secured by Byrd. Failing to settle it in time, he had it transferred to his son.

Nicholson tried to reform these practices, but accomplished little. In his first administration he tried to revoke some land grants, but the Council refused to cooperate; in his second term he prohibited the practice of gaining more headright land by bringing in more Negro slaves. On the other hand, far less helpful were Nicholson's attempts to enforce quitrent payments to the Crown.

During the Nicholson administration, Virginia changed its capital from Jamestown nearby to the newly created city of Williamsburg in the spring

150

of 1700. A more lasting achievement was Nicholson's proclamation in 1703 of the English Act of Toleration in Virginia. Liberty of conscience for all religions was guaranteed. except for non-Protestants. This action guaranteed religious freedom to the new and growing dissenting Protestant sects in Virginia, especially Presbyterians, whose form of worship was quite close to the low Anglicanism of the colony.

The irascible Nicholson soon fell to quarreling with the Blair faction, by now intermarried with the powerful Ludwells. The Blair-Ludwell clique immediately began to plot for Nicholson's recall. Six councillors, led by Blair, submitted such a petition to Queen Anne in 1703, accusing Nicholson of personal bullying and despotic behavior. But the governor took his case openly to the Assembly and the public in the spring of 1705, and the majority of the House of Burgesses, as well as the great majority of the Anglican clergymen of the colony, came to Nicholson's defense. The bulk of the clergy petitioned England, denouncing Blair's attack on the governor and hailing Nicholson's administration. One of Blair's friends published a bitter attack on the convocation of clergymen, the first stanza of which pointedly declared:

> Bless us! What dismal times are these! What stars are in conjunction! When priests turn sycophants to please, And hare-brained passion to appease; Dare prostitute their unction.

Finally, in the summer of 1705 Blair succeeded and Nicholson was removed as governor. He was replaced by a new system. Appointed as governor-in-chief of Virginia was the Earl of Orkney, who remained in England for forty years, drawing a good salary for his post while taking no interest whatever in colonial affairs. As lieutenant governor, in actual charge of Virginia, the Crown appointed Major Edward Nott.

During the short-lived Nott administration, the new governor tried once again to push through a bill forcing Virginia to build ports and to restrict all trade to them. The Port Bill was instigated by English merchants, who would have found it cheaper and more convenient to concentrate their shipments at a few ports rather than having to trade at each planter's wharf. The Crown, however, disallowed the bill and thus finally ended the menace of compulsory ports in Virginia. The Crown also became alarmed that Virginians were shifting from tobacco to cotton or wool raising and manufacturing. In the imperial mercantilist framework, the colonies were not supposed to compete with imperial manufactures; they were supposed only to supply raw material and then purchase the finished product from the mother country. The Board of Trade ordered Nott to discourage any cotton planting in Virginia.

The big dispute of the Nott administration was over the established church. The oligarchic Council, led by Blair, was anxious to put the Anglican Church on a more secure footing by raising ministers' salaries and securing greater tenure in office. Nothing was done, since the relatively liberal

House of Burgesses had opposite objectives. One objective was to reduce the church oligarchy by periodically dissolving the ruling bodies of the church, that is, the vestries, which had become self-perpetuating bodies of church elders. Both parties deadlocked, and neither set of changes could pass, an impasse aggravated by the Anglican clergy's denunciation of the high-handed tactics of the "Scot hireling," Blair. The deadlock meant that the overwhelming majority of Anglican ministers in Virginia—those not officially inducted into office—held office only on the sufferance of the particular board of vestrymen.

Nott died a year after his induction and the next four years were politically uneventful, as the president of the Council served as acting governor of the colony.

While Virginia, in the decades after Bacon's Rebellion, increasingly settled down to a rather placid oligarchic rule, one element in Virginia society persisted in being the reverse of placid about its condition. From Bacon's Rebellion to 1710, the colony seethed with incipient and actual revolts by the Negro slaves. Being an oppressed minority of the populace, the slaves, in revolt by themselves and lacking mass white support, could not hope to succeed, and yet they continued to try to break through to freedom.

In the early 1680s, the Virginia legislature was troubled enough to pass the Act for Preventing Negroes Insurrections. Frequent meetings of Negro slaves were denounced as "dangerous," as conspiratorial activity abounding "under pretext of feast, and burials." Yet, despite such precautions, slave revolts broke out in Virginia in 1687, 1691, 1694, 1709, and 1710, as well as in other years.

The 1687 uprising was centered in Virginia's Northern Neck. The plan of uprising was uncovered, and the leaders executed. The Council, as a consequence, prohibited public slave funerals, which the rebels had used as their meeting ground. But this did not prevent the uprising of 1691, in which the slave Mingoe, having escaped his master in Middlesex County, gathered a guerrilla band and attacked plantations, especially in Rappahannock County.

By 1694 Governor Andros condemned the lack of enforcement of antislave rebellion legislation, thus permitting Negroes to "run together in certain parts of the colony, causing assemblages so dangerous as to threaten the peace of the whole community."

As Negro slaves increased in number after the turn of the century, threats of slave rebellion grew correspondingly. Early in 1709 a plot for rebellion by both Negro and Indian slaves in Surry, James City, and Isle of Wight counties was uncovered. The court inquiry found that the "late dangerous conspiracy [was] formed and carried on by great numbers of . . . Negroes and Indian slaves for making their escape by force from the service of their masters, and for the destroying and cutting off such . . . as should oppose their design." The revolt conspiracy was led by four slaves: Scipio, Peter, Salvadore, and Tom Shaw.

The following year, a slave revolt planned for Easter in Surry and James City counties was betrayed by the slave Will, whose freedom was purchased by the Virginia legislature as a "reward of his fidelity and for encouragement of such services." It was ironic that the informer should be rewarded with the very goal that the rebels were desperately trying to achieve: freedom. The two main rebel leaders were duly executed, said Lieutenant Governor Jennings, "to strike such terror in the other Negroes as will keep them from forming such designs in the future. . . ."

PART III

The Founding of
New England

17

The Religious Factor

Religion was one of the principal traits distinguishing the Northern from the Southern colonies. In the South the state-established Church of England tended to be dominant, but the Northern colonies were largely settled by members of churches dissenting from the established church. These Dissenters came to America largely because they desired to create communities in which they could practice their beliefs undisturbed.

The Protestant Reformation of the sixteenth century had taken two broadly different paths. In the rising absolute monarchies of Europe, the state gained control over the church within the nation (whether Protestant or Catholic) and found it more consonant with its own power-structure to maintain the episcopal system. On the other hand, independent and decentralized cities and provinces, such as Switzerland and the Netherlands, were the home of far more thoroughgoing reform in religious doctrine and structure. In these (Calvinist) countries, bishops were eliminated and ministers appointed directly by the state.

In England, the church, created as a state church by the Crown, not only maintained episcopacy but was far closer than the Lutherans to Roman Catholic doctrine and practice. Protestantizing reforms were soon introduced into the church, but the Catholic church during the reign of Queen Mary drove the more radical of the reformers to Holland and other Continental centers of advanced Protestant theology and practice. When the Church of England was reestablished under Elizabeth in 1559, the returning reformers found the Anglican church even less reformed than before they had gone into exile. They now concentrated on seeking a purification of religious ceremonies within the Anglican church and were thus called

Puritans. The Puritans came to hold important church and university positions and to exercise a strong influence in the government and in Parliament, but the government soon summarily removed them from their posts. Persecution polarized the Puritans, who began to advocate the purification of the church organization (which had blocked the purification of rites) by eliminating the role of the bishops. Some of the reformers (the Separatists, or Congregationalists) doubted the possibility of reforming the state church from within, and illegally withdrew from attendance at church to organize separate reformed churches, vesting autonomous control in each congregation.

The bulk of the Puritans, however, were influenced by the Calvinist or Presbyterian form of church organization dominant in the Netherlands and parts of Switzerland, where their leaders had lived in exile. In the Presbyterian system, first established at Geneva, each church or congregation was, to be sure, ruled by elders—the preaching elder, or minister, and the ruling elder, or leading layman. But to prevent diversity of doctrine, the congregation selected the minister and elder only with the advice and consent of a synod or consistory of the ministers and elders of the churches of the district. While the role of the leading laymen in the church was high, state officials in Geneva were restricted to church members, and this limited the selection of magistrates to laymen who were under the influence of the ministers. Thus, in contrast to Anglicanism, control of the church was partially replaced by church control of the state. This Presbyterian method of church organization, negating the roles of king and bishops, tended to appeal to the ministers and to the local community oligarchs—nobles, gentry, merchants—whose powers over the people would thus be increased at the expense of their political opposition, the king and his officials. In France, England, Scotland, and the Netherlands a large portion of local political leaders became Calvinist and Presbyterian.

Since the English government strongly punished suspected Calvinists, the Presbyterian organization was not directly introduced into England, and the Puritans, aided by their intellectual center at Cambridge University, spread their beliefs from within the Anglican church, by which they influenced the important groups and industrial populations of London, East Anglia, and the West Country.

When James I succeeded Elizabeth in 1603, one of his earliest problems was to face Puritan demands for reform of the Anglican church. The Millenary Petition, signed by about a thousand Puritan ministers of the Church of England (or about one-tenth of all the clergymen of that church), requested modifications in church ceremonies and protection from governmental persecution. Because of its Presbyterian overtones, the petition was rejected and some three hundred of the Puritan clergymen were removed from their positions in the Church of England. The majority of the Puritan clergy, however, continued to conform outwardly to Anglican church ceremonies, in order to continue their reform movement undisturbed. In contrast, some of the Separatists or Congregationalists who had already left the Church of England decided they could no longer bear the persecution and fled England. As Pilgrims, they went to the Netherlands in 1608.

Let us now return to colonization in the early seventeenth century. We remember that the earliest English settlement in America was founded by the London, or "South Virginia," Company in 1606. The "North Virginia," or Plymouth, Company had been granted the American territory from the forty-first to the forty-fifth parallel. The Plymouth Company had landed an expedition in Maine in 1607, but it was forced to return home the following year and then sunk into desuetude. In 1620, Sir Ferdinando Gorges, a favorite of King James, was anxious to secure a monopoly of the fisheries on the northern American coast. To this end, Gorges secured from the king a new charter. Replacing the Plymouth Company was the Council for New England, now completely separate from Virginia, and the territory actually granted to the company was greatly extended to include the land between the fortieth and the forty-eighth parallels. President of the Council was the Duke of Buckingham, an unpopular favorite of King James, and leading members were Sir Ferdinando Gorges and the Earls of Pembroke, Lenox, and Southampton. The Council was granted powers of rule, the subgranting of land in the territory, and a monopoly of shipping on the New England coasts and therefore, implicitly, a monopoly of the fishing rights.

18

The Founding of Plymouth Colony

The mere granting of land by the Crown did not yet create a settlement. The first successful settlement in New England was something of an accident. By 1617 the Pilgrims had determined to leave the Netherlands, where their youth were supposedly being corrupted by the "licentiousness" of even the Calvinist Dutch, who, for example, persisted in enjoying the Sabbath as a holiday rather than bearing it as a penance. Deciding to settle in America, the Pilgrims were offered an opportunity to settle in New Netherland, but preferred to seek a patent from the South Virginia Company, which would provide an English atmosphere in which to raise their children. The Pilgrims formed a partnership in a joint-stock company with a group of London merchants, including Thomas Weston, an ironmonger, and John Peirce, a clothmaker. The company, John Peirce and Associates, received in 1620 a grant from the Virginia Company for a particular plantation in Virginia territory. In this alliance, each adult settler was granted a share in the joint-stock company, and each investment of 10 pounds also received a share. At the end of seven years, the accumulated earnings were to be divided among the shareholders. Until that division, as in the original Virginia settlement, the company decreed a communistic system of production, with each settler contributing his all to the common store and each drawing his needs from it—again, a system of from each according to his ability, to each according to his needs.

Just over a hundred colonists sailed from England on the *Mayflower* in September 1620. Of these, only forty-one were Pilgrims, from Leyden, Holland; eighteen were indentured servants, bound as slaves for seven years to their masters; and the others were largely Anglicans from England, seeking economic opportunity in the New World.

Bound supposedly for the mouth of the Hudson River, the *Mayflower* decided instead to land along what is now the Massachusetts coast—outside Virginia territory. Some of the indentured servants began to grow restive, logically maintaining that since the settlement would not be made, as had been agreed, in Virginia territory, they should be released from their contracts. "They would use their own liberty, for none had power to command them." To forestall this rebellion against servitude, the bulk of the colonists, and especially the Pilgrims, decided to establish a government immediately, even though on shipboard. No possible period without governmental rule was to be permitted to the colonists. The Pilgrim minority straightway formed themselves on shipboard into a "body politic" in the Mayflower Compact, enabling them to perpetuate their rule over the other majority colonists. This, the first form of government in the New World established by colonists themselves, was by no means a gesture of independence from England; it was an emergency measure to maintain the Pilgrim control over the servants and other settlers.

In mid-December 1620 the *Mayflower* landed at Plymouth. In a duplication of the terrible hardships of the first Virginia settlers, half of the colonists were dead by the end of the first winter. In mid-1621 John Peirce and Associates obtained a patent from the Council for New England, granting the company 100 acres of land for each settler and 1,500 acres compulsorily reserved for public use. In return, the Council was to receive a yearly quitrent of two shillings per 100 acres.

A major reason for the persistent hardships, for the "starving time," in Plymouth as before in Jamestown, was the communism imposed by the company. Finally, in order to survive, the colony in 1623 permitted each family to cultivate a small private plot of land for their individual use. William Bradford, who had become governor of Plymouth in 1621, and was to help rule the colony for thirty years thereafter, eloquently describes the result in his record of the colony:

> All this while no supply was heard of. . . . So they began to think how they might raise as much corn as they could, and obtain a better crop than they had done, that they might not still thus languish in misery. At length . . . the Governor (with the advice of the chiefest among them) gave way that they should set corn every man for his own particular, and in that regard trust to themselves. . . . And so assigned to every family a parcel of land . . . for that end, only for present use. . . . This had very good success, for it made all hands very industrious, so as much more corn was planted than otherwise would have been by any means the Governor or any other could use, and saved him a great deal of trouble, and gave far better content. The women now went willingly into the field, and took their little ones with them to set corn; which before would allege weakness and inability; whom to have compelled would have been thought great tyranny and oppression.

The experience that was had in this common course and condition, tried sundry years and that amongst godly and sober men, may well evince the vanity of that conceit of Plato's . . . that the taking away of property and bringing community into a commonwealth would make them happy and flourishing. . . . For this community . . . was found to breed much confusion and discontent and retard much employment that would have been to their benefit and comfort. For the young men, that were most able and fit for labour and service, did repine that they should spend their time and strength to work for other men's wives and children without any recompense. The strong . . . had no more in division of victuals and clothes than he that was weak and not able to do a quarter the other could; this was thought injustice. . . . Upon . . . all being to have alike, and all to do alike, they thought . . . one as good as another, and so . . . did . . . work diminish . . . the mutual respects that should be preserved amongst men. . . . Let none object this is men's corruption . . . all men have this corruption in them. . . .*

The antipathy of communism to the nature of man here receives eloquent testimony from a governor scarcely biased *a priori* in favor of individualism.

Plymouth was destined to remain a small colony. By 1630 its population was still less than four hundred. Its government began in the Mayflower Compact, with the original signers forming an Assembly for making laws, choosing a governor, and admitting people to freemen's citizenship. The governor had five assistants, elected also by the freemen. This democratic setup signified a very loose control of the colony by the Peirce company, which wanted to accelerate the growth of the colony, and saw the Pilgrim dominance as an obstacle to such growth. Religious exclusiveness in a colony necessarily hampers its growth; we have seen that Lord Baltimore soon abandoned the idea of Maryland as an exclusively Catholic colony in order to encourage its rapid development. Thus, persecution of non-Separatists for playing ball on Sunday and for daring to observe Christmas as a holiday was hardly calculated to stimulate the growth of the colony.

To inject some variety into the colony, the English merchants therefore sent the Rev. John Lyford, a Puritan within the Church of England, with a group of colonists to Plymouth. As soon as Lyford began to administer the sacraments according to the Church of England, his correspondence was seized by Governor Bradford, and Lyford and his chief supporter, John Oldham, were tried for "plotting against Pilgrim rule both in respect of their civil and church state." To the charge of Lyford and Oldham that non-Pilgrims were being discouraged from coming to Plymouth, Governor Bradford replied that strangers were perfectly "free" to attend the Pilgrim church as often as they liked. When Bradford spread the stolen letters, critical of the government, upon the record, Oldham angrily called upon the Assembly to revolt against this tyranny, but no one followed his lead. The Reverend Lyford instantly recanted and groveled in his errors before the court.

*William Bradford, *Of Plymouth Plantation, 1620-47* (New York: Knopf, 1952), pp.120-21.

Both men were ordered banished from the colony. Oldham went thirty miles north, with a number of the discontented, to found a settlement at Nantasket (now Hull). Included in this company were Roger Conant and William and Edward Hilton, who shortly traveled further north to join David Thompson, a Scottish trader who had established a settlement at what is now Portsmouth, New Hampshire, at the mouth of the Piscataqua River. The Hiltons were later to found the nearby town of Dover, New Hampshire.

In return for his abasement, the Reverend Lyford was put on six months' probation, but again some critical letters to England were purloined by the government, and this time Lyford was truly expelled and went on to join the Nantasket settlement.

The Pilgrims, however, had not seen the last of the rebellious band. In the spring of 1624, the Pilgrims built a wharf some sixty miles north, on the current site of Gloucester, at Cape Ann in northeastern Massachusetts, only to find the following spring that Lyford, Oldham, and their group had moved there. They had been invited to Gloucester by the Dorchester Company of merchants from western England. The company's founder, the Rev. John White, a Puritan, had already established a fishing village at Gloucester in 1623. Roger Conant was now installed as superintendent of the community, and Lyford became its pastor. Upon returning to Gloucester to find the dissidents established there, the first instinct of Plymouth's military leader, Capt. Miles Standish, was, typically, to demand the surrender of the unwelcome wharf, but cooler heads prevailed and a peaceful compromise was soon reached. The Pilgrims, however, could not make a go of this fishing station and abandoned it at the end of the year.

Upon the bankruptcy of the Dorchester Company the following year, the Conant-Oldham group left Gloucester, and moved fifteen miles down the coast to found the town of Naumkeag, later known as Salem. Lyford was its Anglican minister.

In 1625, Thomas Morton, gentleman lawyer and an agent of Sir Ferdinando Gorges, organized another settlement, Merrymount, north of Plymouth at the present site of Quincy, Massachusetts. Merrymount was an Anglican settlement, and the citizens did not comport themselves in the highly ascetic fashion to which the Plymouth Separatists wished them to conform. Apparently Merrymount was merry indeed, and whiskey and interracial (white-Indian) revelry abounded, including the old Anglican (but denounced by the Pilgrims as pagan) custom of dancing around a maypole, a practice which King James I had urged in his *Book of Sports* (1617). Plymouth had established friendly relations with the Indians, but Merrymount was now threatening to compete most effectively with Plymouth's highly lucrative monopoly of the beaver trade with the Indians. Merrymount was also a place where Morton set his servants free and made them partners in the fur trade, and thus it loomed as a highly attractive haven for runaway servants from Plymouth.

The Pilgrims denounced Morton's colony as a "school of atheism"—"atheism" apparently signifying the use of the Anglican Book of Common Prayer, the maypole, and selling rum and firearms to the Indians (and buying furs in exchange). The sale of rum and firearms was condemned even though relations with the Indians had been perfectly peaceful. Then, in 1628, Plymouth established a virtual New England tradition of persecution by dispatching Captain Standish with an armed troop to eradicate Merrymount. Having surrendered on the promise of safe treatment to himself and the settlement, Morton was assaulted by Standish and his men and almost killed, the Plymouth forces "not regarding any agreement made with such a carnal man." Hauled into a Plymouth court—despite Plymouth's lack of legal jurisdiction over Merrymount—Morton was almost executed; his death was urged at great length by Miles Standish. Finally, he was deported back to England, with Standish still threatening to kill Morton personally before he could leave the colony. Before deportation, Morton was confined alone for over a month of severe winter at the Isles of Shoals without a gun, knife, or proper clothing.

Despite the destruction of Merrymount, and the failure of other attempts at settlement, the 1620s saw several settlements dot the Massachusetts coast. Most important was the Roger Conant group at Naumkeag; another was a settlement at Boston led by the Puritan minister, Rev. William Blackstone.

In 1627 the inherent conflict between colony and company in Plymouth was finally resolved, by the elimination of the company from the scene. In that year, the seven years of enforced communism by the company expired, and all the assets and lands were distributed to the individual shareholders. Grants of land were received in proportion to the size of the stock, so that the larger shareholders received larger gifts of land. This complete replacement of communism by individualism greatly benefited the productivity of the colony. Furthermore, the colonists took the happy occasion to buy up the shares of the Peirce company. Plymouth was now a totally self-governing colony. By 1633 the entire purchase price had been paid and the colonists were freed from the last remnant of company, or indeed of any English, control.

There still remained, of course, the overlord Council for New England. In 1630 the Council granted a new patent to the Plymouth Colony, clearly defining its territory, and recognizing its right to freedom of trading and fishing. But Governor Bradford limited the privileges of trade to the original Pilgrim partners—the Old Comers—and kept the patent in his own possession before relinquishing it in 1641. Plymouth was destined to remain a small colony in which the nominal rulers, the freemen, were rarely consulted, and the governor and the Council imposed an oligarchic rule. But after the Council for New England was dissolved in 1635, Plymouth nevertheless became a fully self-governing colony.

19

The Founding of Massachusetts Bay

When the tiny band of Separatists left England in 1608, the great bulk of English Puritans, despite the persecutions of the early part of the reign of James I, were highly confident of their future in England and of the potential for reform within the English church structure. Why then the intense Great Migration only one generation later? What had happened to sap the confidence of the English Puritans?

At the beginning of the seventeenth century, virtually all of England's export trade consisted of unfinished woolen cloths, which were sent to the Netherlands for finishing and dyeing and to be reexported to the north for grain. In the decade following the conclusion of peace with Spain in 1604, the woolen trade, and hence the English economy, flourished. But parliamentary refusal to approve any further taxes in protest against rising taxation, as well as the persecution of Puritan clergy, led, in 1614, to the Crown's dissolution of Parliament. In its search for revenue, the Crown then decided to create new monopolies—and its meddling in the vital wool trade had disastrous results. On the proposal of Alderman Cockayne of the Eastland Company, the government suspended the charter of the Merchant Adventurers (an attempted monopoly in the export of unfinished cloth), and completely prohibited the export of unfinished cloth upon which the prosperity of England rested. Instead, a new charter was granted to a syndicate of Eastland Company and Levant Company merchants in a new company, the King's Merchant Adventurers, which had a legal monopoly of the export of finished and dyed cloth, half the profits of which were to be paid to the Crown.

The English government failed to realize that the English were not technically equipped for finishing and dyeing cloth; the higher costs of finishing woolens in England left an open field for the emergence of a new competitive cloth industry on the Continent. As a result, English woolen exports fell by a catastrophic one-third in two years, and the repeal of the prohibition in 1616 could not succeed in reviving the cloth trade. Not only did the tax-crippled English industry have to compete with the low-cost industry of the Continent, but the outbreak of the Thirty Years' War in 1618 brought about a Continent-wide debasement of currencies, a debasement that aided exports from the debasing countries at the expense of such other countries as England. Renewal of war in the Netherlands in 1622 further disrupted the vital market there, and the result was a continuing great depression in England in the twenties, a depression and unemployment concentrated particularly in the cloth-making centers of East Anglia and the West Country.

Fearful of rising political opposition sparked by the depression, the government tried desperately to relieve the victims of the depression by maintaining wage rates at a high level and keeping failing companies in operation. The result was only to prolong and intensify the depression the government was trying to cure: artificially high wage rates deepened unemployment in the clothing centers and imposed higher costs on an already high-cost industry; propping up of inefficient producers wasted more capital and ruined their creditors; and the domination of inefficient monopoly companies was tightened at the very time when the industry's salvation could only come from freer competition and escape from the taxation and regulation of government. The overcapitalized monopoly companies were especially hard hit by the depression; the East India and Muscovy companies defaulted to their creditors, and the Virginia Company's difficulties resulting from the government's monopoly of tobacco sales led to its dissolution. Hence the royal assumption of power over the Virginia colony.

One growing light on the economic horizon was the exportation of the lightweight "new draperies," produced free from government control, and over which no monopoly company held sway. Export trade in these new draperies was developing in southern Europe by the 1620s. The contrast in the fortunes of the two branches of cloth trade was too great to be ignored—the connection between free trade and economic growth, and between privileges and decline was becoming evident to contemporaries.

In successive Parliaments the representatives of the people demanded freedom in economic and political affairs and the termination of the government's restrictions, monopolies, and taxes that had brought about the depression engulfing the country. The government responded characteristically by imprisoning the opposition leaders, such as Sir Edwin Sandys and Lord Saye and Sele, for advocating free trade, radicalism, and interference with tax collection. The Parliament of 1624 presented a list

166

of grievances in protest against the moratoria issued to debtors against their creditors, against the increases in government officials and expenses, against extraordinary tariffs and taxes, against the government's use of informers and enforcement of regulations and controls, and against the monopoly trading companies, which were popularly regarded simply as gangs of thieves, from the East India Company to the Council for New England. The Parliament concluded by passing the Act Against Monopolies, by which all monopolies were outlawed and all proclamations furthering them prohibited. Unlike the depression of the 1550s, which had led to the unquestioned creation of monumental government controls over the economy, the depression of the 1620s witnessed an attempt toward liberalization by removing the regulations that had caused the crisis. The movement for the abolition of the government's monopolies and regulations became a major part of the seventeenth-century constitutional struggle in England, and had a significant influence on the American colonists, whose migration was a fruit of the government's controls.

However clear the principles of liberalism had become, the struggle for their realization in the seventeenth century had hardly begun. The accession of Charles I to the throne in March 1625 ushered in a period of conflict that was to span the mid-seventeenth century. The financial difficulties of the new government were greatly increased when England decided to enter the Thirty Years' War by attacking Spain in 1625.

The English government had remained behind the scenes in the early phases of the war, acting through diplomacy and subsidies, despite the pressure of Puritan opinion for greater aid to the Calvinist forces of Germany, which had gone to war with Austria, and to the United Provinces, which had renewed the war with Spain and had suffered heavy defeats by the two Hapsburg powers. When the English government intervened in an alliance of the Lutheran powers of northern Europe with the anti-Hapsburg Catholic powers of southern Europe, it tried to use the excitement of war preparations as a convenient means of gaining taxes from Parliament. However, the Parliament refused to be stampeded by the crisis of European Protestant fortunes, and refused to vote taxes until the government had redressed grievances, especially in church reform. For the major authority in government on ecclesiastical matters was Rev. William Laud, archbishop of Canterbury, who strongly opposed Puritanism in doctrine and in practice, and who had embarked upon a policy of eliminating all churchmen suspected of Puritan sympathies and promoting those whose theology and devotions the Puritans considered Catholic in origin.

The persecution of the Puritan clergy was matched by imprisonment of the opposition leaders and of merchants who refused to pay the taxes that Parliament had refused to approve. Moreover, the people were conscripted or had soldiers quartered in their homes if they refused to pay these taxes. It was this climate of increasing religious and political persecution placed on top of the continuing economic depression that led the Rev. John White, a mildly Puritan minister from Dorchester and founder of the Dorchester Company, to revive the project of a settlement on the coast of New England. A settlement was projected to form a colony of West Country Puritans who would find refuge without having to submit to the tyranny of the religious and social conformity of the Separatists at Plymouth. Surely if the relatively humble Separatists could succeed in America, the far wealthier and more powerful Puritans could succeed all the more. The old Dorchester Company was bankrupt, but in 1628 White formed the New England Company with other Puritans and with old Dorchester associates, and secured a grant from the Council for New England of all the land between three miles south of the Charles River (which runs through Boston) and three miles north of the Merrimack (now the Massachusetts–New Hampshire border). Immediately John Endecott and a major financier of the company, Matthew Cradock, were sent out, with settlers, to take control of the Naumkeag settlement—by then re-named Salem—and for Endecott to supersede Conant as governor.

John Endecott's idea of rule was that God had chosen him as "a fit instrument" for establishing a new Canaan for the chosen people by rooting out all lesser folk, red and white, preferably by means of the pillory and the whipping post. His major struggle was to cripple the livelihood of the old settlers by prohibiting their tobacco culture and beaver trade, turning these over to the New England Company. The "old planters" could only protest in vain that they were becoming slaves to a monopoly company.

During the spring of 1629, still harder-line Puritans immigrated to the New England colony, and their ministers established a quasi-Separatist church based on a congregational covenant. Old planters who refused to go this far from the Church of England and embrace the covenant were persecuted by Endecott as "libertines," and some were deported to England, where the Rev. John White tried vainly to protect them. Many of the old planters expelled from Salem by Endecott moved to Rev. William Blackstone's settlement at Boston and Charlestown.

Migration under the New England Company was small, but the rush of events soon intensified Puritan desires to seek a haven in the New World. Having added a war against France in 1627 to the conflict with Spain, the Crown was obliged to call Parliament into session to provide financing for the war effort. But Parliament took the occasion to present a petition of its grievances to be met before voting taxes for the king's adventures. The Petition of Right (June 1628) denounced taxation without consent of Parliament, arbitrary arrests without benefit of habeas corpus, and the quartering of the government's soldiers upon the people. Insistence upon these libertarian demands before supply of revenue led to the king's dissolution of Parliament in March 1629 and to the Crown's arrest of the leaders of the opposition.

Thus, English Puritans faced the gloomy prospect of greatly intensified repression at home, at the hands of the absolute royal power and its prerogative courts (of the High Commission and the Star Chamber). Puritan gloom was further deepened by the aggravated plight of their fellow Calvinists on the European continent. England's military operations against France and Spain had failed, especially in trying to relieve the French Huguenots (Calvinists) besieged by the French Crown at La Rochelle; the Huguenots were forced to surrender to the French forces in October 1628. Early the following year, the Protestant powers in Germany concluded a humiliating peace issuing from the almost un-interrupted string of losses they had suffered in the first decade of the Thirty Years' War. Finally, the Calvinist United Provinces in the Nether-lands were undergoing serious losses at the hands of the Spanish army. Thus, everywhere in Europe the Catholic powers were triumphant, and the Protestants suffering losses. As the Puritan leader John Winthrop concluded, during 1629, "All other Churches in Europe are brought to desolation, and it cannot be but the like judgment is coming upon us." A secure sanctuary in America seemed to be vital for Puritan survival.

Seeing their plight, the Puritans were able to persuade Charles I to grant a royal charter in March 1629 to the Massachusetts Bay Company, the more powerful successor of the New England Company. Coincidentally, the charter was granted just four days after King Charles' dissolution of Parliament. The old unincorporated company had now become an in-corporated body politic with power to govern its granted territory. The old grant of land was reconfirmed. The new company was to appoint the governor, deputy governor, and council, and make laws for its settlers. The company promptly sent out a fleet of colonists to Salem. With the arrival of this fleet, Salem immediately attained to a larger size than the decade-old Plymouth Colony (by 1630 the Massachusetts Bay colony totaled a little over five hundred people).

Massachusetts Bay Company and colony, however, developed far more rapidly than their founders had foreseen, thanks to the unexpectedly over-whelming interest in emigration among the Puritans of East Anglia. The East Anglians were the most numerous and most extreme of the English Puritans, reaching virtually the point of Separatism from the Church of England. As dedicated Puritans, the East Anglians had been embittered by Archbishop Laud's anti-Puritan movement within the Church of England, and by a widespread growth of a liberal Dutch theology in the universities and among the upper classes, a theology stressing free will and religious toleration. Such doctrines were highly suspect to the Calvinist Puritans bent upon predestination and extirpation of heresy. For a long while, however, the East Anglians had been indifferent to the emigration move-ment, for East Anglia had not been as widely hit by the depression of the 1620s as had the West Country and other manufacturing centers in England. The reason for the relative prosperity was that East Anglia was the center for the production of the lighter new draperies, which had not been crippled by taxation, monopoly privilege, or stringent state regulation. However, the wars with France and Spain interrupted the markets for East Anglian textiles while moving the state, in its frantic search for revenue, to bring taxes and controls upon the new-drapery industry. Production of new draperies in East Anglia dropped by a startling two-thirds between 1628 and 1631, and tens of thousands of spinners and weavers were thrown out of work, increasing the poor-tax burdens upon the country farmers and gentry. Riots and disorders by the workmen made things still worse; they led the government to impose further taxes and minimum-wage rates upon the manufacturers, to force merchants to buy textiles, and to prohibit export competition with the monopoly companies. With sudden economic distress and injustice added to unwelcome political and religious trends, the Puritans of East Anglia were now ripe for mass emigration.

A decisive conference of Puritans took place at the Puritans' intellectual center, Cambridge University, at the end of August 1629. In the Cambridge Agreement, a group of Puritan leaders from East Anglia agreed to join the Massachusetts Bay Company and to immigrate to America if the officers were to be chosen solely from immigrants to New England, and if the company charter were to be carried with them to the New World. Moreover, the Puritan stockholders remaining in England agreed to sell all their shares in the company to the emigrants; the Massachusetts Bay Company could now be completely located in New England as a self-governing Puritan colony. This was a legal action, because the Puritans had cleverly persuaded the king not to specify the location of the company in the charter. John Winthrop, a leading East Anglian attorney was appointed governor of the company and John Humphrey, brother-in-law of the highly influential Earl of Lincoln, deputy governor. When Humphrey decided to remain in England, he was replaced by Thomas Dudley, the steward of the Earl of Lincoln. Although the Rev. John White did send some West Country Puritans to Salem during 1630, the vast bulk of the great Puritan exodus of the 1630s—the Great Migration —came from East Anglia.* The Great Migration of Puritans began immediately, and seventeen ships sailed from England in 1630 alone. They settled not only in Salem, but all along the Massachusetts coast, founding such towns as Watertown, Roxbury, Dorchester, Medford, and Newtown (later Cambridge). During the 1630s, from 20,000 to 25,000 people immigrated to Massachusetts; by 1640, 9,000 remained (deducting emigration from Massachusetts back home or to other lands), while only 1,000 people lived in Plymouth.

Thus, by 1630 the two New England colonies, Plymouth and Massa-

---

*It must be noted that by no means all of the great wave of Puritan emigrants from East Anglia in the 1630s chose to go to Massachusetts Bay. A greater number moved to Barbados, other West Indian islands, and Ireland.

chusetts Bay, had managed to win for themselves virtual self-governing status, independent of English control. Like Virginia, the New England colonies began as chartered companies. But the Virginia Company continued to rule the colony from England, being finally expropriated and superseded by the Crown in 1620. The New England settlements, in contrast, were strongly impelled by religious motives. Hence, the Plymouth Pilgrims and Separatists were only loosely controlled by the parent company, and soon bought out that company completely, while the Puritan Massachusetts Bay Company transferred itself to, and completely blended with, the colony in America.

According to the Massachusetts Bay charter, the governor, deputy governor, and Council of Assistants were to be elected by the whole body of stockholders or "freemen." This sounds highly democratic on paper, but the stumblingblock was that only twelve stockholders migrated to America, and all were officers of the colony. Since any new freemen had to be selected by the existing freemen, the natural tendency was to perpetuate a closed oligarchy and to select few new members. Rumblings of popular resistance occurred as early as the fall of 1630, when 109 settlers petitioned to be made freemen of the company. The freemen gave in to this request, but completely vitiated its effect by mendaciously claiming that the charter had put all power into the hands of the Council of Assistants, who could choose the governor and deputy governor and make all the laws. Moreover, the assistants were to hold office permanently, on good behavior. The *only* function of the body of freemen, it was alleged, was filling vacancies in the council. By thus failing to show the freemen the text of the charter, a dozen Puritan oligarchs managed to keep absolute control of the colony's affairs for great lengths of time. In addition, though in violation of the charter, only Puritans were admitted to the body of freemen, thus insuring domination of the churches and the broad body politic by the church elders.

From the beginning, the authorities had trouble from the newly burgeoning smaller towns. At the beginning of 1631, a tax of sixty pounds was levied upon each settlement, to pay for frontier forts at Newtown. The inhabitants of Watertown promptly refused to pay the tax, assessed by the Council of Assistants, on the great old English ground that no community may be taxed without its own consent. As the Watertown protesters eloquently declared: "It was not safe to pay moneys after that sort, for fear of bringing themselves and posterity into bondage." Here was the first tax strike in America, long anticipating the episode in Surry, Virginia. In 1632 the government bowed to the strike—after an apology was extracted from the resisters and the freemen assumed the power to elect the governor and the assistants (though the governor had to be chosen from the ranks of the assistants), and also to make tax levies. Or rather, this power was assumed by the *representatives* of the freemen—direct democracy now being held impractical in the large colony—and two deputies were elected from each town in Massachusetts. For over a decade, the deputies and the assistants sat in the same house of the legislature (the General Court), but then separated into two houses of that court.

During the following year, political conflicts intensifed in the colony as opinion polarized two camps: Thomas Dudley, backed by the elders, accused Governor Winthrop of "leniency," and of being negligent in instituting the absolute and complete "tyranny of the Lord-Brethren." Dudley called, characteristically, for "heavier fines, severer whippings, more frequent banishments." On the other hand, many of the freemen continued to grow restive at the oligarchical rule, and the leading Puritan divine, Rev. Thomas Hooker, arrived in Massachusetts to stand aghast and protest at the tyranny of the colony's magistrates.

The struggle came to a head in 1634. A paper by Israel Stoughton denounced the government oligarchy for monopolizing power: "They made the laws, disposed lands, raised monies, punished offenders, etc. at their discretion; neither did the people know the portent. . . ." The magistrates responded by burning the paper, but the argument would not thus be stifled. Finally a committee from each of the eight towns in Massachusetts Bay sent representatives to insist on the opening of the hitherto secret charter for the colony. When they then discovered that the lawmaking power was fully and legally vested in the freemen rather than in the assistants, the General Court from then on assumed full jurisdiction for the making of laws. The magistrates made sure, however, that not the *total* body of freemen, but the more malleable deputies in the General Court were actually to make the laws.

For a while, the General Court—especially the deputies in the lower house—was furious at the lengthy betrayal, and, led by Israel Stoughton as speaker of the deputies, it deposed Winthrop as governor and levied fines on some of the assistants. But the number of freemen was still restricted to Puritan church members by an act of 1631, and a law five years later prohibited any new churches from existing in the colony without securing the consent of the authorities. The loosening of the oligarchic rule in Massachusetts was therefore not very great. Indeed, Dudley, who had replaced Winthrop as governor, quickly prohibited Stoughton from any public office for a three-year period. Soon the General Court was all too happy to return Winthrop to office and depose Dudley.

A threat of English overlordship vanished in 1635 upon the dissolution of the Council for New England. The Council had failed financially; its doom had been assured when its fishing monopoly off the English coast was disallowed by the Crown. Sir Ferdinando Gorges and his associates still tried to menace the colony by proposing that the territory of New England be parceled out to individual proprietors in the Council. Gorges also tried his best to have the Massachusetts charter revoked.

The Crown, indeed, was thinking along similar lines. England was getting very worried about the virtual independence of Massachusetts

Bay. In 1634 the lords commissioners for Foreign Plantations in General, as Privy Council committee under the chairmanship of the formidable Archbishop Laud, moved firmly against the colony. Authorized to control the colonies as well as emigration, the commission moved, in the spring of 1635, to revoke the charter of the Massachusetts Bay Company in the courts. The English courts severely rebuked the officer of the Massachusetts colony for not appearing at the trial, and decided to revoke the colony's charter in 1637. Massachusetts prepared to arm to repel an English attack, but it was saved from such a confrontation by the beginnings of the Puritan Revolution the following year, a revolution that hopelessly distracted the English government from Massachusetts affairs for fully a generation.

20

The Puritans "Purify":
Theocracy in Massachusetts

The Puritans had no sooner landed in the New World than they began coercively to "purify" their surroundings. As early as John Endecott's arrival in Salem, the Puritans had surprisingly shifted from their loyal opposition within the Anglican church and had severed themselves from the Anglican communion. In this way, they became to a large extent as Separatist as the Plymouth Pilgrims they had previously despised. This act of separation was accomplished in 1629, with Francis Higginson and Samuel Skelton as the guiding ministers. Two Puritan members of the Council, John and Samuel Browne, balked at this radical departure from Puritan beliefs, and moved to form an Anglican church of their own. This prompted the government to move quickly, in the first act of "purifying" the colony's spiritual atmosphere. Governor Endecott protested that the Brownes' speeches and activities were "tending to mutiny and faction," and promptly deported them to England—thus serving notice that any Anglican worship in Massachusetts would be speedily prosecuted.

The Puritans also proceeded to the final destruction of Thomas Morton's ill-starred Merrymount colony. For Morton, in 1629, had indeed reestablished his colony of the interracial frolic, the Anglican maypole, and brisk and efficient trade in Indian furs that competed with Massachusetts Bay. Massachusetts offered to share the Bay Company's fur trading monopoly with Morton, but the highly efficient Morton refused to do so, judging that he could easily outcompete the Massachusetts monopoly. This he did, far outstripping Massachusetts in the fur trade by over six to one. This the colony could not tolerate, and Captain Littleworth was sent to Merrymount with an armed troop. Littleworth cut down the maypole, burned

174

Morton's house and confiscated his property, and proceeded to destroy the settlement. Morton was charged by the authorities with "alienating" the Indians—the reverse of the fact—and was again deported to England.

Back in England, the embittered Morton protested his persecution and worked for Gorges in trying to void the Plymouth and Massachusetts patents, but to no avail. Years later, returning to Massachusetts, the poverty-stricken Morton was heavily fined, was imprisoned for a year by the authorities, and died in Maine shortly after his release.

The Massachusetts colony was organized in towns. The church congregation of each town selected its minister. Unlike the thinly populated, extensive settlement of Virginia, the clustering in towns was ideal for having the minister and his aides keep watch on all the inhabitants. Although the congregation selected the minister, the town government paid his salary; in contrast to the poorly paid clergy of the Southern colonies, the salary was handsome indeed. Out of it the minister could maintain several slaves or indentured servants and amass a valuable library. The minister—himself a government official—exerted enormous political influence in the community, and only someone whom he certified as "godly" was likely to gain elected office. The congregation was ruled, not democratically by the members, but rather by its council of elders. Also highly important was the minister who functioned as "church teacher," specializing in doctrinal matters.

Since only church members could vote in political elections, the requirements for admission became a matter of concern for every inhabitant. These requirements were rigorous. For one thing, the candidate had to satisfy the minister and elders of his complete adherence to pure doctrine and of his satisfactory personal conduct. And, once admitted, he was always subject to expulsion for deviations in either area.

As the years wore on, the rule of the oligarchy tended to tighten and polarize further, so that a lower proportion of the colony was admitted to church membership. The Puritan leaders made strenuous efforts to exclude the "unsanctified" from the colony. Thus, in 1636 the town of Boston outlawed any person's entertaining strangers for more than two weeks, without obtaining permission from the town government. Salem went one better by hiring an inspector "to go from house to house . . . once a month to inquire what strangers . . . have thrust themselves into the town." To quicken his incentive for snooping, he was rewarded with the fines levied against those whose crime in entertaining "strangers" he had uncovered. In 1637 the Massachusetts government imposed this outlawing of hospitality on all towns, and it was now illegal for any town to permit a stranger to move there without the consent of high government officials. As the years went on, however, and the colony grew, the authorities were forced by the need for labor to admit servants, apprentices, sailors, and artisans, who did not necessarily belong to the body of Puritan "saints."

To the saints and their leaders, any idea of separation of church and state was anathema. As the Puritan synod put it in their *Platform of Church Discipline* (1648): "It is the duty of the magistrate to take care of matters of religion. . . . The end of the magistrate's office is . . . godliness." It is the duty of the magistrate to punish and repress "idolatry, blasphemy, heresy, venting corrupt and pernicious opinions . . . open contempt of the word preached, profanation of the Lord's Day. . . ." Should any congregation dare to "grow schismatical" or "walk incorrigibly or obstinately in any corrupt way of their own," the magistrate was to "put forth his coercive power." And if the state was to be the strong coercive arm of the church, so the church, in turn, was to foster in the public the duty of obedience to the state rulers: "Church government furthereth the people in yielding more hearty . . . obedience unto the civil government." From this attitude, it followed for the Puritan that any rebel against the civil government was a "rebel and traitor" to God, and of course any criticism of, let alone rebellion against, Puritan rule was also a sin against God, the author of the plan for Puritan hegemony. So insistent indeed were the Puritans on the duty of obedience to civil government that the *content* of its decrees became almost irrelevant. As Rev. John Davenport, a leading Puritan divine, put it: "You must submit to the rulers' authority, and perform all duties to them whom you have chosen . . . whether they be good or bad, by virtue of their relation between them and you." Naturally, John Winthrop, who helped govern Massachusetts for twenty years after its inception, agreed with this sentiment. To Winthrop, natural liberty was a "wild beast," while correct civil liberty meant being properly subjected to authority and restrained by "God's ordinances."

Perhaps the bluntest expression of the Puritan ideal of theocracy was the Rev. Nathaniel Ward's *The Simple Cobbler of Aggawam in America* (1647). Returning to England to take part in the Puritan ferment there, this Massachusetts divine was horrified to find the English Puritans too soft and tolerant, too willing to allow a diversity of opinion in society. The objective of both church and state, Ward declaimed, was to coerce virtue, to "preserve unity of spirit, faith and ordinances, to be all like-minded, of one accord; every man to take his brother into his Christian care . . . and by no means to permit heresies or erroneous opinions." Ward continued:

God does nowhere in His word tolerate Christian States to give toleration to such adversaries of His truth, if they have power in their hands to suppress them . . . He that willingly assents to toleration of varieties of religion . . . his conscience will tell him he is either an atheist or a heretic or a hypocrite, or at best captive to some lust. Poly-piety is the greatest impiety in the world. . . . To authorize an untruth by a toleration of State is to build a sconce against the walls of heaven, to batter God out of His chair.

And so the Puritan ministry stood at the apex of rule in Massachusetts, ever ready to use the secular arm to enforce its beliefs against critics and false prophets, or even against simple lapses from conformity.

To enforce purity of doctrine upon society, the Puritans needed a network of schools throughout the colony to indoctrinate the younger generation. The Southern colonies' individualistic attitude toward education was not to be tolerated. Also, the clusters of town settlements made schools far more feasible than it did among the widely scattered rural population of the Southern colonies. The first task was a college, to graduate suitably rigorous ministers, and to train schoolmasters for lower schools. And so the Massachusetts General Court established a college in Cambridge in 1636 (named Harvard College the following year), appropriating 400 pounds for its support. In a few years, after schoolmasters had been trained, a network of grammar schools was established throughout the colony. In 1647, the government required every town to create and keep in operation a grammar school. Thus, Massachusetts forged a network of governmental schools to indoctrinate the younger generation in Puritan orthodoxy. The master was chosen, and his salary paid, by the town government, and, of course, crucial to selecting a master was the minister's intensive inquiry into his doctrinal and behavioral purity. Indeed, in 1654 Massachusetts made it illegal for any town to continue in their posts any teachers "that have manifested themselves unsound in the faith or scandalous in their lives." To feed the network of grammar schools, the colony, in 1645, compelled each town to provide a schoolmaster to teach reading and writing.

There would be no point to government schools for indoctrinating the masses, if there were no masses to be indoctrinated. Vital to the system, therefore, was a law compelling every child in the colony to be educated. This was put through in 1642—the first compulsory education law in America—and was in contrast to the system of voluntary education then prevailing in England and in the Southern colonies. Parents ignoring the law were fined, and wherever government officials judged the parents or guardians to be unfit to have the children educated properly, the government was empowered to seize the children and apprentice them out to others.

One of the essential goals of Puritan rule was strict and rigorous enforcement of the ascetic Puritan conception of moral behavior. But since men's actions, given freedom to express their choices, are determined by their inner convictions and values, compulsory moral rules only serve to manufacture hypocrites and not to advance genuine morality. Coercion only forces people to change their actions; it does not *persuade* people to change their underlying values and convictions. And since those already convinced of the moral rules would abide by them without coercion, the *only* real impact of compulsory morality is to engender hypocrites, those whose actions no longer reflect their inner convictions. The Puritans, however, did not boggle at this consequence. A leading Puritan divine, the Rev. John Cotton, went so far as to maintain that hypocrites who merely conform to the church rules without inner conviction could still be useful church members. As to the production of hypocrites, Cotton complacently declared: "If it did so, yet better to be hypocrites than profane persons. Hypocrites give God part of his due, the outward man, but the profane persons giveth God neither outward nor inward man."

One requisite for the efficient enforcement of any code of behavior is always an effective espionage apparatus of informers. This apparatus was supplied in Massachusetts, informally but no less effectively, by the dedicated snooping of friends and neighbors upon one another, with detailed reports sent to the minister on all deviations, including the sin of idleness. The clustering of towns around central villages aided the network, and the fund of personal information collected by each minister added to his great political power. Moreover, the menace of excommunication was redoubled by the threat of corollary secular punishment.

Informal snooping, however, was felt by some of the towns to be too haphazard, and these set up a regular snooping officialdom. These officers were called "tithing men," as each one had supervision over the private affairs of his ten nearest neighbors.

One Puritan moral imperative was strict observance of the Sabbath: any worldly pleasures indulged in on the Sabbath were a grave offense against both church and state. The General Court was shocked to learn, in the late 1650s, that some people, residents as well as strangers, persisted in "uncivilly walking in the streets and fields" on Sunday, and even "travelling from town to town" and drinking at inns. And so the General Court duly passed a law prohibiting the crimes of "playing, uncivil walking, drinking and travelling from town to town" on Sunday. If these criminals could not pay the fine imposed, they were to be whipped by the constable at a maximum rate of five lashes per ten-shilling fine. To enforce the regulations and prevent the crimes, the gates of the towns were closed on Sunday and no one permitted to leave. And if two or more people met accidentally on the street on a Sunday, they were quickly dispersed by the police. Nor was the Sabbath in any sense a hasty period. Under the inspiration of the Rev. John Cotton, the New England Sabbath began rigorously at sunset Saturday evening and continued through Sunday night, thus ensuring that no part of the weekend could be spent in enjoyment. Indeed, enjoyment at *any* time, while not legally prohibited, was definitely frowned upon, levity being condemned as "inconsistent with the gravity to be always preserved by a serious Christian."

Kissing one's wife in public on a Sunday was also outlawed. A sea captain, returning home on a Sunday morning from a three-year voyage, was indiscreet enough to kiss his wife on the doorstep. For this he was forced to sit in the stocks for two hours for this "lewd and unseemly behavior on the Sabbath Day."

Not only were nonreligious activities outlawed on Sundays, but attendance at a Puritan church was compulsory as well. Fines were levied for absence from church, and the police were ordered to search through the towns for absentees and forcibly haul them to church. Falling asleep in church was also outlawed and whipping was the punishment for repeated offenses.

Gambling of any kind was strictly forbidden. The law declared: "Nor shall any person at any time play or game for any money . . . upon penalty of forfeiting treble the value thereof, one half to the party informing and the other half to the treasury." Yet, as so often happens in this world, what was so sternly prohibited to *private* individuals was permitted to government. Thus, government was permitted to raise revenue for itself by running lotteries. To government, in short, was given the compulsory monopoly of the gambling and lottery business. Cards and dice were, of course, prohibited as gambling. Also prohibited, however, were games of skill at public houses, such as bowling and shuffleboard, such activities being considered a waste of time by the people's self-appointed moral guardians in the government.

Idleness, in fact, was not just a sin, but also a punishable misdemeanor—at any time, not only on Sunday. If the constable discovered anyone, singly or in groups, engaged in such heinous behavior as coasting on the ice, swimming, or sneaking a quiet smoke, he was ordered to report to the magistrate. Time, it seems, was God's gift and therefore always to be used in His service. A sin against God's time was a crime against the church and state.

Drinking, oddly enough, was not completely outlawed, but drunkenness was, and subject to a fine. The practice of drinking toasts was outlawed in 1639, because of its supposedly pagan origin and because, once a man has begun to drink a toast, he is on the road to perdition; "drunkenness, uncleanness, and other sins quickly follow." And yet the stern guardians of the public morality had their troubles, for decades later we find ministerial complaints that the "heathenish and idolatrous practice of health-drinking is too frequent."

Women and children, as might be expected, were treated extremely harshly by the Puritan commonwealth. Children were regarded as the virtually absolute property of their parents, and this property claim was rigorously enforced by the state. If any child be disobedient to his parents, any magistrate could haul him into court, and punish the little criminal with a maximun of ten lashes for each offense. Should the pattern of disobedience persist into adolescence, the parents, as provided by the law of 1646, were supposed to bring the youth to the magistrate. If convicted of the high crime of stubbornness and rebelliousness, the son was to be duly executed. Happily, it is likely that this particular law, on the books for over thirty years, was rarely, if ever, put into effect by the parents.

Women were viewed as instruments of Satan by the Puritans, and severe laws were passed outlawing women's apparel that was either immodest or so showy as to indicate the sin of "pride of raiment." "Immodesty" included the wearing of short-sleeved dresses, "whereby the nakedness of the arm may be discovered"—a practice duly outlawed in 1656.

In outlawing "pride of raiment," women were not discriminated against by the Puritans; men too felt the heavy arm of the state. In 1634 the General Court began the practice of outlawing finery of dress for either sex, including "immodest fashions . . . with any lace on it, silver, gold or thread," hat bands, belts, ruffs, beaver hats, and many other items of adornment. In 1639 more items of sin were added: for example, ribbons, shoulder bands, and cuffs—these nonutilitarian items being of "little use or benefit, but to the nourishment of pride." Excessive finery was subject to heavy fines, and the law was extensively enforced. Thus, in one year, Hampshire County hauled thirty-eight women and thirty men into court for illegal finery, silk being an especially popular sin. One woman was punished "for wearing silk in a flaunting garb, to the great offense of several sober persons."

Even the wearing of one's hair long—an old Cavalier practice condemned by the Puritans, who were therefore called Roundheads—was placed under interdict. The General Court repeatedly condemned flowing hair as dangerous vanity. Many Puritan divines ranked "pride in long hair" fully as sinful as gambling, drinking, or idleness. One citizen, fined for daring to build upon unused government land, was offered a remission of half the amount if he would only "cut off the long hair off his head into a civil frame." Hair righteousness, however, never had much of a chance even in godly Massachusetts, for some of the major leaders of the colony, including Governor Winthrop and John Endecott, persisted in the sin of long hair.

Mixed dancing only came to the colony late in the century, but was promptly condemned as frivolous, immoral and a waste of time. Boston, upon hearing complaints, closed down a dancing school.

The measures of the fanatical Puritan theocracy were not solely motivated by religious zeal. Part of the motivation had an economic-class basis. As the century progressed, the lowly laborers and indentured servants formed an increasing minority of the populace; since they were not admitted to the political and social privileges of church membership, they were naturally the most disaffected members of the social body. The above measures were partly designed to keep the lower classes in their place. Thus, the authorities were *particularly* angered to see servants or the families of laborers having the gall to wear fine apparel. The General Court, in 1658, severely announced "our utter detestation . . . that men or women of mean condition should take upon them the garb of gentlemen, by wearing gold or silk lace, or buttons or silk of taffeta hoods, or scarves, which though allowable to persons of greater estates or more liberal

180

education, yet we cannot but judge intolerable in persons of such like condition." In short, the lower orders must know their place, and the stringent requirements of a fanatical moral code could bend for the upper strata of society.

Similarly, the requirement of compulsory education was enforced particularly upon the indentured servants, as many masters believed that their servants would be less inclined to be independent or "give trouble" if imbued with Puritan teachings.

Indeed, the leaders of the colony did not hesitate to justify the oligarchic rule by the rich over the poor. As Governor Winthrop expressed it in his *A Model of Christian Charity* (1630): "God Almighty in His most holy and wise providence hath so disposed of the condition of mankind as in all times some must be rich, some poor; some high and eminent in power and dignity; others mean and in subjection."

Generally, then, it was the lower orders who had to bear the main brunt of the severely enforced "moral" rules of the Puritan code. Indeed, Massachusetts imposed maximum ceilings on wage rates in order to lower wage costs to employers. The temporarily enslaved indentured servants were particularly oppressed by Puritans trying to maintain them as the efficient property of their masters; they therefore tried to suppress all deviant tendencies from the norm.* Many servants were branded like cattle with their initials and the date of purchase, so as to assure their rapid identification in case of flight. When found unsatisfactory or troublesome, servants were generally punished, whipped, and imprisoned, or had their tenure of servitude extended. Orphan boys were bound out as servants by the state until they reached the age of twenty, while illegitimate boys were especially punished by being bound out until the age of thirty. In addition, indentured servants could, like slaves, be sold by their masters to other masters, and thus be forcibly separated from their families. Servants caught escaping were often punished by having their ears cut off.

---

*The sources of servants in Massachusetts and the other Northern colonies were the same as those of the servants coming to Virginia, as described above.

21

Suppressing Heresy: The Flight of Roger Williams

"The Puritans in leaving England," the historian Thomas Jefferson Wertenbaker wrote, "fled not so much from persecution as from error." It was to build a rigorous theocracy free from dissent that the Puritans built a colony in America. And yet a Protestant theocracy must always suffer from a grave inner contradiction: for one significant tenet of Protestantism is the individual's ability to interpret the Bible free of ecclesiastical dictates. Although particular Protestant creeds may have no intention of countenancing or permitting dissent, the Protestant stimulus to individual interpretation must inevitably provoke that very dissent.

If the Puritans were so rigorous in suppressing idleness and frivolity on the Sabbath, we can imagine their zeal in rooting out heresy. As the Reverend Urian Oakes put it: "The Loud outcry of some is for liberty of conscience . . . I look upon an unbounded toleration as the first born of all abominations." And the Rev. Thomas Shepard echoed that " 'tis Satan's policy, to plead for an indefinite and boundless toleration." The eminent Puritan divine John Norton, in *The Heart of New England Rent,* thundered against liberty: "We both dread and bear witness against liberty of heresy. . . . It is a liberty . . . to answer to the dictate of error of conscience in walking contrary to rule. It is a liberty to blaspheme, a liberty to seduce others from the true God, a liberty to tell lies in the name of the Lord." As for liberty of conscience, Norton speciously claimed to be upholding it, but not the "liberty of the error of conscience"; in short, people were to be "free" to believe what Norton wanted them to, but were not to be free to differ. As early as 1631 the Puritan authorities revealed their position on heresy. In that year Phillip Ratcliffe was whipped, fined forty shillings, had his ears cut off, and was banished for the high crime of "uttering malicious and scandalous speeches against the government and the Church."

The first important case of heresy also came soon after the founding of the colony. To Massachusetts in early 1631 came the young Rev. Roger Williams, who quickly refused the coveted appointment of teacher of the Boston church. An individualist and a fearless logician, Williams had concluded that the Puritan church in Massachusetts, being Separatist *de facto*, should also be Separatist *de jure:* that is, should break openly from communion with the Church of England. In short, he pursued the Puritans' logic further than they were willing to go, and thus embarrassed the Puritans a great deal. Beginning with this dissent, Williams quickly went on to strike hammer blows against the entire political structure of the colony. First he proceeded to deny the right of the civil authority to punish the infraction of religious rule or doctrine. This struck at the entire theocratic principle, and the General Court of Massachusetts declared in reply that it was clearly absurd to maintain that "a Church might run into heresy . . . and yet the civil magistrate could not intermeddle." To the Puritans this was clearly a puzzling and astonishing doctrine.

Williams now accepted appointment as teacher of the Salem church, but his appointment was overruled by the General Court on account of Williams' Separatist views and his dedication to religious liberty. Williams thereupon moved to the fully Separatist Plymouth, where he became assistant to the Reverend Ralph Smith, who had also been ejected from Salem for his pure Separatist views. But Plymouth itself was becoming less Separatist, and could not tolerate Williams' libertarianism. As a result, Williams accepted in late 1633 a second call from Salem to be a teacher of the church. There he joined the senior pastor, Samuel Skelton, in attacking the growing practice of ministers in holding periodical joint discussions—a practice which they perceptively feared would grow into a form of snyodal quasi-Presbyterian control over the individual congregations. Only four years later, Skelton and Williams were proved right by the erection of a system of synods, which also resulted in joint ministerial advice to the civil power.

Williams proceeded to strike another fundamental blow at the social structure of Massachusetts Bay. He denied the right of the king to make arbitrary grants of the land of Massachusetts to the colonists. The Indians, he maintained, properly owned the land and therefore the settlers should purchase the land from them. This doctrine attacked the entire quasi-feudal origin of American colonization in arbitrary land grants in the royal charters, and it also hit at the policy of ruthlessly expelling the Indians from their land. Williams, indeed, was the rare white colonist courageous enough to say that full title to the soil rested in the Indian natives, and that white title could only be validly obtained by purchase from its true owners. The whites, charged Williams, lived "under a sin of usurpation of others' possessions." The denial of the king's right to grant title to land he did not justly own, of course, hit directly at the basis of the Massachusetts charter itself, which, Williams argued, the colonists had a moral duty to turn from and renounce.

The infuriated authorities now moved in on Williams, charging him with subversive doctrine. Bowing to *force majeure,* Williams recanted and offered to burn the tract expressing his dissenting views.

But Williams was too much a man of principle to be suppressed for long, and by late 1634 news reached Boston that Williams was repeating his old subversive doctrines as well as adding the purist religious deviation from Puritan orthodoxy that oaths should not be administered by magistrates to unregenerate sinners. Williams also denounced the loyalty oaths coerced upon the mass of nonfreemen residents of the colony, in April 1634, as blasphemous; he refused to subscribe to the oath and urged his congregation to do the same. Williams did this despite the punishment for refusal having been announced as banishment from the colony.

A crackdown by the Massachusetts authorities was precipitated by Salem church's appointing Williams as its chief minister in place of the deceased Skelton. The Massachusetts authorities now unanimously condemned Williams' views as "erroneous and very dangerous" and denounced Salem's action as "a great contempt of authority." The Massachusetts clergy recommended to the General Court that this dangerous advocate of religious liberty "be removed." Hauled into General Court in July 1635, Williams now remained adamant, even after several confrontations with church authorities.

The General Court now openly moved to undermine Williams with his home base at Salem, punishing that town by refusing to grant it title to land that it claimed at Marblehead Neck. Salem church struck back with an indignation meeting, which sent letters to the congregations of the other churches of the colony, urging them to "admonish" the magistrates and deputies for their "heinous sin." The elders of the other churches made certain to suppress any potential upsurge of popular sympathy for Williams and Salem by not reading the letters to their congregations. Williams continued to strike hard, denouncing the oligarchy of elders for keeping information from the body of church menbers.

As the fierce conflict continued, Williams' fearless spirit, the logic of Protestantism, and the dynamics of the conflict itself drove Roger Williams to the ultimate conclusion of Separatism: calling upon Salem church to separate clearly from the other churches of the colony, as well as from the Church of England. This was the straw that broke the Massachusetts camel's back. The Puritan oligarchy now brandished its temporal sword, sending to Salem its *Model of Church and Civil Power.* The *Model* gave grave warning that the civil magistrates would strike down any "corrupt" or schismatic church. Independent churches would be suppressed; religious toleration could only end by dissolving the state as well as the church.

In September the civil power followed this by subduing Salem: the General Court expelled the Salem deputies and reiterated its refusal to grant the town's land claims. The assistant ruling Salem, John Endecott, defended the Salem church but was promptly imprisoned until he recanted and was discharged. Under the severest pressure by the Puritan oligarchy, the majority of Salem church, as Williams was later to write, "was swayed and bowed (whether for fear of persecution or otherwise) to say and practice what, to my knowledge . . . many of them mourned under."

With Salem brought to heel, it now remained only to suppress the isolated Roger Williams himself. Yet, when brought again into General Court in October 1635, Williams stoutly maintained all of his heretical and libertarian opinions. He refused to recant even when forced to debate with the Rev. Thomas Hooker, a leading Puritan divine. Thereupon the General Court ordered Williams expelled from the colony within six weeks. The sentence of banishment declared:

> Whereas Mr. Roger Williams . . . hath broached and divulged divers new and dangerous opinions, against the authority of magistrates, has also written letters of defamation, both of the magistrates and churches here . . . and yet maintaineth the same without retraction, it is therefore ordered that the said Mr. Williams shall depart out of this jurisdiction.

The court agreed to extend the deadline for Williams' banishment provided that he would not "go about to draw others to his opinions." But the authorities were chagrined to find that even Williams in private was having a subversive effect. While Salem bowed reluctantly to the decision of the authorities—and received the Marblehead land in return—Williams himself separated from the Salem church, and others were moved to do the same.

Over twenty Salem families now prepared to follow Williams southward into exile and there build a haven of religious liberty. With the disappearance of the Council for New England in 1635, Massachusetts Bay and Plymouth were both virtually self-governing, and what is more, the land south of the Massachusetts grant and west of Plymouth became a tempting vacuum, not having been parceled out to any person or group. It was in this free area that Williams now prepared to found a new colony.

The Massachusetts authorities were greatly dismayed, because they had expected that Williams would be forced back to England. It was not enough to oust Williams forcibly from the land area assigned to Massachusetts; should he merely move southward, there would still be a danger that, in the words of Governor John Winthrop, "the infection would easily spread" to Massachusetts Bay. The General Court hastily sent a ship to Salem to arrest Williams and send him speedily back to England. But Williams bested his persecutors and fled alone into the wilderness. He trudged south through the snow and spent the winter among the friendly Narragansett Indians.

In the spring Williams was joined by four friends, and they proceeded to the northern tip of Narragansett Bay, where they founded the settlement of Seekonk. There they were soon joined by several more families from Salem. The great southward flight from Massachusetts had begun.

Williams' travail had scarcely ended, however. Soon the governor of Plymouth Colony wrote to Williams regretfully advising him that Seekonk was still inside the Plymouth boundaries, and that Plymouth could not dare displease Massachusetts by allowing the little band to remain. So Williams was now banished from Plymouth as well; and the purchase of the Seekonk land from the Indians, the clearing of land, and the planting of crops had all been in vain.

Moving west across the Seekonk River, Williams left the jurisdiction of Plymouth and founded the settlement of Providence. In Providence Plantations, Williams and the others scrupulously purchased the land from the Indians, and determined to allow religious liberty in their new and spontaneously formed colony.

How Roger Williams was regarded by the frightened Puritan oligarchs of Massachusetts Bay may be seen from the historical account of the Rev. Cotton Mather, one of the main leaders of the later generation of Puritan divines: "There was a whole country in America like to be set on fire by the rapid motion of a windmill in the head of one particular man, Roger Williams." And Mather realized that Williams' doctrines were aimed at "the whole political, as well as the ecclesiastical, constitution of the country." The reaction of the Massachusetts authorities to Williams' flight was to step up their persecution of Salem Separatism. All meetings of Separatists were now outlawed.

Williams' views, at least in these early days of his career, were notably libertarian, especially in contrast to those of other Americans of his time. But it must be recognized that Williams emerged as an embattled leader within the context of a Puritan and Dissenter movement in England, which in the 1630s and 1640s was rapidly becoming radicalized and increasingly libertarian. The libertarian movement reached its culmination —and was not to reach the same height again for well over a century—in the Leveller movement of the 1640s. Williams himself had participated in the emerging Puritan cause. A protégé of the great liberal jurist Sir Edward Coke, Williams owned opinions that had brought him into conflict with the ultra-Anglican and minion of the Stuarts, Archbishop Laud. Williams thus received his early ideological training in the liberal Dissenter movement.

Free and safe in a Providence enjoying religious liberty and separation of church and state, Roger Williams was later able to elaborate on his doctrines of religious liberty. His most famous theoretical work, *The Bloody Tenent of Persecution for the Cause of Conscience Discussed,* appeared in 1644. A sequel, *The Bloody Tenent Yet More Bloody,* rebutting the reply of the leading Massachusetts divine, Rev. John Cotton, appeared eight years later. Compulsory religion, Williams pointed out, violated the

Christian tenet of love and, by "ravishing and forcing souls" and consciences, led to hypocrisy for fear of state punishment. Coerced religion, Williams declared, leads to sects "slaughtering each other for their several respective religions and consciences." Again unusual for his time, Williams insisted that not only Protestants, but *all* religions must be completely free, including "the most paganish, Jewish, Turkish, or anti-Christian consciences and worships." He added, "To molest any person, Jew or Gentile, for either professing doctrines or practicing worship. . .is to persecute him and such a person (whatever his doctrine or practice be true or false) suffereth persecution for conscience." And this man of courage and principle nobly proclaimed the importance of cleaving to truth: "We must not let go for all the flea-bitings of the present afflictions. . .having bought Truth dear we must not sell it cheap, not the least grain of it for the whole world . . . least of all for a little puff of credit and reputation from the changeable breath of uncertain sons of men."

While Williams' heart was in the right place in insisting on purchasing all land voluntarily from the Indians, there were important aspects of the land problem that he had not thought through. While the Indians were certainly entitled to the land they cultivated, they also (1) laid claim to vast reaches of land which they hunted but which they did not transform by cultivation, and (2) owned the land not as individual Indians, but as collective tribal entities. In many cases the Indian tribes could not alienate or sell the lands, but only lease the use of their ancestral domains. As a result, the Indians also lived under a collectivistic regime that, for land allocation, was scarcely more just than the English governmental land-grab against which Williams was properly rebelling. Under both regimes, the actual *settler*—the first transformer of the land, whether white or Indian—had to fight his way past a nest of arbitrary land claims by others, and pay their exactions until he could formally own the land.

Williams, always a friend of the Indians, bought from the sachems, or chiefs, a grant of the large amount of land called the "Providence Purchase." Williams then donated the land to a Town Fellowship, a joint property held equally by himself and five of his followers—the Fellowship shortly enlarged to thirteen. As long as only the original settlers lived in Providence, all was peaceful, and virtually no government arose at all. As Williams described it, "The masters of families have ordinarily met once a fortnight and consulted about our common peace, watch and plenty; and mutual consent have finished all matters of speed and pace." But it was inevitable that new settlers would come, and then that the arbitrary nature of the land allocation should give rise to conflict. Indeed, recriminations and tensions rapidly developed. Not realizing the inherent injustice of any arbitrary claims to unsettled land, and therefore not realizing that he and the others of the Fellowship were taking on the aspect of quasi-feudal land monopolists, Williams naturally believed he had acted generously in giving the land to the Fellowship. But the later settlers, forced to purchase the land from the Fellowship, properly resented this feudalistic proprietary.

The Fellowship, later enlarged to fifty-four, assigned eleven acres to each member, plus the right to an additional 100 acres apiece. In this way some of the land passed quickly to the individual members of the Fellowship. If their acreage was not in precise proportion to the degree of settlement, at least this land was now in the hands of its just owners, the individual settlers. But, unfortunately, the great bulk of the Providence tract still remained in the hands of the collective Fellowship proprietary, and in 1640 the Fellowship moved to formalize its claim, and to establish a proprietary oligarchy over future settlers. In that year, the Fellowship drew up a "Plantation Agreement at Providence," and appointed a board of five "disposers" that would take charge of disposing of the land, managing the land held in common, and passing judgment on the qualification of new settlers. Taught little humility by their own sufferings, the disposers tended to be rigorous in their judgments. Before a man was permitted to settle and buy land in Providence, even the land of an individual settler willing to sell, the Fellowship had to approve, and a veto by one Fellow was sufficient to bar the newcomer. The original Fellows soon admitted more members, but the number of Fellows never exceeded 101, and the later members received only twenty-five rather than 100 acres of collectively owned land. Positions in the Fellowship descended to the heirs of the original members; the other settlers who were permitted to become landowners in Providence were excluded from the select circle of the Fellowship proprietary, which thus controlled the land and government. The Fellowship kept a sharp check on its five disposers, but this hardly made the government of Providince less oligarchical.

The most oligarchic feature of the Plantation Agreement dealt with Pawtuxet, a tract of land immediately south of Providence. Pawtuxet had been purchased from Indian sachems in the spring of 1638 and turned over by Williams to the Fellows, then numbering thirteen. Overriding Williams' wishes, the Fellows, led by William Arnold and William Harris, decided in October of 1638 eventually to divide the Pawtuxet lands among themselves, without even providing for any new settlers. The Agreement of 1640 confirmed Pawtuxet as a closed proprietorship.

Roger Williams carried his principles of religious liberty into practice. There was no state church, and no one was forced to attend church. Williams himself was to change his religious views several times, becoming a Baptist for a few months, and then ending as a Seeker, who held to no fixed creed. Liberty has its own inner logic, and so Williams' religious liberty in Providence extended also to women. One of Williams' Salem adherents who had followed him to Providence, Joshua Verin, tasting the heady wine of religious liberty, grew disenchanted with Williams' sermons and stopped attending church. This was perfectly legitimate in his newfound home, but Verin went so far as to prevent his wife from attending, even beating her to prevent her from going. Verin was therefore disfranchised by Providence in the spring of 1638 for restraining his wife's conscience; he soon returned to Salem, where he could again exercise the Puritan role of despotic paterfamilias.

The logic of liberty had, as we shall see, even more drastic implications. For, as some citizens of Providence began to reason, if the conscience of the individual was to be supreme in religious matters, if the state was to have no power to interfere with any actions determined by his religious conscience, why shouldn't his liberty extend to civil matters as well? Why shouldn't the individual's conscience reign supreme in all civil as well as religious affairs?

22

Suppressing Heresy: The Flight of Anne Hutchinson

Very shortly after the expulsion of Roger Williams, the Massachusetts Bay Colony was rent far more widely by another heresy with roots deep in the colony—the "antinomianism" of Mrs. Anne Hutchinson. A major reason for the crisis that Anne Hutchinson's heresy posed for Massachusetts was that she occupied a high place in the colony's oligarchy. Arriving in Massachusetts in 1634, she and her husband lived close to Governor Winthrop's mansion in Boston and participated in Boston's high society. A friend of the eminent Rev. John Cotton, she first confined her religious activities to expatiating on Cotton's sermons. Soon, however, Mrs. Hutchinson developed a religious doctrine of her own, now known as antinomianism. She preached the necessity for an inner light to come to any individual chosen as one of God's elect. Such talk marked her as far more of a religious individualist than the Massachusetts leaders. Salvation came only through a covenant of grace emerging from the inner light, and was not at all revealed in a covenant of works, the essence of which is good works on earth. This meant that the fanatically ascetic sanctification imposed by the Puritans was no evidence whatever that one was of the elect. Furthermore, Anne Hutchinson made it plain that she regarded many Puritan leaders as *not* of the elect. She also came to assert that she had received direct revelations from God.

In contrast to Williams' few Salem followers, Anne Hutchinson had rapid and sweeping success in converting her fellow citizens. John Cotton now became a follower of hers, as did young Sir Henry Vane, chosen governor by the General Court in 1636, and Anne's brother-in-law, Rev. John Wheelwright. Indeed, John Winthrop (deputy governor in 1636) wrote disgustedly that virtually the entire church at Boston had become her converts. As bitter enemies of Anne, there remained especially Winthrop and the senior minister of Boston, John Wilson. Mrs. Hutchinson failed in her attempt to oust Wilson from his post, but she did succeed in having him censured by his own congregation.

The Hutchinsonian movement began, if inadvertently, to pose political problems for the oligarchy as well. The conscription of soldiers for a war against the Indians met resistance from Boston Hutchinsonians, on the ground that the military chaplain, Rev. John Wilson, was under a "covenant of works" rather than of grace.

The anti-Hutchinson forces moved first against the fiery Reverend Mr. Wheelwright; the General Court narrowly convicted him of sedition and contempt in March 1637. But the sentencing of Wheelwright was postponed. The turning point of the Hutchinson affair came with the May election of 1637, which the Winthrop forces managed to win by shifting its site from pro-Hutchinson Boston to Newtown (now Cambridge). The election pitted Sir Henry Vane against former governor Winthrop and Thomas Dudley, running for his old post of deputy governor. With the election turning on the Hutchinson issue, Vane carried Boston but lost the other towns heavily. Winthrop, Dudley, and the majority of the magistrates, or assistants, were carried by the conservative, anti-Hutchinson faction—a not surprising victory when we consider that suffrage was restricted to the ranks of accepted church members.

This overwhelming defeat spelled swift suppression for the antinomian heretics. Quickly the new General Court passed a law that penalized strangers and was directed against a group of Hutchinsonians known to be on their way from England. Disheartened, Sir Henry Vane gave up the struggle and returned to England. Seeing the way the wind was blowing, John Cotton promptly deserted his old disciple, abjectly recanted his "heresies," and at a Newtown synod denounced ninety-one antinomian opinions as unwholesome or blasphemous. Vane was gone and Cotton an apostate, but there was still the Reverend Mr. Wheelwright. The already convicted Wheelwright was again hauled before the General Court and sentenced to banishment from the colony. Wheelwright walked through the snows to New Hampshire in the north, where he founded the settlement of Exeter. When by 1643 Massachusetts had appropriated the New Hampshire towns, Wheelwright fled to Maine. But by 1646 Wheelwright had recanted, bewailed his own "vehement and censorious spirit," and was allowed back into Massachusetts.

Having vented their fury on the major followers and isolated the leader, the Puritan oligarchs proceeded to the culminating point of the drama: the trial and persecution of Anne Hutchinson herself. There was no independent judiciary in the colonies; the supreme judicial arm in Massachusetts was the legislative body, the General Court, at this time a unicameral legislature presided over by the governor. Anne Hutchinson was hauled up for "trial," or rather public examination, before the General Court in November 1637. Anne's enemies on the General Court duly "tried" her, convicted her of sedition and contempt, and banished her from the colony. Governor Winthrop summarized the proceedings thus: "The Court hath already declared themselves concerning . . . the troublesomeness of her spirit, and the dangers of her course amongst us, which is not to be suffered." Winthrop then called for a vote that Mrs. Hutchinson "is unfit for our society—and . . . that she shall be banished out of our liberties and imprisoned till she be sent away. . . ." Only two members voted against her banishment.

When Winthrop pronounced the sentence of banishment Anne Hutchinson courageously asked: "I desire to know wherefore I am banished." Winthrop refused to answer: "Say no more. The court knows wherefore, and is satisfied." It was apparently enough for the court to be satisfied; no justification before the bar of reason, natural justice, or the public was deemed necessary.

The General Court now proceeded against all the leading Hutchinsonians, concentrating on sixty Bostonians who had previously signed a moderate petition denying that Reverend Wheelwright had stirred up sedition among them. Two members of the General Court, both of whom had spoken up for Mrs. Hutchinson at the trial, were expelled from the court and banished from the colony. Many people were disfranchised, and seventy-five citizens were disarmed, on the pretext that the Hutchinsonians were plotting to follow the path of the German Anabaptists of old and rise up in armed revolt. The "reasoning" as expounded by Dudley at the Hutchinson trial was that the German Anabaptists had *also* claimed to enjoy private revelations. Hutchinsonian military officers were forced to recant, but the determined Capt. John Underhill refused to do so and was duly banished.

Anne Hutchinson's ordeal was still not ended. Spared banishment during the rugged winter, she was imprisoned at the home of one of her major enemies, and the elders attempted, throughout the winter, to argue her out of her convictions. Finally, they subjected her to an ecclesiastical trial the following March. Tormented, ill, and exhausted, Mrs. Hutchinson momentarily recanted, but as she continued to be denounced, her spirits returned and she put forth her views again.

To save himself from the fate meted out to the other Hutchinsonians, John Cotton now apparently felt that his personal recantation was not enough, so he joined the pack rending Mrs. Hutchinson at the ecclesiastical trial. This man, whom Anne Hutchinson had revered and followed to the New World, now turned on her savagely, wailing that he had been duped, denouncing her as a liar and for conduct tending eventually to infidelity.

The Boston ecclesiastical court then pronounced excommunication upon Anne, and it was the peculiar satisfaction of the Rev. John Wilson, her most bitter enemy, to deliver the sentence:

John Winthrop

Increase Mather

Edmund Andros
(Engraved by E. G. Wilhams & Bros., New York)

Governor Berkeley and the Insurgents (Bacon's Rebellion, 1676)

Cotton Mather

William Penn
(Engraved by J. Posselwhite)

Statue of Roger Williams in Providence, Rhode Island

Statue of Anne Hutchinson

I do cast you out and in the name of Christ, I do deliver you up to Satan, that you may learn no more to blaspheme, to seduce and to lie, and I do account you from this time forth to be a heathen and a Publican . . . therefore I command you in the name of Christ Jesus and of His Church as a Leper to withdraw yourself out of the Congregation. . . .

The undaunted Anne Hutchinson had the last word: "Better to be cast out of the Church than to deny Christ."

While Anne was undergoing imprisonment and subsequent excommunication, the leaders of the Hutchinsonian movement gathered together to flee the colony, and to prepare a home for themselves and Anne away from the developing reign of terror in Massachusetts. On March 7, 1638, nineteen men, including Anne's husband, William Hutchinson, gathered at the home of the eminent Boston merchant William Coddington, one of the wealthiest men in the colony and its former treasurer. In a solemn compact, the nineteen formed themselves into a "Bodie Politick," choosing Coddington as their judge.

The Hutchinsonians first intended to go to Long Island or Jersey to make their home, but they were persuaded by Roger Williams to settle in the Rhode Island area. On Williams' friendly advice, Coddington purchased the island of Aquidneck from the Indians, and founded on the island the settlement of Pocasset (now Portsmouth). Anne, ill and exhausted, joined her husband at Aquidneck in April as soon as her trial was over.

The enormous significance of Roger Williams' successful flight and settlement of Providence two years before was now becoming evident. For Williams' example held out a beacon light of liberty to all the free spirits caught in the vast prisonhouse that was Massachusetts Bay. By the happy accident of the demise of the Council for New England, the land south of Massachusetts Bay and west of Plymouth was free land, free of proprietary and effective royal government alike. It was a haven for religious liberty and for diverse sects and groupings, and for an extension of the logic of liberty as well; for once liberty is pursued and experienced, it is difficult to hobble its uttermost expansion.

When the ill Anne Hutchinson arrived at her haven in Aquidneck, the many months of persecution had left their mark and she suffered a miscarriage, as did her beautiful young follower Mary Dyer, who had stood up to walk out of the Boston church with the excommunicated Anne. The Puritan leaders of Massachusetts Bay, preoccupied for years afterward with the Hutchinsonian menace, characteristically gloated in righteous satisfaction at the misfortunes of Anne and Mary. The theocrats were jubilant and the Rev. John Cotton, Governor Winthrop and the Rev. Thomas Weld all hailed Anne's and Mary's sufferings as the evident judgment of God. It was typical of the Puritans to hail the misfortunes of their enemies as God's judgment, and to dismiss any kindness shown them by others as simply God's will and therefore requiring no gratitude to those showing it.

Massachusetts Bay continued, indeed, in a state of hysteria over the Hutchinsonian heresy for a number of years. Anne's followers and sympathizers were fined, whipped, and banished, and five years later Robert Potter was executed for being a Hutchinsonian. It was also typical that, with Anne outside their jurisdiction, the Boston church leaders should send a committee to Aquidneck to try to persuade her of the error of her ways. If they could no longer inflict violence upon Anne, they could at least badger and harass her. It is not surprising that the beleaguered Anne gave the committee short shrift, kicked it out of her home, and denounced the Boston church as a "whore and a strumpet."

In Pocasset, Anne was spiritual leader of the flock and Coddington temporal leader. The Pocasset government was chosen by the assembled freeholders, and, like Providence, the government had to consent to the arrival of any newcomers to the colony. But Anne Hutchinson was becoming more and more concerned for the principle of freedom of conscience rather than for propagating her own religious views. She began to see that Coddington and his associates were launching a new theocracy of their own in the infant colony. For Coddington was "judge" of the settlement, basing his decrees and decisions on the "word of God," as interpreted by himself. And Anne began to chafe at the state control that Coddington was increasingly imposing.

Coddington based his seizure of power on the flimsy legalism of his being the sole name on the deed of purchase of Aquidneck from the Indians. Therefore, he claimed for himself all the rights of a feudal lord owning the whole island, owning and renting out the lots of all the settlers, and asserting authority over all land grants.

At the beginning of 1639, Anne Hutchinson led a movement that successfully modified the Pocasset constitution; the change gave the body of freemen a veto over the actions of the governor, and the right to elect three "elders" to share the governor's powers. Thus, the increasingly dictatorial rule of Coddington was checked.

Coddington reacted most ungraciously to this limitation on his power, and he appointed a constable to keep watch on any "manifest breaches of the law of God that tend to civil disturbance." Had Anne Hutchinson fled the theocracy of Massachusetts only to see a miniature raise its head in her new home? Finally, in April, the Hutchinson forces insisted, at the Pocasset town meeting, on a new election for governor—a demand that startled Coddington, who expected to remain in office indefinitely and without the fuss and bother of elections. Vigorous pressure by the freemen on Coddington finally won the demand for elections, and William Hutchinson was elected by a large majority. Coddington and his followers, including Nicholas Easton, John Coggeshall, William Dyer, and John Clarke, abandoned Pocasset and founded the new settlement of Newport, at the southern end of Aquidneck Island.

The victorious Hutchinsonians adopted a new compact of government and changed the name of the town to Portsmouth. Oligarchical distinctions were eliminated, and all the male inhabitants signed the new compact. Provision was made for jury trial, and church and state were at last separated. There was no provision, for example, in the new civil compact about the "word of God," the only rule by which Coddington had made his decisions. Anne Hutchinson had been rapidly learning firsthand about state persecution, and freedom of religion for all Christians was now guaranteed. William Hutchinson was chosen new chief judge of the colony.

The power-hungry Coddington now mounted an armed attempt to rule over Portsmouth, but was forcibly ejected by the Hutchinsonians. Soon, however, Coddington was able to arrest William Hutchinson and order his disfranchisement. Anne and her husband were again victims of harassment and persecution.

A year later, on March 12, 1640, the two groups came to an agreement and the settlements of Portsmouth and Newport (the latter by now being the larger of the two) united, primarily on the libertarian principles of Portsmouth. Coddington was chosen governor, however, and William Hutchinson one of his assistants. The separate towns were allowed to retain their autonomy, and the laws were to be made by the citizens rather than by an oligarchy. And a year later, in May 1641, the Aquidneck government declared: "It is ordered that none shall be accounted as delinquent for doctrine." Religious liberty had been officially decreed in Aquidneck. The settlements of Providence and Aquidneck had raised the banner of freedom for all religious creeds. In this free air, diversity of religion came to proliferate in the colony.

Soon, however, Mrs. Anne Hutchinson, ruminating in the free air of Rhode Island on the meaning of her experience, came to an astounding and startling conclusion—and one that pushed the logic of Roger Williams' libertarianism far beyond the master. For, as Williams reported in bewilderment, Anne now persuaded her husband to give up his leading post as assistant in the Aquidneck government, "because of the opinion, which she had newly taken up, of the unlawfulness of magistry." In short, the logic of liberty and a deeper meditation on Scripture had both led Anne to the ultimate bounds of libertarian thought: to individualist anarchism. No magistracy whatever was lawful. As Anne's biographer Winifred Rugg put it: "She was supremely convinced that the Christian held within his own breast the assurance of salvation. . . . For such persons magistrates were obviously superfluous. As for the other, they were to be converted, not coerced."*

To the Puritans of Massachusetts, Aquidneck was an abominable "Isle of Errours" and the Rhode Island settlements were "Rogue's Land." Massachusetts began to plot to assert its jurisdiction over these pestiferous settlements and to crush the havens of liberty. Indians were egged on to

---

*Winifred K. Rugg, *Unafraid, A life of Anne Hutchinson* (Boston, 1930).

raid the Providence and Aquidneck territories. Massachusetts then shut off all trade with the Rhode Islanders, who were thus forced to turn to the neighboring Dutch settlements of New Netherland for supplies. A son and son-in-law of Anne's, visiting Boston, were seized and very heavily fined by the authorities, and then banished from Massachusetts on pain of death.

In 1642, soon after his resignation from public office, William Hutchinson died. Deprived of her husband and mainstay, disgusted with all government, and deeply worried about Massachusetts' threatened encroachments on Rhode Island (and knowing also that the Bay Colony was now regarding her as a witch and therefore deserving of death), Anne decided to leave once more. Taking a few members of her family and a few dozen disciples, Anne Hutchinson left Rhode Island to go to Long Island, in New Netherland, and finally to settle in the wilderness of Pelham Bay. There, in late summer of 1643, Anne and her family were murdered by a band of Indians, engaged in armed struggle with the Dutch. William's and Anne's deaths were hailed and gloated over by the Puritan oligarchy of Massachusetts Bay. To the unconcealed delight of the divines of Massachusetts, Anne Hutchinson had, finally, been physically destroyed; but the spirit of liberty that she embodied and kindled was to outlast the despotic theocracy of Massachusetts Bay. Perhaps, in the light of history, the victory in the unequal contest was Anne Hutchinson's

Even in the short run, Massachusetts Bay was soon to meet again the spirit of Anne Hutchinson—the emphasis on the inner light, on individual conscience, on liberty—in the new sect of Quakers, a sect joined by many Hutchinsonians, including William Coddington and Mary Dyer, and in the Baptists, headed by Anne Hutchinson's sister, Catherine Scott, and by the Hutchinsonian Dr. John Clarke.

23

The Further Settlement of Rhode Island: The Odyssey of Samuell Gorton

In the meanwhile, religious liberty, and hence diversity, was flourishing in nearby Providence. An Anglican minister who had been living in the vicinity before the Williams settlement continued to preach there. Baptists came also to the colony and exerted great influence. The first Baptist minister was Dr. John Clarke, a physician, who had arrived in Massachusetts from England just in time to join with Anne Hutchinson and leave for Aquidneck. William Harris also was a leading Rhode Island Baptist from the earliest days. The brilliant Baptist leader and sister of Anne Hutchinson, Mrs. Catherine Scott, even succeeded in temporarily converting Roger Williams (along with many other leaders) to the Baptist faith in early 1639. The inveterate Baptist insistence on individual conscience and the right of religious liberty was very close to Williams' views. In addition, each Baptist church was separate and completely autonomous; the officers were democratically elected by the entire congregation. In a few months, however, Williams shifted again to become a Seeker, which he continued to be for the rest of his life. Williams had arrived at the point of questioning the claims of all churches to apostolic authority or to correctness of ritual.

In addition to religious liberty, and apart from land allocation, the powers of government in Providence were limited. Disputes were to be settled by arbitration, but the arbitration was compulsory, enforced by the ruling "disposers." And, in contrast to Massachusetts, there was no establishment of government schools.

One of the most repeatedly and consistently persecuted Americans of the seventeenth century was Samuell Gorton, an individualist and a free spirit who had been a clothier in London. Gorton, a "Professor of the Mysteries of Christ," challenged not only the right of theocracy, but the wisdom of all priests and formal religious organizations. Politically, this individualist argued that any transgressions of government beyond the rights guaranteed by the English common law were impermissible. Gorton also opposed theocratic laws against immorality, and questioned the existence of heaven and hell, the truth of the Scriptures, baptism, and the taking of oaths.

Chafing at the restrictions of Anglican England, Gorton left London for Boston in 1636 "to enjoy liberty of conscience, in respect to faith towards God." It did not take Gorton long to see that he had only moved from the frying pan into the fire; he arrived just in time to see the expulsion of the Reverend Wheelwright to Exeter, and he realized that if Massachusetts would not tolerate the presence of the relatively orthodox Wheelwright, it could surely have little place for the likes of him.

Gorton therefore left quickly for Plymouth, where he began to attract considerable following for his views. Adopting Anne Hutchinson's device of prayer meetings in his parlor, Gorton began to arouse the ire of the colony's oligarchs by making a convert of the wife of the Rev. Ralph Smith, the respected retired minister of Plymouth. Another inconvenient convert was a sewing maid of the current minister of the colony, the Reverend Mr. Rayner. Reverend Mr. Smith began a campaign to expel Gorton from the colony, and a suitable excuse came shortly to hand. Employed as Mrs. Gorton's serving maid was a widow newly arrived from England, Ellen Aldridge. Charges began to be whispered about Plymouth Colony that Ellen had committed the grievous offense of "smiling in church." Complaints were duly lodged against her, and the Plymouth fathers summarily ordered Ellen to be promptly expelled from the colony as a "vagabond." Gorton spoke up heatedly in protest over these high-handed proceedings, for which high crime Gorton himself was hauled into court in late 1638. In a pretrial hearing, Gorton accused one of the magistrates of lying, a charge which only added to his crimes. At this trial Gorton denounced the grave violation of English common law in uniting the offices of prosecutor and magistrate in the same man. Protesting against the injustice of the trial, Gorton addressed the crowd: "Ye see good people how you are abused! Stand for your liberty; and let them not be parties and judges." The frightened church elders, on hearing this plea, urged the court to inflict summary punishment to remove this libertarian troublemaker from the colony. Gorton was duly prohibited from speaking in his own defense, and the court swiftly fined Gorton and gave him fourteen days to leave Plymouth. Gorton was thereby forced to walk through the wilderness in the snow, and was barely able to finish the journey southwestward to Portsmouth, where he settled.

In Portsmouth, Gorton found political rule centered in William Coddington, the sole magistrate. Joined there by his main Plymouth disciple, John Wickes, Gorton promptly amassed a large following, and formed an alliance with Anne Hutchinson to overthrow Coddington's dictatorial rule and to repulse Coddington's armed attempt to impose his rule in Portsmouth.

A year later, however, with Newport joined to Portsmouth, Coddington was back in command, even though opposed by the majority of Portsmouth residents. Again Samuell Gorton, who had steadfastly refused to enter into the agreement to join Newport, felt the lash of persecution, and again Gorton's defense of someone in his employ was the catalyst used.

At the end of 1640 an old woman's cow invaded Gorton's land. Coming after the cow, the trespassing old lady got into a fight with a serving girl of Gorton's, after which the woman hauled the servant into court. Gorton defended his servant, and strongly protested the unfair trial, attacking the justices as "just asses." He also denied the authority of the constituted court and government. Since no royal charter covered Rhode Island, it was free territory, and therefore no authority to set up a government could exist. Coddington, the chief justice at the trial, ordered Gorton arrested forthwith, crying out, "You that are for the King, lay hold on Gorton"; to which the defiant Gorton instantly riposted: "All you that are for the King, lay hold on Coddington." A hand-to-hand fight ensued, with Coddington's armed guard gaining the victory. Gorton was arrested and John Wickes, who had also defended the servant, was put into the stocks, Gorton himself was soon whipped and banished from Aquidneck; Wickes and several Gortonites were banished as well.

What next? The only place left for Gorton to go was Providence, and so he and a dozen families of disciples arrived there in the winter of 1640–41. In Providence, Gorton found two major factions: the owners of Pawtuxet, headed by William Arnold and William Harris, and Providence proper, led by Roger Williams. The oligarchical Pawtuxet clique was particularly fearful that Gorton might convert a majority of townsmen and overturn its rule, and so the Pawtuxet rulers refused to allow the Gortonites to use the town commons. The Arnold faction urged that the "turbulent" Gorton and his followers be expelled immediately from the settlement. But Gorton expanded his following, and they soon became a third force in the little colony,

And what of Roger Williams? Enjoying increasing political power, Williams was beginning to lose the edge of his libertarian principles. He became alarmed that Gorton, far more individualist and libertarian than himself, was "bewitching and bemadding poor Providence . . . with his unclear and foul censures of all the ministers of this country. . . . " Williams tried to violate, *sub rosa*, his own principles of religious liberty by simply excluding Gorton from Providence, an exclusion which was in the power of the landed oligarchy of the town. Or rather, Williams, more moderate than Arnold, wanted to grant Gorton admission *only* if he pledged to respect the authority of the government, and if he abandoned such "uncivil" protests as had gotten Gorton expelled from Portsmouth.

Finally, in November 1641 some of the Pawtuxet faction seized some cattle owned by a Gortonite, to satisfy a debt judgment the Gortonites believed to be arbitrarily decreed by the disposers. This led to a full-fledged riot between the two factions (the Gortonites being led by Randall Holden and John Greene) and the Gortonites managed to save their friend's property from the "cattle stealers."

Because of the riot, thirteen of the Pawtuxet oligarchs made a desperate and treacherous call for the Massachusetts government to intervene with force to expel the "anarchist" Gortonites. The oligarchs pulled out all the stops against their enemies, accusing the Gortonites of being anarchists, and leaning toward communism and free love, or "familism." Their appeal to Massachusetts was a direct threat to all the precious liberties that the men of Providence had fled Massachusetts to preserve. And thus began an active threat to Rhode Island liberty from Massachusetts that was to last and be of great significance for the little settlements for years to come.

Massachusetts replied haughtily to the Pawtuxians that it would intervene only if Providence would first submit to its authority, which Providence would not do. Indeed, less than a third of the Providence citizens supported the Arnold-Harris petition.

Williams, however, now joined the Pawtuxians in obtaining the expulsion of Gorton from Providence. Gorton was now banished even from this relative haven of religious liberty. His only consolation was that *this* time he wasn't whipped out of town. Gorton and his followers now moved to West Pawtuxet, an unused tract of land which Gorton had purchased the year before. But once again, the alarmed Arnold-Harris forces in September 1642, requested coercive intervention by Massachusetts and in return offered the submission of Pawtuxet to Massachusetts authority. Delighted, Massachusetts accepted with alacrity, and their declamations thoroughly alarmed the Gortonites. Governor Winthrop, for example, exulted that Samuell Gorton "was a man not fit to live upon the face of the earth," and Massachusetts troops made ready, it appeared, to put that harsh value judgment into effect.

There was, it seemed, no place in America that would tolerate the existence of Samuell Gorton—not even the relatively free Providence and Aquidneck settlements. There was but one course left: Gorton determined to found an entirely new settlement of his own. Gorton, a friend of the Indians and of Indian rights, moved with his flock south of Providence to purchase Indian land and found the settlement of Shawomet in November 1642.

Tasting the heady wine of freedom at last, the Gortonites sent a defiant letter to the Massachusetts authorities, which the diligent Boston synod discovered to contain no less than twenty-six 'blasphemies." Massachusetts and its Pawtuxian underlings now formed a secret alliance with some marauding Indian chiefs to lay claim to Shawomet territory in order to charge that the Gortonite land purchase was null and void. Massachusetts, suddenly and for the first time championing Indian land rights and implicitly assuming jurisdiction in an area not covered by its charter, ordered Gorton to appear before the Massachusetts courts to defend his land claims. Gorton of course refused.

In the summer of 1643, Massachusetts shamefully arranged the murder of the high Indian chief Miantonomo, who had sold Shawomet to Gorton. Again the Massachusetts General Court wrote to the Shawomet settlers, ordering them all to appear at Boston, ostensibly to settle the land claims. Randall Holden wrote the defiant reply for the Gortonites on September 15, a reply filled, of course, with what the Bostonians called blasphemies. Addressing himself to "the great and honoured Idol General, now set up in the Massachusetts," Holden denounced the submitting Indian sachems (headed by one Uncas) as thieves, pointing out that Shawomet was outside Massachusetts jurisdiction, and proceeding to talk to the Massachusetts oligarchy, at long last, in terms which none had yet dared to use. Calling them a generation of vipers, murderers of Anne Hutchinson, and companions of Judas Iscariot, Holden and the Gortonites heroically declared that they would henceforth treat Massachusetts precisely as Massachusetts treated them:

According as you put forth yourselves towards us, so shall you find us transformed to answer you. If you put forth your hand to us as country-men, ours are in readiness for you; if you exercise the pen, accordingly do we become a ready writer; if your sword be drawn, ours is girt upon our thigh; if you present a gun, make haste to give the first fire, for we are come to put fire upon the earth, and it is our desire to have it speedily kindled.

To this valiant defense of the rights of Shawomet, Massachusetts replied instantly in the way it knew best: by declaring the Gortonites "fitted for the slaughter" and by dispatching an armed troop. The Massachusetts troop having laid siege to Shawomet, Gorton asked Massachusetts to accept an offer of Providence ministers to arbitrate the dispute. Winthrop quickly refused, charging that this was just a ruse to delay matters while Gorton stirred up the Indians. After the soldiers plundered the houses and seized the cattle of the Gortonites, the settlers surrendered, but only on the pledge of the soldiers that they would be treated, en route to Boston, as guests rather than as captives. As soon as the surrender was completed, however, the Massachusetts soldiery reneged on the agreement and the Gortonites were marched to Boston under orders that anyone who spoke on the way would be knocked down and anyone who dared to step out of the column would be run through with a bayonet.

Arriving in Massachusetts, the Gortonites found that that colony had now conveniently forgotten about the dispute over the Indian land claims. With the Gortonites at last in its power, Massachusetts held them exultantly without bail on charges of heresy, blasphemy, and opposition to the authority of Massachusetts. According to now hallowed Massachusetts custom, it was not enough of a scourge upon the Gortonites to be charged with heresy, blasphemy, and treason; in addition, they had to be constantly pursued and harassed by the church elders and ministers trying to convert them to the Puritan faith. Once—only once—was Gorton allowed to speak in a Massachusetts church, to the great regret of the theocracy. Courageously he proclaimed: "In the church now there was nothing but Christ, as that all our Ordinances, Ministers, and Sacraments, etc. were but men's inventions, for show and pomp."

On hearing this, some of the ministers urged the magistrates speedily to "hew" Gorton "in pieces." The Rev. John Cotton urged death for the heretics; indeed, the cry for death was joined by all but three ministers of the colony. Happily, the death vote lost (by two votes) in the General Court— the supreme judicial as well as legislative arm of the colony. Not that the court's sentence was not severe. On November 3, 1643, the General Court condemned the Gortonites to indefinite terms of hard labor in chains and forbade them to speak any of their "blasphemous and abominable heresies" on pain of death.

The indomitable Gortonites, however, did not let their sentence faze them in the least. Working at hard labor rather than languishing in prison meant that they traveled throughout the colony, working in different towns. Defiantly ignoring the death threat, the Gortonites preached their view of the Gospel wherever they went, and made numerous converts all over the colony, especially among women. Before long a majority of the colony was at the least sympathetic to their plight. Many influential leaders, including former governor John Endecott, urged death for the disobedient Gortonites, and Rev. John Cotton recommended that they be starved into submission. But finally, the alarmed and perplexed authorities decided that the safest course was to get the resisting Gortonites out of the country. They freed the prisoners, giving them fourteen days to leave the colony on pain of death. The Massachusetts authorities assumed that the banishment order covered Shawomet; acting on the technicality that the town was not explicitly mentioned in the order, the Gortonites returned home to Shawomet.

They were not long allowed to remain there, however. On hearing of their return, Governor Winthrop ordered the Gortonites out, and the hapless settlers fled back to Portsmouth, where they rented houses and land, despite the opposition of Governor Coddington to their immigration. But the trials and tribulations of Samuell Gorton and his flock were far from over.

Much as Roger Williams continued self-government free from English rule, the threat of Massachusetts imperialism, brought on by the Pawtuxet oligarchs, had driven him to realize that it was now necessary to gain an English charter to protect the Rhode Island settlement, once and for all, from Massachusetts aggression. Sailing in 1643 for England, now in the midst of the exhilarating ideological ferment of the Puritan Revolution,

Williams persuaded Parliament, in the spring of 1644, to grant Providence and Aquidneck a charter as the united "Providence Plantations."

While in England, Williams happily associated with the radical liberal wing of the revolution—especially with Sir Henry Vane, the former ally of Anne Hutchinson in Massachusetts—and with its struggle against any established Presbyterian or Puritan church. It was in England, indeed, that Williams was inspired to elaborate his principle of religious liberty and to publish his famous *Bloody Tenent*. His writings were hailed by the British liberals, who used Williams' arguments in their own struggle against any budding theocracy.

The new Rhode Island charter was happily loose and vague, allowing any sort of self-government generally and vaguely compatible with English laws. On Williams' triumphal return to Providence in late 1644, the colony's General Assembly met for the first time and formed a loose and informal organization, with Williams chosen as "chief officer." Bitterly opposed to the charter, however, was William Coddington, whose increasingly pressed claim to sole ownership of all of Aquidneck Island was now permanently in jeopardy. Coddington treacherously followed the Pawtuxet lead by seeking to bring in the force of Massachusetts (and also the newly formed New England Confederation) against the new charter. Forgetting his former fight for liberty alongside Anne Hutchinson, Coddington actually wrote Winthrop that he believed wholeheartedly in the Massachusetts system, "both in Church and Commonwealth."

Samuell Gorton returned to Portsmouth just in time to throw himself into the defense of the charter against Coddington's attempted usurpation. Gorton was, in fact, made a judge by the anti-Coddingtonians of Portsmouth.

Despite the protective charter of 1644, Massachusetts continued, in the next two years, to claim authority over all of the Rhode Island settlements. Thus, in 1645 Massachusetts and its sister colonies of the United Colonies, or New England Confederation, declared war against the peaceful Narragansett Indians and dispatched a military force to Rhode Island. Upon hearing of Roger Williams' negotiation of neutrality with the Narragansetts, Massachusetts and Plymouth thundered to the Providence Plantations that if they persisted in their neutrality they would be treated as enemies, and also forbade them to operate under their 1644 charter.

Moving specifically against the Gortonites, Massachusetts, in autumn 1645, authorized a group of families to settle at Shawomet, on the lands seized from the Gortonites. Plymouth, however, felt that it too had a claim to the territory and warned off the new settlers from Massachusetts. The United Colonies of New England promptly proceeded to assume jurisdiction and presumed to award the territory to Massachusetts.

Alarmed at the developing aggression of Massachusetts, Samuell Gorton decided to go to England to seek definite English protection for his rights to Shawomet. Holding also an impressive commission from his friends, the Narragansett Indians, who declared themselves willing to submit to an English charter, Gorton, along with Holden and Greene, left for England in late 1645.

After a decade of odyssey and persecution, it was highly gratifying for Samuell Gorton to arrive in England at the height of the great libertarian ferment spawned by the Levellers and other radical individualist groups. Gorton had the time of his life for two years, spoke throughout England, was widely hailed, and wrote and published two books—his literary output being inspired, evidently, by the radical libertarian ferment in England.

In the fall of 1646, Randall Holden and John Greene returned triumphantly to Boston, armed with an order from the Earl of Warwick, head of the Commission for Foreign Plantations, to allow the Shawomet settlers to return home in freedom and to remain there without molestation. The submission of the Narragansett Indians to England also successfully kept the potentially bountiful Narragansett country out of Massachusetts' hands. The incensed Massachusetts authorities seriously considered jailing Holden and Greene and ignoring Warwick and Parliament. But cooler heads finally prevailed, and the two Rhode Islanders were allowed to proceed on their way.

Samuell Gorton himself exultantly returned to Boston in the spring of 1648. The infuriated General Court of Massachusetts immediately decided to lock up Gorton "to prevent the infection of his pestilent doctrine," but Gorton triumphantly produced a letter of safe conduct from the Earl of Warwick. The disgruntled General Court had been stopped from arresting Gorton, but it gave him a week to get out of the colony. Gorton returned to Shawomet, which he gratefully renamed Warwick. William Arnold, the leading Pawtuxet oligarch, continued to complain about Gorton to Massachusetts and urge intervention, but Massachusetts was now chastened and decided, at long last, to leave the Gortonites alone. The saga of violent Gortonite persecution was finally over.

Shawomet, and later Warwick, had no government at all until it united with the other towns to form the colony of Providence Plantations in 1648. Until then, the little settlement, in the words of Gorton, "lived peaceably together, desiring and endeavoring to do wrong to no man, neither English nor Indian, ending all our differences in a neighborly and loving way of arbitration, mutually chosen amongst us." But this anarchist idyll soon came to an end. Beginning in 1647 and completed the following year, the four Rhode Island Towns of Providence, Portsmouth, Newport, and Warwick were united into the colony of the Providence Plantations. From a persecuted outcast, Samuell Gorton had now become a respected leader of the colony. As the undisputed leader of Warwick, Gorton was chosen town magistrate and for numerous other posts, and he was Warwick's main representative in the new colony.

The code of the united colony, drawn up in 1647, followed Gorton's insistence on conforming judicial procedure to English Law. The code had been largely drafted by Roger Williams, acting as moderator of the Providence town meeting, and discussed in detail both by committees of correspondence in the various towns and by the Assembly. Numerous safeguards were included against the exercise of power by the central government of the colony. The selected officers, who constituted the supreme judicial power, did *not*, as in other colonies, constitute also an upper legislative house. Instead, they had no position in the legislature, which was in fact a General Assembly of *all* the freemen of the colony. The only representative body was a General Court—a committee of six from each town, meeting in between the meetings of the larger General Assembly. Laws passed by the General Court were subject to the approval of the towns. If a majority of the towns approved, then the law would stand, but only until confirmation by the next General Assembly. Popular elections were to be annual, for all representatives *and* executive officers. The duties of each official were carefully defined and every officer was warned not to go "beyond his Commission." Wrongdoing by any official made him liable to impeachment and trial in the General Assembly. In addition, the towns were empowered to make their own apportionment of the taxes levied upon them by the central government, and to do their own collecting.

One of the crucial safeguards raised in the code against the central government was the guarantee of home rule to each town. To guard against the supremacy of any one town, the General Court and Assembly were to rotate their meeting place among the towns. Moreover, the code provided for initiative and referendum, and nullification by the towns. Initiative permitted the "agitation" and passage of new legislation by a majority of the town meetings themselves, thus completely bypassing the General Court. The referendum-and-nullification provision forced the General Court, as we have seen, to refer its enactments to the towns, a majority of which could veto any legislation. In accordance with Rhode Island's role of providing asylum, there were (unlike Massachusetts) no "stranger" laws preventing persons or towns from receiving newcomers without the consent of the central government.

The code also provided no mitigation of legal penalties for "gentlemen" criminals, and there was no primogeniture in the law of inheritance. In contrast to the brutal edicts of Massachusetts, punishments for crime were restricted, and were far more proportional to the gravity of the crime. Only once did Rhode Island under the code whip or brand anyone, and branding was abolished by 1656. And in contrast to the scores of capital crimes in England and Massachusetts, Rhode Island listed only nine crimes as capital. More important, only two criminals were executed in Rhode Island during Roger Williams' long lifetime—and both of these were murderers.

Religious liberty was guaranteed in the Rhode Island code, and the laws against personal immorality, though not completely absent, were relatively mild. There was neither sumptuary legislation against "unseemly" adornment nor any attempt to regulate a person's church life, though laws restricting drinking and gambling were imposed. And while witchcraft was technically illegal, the law against supposed witches was never enforced in Rhode Island.

After several years of this system, the General Assembly in 1650 dissolved itself, thereby ending the democratic veto of the body of freemen. A newly strengthened unicameral General Court of six from each town now constituted the legislature of the colony. Provision for veto of any law by a majority of towns was, however, retained.

In the new government, it might be added, Samuell Gorton was especially selected to serve on committees of defense against Massachusetts' encroachments, a task which Gorton was certainly happy—and well fitted—to pursue.

Let it not be thought, however, that Rhode Island was in any sense out of the woods. For one thing, it still faced the Coddington threat. Thwarted in his claim to unfettered rule in Aquidneck, Coddington spurned Williams' offers to arbitrate their differences, and turned again to an outside colony to practice subversion—this time to Plymouth. Aquidneck would not agree to the scheme, however, and Coddington left for England in late 1648 to plead his case there.

In the meanwhile, Massachusetts Bay continued its pressure on Rhode Island, and especially on Warwick and the Gortonites. Massachusetts and Plymouth stirred up the Indians to plunder Warwick. And then Massachusetts returned to its imperialist course by meddling in behalf of William Arnold and the Pawtuxet oligarchy. Arnold embarked on an aggressive campaign of land-grabbing, and forcibly seized the land of William Field of Pawtuxet. When Field sued in the Providence courts, Arnold refused to appear, and produced obviously mutilated documents of title to try to prove that Providence had no jurisdiction. These documents would, in effect, have ejected many Pawtuxians from their homes and lands, which would then become the property of Arnold and his friends. At this point, spring 1650, Massachusetts suddenly intervened and ordered Rhode Island to end its prosecution of this case, thus throwing its cloak of protection over the land theft by William Arnold and his friends, and moving to extend its suzerainty over Rhode Island.

To add to Rhode Island's and Gorton's troubles, Massachusetts quickly followed this intervention by granting to Arnold and his Pawtuxet friends the right to encroach on Gortonite land in Warwick. It did this by decreeing the forced merger of Pawtuxet and Warwick into one county of Suffolk. Shortly afterward, in the fall of 1650, Massachusetts troops arrived in Rhode Island and prevented the Warwick citizens from prosecuting Arnold. Finally, to make the little colony's cup overflow, Coddington returned from England in the spring of 1651 with an astounding new charter, granting Coddington the right to rule Aquidneck Island as its sole feudal lord and ruler for life, to be aided only by six appointed assistants.

The hammer blows against Rhode Island were now falling thick and fast. Massachusetts sent an official warning to Roger Williams that any attempt to collect taxes from William Arnold and his Pawtuxet oligarchs would lead the Bay magistrates to intervene "in such manner as God shall put into their hands." And, what is more, the United Colonies of the New England Confederation authorized Plymouth to assume complete jurisdiction over Warwick.

Little Rhode Island was clearly in desperate straits. Its plight was reinforced by Massachusetts' persecution of the growing sect of Rhode Island Baptists. As early as 1646, the United Colonies had ordered the vigorous suppression of Baptists for rejecting infant baptism. The Baptists proceeded to aggravate the Puritan theocracy all the more by adopting the practice of baptism by immersion. Dr. John Clarke, the Baptist leader in Rhode Island, infuriated the Massachusetts authorities by converting some citizens of Seekonk, on the Plymouth side of the border, and Massachusetts went so far as to threaten armed action against Plymouth if it did not suppress the invading Baptists. By the fall of 1651, Massachusetts was negotiating with William Coddington for forcible extradition of all those refugees from Massachusetts who had found shelter at Aquidneck, and it began to contemplate the invasion of Rhode Island for the armed suppression of the Rhode Island Baptists.

During this time, John Clarke and Obadiah Holmes, the successful Baptist missionaries to Seekonk, had fallen into the hands of the Massachusetts oligarchy. Visiting a sick old communicant at Lynn, Clarke and Holmes were arrested and sentenced to a heavy fine. The eminent Clarke protested that Massachusetts proceedings violated traditional rights under English law; the report of Governor Endecott held—characteristically— that Clarke "deserved death" and "was worthy to be hanged." Obadiah Holmes refused to sanction the legitimacy of his sentence by not paying the fine, at which point the enraged Rev. John Wilson, minister of the Boston church, struck Holmes in a fury and called down "the curse of God" upon him. Holmes received an extremely severe whipping of thirty lashes, scarring him for life. After this additional fines were levied on the two men, with promise of another severe whipping in case of default.

Roger Williams protested fervently against this brutal treatment, but to no avail. Deeply moved, Williams asked Massachusetts how it was that "he that speaks so tenderly for his own, hath yet so little respect, mercy or pity to the like conscientious persuasions of other men." And Williams cried out:

> It is a dreadful voice from the King of Kings, and Lord of Lords: "Endicot, Endicot why huntest thou me? Why imprisonest thou me? Why finest, why so bloodily whippest, why wouldest thou . . . hang and burn me?"

There was rising disgust in England as well. The English Puritans had come increasingly under the influence of libertarian views, emanating from the revolutionary ferment. As Massachusetts tightened its theocratic rule, the English Puritans became more and more horrified. Sir Richard Saltonstall, himself a former Massachusetts oligarch who had long since returned to England, wrote to Massachusetts in eloquent and aggrieved reaction to the prolonged whipping of Holmes:"It doth not a little grieve my spirit to hear what sad things are reported daily of your tyranny and persecutions in New England, as that you fine, whip and imprison men for their consciences." English Puritans, Saltonstall reminded them, had hoped that "you might have been eyes to God's people here, and not practice those courses in a wilderness, which you went so far to prevent."

Rhode Island was clearly hemmed in on every side, with Plymouth seizing Warwick, Coddington seceding to become sole overlord of Aquidneck and allying himself with the colony's enemies in Plymouth and Massachusetts, and Massachusetts assuming jurisdiction to protect the Pawtuxet land-grab and threatening suppression of Rhode Island Baptists—indeed the crushing of the colony altogether. It was more than high time for a final desperate attempt to save the little colony. Obviously, the only thing to do was to send respected agents immediately to England, to try to obtain firm parliamentary protection for Rhode Island's charter. Samuell Gorton, now president of Providence Plantations (a truncated colony including only Warwick and Providence), was the active force in raising 200 pounds to send Roger Williams to England. The majority of citizens of Aquidneck, bitterly opposed to Coddington's usurpation, raised the money to send Dr. John Clarke of Newport along with Williams, to represent the island. The Gortonites quickly informed the United Colonies that Williams was going to England on their behalf, among other things to detail the numerous wrongs they had been suffering at the hands of Plymouth and Massachusetts.

Alarmed by this decision, the determined William Arnold pleaded with Massachusetts to send troops immediately and take over Rhode Island before the opportunity was lost. Asking Massachusetts to keep his letter secret, Arnold—not noted for his own personal piety—warned that should Rhode Island be allowed to continue in existence "under the pretense of liberty of conscience . . . thee comes to live all the scum the runaways of the country." Arnold pointed to a horrible example: a man imprisoned in Connecticut (New Haven) for adultery had escaped prison and fled to Rhode Island, where he was *not* executed, although the guilty woman, having failed to escape, was properly put to death. Arnold also charged indignantly that some of the Gortonites "cryeth out much against them that putteth people to death for witches; for they say there be no other witches upon earth . . . but your own pastors and ministers."

Massachusetts, however, growing a bit cautious, did not take Arnold's tempting advice. Instead, it went so far as to permit Williams and Clarke free passage to Boston, where they set sail for England in November 1651.

With Williams gone, Samuell Gorton was the dominant force in the

Providence-Warwick government. As president, and then as moderator of the Assembly the following year, Gorton was able to enact the outlawing of slavery in the colony, and also to limit the term of any indentured service to ten years. Unfortunately, the former law remained a dead letter, but it was the first act of abolition of slavery in American history. Gorton also secured the elimination of imprisonment for debt. Samuell Gorton had successfully completed his odyssey of persecution to become one of the foremost leaders of the colony.

24

Rhode Island in the 1650s: Roger Williams' Shift from Liberty

With Williams gone to England, William Coddington discovered that it was not easy to impose absolute feudal rule upon a free people. The citizens of Aquidneck, led by Capt. Richard Morris and Nicholas Easton, launched an armed revolt against Coddington in early 1652, threatening him and ordering his feudal court to disperse. Coddington, searching for yet another imperial armed force that he could rule and hide behind, turned in desperation to the Dutch, asking vainly for a troop of New Netherland soldiers to suppress the revolt. When Coddington's chief aide, Captain Partridge, seized the home of one of the citizens to enforce a Coddingtonian court order, the enraged populace rose up, occupied the house, and hung the captain then and there. The voice of the people had been heard, and Coddington, speedily taking the lesson to heart, reversed New England custom by fleeing *to* Massachusetts. He dared return only when he had signed an agreement relinquishing all claims to any greater ownership of Aquidneck than had any other freeman.

In the meantime, Williams and Clarke easily convinced the English government of the spuriousness of Coddington's claim, and obtained an order vacating the Coddington charter. Soon William Dyer returned to Aquidneck from England with the good news. The Coddington threat was finally over.

Williams arrived in England at the moment of Puritan victory and at the peak of the revolutionary intellectual ferment. The great libertarian Leveller movement was at the peak of its influence, and religious freedom had given rise to many diverse and enthusiastic sects. Williams plunged again into intimate association with such liberal Puritan leaders as Sir Henry Vane and John Milton. The upsurge of libertarian views had led to a polarization of ideas among the Puritans, a polarization accelerated by the disruption that always follows the victory of a revolutionary coalition. The orthodox Puritans, or Independents, headed by the Rev. John Owen, began to move toward a new state church of their own and toward the suppression of other religious views. The liberal wing of the Puritans, including Vane and Milton, moved in to battle this essentially counterrevolutionary trend, and Williams enthusiastically joined in this struggle.

Eight years before, Williams' *Bloody Tenent* had been ordered burnt by the Presbyterians then in control of Parliament. Now his writings in behalf of religious liberty received great acclaim in Parliament and in the victorious New Model Army. This was especially true of his published reply to the Rev. John Cotton's attack on the *Bloody Tenent*. Williams' rebuttal was *The Bloody Tenent Yet More Bloody,* in which he denounced Massachusetts' persecution of men for their consciences. Williams also proceeded to a keen attack on the Massachusetts oligarchy: a forced payment of tithes created a church leadership "rich and lordly, pompous and princely," and gave it a monopoly on public office. Wasn't the insistence on compulsory church attendance a reflection of the fear of the rulers that, given a free choice, people's attendance in their churches would fall off? Williams pointed also to Holland's commercial greatness continuing side by side with its practice of religious toleration. And he warned prophetically that the Irish question would never be settled so long as the laws persecuting Roman Catholics remained. Only full religious freedom, "free Conferrings, Disputings and Preachings," could reduce civil strife and bloodshed.

Williams even pressed on from his insight into religious liberty to a much wider politico-economic libertarian view: the kings of the earth, he declared, used power "over the bodies and goods of their subjects, but for the filling of their paunches like wolves." These rulers, employing "civil arms and forces to the utmost," pressed for "universal conquest" to establish "rule and dominion over all the nations of the Earth." But, on the contrary, government's proper function is to secure to each individual his "natural and civil rights and liberties . . . due to him as a man, a subject, a citizen."

In another tract written in that exhilarating spring of 1652, *Hireling Ministry None of Christ's,* Williams defended the idea of voluntary rather than compulsory donations to churches. He also declared: "I desire not that liberty to myself, which I would not freely and impartially weigh out to all the consciences of the world beside." Government's "absolute duty" was to insure "absolute freedom" for each religious group.

Williams' new writings had a twofold thrust and purpose: to advance the cause of Rhode Island liberty against Massachusetts, and at the same time to wage the good and general fight for liberty against tyranny in England itself. The major complementary tract, setting forth the specific case for Rhode Island, as well as a Baptist defense of religious liberty, was John Clarke's newly published *Ill Newes from New-England.*

Although Williams and Clarke had no difficulty disposing of Coddington's

211

claims, the larger problem of Rhode Island *vis-à-vis* Massachusetts was far more difficult. For the crucial decision on which way the Puritan Revolution would turn rested not with Williams' friends but with Oliver Cromwell, head of the New Model Army and a centrist torn between the flaming principles of the liberals and a conservative yearning by orthodox Independents and Presbyterians for a swing back to statism. Cromwell, furthermore, was friendly with the oligarchs of Plymouth and Massachusetts Bay, as well as with Roger Williams. Moreover, the Protector was, fatefully, balking increasingly at the obvious next task of the revolution: the smashing of feudal landholding. The libertarian groundswell of the revolution could not be sustained unless the feudal oligarchy was dispossessed of political power as well as of its restrictive hold of the land of England created by that power and on which that power was now based.

Events moved swiftly, as happens in revolutionary situations, and by May 1653 Cromwell had made his fateful decision—for the landed oligarchy, for statism, and for counterrevolution. Parliament was forcibly dissolved, and military dictatorship assumed by Cromwell. The great Leveller leader John Lilburne was jailed for his libertarian views and the Leveller movement broken up. Only the courageous Sir Henry Vane continued to cry out in protest, charging that Cromwell was plucking up liberty by its very roots. Williams too joined Vane in opposition, at least privately denouncing the Protector as a "usurper" and also attacking Cromwell's aggressive imperialism, typified by his war against the Dutch.

Proceeding skillfully, however, Williams was able to procure an at least tentative confirmation by the English government of Rhode Island's charter claims. Short of funds and discouraged by the new turn on the English scene, and spurred by the turmoil in Rhode Island, Williams returned home in the summer of 1654, leaving John Clarke in London to continue the negotiations.

Williams arrived to find a highly troubled colony. In particular, his beloved Providence was again in great danger. William Coddington had been successfully overthrown, but this by no means ended trouble from Aquidneck. Instead, the Aquidneck government, headed by William Dyer and including Nicholas Easton, had embarked on an aggressive, imperialist course of its own. It had launched piratical attacks on the Dutch of New Netherland, and simultaneously, in spring 1653, combined with a minority of Providence-Warwick people to claim that theirs was the true government of the Rhode Island colony. The Providence-Warwick government had protested, and charged that Aquidneck aggression against the Dutch would "set all New England on fire." At the same time, the Pawtuxet oligarchy again refused to pay taxes to Providence, and once again Massachusetts threatened armed intervention and prevented Providence from pressing its claim.

Any lesser man than the great founder of Rhode Island would have been discouraged enough to give up. For almost two decades Roger Williams had fought for individual liberty, in England, in New England, and especially for his Rhode Island. And now England was retrogressing and Rhode Island was rent in civil strife. But the great peacemaker, who had conciliated so many disputes and conflicts with the Indians, now used his powerful influence to bring the various factions into conciliatory negotiations. Rational persuasion and not force was his instrument in obtaining agreement and a new unity in the colony. Williams' main task was to bring into the negotiations a reluctant Providence, disgusted by the piracy conducted by the Dyer-Easton rulers of Aquidneck against the Dutch. Finally, each of the four towns agreed to choose six commissioners for a conciliation conference, which met at Warwick at the end of August 1654. The decision of the conference was at once a victory for Williams and unity, and a complete defeat for the Easton-Dyer faction. Reunion of the Rhode Island colony was achieved, and all the laws of Aquidneck since the Coddington usurpation were eliminated, thus restoring the old pre-Coddington dispensation to the colony. Coddington himself formally submitted to Rhode Island authority two years later. Roger Williams was then elected president of the reunited colony.

Even the Pawtuxet troubles were finally fading. Benedict Arnold, son of William and leader of the Pawtuxet oligarchy, finally abandoned the oligarchy's long search for outside armed intervention, renounced Massachusetts, submitted himself to Rhode Island, and moved from Pawtuxet to Newport. However, the actual reunion of the rest of the colony with Pawtuxet did not take place for five more years.

A year later, 1655, Oliver Cromwell greatly helped settle the outstanding issues by sending a formal message to Rhode Island, confirming its right to self-government under the charter of 1644.

On this happy event, Williams wrote to Vane on behalf of the town of Providence. Vane had written to Rhode Island wondering why the colonists had fallen into such disorder. Williams replied for Providence that Rhode Island has "long drunk of the cup of as great liberties as any people that we hear of under the whole heaven." Possibly this "sweet cup hath rendered many of us wanton and too active." Rhode Island, Williams pointed out, had been spared the civil war of England, the "iron yoke of wolfish bishops," and the "new chains of Presbyterian tyrants . . . nor in this colony have we been consumed with the over-zealous fire of the so-called godly Christian magistrates." Williams expanded this recital of Rhode Island liberties to include the political and economic: "Sir, we have not known what an excise means; we have almost forgotten what tithes are, yea, or taxes either, to church or commonwealth."

It was at this very moment, the moment of triumph, that Roger Williams made a radical and fateful shift in his thinking and actions. From a fighter for liberty, Williams suddenly became a statist and an invader of liberty; from a devoted advocate of freedom of conscience, Williams became himself a persecutor of that very conscience. What was the reason or reasons for this sudden turnabout, this betrayal of the causes for which Roger Williams had so long devoted his very life?

No historian can ever look completely into the soul of another man, but he can make some judicious estimates. We may note several probable reasons for the shift. First, there is the subtle corruption wrought by power, even upon the staunchest libertarian. In the last analysis, power and liberty are totally incompatible, and when one gains the upper hand, the other succumbs. The heroic fighter for liberty *out* of power is often tempted, once the reins of command are in his hands, to rationalize that *now* "order" must be imposed—by him; that "excessive" liberty must be checked—by him. Williams had been president of Rhode Island only once before, in the 1644–47 period when there was hardly any government in the colony. As soon as the colony was formally organized in 1647, Williams had been happy to retire to the private life of a successful fur trader. He had then only emerged from private life to go to England to save the colony. It was only now, in effect, that he was assuming the political post of head of Rhode Island.

A second reason was the coinciding theoretical error that Williams had made in his letter to Vane, that what Rhode Island had been suffering from was an excess of liberty—the "sweet cup hath rendered many of us wanton. . . ." On the contrary, the conflicts in Rhode Island had been caused not by too *much* liberty, but by too *little:* the land monopoly and the treachery of the Pawtuxet oligarchs, the Coddington attempt to impose feudal rule, the continuing imperialist pressure of Massachusetts and the United Colonies. It had only been the remarkable sturdiness of the libertarian tradition in Rhode Island that had kept the colony free despite all these dangers, and had enabled it to escape them at last; and the thought and life of Roger Williams had been perhaps the chief ingredient in that tradition. But that great tradition, strong enough to surmount other periods, was not strong enough to survive its betrayal by its own leading architect.

A third reason for Williams' shift was undoubtedly his discouragement at the retrogression of the libertarian movement in the mother country. Williams had been one of the great lights of that movement, and it in turn had inspired and nourished him—in the 1630s, the 1640s, and on his last visit to England. But then it had been an exciting, rising movement; now, because of Cromwell's betrayal, it was rapidly losing heart and being put to rout. Was the now aging Williams strong enough to keep his convictions at the same burning pitch? Was he strong enough to resist all the temptations to follow the Cromwellian path? Evidently the answer is no. We may consider, also, Williams' earlier lapse from the libertarian principle in the days of the Gorton persecution—and Williams' eventual siding with the Pawtuxet faction to expel Gorton from Providence. Purity of principle had been cast aside even then. And this indicates a fourth contributory reason for Williams' change of heart: a tendency to react testily when people more radically individualist than himself appeared upon the scene.

Williams' shift from liberty to tyranny was first revealed, sharply and startlingly, in his imposing upon the people of Rhode Island compulsory military service. The other colonies underwent conscription, but this was a strong blow to the libertarian movement of Rhode Island. Driving through a compulsory-militia bill and the selection of military officers in a Providence town meeting, Williams precipitated vehement opposition. The leaders of this libertarian opposition were the Baptists, who denounced the bearing of arms as un-Christian and conscription as an invasion of religious liberty and of the natural rights of the individual. This opposition was itself radicalized by the crisis precipitated by Williams, and the logic of the pacifist opposition to conscription and arms-bearing led them straight to the *ne plus ultra* of libertarianism: individualist anarchism. The opposition—led by Rev. Thomas Olney, former Baptist minister at Providence, William Harris, John Field, John Throckmorton, and Williams' own brother Robert—circulated a petition charging that "it was blood-guiltiness, and against the rule of the gospel, to execute judgment upon transgressors, against the private or public weal." In short, government itself was anti-Christian.

The emergence of William Harris as an anarchist was a particularly striking phenomenon. This contentious man, who had been one of the original few to accompany Williams to Providence and had then joined the Pawtuxet oligarchy, had been suddenly aroused by William Arnold. Harris had been one of the victims of Arnold's attempted land-grab under the aegis of Massachusetts. Apparently this sobering experience of how the state can be used to oppress as well as to confer privileges, added to his disfranchisement by Providence a dozen years before for street brawling, had set Harris on the individualist path. His Baptist pacifism completed the process.

Roger Williams bitterly condemned the "tumult and disturbance" caused by the anarchist petition—conveniently failing to place any blame for the tumult on his original imposition of conscription. And Williams sneered at the "pretense" that arms-bearing violated the petitioners' conscience. He then came up with a famous analogy to support his newfound statist philosophy. He likened human society to a ship on which all people were passengers. All may worship as they pleased, he graciously declaimed, but none is to be allowed to defy "the common laws and orders of the ship, concerning their common peace or preservation." And if any should mutiny against their "officers" or "preach or write that there ought to be no commanders or officers because all are equal in Christ, therefore no masters nor officers, no laws nor orders, no corrections nor punishments . . . the commanders may judge, resist, compel and punish such transgressions. . . ." In short, not only were "mutinous" actions to be punished by the state, but even the very *advocacy* of anarchist principles.

Williams' analogy was superficially attractive, but of dubious relevance. If society inhabits a ship and must obey "its" officers, who are the *owners* of the social "ship"? What gives one set of men in a country the right to claim "ownership" of that country and the people in it, and therefore the right to command and force others to obey? These were questions that Williams never bothered to raise, let alone answer. He might also have pondered in what way individual persons, pursuing their separate ways on land, were in any way comparable to a ship—and a *single* ship at that— which has to go in one direction at a time. Why must everyone be on *one* ship?

Williams' pronouncement did not convince the opposition either. The anarchists rose in rebellion against Williams' government, but were put down by force. Despite this failure, at the 1655 elections a few months later, at which Williams was reelected president, Thomas Olney was elected an assistant, and was seated even though he had participated in the uprising.

Williams now began a systematic campaign of statism in the colony. The central government was aggrandized at the expense of the home-rule rights of the towns. In May 1655 the Assembly decided to bypass its financial dependence on funds raised by the towns, and to appoint officials to levy general taxes directly on the people. The following year it was decreed that no laws of the colony may be "obstructed or neglected under pretense of any authority of any of the town charters."

Williams also moved to stiffen the laws against immorality. The Assembly decreed the compulsory licensing of liquor dealers and an excise tax on liquor. Sales of spirits to Indians were restricted severely. Punishments were intensified. The four towns had, until then, failed to provide prisons or stocks, so little was the need and so pervasive the spirit of freedom. But the colonial Assembly now moved to fill this gap and also to outlaw "verbal incivilities," which were to be punished by the stocks or payment of a fine. Adultery, which had not been subject to express penalty in the code of 1647, was now to be punished by whipping and a fine. Corporal punishment was to be levied for "loose living" and masters were to be held responsible for the "licentious careers" of servants or minor sons. On the other hand, divorce laws were liberalized, to allow for divorce for reasons of incompatibility.

It is clear that a large part of the motivation for the new statist trend was a desire to curry favor with Cromwell. It was shortly after receipt of Cromwell's official reconfirmation of Rhode Island's charter, in June 1655, that the Assembly passed the law against loose living, on information that Cromwell was restive at the state of morality in the colony. Furthermore, Cromwell in his message had ordered Rhode Island to provide against "intestine commotions." The colony swiftly passed a law against "ringleaders of factions," providing that such ringleaders, when found guilty by the General Court, were to be sent to England for trial. Here was the fulfillment of the ominous hints of Williams' ship analogy.

But Baptist anarchism continued to multiply in Rhode Island. One of the new adherents was none other than Catherine Scott, the leading Baptist minister and a sister of Anne Hutchinson. Anne Hutchinson's lone pioneering in philosophical anarchism before her death had planted a seed that came to fruition a decade and a half later. Also adopting anarchism were Rebecca Throckmorton, Robert West, and Ann Williams, wife of Roger's brother Robert. Catherine Scott and Rebecca Throckmorton were soon to espouse the Quaker faith. Finally, in March 1657 the crackdown arrived, and the four individualists were summoned into court by Williams, as being "common opposers of all authority." Williams relented after this public intimidation, however, and the charges were dismissed.

Meanwhile, Williams' relations with Pawtuxet had undergone a subtle but significant change. A former aggressor that many times had called on Massachusetts to crush the colony, Pawtuxet now became a relative island of liberty resisting encroachment from Providence. Apart from its oligarchy in land, Pawtuxet had managed to avoid paying taxes either to Rhode Island or to Massachusetts Bay, and was content to live in liberty from immorality laws or from laws against trading with the Indians. It was now Williams who began to agitate aggressively for a joint Massachusetts-Providence suppression of Pawtuxian liberties and for the forcible end to Pawtuxet secession.

This entire Pawtuxian experience with governments served to confirm William Harris in his anarchism, and also to embitter Williams against Harris more than against his fellows. Harris was particularly vehement in opposition to taxation—all taxation—and circulated to all the towns a manuscript denouncing "all civil government," and urged the people to "cry out no lords, no masters." Harris predicted that the state, the "House of Saul," would inevitably grow "weaker and weaker," whereas the "House of David," Harris and his followers, would grow "stronger and stronger." Harris also condemned all punishments and prisons, all officials and legislative assemblies.

William Harris was now hauled into court, charged with "open defiance under his hand against our Charter, all our laws . . . parliament the Lord Protector and all government." Harris, instead of quieting down under intimidation as had Mrs. Scott and the others, swore that he would continue to maintain his anarchism "with his blood." Persistently refusing to recant, Harris repeated his interpretation of Scripture that "he that can say it is his conscience ought not to yield subjection to any human order amongst men." The General Court found that Harris was guilty of being "contemptuous and seditious" and he and his son were heavily bonded for 500 pounds. The evidence was sent to England in preparation for a trial there for treason.

The treason trial never materialized, but only because the ship carrying the evidence to England was lost at sea. Harris was finally sufficiently cowed, however, to abandon his anarchism and he turned instead to a lifelong harassment of the hated Roger Williams through litigation of land claims.

Williams retired from the presidency in 1657, and a year later Pawtuxet was reunited with the rest of the colony.

25

The Planting of Connecticut

Rhode Island was not the only New England colony settled by former residents of Massachusetts Bay. But whereas Rhode Island was peopled by exiles and refugees, the exodus to Connecticut—the other area of southern New England not covered by charter or other royal grant of ownership—was largely voluntary.

From the early 1630s the Connecticut vacuum proved to be a magnet for settlers from several of the colonies. The first settlers were Dutch from New Amsterdam, who in mid-1633 established a trading post—for trade with the Indians—at Fort Good Hope (now Hartford). The preceding fall, Edward Winslow, a leader of Plymouth, had explored the Connecticut River Valley; after unsuccessfully trying to promote a joint Plymouth-Massachusetts expedition in the summer, he organized a trading post on the river at Windsor, north of Hartford, in the fall of 1634. John Oldham, from Massachusetts, founded a small settlement, at about the same time, at Pyquag (Wethersfield), south of Hartford on the Connecticut River. In the following year, other groups from the Bay settled around Hartford and even at Windsor, in defiance of Plymouth's claim to engrossment of the area.

In the summer of 1635, a Dutch vessel, erecting a fort and trading post at the mouth of the Connecticut River, was forcibly driven off by John Winthrop, Jr., a son of the Massachusetts governor and an agent of Lord Saye and Sele, Lord Brooke, and other lords who had jointly received a grant of the territory from the Council for New England. Winthrop named the conquered settlement Saybrook in his patron's honor.

One of the most important founders of Connecticut was Rev. Thomas

Hooker, minister at Newton in the Bay Colony. While Hooker was scarcely a libertarian, he was a moderate who was highly critical of the rigors of the Massachusetts theocracy. Hooker especially objected to the policy of admitting only a minority to membership in the approved Puritan churches, and of the virtually automatic reelection of state officials that had been instituted by the ruling oligarchy. Hooker also urged a clearer definition of the laws in order to limit the arbitrary rule of the magistrates. Finally, Hooker and his followers left Massachusetts in 1636 to settle at Hartford, his associates being led by the wealthy John Haynes and the lawyer Roger Ludlow, who moved southwestward in three years to found the Connecticut towns of Fairfield and Stratford. These and the previous river towns had all been settled with the permission of Massachusetts. But now a conflict arose between the claims of the English lords to the entire Connecticut Valley (as well as to Saybrook), and the right of the settlers themselves. In March 1636 the Massachusetts General Court, in a decision agreed upon by Hooker, the Connecticut settlers, and Winthrop—who had been regarded as governor of the territory—created a commission to govern the Connecticut River towns. In the joint agreement, Massachusetts—and Winthrop—ceded all governmental powers to the commission (all commissioners were to be residents of the territory), which was empowered to govern with the consent of all the inhabitants—thereby at least formally widening the base of government beyond the body of church membership. The commission was to be temporary, lasting only a year, but the effect was to relinquish all of Massachusetts' and Winthrop's claims to the river towns, and to leave Winthrop in charge of Saybrook.

Early the following year, three river towns—Hartford, Windsor (which had bought out Plymouth's claim), and Wethersfield—elected three men from each town to meet as a General Court and act as the sovereign governmental authority. In the spring of 1638, the Reverend Mr. Hooker declared in an election-day sermon that the "foundation of authority is laid . . . in the free consent of the people"; in January 1639 the three towns established their own permanent government based on a written constitution, the Fundamental Orders of Connecticut. The most northerly river town of Agawam (Springfield), led by William Pynchon, refused to join in this constitution, and instead submitted itself (permanently, as it eventually turned out) to Massachusetts' rule.

The Fundamental Orders, largely inspired by Hooker, provided for a unicameral General Court of four deputies from each of the towns, as well as an annually elected governor and assistants. The governor was to be subordinate to the General Court, which had the legislative power not subject to any gubernatorial veto. Furthermore, the governor and the assistants could not serve for two consecutive years. These provisions, however, did not prevent the assistants from forming an oligarchy, by obtaining a veto power over the General Court. Yet the united colony of Connecticut still remained a federation of independent towns, since all power not expressly granted to the General Court continued to be reserved to the separate towns.

Let it not be thought, however, that the more democratic Connecticut framework was significantly less intolerant than Massachusetts Bay. The Connecticut leaders agreed with Massachusetts that a major task of the state was to compel uniformity of religious creed. Connecticut's law of 1642 provided that if "any man after legal conviction shall have or worship any other God but the Lord God, he shall be put to death." In 1644 the General Court established the Puritan church by taxing all residents for its support. And failure to attend a Puritan church, or speaking critically of its official doctrine, was outlawed and punished by stiff fines. While there was no official religious test for voting in Connecticut, as there was in the Bay, suffrage was restricted to freemen. Admission to the ranks of freemen was, in effect, restricted to orthodox churchmen, the admission being decided by the General Court itself. And one of the requirements for admission was that the person be of "peaceable and honest conversation"; interpretation of this vague test rested with the authorities. The chief difference between Massachusetts and Connecticut rule was that Hooker and Connecticut based the government of the colony on the body of orthodox church members, while Massachusetts government was far more centered in the hands of an oligarchy of magistrates and ministers.

Whereas local town government was guarded against any invasion by central government power, the same cannot be said for the liberty of the individual in Connecticut. Land allocation was, as in Massachusetts, under the control of the local oligarchy; land reverted to the ownership of the town if the individual owner moved away; forced labor was imposed for road building; and strangers had to be admitted by the town government. Blasphemy, drunkenness, and the like were outlawed and indentured servants jealously guarded. Speech critical of the government was severely punished. One woman was duly executed for expressing anti-Christian sentiments. A score of women were punished for alleged witchcraft and several hanged—the persecution of "witches" reached a peak in the early 1660s. Repeatedly, in the late 1640s and 1650s, the Connecticut government took steps to overrule the towns so as not to admit supposed "undesirables" to residence. Minimum requirements of property for "freemen" and for "admitted inhabitants" were imposed. By the 1660s oligarchy in Connecticut had grown considerably and at the expense of the originally more democratic framework envisioned by Thomas Hooker.

Meanwhile, what of Saybrook? By the early 1640s, the English lords had lost interest in their claims and had, at least *de facto,* abandoned them. The only proprietor living at Saybrook was George Fenwick, who illegally and without consulting his partners sold the ownership of Saybrook to Connecticut in exchange for the privilege of exacting tolls on goods passing through the mouth of the Connecticut River. From the time of this agreement, in 1643–44, Connecticut assumed complete jurisdiction over Saybrook.

By 1662 fifteen towns had associated themselves in the Connecticut colony. Most of them were situated on the Connecticut River; the others were in the Fairfield-Stratford area to the southwest, on Long Island Sound, or eastward in the New London area. In addition, several townships on Long Island had joined Connecticut, including Southampton, Huntington, and Oyster Bay.

Completely separate from the Connecticut towns, for over a generation, was the Colony of New Haven. The founder of New Haven was the Reverend John Davenport, who arrived in Boston from England with his followers just in time to play a leading role in the persecution of Anne Hutchinson. To Davenport, *mirabile dictu,* Massachusetts Bay was lax and soft and not nearly theocratic enough. And so the Reverend Mr. Davenport, along with the wealthy merchant Theophilus Eaton, founded New Haven as an independent town in the spring of 1638. The land was purchased from the Indians. Davenport and Eaton made sure that *their* ruling theocracy would be *really* oligarchic, without any of the Bay Colony's democratic taint. In mid-1639, they selected twelve men, who in turn chose seven men, to begin the church, and government, of the town. This committee of seven had absolute power over admission of any member to the church, and only church members, of course, could vote in governmental elections. The result was that at the outset over one-half of the inhabitants of New Haven town were disfranchised, an achievement which Massachusetts took a score of years of growth and immigration to emulate.

The laws of New Haven were expressly to be confined to the "laws of God," as interpreted by the ruling clique. The seven committeemen, known as the "pillars of the church," chose nine or more additional men to constitute the General Court of the town. This court elected a magistrate and four deputies who served as judges. There was no need for jury trial, as the answers were to be found by the judges in the Bible. The town's General Court *was* the sole "town meeting." In short, there was little for even the restricted voting list to vote about.

The New Haven settlers soon founded other towns: in 1639, nearby Milford and Guilford on the coast, followed by Stamford, some distance to the southwest, in 1641. Milford, founded by Rev. Peter Prudden, was more democratic than the other towns. The rules on church membership and voting were relaxed, so that only less than one-fifth of the populace was disfranchised, and at least a handful of local leaders remained outside the church. A more rigid deviation from the New Haven norm characterized the town of Guilford, founded by Rev. Henry Whitfield, a friend of Hooker and Fenwick. In Guilford, political privileges were restricted not simply to Puritan church members, but to members of Whitfield's *own* church.

Stamford was settled in a manner completely different from the settling of other towns. New Haven had recently acquired a tract of land via one of the usual arbitrary purchases from the Indians. Anxious to settle the land, Davenport persuaded a group of dissidents in Wethersfield, Connecticut, headed by Rev. Richard Denton, to found a settlement (Stamford) there. In return, Stamford would submit to the jurisdiction of New Haven, send deputies to New Haven's town court, and accept magistrates and officials chosen by the New Haven court.

Another town settled by New Haven was Southold, in 1640, on the northeastern tip of Long Island. The tract had been purchased from someone who had a dubious grant from the old Council for New England. On that tract Southold was founded by Rev. John Youngs. Again, New Haven retained jurisdiction.

In 1643 these five towns—New Haven and its cluster of two (Stamford and Southold), and the two independent towns of Milford and Guilford—united to form the Colony of New Haven. The Frame of Government of the colony restricted suffrage in the same way as in the original New Haven town; indeed, each town's government was similar to New Haven's. Over each government was the central government of the colony. The approved church members—the freemen—elected the deputies from each town, a governor, and a court of magistrates; all of these constituted the unicameral General Court, which exercised the colony's legislative, executive, and judicial functions. The colony, however, was a loose confederation of towns, each town being autonomous in its own affairs.

So entrenched was the original oligarchy that Theophilus Eaton had no difficulty in remaining magistrate of New Haven town and governor of the colony from the beginning until his death in 1658.

Other towns added later to New Haven Colony were Branford, near New Haven, and Greenwich, as an addition to Stamford. No further foothold was gotten on Long Island; the towns there decided to join Connecticut. The failure of Southampton, Huntington, and Oyster Bay to join New Haven Colony was a particularly bitter blow, since New Haven had helped finance their settlement. The Long Island towns, however, objected particularly to New Haven's highly restrictive franchise.

As we might expect, the theocratic rigors of New Haven Colony were severe indeed. Drunkenness and sexual misdeeds were not only outlawed, but regulated minutely by the authorities. Even card playing, dancing, and singing were partially prohibited, because they tended to corrupt the youth and were a "misspense of precious time." Smoking in public was prohibited. The laws were enforced with particular severity against the lower classes—servants and seamen especially. Punishment was inflicted by stocks, pillories, whipping, and imprisonment, and some persons were executed for the crime of adultery. In a typical sentence in New Haven town, Goodman Hunt and his wife were banished from the town because he allowed someone else to kiss Mrs. Hunt on a Sunday.

New Haven did not turn out to be a flourishing colony, and much of the capital of the merchants was dissipated in unprofitable ventures. Not the least of these were the repeated and unsuccessful attempts to plant New Haven colonies far to the southwest, along the banks of the Delaware River.

One trouble was that the Delaware already had settlements, and non-English ones at that. Sweden's New Sweden Company had planted a settlement at Fort Christina (Wilmington) in 1637, headed by the Dutchman Peter Minuit. The Dutch established their own settlements on the river shortly thereafter. New Haven merchants organized the Delaware Company, and in 1640 their expedition, headed by Capt. George Lamberton and Capt. Nathaniel Turner, settled at Salem Creek, on the east bank of the river. Swedish and especially Dutch pressure against the colonists, added to the severe conditions, forced the closing of the settlement. Many years later, in the mid-1650s, New Haven projected a much larger, better-organized settlement on the Delaware, but this too never materialized. New Haven was anxious for others to make war upon the Dutch, to oust them from the Delaware and pave the way for their own colonial expansion. Massachusetts, however, wisely refused to be persuaded to war upon the Dutch for New Haven's advantage, and the New Haveners were bitterly disappointed when Cromwell made peace with Holland.

Discontent against the tight oligarchic rule was manifest in the colony by the 1650s especially outside the town of New Haven. When war loomed against the Dutch in the mid-1650s, citizens of Stamford, Milford, and Southold demanded an extension of the highly restricted suffrage and the substitution of regular English law for the rigors of the "Bible Commonwealth." Robert Basset of Stamford was a particularly vocal dissident, attacking the government as tyrannical, and one under which justice could not possibly be obtained. The colony cracked down severely on all dissidents, hauling them into court and charging them with an attempt to change, undermine, and overthrow constituted authority, and with breaking their loyalty oaths by stirring up rebellion. All were convicted and heavily fined, and made haste to confess their sins. After this suppression, loyalty oaths were more widely imposed upon the inhabitants. Even so, grumbling continued against the high taxes and heavy debts stemming from increased governmental expenses for schools, meetinghouses, watchhouses, etc., and there was widespread tax evasion in the colony.

26

The Seizure of Northern New England

By the 1650s, then, five colonies were established in New England, as virtually self-governing entities: Massachusetts Bay and Plymouth in central New England, and Rhode Island, Connecticut, and New Haven in the south. The estimated total population of these colonies in 1650 was: Plymouth, 1,500; Rhode Island, 800;* Connecticut and New Haven combined, 4,100; Massachusetts Bay, with twice as much as the others combined, 14,000.

What, however, of northern New England—the region north of Massachusetts Bay? The first settlements there had been made by "unauthorized" private groups of fishermen. In 1621 a group settled at the mouth of the Piscataqua River, near the site of what is now Portsmouth, New Hampshire, on the Maine border. Two years later, another fishing group settled at Dover, up the bay from Portsmouth. More formal colonizing came later when, in August 1622, the Council for New England jointly granted to John Mason (a friend of the Duke of Buckingham, a favorite of King Charles I) and Sir Ferdinando Gorges all the land between the Merrimack and the Kennebec rivers (the former is now approximately at the New Hampshire—Massachusetts border, the latter is in western Maine). Small special subgrants of land were now made. In 1622 to David Thompson, who the following year founded the settlement of Rye (south of Portsmouth on the coast). In 1623 Christopher Levett received

*Of the distribution of population in the Rhode Island settlements, the breakdown in 1655 was approximately: Newport, 38 percent; Portsmouth, 29 percent; Providence, 17 percent; Warwick, 16 percent. In short, two-thirds of the Rhode Islanders lived in Aquidneck and one-third on the mainland.

a small grant and founded a settlement at the mouth of the Casco River (west of the Kennebec in Maine). And the following year John Oldham and Richard Vines settled Biddeford, on the south side of the Saco River, in what is now southern Maine. In 1629 Mason and Gorges agreed to divide their granted territory, Gorges obtaining all the land north of the Piscataqua, which he called Maine, and Mason all the land to the south, now called New Hampshire. In the early 1630s, Walter Neale founded two settlements on the Piscataqua, expanding Portsmouth further to the south, and adding the Rye settlement, and South Berwick on the north side. Gorges concentrated his colonizing in the area of York, a bit north of the border.

By the mid-1630s, then, northern New England was split in two, with small settlements along the coast: Casco, Biddeford, South Berwick, and especially York in Maine; Portsmouth and Dover in New Hampshire. John Mason had every intention of becoming lord proprietor of New Hampshire. Asserting that all the land was his own, he gave orders to arrest or shoot any persons daring to hunt animals on "his" territory. Mason also intended to establish the Anglican church in New Hampshire and to outlaw Dissenters. Stern resistance by the populace thwarted his designs, and when Mason died at the end of 1635, the colonists rebelled and announced the vacating of Mason's claims. They declared Mason's lands appropriated, and from then on they refused to recognize the sovereignty of his heirs. New Hampshire territory was now, like Rhode Island, a vacuum for free and unhampered settlement. Two years later, Rev. John Wheelwright, the first Hutchinsonian to be expelled from Massachusetts, walked northward through the snows to found the town of Exeter, New Hampshire. Wheelwright and his followers drew up the Exeter Compact in founding the town; it was modeled after the original Mayflower Compact. More orthodox Puritans, sent from Massachusetts Bay shortly afterward, founded Hampton, in New Hampshire.

Maine, however, was not that lucky with its proprietary feudal overlord. In 1639 Gorges obtained a royal charter that confirmed his position as proprietor and governor of Maine. Gorges sent his cousin Thomas Gorges to Maine to rule the colony, and he established a provincial court at York.

But if New Hampshire territory was a vacuum, it was, again, a vacuum that invited seizure by the ambitious, expansionist Massachusetts power. Massachusetts not only was impelled by the territorial drive endemic to all states, but also was attracted by the rich prospect of timber, fur, and fishing resources in the north. Unlike Rhode Island, New Hampshire and Maine had no influential Puritan friends in England; indeed, Mason and Gorges had been royal favorites and the settlers were largely Anglican. Hence, when the Puritans came to power in England, northern New England was looked upon as a ripe plum for Massachusetts' designs.

The New Hampshire towns were the first to go. Hampton, founded as an outpost of Massachusetts Bay, had always been under its jurisdiction, and had been sending a representative to the Massachusetts General Court. The other towns, beginning with Dover, were appropriated by Massachusetts during 1641–43, a circumstance forcing Reverend Mr. Wheelwright to flee once more, this time to Maine. Also appropriated were scattered New Hampshire towns far to the west of the Piscataqua towns: Merrimack and Salisbury on the Merrimack River, and Haverhill far to the northwest.

Fortunately, Massachusetts' rule over the New Hampshire towns was relatively enlightened—due partly to the religious diversity of the towns and the numerous Anglicans living there. A large measure of home rule was allowed; the towns governed their local affairs in town meetings and elected deputies to the General Court at Boston. Significantly, the New Hampshiremen were exempt from the church-membership qualification for voting, a qualification strictly enforced in Massachusetts proper.

Massachusetts' grab of Maine came a decade later and encountered stiffer resistance. Gorges' death in 1647, coupled with the rise of Puritanism in England, left a vacuum in Maine. The three towns at the southern tip of Maine—York, Wells, and Kittery—attempted to form a free and independent union like that in Rhode Island, but Massachusetts did not permit it to come to fruition. Ignoring an appeal by Maine to Parliament, Massachusetts seized the towns in 1652 and then proceeded to annex the Saco and Casco settlements as well. Fortunately, the Maine towns received the same home-rule privileges as the towns of New Hampshire. Thus, both New Hampshire and Maine had by the 1650s been swallowed up by Massachusetts Bay.

27

Joint Action in New England: The Pequot War

It was characteristic of the New England colonies that their first exercise in united action came in a joint slaughter of Indians; specifically, the Pequot War of 1636–37. The Pequots, who were the dominant tribe in the Connecticut area, had had difficulty with the Dutch in Connecticut and were therefore eager at first to welcome the English colonists. Unfortunately, Lt. William Holmes, commanding the first English settlement—the Plymouth expedition to Windsor—started off on the wrong foot; in late 1633 he purchased the land from dissident sachems whom he had brought back with him, and who had been expelled by the Pequots. Another unfortunate incident was the murder by the Pequots of a drunken Virginian sea captain named Stone, in the summer of 1633, in the mistaken belief that he was Dutch. Yet, the following year, the Pequot grand sachem Sassacus made with Massachusetts Bay a treaty that amounted to surrender to white wishes: the English were to be allowed to settle in Connecticut. The murderers of Stone were also to be surrendered to the English, but the latter thoughtfully made no demands for enforcement of this provision.

This peaceful state of affairs was disrupted by the murder of a prominent New England trader. In 1636, John Oldham was killed by the Block Island Indians on Block Island in the Atlantic Ocean east of Long Island. Now there were several things that characterized white treatment of the Indians in North America: (1) Indian guilt was always treated as collective rather than individual and punishment was never limited to the actual individual criminals; (2) the punishment was enormously greater than the original crime; (3) no careful distinctions were made between Indian tribes, the collective guilt being extended beyond the specific tribe involved; and (4) surprise attacks were used extensively to slaughter men, women, and children of the tribe. All these characteristics marked the white reaction to the murder of Oldham. In the first place, immediately after the death of Oldham, a party of whites under John Gallop shot at and rammed the unarmed Indian crew that had committed the crime, until all but four of the Indians were drowned. Of the four, two surrendered and one of them was promptly thrown overboard by Gallop.

But this swift punishment of the actual criminals was of course thought insufficient. Governor Vane of Massachusetts Bay quickly outfitted the tough John Endecott with an armed troop to slaughter more Block Island Indians. Now the Block Islanders had nothing to do with the Pequots. But somehow even the relatively liberal Vane concluded *a priori* that the Pequots *must* be harboring some of the murderers and he ordered Endecott to include the Pequots in the rigors of collective "punishment." Specifically, Endecott was instructed to massacre every male Indian on Block Island whether guilty or innocent of the crime, and to kidnap all the women and children—in short, to depopulate Block Island of native Indians. He also instructed to demand from them a thousand fathoms of wampum and to seize a few Pequot children as hostages for their good behavior.

Endecott found that he could not catch the Block Island Indians, but he partially compensated by burning all their crops and wigwams and by destroying their property. Returning from the island, he could not persuade the supposedly ferocious Pequots to fight, but he nevertheless managed to kill some of them and to burn many Pequot crops and wigwams.

The Pequots, understandably rather bitter at this undeserved plunder, urged the Narragansett Indians, the leading tribe in Rhode Island, to join with them in warring against the white invaders. The Narragansetts, however, were very friendly with Roger Williams and, under his influence, refused the offer (for which friendship, as we have seen, the Narragansett grand sachem was later murdered by Massachusetts). The Pequot reprisal was to besiege Fort Saybrook, whose leader, Lt. Lyon Gardiner, had warned the exuberant Endecott in his plunder that "you come hither to raise these wasps about my ears, and then you will take wings and flee away." Still, the situation was not yet out of hand, as only the military had been attacked, and not the settlers. But then, in the spring of 1637, amidst this explosive situation, the settlers at Wethersfield violated a solemn agreement they had made with a friendly chief named Sequin. When they bought the land from Sequin, they agreed to allow him to remain within the town limits. But now Wethersfield violated the agreement and expelled Sequin from the town. For the Pequots this was the last straw and they attacked Wethersfield and killed some of the inhabitants.

In the minds of the white men of that era, the deaths of a few white settlers were enough to justify the immediate extermination of an entire Indian nation—and it was precisely on such a course that the New England colonies now embarked. The first meeting of the General Court of

Connecticut in May resolved upon an "offensive war against the Pequot," and ninety men were conscripted from the three river towns under the command of Capt. John Mason (no relation to the Mason of New Hampshire). Joined by some dissident Indians, Mason launched a sneak attack on the Pequot camp, surrounding and burning the entire camp and slaughtering some six hundred Indians, the bulk of them old men, women, and children.

The remnant of the Pequot tribe, under Sassacus, attempted to flee westward, but they were now pursued by a combined force of Mason's troops and over a hundred men from Massachusetts and Plymouth. Stragglers from the Pequots were slaughtered; of over a hundred Pequot men, women, and children hiding in a swamp, all the men were murdered in cold blood by the Massachusetts troop. Two Pequots, spared when they promised to take the whites to Sassacus, were murdered when they failed to do so. The Pequot women were all either turned over to the ungracious hands of the dissident Indians, or sold into slavery in Massachusetts. Finally, the remainder of the Pequots were trapped in a swamp near the site of Fairfield. The men were wiped out and the women sold into slavery, in which, not making successful slaves, they died soon after. Roger Williams' pleas to Massachusetts for mercy for the Pequot prisoners were unheeded—despite his great service in keeping the Narragansetts out of the war. As for Sassacus, he managed to escape across the Hudson, but there the Mohawks—one of the Iroquois tribes allied to the Dutch and English—killed him and sent his scalp back to Boston as a token of their friendship with the English. The extermination of the Pequot people had been successfully accomplished.

28

The New England Confederation

The experience of the Puritan colonies in the joint aggression against the Pequots, added to the continuing drive of Massachusetts Bay for domination over its neighbors, led to a more formal bond between them.

As early as 1634 Massachusetts had moved in to establish control over a wholly Pilgrim trading post on the Kennebec in Maine. It arrested a Plymouth magistrate there and forced Plymouth leaders to go to Boston to settle the matter. Similarly, the following year Massachusetts forced Pilgrims out of land that they had settled on the Connecticut River, to permit Bay settlers to occupy the land. Massachusetts also pressed claims for large portions of Connecticut and Plymouth territory, and we have seen its designs on Rhode Island.

The first discussion of a confederation between the Puritan colonies occurred at the synod of August–September 1637 for the condemnation of Anne Hutchinson. The synod was attended by ministers from Connecticut and Massachusetts. Governor Winthrop of Massachusetts suggested to the Connecticut ministers that the synod become a regular annual meeting of the ministers of both areas because of their mutual "distaste for unauthorized interpretation." In the spring of 1638 Roger Ludlow, an advocate of strong government in Connecticut, inquired further about a confederation, as did John Davenport and Theophilus Eaton of New Haven. Connecticut sent John Haynes to Massachusetts to confer on the matter, but Massachusetts insisted on control of the upper Connecticut Valley about Springfield—crucial to the fur trade—which Connecticut refused to acknowledge. Massachusetts proposed setting up a commission with absolute power to settle all disputes between the colonies, and without reference to the separate assemblies. In this way, Massachusetts hoped to gain control of the sister colonies, deeming it far easier to dominate a group of magistrates than the elected General Courts of the various colonies. But Thomas Hooker pointed out that the terms proposed by Massachusetts exceeded the "limits of that equity which is to be looked at in all combinations of free states." To prevent oligarchic control by the joint magistrates of the colonies, Hooker insisted that any such commissioners be elected.

The confederation proposed at this time therefore proved abortive. The joint Pequot War effort and the growing united interest in preventing asylum from being granted to runaway indentured servants, however, caused the Puritan colonies to draw closer together. Despite this, Massachusetts continued its aggressive expansion, seizing, as we have seen, the New Hampshire settlements. Similarly, Connecticut and New Haven were settling in territory claimed arbitrarily by the Dutch and liked the idea of a confederation for defending it. Furthermore, the civil strife in England was making the New England colonies even more self-governing than before and giving them an opportunity to carry more weight by acting jointly.

Finally, in the fall of 1642 Plymouth proposed a confederation provided that the General Court of each colony ratify all agreements. Connecticut also agreed to send delegates to a meeting in the spring, quickly making sure that Saybrook was incorporated within its realm before the confederation was formed. In May 1643 Massachusetts, Connecticut, Plymouth, and New Haven colonies agreed to form the "Confederation of the United Colonies of New England."

The Articles of Confederation declared its purpose to be "a firm and perpetual league of friendship, for offense and defense . . . both for preserving and propagating the truths of the Gospel and for their mutual safety and welfare." The General Court of each colony was to elect two commissioners to meet once a year and on special occasions. These eight commissioners had the power to declare war, make peace, and allocate military expenses among the colonies in proportion to their population. But approval of each colony's General Court was needed to levy the tax. For commissioners to reach any decision whatever required an affirmative vote of six of the eight. The commissioners were also to make recommendations to the specific colonies, settle boundary disputes, and provide for the capture of fugitives—for example, runaway servants. There was no executive; annually one of the commissioners was chosen president, and he served merely as moderator of the proceedings. All the commissioners had to be Puritan church members.

No colony was bound by the commissioners' decisions unless its General Court approved. Thus each colony could nullify any decisions affecting it, and insure against aggrandizement by the new centralized power.

One important provision of the confederation was to guarantee the independence and given territory of each member colony. For this reason,

Massachusetts moved to reject a proposal to admit the Maine settlements to the confederation, since Massachusetts was preparing to confiscate them. Rhode Island was not admitted for similar reasons, and also because its individualistic policies were a standing reproach to the other colonies. Thus, Rhode Island's continual refusal to coerce the return of fugitives and runaway servants from the other colonies—the colony was preserving itself as a haven for the oppressed—was itself a vital blow to the structure of caste and persecution in the other New England colonies. Hence, Rhode Island's application for admission in 1648 was rejected unless it agreed to become part of Massachusetts Bay—a condition that Rhode Island, of course, angrily rejected.

This first confederation of colonies in the New World was modeled on the United Provinces of the Netherlands, which had been established by the Union of Utrecht in 1579. The United Provinces was a loose confederation of seven provinces for purposes of defense. Deputies were selected by the autonomous provinces, each of which had to approve the decisions of the union for it to be bound by the union's actions. Many New Englanders had experienced the workings of such a confederation during their previous exile in the Netherlands.

From the start, the commissioners were clearly extensions of the ruling magistracy of the colonies. First president of the confederation was Governor John Winthrop, and his sons and grandsons became commissioners as well as magistrates in Massachusetts and Connecticut. The same was true for the other Massachusetts signatory of the Articles of Confederation, Thomas Dudley; he and his sons-in-law were to become governors and commissioners. Similarly Theophilus Eaton, governor and commissioner from New Haven; his sons-in-law became magistrates and commissioners from New Haven and Connecticut.

The requirement that commissioners belong to the Puritan church soon bore fruit. One of their earliest proposals, in 1646, was in answer to a request of Massachusetts for a meeting of the elders of the New England churches "to consider some confession of doctrine and discipline with solid grounds to be approved by the churches." After the Westminster Assembly in England adopted the Westminster Confession of Faith (1647), which espoused presbyterianism, a synod was held at Cambridge, Massachusetts, in 1648, the same year in which the Cambridge Platform of the church was issued. The Platform accepted the Westminster Confession and provided that "idolatry, blasphemy, venting corruption and pernicious opinions are to be restrained and punished by the civil authority," and "if any church one or more shall grow schismatical, rending itself from the communion of other churches, or shall walk incorrigibly or obstinately in any corrupt way of their own, contrary to the rule of the Word; in such case, the Magistrate is to put forth his coercive power, as the matter shall require." The Massachusetts path of persecution had been confirmed by the

United Colonies. The commissioners of the confederation also levied an annual contribution on the towns of the colonies for the support of Harvard College.

After the massacre of the Pequots, the Narragansetts became the main body of Indians in southern New England. We have seen how Massachusetts and the United Colonies tried to take over Warwick and the Narragansetts, only to be foiled by the submission of the Narragansetts to England through Samuell Gorton. The United Colonies, however, struggled hard to conquer the Narragansetts. In 1645 Miles Standish led a confederation force into Rhode Island to beat the Narragansett Indians into a "sober temper." Foiled by Roger Williams' negotiation of peace and neutrality with the Indians, the enraged Standish threatened to seize any settler helping the Indians.

The confederation scarcely fulfilled the high hopes of its founders, and largely because of continuing difficulties between Massachusetts and its fellow colonies, with Massachusetts aggressively pressing its claims against the others. Thus, Massachusetts and Connecticut quarreled over the land taken from the Pequots. For years, Massachusetts claimed the lands, granting large tracts to Governor Winthrop's son John Jr., an assistant of the colony. Young Winthrop was even granted governmental power over his plantation. Finally, after the senior Winthrop's death in 1649, his son accepted Connecticut jurisdiction and was soon to become a long-term governor of his adopted colony. A more important rift occurred over Springfield, the northernmost settlement on the Connecticut River. Geographically one of the Connecticut towns, Springfield, as the uppermost town on the river, was critically important in the beaver trade with the Indians. In the late 1640s, Connecticut levied a river tax on the various towns to finance its hastily purchased Fort Saybrook. Springfield, led by its virtual manorial lord, William Pynchon, refused to pay the tax, pointing out that it had joined Massachusetts upon the creation of the New England Confederation, and was therefore outside Connecticut's jurisdiction. Massachusetts had appointed Pynchon as chief judge and magistrate; he ruled Springfield, and had a right of appeal to the court of assistants of the colony at Boston. To strengthen its claim on Springfield, Massachusetts now accepted deputies from the town to its General Court. Massachusetts of course backed Springfield's refusal to pay and persisted in defying the confederation agreement to submit all such disputes to arbitration. Massachusetts also retaliated by taxing products of the other New England colonies entering Boston. For the remainder of the century, Springfield continued as a virtually independent republic, loosely under Massachusetts, and governed by Pynchon and his son John. Springfield, indeed, set up its own frontier trading posts at such new settlements as Westfield, Hadley, and Northampton.

Massachusetts also took the lead in aggressive actions of the United Colonies against other English colonies—for example, breaking off trade with Virginia, Bermuda, and Barbados for daring to continue their support of the royalist cause.

Most of the friction between Massachusetts and the other colonies occurred over acts of imperial aggression by one or the other against their French neighbors to the north or the Dutch to the south. The first confrontation occurred with the French. After the Virginians had sacked the French Jesuit settlement at Port Royal in 1613, the French created the Company of New France, with Cardinal Richelieu, chief minister to Louis XIII, as president. Richelieu granted his own company feudal rule of the land and a monopoly of the fur trade. England conquered the Acadian and some other Canadian settlements from France in the war of 1627–29, but these areas were restored in 1632 in return for a large dowry from the French bride of the English king Charles I.

By 1643 a virtual war had broken out between two French claimants to the rich prize of Acadia—especially to the fur monopoly and the feudal tenure. The losing claimant, Claude de la Tour, appeared at Boston in 1643, and Governor Winthrop and a few of the ruling oligarchs decided to give de la Tour secret support for an expedition against the French governor. In defiance of legality this crucial matter was referred neither to the General Court nor to the commissioners of the new Confederation of the United Colonies. Winthrop and the others did not submit the issue because they knew that this rash interference in French affairs would have been rejected. The purpose of the affair was to have a clique of Boston merchants join in plunder, and gain a share in the fisheries and the tempting Acadian fur monopoly.

The ignominious failure of the expedition swelled the rising opposition to the scheme in Massachusetts—an opposition led by the competing merchants from Salem and other outlying towns—and Winthrop was temporarily deposed in the 1644 election. Leader of the opposition to the Acadian adventure was Richard Saltonstall, a merchant of Ipswich, north of Salem. Still, the raiders did manage to plunder the plantation of the French governor, Charles d'Aulnay, and to bring back the booty to be sold at auction in Boston. The proceeds of the auction were divided among the raiders. The new governor, John Endecott, however, proclaimed the neutrality of Massachusetts in the intra-French war and offered d'Aulnay satisfaction. The commissioners of the United Colonies met in the fall of 1644 and sternly forbade all such secret plundering expeditions in the future. Finally, Massachusetts signed the Treaty of Boston with d'Aulnay in the fall of 1644, providing that the English in Massachusetts and the French in Acadia have a right to trade freely with each other and with any other peoples, and also providing that any disputes between the two parties be settled by peaceful means.

In the conflicts with the Dutch, on the other hand, it was the southern New England colonies that yearned to plunder the Dutch, and it was Massachusetts that held back from a war in which it was not economically concerned.

Connecticut and New Haven were early embroiled in problems with the Dutch. The original Dutch fort at Hartford was surrounded by English settlers, and the English pressed on to eastern Long Island. Such settlement was in itself highly legitimate, but this was not true of the accompanying *political* claims for governing these areas. New Haven also clashed with the Dutch and Swedes in the Delaware settlements, and was bitter not only at the Swedish and Dutch fur monopoly, but also at the Dutch for granting of asylum to runaway servants of the New Haven colonists.

The governor of Dutch New Netherland, Peter Stuyvesant, and the commissioners of the United Colonies, concluded the Treaty of Hartford in 1650, supposedly settling the large part of the disputes between them. The English were granted sovereignty over all land east of Greenwich, Connecticut, except for Fort Good Hope (Hartford), and over all of Long Island east of Oyster Bay. England, however, refused to ratify the treaty or to recognize any Dutch territory in America, and within a year, New Haven—backed by the United Colonies—attempted further expansion on the Delaware. What is more, the commissioners played a role in the passage of the anti-Dutch Navigation Act of 1651 in the English Parliament.

The following year, Cromwell launched his war of aggression against Holland, and New Haven and Connecticut whooped for war in earnest. They even stirred up false rumors of an alleged plot by Stuyvesant to incite the Indians to attack. Violating the treaty of 1650, Connecticut seized the Dutch fort at Hartford and forcibly incorporated the territory. And even Aquidneck, as we have seen, engaged in piracy against Dutch shipping. Furthermore, the English settlers in the New Netherland portion of Long Island—in the towns of Oyster Bay, Hempstead, Flushing, Jamaica, Newtown, and Gravesend—formed their own independent union.

Connecticut and New Haven, yearning for war, swung all but one of the commissioners to declare war against the Dutch, but Massachusetts coolly vetoed the scheme. Massachusetts asserted in its own curious but convenient interpretation of the Articles of Confederation, that the commissioners had no power to declare an *offensive* war. However, the Bay Colony was on completely sound legal ground in insisting on its right of nullification of the war decision as applied to itself. The Dutch model of the confederation, incidentally, had also stressed this right of nullification by each constituent province.

Why did Massachusetts balk at war? For one thing, it had no desire to put up two-thirds of the forces and the bulk of the finances for a war in which it could not gain. In fact, any Connecticut or New Haven accession to the lucrative Dutch fur trade with the Iroquois might well have been detrimental to Massachusetts' trading interests.

Massachusetts was successful in blocking the war and the English war with the Dutch ended in 1654 without New England's entering the fray.

Ironically, a British fleet, sent to America to act against the Dutch, arrived after the end of the war; thwarted, it decided not to waste its preparations and it promptly seized Acadia from the French. It is no coincidence that the leader of the Massachusetts force that helped conquer Acadia was Major Robert Sedgwick, a prominent Boston fish merchant, eager to obtain access to the Acadian fisheries.

29

Suppressing Heresy:
Massachusetts Persecutes the Quakers

After its persecution of the Hutchinsonians and the Gortonites, Massachusetts continued on its path of suppressing all deviations from the Puritan norm. The next important case was that of Dr. Robert Child. As early as 1644 a growing number of people subjected to oligarchic Puritan rule had found expression in an unsuccessful petition whose purpose was to widen the highly restricted civil privileges of nonmembers of the Puritan church. Two years later, in May 1646, Dr. Robert Child, a Presbyterian minister and graduate of the University of Padua, and Samuel Maverick, a very wealthy founder of the colony, headed a petition of seven important men of the colony protesting existing rule. The petition noted that there were many thousands of residents of Massachusetts who were disfranchised even though they were taxpayers and subject to all the levies and duties of the colony. The signers of the petition were leading merchants and property owners; they included Presbyterians, Anglicans, and men of diverse religious and political views, united only by their desire for a freer society.

The petitioners asked that Anglicans and Presbyterians either be admitted to church membership or be allowed to establish churches of their own. They also urged that "civil liberty and freedom" be speedily granted to all Englishmen, and that they no longer be compelled to attend Puritan service under penalty of a heavy fine. As Englishmen, they deserved to be treated "equal to the rest of their countrymen, and as all freeborn enjoy in our native country." The petition also attacked the ruling "overgreedy spirit of arbitrary power" and the suppression of liberty in Massachusetts Bay—like "illegal commitments, unjust imprisonments, taxes . . . unjustifiable presses, undue fines, immeasurable expenses . . . non-certainty of all things . . . whether lives, liberties, or estates."

The Child petition was denounced from numerous Puritan pulpits as sedition, "full of malignancy, subversive both to church and commonwealth." Winthrop, Thomas Dudley, and the General Court also angrily rejected the petition, and the signers were taken into court, heavily fined, and warned "to be quiet and to meddle with your own business"—an injunction which the Puritan oligarchy itself had never been conspicuous for heeding. When the petitioners had the audacity to appeal to Parliament to attain in Massachusetts the degree of freedom enjoyed in the home country, Winthrop had them fined and imprisoned for criticizing and opposing the government. When Child and some of the others attempted to leave, to present their case to England, they were seized, searched, and imprisoned.

Child managed to escape to England, but proved to be the unfortunate victim of poor timing. Having made his appeal originally to a predominantly Presbyterian—and therefore presumptively sympathetic—Parliament, Child's case now came before a body dominated by Cromwell and his Independents, far more sympathetic to Massachusetts Bay. Furthermore, Child made the mistake of getting involved in an altercation with a Massachusetts Puritan then influential in England. Child was arrested by Parliament and was freed only on a written promise never to speak badly of New England again.

The Child opposition had thus been quickly and efficiently suppressed by Massachusetts, even though it had the support of a large part of the population of the colony. But Massachusetts was soon to reach the turning point in its previously unchecked highroad of persecution; despite a frenzy of zeal, it was never able to suppress the determined and courageous Quakers—the individualist champions of the inner light and the next great wave of heretics in the colony.

The first Quakers to arrive in America came to Boston in July 1656. They were two Englishwomen, Ann Austin and Mary Fisher. Although no law had yet been passed in Massachusetts prohibiting the arrival of Quakers, the two women were immediately imprisoned and searched carefully for "witch-marks." Deputy Governor Richard Bellingham sent officers to the ship, searched the ladies' baggage, seized their stock of Quaker literature, and had it summarily burned. The women were imprisoned for five weeks, during which time no one was allowed to visit or speak to them. No light or writing material was allowed in their cell, and the prisoners were almost starved to death. At the end of this ordeal, they were shipped back to Barbados.

Bellingham denounced the two Quakers as heretics, transgressors with "very dangerous, heretical, and blasphemous opinions" and "corrupt, heretical, and blasphemous doctrines." Bellingham's litmus test for deciding if the ladies were Quakers was brusque indeed; one of them happened to say "thee," whereupon Bellingham declared that "he needed no more; now he knew they were Quakers."

Governor Endecott's only criticism of Bellingham's treatment of the two Quaker ladies was to say that if *he* had been present, the prisoners also would have been "well whipped."

A few days after the Austin-Fisher "threat" had been disposed of, nine more Quakers arrived in Boston. They were summarily arrested, imprisoned for eight weeks, and then shipped back; the master of the ship that brought them was also jailed, no doubt as an instructive moral lesson to future ship captains. If the existence of the two ladies had driven the Massachusetts authorities to fury, this was nothing compared to the effects of the new goad. Governor Endecott, repeatedly haranguing the hapless prisoners, kept threatening to hang them; for example: "Take heed ye break not our ecclesiastical laws for then ye are sure to stretch by a halter." Since it was very difficult for a Puritan in good standing, let alone a Quaker, *not* to break some ecclesiastical law, the halter was close indeed. It is no wonder that Mary Prince, one of the prisoners, was impelled to denounce Endecott as a "vile oppressor" and "tyrant," and the Massachusetts ministers as "hirelings" and "Baal's priests." At their trial the Quakers had the impudence to ask for a copy of the laws against them, which request Endecott angrily refused—causing a murmur of sympathy in the audience for the prisoners. For, it was openly asked, "How shall they know when they transgress?"

From this point on, the persecution of Quakers was savage and fanatical, but the determination of the Quakers to keep coming and spreading their Gospel remained remarkably steadfast. In October the General Court passed a law providing for the fining of any shipmaster bringing a known Quaker to Massachusetts; the Quaker was to be imprisoned, severely whipped, "kept consistently to work" and not permitted to speak to anyone. Any existing resident of Massachusetts who dared defend any Quaker opinion was to be fined and banished on the third offense; any criticism of a magistrate or minister was to be met with a whipping and a heavy fine. Thus, not only the Quakers but anyone presuming to defend their rights or to criticize the brutally repressive acts of the authorities was to be dealt with as a criminal. An early example was Nicholas Upshall, a weak old man who had bribed the jailer to give Ann Austin and Mary Fisher some food while they were starving in prison. Upshall protested against the oppressive anti-Quaker law, and for this offense he was fined, imprisoned, and banished from the colony. From Plymouth, old Upshall was forced to walk to Rhode Island in the winter snows. The old man was given shelter by an Indian who exclaimed: "What a God have the English who deal so with one another about the worship of their God!" Upshall finally found sanctuary in Warwick.

In succeeding years, Quakers were repeatedly stripped (to be searched for witch marks) and whipped, the ears of the men were cut off, and mere attendance at a Quaker meeting was deemed by the authorities as automatic proof of Quaker belief. In 1661 the Cart and Whip Act decreed that all Quakers, men and especially women, were to be stripped, tied to a cart's tail, branded on the left shoulder, and then whipped through every town until they had reached the borders of the colony.

Later apologists for Massachusetts Bay have maintained that all this was nothing more than a perhaps overzealous means of enforcing immigration restrictions. Among other things, this overlooks the fact that the persecutions were conducted as much against "native" converts to Quakerism as against new arrivals. Thus the Southwick family in Salem, converts to Quakerism, were repeatedly persecuted. Edward Batter, the treasurer of Salem and indefatigable Quaker hunter, had two children of Lawrence Southwick sold into servitude to Virginia and Barbados, in order to satisfy fines levied for aiding the Quakers.

Massachusetts lost no time after the first Quaker arrivals in urging the United Colonies to pass a general regulation prohibiting any "such pests" from being admitted into any New England colony. Generally, the sister colonies enthusiastically complied. New Haven, as we might imagine, was especially eager, and its torture methods were a match for Massachusetts Bay's. Plymouth and Connecticut followed some distance behind. In 1658 the commissioners of the United Colonies urged the several colonies to decree the death penalty for all Quakers who dared return after banishment. Only Massachusetts, however, followed this advice. Plymouth, though not passing the death penalty, was hardly reluctant to persecute the Quakers, and one of its magistrates was deposed for being willing to tolerate the Friends. Most reluctant was Connecticut, Governor Winthrop virtually begging the Massachusetts magistrates not to enforce the death penalty. Connecticut did, however, outlaw heresy, but left it to the magistrates or elders to determine if heresy existed, and if so, what punishment was to be meted out.

Of all the New England colonies, we might expect that if any gave haven to the Quakers it would be doughty little Rhode Island, and this was the case. Rhode Island was happy to receive the Quakers, the first of whom arrived at Newport in 1657. On the Quakers' arrival, the commissioners of the United Colonies immediately wrote to the Rhode Island government, demanding that it follow the "prudent" course of Massachusetts and banish all the present Quakers and prevent any new arrivals, so that this "devilish contagion" might not spread. Finally, the commissioners darkly threatened intervention if Rhode Island failed to comply. Interestingly, Massachusetts also warned that the Quakers were not only seditious but also "anarchistic"; their doctrines "turned the hearts of the people from their subjection to government."

Rhode Island's reply reasserted its religious freedom: "As concerning these Quakers . . . we have no law among us, whereby to punish any for only declaring by words, etc., their minds and understandings concerning the

240

things and ways of God. . . ." The General Assembly of Rhode Island also replied that freedom of conscience was the keystone of their charter, "which freedom we still prize as the greatest happiness that men can possess in this world." The Assembly pointedly added that Quakers were being allowed their freedom in England. The United Colonies answered by threatening to embargo all trade to and from Rhode Island.

Quakerism found in Rhode Island not only a refuge, but also a ripe field for conversion. Its individualism made a deep impress on the colony, and in a decade it had even secured a majority. The Newport leaders—William Coddington and Nicholas Easton, and others—were converted and Quakerism completely dominated that town. The redoubtable Catherine Scott and many others of the numerous Baptists were now converted to the Quaker faith. William Dyer, one of the leading Quakers, soon became the secretary of Rhode Island.

As Massachusetts had fearfully predicted, the Quakers used Rhode Island as the base of their missionary operations in Massachusetts. As the Bay Colony had warned in its message to Rhode Island, the Quakers were using the base to "creep in amongst us" and to "infuse and spread their accursed tenets."

The Quaker influx was met, predictably, by an accelerating ferocity. The Puritan divines were the zealous theoreticians of the persecution. The Reverend Urian Oakes denounced the Quaker principle of liberty of conscience as a "liberty of perdition" and "the firstborn of all abominations." And just as many former Hutchinsonians were becoming Quakers, so the Massachusetts campaign of suppression drew echoes of the old Hutchinsonian battles. In the forefront of the Quaker hunt was none other than the fiery Rev. John Wilson, leading persecutor of Anne Hutchinson. Wilson thundered in a typical sermon that "he would carry fire in one hand and faggots in the other, to burn all the Quakers in the world."

After the expulsion of old Nicholas Upshall, the next important Quaker case was Mary Dyer, wife of the secretary of Rhode Island. Two decades earlier, the beautiful young Mary had walked down the aisle with Anne Hutchinson when Anne was condemned. Now a determined Quaker, Mary arrived in Massachusetts and was quickly banished to Rhode Island. Mary Clark, entering Massachusetts on her Quaker mission, was given twenty lashes "laid on with fury," was imprisoned for three months, and then banished in the snows of midwinter. Yet, alarming Quaker inroads were being made in Salem, led by Christopher Holder and John Copeland, who were seized by the authorities and lashed very severely. Thomas Harris, entering from Rhode Island, was denounced by the deputy governor of Massachusetts as deserving of being hanged, and was lashed unmercifully before being expelled.

The culmination of this first, pre-death-penalty phase of the Quaker persecutions was the torture of the venerable William Brend. Brend had landed at Newport in 1657 and became one of the leading Quakers in

Rhode Island. He went to Salem in 1658. Along with other Quakers, Brend was imprisoned. At this point, the Quakers put into practice the now famous technique of nonviolent resistance, of refusing to cooperate with injustice, of refusing to grant to the oppressor the sanction of the victim. Commanded to work in prison, Brend and the others refused. To force them into submission, the authorities proceeded to a frenzy of torture against Brend. The old man was kept four days without food, then whipped ten lashes, starved again, then put into irons and starved for over a day, and finally given 117 blows with a pitched rope. And yet, despite this fever pitch of brutality, the weak and old Brend heroically refused to yield.

The people of Massachusetts had been getting increasingly restive at the reign of terror against the peaceful Quakers, but this treatment was, for many, too much to bear. Protests swelled; a large and angry crowd gathered outside the jail and began to storm the building, calling for the punishment of the jailer. At this point, the incipient revolt was quieted by the eminent theoretician of the anti-Quaker terror, Rev. John Norton. Stretching a metaphor, Norton declaimed: "William Brend endeavored to beat our gospel ordinances black and blue, and if he was beaten black and blue, it was just upon him."

Soon, the Massachusetts authorities pressed on to mutilation of the Quakers. When in the summer of 1658 Christopher Holder and John Copeland were arrested, the magistrates ordered the cutting off of one ear each. Governor Endecott, however, was less successful at besting the Quakers at public argument than in using his superior force to mutilate them. Endecott denounced the Quakers for their custom of keeping their hats on in court and for addressing him by name instead of by title, and thus showing contempt for constituted authority. The Quakers quickly replied that the only honor due to all men is love, and that the Bible never required people to take off their hats before magistrates.

Witness to the mutilation of her friends was none other than Catherine Scott, the sister of Anne Hutchinson and future mother-in-law of Holder. For making critical comments at the execution, Mrs. Scott herself was seized and given ten lashes, and then warned by Endecott that she might be hanged if she returned: "We shall be as ready to take away your lives as you will be to lay them down."

Since even mutilation could not stop the intrepid Quaker missionaries, the Massachusetts authorities decided to accelerate further their campaign of terror. After the Brend case, the Reverend Mr. Norton, the other divines, and the magistrates, decided to react to the popular resistance by decreeing the death penalty should any Quaker return after banishment. Norton instigated a petition signed by twenty-five citizens, urging banishment for all Quakers and death upon return, for the second "offense" of being a Quaker in Massachusetts. Resisting the oligarchy of magistrates and divines was the more democratic House of Deputies, which finally consented to the new law in October, by a hairline majority of one. To make sure that the death penalty would be enforced without shilly-shally-ing, the bill removed the right of a trial by jury, and left Quaker cases to the not too tender mercies of a court of three magistrates, two of whom would suffice for imposing the death penalty.

To defend the new law against rising popular opposition the General Court appointed the colony's leading divine, and the foremost champion of the Quaker hunt, Reverend John Norton, to write its definitive apologia. The following year, 1659, Norton published his findings in *The Heart of New England Rent at the Blasphemies of the Present Generation*—a revealing title. Norton warned that the Quaker claim of individual divine inspiration made the authority of ministers and magistrates equally unnecessary—thus challenging the basic rule of church *and* state. And the temptation held out by the prospect of such overthrow was bringing many converts to the Quaker creed. Religious liberty, to Norton, was simply "a liberty to blaspheme, a liberty to tell lies in the name of the Lord." Norton concluded that the Bible pointed to the proper path: "And he that blasphemeth the name of the Lord, he shall surely be put to death, and all the congregation shall certainly stone him."

With the persecution of the Quakers mounting to a critical pitch, the stage was now set for the tragic climax: murder. No one had long to wait. Defying the death penalty threat, Mary Dyer returned to Boston and was imprisoned, and was there joined by William Robinson, a merchant from London, and Marmaduke Stevenson, two Quakers who had crossed the border from Rhode Island. The three were released and ordered again to leave the colony on pain of death. Robinson and Stevenson refused to bow to oppression and remained. Mary left but returned again to comfort the imprisoned Christopher Holder.

Seized again, the three defiant Quakers were hauled into court in October 1659. Robinson asked permission to read a statement explaining their defiance of Massachusetts law but the fiery Governor Endecott thundered: "You shall not read it!" Endecott charged that "neither whipping nor cutting off ears, nor banishment upon pain of death will keep ye from among us." He therefore sentenced them to hang. The death penalty had now passed from threat to reality. Marmaduke Stevenson retorted: "The Lord hath said . . . the same day ye put his servants to death shall . . . you be curst forevermore. . . . Therefore in love to you all I exhort you to take warning before it be too late."

Nine days later, on October 27, the three condemned Quakers were led to their public hanging—the first execution for religion on American soil. It was a dramatic day on Boston Common and angry opposition among the people led the authorities to bring out a hundred armed soldiers to stand guard over the proceedings. When the condemned trio were led out of the prison, the soldiers deliberately drowned out the prisoners when they attempted to address the restive crowd. Reverend John Wilson contributed to the day's festivities by taunting Robinson. As Robinson and Stevenson

243

were about to be hanged, the former addressed the throng: "We are not evil doers," he cried, "but witnesses to the truth and to the inner light of Christ." Vigilant to the end, the Reverend Mr. Wilson shouted: "Be silent, thou art going to die with a lie on thy mouth." "Hang them or die!" Wilson exhorted and the two Quakers were duly killed. Mary Dyer had gained a reprieve, but with calculated brutality the authorities did not tell her this until the halter was around her neck.

Driven back to Rhode Island, Mary Dyer remained undaunted, and again went back to Massachusetts Bay. Again condemned to death, Mary denied the validity of the law and declared that she had returned to bear witness against it. Upon refusing to agree to return to Rhode Island to stay, Mary Dyer was hanged on June 1, 1660. Perhaps the contemporaneous Quaker historian George Bishop was right and Mary Dyer indeed had the last word. For Bishop wrote, addressing the Massachusetts Bay: "Your bloody laws were snapped asunder by a woman, who, trampling upon you and your laws and your halter and your gallows and your priests, is set down at the right hand of God."

And still the indomitable Quakers kept coming. Among the most determined to bear witness was William Leddra. Again and again, Leddra had visited Massachusetts, had been whipped, starved, and driven out, only to return. Now Leddra was being dragged into court in his shackles, having been chained to a log of wood all winter. He was charged with sympathizing with the executed Quakers, with using "thee" and "thou," with refusing to remove his hat—in sum, with being a Quaker. Promised his life if he recanted his faith, Leddra answered: "What, act so that every man who meets me would say, 'this is the man that has forsaken the God of his salvation!'" When a magistrate asked Leddra if he would agree to go to England if released, the prisoner coolly replied, "I have no business there." "Then you shall be hanged," retorted the magistrate. Leddra appealed to the laws of England, but the court held—as might be expected—that England had no jurisdiction in the case, and pronounced the sentence of death.

Still chained to the log, Leddra calmly wrote shortly before his execution:

I testify . . . that the noise of the whip on my back, all the imprisonments, and banishments on pain of death, and the loud threatenings of a halter did no more affright me, through the strength and power of God, than if they had threatened to bind a spider's web to my finger. . . . I desire to follow my forefathers in suffering and in joy. My spirit waits and worships at the feet of Immanuel.

On March 14, 1661, William Leddra was led out to his execution on Boston Common. Once again, the heavily armed guard prevented him from addressing the crowd. But as the officers were taking him to the gallows, Leddra cried out: "For bearing my testimony for the Lord against deceivers and the deceived I am brought here to suffer." The people were so moved by Leddra's calmness and nobility that again the crowd threat-

244

ened and once again the vigilant Reverend Mr. Wilson stepped into the breach, explaining to the people that many such criminals are willing to die for their "delusions."

Leddra was destined to be the last American martyr, although there were to be a number of close calls. Wenlock Christison, a banished Quaker, returned to Massachusetts during the Leddra trial in order to protest it in court. In the midst of the trial, Christison had appeared in court and warned Endecott: "I am come here to warn you that you shed no more innocent blood, for the blood that you have shed already, cries to the Lord for vengeance to come upon you." Christison was, of course, arrested immediately, and protested at his own trial that the law violated the laws of England. Given a chance to recant, Christison defiantly replied: "Nay, I shall not change my religion, nor seek to save my life. I do not intend to deny my Master, and if I lose my life for Christ's sake, then I shall save it."

Governor Endecott summoned the magistrates for the usual death sentence, but by now the groundswell of popular resentment against the blood-bath was becoming menacing and several magistrates, led by Richard Russell, refused to vote for death. Enraged at two split votes, and two weeks of determined opposition to the "bloody course," Endecott shouted: "You that will not consent, record it. I thank God I am not afraid to give judgment," whereupon he summarily and illegally declared the death sentence himself. Upon hearing his sentence, Christison warned the court: "What do you gain by it? For the last man that you put to death here are five come in his room; and if you have power to take my life from me, God can raise up the same principle of life in ten of his subjects and send them among you in my room, that you may have torment."

By early 1661 two Quakers were under sentence of death. Beside Christison, Edward Wharton of Salem had been a fellow prisoner and cellmate of Leddra throughout his final ordeal. Wharton had been fined heavily and whipped with twenty lashes for denouncing the killing of Robinson and Stevenson and was later arrested for being a Quaker. When Leddra was sentenced to death, Wharton was banished on pain of death and given ten days to leave the colony. Instead, Wharton accompanied his friend to the gallows and buried Leddra's body. He then went to Boston and wrote the authorities that he was there and there he would remain!

Yet these two courageous men, plus twenty-seven other Quakers awaiting trial, were never executed. For word now reached Massachusetts of an event that was to prove momentous in the history of New-England—and to spell the beginning of the long drawn-out end to the reign of the Puritan theocracy in Massachusetts Bay: the reestablishment of the monarchy in England. Now there was no longer an indulgent Puritan rule in England or a civil war to distract the imperial power from the knowledge that Massachusetts and the other New England colonies were totally self-governing.

Knowledge of the Restoration therefore gave the Massachusetts authorities pause. The year before, rising internal protest within Massachusetts had led them to free a Quaker couple from the death sentence. They also knew that English and banished American Quakers had been protesting the persecution to the home government. Indeed, George Bishop's *New-England Judged** had just been published, and had made a deep impression on Charles II.

The king was particularly incensed at Massachusetts' scornful refusal of appeal to the laws of England. The banished Quakers presented a petition to the king detailing the persecution that they had suffered to date. Massachusetts countered with the charge that the Quakers were "open blasphemers" and "malignant promoters of doctrines tending to subvert both our church and state." Edward Burrough replied for the Quakers that they had never "lifted up a hand or made a turbulent gesture" against church or state, but had only warned sinners to repent. It was at this point that the news arrived in England of the martyrdom of William Leddra. Burrough gained a personal interview with the king and told him the news. Burrough warned: "There is a vein of innocent blood opened in thy dominions which will run all over, if it is not stopped." To the king this was the last straw: "I will stop that vein." "Then stop it speedily," Burrough implored, "for we know not how many may soon be put to death." The king promptly dispatched the banished Quaker Samuel Shattuck to Massachusetts with the order to stop all further execution and torture of the Quakers and to permit all imprisoned Quakers to leave for England.

Prudently, Massachusetts released all Quakers, and ordered them to leave for England or else leave the border of Massachusetts within eight days. Two recalcitrant prisoners were tied to a cart's tail and whipped out of the colony. Among the Quakers released were Christison and old Nicholas Upshall, who had been imprisoned for two years.

Massachusetts, however, refused to obey the order to transfer Quaker prisoners to England for trial as an infringement of its charter rights and privileges. Furthermore, the General Court sent two of the colony's most prominent leaders, Simon Bradstreet and Rev. John Norton, to England to justify persecution of the Quakers. The two denounced the Quakers' "dangerous, impetuous and desperate turbulence, both to religion and the state civil and ecclesiastical." The king now changed his mind and in effect rescinded his order, except for stopping the death penalty: "We have found it necessary . . . here to make a sharp law against them and we are well contented that you do the likewise there." Charles added the acknowledgment that Quaker principles were basically incompatible with the existence of any kind of state.

The Massachusetts authorities needed no more encouragement to resume their campaign against the Quakers—of course, stopping short of execution. It was at this point that the Cart and Whip Act was passed. This provided for tying Quakers to the tail of a cart and whipping them out of the

---

*Published in 1661 as *New-England Judged, Not by Man's, but the Spirit of the Lord.*

colony. Death was now only the penalty for the sixth offense, but this was never to be enforced. The peak of the terror campaign had passed.

Massachusetts proceeded to enforce the Cart and Whip Act as thoroughly as it could, particularly against Quaker women. Many Quakers, including several of the released prisoners, were whipped out of the colony only to return. Public pressure forced a modification of the terms of the Cart and Whip Act in the fall of 1662, but the persecution continued undiminished. Particularly important was the case of three English Quaker women— Alice Ambrose, Mary Tomkins, and Ann Coleman—who had, along with the released Edward Wharton, gone to the annexed New Hampshire town of Dover and made considerable progress there among former Hutchinsonians and Baptists, as they did also in Maine. Finally, the Reverend Mr. Rayner, Puritan minister of Dover, induced the Massachusetts magistrates to apply the Cart and Whip Act to the three women. The women were duly stripped to the waist, tied to a cart's tail, and whipped through eleven towns, through deep snow, and lashed up to ten times apiece in each town. And yet the tortured women met their fate by singing hymns as they went. Finally, Walter Barefoot of Salisbury could stand the sight no more. Barefoot had himself made deputy constable and took it upon himself to liberate the three women—this despite the urging of old Rev. John Wheelwright, now residing in Salisbury, to continue the whippings. Wheelwright had now evidently made his peace with Massachusetts in every way and was busy repudiating his heretical and libertarian past.

As soon as they were freed, the three courageous women returned to Dover to continue their prayer meetings. Alice Ambrose and Mary Tomkins were promptly seized, dragged through the snow, imprisoned, and then tied to the tail of a canoe and dragged through deep and freezing water, almost being killed in the process.

Another important case was that of the unfortunate Elizabeth Hooton, an aging lady who had been the first woman Quaker in England. Her whole life a bloody hegira of persecution and torture, Elizabeth had walked virtually from Virginia to Boston where she was immediately jailed, taken to the border, and left in the wilderness, from which she walked to Rhode Island. Sailing back to Boston, she was arrested and shipped to Virginia. After being persecuted in Virginia, she went to England. Obtaining a special license from the king to build a house in America, she sailed to Boston once more. Here Massachusetts refused to allow Friends to meet in her home, and she left for the promising Piscataqua towns. At Hampton she was imprisoned, and in Dover put into the stocks and imprisoned. Then Elizabeth Hooton returned to Cambridge where she was thrown into a dungeon and kept two days without food. A Quaker, hearing about her sufferings, took her some milk, for which she was fined the large sum of five pounds. Despite her letter from the king, Elizabeth was given ten lashes in Cambridge, then taken to Watertown and lashed ten times more, and, finally, tied to a cart in Dedham and whipped through the town with ten more lashes. At the end of this travail she was left at night in the woods; from there she managed to walk to Seekonk and thence to Newport.

Incredibly, and notwithstanding this bloody odyssey, Elizabeth Hooton did not give up. Once again she returned to Cambridge, where after being subjected to verbal abuse by a group of Harvard scholars she was whipped through three towns to the Rhode Island border. Yet again Elizabeth returned to Massachusetts to bear witness to her faith. Again she was lashed ten times, put in prison, then whipped at a cart's tail through three more towns, and left in the woods. Back again, she went to Boston, was whipped out of town once more and threatened with death if she returned. But Elizabeth continued to return and the authorities did not dare go all the way; she was whipped out of several more towns, and walked again to Rhode Island.

In protest against these punishments, many Quaker women began appearing naked in public as a "naked sign" of the persecution, for which behavior they were, of course, whipped through the towns.

Another turning point in the Massachusetts persecution of the Quakers came in the mid-1660s. As will be treated further below, King Charles II sent a commission to New England in 1664 with instructions to reestablish the royal power. The commissioners promptly ordered Massachusetts to stop all persecution of the Quakers, so that they might "quietly pass about their lawful occasions." They added that it was surprising that the Puritans, who had received full liberty of conscience themselves, should refuse it to other religious groups. Although Massachusetts by no means submitted to commission rule, the Puritans dared not go too far in persecuting the Quakers for fear of losing their precious charter. Furthermore, the bloodstained older generation of the Puritan oligarchy had begun to die off, and to be replaced by a far more moderate generation. In 1663 the spiritual leader of the colony and of the persecutions, the Reverend John Norton, died at the age of fifty-seven, and the Quakers may be pardoned for exulting that this took place "by the immediate power of the Lord." Two years later, the temporal leader of the colony, Governor John Endecott, followed Norton in death. It is ironic, incidentally, that none other than Elizabeth Hooton turned up at Endecott's funeral and attempted to address the throng.

And so the ruthless attempt to eradicate Quakerism from Massachusetts Bay had signally failed. As Roger Williams had warned Massachusetts when the Quakers first arrived, the more savage the persecution the more adherence to the Quakers would multiply. Not only did this happen, but internal opposition to the oligarchy multiplied as well. By the 1670s, troubled by their failure and by the growing internal and external opposition, the Massachusetts authorities decided to slacken their campaign of terror. Despite the urgings of such diehards as the Reverend Thomas Shepard, an open Quaker meeting in Boston in 1674 was allowed to be held. By

1676 the Reverend Mr. Hubbard was concluding that "too much severity" in persecution could only lead to "incurable opposition and obstinacy." The last case of Quaker persecution occurred in 1677, when Margaret Brewster came out from a sick bed in sackcloth and ashes "to bear a testimony and be as a sign to warn the bloody town of Boston to end its cruel laws." She was duly whipped through Boston at the tail of a cart.

The bloody persecution of the Quakers was over. The Massachusetts theocracy, while succeeding in driving out Roger Williams and the Hutchinsonians, had failed completely to extirpate the indomitable Friends.

Massachusetts Bay also pursued the newly burgeoning sect of Baptists in the 1660s, but not with the same intensity with which it pursued the Quakers. The founder of the Baptists in Massachusetts was Thomas Gould of Charlestown, who was repeatedly harassed by ministers, elders, and high authorities to bring his infant for baptism. Refusing to do so because of his opposition to infant baptism, Gould tried to organize his own congregation. They were immediately hauled into court, convicted of heresy, fined, and imprisoned.

The Massachusetts authorities, fond of interminable argumentation, then arranged a public debate in Boston between six leading Puritan ministers and some of the humble Baptists, who were bolstered by several emissaries from the strong contingent of Baptists from Newport, Rhode Island. The debate, which took place in April 1668, lasted through two days, during which the Baptists were repeatedly denounced as enemies of the church and state. One of the leading Puritans, the Reverend Jonathan Mitchell, ended the debate on an ominous note—the injunction from Deuteronomy that "the man that will do presumptuously and will not hearken unto the priest . . . even that man shall die."

But this time the threat remained only a threat. The authorities did proceed with further trial of Gould and two associates, who were charged with organizing a church without approval of the government and whose denial of infant baptism undermined the authority of "unbaptised" ministers and congregations. The court sentenced the Baptists to banishment, and when they refused to leave, they were imprisoned for many months.

However, as we have seen with the Quakers, sentiment against religious persecution was now growing in Massachusetts, even among Puritans. This was increased by a post-Restoration immigration of English Puritans, who were far more tolerant than the Old Guard of Massachusetts Bay. A group of sixty-six, including prominent men of the colony, pleaded for freedom for the Baptists. The oligarchy reacted, as was their habit: seizing and convicting the petitioners for contempt of authority. The petitioners were fined and forced to apologize.

But, as in the case of the Quakers, persecution only swelled the ranks of the persecuted. In 1679 the Baptists were strong enough to build their own meetinghouse. The General Court immediately passed a law confiscating all churches built without government permission. The authorities promptly seized the building, and banned services there "without license from authority." The congregation continued to meet in the yard, and finally the General Court gave up, fearful of defying the king, who was leaning increasingly toward religious freedom. The court eventually returned the church to its owners. The Baptists too had won their right to worship in their own way.

30

Economics Begins to Dissolve the Theocracy: Disintegration of the Fur Monopoly

As happens on every new continent, the vast majority of Americans were engaged in transforming natural resources into use; in the case of New England, farming, fish, timber, and furs purchased from Indians located deep in the interior. Merchants and shippers largely exported this produce and in return imported other desired goods from abroad. It should be noted that, in contrast to the glib assumptions of many critics, there is no inherent "class conflict" between farmers and merchants in the market economy. There is no "agrarian interest" in a *per se* clash with a "commercial" or "mercantile" interest. Both groups play an intermeshing and complementary role in the processes of production and exchange. How, indeed, could "agrarians" find a market for their produce without merchants, and without farmers, in *what* goods would the merchants trade and *to whom* would they sell?

New England, indeed all of America north of the Potomac, had not the monoculture of the South (tobacco in the Chesapeake area and, later, rice in South Carolina), but a variety of products. The first products of New England were fish and furs, and the bulk of the earlier settlements began as fishing stations or fur trading posts. From the Indians, the whites soon learned two techniques indispensable to carving a living out of the new land: how to clear these unfamiliar woods, and how to grow that new product, Indian corn (maize), which soon became the North's leading agricultural product. Other important agricultural commodities in the North were wheat, rye, and barley.

To the first generation of devout Puritans migrating en masse to Massachusetts, intent on founding their "Bible Commonwealth," trade

251

was more than slightly suspect. Trade was something to be watched, regulated, controlled—a standing distraction from "godly" concerns. There was little conception that the market has laws and workings of its own.

And yet, economic reality had, as always, to be dealt with—and even in the godliest of commonwealths there was often chicanery afoot. When the Puritans began to arrive in the late 1620s, the most highly developed enterprise in New England was the Plymouth fur trade with the Indians. But within a decade the Plymouth fur trade had virtually disappeared, and the economically declining Pilgrims had to content themselves with sending their agricultural produce to Boston to sell. How did this happen? How did Plymouth so swiftly become a sleepy backwater of Massachusetts Bay?

It is misleading to say that Massachusetts, with its influx of Puritans, was larger and wealthier. For this would not automatically have effected such a drastic revolution in fortunes. Moreover, Massachusetts supplanted Plymouth in the fur trade even though very few furs were native to the Massachusetts area.

The swiftness of this turnover is explicable only by contrasting the workings of governmental monopoly privilege with free private enterprise. In 1627 Plymouth owed £1,800 to its English financiers. Taking advantage of this opportunity, a group of eight leading rulers of the colony —as key members of the ruling oligarchy—in effect granted themselves a monopoly of the Plymouth fur trade in exchange for assuming the Plymouth debt. Also drawn into the monopoly scheme were four of the English merchant-creditors. The monopoly was to run for six years, but was annually renewed for several years afterward. Monopoly never spurs enterprise or initiative, and this was undoubtedly a major factor in the swift decline of the trade in the late 1630s, when competition from Massachusetts had to be faced. Plymouth could not, after all, deal with Massachusetts Bay as it had dealt with the competition of the highly efficient fur trader Thomas Morton, that is, by wiping out his settlement and deporting him back to England. Furthermore, the London creditors, while ingesting monopoly profits, fraudulently failed to reduce the Plymouth debt by that amount; the debt thus remained a heavy burden on the colony. So swiftly did the Plymouth fur trade collapse that virtually no one remained in it by 1640 and the monopoly was allowed to lapse.

It is true that the Massachusetts settlers helped this process along by such acts as seizing the Windsor trading post on the Connecticut River in 1635, but these were scarcely decisive. Instead, it was private, independent settlers, building trading posts in the interior—especially on the Connecticut River—building at their own risk and on their own initiative, who developed the New England fur trade. The most important fur trader was William Pynchon, who founded Springfield, the strategic northernmost settlement on the Connecticut River. Pynchon became a virtual manorial lord of Springfield, functioning as landed gentry and chief magistrate.

While the fur trade in Massachusetts and Connecticut was relatively free in contrast to Plymouth's, it was hardly a pure free enterprise. The governments regulated the prices of furs, taxed income from the trade, and moreover, insisted on licensing each entry into the trade. Indeed, entrance into the vital fur trade became a lucrative monopolistic privilege restricted to influential men with connections in the government of the colony. William Pynchon was granted the exclusive monopoly of the entire fur trade in the crucial Springfield region. As a result, he was able to expand greatly and establish branch trading posts of Springfield in the new settlements at Hadley and Westfield. In 1644 Massachusetts granted a twenty-one-year fur monopoly to one company that included Boston importers William Tyng and Robert Sedgwick. The monopoly quickly went bankrupt, as did another attempt at a fur monopoly the following year.

In Rhode Island, meanwhile, Roger Williams was the first leading fur trader. One of the secrets of his success was that his social philosophy of peace and friendship with the Indians was complemented by concrete peaceful trading relations.

But New England, in the final analysis, was fur-poor, and by the late 1650s even the Massachusetts fur trade was beginning to decline rapidly. In New Haven it was a drive for scarce furs that lay at the root of New Haven's desperate attempts to colonize the Delaware Valley. As New England furs became scarcer, Indian trade concentrated deeper into the interior, and was increasingly centered around the Dutch post of Fort Orange at the current site of Albany. New England fur interests gave way to interests in land, agriculture, and other types of trade.

31

Economics Begins to Dissolve the Theocracy: The Failure of Wage and Price Control

From the first, the Massachusetts oligarchy, seeing that in the New World land was peculiarly abundant in relation to labor, tried by law to push down the wage rates that they had to pay as merchants or land-owners. Maximum-wage controls were persistently imposed. John Winthrop set the tone in 1633, complaining that "the scarcity of workmen had caused them to raise their wages to an excessive rate. . . ." What else was supposed to happen with a scarce product?

As in the South, there were at the base of New England's economic structure indentured servants and Negro slaves, who sometimes were farm labor but mostly were artisans, helpers, and domestic servants. After the servants' terms expired, they received small grants of land and became farmer-settlers. The Massachusetts gentry also supplemented this system of labor with general compulsory service in harvesting neighboring farms—a neat way of exploiting the local citizenry at wage rates far below the market.

Maximum-wage control always aggravates a shortage of labor, as employers will not be able to obtain needed workers at the statutory price. In trying to force labor to be *cheaper* than its price on the free market, the gentry only made it more difficult for employers to obtain that labor. By 1640 Winthrop was admitting that Massachusetts had "found by experience that it would not avail by any law to redress the excessive rates of laborers' and workmen's wages, etc. (for being restrained, they would either remove to other places where they might have more or else being able to live by planting or other employments of their own, they would not be hired at all). . . ."

254

Of course, one method of alleviating this induced shortage was by using the *forced* labor of slavery, servitude, and compulsory harvest service. Thus, one intervention by violence in the market created conditions impelling a further and stronger intervention. But apart from forced labor, the Massachusetts authorities, as we have noted, found it extremely difficult to enforce maximum-wage control.

The first maximum-wage law was enacted by Massachusetts as early as 1630. Due to the high wages commanded by the scarcity of construction craftsmen, the law concentrated on maximum-wage rates in the building trades. Carpenters, bricklayers, etc., were limited to two shillings a day and any payment above this rate would subject both the employer and the worker to punishment (for instance, a buying-cartel of employers established by the law punished the recalcitrant employer who decided to break ranks). Almost immediately, the magistrates decided to imbibe more of the magic medicine, and legal wage rates were pushed down to sixteen pence a day for master carpenters and bricklayers, and correspondingly lower for other laborers.

But the economic laws of the market made enforcement hopeless, and after only six months, the General Court repealed the laws, and ordered all wages to be "left free and at liberty as men shall reasonably agree." But Massachusetts Bay was not to remain wise for long. By 1633 the General Court became horrified again at higher wage rates in construction and other trades and at the propensity of the working classes to rise above their supposedly appointed station in life by relaxing more and by spending their wages on luxuries. Denouncing "the great extortion . . . by divers persons of little conscience" and the "vain and idle waste of precious time," the court enacted a comprehensive and detailed wage-control program.

The law of 1633 decreed a maximum of two shillings a day without board and fourteen pence with board, for the wages of sawyers, carpenters, masons, bricklayers, etc. Top-rate laborers were limited to eighteen pence without. These rates were approximately double those of England for skilled craftsmen and treble for unskilled laborers. Constables were to set the wages of lesser laborers. Penalties were levied on the employers and the wage earners who violated the law. Sensing that maximum controls below the market wage led to a shortage of labor, the General Court decreed that no idleness was to be permitted. In effect, *minimum hours* were decreed in order to bolster the maximum-wage law —another form of compulsory labor. Workmen were ordered to work "the whole day, allowing convenient time for food and rest."

Interestingly, the General Court soon decided to make an exception for the *government* itself, which was naturally having difficulty finding men willing to work on its public-works projects. A combination of the carrot and the stick was used: government officials were allowed to award "such extraordinary wages as they shall judge the work to deserve." On the other hand, they were empowered to send town constables to conscript laborers as the need arose.

Although merchants were happy to join the landed oligarchy and the Puritan zealots in forcing down the wage rates of laborers, they were scarcely as happy about maximum controls on selling prices. The gentry were eager, however, to force downward the prices of products they needed to buy. A blend of mercantilist fallacies and Puritan suspicion of commerce, the result was persistent attempts to force commodities below their market prices. Having little conception of the function of the price system on the free market, the Massachusetts authorities also felt that maximum-price control would bolster the maximum-wage-rate program. There was no understanding that general movements in prices and wages are governed by the supply of and demand for money, and that this too can best work itself out on the free market.

Corn was the major monetary medium of the North, and in 1630 Massachusetts set the sterling price of corn at six shillings per bushel. Failing to work, this control was repealed along with the wage laws of 1631, and corn was "left at liberty to be sold as men can agree." In 1633, however, maximum-price controls were reimposed as an auxiliary to the wage controls.

The massive wage laws of 1633 were quickly discovered to be a failure; once again the quiet but powerful economic laws of the market had triumphed over the dramatic decrees of the coercive state. After one year the actual wage rates were fifty percent higher than the statutory levels. At that point, the General Court repealed the penalties against *paying*, but retained those against *receiving*, wages above the fixed legal rate. While, in fact, no *employer* had ever been tried or penalized under the old act, the wage law was now an open and flagrant piece of class legislation. This was nothing new, however, as there were ample precedents in English maximum-wage laws since the early fifteenth century.

Another change made in 1634 allowed a little flexibility in decreed prices and wages by permitting each town to alter the legal rate in case of disputes. Only a year later the General Court, despairing of the continued failure of the law to take hold, repealed the comprehensive wage controls and the auxiliary price controls. Just before this comprehensive repeal, the courts had apparently been driven by the failure to inflict ever harsher penalties; fines had been so heavy that two workers were imprisoned for failure to pay. The authorities were at the crossroads: should they begin to impose on workers violating clearly unworkable economic decrees the sort of punishment meted out to heretics or to critics of the government? Happily, common sense, in this case, finally prevailed.

Made wary by its thundering failure, the theocracy no longer attempted a comprehensive planned economy in Massachusetts Bay.

From then on, it was content to engage in annoying, but not fatal, hit-and-run harrassments of the market. Penalties were made discretionary, and in 1636 wage and price regulations were transferred by the provincial government to the individual towns, as suggested by the leading Puritan divine, Rev. John Cotton. The General Court was supposed to exercise overall supervision, but exerted no systematic control. Control by each town, as had been anticipated, was even more ineffective than an overall plan, because each town, bidding against the others for laborers, competitively bid wages up to their market levels. The General Court wailed that all this was "to get the great dishonor of God, the scandal of the Gospel, and the grief of divers of God's people." A committee of the most eminent oligarchs of the Bay colony was appointed to suggest remedies, but could think of no solution.

Of the towns, Dorchester was perhaps the most eager to impose wage controls. During the Pequot War, and again in 1642, it combined maximum wages with conscription of any laborer unwilling to work and to work long enough at the low rates. Hingham also enacted a maximum-wage program in 1641, and Salem was active in prosecuting wage offenders.

In 1635, the year of the repeal of the wage and price plan, the Massachusetts authorities tried a new angle: under the cloak of a desire to "combat monopolizing," the Massachusetts government created a legal monopoly of nine men—one from each of the existing towns—for purchasing any goods from incoming ships. This import monopoly was to board all the ships before anyone else, decide on the prices it would pay, and then buy the goods and limit itself to resale at a fixed five percent profit. But. this attempt to combine monopoly with maximum-price control failed also. The outlawing of competing buyers could not be enforced and the import monopoly had to be repealed within four months. What ensued was far better but was still not pure freedom of entry. Instead, licensing was required of all importers, with preference usually given to friends of the government.

Generally, the merchants were the most progressive, wordly, and cosmopolitan element in Massachusetts life. The merchants were able to gain political control of the growing commercial hub of Boston by the mid-1630s. But the rest of Massachusetts remained in the hands of a right alliance of Puritan zealots and landed gentry who dominated the magistrates' council and the governorship. During the decade of the 1630s only two out of twenty-two magistrates were merchants, one of these being the Hutchinsonian leader William Coddington. This reflected the occupational differences of their native England. The gentry had, by and large, been minor gentry in rural England, while the merchants usually hailed from London or other urban centers. In contrast to the authoritarian and theocratic gentry, the merchants had a far more individualist and independent spirit and often opposed the Massachusetts oligarchy.

It was no accident that almost all the merchants championed the Hutchinsonian movement—including Coddington, John Coggeshall, and the Hutchinson family itself. In spite of the earlier failures, Massachusetts tried to resume its harassment and regulation of the merchants, but even more sporadically than in the case of wages. Millers were fined for charging what were arbitrarily termed "excessive" prices for their flour. A woodmaker was fined in 1639 for charging the Boston government "excessive" prices for making Boston's stocks, and, as Professor Richard Morris notes, the General Court "with great Puritan humor sentenced him, in addition, to sit in the stocks he himself had made."* Heavy fines and Puritan denunciations were also the lot of merchants supposedly overcharging for nails, gold buttons, and other commodities. The Puritan church was quick to condemn these merchants, and insisted on penitence for this "dishonor of God's name" in order to regain membership in the church.

The most notable case of persecution of a merchant occurred in 1639. Robert Keayne, a leading Boston importer and large investor in the Massachusetts Bay Company, and the devout brother-in-law of Rev. John Wilson, was found guilty in General Court of gaining "excess" profit, including a markup of over one hundred fifty percent on some items. The authorities displayed once more their profound ignorance of the functions of profit and loss in the market economy. Keayne was especially aggrieved because there was no law on the books regulating profits. In contrast, the Maine court, in the case of *Cleve* v. *Winter* (1640), dismissed charges against a merchant for setting excessive prices, on the grounds that it was not legitimate to regulate a man's profit in trade. So a sounder strain of thought did exist despite the official view.

Massachusetts' sister colonies also tried to impose a theocratic planned economy. As we might have expected, the effort of New Haven Colony, founded in distaste for the alleged laxity of Massachusetts Puritanism, was the most comprehensive. New Haven's Act of 1640 established fixed profit markups of varying grades for different types of trade: three pence in the shilling, for example, for retail of English imports, and less for wholesale. Prices were supposed to be proportionate to risk for colonial products. Above all, a highly detailed list of maximum-wage rates for each occupation was issued. A year later, an ambitious new schedule was decreed, pushing down wage rates even further.

But even fanatical New Haven could not conquer economic law, and only nine months later the authorities were forced to admit defeat, and the entire program was repealed. After that resounding failure, no further comprehensive controls were attempted at New Haven, although there were a few sporadic attempts to regulate specific occupations.

*Richard B. Morris, *Government and Labor in Early America* (New York: Columbia University Press, 1946), p. 74.

Comprehensive wage control was also attempted in Connecticut. An abortive regulation of wages was imposed in early 1640, but repealed later the same year. The following year Connecticut, again alarmed about "excessive" and rising wages (with men "a law unto themselves"), enacted a maximum-wage scale for each occupation. However, instead of the heavy fines imposed by Massachusetts, the only prescribed penalty was censure by the colony's General Court.

Because the monetary medium of Connecticut was corn, wheat, or rye, maximum-wage legislation, to be effective, depended on *minimum* rates of exchange of these commodities in terms of shillings—otherwise, maximum wages in shillings would be effectively negated by declines in the shilling prices of corn. Minimum corn, wheat, and rye prices were, accordingly, fixed at legal tender for wage and other contracts. A slight reduction of wheat and corn prices, however, was allowed in 1644, and, finally, in 1650 Connecticut also abandoned the foolhardy attempt to plan the price and wage structure of the colony's economy.

32

Mercantilism, Merchants, and "Class Conflict"

The economic policy dominant in the Europe of the seventeenth and eighteenth centuries, and christened "mercantilism" by later writers, at bottom assumed that detailed intervention in economic affairs was a proper function of government. Government was to control, regulate, subsidize, and penalize commerce and production. What the *content* of these regulations should be depended on what groups managed to control the state apparatus. Such control is particularly rewarding when much is at stake, and a great deal *is* at stake when government is "strong" and interventionist. In contrast, when government powers are minimal, the question of who runs the state becomes relatively trivial. But when government is strong and the power struggle keen, groups in control of the state can and do constantly shift, coalesce, or fall out over the spoils. While the ouster of one tyrannical ruling group *might* mean the virtual end of tyranny, it often means simply its replacement by another ruling group employing other forms of despotism.

In the seventeenth century the regulating groups were, broadly, feudal landlords and privileged merchants, with a royal bureaucracy pursuing as a superfeudal overlord the interest of the Crown. An established church meant royal appointment and control of the churches as well. The peasantry and the urban laborers and artisans were never able to control the state apparatus, and were therefore at the bottom of the state-organized pyramid and exploited by the ruling groups. Other religious groups were, of course, separated from or opposed to the ruling state. And religious groups in control of the state, or sharing in that control, might well pursue not only strictly economic "interest" but also ideological or spiritual ones,

260

as in the case of the Puritans' imposing a compulsory code of behavior on all of society.

One of the most misleading practices of historians has been to lump together "merchants" (or "capitalists") as if they constituted a homogeneous class having a homogeneous relation to state power. The merchants either were suffered to control or did not control the government at a particular time. In fact, there is no such common interest of merchants as a class. The state is in a position to grant special privileges, monopolies, and subsidies. It can only do so to *particular* merchants or groups of merchants, and therefore only at the expense of other merchants who are discriminated against. If X receives a special privilege, Y suffers from being excluded. And also suffering are those who would have been merchants were it not for the state's network of privilege.

In fact, because of (a) the harmony of interests of different groups on the free market (for example, merchants and farmers) and (b) the lack of homogeneity among the interests of members of any one social class, it is fallacious to employ such terms as "class interests" or "class conflict" in discussing the market economy. It is only in relation to *state* action that the interests of different men become welded into "classes," for state action must always privilege one or more groups and discriminate against others. The homogeneity *emerges from* the intervention of the government in society. Thus, under feudalism or other forms of "land monopoly" and arbitrary land allocation by the government, the feudal landlords, privileged by the state, *become* a "class' (or "caste" or "estate"). And the peasants, homogeneously exploited by state privilege, also become a class. For the former thus constitute a "ruling class" and the latter the "ruled."* Even in the case of land privilege, of course, the extent of privilege will vary from one landed group to another. But merchants were not privileged *as a class* and therefore it is particularly misleading to apply a class analysis to them.

A particularly misleading form of class theory has often been adopted by American historians: inherent conflicts between the interests of homogeneous classes of "merchants" as against "farmers," and of "merchant-creditors" versus "farmer-debtors." And yet it should be evident that these disjunctions are extremely shaky. Anyone can go into debt and there is no reason to assume that farmers will be debtors more than merchants. Indeed, merchants with a generally larger scale of operations and a more rapid turnover are often heavy debtors. Moreover, the same merchant can

*The differences between the Marxian attribution of "classes" to the market, and the confining of the concept to the "caste" or "estate" effects of state action, have been brilliantly set forth by Ludwig von Mises. See his *Theory and History* (New Haven: Yale University Press, 1957), pp. 112ff; and *Socialism* (New Haven: Yale University Press, 1951), pp. 328ff. Contrast the confusion in Lenin's attempt to defend the Marxian jumble of estate and non-estate groups by the same concept of class. See V. I. Lenin, "The Agrarian Programme of Russian Social-Democracy," *Collected Works* (Moscow: Foreign Languages Publishing House, 1961), 6:115.

shift rapidly from one point of time to another, from being a heavy net debtor to net creditor, and vice versa. It is impermissible to think in terms of fixed persisting debtor classes and creditor classes tied inextricably to certain economic occupations.

The merchants, or capitalists, being the peculiarly mobile and dynamic groups in society that can either flourish on the free market or try to obtain state privileges, are, then, particularly ill-suited to a homogeneous class analysis. Furthermore, on the free market no one is fixed in his occupation, and this particularly applies to entrepreneurs or merchants whose ranks can be increased or decreased very rapidly. These men are the very opposite of the sort of fixed status imposed on land by the system of feudalism.

33

Economics Begins to Dissolve the Theocracy: The Failure of Subsidized Production

To return to the New England scene, the flourishing but harassed Massachusetts merchants received a severe economic shock in 1640. Much of the capital and credit for expanding their commerce had come from the wealthier emigrants from England, but by 1640 the great exodus had dried up. Realization of this change further cut off the vital flow of English credit to Massachusetts merchants, since the credit had been largely predicated on a continuing flow of immigrant funds. In addition, the fur trade was already declining from the drying up of nearby sources and the restrictions of the licensing system. A result of these factors was a severe economic crisis in 1640 with heavy declines in prices—of cattle, land, and agricultural products. Credit and confidence also collapsed, and the consequent calling in of debts aggravated the crisis. (There can be little doubt that the panic was also aggravated by the crisis in the English economy in 1640, a crisis sparked by Charles I's seizure of stocks of bullion and other commodities.) As is usual in an economic panic, the debtors faced a twofold squeeze: falling prices meant that they had to repay their debts in currency worth more in purchasing power than the currency they had borrowed; and the demand to pay quickly at a time when money was hard to obtain aggravated their financial troubles.

Almost immediately, the debtors turned to the government for aid and special privilege. Obediently, the Massachusetts General Court passed, in October 1640, the first of a series of debtors-relief legislation that was to plague America in every subsequent crisis and depression. A minimum-appraisal law compelled the appraisal of insolvent debtors' property at an artificially inflated price and a legal-tender provision compelled creditors to accept all future payments of debts in an arbitrarily inflated and fixed rate in corn, cattle, or fish. Additional privileges to debtors were passed in 1642 and 1644; in the latter, for instance, a law was passed permitting a debtor to escape foreclosure by simply leaving the colony. Most drastic was a law passed by the upper chamber of magistrates, but defeated by the deputies, which would have gone to the amazing length of having the Massachusetts government assume all private debts that could not be paid!

The fact that this general debt-assumption bill was passed by the council of magistrates, the organ par excellence of the ruling oligarchy, and rejected by the substantially more democratic chamber of deputies, indicates the need for drastic revision of the common historical stereotype that debtors are *ipso facto* the poor. For here we find the debtors' interest represented especially by the ruling oligarchy and not by the more democratic body.

Further debtors-relief legislation—again at the behest of merchants—was passed in 1646, compelling creditors to accept barter payments for money debts, and in 1650, compelling outright moratoriums on debt payment.

With fur production declining badly, the Massachusetts government turned desperately to artificial attempts to create industry by state action. The motives were a blend of the mercantilist error of attempting self-sufficiency and cuts in imports and the shrewd granting of privileges to favorite businessmen.

Hence, the colony decided to turn to the subsidization of iron manufactures. Early iron mines in America were small and located in coastal swamps ("bog iron"), and the primary manufactured or wrought iron was produced cheaply in local "bloomeries" at an open hearth. The Massachusetts government, however, wanted to force the use of the more imposing—and far more expensive—indirect process of wrought-iron manufacture, a process that required the erection of a blast furnace and a forge. Such an operation required a far larger plant and much more skilled labor.

In 1641, John Winthrop, Jr. found bog-iron ore at Braintree. He decided to embark on the ambitious construction of a furnace and forge—the first in the colonies. The Massachusetts General Court had offered any discoverer of an iron mine the right to work it for twenty-one years; yet it insisted that within ten years an iron furnace and forge be erected at each bog mine—thus repressing the cheaper open-hearth process. The court also insisted that the Winthrop Company—soon organized as the Company of Undertakers for an Iron Works in New England, with English capital—transport iron to churches, and keep a minimum of its production at home rather than export the iron. In 1645 the company was granted a twenty-one year monopoly of all iron manufacturing in Massachusetts as well as subsidies of timberland, provided that within a few years the company would supply the colonists with iron at a price of no more than twenty pounds a ton.

However, even with these privileges, plus large grants of timberland that Winthrop managed to wangle from the towns of Boston and Dorchester, the venture at Braintree was too expensive and failed almost immediately. Ousting Winthrop, the company moved its operation northward to Lynn, where it managed to build a furnace and forge and to produce some quantities of bar iron. Here again, economics caught up with the venture, and costs rose faster than revenues. In addition, the company owners wanted to sell the iron for cash but the Massachusetts court insisted that the company accept barter for its iron, thus "keeping the iron in the colony"; otherwise, the court argued, the iron would redound to the benefit of foreign buyers and the cash profits would be siphoned off to the owners in England. The wages paid at the ironworks were apparently not enough of a benefit for the court. In its unsuccessful petition to the General Court, the company pointed to the benefits to the colony of its payment of wages and purchase of supplies, and argued that it had a right to export as it chose and to obtain cash in return. What in the world would it do with crops paid in barter? With this sort of harassment added to its other troubles, the company finally went bankrupt in 1653, and the ironworks itself closed down less than a decade later.

This was not the last of younger Winthrop's ventures into subsidized, uneconomic, and failing enterprises. In 1655 he discovered a bog-iron deposit at Stony River in New Haven Colony. The New Haven authorities, finding their colony increasingly a sleepy backwater rather than the expected commercial success, eagerly welcomed the chance to subsidize an ironworks. Raising the capital locally to avoid colonial harassment from foreign owners, Winthrop was granted a host of special privileges by colony and town governments including land grants, payment of all costs of building the furnace, a dam on the river, and the transport of fuel. One of the owners was the deputy governor of New Haven, Stephen Goodyear, who was thus able to use the power of the government to grant himself substantial privileges. Yet this ironworks quickly began to lose money and little iron was ever produced at Stony River. The works was abandoned altogether in the 1660s.

The sorry record of forced iron production was matched by that of compulsion in textiles. The New England governments, heedless of the fact that the growth of hemp was largely uneconomic, decided that not enough hemp was being grown by private farmers and that something had to be done about it. Connecticut went to the length of compelling every family to plant a minimum of hemp or flax, but soon had to abandon the attempt. Massachusetts decided, in 1641, to grant a subsidy of twenty-five percent for all linens, cottons, and woolens spun or woven in the colony. It also decreed that all servants and children must spend *all* their leisure time on hemp and flax. So speedily did all this spur the growth of hemp that only one year later, Massachusetts rescinded its subsidy and felt it had to legislate against the "hoarding" of stocks of hemp.

Massachusetts also felt that not enough warmer woolen clothes were being produced at home. In 1645 it ordered the production of more sheep, and in 1654 prohibited all further exports of sheep. Finally, in 1656 Massachusetts brought its fullest coercive powers into play: all idle hands, especially those of "women, girls, and boys," were ordered to spin thread. The selectmen of each town were to appoint from each family at least one "spinner" and each spinner was ordered to spin linen, wool, or cotton, at least half the year, at a rate of three pounds of thread per week. For every pound short of the decree, the family responsible was to pay a fine of twelve pence to the state. Still, all these stringent mercantilist attempts to coerce self-sufficiency were a failure; economic law prevailed once more over statute law. By 1660 the attempts to found a textile industry in Massachusetts were abandoned. From then on, rural western Massachusetts made its clothes at home ("homespun" household manufacturers), while the urban citizens were content to import their clothing from England.

John Winthrop, Jr. also tried to found a saltworks in Massachusetts, again subsidized by a government eager to promote self-sufficiency in salt. These subsidies continued intermittently over a twenty-year period. In the 1630s free wood for fuel was donated to Winthrop's salthouse; in the 1640s Massachusetts agreed to buy 100 tons of salt from Winthrop; in the mid-1650s the General Court granted him a twenty-one-year patent. But Winthrop never succeeded in producing any salt.

34

The Rise of the Fisheries
and the Merchants

Attempts of the government to subsidize the beginning of fisheries also proved fruitless. During the 1630s, fish were either imported or came from Englishmen fishing off Newfoundland and the Maine coast. But the civil war of the 1640s crippled the English fishing fleet. New England fishermen, without need of government coercion, expanded their activities to fill the gap. There sprang up along the New England coast communities of fishermen-farmers, who fished and farmed in alternate seasons. These settlements, in such towns as Marblehead, Nantucket, and the Isles of Shoals, were conspicuously *non*-Puritan. In 1644, for example, *not one* resident of Marblehead qualified as a freeman; in short, not one was a church member. In 1647, in fact, so solicitous was the General Court of the morals of the Isles of Shoals that no women were allowed to live in the town.

The growth of the fisheries greatly expanded the opportunities for trade, and merchants came in to market the catch and equip the cargoes. Indeed, the Navigation Act of 1651, extending to fish the ban against foreign vessels carrying colonial products, was put through by the London merchants to seize the lucrative carrying trade from Dutch and French vessels. The New England merchants purchased the catch from the fishermen and shipped it to London importers. These importers were the major entrepreneurs of the trade; they owned, planned, and financed the shipment from the beginning. Similarly, London exporters of manufactured goods to New England financed the retained ownership of the shipments until sold in the colony. So important were close ties to London, that those New England merchants who had family or friendship connections with London merchants were the ones who flourished in the trade. New England merchants themselves financed fish exports to the Southern colonies.

By 1660 New England was the fish leader of the colonies, and fish production was flourishing. From the fisheries, the newly burgeoning body of Massachusetts merchants expanded the carrying trade to many other products. The merchants shipped New England agricultural products, including horses, cattle, and timber, abroad. They imported wine from Spain and east Atlantic islands, and sugar from the West Indies. They carried English manufactured goods to Virginia and North Carolina, buying in turn the tobacco of the South and exporting it. A particular feature of New England shipping was the "triangular trade": exporting timber and agricultural products to the Canaries, transporting slaves from there to the West Indies, and then importing sugar from those islands.

During the 1640s and 1650s, the impact of the English civil war on New England trade was a shifting one. In 1645 the merchants drove a free-trade bill through the Massachusetts General Court, allowing trade with ships of all countries. This was accomplished over the protests of many of the leading magistrates of the colony, who were interested more in the Puritan cause than in freedom of trade. Later, however, the Navigation Acts forced Massachusetts to prohibit trade with France and Holland. And over merchants' protests, Massachusetts obeyed Parliament by outlawing trade with those colonies that remained royalist: specifically, Virginia and the West Indies. Returning the favor, Parliament in 1644 exempted New England trade from all English import and export duties.

One of the most important economic consequences of the Puritan Revolution for New England was its impact upon the timber industry. The expansion of New England shipping had given rise to a flourishing shipbuilding industry. It had also spurred the growth of one of the most important New England industries: timber, especially *mast trees* for ships, which flourished particularly on the Piscataqua, a region of Massachusetts now in New Hampshire. But the biggest single impetus to the growth of the mast tree industry was not so much the natural growth of shipbuilding as the huge war contracts suddenly begun in 1655. In that year, Oliver Cromwell launched the expedition that captured Jamaica from Spain. Fearful that the Baltic trade—the largest source of timber and mast trees for England—would be cut off by the war, Cromwell gave orders for the stockpiling of timber in New England.

But more than excessive caution lay at the root of this stockpiling program; the appropriation of special privilege was even more in evidence. For, during the Commonwealth era, many Puritan merchants of New England returned home to England and rose to leading positions in the government. Several were even involved with the awarding of contracts for the Jamaica expedition. These merchants, still deeply connected with New England trade, took care to grant themselves and their associates enormous and lucrative timber contracts. Thus, the head of the Jamaica expedition was Maj. Gen. Robert Sedgwick, one of New England's biggest merchants. The commissioner of the English navy was Edward Hopkins, another leading Massachusetts merchant. Commissioner of trade was Rear Admiral Nehemiah Bourne, a leading Massachusetts shipwright. Another commissioner of the navy was the Massachusetts shipwright Francis Willoughby. And treasurer of the navy and direct awarder of the naval contracts was Richard Hutchinson, London merchant and brother-in-law of the martyred Anne.

By 1660 all the general patterns of New England trade and production were set for more than the next hundred years. These included not only the trade and production outlined above, but also the emergence of Boston as the overwhelmingly dominant trading center, for Massachusetts and for all of New England. The produce—of agriculture, fish, and forest—from the rest of New England was sent to Boston, whence it was shipped abroad. The other towns became secondary and subsidiary centers, feeding the main metropolis from the produce gathered from their outlying areas. Similarly, almost all imports into New England came to Boston; from here they were shipped to the rest of the colony. Of the 20,000 residents of Massachusetts, fully 3,000 lived in Boston. To a lesser extent Charlestown and Salem were also leading trade centers. In these three towns, being a merchant was a full-time occupation, whereas in the smaller urban areas trade was a part-time calling.

As early as the mid-1640s, the expanding and influential merchants tended to be restive about the theocracy and its persecution of heresy. Trade and fanatical intolerance do not mix well. The trader tends to want peace, wider markets, and freedom of movement. Anything else, any blocking of these channels, is bad for business, bad for trade. In Massachusetts, the merchants saw that persecution blocked immigration—therefore, the expansion of trade—and injured Massachusetts' reputation in England regarding credit and connections. In 1645, it was a group of eminent merchants, headed by Sedgwick, Bourne, and Emmanuel Downing, who led a petition for repeal of the virtual ban against strangers unacceptable to the government, and against the expulsion of the Baptists. But the church elders thundered against leniency and prevailed.

We have seen the brusque fate meted out by Massachusetts to the petition in 1646 for greater religious freedom and broader franchise by Dr. Robert Child and other merchants and eminent non-Puritan church members of the colony. Six years later, the powerful manorial lord of Springfield, the fur trader William Pynchon, returned to England after his book, critical of the Massachusetts persecutions, was publicly burned by the authorities. And the Boston merchant Anthony Stoddard was jailed for "insolence" to the government. The merchants generally opposed the official adoption of theocracy by the General Court when in 1651 it endorsed the Puritan Confession of Faith and Discipline that had been drawn up by the Synod of Massachusetts five years earlier.

This does not mean that the merchants were flaming libertarians; indeed, they heartily endorsed the brutal persecution of the Quakers. But all in all, the merchants were the liberal wing of the Massachusetts community. Their "softness" was duly denounced by the Puritan zealot Edward Johnson: "Being so taken up with . . . a large profit . . . they would have had the commonwealth tolerate divers kinds of sinful opinion to entice men to come and sit down with us, that their purses might be filled with coin, civil government with contention, and the Churches of our Lord Christ with errors. . . ."

And so trade, economics, became increasingly a solvent of fanatical zeal. By their very presence alone, the merchants were a disrupting element in the would-be Puritan monolith. Many of the new merchants of the 1650s were not even Puritans at all (for example, Thomas Breedon, Col. Thomas Temple, Richard Wharton); whether inside or outside the church, they brought with them a worldly, urbane, and cosmopolitan spirit that weakened what the Puritans regarded as the moral fibre of the younger generation. It is no wonder that in 1659 the General Court was so concerned as to proclaim a "day of humiliation" because of the great "sensuality under our present enjoyments."

35

Theocracy Begins to Wither: The Half-Way Covenant

The Puritan theocracy faced not only the direct problem of the merchants and their worldly spirit, but also the withering of their dominion from within the very bosom of the church itself. First, the Puritans had to bear the cross of their own brethren in England, who had come increasingly under the influence of liberal ideas in the 1640s and were reproaching Massachusetts for its intolerance. Even the former firebrand and persecutor of Anne Hutchinson, Rev. Hugh Peter, having returned to England, now urged religious toleration in Massachusetts. Shortly before his death in 1649, Governor Winthrop received the sad and deeply puzzling news that his own son Stephen, fighting in Cromwell's New Model Army, was actually advocating liberty of conscience. "I hope his heart is with the Lord," said Winthrop wistfully.

But even within Massachusetts itself, theocratic rule was beginning to slacken. During the 1650s opinion grew rapidly in the New England church that the requirements for being chosen a member of the "elect" should be greatly loosened. The issue was aggravated by the fact that only church members could become freemen, and hence vote in Massachusetts Bay. Therefore, the growing pressure for a broader and more democratic franchise could only be satisfied by softening the requirements for church membership—in short by weakening Puritan tenets themselves.

The crisis was precipitated in the Hartford church in Connecticut where the practice of Rev. Samuel Stone in admitting church members was thought lax by many of the church elders. In 1657, the General Court of Massachusetts proposed a synod of all the New England colonies.

Rhode Island, of course, would take no part, not being a Puritan colony. New Haven, most rigorously wedded to theocracy and opposed to any change, also refused to participate. From the other end of the spectrum, Connecticut accepted and its authorities sent four ministers to the synod; Massachusetts appointed fifteen. Over the bitter opposition of the conservative ministers, the synod adopted the "Half-Way Covenant," which automatically allowed all those baptized in the church to become church members and to have their children baptized as well. Their membership would only be associate, or "half-way," but the important point was that this partial membership entitled them to vote and therefore to political rights. This was a drastic change and could only weaken theocratic rule and considerably democratize oligarchic rule in Massachusetts. In 1662 another intercolonial synod reaffirmed the Half-Way Covenant, and the General Courts of Massachusetts and Connecticut advised its adoption by all the churches. From all sides and on many fronts the pressures were multiplying for dissolution of theocratic rule.

36

The Decline and the Rigors
of Plymouth

What, in all this time, was happening to Plymouth, the mother colony of all New England? Succinctly, it was rapidly and irretrievably declining. As we have seen, its fur trade had virtually disappeared by 1640. And for the next twenty years, only further decline ensued. By the mid-1640s the town of Plymouth was virtually a ghost town; and economically the colony had become a backwater of Massachusetts Bay.

By the 1640s Plymouth, like Massachusetts, found the intensity of its religious zeal on the wane, and heresy and "moral" laxity were increasing. Plymouth faced a crossroads on how to react to this development: by liberty and toleration or by following Massachusetts' path of persecution? The critical point came in 1645 when William Vassall, a leading merchant, presented to the General Court of Plymouth as well as to that of Massachusetts Bay a petition for complete religious liberty—to grant "full and free tolerance of religion to all men that will preserve the civil peace and submit unto the government." "All men" meant exactly that, including Familists, Roman Catholics, and Jews. There was great sentiment in the General Court in favor of the Vassall petition. It commanded the support, in fact, of a majority of the chamber of deputies, and even of such an old roustabout as Capt. Miles Standish. But the ruling oligarchy of the colony, headed by Governor Bradford, Thomas Prence, and Edward Winslow, strongly opposed religious liberty and was able to block its approval.

This was the turning point and for the next two decades Plymouth accompanied its economic decline by following the lead of Massachusetts in increased theocracy and religious persecution. The colony proceeded to impose fines for failing to attend church, corporal penalties for denying the Scripture, and denial of the rights of citizenship to all critics of the laws of Plymouth or of the "true religion."

One of the persistent troubles of Plymouth was a shortage of ministers, aggravated by its poverty, decline, and increased intolerance. To deal with this scarcity, Plymouth took another fateful step down the theocratic road: it established a state church supported by taxation. Protests against this new establishment were led by Dr. Matthew Fuller, of the town of Duxbury, who for his pains was denounced as "wicked" by the Plymouth authorities and forced to pay a steep fine.

Despite this establishment, the Pilgrim ministers remained poor, as they had to collect the pulpit taxes themselves and the parishioners were usually far in arrears.

Religious persecution continued to tighten. The colony did not believe itself too poor to afford inspectors of youth; one was appointed in each parish to supervise and birch any boy unruly in church. When this procedure failed, the inspectors intensified their birching penalties and included girls in this corporal punishment as well.

Governor William Bradford died in 1657 at the age of sixty-seven. He left the colony impoverished, though he himself died a rich man, the richest in Plymouth. He was succeeded by Thomas Prence, who liked to think of himself as a "terror to evildoers." When the Quaker influx arrived in Plymouth, Prence was as good as his word. Laws passed against Quakers provided for the summary arrest of suspected heretics, in order to keep "corrupt" would-be freemen from the colony. And as a special slap at any Anglican deviation, the vicious practice of celebrating Christmas was outlawed.

In 1659 six Quakers were banished and Governor Prence thundered that all Quakers deserved "to be destroyed, both they, their wives, and their children, without pity or mercy." But most Pilgrims balked at this call for total victory. As a result, the colony did not flay, brand, or mutilate—let alone kill—its Quakers, as did Massachusetts Bay.

The leading case of Quaker persecution in Plymouth was that of Humphrey Norton, who was banished and then returned. Though denounced by Governor Prence, Norton refused, according to Quaker principles, to take an oath of allegiance. Sentenced to be whipped, Norton managed to escape the punishment by refusing to pay the customary marshal's fee for the "service" of being whipped, and was again expelled.

As in Massachusetts Bay, there was widespread public opposition to the persecution; the persecution itself multiplied the number of Quaker converts. Thus, almost the entire town of Sandwich at the entrance to Cape Cod was converted to the Quaker faith. Barnstable, further along the Cape, liberally harbored and protected Quakers. Indeed, Barnstable's Pilgrim minister, Rev. John Lothrop, accepted as church members all who promised to keep the Ten Commandments.

To deal with the troublesome Sandwich problem, the colonial government of Plymouth sent there as special colonial constable one George Barlow, soon to be notorious as the "Quaker Terror." Barlow was paid on a commission basis by Plymouth Colony for finding heretics. Naturally his zeal was unbounded. Barlow ruthlessly plundered the town of Sandwich, finding all suspects and disfranchising eight freemen. The people of Sandwich dealt with Barlow in their own good way: resisting, harassing him and his family, and putting him into the stocks. Finally the people triumphed, and Barlow was driven out of town.

Another leading center of resistance and heresy was Duxbury, north of the town of Plymouth. Duxbury was a town filled with Baptist and Quaker converts. Here resistance to the tyranny of the Plymouth authorities was led by Rev. John Holmes and the Howland family. Zoeth Howland was put into the stocks by the authorities for criticizing the persecuting ministers and many citizens of Duxbury joined him in choosing to pay the fine rather than attend the Pilgrim church. Particularly galling to the despotic Governor Prence was the fact that his own daughter Elizabeth had fallen in love with Arthur Howland, the leading opponent of his tyrannical rule. Repeatedly, Prence had Howland arrested and heavily fined for the crime of courting Elizabeth, but Prence finally, after a decade, broke down and permitted their marriage.

One of the strongest centers of liberal resistance in Plymouth was the town of Scituate, at the extreme north of the colony. Here the resistance was led by two eminent leaders of the colony, the veteran assistant governor, Capt. James Cudworth, and Timothy Hatherly, a member of the General Court for twenty years. Hatherly was summarily expelled from the General Court and disfranchised by the province, but the town of Scituate stubbornly reelected him as a deputy. The General Court, however, refused to seat the intractable Hatherly. Cudworth, in his turn, was dismissed from his high post as one of Plymouth's two commissioners of the United Colonies. Bitterly, Cudworth denounced the actions: "Our civil powers are so exercised in matters of religion and conscience that we have no time to effect anything that tends to the promotion of the civil weal." Cudworth also attacked the establishment of a state religion as well as the persecution of the Quakers. But even Cudworth's protest was met in the familiar way: he was dismissed as assistant governor, deprived of his military command, and disfranchised.

This treatment of Cudworth only swelled the tide of protest. The frightened magistrates decided to appoint sound and reliable Pilgrims in each town to argue with the Quakers and convert them. But this policy turned out disastrously. Deacon John Cooke, officially appointed to spy upon heretics, was himself converted to the Baptist faith and excommunicated by the Pilgrims. A much more telling blow to the authorities was the case of Isaac Robinson. Robinson, son of the beloved Rev. John Robinson, the founder of the Pilgrim sect, who had never left Leyden, Holland, for America, was appointed the official convincer at Sandwich.

Instead, the would-be converter was himself converted and became a Quaker. The embittered magistrates denounced Robinson for "sundry scandals and falsehoods," dismissed him from all his offices, and deprived him of his rights as a freeman.

In the end, the Quakers emerged victorious, as they did in Massachusetts Bay. Town after town in Plymouth Colony eventually took it upon itself to grant full civil rights to the Quakers. The death of old Governor Prence in 1673 brought the more liberal younger generation to the fore, and the new governor, Major Josiah Winslow, restored all civil rights to the Quakers and their supporters. James Cudworth, too, was renamed assistant governor. The old persecuting zeal in Plymouth Colony was ended.

37

The Restoration Crisis
in New England

The Restoration of the Crown in May 1660 was a fateful event for New England. The destruction of the Puritan Revolution had ended, and the home country could now turn its full attention to the state of the American colonies. From the royal point of view the Southern colonies were in satisfactory order: Virginia, always of royal sympathies, had already restored the royal Governor Berkeley to his post; and the Calverts had quickly returned to control of Maryland. But in the north, the New England colonies appeared chaotic. Not one colony had a royal governor; all were self-governing, and three—Rhode Island, New Haven, and Connecticut—didn't even have a proper charter. Connecticut and New Haven were completely without a charter, and Rhode Island's perfunctory charter had been granted by the Commonwealth Parliament and thus could hardly be deemed valid by the restored Crown. And though Charles II in his Declaration of Breda, preceding the Restoration, had pledged religious liberty, none of the Puritan or dissenting colonies of New England anticipated warm treatment.

Neither were the New England colonies reassured by the English condemnation of those implicated in the death of Charles I. Of those implicated fourteen, including Henry Vane and Hugh Peter, were executed, twenty-five committed to life imprisonment, and many others exiled or excluded from public office. Two of the regicides, Whalley and Goffe, escaped to New England, where they were protected and became the objects of constant complaint by the English government, which was convinced that the two were plotting to restore the Commonwealth. The news of the Restoration was, indeed, received as a calamity in New

England, signifying at the least the end of the Puritan republic, which had treated these colonies almost as self-governing allies. Typical of New England's response to the Restoration was the comment of Roger Williams: "The bloody whore is not yet drunk enough with blood of the Saints." But the New England colonies prudently decided to recognize the Restoration government: Rhode Island in October 1660, Connecticut and New Haven in March and June of 1661, and Massachusetts trailing them all in August 1661.

The first order of business for the three New England charterless colonies was to preserve their self-government by obtaining royal charters. Connecticut, one of the three, determined to seize the occasion to annex some or most of the territory of its neighbors. John Winthrop, Jr. was sent to London as Connecticut's agent to try to annex all of Rhode Island, New Haven, and even New Netherland to the west, still in the hands of the Dutch. If not all of Rhode Island, then Connecticut at least tried to seize the Narragansett Country, about one-third of present Rhode Island— the territory to the southwest of Warwick and west of Narragansett Bay. Winthrop was particularly eager to acquire the Narragansett Country as he was a leading partner of the Atherton Company of Massachusetts, speculators whose arbitrary claims to the land were backed by Connecticut. This backing was quite understandable: the Atherton Company had been recently formed, in 1659, and had engaged in a spurious purchase of the choicest areas of the Narragansett Country, near Boston Neck, from the sachem of the Narragansett Indians. Winthrop had then proceeded to use his power as governor of Connecticut to add greatly to the possessions of himself and his partners. In the fall of 1660 Winthrop induced the New England Confederation to order the Narragansett Indians to pay Connecticut a huge fine in wampum in compensation for various disturbances in the border regions. The gracious alternative offered the Indians was to mortgage the entire Narragansett Country to the Connecticut government. Captain Humphrey Atherton, a major partner of the Atherton Company, now in turn graciously paid the Indian fine, provided that Connecticut transfer the mortgage of the Narragansett Country to the company. By treading this path of chicanery and coercion, the Atherton Company managed to acquire a claim—unrecognized by Rhode Island—to the Narragansett Country of Rhode Island. Only Connecticut jurisdiction guided by the company's own Winthrop could guarantee the land to the company.

Connecticut's designs on New Haven were also made clear before Winthrop arrived in London. It had sent an arrogant message to the latter colony in early 1661, asserting "our own real and true right, to those parts of the country where you are seated, both by conquest, purchase and possession. . . ."

Winthrop managed, by judicious distribution of money in London, to obtain for Connecticut a royal charter in May 1662. The charter confirmed Connecticut's powers of self-government and left its political structure intact, except for restricting the franchise completely to freemen of the colony. The royal charter granted to Connecticut all land west of Narragansett Bay and south of Massachusetts. By this, Rhode Island territory was reduced to the tiny area of existing settlement and New Haven Colony, whose existence was not even mentioned by Connecticut in its negotiations at London, was wiped out altogether. It is quite probable that the new English government, in the confusion of the day, had never heard of New Haven Colony, and that its grant of New Haven's territory to Connecticut was entirely unwitting. The problem was that New Haven, a fading colony with an economy in decline, felt itself too poor to afford the expense of maintaining an agent in London, and it believed that either Connecticut or Massachusetts, its brothers in the New England Confederation, would look after its interests. Very fortunately, Rhode Island did have an agent in London to speak up for its interest. Dr. John Clarke had remained there after Roger Williams' return to Rhode Island years before. When Charles II assumed the throne, Clarke had urged a new charter for Rhode Island, stressing its great principle of "soul liberty," or freedom of conscience, and shrewdly emphasizing the similarity of that principle to Charles' views in his Declaration of Breda. Now as soon as Clarke heard of the aggressive Connecticut charter gained by Winthrop, he appealed to the king for a charter and for review of the Connecticut document, which had "injuriously swallowed up one half of our colony." In response, Edward Hyde Clarendon, the lord chancellor, blocked the Connecticut charter and the dispute raged between Winthrop and Clarke, with Winthrop continuing to insist that the Narragansett lands belonged to Connecticut. Finally they submitted the dispute to five arbitrators, who awarded the entire Narragansett Country to Rhode Island; the Pawcatuck River was to be the latter's western boundary, as in the original Rhode Island patent in 1644. The award also provided, however, that the Atherton Company was free to shift the jurisdiction over its land to Connecticut. John Winthrop, Jr.'s personal property on Fishers Island, on the boundary, was also carefully given to Connecticut. With Winthrop and Clarke both accepting the settlement in April 1663, Winthrop now joined in support of a royal charter for Rhode Island. Finally, in July 1663, the Crown granted Rhode Island its charter as a self-governing colony, including the Narragansett land.

Particularly remarkable in the charter was the explicit guarantee of religious freedom for Rhode Island: "No person within the said colony was to be anywise molested, punished, disquieted or called in question for any differences in opinion in matters of religion, and do not actually disturb the civil peace." Furthermore, Rhode Island was protected from encroachment by Massachusetts by guarantees of freedom to trade with the Bay Colony. In general, the governmental changes made by the new royal charter were minor: the president's name was changed to governor, and the number of assistants or magistrates expanded from four to ten. The new charter, however, did cause the removal of the important nullification check on central government power in Rhode Island, by rescinding the law requiring a majority of towns to approve the laws of the General Court. Two years later the Crown restricted democracy further by requiring that suffrage in Rhode Island, as well as in the rest of New England, be limited to those with "competent estates."

The Narragansett land dispute was far from over. As soon as Winthrop had concluded his agreement with Clarke in April, he joyfully sailed for home, convinced that he had outsmarted Rhode Island. By the agreement the Atherton Company was recognized as the owners of the Narragansett lands and it was granted a free choice of jurisdiction. Winthrop had no doubt which path his associates would choose. As soon as he landed, Winthrop and his partners voted to shift jurisdiction of the Narragansett Country from Rhode Island to Connecticut and Connecticut eagerly accepted the gift. But, in the meanwhile, in the course of drafting the Rhode Island charter, Clarke had shrewdly neglected to include any mention of a free option to the Atherton Company. Thus, Rhode Island obtained a charter with unconditional jurisdiction over the Narragansett lands.

But if Dr. Clarke did a superb job of winning rights for Rhode Island in the turbulent years following the Restoration, hapless New Haven suddenly found itself blotted from the map. Here was a treacherous blow indeed from its neighbor colony, and a clear violation of the terms of the New England Confederation.

In addition to treachery without, New Haven was suffering increasing opposition within—rebellion against its extreme theocratic and oligarchic rule. The opposition denounced the severe limitations on suffrage and longed to join the more liberal and prosperous Connecticut. Francis Browne, for example, denounced the New Haven government and magistrates and refused to obey laws not in conformity with the laws of England.

When news of the royal grant of New Haven to Connecticut arrived in the fall of 1662, Connecticut issued an ultimatum to New Haven Colony to surrender its jurisdiction to it. The colony refused, but town after town now took advantage of the opportunity to shift its allegiance from New Haven to Connecticut. First came Southold on Long Island and then part or all of Stamford, Greenwich, and Guilford. By the end of 1662, the jurisdiction of New Haven had shrunk to a fraction—to its hard core. Only the towns of New Haven proper, Milford, and Branford remained.

The core of New Haven, headed by Governor William Leete and Rev. John Davenport, remained adamant. The freemen of the colony voted to keep its independence, and to appeal the decision to the king and ask for a charter for the colony. New Haven then took its case to the New England Confederation, charging Connecticut with gross violation of its terms. In September 1663 the Commissioners of the United Colonies voted in favor of New Haven and its continued independence. Connecticut, however, blithely ignored the verdict of the commissioners and continued to demand unconditional submission. New Haven, for its part, took heart in the winter of 1664 when the Crown's order to the colonies enjoining enforcement of the Navigation Acts included New Haven in its address. This seemed to accord implicit royal recognition of New Haven's autonomy. Even the defection of the town of Milford to Connecticut could not dampen New Haven's hopes for survival.

But in 1664 the crisis reached its culmination. The king took the first step down the path of ending the right of self-government in New England by sending four commissioners to New England in mid-1664 to try to enforce the navigation laws, settle disputes, and generally begin the process of taking over the colonies. In the meanwhile, in March the king decided to give to his brother James, the Duke of York, the entire huge area of New Netherland, which England was in the process of seizing from the Dutch: from the Connecticut River all the way south to Delaware Bay—virtually the entire middle area between New England and the Southern colonies of Chesapeake Bay. For good measure, James was also granted all of central and eastern Maine, from the Kennebec River east to St. Croix on the Canadian border.

The huge grant to the Duke of York startled Connecticut, for all of Long Island now belonged to the duke. In 1650 New England had come to an amicable agreement with the Dutch for partitioning Long Island: three-quarters of the island east of Oyster Bay went to Connecticut or New Haven, and Dutch sovereignty was virtually limited to Long Island areas that now are Nassau County and part of New York City. Now, suddenly, the Long Island towns had been transferred to the Duke of York. But far more dangerous was the fact that James was now granted all land west of the Connecticut River. This meant the virtual eradication of the colony of Connecticut; all the significant towns in the colony, except New London, were located west of this river. Its charter thus completely negated, and being anxious to present the royal commission with a *fait accompli*, Connecticut again demanded total submission from New Haven and sent its agents to that colony to take over the government.

The other colonies also wanted to settle matters as quickly as possible. The commissioners of the United Colonies reversed their stand in September and endorsed Connecticut's appropriation of New Haven. Finally, in November the royal commissioners agreed and decided that all the New Haven area belonged to Connecticut.

The blow was final. The Crown had decided. In December 1664 the New Haven General Court surrendered but under bitter protest to the last, denouncing the injustice imposed by Connecticut. New Haven Colony was ended, and the towns became part of the considerably more liberal colony of Connecticut.

The most extreme and rigid Puritan theocracy in New England was thus no more. The Reverend John Davenport, founder and spiritual chief of New Haven, moved to the ministry of First Boston Church, there to end his days in bitter controversy, as the foremost and most relentless enemy of the Half-Way Covenant. As for Branford's zealous minister, Rev. Abraham Pierson, he had led his flock there from Southampton, Long Island, two decades before, when that town had decided to join the lax rule of Connecticut. He was not now prepared to give up the strict theocratic ideal, and so he moved his flock once more, this time to found another theocratic settlement in former Dutch territory at New Ark, on the banks of the Passaic River.

With New Haven seized by Connecticut, the New England Confederation came to a virtual end. Although it formally existed for twenty more years, its annual meetings ceased and it no longer played a significant role in New England affairs.

The Massachusetts Bay Colony's authorities, with their old self-governing charter, had good reason meanwhile to fear the onset of the Restoration. Already a British command had forced Massachusetts Bay to slacken its persecution of the Quakers. What further encroachments might follow?

King Charles, for his part, was determined to bring his most recalcitrant and independent colony to heel. Its virtual independence, its widespread flouting and evasion of the recently passed Navigation Acts, its oligarchic rule by a Puritan theocracy, its grabbing of the New Hampshire and Maine settlements, could only infuriate an Anglican monarch. In mid-1662 the king confirmed the Massachusetts charter but, vaguely and ominously, stressed the invalidity of all laws contrary to the laws of England. More substantively, the king ordered Massachusetts to permit the use of the (Anglican) Book of Common Prayer, and to grant the franchise to all freeholders of "competent estate" *whether or not* they were members of a Puritan church. By this last command, of course, the king struck at the heart of theocratic rule in Massachusetts. Massachusetts was able to obey the letter of this demand, but not the substance: in place of restricting voting to church members, the Bay Colony substituted the requirement that each nonmember must obtain confirmation from the local minister, the town selectmen, and the General Court itself, that he was orthodox in religion—a gantlet that no one was able to run.

Eventually, King Charles saw his opportunity to take the first fateful step for bringing Massachusetts to heel. In 1664 he sent an expedition under Col. Richard Nicolls, a veteran royalist, to America to conquer and seize New Netherland from the Dutch. Nicolls was to remain to govern New Netherland—now renamed New York—as the Duke of York's deputy. The king took the opportunity to name Nicolls as head of a four-man commission to subdue New Netherland and to inspect, regulate, and settle disputes in New England.

Here was the first intrusion of English authority on New England. Both Massachusetts and the king saw the commission correctly—the entering wedge of British rule and the end of self-government, as well as the overthrow of the Puritan oligarchy in Massachusetts. And neither was Massachusetts reassured by the fact that one of the royal commissioners was Samuel Maverick. A former Boston merchant and veteran rebel against Massachusetts tyranny, and a signer of the Child petition, Maverick was a man eager to wreak vengeance against his old enemy. Professor Oliver Chitwood points out that in this emerging "fight between the Massachusetts oligarchy and the Crown, the people stood to lose regardless of the outcome. If the king won, the rights covered by the charter would be lost to the colony as a whole. On the other hand, if the oligarchy won, it would be strengthened in its position and the old policy of intolerance and limited suffrage would continue."* Apparently Chitwood does not see the other side of the coin; for upon either outcome, the people also stood to gain—self-government and freedom from imperial rule on the one hand, liberation from theocracy on the other.

The commission came armed with two sets of royal instructions: public and secret. The public instructions were to hear complaints, settle disputes between the New England colonies, and enforce the Navigation Acts. They also conveyed the king's good intentions to Massachusetts. The secret instructions, however, were to press for the election of more amenable deputies and magistrates who would approve the idea of a royal governor in Massachusetts. Nicolls himself was the king's preference for this post. The king also instructed the commissioners to insist upon religious toleration in New England, especially, of course, for Anglicans.

Upon the commissioners' arrival in July 1664, Massachusetts delivered a ringing reply to their pretensions: Massachusetts' enemies had evidently persuaded the king to send a commission that could on its own discretion revoke the colonists' fundamental right of self-government, a right granted in their patent. In addition to these arguments from principle, the royal commissioners were subjected to personal denunciation in the colony. One of the commissioners, the ambitious Sir Robert Carr, was accused of keeping a mistress, while Col. George Cartwright was suspected of being a "papist." In the Puritan climate of Massachusetts Bay, it was difficult to know which crime was deemed the more heinous.

The commission proceeded first to the rapid accomplishment of its top-priority mission—the conquest of New Netherland. The commissioners' next step, according to their instructions, was to outflank Massachusetts by bringing the weaker New England colonies into submission before confronting their most difficult task, Massachusetts Bay. Accordingly, their first step, in early 1665, was Plymouth, where the commissioners demanded that the franchise no longer depend on religious opinion, and that there be religious liberty, at least for "orthodox" Christians. In contrast to Massachusetts Bay, Plymouth quickly succumbed, thus greatly weakening the theocratic and oligarchic rule. The king warmly commended Plymouth for its ready compliance, but not without a pointed

*Oliver P. Chitwood, *A History of Colonial America,* 3rd ed. (New York: Harper, 1961), p. 219.

reference to her errant sister: "Your carriage seems to be set off with the more lustre by the contrary deportment of the colony of the Massachusetts. . . ."

The next step was to settle the still raging boundary dispute over the Narragansett Country; the commission was granted power to override any previous royal charter. Connecticut and the Atherton Company were still actively claiming the land. The Crown had advised the commissioners to take the Narragansett Country away from both Connecticut and Rhode Island and to make it a direct royal province, with the Atherton claim continuing in force. At the end of March the commissioners rendered their decision, amending their instructions significantly. For although the Narragansett Country was indeed awarded directly to the Crown and called "King's Province," the commissioners decided to compensate Rhode Island for the loss by authorizing it independently to govern the province in the king's stead. Moreover, they were convinced by Rhode Island's demonstration of the fraudulent nature of the Atherton Company's purchase of the tract from the Indians. The commissioners, therefore, boldly vacated the arbitrary Atherton claim and ordered the company proprietors off the territory. (Sir Robert Carr, however, demonstrated his buccaneering bent by asking the Crown to grant him title to a large tract of the best Narragansett grazing land.) Winthrop, however, managed to persuade Nicolls, who had not been present, to get the Atherton decision reversed. But at least Rhode Island was left in charge of the territory.

The commissioners' other major impact on Rhode Island was, as we have seen, the compulsory narrowing of suffrage to those of "competent estates." Rhode Island needed no prodding, of course, to agree to what they already had: permission for all the orthodox to have churches of their own choosing.

Apart from the Atherton decision, the commissioners' rulings were quite satisfactory to Connecticut. We have already seen the commissioners' role in the liquidation of New Haven. The commissioners were told by Connecticut that it already met the requirements of giving the right to vote to all "men of competent estates," even if not church members, and of permitting full religious liberty to those of orthodox belief and "civil lives." While it was true, however, that Connecticut had been far more democratic than Massachusetts in granting the vote to nonchurch members, it had hardly permitted full religious freedom to non-Puritans. In return for their ready compliance with the commissioners' requests, Connecticut and Rhode Island were, like Plymouth, favored with a message from King Charles complimenting them on their good behavior.

Their business with the southern New England colonies speedily and satisfactorily concluded, the commissioners turned their attention to their major problem—Massachusetts Bay. Confronting the Massachusetts General Court in May 1665, the commissioners soon realized that this colony would be winning no good-conduct medals from the king. The commissioners put forth their demands: that they proposed to act as an appeals court for Massachusetts cases; that, as the other colonies had done, Massachusetts adopt an oath of allegiance to the king; that it grant full religious liberty to Anglicans; and that it observe the Navigation Acts. The commissioners also demanded that Massachusetts *really* eliminate its prohibition against voting by nonchurch members.

Led by Governor Richard Bellingham, Massachusetts flatly refused each one of these royal demands. Massachusetts' charter, it further declared, gave the Bay Colony absolute power to make laws and administer justice; therefore, any appellate activity by the commission would be an intolerable breach of Massachusetts' rights. The commissioners angrily retorted that they were the direct agents of the king, the very royal authority responsible for the charter. Does Massachusetts deny the authority of the royal commission? Massachusetts answered, in a masterpiece of evasion and pseudohumility, that it was beyond its capacity or function to pass on the validity of the commission.

The commissioners decided to take the bull by the horns, and set themselves up as an appellate court, in the house of Capt. Thomas Breedon, to hear grievances against Massachusetts. But the General Court moved swiftly, proclaiming "by the sound of the trumpet" outside the Breedon house that this action was a breach of the royal charter and of Massachusetts' rights, and could not gain the General Court's consent.

Defeated and frustrated, the commissioners left Boston, but with this warning of things to come: "The King did not grant away his sovereignty over you when he made you a corporation. When His Majesty gave you power to make wholesome laws and to administer justice by them, he parted not with his right to judge whether the laws were wholesome . . . 'tis possible that the charter that you so much idolize may be forfeited, until you have cleared yourselves of those many injustices, oppressions, violences, and blood for which you are complained against."

With Col. Richard Nicolls returning to New York to take up his post as governor, the other commissioners proceeded northward, to try to disrupt Massachusetts' rule over the New Hampshire and Maine settlements. Beyond obtaining a few signatures on a petition to the king for relief from Massachusetts' rule, the commissioners accomplished little in the New Hampshire towns, even though accompanied by agents of the proprietary claimant to New Hampshire, Robert T. Mason. The towns of Portsmouth and Dover, in fact, sent for some Massachusetts magistrates to emphasize their solidarity with Massachusetts. This was not surprising because New Hampshire was dominated by an oligarchy of Massachusetts merchants—for example, Valentine Hill and the Waldron family—who had moved to the Piscataqua to engage in the flourishing timber and fish trade. The oligarchy was either appointed by the Massachusetts General Court or elected by a highly limited franchise. A dozen petitioners from Portsmouth complained to the commission that under Massachusetts "five or six of the richest men of this parish have ruled and ordered all offices, both civil and military, at their pleasure, and none durst make opposition for fear of great fines or long imprisonment." In particular, the opposition attacked the theocratic Puritan rule and pleaded for the right to worship as Anglicans and for the right to vote. The greatest fire of the petitioners was leveled at Dover's Puritan minister, Rev. Joshua Moody. The petitioners also asked for a union of New Hampshire with Maine, where the settlements had similar problems.

If some merchants were privileged members of the New Hampshire oligarchy, so also merchants like Francis Champernowne headed the petition and merchants like Pynchon and Bradstreet defended the petitioners in the Massachusetts court. But all to no avail. For as soon as the commissioners left, the Massachusetts authorities began to arrest the leading petitioners and complainants. Thus, the Portsmouth distiller Abraham Corbett was hauled into court "to answer for his tumultuous and seditious practices against his government."

Pickings were more fruitful for the commission, however, in the Maine towns, which had been seized by Massachusetts only a decade before, and where the preponderance of anti-Puritan settlers and fishermen kept resentment high. Finding Maine discontented with Massachusetts' rule, the commissioners proceeded to organize an independent government at York for the eight Maine towns. The commissioners were armed with a royal letter commanding the surrender of the Maine towns to the jurisdiction of Ferdinando Gorges, grandson and heir of the previous proprietor, and John Archdale accompanied the commission as an agent of Gorges to see that the order was carried out.

Traveling further east to the Duke of York's new province east of the Kennebec river (now central and eastern Maine), the commissioners then organized a government, under the duke, of the few scattered inhabitants, and named the territory Cornwall.

Before disbanding, the commissioners sent their report to the Crown in December 1665. In it they attacked Massachusetts' intransigence and recommended revocation of the Bay Colony charter. They also recommended direct royal government for New Hampshire and Maine, and praised the cooperative attitude of other New England colonies.

The commissioners' report, however, proved to be ill-fated. One ill omen: none of the commissioners arrived home with the report. Maverick settled down in New York, Carr died shortly after, and Cartwright, traveling to England with the report, was captured at sea by the Dutch. More significantly, the king found this an inopportune time to tangle with Massachusetts.

The Dutch had naturally taken umbrage at England's sudden seizure of New Netherland at a time when the two countries were at peace. And in the ensuing war with the Dutch, England bore heavy losses and expenses, especially as the French entered on the side of the Dutch. A great plague also devastated London and southern England, and later in the year a great fire destroyed two-thirds of the housing of London. Furthermore, clamor was rising against the king's lord chancellor, the despotic Earl of Clarendon, soon to be ousted and to flee into exile. With all the turmoil in England, Charles decided to let the Massachusetts matter go for the time being. In April 1666 he asked Massachusetts to send an agent to England to answer the commissioners' charges. Massachusetts brusquely replied that it had already given all its explanations to the commissioners and now had nothing to add. The Bay Colony did, as a sweetener, send to the Crown for the royal navy a gift of two large expensive masts, worth about two thousand pounds, from the New Hampshire forests.

Massachusetts' refusal had not been decided upon without opposition. Leading citizens of a few Massachusetts towns counseled obedience to the king's order. Of the Boston petitioners against defiance, the overwhelming majority were: (a) merchants, and (b) nonfreemen, and hence nonvoters and non-Puritan church members. Thus, the counsel of caution came largely from the groups most prominent in strong opposition to the rule of the existing oligarchy.

Despite the defiance of Massachusetts, the king now dropped the matter and pursued the colony no further. At home the hated Earl of Clarendon fell from power in 1667, to be succeeded by the Cabal ministry, in which Anthony Ashley Cooper, later Earl of Shaftesbury, was the most influential official on colonial affairs. And since Lord Ashley was himself an active proprietor of the new Carolina grant, it was to his interest to minimize royal interference in the colonies. Influential fellow colonial proprietors like the Duke of York, furthermore, were interested more in exploring their own proprietary claims than in bringing the colonies to heel. The Massachusetts government had triumphed—for the short run.

Even the one victory of the commissioners over Massachusetts Bay—the separation of Maine—turned out to be short-lived. During the Anglo-Dutch war, support for Massachusetts in Maine increased out of fear of the Indians friendly to the French and French-Catholic missionaries. Also, realizing that England, in the wake of war and the fall of Clarendon, was in no mind to intervene, Massachusetts, in the spring of 1668, took steps forcibly to reincorporate the Maine towns into the Bay Commonwealth. Four leaders of the General Court went to York and there reimposed Massachusetts' rule on Maine. Massachusetts now ruled triumphant, without a single defeat at the hands of the Crown.

One of the most far-reaching actions of the first years of the Restoration was a series of Navigation Acts, by which England imposed mercantilist restrictions on its empire. Attempting to eliminate the more efficient Dutch shipping from the American trade for the benefit of the London merchants, the Puritan Parliament in 1650–51 had prohibited foreign vessels from trading with America; goods to and from the colonies could only be carried on English or colonial ships, or on ships of the home country of growth or manufacture. Fish imports and exports from England were limited to English ships alone. As part of the Restoration compromise, Charles II continued to gratify the London merchants and passed a series of Navigation Acts in 1660–63. Part of the commissioners' instructions, indeed, was to see to the enforcement of these acts.

The new Navigation Acts drastically restricted and monopolized American colonial trade, to the detriment of the colonies. The Navigation Act of 1660–61: (1) restricted all colonial trade to "English" ships (English and American), that is, ships built, owned, and manned by Englishmen; (2) excluded all foreign merchants from American trade; and (3) required that certain enumerated colonial articles be exported *only* to England and English colonies. We have already seen the havoc caused in the Southern colonies by tobacco being made one of the enumerated goods. Among the others were sugar, cotton-wool, and various dyes. The second important Navigation Act was the Staple Act of 1663, which provided that all goods exported from Europe to America must first land in England. Only a few colonial imports were exempt from this prohibition: salt, servants, various provisions from Scotland, and wine from Madeira and the Azores. The Staple Act meant that English ships and merchants would monopolize exports to America, while English manufacturers selling to America would be privileged by extra taxes being levied at English ports on foreign exports to the colonies. The enumerated-articles provision insured that these staples would be exported only by English merchants and in English ships. The English seizure of New Netherland was partly designed to complement the Navigation Act by crushing the Dutch freight trade with the New World.

The *immediate* impact of these acts on New England merchants and the New England economy was not great. New England imports were largely manufactured goods from England anyway, and thus were not greatly affected. And the restrictions—such as the enumerated articles and the prohibition of direct imports of wines from the Canary Islands—were simply ignored. The Massachusetts merchants blithely continued to ship enumerated articles direct to European ports—for example, tobacco to Holland—and to import goods direct from Europe. The New England merchants were happily able to save the South from immediate devastation at the hands of the Navigation Acts by first importing Southern tobacco to Boston and then exporting it direct to foreign countries. In this way, the South, for a time, was enabled to avoid the drastic burden of the Navigation Acts. The distracted English government did not attempt to enforce any of these restrictions until the Anglo-Dutch wars were over in the mid-1670s. The position of the merchants was backed fully by the Massachusetts General Court, which declared that it simply was not subject to "the laws of England any more than we live in England." On this issue the Boston merchants and the Puritan theocracy were allied: the former to prevent British restrictions on their trade, the latter to keep England from interfering with the Puritan regime in Massachusetts.

Indeed, the Massachusetts merchants, able to avoid the restrictions of the Navigation Acts, were also able to take advantage of the provisions driving out their efficient Dutch competitors. The London merchants, having used governmental power to crush Dutch competitors, suddenly found to their dismay the Massachusetts merchants outcompeting them in marketing colonial products in Europe, in shipping, and in supplying the colonies with imported manufactures—including European products competing with English goods. The king's revenue was of course diminished by direct trade with Europe, because the taxes levied at English ports were avoided.

The most flourishing trade in New England during the Dutch wars of the 1660s and 1670s was the essentially uneconomic supplying of war contracts to provision the English attempts at conquest. Massachusetts' major provisions were naval stores, especially masts, channeled through Portsmouth, New Hampshire. This became the biggest business seen in New England up to that time. Once again, London merchants were the key entrepreneurs in this trade, using their influence to obtain government war contracts. The most favored Massachusetts merchants were those with connections to the London contractors. The leading New England mast supplier was Peter Lidget, but the Massachusetts mast industry was able to flourish largely because it was highly competitive and not centrally organized. In 1670, for example, Richard Wharton was able to obtain for his company a ten-year monopoly of the supply of naval stores (including masts) in Massachusetts and Plymouth, but the endeavor quickly failed because the grant of privilege was impossible to enforce. Once again the market process was able to dissolve even a monopoly created by government privilege.

PART IV

The Rise and Fall of New Netherland

38

The Formation of New Netherland

The British seizure of New Netherland—the vast if thinly settled Dutch territory in North America—wrought a permanent change in the pattern of English colonization in the New World. The grant of this vast area to the proprietorship of the Duke of York, younger brother of Charles II, and its seizure by Col. Richard Nicolls in 1664, brought under English control a great land area that much later was to constitute the "middle colonies."

How had New Netherland been formed? Seventeenth-century Dutch policies cannot be fully comprehended without recognizing the fierce and continuing political divisions within the Dutch republic over constitutional and foreign policies. Early in their long revolutionary struggle against Spain for religious toleration, freedom from taxation, and independence from central imperial rule, the seven northern Dutch-speaking Calvinist provinces of the Netherlands had established a loose confederation. Governing these United Provinces was a States-General representing the completely autonomous provincial legislatures or states. Not being burdened by the overweening state power of the other European countries, the Dutch maritime cities, especially those in the provinces of Holland and Zeeland, were able to forge the greatest economic progress in Europe. The Dutch freely engaged in trade throughout Europe, even after Spain's union with Portugal had cut off their supplies of spices, sugar, and salt from the East Indies, Brazil, and the West Indies. The war against Spain, however, continued even after Spanish troops had been driven from the northern provinces, after the ten Catholic southern provinces had gained recognition of their rights by Spain, and after France and then England had determined to make peace with Spain. The struggle for national liberation thus became transformed into a war of Dutch aggression against the southern provinces. A regular standing army was developed, serving to expand the executive power in the central government, as well as central government power over the constitutionally independent provincial governments. Thus, the central executive, not to mention the officer class of the army, had a vested interest in continuing the war. This continuation of the war for the benefit of the executive-military authorities forced the syndicates of merchants who had successfully and rapidly developed private trade to the East Indies to seek a means of mutual defense from attacks by the Spanish or Portuguese fleets. Under the leadership of Amsterdam, these syndicates or chambers created the United East India Company in March 1602. This company, under the control of the local chambers, organized joint voyages to the East Indies for their mutual protection during wartime. After the war, however, the company became a monopoly for governing Dutch settlements in the Indies.

The fundamental cleavage in the politics of the United Provinces developed when the merchants of the cities of Holland and of other provinces, led by the foremost Dutch statesman, Johan van Oldenbarneveldt, successfully pursued peace negotiations with Spain despite the complete opposition of the Dutch military leaders. The Dutch merchants desired peace in order to end the threat of military dictatorship and the burden of taxes, and to gain access to world markets through free and peaceful trade. These merchants formed the basis of the Republican party, standing for liberal principles of peace, free trade, liberty, and, in particular, the maintenance of the original Dutch confederation of towns and provinces. In that confederation, each level of governmental power was strictly limited by the application of a virtual unanimity principle. The Republicans, furthermore, tended to be Arminians, following the liberal Dutch Protestant theologian Jacobus Arminius, who emphasized free will, natural law, and religious toleration as over against the Calvinist doctrines of predestination and state enforcement of religious conformity.

Opposition to the peace negotiations with Spain was centered in the Orange party, composed largely of gentry dependent upon their lucrative and powerful military positions and whose leader was the Prince of Orange, the military commander of the Netherlands. The Orange party sought greater powers for the central government, a strong standing army, and ultimately the substitution of an Orange monarchy for the republican confederation. Allied with the nobility and military in the Orange party was the great part of the Calvinist ministers; the Orange party, in fact, was often termed the "Calvinist party." The Calvinist ministers found the discipline of war more suitable to Calvinist practices than was the increased standard of living resulting from peaceful trade. Furthermore, a strong central government, resulting from war, was seen as the best means of enforcing religious conformity, especially against the Arminians, who were protected by the provincial independence of Holland.

Holland was the center of strength of the Republican party, containing as it did the least influence by nobles or the military and the greatest commercial and maritime strength. The Orange party, however, had strong support even in the cities of Holland from Calvinist emigrés from southern Netherlands, largely French-speaking Walloons who formed an important and wealthy part of the population. Like most emigrés throughout history, the bulk of the southerners were not content to live in the free atmosphere of their newfound home. Instead, unable to persuade the majority of their original countrymen of the justice of their cause, they tried to win by dragging their new fellow citizens into war and thus riding to power on the backs of foreign troops and guns. Emigrés always tend to constitute a menace to those who graciously welcome their migration. In the Dutch republic, the Orange party had strong support from the southern emigrés, whooping for a war of aggression against the Spanish Netherlands to "liberate" the reluctant Catholics in behalf of Calvinism.

The peace negotiated by the Dutch Republicans, the Twelve Year Truce of Antwerp (April 1609), gained the recognition by Spain of the virtual independence of the United Provinces and of the right of the Dutch to engage in Eastern trade similar to the right won by England in the treaty of 1604. Also in 1609 the Dutch East India Company hired the English explorer Henry Hudson to find a northeast arctic route to the Orient. Hudson was instructed not to seek a northwest passage through North America, as the Republican-run company was anxious to avoid any danger to peace with Spain by challenging Spain's imperial claims in the New World. Disobeying his instructions, Hudson, on failing to find a northeast route, sailed to North America and explored, among other areas, Delaware Bay and the Hudson River as far north as the fur trading region near Albany.

Since fur was a leading commodity in Dutch trade from Scandinavia and Russia, the new possibility of a cheaper American source spurred the remarkably enterprising Amsterdam merchants into action. During the next four years many Amsterdam merchants outfitted small ships and engaged in a very profitable fur trade with the Indians, in exchange for beads and cloth. These individual traders also founded a settlement on Manhattan Island, explored first by Adriaen Block in 1613. In 1614 thirteen of the Amsterdam merchants there engaged in the America trade, banded together, and managed to secure from the states of Holland and Friesland a monopoly of all trade in America for the space of six voyages. Soon afterward, these merchants strengthened their hold by forming the United New Netherland Company and obtaining from the States-General a three-year monopoly of all American trade in the area between New France in the north and the Delaware River.

One of the first acts of the New Netherland Company was to found a settlement vital to the fur trade, far up the Hudson River at Fort Nassau (later Fort Orange, now the site of Albany), near the junction of the Hudson and Mohawk rivers. The fort was built on the site of an old ruined trading post, which had been erected about 1540 by French fur traders and soon abandoned. In 1618 the commandant of Fort Nassau came to a significant agreement with the chiefs of the mighty Iroquois Indians—the Five Nations. In this durable treaty, the Dutch and Iroquois agreed to trade peacefully in muskets and ammunition in exchange for fur.

The New Netherland Company tried to renew its monopoly in 1618, but heated opposition by excluded merchants blocked an extended grant, and the American fur trade was then thrown open again to the competition of individual merchants, albeit under license of the government. To its pleased surprise the New Netherland Company found that it prospered even more under the bracing air of competition, and the company now laid plans for further expansion.

At this point, however, Dutch affairs took a fateful turn. The Orange party, rallying the army officers (largely gentry dependent upon military posts), used the theological disagreements between Arminians and Calvinists to effect a coup and overthrow the republican constitution in 1619. Using its narrow 4-3 majority in the States-General, based on control of the rural Calvinist provinces, the Orange party had convoked a national synod of the Dutch Reformed Church. When the synod condemned and ordered the persecution of the Arminian theologians, the state of Holland refused to approve, using its well-founded constitutional independence to safeguard the principle of religious toleration. At that point, Prince Maurice of Orange and his army attacked Holland and arrested Oldenbarneveldt and other Republican leaders, including Hugo Grotius, the founder of international law. A reign of terror was instituted by the Orange party: the venerable Oldenbarneveldt was tried illegally, with no provision for defense, and executed for treason in May 1619. The Arminian leaders, moreover, were persecuted and exiled.

The now dominant Orange party proceeded to renew its aggression against the southern Netherlands upon expiration of the truce in 1621, and proposed to carry the war to the American possessions of Spain and Portugal. At this point there came to the fore an eminent Walloon emigré merchant, William Usselincx, who for thirty years had propagandized for the establishment of a Dutch West India Company to establish colonies in South America for reaping such valuable tropical products as sugar and tobacco. In June 1621 the States-General chartered the Dutch West India Company under Orange control with the aim of plundering and conquering the Spanish and Portuguese colonies and monopolizing the slave trade. Although modeled on the Dutch East India Company, the West India Company was a pure creation of the state to achieve military objectives; the state contributed half the capital and ships and forced the rest of the capital and ships from reluctant Dutch merchants. In place of the independent Dutch merchants (such as the New Netherland Company), who had gained an important smuggling trade to Brazil and the Caribbean and a free trade to the Hudson River, a monopoly of Dutch trade with and between the Atlantic coasts of Africa and the Americas was now granted to the new company. The company was also granted a monopoly of all colonization in America. A government in the form of a commercial company, this overseas instrument of Orange aggression possessed governmental and feudal powers—to rule its arbitrarily granted territories, to legislate, to make treaties, to make war and peace, to maintain military forces and fleets of warships in order to plunder, conquer, and colonize. Only the company's appointed governor general had to be approved by the States-General. Dominant on the board of nineteen directors was the Amsterdam Chamber of the Company, which owned over forty percent of the capital and thus became the effective ruler of New Netherland.

Engaged in forming the huge Dutch West India Company, the States-General had no interest in granting the request made in 1620 by the English Pilgrims residing in Leyden, Holland, for founding a colony on Manhattan Island. Their proposal rejected, the Pilgrims soon ended their wanderings by landing at Plymouth, Massachusetts.

The Dutch West India Company mostly concentrated on the Atlantic colonies of Portugal in Brazil and Angola, for Brazil was the major source of European sugar and Africa supplied the slaves who produced that sugar. The company, in fact, temporarily captured Bahia in Brazil in 1624. When a company fleet captured the Spanish silver fleet in 1628, the money was used to finance the Dutch conquest of northeastern Brazil, beginning with Recife in 1630, and of the Portuguese ports of Luanda (near the lower Congo) and Benguela in Angola, Goree and Elmina in West Africa. The company established colonies on the Guiana coast and in the unoccupied islands in the Caribbean, St. Eustatius, and Tobago in 1632 and Curaçao in 1634. The governor at Curaçao for the next decade was Peter Stuyvesant, who had been in the military service of the company for many years. Thus, the Dutch West India Company had many valuable and important interests, of which the colony of New Netherland was one of the least valued.

39

Governors and Government

The Dutch West India Company began operations in 1623, and in the same year the first party of permanent Dutch settlers landed in the New World—apart from a settlement near Cape May on the Delaware Bay in 1614. The new colonists landed in Manhattan. Others in the party settled in Fort Orange. The settlers, significantly, were a party of Walloon emigrés. Appointed governor, or director general, of New Netherland was Capt. Cornelis May. Under May's aegis the Dutch quickly began to expand over the vast virgin territory. Fort Nassau was built on the east bank of the Delaware River (now Gloucester, New Jersey, opposite Philadelphia). Another Dutch party built Fort Good Hope on the Connecticut River, and we have seen the fate meted out to it by the English "planters" of Connecticut. Still other Dutchmen settled on what is now the coast of Brooklyn and on Staten Island.

Why didn't the English, who had laid claim to the whole coast, seriously molest the Dutch settlements? For the first decade the English were busy fighting with Spain and France. After that came the troubles and distractions of the Puritan Revolution. It was only the advent of the Restoration period that enabled England to turn serious attention to exerting its power over New Netherland—as well as over Massachusetts.

In the spring of 1626 Peter Minuit took over as director general, and it was he who, in a series of fateful decisions, laid the pattern of social structure for New Netherland. In the English colonies the chartered companies and proprietors tried to gain immediate profits by inducing rapid settlement. The need for these inducements led to the inevitable dissolution of original attempts to maintain feudal land tenure, as lands were divided up and sold, and halfhearted attempts to collect feudal quitrents from the settlers were

298

abandoned in the face of their stubborn evasion and resistance. Moreover, the need for inducing settlement also led the companies or proprietors to grant, from the beginning, substantial rights of democracy and self-government to the colonists. Happily, none of the English settlements *began* as royal colonies; either they were settled by individuals, for individual temporal or spiritual gain, or they were governed by profit-seeking companies or proprietors who were induced by hopes of profit to grant substantial or even controlling rights of property and self-government to the settlers. North Carolina, New Hampshire, Maine, Rhode Island, and Connecticut began as individual self-governing settlements; Virginia and Massachusetts as chartered companies; Maryland and South Carolina as proprietorships.

But the Dutch West India Company and Minuit decided quite differently. As profit seekers they first concentrated on their monopoly of the lucrative fur trade, and for this trade extensive settlements were not needed. Whether by design or not, the effect of Dutch policy was to discourage settlement greatly, and to hamper the development of the vast area over which the Dutch West India Company had been assigned its monopoly. For example, one of Minuit's first actions was to order the colonists back, to concentrate them around the fort in New Amsterdam on the tip of Manhattan, which had been purchased from the Indians. This arbitrary policy left only a few traders at Fort Orange and only one vessel on the Delaware, Fort Nassau being completely abandoned. This action stemmed from the company's high-handed decision to retain its exclusive monopoly of trade; to leave too many individuals in the interior would foster illegal, competitive trading. Second, the Dutch perpetuated a feudal type of land tenure by insisting on *leasing*, rather than *selling*, land to the settlers. It is no wonder that with no settler permitted to own his land and thus help to dissolve feudalism and land monopoly—and with no one permitted to trade on his own account—the pace of settlement was very slow.

Furthermore, the form of government was by far the most despotic in the colonies. There was no self-government or democracy, no limitation whatever on the arbitrary rule of the company and its director general. The director, along with a Council of Five appointed by the Amsterdam Chamber, ran the entire government; its legislative, executive, and judicial functions. They were joined by two other officials appointed by the company: the *Schout-Fiscal,* who made arrests and collected revenue, and the *Koopman,* the secretary of the colony. There were no legislatures or town meetings of any sort.

By 1629 it was evident that the colony was growing very slowly, only 300 persons, for example, lived in New Amsterdam. The company therefore decided to spur settlement, but instead of dissolving its land monopoly into a system of true private property for landed settlers, it decided to make the monopoly into a more elaborate feudal structure, sub-land monopolists placed over large particular areas in New Netherland. In the Charter of Privileges and Exemptions of 1629, the company decided to grant extensive tracts of land to any of its members who should bring over and settle fifty or more families on the tract. The tracts were required to lie along the banks of the Hudson (or other navigable rivers) and were granted in huge lots of sixteen miles along one shore of the Hudson, or eight miles on both shores. The depth on either side of the Hudson was indefinite. The grantee was termed a "patroon," or lord of the manor. In imitation of the feudal lord, the patroon was to possess civil and criminal jurisdiction over his tenants, or "peasants." The tenants had the formal right of appeal from the patroon's manorial courts to the feudal overlord—the company's government—but in practice the tenants were forced to forgo this right. The property of any tenant dying intestate reverted to the patroon, and the tenant was forced to grind his grain at his patroon's mill. The tenants were exempted from colonial taxation for ten years, but in return they were compelled to stay on the original estate for the entire period. To leave was illegal—an approximation of medieval serfdom.

Aside from being a temporary serf and having no hope of owning the land he tilled, the tenant was also prohibited from weaving any kind of woolen, linen, or cotton cloth. Even the patroons were prohibited from weaving, in order to keep the monopoly of the trade in the hands of the company government and to maintain a monopoly of the colonial market for Dutch textiles. This provision, however, was continually evaded and led to numerous conflicts. Neither tenant nor patroon could engage in the fur trade, which was still reserved to the company and its agents. Apart from these commodities, the patroons were at liberty to trade, but were required to pay a five percent duty to the government at New Amsterdam for exporting their goods. The use of slaves in domestic service or in tilling the soil was also sanctioned. The patroons were required, however, to purchase the granted land from the local Indians. It should be noted that Manhattan Island was exempted from the granting of patroonships: the land of that valuable island was to be reserved for the direct monopoly of the company government of the province.

While the incentive to become a tenant remained minimal, the incentive to become a patroon was now considerable. It should not be surprising that the receivers of these handsome grants of special privilege were leaders or favorites of the company itself. Thus, the first patroonship was granted by the company to two members of its own board of directors, Samuel Godyn, president of the Amsterdam Chamber of the Company, and Samuel Blommaert, who granted themselves a large chunk of what is now the state of Delaware, as well as sixteen square miles on Cape May across the Delaware Bay. Godyn and Blommaert took five other company directors into partnership to expand the capital of the patroonship, and one of the partners, Capt. David De Vries, was sent with a group of settlers to found the patroonship of Swanendael (now Lewes), near Cape Henlopen in Delaware.

The Swanendael manor was settled in 1631, but the settlement soon ran into difficulties. For one thing, it was chiefly designed as a whaling station, but De Vries soon found that whales were scarce along the Delaware coast. Furthermore, the Swanendael settlers managed to provoke the Indians into attacking and massacring them. The settlers had emptied a pillow, leaving the remains as waste, which happened to contain a piece of tin embossed with the emblem of the States-General of New Netherland. An Indian chief found the abandoned tin and used it for his tobacco pipe, whereupon the settlers, in an act unexcelled for stupidity even in the sordid history of white treatment of Indians, executed the hapless chief for "treason" to the Netherlands. It is hardly puzzling that the Indians proceeded to attack and wipe out the settlement. In addition to these calamities, the patroons then quarreled and dissolved their partnership. They sold the land back to the company government in 1634 for a handsome 15,000 guilders. The first patroonship in New Netherland had proved to be a failure.

The second patroonship was also a failure. Michael Pauw, another of the grasping company directors, managed to obtain a grant for himself of the area that now includes Hoboken, Jersey City, and the whole of Staten Island. Pauw called his colony Pavonia, which he organized on the site of Jersey City for a few years. The Indians, however, proved troublesome and the patroonship was losing money, and so in 1637 Pauw sold the land back to the obliging company for 26,000 guilders (land, of course, that the company had originally granted Pauw as a gift).

The first successful patroonship—and the only one that continued past the demise of New Netherland and through the eighteenth century—was the grant to yet another Amsterdam Chamber director, the wealthy jeweler Kiliaen van Rensselaer. Van Rensselaer's domain, Rensselaerswyck, prospered because of superior management and because its area was strategically located for fur trade with the Iroquois. It included virtually the entire area around Albany (now Albany and Rensselaer counties) except Fort Orange itself, which remained the property of the company government.

Immediately there began conflicts between the Hudson River patroons and the government. For the patroons began to ignore the Dutch West India company's legal monopoly of the highly lucrative fur trade, and the company began to tighten its regulations to enforce its monopoly. The patroons' illegal fur trade not only endangered the company monopoly; it also led them to concentrate on furs rather than encourage a large agricultural population, which the company government was now trying to foster. As a consequence, Peter Minuit was fired as director general by the company in 1632, on charges of being too soft on the patroons.

Succeeding Minuit was Wouter Van Twiller, a clerk in the company's Amsterdam warehouse, chosen because he had married into the powerful Van Rensselaer family. Conflicts with the patroons over fur trading continued in the Van Twiller regime. Externally, New England began the process of overrunning Fort Good Hope on the Connecticut River. However, the English occupation of the abandoned Fort Nassau, on the east bank of the

Delaware, was ended as Van Twiller reoccupied the fort and drove out the settlers. Further Dutch expansion took place during the Van Twiller administration: Arendt Corssen erected Beaver Road Fort on what is now the Pennsylvania side of the Delaware.

A good part of the expansion of land was accomplished for the benefit of Governor Van Twiller himself. He and his friends were given land grants and purchased large speculative tracts of land from the Indians. The tracts were concentrated on western Long Island, notably in the present Flatlands of Brooklyn. Van Twiller himself purchased Governors Island. None of these purchases was approved, as was legally required, by the Amsterdam Chamber of the Company. What is more, the director saw to it that his own farms received the best services from the government.

In addition to the conflicts over land irregularities and fur trading, the *Schout-Fiscal* opposed the director's methods. When Van Twiller fired the *Schout-Fiscal,* Lubbertus Van Dincklagen, the latter complained to the States-General. Furthermore, although some tobacco was now growing on Manhattan Island, the emphasis on the fur trade was helping to discourage agriculture and permanent settlement. The States-General, perturbed that emphasis on fur was discouraging permanent settlement in New Netherland, ordered the dismissal of Wouter Van Twiller in 1637.

But if the Dutch colonists had been chastised with whips, they were now to be chastised with scorpions. Arriving in 1638, the new director, Amsterdam merchant Willem Kiefft, proceeded to impose an absolute despotism upon the colony. First, he reduced his council of advisers from five to one, and on this rump council of his adviser and himself, he had two votes. To appeal his decisions to the Netherlands was now made a high crime. Assured of absolute power to issue his decrees, Kiefft outlawed virtually everything in sight. *All* trade, of any commodity whatsoever, was outlawed, except by special license issued by Kiefft. Any trader doing business without a license had his goods confiscated, and was subject to further punishment. To guard against possible trade, all sailors were prohibited from being on shore at night, under penalty of forfeit of wages and of instant dismissal on second offense. All sales of guns or ammunition to the Indians were prohibited on pain of death. All sorts of "immoralities" were prohibited. Heavy restrictions were placed on the sale of liquor; any tavern keeper selling liquor to tipsy customers was subject to a heavy fine and to confiscation of his stock. A tax was placed on tobacco. It is no wonder that De Vries, who had strongly opposed the tyranny of Van Twiller, had far more to resent now.

At the very time that Kiefft was imposing his despotism on New Netherland, however, overall company policy for the colony was changing drastically for the better. It was becoming increasingly evident to all that *something* needed to be done to obtain permanent settlers for this very thinly peopled territory. Characteristically, the patroons suggested a stronger dose of the medicine on which they were prospering: feudalism. The patroons, in their proposed "New Project," suggested that the Netherlands take the path by which England was insuring the profitability of Virginia's large plantations: furnishing them with white indentured servants—paupers, convicts, and vagabonds. Instead, the West India Company made the vital decision in the fall of 1638 to liquidate and abolish all of its monopolies in the New World, including fur, manufacturing, and the right to own land. Even foreigners were to have the same liberties as Dutchmen. The only monopoly retained by the company was that of transporting the migrating settlers to America. Furthermore, the new freedom to own land was made effective by granting every new farmer the right to a farm he could cultivate, although the company did insist that the farmer pay it rent for a half-dozen years, as well as the more reasonable provision that the farmer repay it the capital it had borrowed. And in 1640 the company liberalized the patroon system further, in a new Charter of Privileges and Exemptions. The size of patroon grants was greatly reduced—two hundred acres being awarded to anyone bringing over five settlers—and freedom of commerce was strengthened.

This liberalization led to an immediate and pronounced influx of settlers into New Netherland. In one year the number of farms on Manhattan Island more than quadrupled. De Vries arrived with organized parties of settlers who went to Staten Island. Jonas Bronck made a settlement on the Bronx River. Englishmen, taking advantage of the full rights for foreigners, also poured in to settle on the vast land available: some came from Virginia and raised tobacco, others fled from Massachusetts Bay. The only requirement was that they take an oath of allegiance to the Dutch Netherlands.

But while relations between *individual* settlers of the two countries were harmonious and naturally so, the relations between the two governments, each rapaciously claiming sovereignty, were equally naturally, quite troublesome. An individual settler of whatever nationality can clearly and evidently demarcate for himself a tract of land by transforming it by his labor, but there is no such clear-cut criterion for imposing governmental sovereignty. Therefore, while individuals of different nationalities can peacefully coexist within any given geographic area, governmental territorial conflicts are perpetual.

Thus, Director Kiefft, alarmed at the growth of Connecticut, seized the English town of Greenwich and forced the citizens to acknowledge Dutch jurisdiction. Angered also by New Haven and Connecticut settlements on eastern Long Island, Kiefft laid claim to all of what now are Kings and Queens counties, in another convenient purchase from the Indians. When in 1639 a group of settlers from Lynn, Massachusetts, landed in Cow Bay, Queens, they tore down the arms of the Dutch States-General from a tree and carved on it a fool's head. But Kiefft drove the New England settlers away, and they went east to found the town of Southampton.

Long Island was particularly important as a source of wampum, beads from sea shells which had long served the Indians as their monetary medium of exchange. Wampum was particularly important to the white man as the best commodity to trade with the Indians for furs.

Until the advent of the Kiefft administration, relations with the Indians had been cordial. But now they began to deteriorate. For one thing, ofttimes the cattle of the many new agricultural settlers strayed onto Indian property and ruined Indian corn fields. When the Indians very properly protected their corn by killing the white man's invading cattle, the white settlers, instead of curbing their cows, exacted reprisals upon the Indians.

Moreover, the Indians of the lower Hudson, Connecticut, and what is now New Jersey were all members of the Algonquin Confederacy. The Algonquins' traditional enemies were the powerful and aggressive Iroquois, of upstate New York. Now the new Kiefft ruling that no arms may be sold to any Indians on pain of death was vigorously enforced in the neighborhood of Manhattan, but not against the valuable fur-supplying Iroquois to the north. The Algonquins were naturally embittered to find the Dutch eagerly supplying their worst enemies with arms while they were rudely cut off. To meet the Algonquins' problems, Director Kiefft did not take the sensible course of repealing the prohibition against selling them arms. Instead, he had what seemed to him a brilliant idea: Fort Amsterdam was really a protection for the Algonquins as much as for the Dutch; therefore, *they* should also be taxed to pay for its upkeep. Therewith, Kiefft's despotism reached out to the Indians as well, except that they were not so helpless to resist as were his hapless Dutch subjects.

For sheer gall, Kiefft's demand upon the Indians for taxes in corn, furs, and wampum was hard to surpass. The Tappan tribe of Algonquins was properly sarcastic, and denied that the fort was any protection to it. The Tappans had never asked the Dutch to build their fort, and they were therefore not obliged to help maintain it.

At this point of growing tension, some employees of the West India company, retraveling to the Delaware River in 1641, landed on Staten Island and stole some pigs belonging to David De Vries. As often happened in the colonies, the hapless Indians were blamed *a priori* for the theft. In this case, Kiefft, without bothering to investigate, decided that the Raritan Algonquins were to blame. He promptly sent out an armed troop that murdered several Raritans and burned their crops. The Raritans, having no recourse in Dutch courts, had only one means of redress: violence. In reprisal, they destroyed De Vries' plantation and massacred his settlers. Kiefft, always ready to escalate a conflict, proclaimed a bounty of ten fathoms of wampum for anyone who brought in the head of a Raritan Indian.

At this juncture, an Indian from Yonkers who as a little boy had seen his uncle murdered in Manhattan by a gang of white servants of Peter Minuit, now murdered a Dutch tradesman in revenge. When Kiefft demanded the murderer, the Indian sachem refused to surrender him, reasoning that the balances of justice were now even.

Kiefft was now building up to an Indian war on two fronts, but the people were refusing to bear arms or to pay for a looming, dangerous, and costly conflict. To raise funds and support for a war, Kiefft in 1641 called together the first representative group of any kind in New Netherland: an assembly of heads of families, who chose a board of twelve men, headed by De Vries, to speak for them.

Although De Vries had more personal reasons to be anti-Indian than the director, he advised caution: the surrender of the murderer must be insisted upon, but the colony was not ready for a war. Moreover, De Vries adopted the great English tradition of redress of grievances before supply: when a despotic king was finally forced to call an assembly in order to raise expenses for a foreign war, the assembly would drive a hard bargain and insist first on liberalization of the tyranny. This is what the Twelve Men did before consenting to war in 1642. They demanded that Kiefft restore the council to five members, of whom four would be chosen by popular vote. They also demanded popular representation in the courts, no taxes to be levied without their consent, and greater freedom of trade. One of their demands, however, was the reverse of liberal: that importation of English cattle be excluded—clearly a desire for further privilege by the patroons. Kiefft finally responded in characteristic fashion, by dissolving the Twelve Men and proclaiming that no further public meetings might be held in New Amsterdam without his express permission.

Although the Dutch had failed to obtain the murderer from the Westchester Indians, a year's truce had been arranged by Jonas Bronck. Then, in 1643 an Indian was made drunk and robbed by some Dutch at the Hackensack settlement. In revenge, the Indian killed a Hackensack settler. The chiefs of the Indian's tribe hastily told De Vries, the patroon of Hackensack, that they would pay two hundred fathoms of wampum to the victim's widow, which they felt was reasonable compensation. De Vries advised acceptance of the offer, but Kiefft insisted on surrender of the murderer. The murderer, however, had fled up river to the Haverstraw Indians. Kiefft immediately demanded that the Haverstraws surrender him.

At this point a new factor intervened; a force of aggressive Mohawks of the Iroquois confederacy, each armed with Dutch muskets, descended upon the Hudson River tribes to terrorize and exact tribute. Although the Dutch would not break their treaty with the Iroquois by fighting them, De Vries did agree to give shelter to the Algonquin refugees at his main patroonship of Vriesendael at Tappan, and other refugees took shelter at Pavonia and on Manhattan Island.

Counsel was now divided among the Dutch. De Vries, backed by councilman Dr. La Montague and Rev. Everardus Bogardus, advised peaceful mediation in the Indian conflict. But Kiefft, over their passionate protests, saw only a Heaven-sent chance to pursue his grand design of liquidating the Indians. In this he was supported by Van Tenhoven, the secretary of the colony, and especially by Maryn Adriaensen, a member of the Twelve Men and a former freebooter in the West Indies. In an extraordinarily vicious sneak attack, Dutch soldiers, at midnight of February 25, 1643, rushed into the camps of sleeping refugees at Pavonia and Corlears Hook on Manhattan Island and slaughtered them all. In all, well over a hundred Indians were massacred, including the hacking to pieces of Indian babies. Led by Adriaensen, the soldiers exultantly marched back to Fort Amsterdam in the morning, bringing back many Indian heads. Director Kiefft rather aptly called it a truly Roman achievement. Taking their cue from this treacherous official massacre of peaceful and friendly Indians, some settlers at Flatlands fell suddenly on a group of completely friendly Marechkawieck Indians, murdered several, and stole a large amount of their corn.

The Algonquins could give but one answer to this outrage—all-out war on the Dutch. The entire Algonquin peoples, led by the Haverstraws, rose up against their tormentors. It was during this total conflict that poor Anne Hutchinson was killed by Indian raiders. The English settlements of Westchester were all wiped out. Even Vriesendael was attacked but, notably, while the destruction of Vriesendael was under way, an Indian spoke in praise of De Vries and the Indians departed after expressing regrets for their action. The Long Island settlements were also destroyed, as well as those on the west bank of the Hudson. The only Long Island settlement spared was Gravesend, a colony organized by Lady Deborah Moody, a Baptist refugee from Massachusetts. Only a half-dozen farms on Manhattan Island remained intact. By 1644, almost all the Dutch settlers were forced to abandon their homes and fields to destruction and to retreat behind the wall of Fort Amsterdam (now Wall Street), at the southern tip of Manhattan Island, around which fort the village of New Amsterdam had grown. Fort Orange and Rensselaerswyck, in friendly Iroquois country around Albany, remained unmolested. One of Kiefft's contributions to the struggle was to be the first white man to offer a bounty for Indian scalps.

The disastrous consequences of Willem Kiefft were now becoming fully evident. A needless and terribly destructive war had been inflicted upon the Dutch as the sole result of Kiefft's tough, hard-line policy toward the Algonquins. Popular indignation against Kiefft now rose insistently, and demands grew for his expulsion. De Vries, embarking for Holland, bitterly warned Kiefft that "the murders in which you have shed so much innocent blood will yet be avenged on your own head." Typically, Kiefft tried to disclaim all responsibility by throwing all the blame on his adviser in slaughter, Maryn Adriaensen. Adriaensen, whose farm had just been destroyed, naturally grew somewhat bitter at this treachery, and with a few comrades rushed into Kiefft's room to try to shoot the director. The assassination attempt failed; the man who fired the shot was instantly killed and his head publicly displayed.

With the Dutch community facing disaster, the despotic Kiefft, his treasury empty, was again forced to consult the leading colonists in order to raise money to fight a war of his own creation. In late 1643 he chose a board of Eight Men for this purpose. No funds could be obtained from the West India

Company because it was in the process of going bankrupt. And money raised by piratic attacks on Spanish shipping could only be highly irregular. Regular funds were also needed to maintain a company of soldiers, recently sent by the company and peremptorily quartered upon the town. Faced with this problem, Kiefft turned to one of his favorite devices: the imposition of a crushing tax. Kiefft proclaimed an exise tax on the brewing of beer, on wines and spirits, and on beaver skins. The Eight Men strongly objected, arguing rather lamely that taxes could be levied only by the home company itself, and, more cogently, that it was the business of the company and not of the settlers to hire and maintain soldiers. Furthermore, they protested that the settlers were ruined and could not pay taxes. (The suggestion of the Eight Men to tax speculators and traders was not, however, very constructive.) Kiefft replied in his usual brusque fashion, "In this country, I am my own master and may do as I please."

The people of New Amsterdam now had to confront not only Indians on the warpath, but further tyranny and exactions at home. Naturally, their grumbling opposition to Kiefft redoubled, and it was hardly allayed when Kiefft made an appointment with some of the Eight and then failed to keep it. The brewers refused to pay the tax. The matter was taken into court, but in essence Kiefft *was* the court and speedy judgment was rendered against the brewers, whose product was confiscated and given to the soldiers. Hostility to Kiefft now filled the colony and he was generally reviled as a villain, a liar, and a tyrant.

Finally, the long-suffering colonists could bear Kiefft no longer. Speaking for the colonists, the Eight Men in October 1644 directly petitioned the States-General in the Netherlands to remove Kiefft forthwith. The Eight Men wrote eloquently of their plight under Kiefft:

> Our fields lie fallow and waste; our dwellings and other buildings are burned; not a handful can be either planted or sown . . . we have no means to provide necessaries for wives or children. . . . The whole of these now lie in ashes through a foolish hankering after war. For all right-thinking men here know that these Indians have lived as lambs among us until a few years ago. . . . These hath the Director, by various uncalled-for proceedings, so embittered against the Netherlands nation, that we do not believe that anything will bring them and peace back. . . .
>
> This is what we have, in the sorrow of our hearts, to complain of; that one man . . . should dispose here of our lives and property according to his will and pleasure, in a manner so arbitrary that a king would not be suffered legally to do . . . We pray . . . that one of these two things may happen—either that a governor may be speedily sent with a beloved peace to us, or that [the company] will . . . permit us to return with wives and children to our dear Fatherland. For it is impossible ever to settle this country until a different system be introduced here, and a new governor be sent out. . . .

The petitioners also asked for greater freedom and more representative institutions to check the executive power.

This *cride coeur* of the oppressed people of New Netherland was heeded by the West India Company and Kiefft was removed in May 1645. It was perhaps not coincidental that the Algonquins and the Dutch were able to conclude a peace treaty soon afterward, in August, under pressure, to be sure, of the pro-Dutch Mohawk tribe. The parties sensibly agreed that whenever a white man or an Indian should injure the other, the victim would apply for redress to the juridical agencies of the accused. An ironical part of this peace treaty was the Algonquin agreement to return the kidnapped granddaughter of Anne Hutchinson, who now liked Algonquin life and who was returned against her will. Even a peace treaty could not be carried out, it seems, without someone being coerced.

Unfortunately, the company was delayed two years in sending the new governor, and Kiefft continued to oppress the citizenry in the meanwhile. Even the coming of peace did not completely lift the burdens of the people. The people had happily rejoiced when they heard the glad tidings of Kiefft's ouster. Kiefft immediately threatened all of his critics with fines and imprisonment for their "sedition." He continued to prohibit any appeals of his arbitrary decisions to Holland. The director was thereupon denounced by the influential Rev. Mr. Bogardus, in his sermons: "What are the great men of this country but vessels of wrath and fountains of woe and trouble? They think of nothing but to plunder the property of others, to dismiss, to banish, to transport to Holland!" To counter this courageous attack, Kiefft decided to use the minions of the state to drown out Bogardus' sermons—by soldiers' drum rolls, and even by roar of the fort's cannon. But Bogardus would not be silenced. Kiefft then turned to the method of violence to stop his critic—to the legal proceedings of his own state. Kiefft's charges against Bogardus in Kiefft's court included "scattering abuse," drinking alcohol, and defending criminals (such as Adriaensen in his attempt to assassinate the director). When these charges were served on Bogardus, he defiantly refused to appear, challenging Kiefft's legal right to issue the summons; with the people solidly on the minister's side, Kiefft was forced to yield.

Finally, at long last, Kiefft's replacement, Peter Stuyvesant, arrived in May 1647. So great was the jubilation of the people in getting rid of this incubus, that almost all of the fort's powder was used up in the military salute celebrating the arrival of the new director. When Kiefft handed over the office, the conventional vote of thanks to the old director was proposed, but two of the leading Eight Men, Cornelis Melyn, the patroon of Staten Island, and the German Joachim Kuyter, refused to agree, saying that they certainly had no reason to thank Kiefft. Moreover, they presented a petition for a judicial inquiry into Kiefft's behavior in office. But apart from being no liberal himself, Stuyvesant saw immediately the grave threat that a precedent for inquiry into a director's conduct would hold for any of his own despotic actions. The late nineteenth-century historian John Fiske aptly compared Stuyvesant's position to that of Emperor Joseph II of Austria-Hungary during the American Revolution over a century later: "Stuyvesant felt as in later days the

Emperor Joseph II felt when he warned his sister Marie Antoinette that the French government was burning its fingers in helping the American rebels. I, too, like your Americans well enough, said he, but I do not forget that my trade is that of king—*c'est mon metier d'etre roi!* So it was Stuyvesant's trade to be a colonial governor. . . ."*

Stuyvesant loftily declared that government officials should never have to disclose government secrets on the demand of two mere private citizens. And furthermore, to petition against one's rulers is *ipso facto* treason, no matter how great the provocation. Under this pressure, the petition of Melyn and Kuyter was rejected in the council, even though the company, in a mild gesture of liberality, had agreed to vest the government of New Netherland in a three-man supreme council (instead of Kiefft's one-man rule): a director general, a vice director, and the *Schout-Fiscal.* All, however, were company appointees.

The Dutch soon found that their jubilation at the change of directors should have been tempered. From his speech upon arrival, "I shall govern you as a father his children" Stuyvesant indicated no disposition to brook any limits to his rule. Even on the ship coming over, he had angrily pushed the new *Schout-Fiscal* out of the room because the latter had not been summoned. When Stuyvesant assumed command, he sat with his hat on while others waited bareheaded before he deigned to notice them, a breach of etiquette; he was, as one Dutch observer exclaimed, "quite like the Czar of Muscovy." Furthermore, Stuyvesant was not willing to let the Melyn-Kuyter matter rest with the rejection of their petition. He now summoned *them* to trial; and Kiefft eagerly accused these two "malignants" of being the real authors of the "libelous" Eight Men petition. Kiefft suggested that the two defendants be forced to produce all their correspondence with the company, and to show cause why they should not be summarily banished as "pestilent and seditious persons." Stuyvesant agreed, but Melyn and Kuyter showed so much damning evidence against Kiefft that *these* charges were quickly dropped. But if one charge fell through, another must immediately be found. Melyn and Kuyter were now indicted on the trumped-up charge of treachery with the Indians, and of attempting to stir up rebellion. Without bothering about evidence this time, Stuyvesant rushed through the prearranged verdict of guilty.

Stuyvesant was eager to sentence Melyn, as the leader of the two, to death, and he seriously pondered the death sentence for Kuyter also. For Kuyter had also committed two grave crimes: he had dared to criticize Kiefft, and he had shaken his finger at the ex-director. And Stuyvesant remembered the philosophizing of the Dutch jurist Josse de Damhouder: he who so much as *frowns* at a magistrate is guilty of insulting him. He also recalled the admonition of Bernardinus de Muscatellus: "He

---

*John Fiske, *The Dutch and Quaker Colonies in America* (Boston: Houghton Mifflin Co., 1899), 1:202.

who slanders God, the magistrate, or his parents, must be stoned to death." Stuyvesant was persuaded by his more cautious advisers, however, not to execute Melyn and Kuyter; instead, both were heavily fined and banished. Banishment, however, raised the danger that they would spill their tales of woe to the authorities in Holland. So Stuyvesant warned Melyn: "If I thought there were any danger of your trying an appeal, I would hang you this minute from the tallest tree on the island." This was in line with Stuyvesant's general view of the right to appeal: "If any man tries to appeal from me to the States-General, I will make him a foot shorter, pack the pieces off to Holland and let him appeal in that fashion."

The ironic climax of the Kiefft saga occurred when Kiefft finally left for Holland in August 1647 with a large fortune of 400,000 guilders, largely amassed from his term in office, and with Melyn and Kuyter in tow as his prisoners. The ship was wrecked and Kiefft drowned, in seeming confirmation of De Vries' prophecy. Before his death, he purportedly confessed his wrongdoing to Melyn and Kuyter, who were rescued and who were able to gain their freedom in Holland.

40

The Dutch and New Sweden

The Kiefft administration had witnessed another development annoying to the Dutch West India Company and to the Dutch government: the settlement by Sweden of arbitarily proclaimed Dutch territory on the Delaware. The Delaware, and indeed America as a whole, presented a vast virgin territory for virtually any settlers of any nationality who wished to emigrate. But government sovereignty is always jealous of its self-trumpeted monopoly. In 1633 the New Sweden Company was formed, of equal parts of Dutch and Swedish capital, as a successor company to one of William Usselincx's projects. The idea was the creation of Peter Minuit, the disappointed, ousted governor of New Amsterdam, and of Samuel Blommaert, a director of the Dutch West India Company at odds with the controlling interests of that company. Blommaert, who became an agent of the Swedish Crown, was by far the largest Dutch investor. Of the Swedish investors, three were of the family of Oxenstierna, the prime minister of Sweden.

In the spring of 1638, the first small party of Swedish settlers, led by Minuit, landed on the west bank of the Delaware and built Fort Christina (now Wilmington). Land was purchased from the local Indians. The Swedes lived in uneasy coexistence with their neighbors. The Dutch quickly protested the infringement of their monopoly, and Virginia carped at the competition of Swedish fur trade with the Indians. But the Dutch were constrained from war against New Sweden by the fact that the two countries were allies in the Thirty Years' War, then raging in Europe. Dutch colonists planted a settlement twenty miles north of Fort Christina, but, characteristically, the Dutch area was thinly populated; those who did settle there were soon outnumbered by the Swedes. By 1640 the Swedish colony had a Lutheran minister, Rev. Reorus Torkillus.

The Dutch were less tender, however, with the English settlers. In 1640 the leaders of New Haven Colony, including Governor Theophilus Eaton, formed the Delaware Company in an attempt to secure prosperity for the colony by promoting settlements on the Delaware. The effort was supported financially by the General Court of New Haven Colony. The first New Haven settlement on the Delaware took place in the summer of 1641, in southwestern New Jersey. The small group of settlers began to grow tobacco and to trade with the Indians. Promptly, the Dutch troops at Fort Nassau, aided by a Swedish force, invaded the New Haven land, burned the houses of the settlers, and shipped the prisoners to Manhattan.

Meanwhile, Sweden asserted its rampant nationalism by moving to put the New Sweden Company under Swedish governmental control. In 1641 the Swedes bought out the Dutch investors in the company and the following year the Swedish Crown moved in to exert full control over the company's affairs. By 1642 New Sweden was under the direct rule of the Swedish Council of State, which appointed as the new governor the veteran soldier of fortune, Johan Printz.

Printz immediately began a campaign of harassment of the small New Haven settlement and its leader, George Lamberton, whom he forbade to trade without a license. Under this treatment, the New Haven settlement soon collapsed. Flushed with the victory, Printz established a series of forts, including Fort Elfsborg, near Salem Creek, and Fort New Krisholm at the mouth of the Schuykill River on the west bank of the Delaware.

By 1644 New Sweden reached its peak of population, less than three hundred. This contrasted to a population in all of New Netherland of 2,000. But from that point on, this already small colony entered into a decline. For one thing, Sweden was interested in tobacco, and not in the fur available in the Delaware Valley.

To return to New Netherland proper, we have seen that Peter Stuyvesant was every bit as rigorous a tyrant as his predecessor, albeit more sophisticated and systematic in his depredations. As soon as he took office he persecuted the critics of Kiefft, and threatened to hang anyone appealing his decisions to Holland. He also decreed that no liquor be sold to any Indians, and that none at all be sold on Sunday mornings or after nine o'clock curfew. Taxes were raised sharply, a new excise was laid on wines and spirits, and export taxes on furs increased to thirty percent. When these laws were not observed, Stuyvesant added corporal punishment to the usual fines. All forms of smuggling and illegal trading were, of course, forbidden on pain of heavy penalties.

Stuyvesant, therefore, was rapidly acquiring the reputation in the colony of being little different from the hated Kiefft. But Stuyvesant elaborated a sophisticated refinement. After enmeshing the economy in a network of restrictions and prohibitions, Stuyvesant in return for heavy fees sold *exemptions* from these regulations. In short, Stuyvesant saw that the key to wealth for a government ruler is to create the opportunity for monopoly privilege (for example, by outlawing and regulating productive activities) and then to sell these privileges for what the traffic can bear. Stuyvesant's sales yielded him a fortune during his term in office, in currency and in land.

To levy increased taxes, Stuyvesant, too, was forced to call together representatives of wealthy families of the colony—in this case a group of Nine Men. The Nine Men were chosen as advisers and judges by eighteen men, who in turn had been elected by Dutch householders of Manhattan, Flatlands, and Breukelen (now northwestern Brooklyn), in September 1647. Stuyvesant realized that, rather than rule totally alone, it would be far shrewder to *share* his monopoly gains with the Nine Men, thus cementing them to his rule and warding off the rise of the sort of serious opposition that had ousted Kiefft. And so Stuyvesant pleased the Nine Men by restricting the crucial fur trade of the Hudson Valley to the old residents, the new ones needing considerable property to be admitted. This was later expanded, however, to a fee requirement for all residents, with the fee being a purchase of the approval of Governor Stuyvesant. After this expansion, there was no incentive for the Nine Men to continue to back the director. All these various taxes and regulations, however, were generally evaded by shippers and traders—the reaction of traders to harassment and depredation from time immemorial. These successful evasions benefited the traders and the mass of consumers alike.

The honeymoon with the Nine Men did not last long. For one thing, Stuyvesant had refused to permit New England ships in New Netherland ports, even though New England permitted entry of the ships from New Netherland. In 1648, New England retaliated against all Dutch trade with the Indians, causing considerable economic distress in the Dutch colony. Another important factor in this distress was the high customs in New Amsterdam and the heavy penalties for evasion imposed there. Spurred by the withering of commerce subsequent to the New England regulation, the Nine Men, led by their president, Adrien Van der Donck, patroon of Yonkers, appealed the Stuyvesant ruling to Holland. Stuyvesant seized the papers of the Nine Men, arrested Van der Donck, and expelled him from their membership.

At this point, none other than Cornelis Melyn arrived from Holland, brandishing a safe-conduct from the States-General as well as a condemnation of Stuyvesant's harsh treatment of Melyn and Kuyter. Chastened temporarily, Stuyvesant released Van der Donck, and allowed the Nine Men to send their petition to the States-General. The petition, sent in the fall of 1649, asked the States-General to take over the government of New Netherland from the West India Company, in order to allow local self-government in New Amsterdam and to encourage rather than restrict trade. The petition also included a severe indictment of the government of Peter Stuyvesant and of the Dutch West India Company. As the petition charged: "Nobody is unmolested or secured in his property longer than the Director pleases, who is generally inclined to confiscating." The petition wisely noted, "A covetous chief makes poor subjects."

Oddly enough, Stuyvesant's main support at this time came from a group of English settlers on Long Island, headed by George Baxter of Gravesend, who was Stuyvesant's appointed English secretary of state. The magistrates of the English settlements of Gravesend and Hempstead fawningly expressed the fervent hope for no change of government, praised the existing strong government, and warned that any democratic procedure in New Netherland would surely lead to anarchy and ruin. Three years after the petition, the company's sole concession was to order Stuyvesant to grant a municipal government to New Amsterdam. However, this was only a *pro forma* victory for the idea of limiting government; Stuyvesant insisted on retaining the power to appoint all of the municipal officials, and to decree the municipal ordinances.

In foreign affairs Stuyvesant was cautious and conciliatory regarding the power of the English colonies, realizing as he did that Connecticut's and New Haven's activities on the Connecticut River, Westchester, and Long Island constituted a potential threat to Dutch rule. In 1650, Stuyvesant negotiated a boundary settlement with the New England Confederation, partitioning Long Island at Oyster Bay. This partition continued to be upheld even after the outbreak of the first Anglo-Dutch War (1652-54). Indeed, the only loss suffered by New Netherland in that war was Connecticut's seizure of Fort Good Hope, which had been a hopeless enclave in hostile territory for a long while. The Dutch West Indies Company, however, suffered very seriously from the Anglo-Dutch War. For England was allied with newly independent (1640) Portugal, which proceeded to reconquer Angola and northern Brazil, the company's most lucrative possessions (England was rewarded with rights in the slave trade by the Portuguese). The company's financial problems were compounded by lack of support from the government and the merchants, who preferred private trade to the expenses of monopolies and colonial government.

Stuyvesant's own problems during the war were chiefly internal rather than external. On the outbreak of the war, the English settlers were alienated by the company's prohibition of any but Dutchmen in public office. Captain John Underhill organized a one-man rebellion at Hempstead and Flushing, claiming allegiance to England and denouncing Stuyvesant's tyranny: his seizure of private land, imposition of heavy taxes, religious persecution, banning of any election procedures, and imprisonment of men without trial. Underhill was forced to flee to Rhode Island.

More significant was the disaffection of such former lieutenants of Stuyvesant as George Baxter. Baxter's opposition forced the reluctant director to agree to a "landtag," or popular convention, to meet to discuss public affairs. The landtag met in December 1653 with four Dutch and four English towns represented by nineteen delegates. (The Dutch towns: New Amsterdam, Breukelen, Flatlands, and Flatbush; the English: Flushing, Gravesend, Hempstead, and Middleburg.) Despite the partition treaty of 1650, most of the new settlers of western Long Island were English, and many of these settlements had acquired some rights to local self-government from the charter of 1640. Now they were in the forefront of the complaints of arbitrary government. Ostensibly called to concentrate on the English war, the landtag's meeting was turned by Baxter—attracted out of office to the liberal cause—to the most pressing problem, Stuyvesant's own tyranny. Baxter drew up, and the landtag unanimously approved, a Remonstrance and Petition attacking all the despotic evils of the existing regime: especially arbitrary government by the director and his council, appointment of officials and magistrates without consent of the people, and granting of large tracts of land to favorites of the director. They also demanded a permanent landtag with power to raise taxes and help select officials, and they asserted that "the law of nature" authorized all men to associate in defense of their liberty and property. Here were the very "rights of man" which Peter Stuyvesant had always despised.

Stuyvesant, like Kiefft, had thought his subjects would come together to meet an "external threat"; he found them instead seizing the opportunity to challenge the threat to their life, liberty, and property that they were suffering chronically at home. Stuyvesant, of course, brusquely rejected the Remonstrance and promptly declared the assembly illegal and ordered it dissolved. Stuyvesant poured his scorn on the "law of nature"; only appointed *magistrates,* not private individuals, had the right to hold political meetings: "We derive our authority from God and the company, not from a few ignorant subjects, and we alone can call the inhabitants together." Moreover, charged the director, the whole proceedings "smelt of rebellion."

Stuyvesant was able to continue the arbitrary rule that was crippling and greatly slowing down the development of the colony. Indeed, the company not only approved the director's treatment of the landtag, but gently chided him for engaging in any sort of dialogue with "the rabble." Encouraged, Stuyvesant expelled Baxter and James Hubbard of Gravesend from their civil offices. When the latter raised the English flag at Gravesend and both proclaimed their allegiance to Cromwell, Stuyvesant sent a troop to imprison Hubbard and Baxter. The director's victory over his opposition was complete.

As we have noted, Stuyvesant's foreign policy, in welcome contrast to Kiefft's, was cautious and conciliatory. When Stuyvesant assumed office, he found Governor Printz of New Sweden constructing many forts on the Delaware River. To counter this expansionist policy, Stuyvesant built Fort Beversrede (now Philadelphia) in the spring of 1648, across the Schuylkill River from the new Swedish Fort New Krisholm. But the rambunctious Swedes twice burned Fort Beversrede during that year, and each time the Dutch simply rebuilt, without retaliation. Then, in 1651 the Dutch built Fort Casimir (New Castle) below Fort Christina; strategically located, it commanded the river approaches to most of New Sweden.

During the early 1650s, friction was building up in Europe between Sweden and the United Provinces. The Thirty Years' War had ended in 1648, and now the two countries would soon erupt into open conflict over Sweden's interventions in Denmark. In this delicate situation, the new governor of New Sweden committed the enormous blunder of launching a surprise attack on Fort Casimir, and thus helped end New Sweden forevermore. Surely this governor, Johan Rising, an associate of the powerful Oxenstierna family, must have realized that his tiny colony of less than a few hundred souls could hardly have held its own in a war with New Netherland. And yet, inexplicably, Rising suddenly attacked and seized Fort Casimir in 1654, renaming it Fort Trefaldighet. This provocation was the last straw for the hitherto patient Dutch, who decided to wipe out New Sweden for good.

The following year the Dutch sent seven ships, headed by Stuyvesant, and quickly forced the surrender of the two Swedish forts. The Swedish governor was returned to Sweden. Most of the Swedish settlers elected to remain, but were forced to take a loyalty oath to Holland. New Sweden had ended. It was now a part of the enlarged New Netherland.

The Delaware Bay area was now governed by the Dutch, who provided the officialdom and the fur traders, but the bulk of the settlers—amounting to about six hundred by 1659—were Swedes and Finns, who provided the farmers and village governments. (Finland was, in those years, under Swedish rule, and hence many of the "Swedish" immigrants were Finns.) In 1656 there occurred the fateful separation of the west bank of the Delaware River—from Fort Christina (Wilmington) southward—from the rest of the Delaware River settlements. In short, a separate life began for the future colony of "Delaware." As a direct result of the highly expensive expedition to conquer New Sweden, the heavily indebted Dutch West India Company in 1656 transferred its sovereignty over part of this area to its creditor, the city of Amsterdam. Three years later, the company transferred the entire west bank, from Fort Christina southward, to Amsterdam.

The city of Amsterdam sent out more settlers to its new land; renamed Fort Christina, Altena; and named its new colony New Amstel, which was headed by one Alrichs. In 1659 Alrichs was succeeded by Alexander d'Hinoyossa, who became the sole governor of what was later to be Delaware.

The Swedish and Finnish settlers soon found that their lot under Amsterdam rule was much worse than under New Netherland, and the Dutch West India Company. Their freedom of trade was far more restricted, and the city of Amsterdam's officials arrogated to themselves a tight monopoly of all trade. Stuyvesant was also bitter at this governmental rival in his former domain.

41

New Netherland Persecutes
the Quakers

As Swedish and Finnish Lutherans were incorporated into the domain of New Netherland, the problem of theocracy and religious persecution became acute. We have indicated that New Netherland was largely governed by that wing of Dutch opinion that advocated Calvinist theocracy, as over against the libertarian approach of their Republican rivals. The Dutch West India Company in general and Peter Stuyvesant in particular hated the idea of religious toleration and desired theocracy under the Dutch Reformed Church, as directed by the synod, or classis, of Amsterdam. In 1654 Stuyvesant forbade any Lutheran minister from holding services, and the company decreed that only Dutch Reformed services were permissible in the colony. In 1656 all other religious meetings were prohibited under heavy fine and no baptism was permitted except that of the Dutch Reformed Church. Indeed, Stuyvesant went so far as to imprison several persons for attending private Lutheran meetings. But for this he was censured by the States-General. And in 1657 even a commission from Amsterdam to serve as a Lutheran pastor did not save the newly arrived Rev. Ernestus Goetwater from being shipped back to Holland by the authorities. Leading the campaign of persecution was the influential Dutch Calvinist minister, the Reverend Mr. Megapolensis.

It was at this time that the great wave of Quaker persecutions began in New England and Peter Stuyvesant was not to be caught lagging. New Netherland, indeed, was distinguished, even among the colonies, for its extensive use of torture—particularly the rack—to extract confessions and to whip and mutilate runaway servants and slaves. Now, in 1656, Stuyvesant decreed that Quakers could be tied to a cart's tail and assigned hard labor for two years.

The first Quakers in New Netherland arrived from England in 1657. Two women, Mary Weatherhead and Dorothy Waugh, were thrown into a dungeon as soon as they began to preach and after a week were sent, tied up, to Rhode Island—that "sewer of heretics." Robert Hodgson, another English Quaker, found many receptive hearts in Long Island and prepared to preach at Hempstead. There he was seized by a local magistrate, Richard Gildersleeve, and imprisoned in the latter's house. But Hodgson was able to preach even under house arrest. Governor Stuyvesant now sent an armed guard to Hempstead, bound Hodgson closely, and arrested two women for the crime of giving space to the Quaker. The three were taken by cart, Hodgson dragged at the tail, to New Amsterdam. Prevented from speaking in his own defense, Robert Hodgson, for the crime of being a Quaker, was fined 600 guilders and sentenced to two years at hard labor. But Hodgson courageously refused to cooperate in this unjust sentence; he refused to work or pay. Whereupon he was chained to a wheelbarrow and beaten with a tarred rope. This treatment continued for three days, and Hodgson still refused to work or pay. For speaking out of turn, the Quaker was hung up and whipped at Stuyvesant's order. The director then told him that he would be beaten every day until he worked and paid the fine. Finally Hodgson yielded and agreed to work in prison. However, pressures on the director led him to waive the fine and eventually Hodgson was permitted to leave the colony for Rhode Island.

A fine of fifty pounds was now proclaimed for anyone found sheltering a Quaker for so much as one night, and the law against meetings was revived. The first enforcement was against Harry Townsend of Flushing Town on Long Island. He was thrown into prison when he refused to pay a heavy fine for attending a Quaker meeting. This spurred a complaint by the English settlers of Flushing. They protested that they were obliged to do good to *all* Christians, including Quakers, and that they would therefore continue to shelter them as "God shall persuade our conscience."

The receptivity of Flushing and other western Long Island towns to religious freedom, and even to the Quaker creed itself, deserves explanation. These towns were settled by New Englanders, but the settlers were not the Puritans who peopled the Connecticut and New Haven towns of eastern Long Island. The fountainhead of this different migration was Lady Deborah Moody. Born in England and persecuted by the Church of England, this widow had been invited by her friends the Winthrops to move to Massachusetts to gain her religious freedom. Settling at Lynn, Massachusetts, in 1640, but belonging to the Salem church, Lady Moody and a few followers were harassed by Massachusetts for opposing infant baptism and adopting the Baptist creed. Hence Lady Moody, like other heretics, left Massachusetts in 1643. She bought an estate at Gravesend, Long Island, where she was followed by many other families from Lynn. We have seen that Gravesend, alone, survived the Indian war against Willem Kiefft. In the next decade other Lynn Baptists as well as Seekers organized more settlements on west Long Island: Flushing, Jamaica, Hempstead, and Oyster Bay. By 1653 Peter Stuyvesant was complaining that the Long Island towns were selecting local magistrates without regard to their Calvinism, and that Gravesend in particular was electing Baptists and freethinkers.

The persecution of the Quakers now worked, as in New England, to multiply greatly the number of Quaker converts. Lady Moody and many of her followers from Lynn became Quakers at this time.

To return to the Flushing protest, this was a remonstrance drawn up in a public meeting and signed by thirty-one men, headed by the town clerk, Edward Hart, and the sheriff, Tobias Feake. The remonstrance pointed not only to Christian conscience but also to the fact that their town charter "grants liberty of conscience without modification" and that they intended to stand by these rights. Many of the signers were originally from Lynn; others were English Pilgrims who had lived in Leyden, Holland.

For this heroic act of defiance, Stuyvesant dismissed Feake and Hart from their official positions, harshly imprisoned the latter and heavily fined the former, and deprived Flushing of the right to hold town meetings. But this tyranny was in vain, as the illegal sheltering of Quakers and the conversion to their creed continued and intensified. Also in vain were the jailings of Quakers, of whom there were at one time nine imprisoned in New Amsterdam. The Dutch Calvinist ministers Megapolensis and Drosius despairingly reported in 1658: "The raving Quakers . . . continued to disturb the people of this province. Although our government has issued orders against these fanatics, nevertheless they do not fail to pour forth their venom. There is but one place in New England where they are tolerated and that is Rhode Island, which is the sewer of New England."

The persecution of the Quakers in New Netherland was finally ended by the case of John Bowne. Bowne, a Quaker convert in Flushing, had been fined twenty-five pounds for holding a meeting, and threatened with banishment for nonpayment. After three months in prison, Bowne was deported to Amsterdam, the council deciding on banishment "for the welfare of the community and to crush as far as it is possible that abominable sect who treat with contempt both the political magistrates and the ministers of God's holy Word and endeavor to undermine the police and religion." But Bowne put his case before the Dutch West India Company in Amsterdam. Shocked at the excesses, the company directed Stuyvesant that "the consciences of men ought to remain free and unshackled. *Let everyone remain free* so long as he is modest, moderate, and his political conduct irreproachable." Bowne returned to Flushing a free man in 1663, and the Quakers were not persecuted again. As in New England, the Quakers had by the early 1660s triumphed over persecution.

42

The Fall and Breakup
of New Netherland

New Amsterdam functioned as the major center of an illegal but free trade for the English colonies in America, for the purchase of European manufactures and for the sale of enumerated commodities, especially tobacco. Following the Restoration of Charles II, and the elaboration of the Navigation Act structure, England began to find New Netherland to be a major irritant, a major loophole in its attempt to mold and restrict colonial trade.

The English Council of Trade, established in the autumn of 1660, complained regularly to the government that New Netherland was the center of free trade in America in violation of the acts of trade. Furthermore, English ire was drawn toward New Netherland because the latter vigorously competed with the English colonies for settlement by Englishmen. The colonial concern of the English government was reflected in its continuation of the Protectorate project for settlement and development of the island of Jamaica. The colonial government there would be completely dominated by the English government and was to be the standard form imposed on the colonies. Since an elected assembly such as Virginia's would be attractive to settlers, this form of government was pressed on Jamaica. And the fear that Dutch toleration would attract English settlers to Long Island instead of to Jamaica caused the English government to exempt the English colonies from the principal religious act of the Restoration—the Act of Uniformity of May 1662. In February 1662 the Dutch West India Company had invited all those "of tender conscience in England or elsewhere oppressed" to settle on Long Island, where the major English settlements in New Netherland were located.

Since this threatened to attract Dissenters from England, where repression of the Puritans was increasing, and especially Dissenters from New England, the 1662 Act of Uniformity did not apply to the colonies, which had been included in the 1559 Act. Thus, Dutch colonial competition provided the New England colonies with religious benefits as well as economic and political ones.

The Dutch West India Company, furthermore, was a point of special animosity to the English imperialists, as it was a major competitor of the principal instrument of English speculation and expansion, the Company of Royal Adventurers into Africa, which had raided the Dutch slave ports in West Africa. When the Spanish government sold the slave-trade contract, or Asiento de negros, to a Genoese company, which subcontracted the Asiento to the Dutch West India Company and the Company of Royal Adventurers into Africa, the English company was granted a new charter (January 1663) and the monopoly of trade in slaves from West Africa to the English colonies, as well as the exclusive right to occupy ports in West Africa.

In 1650 New Netherland and the New England Confederation had come to an agreement by which the English towns of eastern Long Island came under Connecticut or New Haven government, and the western quarter of the island remained Dutch. Connecticut, emboldened by its new royal charter, now also pressed its presumptuous claims to Dutch territory, specifically to Westchester County and to the towns of western Long Island, where Englishmen had continued to settle. Peter Stuyvesant realized that in any conflict, New Netherland would be hopelessly beaten by the English colonies alone. Its population of 5,000 contrasted with one of 8,000 in Connecticut, over 20,000 in Massachusetts, and 27,000 in Virginia. As early as 1655, Stuyvesant had displayed his caution in relations with the English when the New Englander, Thomas Pell, purchased and settled the Westchester land of Pelham Manor, formerly Anne's Hoeck, where Anne Hutchinson had been murdered. Stuyvesant ordered Pell to leave, bag and baggage, but did nothing when Pell failed to comply. And now, in late 1663, the English towns of Long Island rebelled and proclaimed King Charles as their sovereign. They formed themselves into a league (consisting of Hempstead, Gravesend, Flushing, Oyster Bay, Middleburg, and Jamaica) and chose the veteran adventurer John Scott of Hempstead as their president. The rebels thereupon called upon England for action to crush the colony of New Netherland. Stuyvesant again pursued the course of prudence, and agreed to Connecticut demands to give up Westchester and the Long Island towns. When interethnic riots ensued on Long Island, however, Stuyvesant sent an armed force to protect the Dutch Long Island towns of Breukelen and Flatbush.

Amid this growing crisis, a landtag met in New Amsterdam in April 1664, but could only bow reluctantly to *force majeure* and agree to yield to Connecticut's terms. But in the meanwhile, a special committee of the

Privy Council found a solution (in January 1664) to the problem of the English settlers in New Netherland and the threat of free trade to England that New Netherland's existence posed: it would end New Netherland's existence by conquest. Consequently, in February a grant and on March 12 a patent were issued to the Duke of York, giving him the territories along the Hudson and Delaware rivers where the Dutch had settled, plus a governmental appropriation of money to cover the expenses of seizing them as well as the Dutch ports of West Africa. The seizure was to be accomplished by the English navy, of which the Duke of York was commander. Of the three-man special committee that had submitted this recommendation to the Privy Council, it should be noted that all were officials of the Admiralty under the Duke of York, and two of them, Lord Berkeley and Sir George Carteret, were promptly rewarded (June 1664) by the grateful Duke with a subgrant of the territory between the Hudson and the Delaware rivers.

In April 1664 the Duke of York appointed Colonel Richard Nicolls to head a commission of four to direct the conquest of New Netherland and to establish English government there. The commissioners, as we have seen, were instructed to arrange for the aid of New England in the conquest of New Netherland, to gain the enforcement of the Navigation Acts, and to settle the disputes in New England. Colonel Nicolls promptly launched an armed expedition to seize New Netherland.

To meet the English force of 1,000 men that arrived at the end of August, Stuyvesant had only 150 soldiers and 250 citizens capable of bearing arms. Not only were the Dutch outnumbered, but disaffection had been strong for years and the burgomasters were strongly inclined to submission. This inclination was greatly intensified by Nicolls' generous terms to the Dutch, offering liberty of conscience, the retention of property rights, and freedom of trade and immigration. Furthermore, the Dutch citizens were promised freedom from conscription and guaranteed against any billeting of soldiers in their homes.

It was not lost on the realistic Dutch people that they would be enjoying far more liberty under English rule than they ever had under the despotic company government. The burgomasters and even the magistrates now clamored for submission. In a tantrum at surrendering his power, Stuyvesant tore the English message to bits, but the people demanded to hear it and Nicholas Bayard, one of the leaders of the Dutch community, pieced it together and read it to the crowd, which now called exuberantly for submission. The people were intelligent enough to regard their lives and liberties more highly than they did a remote and artificial patriotism. As the historian John Fiske pointed out: "There were many in the town who did not regard a surrender to England as the worst of misfortunes. They were weary of [Stuyvesant's] arbitrary ways . . . and in this mood they lent a willing ear to the offer of English liberties. Was it not better to surrender on favorable terms than to lose their lives in behalf of—what? Their homes and families? No indeed, but in behalf of a remote government which had done little or nothing for them! If they were lost to Holland, it was Holland's loss, not theirs."*

Yet, Stuyvesant, a hard-liner to the last, desperately tried to rouse the rapidly defecting Dutch to resistance to the death. Even his closest supporters turned against him. His councillor, Micasius de Sille, warned that "resistance is not soldiership, it is sheer madness." The rigorous Calvinist minister Reverend Mr. Megapolensis urged that "it is wrong to shed blood to no purpose." Even Stuyvesant's own son, Balthazar, affixed his name to a remonstrance, signed by nearly a hundred leading citizens, that pled for surrender. Finally, left alone in his colony, Peter Stuyvesant gave in, and on September 7 surrendered to the English. Colonel George Cartwright, a fellow royal commissioner of Nicolls', obtained the peaceful surrender of Fort Orange on September 20. The English promptly assumed and continued the understanding the Dutch had with the Iroquois. New Netherland had disappeared.

The English had one last military task: the conquest of the separate colony of New Amstel. Nicolls sent another royal commissioner, Sir Robert Carr, to the Delaware. Once again the sensible Dutch burghers of New Amstel were eager to surrender. But the autocratic governor d'Hinoyossa insisted on hopeless resistance. The English finally stormed and captured Fort Casimir on October 10, and English troops took revenge by plundering and killing some of the citizenry. The Atlantic coast from Maine to South Carolina was now in the hands of the English.

It is an ironic footnote on Peter Stuyvesant's frenzy at the idea of surrender that he passed his last days, in the late 1660s and early 1670s, in peaceful contentment on his farm in Manhattan, not only unmolested but in friendship with Governor Nicolls. Shorn of power, Peter Stuyvesant was a happier and perhaps a wiser man.

The first step of the new governor, Colonel Nicolls, was to change important names from Dutch to English: and so New Amsterdam became the city of New York, New Netherland became New York Province, and Fort Orange was renamed Albany, after one of the Duke of York's titles. West of the Delaware, New Amstel was changed to New Castle, and Altena to Wilmington.

Trouble in Delaware began immediately, as Sir Robert Carr plundered the Dutch settlements unmercifully, confiscating property for the use of his family and friends, plundering houses, and selling Dutch soldiers into servitude in Virginia. Nicolls rushed down to Delaware, removed Carr, and placed his son, Capt. John Carr, in command of the district and at the head of a council of seven.

Boundary and jurisdiction offered a longer-range problem in the Delaware district. For Lord Baltimore claimed all of the west bank of the Delaware on behalf of Maryland, under Maryland's charter from Charles I. But the Duke

*John Fiske, The Dutch and Quaker Colonies in America, 1:289.

of York refused to remove his troops, and the Delaware region remained as part of New York Province. Another boundary dispute requiring settlement was the conflict with Connecticut. According to the Duke of York's charter, New York could have claimed all of Connecticut up to the Connecticut River, thus almost obliterating the colony, but Nicolls amicably settled for Westchester County, and Connecticut obtained the land to the east. This territory included the town of Stamford, which had tried to proclaim itself an independent republic. On the other hand, New York, according to the clearcut terms of the charter, obtained jurisdiction over all of Long Island. In imitation of Yorkshire in England, Nicolls promptly organized Long Island, Staten Island, and Westchester, with their preponderant English population, into one district called Yorkshire. The new district contained three subdistricts or "ridings": the East (now Suffolk County and most of Nassau County); the West, including what is now Kings County and Staten Island; and the North, including what is now Westchester, Bronx, and Queens counties.

As a result of the king's grant to the Duke of York, New York now included Delaware, the County of Cornwall (all of Maine east of the Kennebec), and such islands off Massachusetts as Nantucket and Martha's Vineyard. But one breakup of the old New Netherland territory was a bitter blow to Nicolls' hopes of power. In June 1664, before New Netherland had even been won, the Duke of York had granted the territory between the Hudson and Delaware rivers, bounded at 41° on the north, to the proprietorship of two of his court favorites, John Lord Berkeley and Sir George Carteret. This new province of New Jersey now lay outside New York jurisdiction.

As proprietors of New Jersey, Berkeley and Carteret were anxious to promote rapid colonization. Hence, in February 1665 they promulgated the liberal Concessions and Agreements, which granted religious freedom to the inhabitants and which offered one hundred fifty acres of land for each indentured servant brought over—subject to quitrents of one-half pence per acre to the proprietors. Each servant, upon completing his term, was to receive seventy-five acres of land. Furthermore, the concessions granted the right of freeholders to form their own representative assembly. The governor and council were to be appointed by the proprietary, but no taxes could be levied without the approval of the assembly. (These particular provisions were virtually identical with the abortive Concessions and Agreements promulgated by the Carolina proprietary six weeks earlier.) Appointed as first governor of New Jersey was Philip Carteret, a distant relative of the proprietor. Carteret set up his capital at the new settlement of Elizabethtown. Attracted by the guarantee of religious liberty and by the open land, New Englanders soon poured into New Jersey, adding such settlements as Piscataway, Woodbridge, Middletown, and Shrewsbury to the older Dutch town of Bergen, which included Pavonia and Hoboken. In particular, many citizens of New Haven, disgruntled at the seizure by Connecticut, came to New Jersey. The Reverend Abraham Pierson, the arch-Calvinist minister of Branford, led his flock, as we have seen, to found New Ark. Attempting to duplicate the theocracy of New Haven, they provided in the town constitution that only Puritan church members could vote.

Meanwhile, after temporarily leaving the Dutch officials in office, Governor Nicolls of New York drew up, for the largely English-speaking district of Yorkshire, a set of fundamental laws known as the "Duke's Laws." The Duke's Laws did not grant anything like the degree of representative government achieved in the other English colonies. There was no elected assembly. Instead, the legislative power was exercised by a Court of Assizes, a body of judges appointed by and subject to the veto of the governor. On the other hand, trial by jury was introduced into a colony that did not have the safeguard before. The Anglican church was now established, with the church supported in each town, but freedom of conscience was granted to all of the sects. Neither were there any town meetings of the old New England model, but the towns were allowed to elect a ruling constable and a board of eight overseers, who were, however, accountable to the governor. The patroons were confirmed in their domains, now called "manors," and the militia was to be under the control of the provincial government.

In general, we may say that the Duke's Laws were more liberal than the old despotic Dutch rule, but far inferior to New England's. For the Long Island towns, used to a considerable amount of self-government, the Duke's Laws were a decidedly backward step. In March 1665 a convention of thirty-four delegates from seventeen Yorkshire towns of Westchester and Long Island (thirteen English and four Dutch) was called to approve the Duke's Laws. The Long Islanders, who had been promised by Nicolls their original New England town autonomy and a popular, self-governing assembly, were understandably bitter at this about-face. However, to their great regret, the convention finally gave its approval to the laws. But the Long Island townsmen continued to balk, and to object bitterly to what they believed to be a betrayal by their own deputies. John Underhill attacked the new laws as "arbitrary power." They also objected vehemently to Nicolls' decree forcing all settlers and landowners in the province to pay a fee to the government to have their land titles reconfirmed. The object of the government was not only to obtain the fine, but to force the lands to enter the rolls to become subject to payment of quitrents. So strong were the protests that the new Court of Assizes decreed that anyone criticizing the Hempstead deputies would be punished for "slander." Three protesters from Flushing and Jamaica were duly fined and placed into the stocks. The townsmen even practiced a form of nonviolent resistance, refusing to accept the governor's appointments as town constables. The governor finally imposed a fine of five pounds to force the appointees to accept their posts.

Flushing was in such a rebellious state in 1667 that Nicolls finally disbanded its militia and disarmed all of its citizens. And so bitter were the Long Island towns about reconfirming their land titles for a fee, and for subjection to quitrents, that they did not confirm the titles for the entire first decade of English rule. These New Englanders had always been able to own their land in full without having to pay feudal quitrents.

Another deep economic grievance of the Long Islanders was Nicolls' attempt to enforce the payment of customs taxes on direct trade with Long Island—a threat that was countered by extensive smuggling. Nicolls' attempt included the hated appointment of a deputy collector of customs for Long Island to supplement the collector at New York City.

In New York City a similar but even less democratic system was imposed; all the municipal officials were appointed annually by the governor. The English offices of mayor, alderman, and sheriff replaced such Dutch posts as the *Koopman* and the *Schout-Fiscal.* The Dutch population of the city protested this arbitrary rule at length and asked at least for the right of the judicial and legislative New York City Council to present two lists, from which the governor would have to choose the next council. This concession was finally granted in 1669. In 1668 the Duke's Laws were extended to Delaware and to the remainder of New York, excluding such predominantly Dutch areas as Kingston, Albany, and the new western settlement of Schenectady, where the Dutch laws and institutions were allowed to remain.

During the second Anglo-Dutch War of 1664–67, in which the French took the side of the Dutch, Nicolls, as the king's spokesman in America, called repeatedly for joint New York–New England action against Dutch and French America. But New England and especially Massachusetts pursued a wise course of peace and neutrality. In February 1666 England, joined by Nicolls, instructed the New England colonies to organize an expedition for the purpose of seizing Canada from the French. But the New Englanders stalled and the project came to nothing, much to the annoyance of Governor Nicolls, who had to be content with depriving the Dutch citizens, the great majority of the population of the province, of all their arms.

The Dutch citizens suffered considerable grievances from the English troops, especially during the war. Nicolls imposed heavier taxes upon them to maintain these troops, and billeted the troops in the homes of the unwilling Dutch burghers. Tax delinquency rose sharply during the war period, and when Nicolls requested aid in fortifying New York City, the Dutch balked so long as their own arms were not returned to them—certainly a telling point. Even Governor Nicolls recognized that the English soldiers tended to treat the Dutch citizens very badly. One important incident occurred at the Dutch town of Esopus (now Kingston) in 1667. Here the English Captain Brodhead ruled the citizenry in high-handed and dictatorial fashion. One time, Brodhead denounced a man for celebrating Christmas in the Dutch rather than in the Anglican manner. Finally, Brodhead refused to obey the wish of the civil authorities of the town to set a certain prisoner free. When the Kingstonians protested, Captain Brodhead threatened to burn down the town. The threat was enough to cause a riot, and finally an attack on Brodhead; a Dutchman was killed in the melee by one of Brodhead's troop. The governor then stepped in to suspend Brodhead and also punish the leading Dutch resisters.

The Dutch citizens of New York City also had an important economic grievance, and good reason to deem themselves economically betrayed by the new regime. In the surrender treaty of New Netherland, the English had made various promises that trade with Holland and in Dutch ships would continue freely. But this was in direct conflict with the English Navigation Acts. What was to be done? Nicolls at first allowed a few selected New York merchants to trade with Holland. After the war was over, agitation for permission to trade with Holland was renewed. To avoid a decline in the Indian fur trade (the Indians preferred Dutch goods), and wholesale emigration by the Dutch citizens, Nicolls persuaded the Duke of York in 1667 to permit Dutch trade with New York. And yet, in late 1668, this right was abruptly canceled, despite strong protests from the Dutch officials of the city government, as contradictory to basic English imperial policy.

PART V

The Northern Colonies in the Last Quarter of the Seventeenth Century

43

The Northern Colonies, 1666-1675

By the mid-1660s the enormous impact of the Restoration crisis in the northern colonies was over, and the colonies began to settle down to their changed conditions. In New England, Connecticut, and Rhode Island not only self-governing remained, but confirmation of this role was won by royal charter. Rhode Island also retained its control over Narrangansett Country despite Connecticut's attempted seizure. Connecticut succeeded in seizing and annexing the Colony of New Haven, thus eliminating the last major bastion of Calvinist ultraorthodoxy in New England. Massachusetts triumphed over the attempts of the royal commission to bring it to heel, and it remained defiant and self-governing. The Maine towns were organized into a separate government by the commissioners, but they were soon reannexed by Massachusetts Bay. But the rigid rule of the Massachusetts theocratic oligarchy was steadily weakening from within as the more liberal merchants rose to greater influence with the rise of Boston as a crucial trade center of New England. The Half-Way Covenant demonstrated the weakening of the Puritan zeal of the younger generation of the Bay Colony, and the persecution of the Quakers was virtually over.

In the Middle Colonies, the critical event was the almost bloodless seizure of New Netherland by the English, and its transformation into the proprietary colony of New York, owned by the Duke of York. The province included the district of New Castle (now Delaware) but the intermediary area of New Jersey was granted to two of the Duke's favorites, who introduced a representative government far more liberal than that of New York in order to encourage rapid settlement. And the principle of religious liberty, Quakers included, spread through the colonies upon its triumph in New York and New Jersey.

The accession of English rule in New York touched off the second Anglo-Dutch War (1664–67), and the Treaty of Breda (July 1667) formally ceded

New Netherland to England. Free trade between New York and Holland was also agreed upon for a seven-year period. Nicolls' successor as governor, Col. Francis Lovelace, won the approval of the people in 1668 by abolishing New York City's two social castes, created by Peter Stuyvesant a decade before. These were the "great burghers" (including government officials, officers of the militia, ministers, and others paying fifty guilders into the city treasury) and the "small burghers" (including all others in the city, and strangers paying a fee of twenty-five guilders). Only great burghers had been eligible for public office and had been exempt from certain penalties in criminal cases. The abolition of this caste system was applauded, but the conflict with the Long Island towns continued and intensified. New York was now the only colony imposing taxes without the consent of a representative assembly, and the New Englanders on Long Island were used to far better treatment. And as we have seen, the Long Islanders deeply resented the requirement of paying customs duties at the same rate as New York City. In addition, they protested bitterly a tax that was levied on them in 1670 by Governor Lovelace to pay for repairs to the fort on Manhattan— formerly Fort Amsterdam, now Fort James. The Long Island towns drew up a remonstrance at Huntington that declared their refusal to pay such a tax and that rested their case on the time-honored principle of English liberties and of "no taxation without representation." We have seen that a similar tax protest had wrung representative government (albeit an oligarchic one) from Massachusetts in 1631; but now the resistance was dealing with royal authority. Lovelace denounced the protest as seditious, ordered the signers prosecuted, and had the petition publicly burned at the city hall. And the people, who had so recently been promised "English liberties" instead of arbitrary Dutch rule, were now told that their "liberty" should consist of thinking of nothing but "how to pay taxes."

In 1673 the embittered eastern Long Island towns of Southampton, Southold, and East Hampton petitioned the king for separate English charters for themselves. These rejected, they asked the king, unsuccessfully, to be allowed to return to the jurisdiction of Connecticut. Their reasons: the lack of a representative assembly, the lower tax rates in Connecticut, and their natural trading ties with New England (including exchange of Long Island whale oil for New England goods).

Another cause of discontent lay in New York City. There the government organized the cartmen into a monopoly cartel or guild: the guild was granted the monopoly of the carting business in the city. In return, the carters were forced to work for the city one day a week. As guaranteed monopolists, the cartmen naturally felt that they no longer had to supply their customers with efficient or courteous service; and the courts of the city tried to correct the matter by threatening to allow nonguild carters to operate. But these threats did not overcome the unfortunate consequences of the government's original intervention: the guild monopoly.

In New Jersey the new settlers from New England, used to democratic self-government, quickly began chafing at the rule of Governor Philip

Carteret. Even though the regime was far more liberal than New York's, this was the New Englanders' first encounter with a proprietary governor and his appointed Council, able to veto their decisions. When New Jersey's first Assembly opened in 1668, trouble began almost immediately as the people of Middletown repudiated the election of their deputies, asserting that it was invalid. Their basic complaint was that the deputies, John Bowne (not the same Bowne who had led the protest in Flushing) and James Grover, violated their liberties by voting for an onerous five-pound tax on townships. Middletown rested its legal case on a land grant that had been made to it by Governor Nicolls, before the proprietary grant of New Jersey to Berkeley and Carteret had become known. Middletown then chose two others as their successors, and the nearby townsmen of Shrewsbury selected still others to replace Bowne and Grover, who had also represented them. But Middletown and Shrewsbury insisted that their representatives add to their oath of allegiance the proviso that they could recognize the validity of no act impinging on the liberties of their original patent, which included a seven-year exemption from township taxes.

The Assembly, however, disqualified the proviso and the next delegates and the two towns refused to pay the five-pound township tax. And so Middletown prepared for rebellion. A town meeting in February 1669 ordered its citizens on pain of penalty to aid anyone resisting removal of their possessions, especially by agents of the Assembly. Middletown acknowledged its allegiance to the king, but disclaimed any interest in, or knowledge of, the proprietors. It also objected to paying any feudal quitrents to the proprietors. Middletown had already received the land from Nicolls and had purchased it from the Indians. What did Berkeley and Carteret have to do with it? Even before the Assembly had met, Governor Carteret had forbidden Middletown and Shrewsbury from electing any officials, and now they were warned against exercising any functions. But Middletown and Shrewsbury, undaunted in the face of being declared in contempt of "lawful authority," remained in open defiance of the government and refused to pay the township tax or quitrent.

This was only one of the mounting troubles faced by the New Jersey authorities. The Assembly itself had broken up in disorder when the governor refused to allow his Council and the larger elected Assembly to meet in joint session, a meeting that could have meant surrender of his veto power. The former New Netherland's first attempt at a representative assembly had collapsed.

With no continuing Assembly and Middletown in tax rebellion, the governor soon found Elizabethtown joining the fray. In the spring of 1670 Elizabethtown, maintaining that its land grant from Nicolls exempted it, refused to pay the quitrent. A further grievance of Elizabethtown was that Carteret, one of its residents, insisted on making town decisions without consulting the town meeting. For example, Carteret had revoked the militia commissions of two popular leaders of the town, Luke Watson and John Woodruff, because they had disobeyed him. The following year Elizabethtown engaged in more open defiance: Carteret, without consulting the town meeting, granted town land to Robert Michel, one of his indentured servants now at the end of his term. In protest, the town leaders pulled down Michel's fence and part of his house. Carteret could do nothing in retaliation, and the son of one of the protesters was defiantly chosen as town constable. Finally, a court fined the town leaders for their part of the protest.

Thus, by 1670–71 many of the New Jersey settlements were in revolt against the payment of quitrent. The New England settlers, used to absolute private freehold landed property, were not about to yield supinely to an attempt to impose feudal land tenure upon them. It is characteristic, however, that New Ark, or Newark—the heir of New Haven's absolute theocracy—did not join in the tax strike. Instead, Newark reaffirmed "the renewal of a solemn agreement to submit to law and authority. . . ."

By the spring of 1672 a familiar situation in the history of rebellion had come about: the dynamics of a revolutionary situation had proceeded beyond its original founders. On May 14, deputies from all the towns, even Newark, met in a completely illegal and unrecognized assembly, and formed an openly revolutionary government. All towns were represented except the original rebels, Middletown and Shrewsbury, which decided to keep ignoring any assemblies. Of all the towns, only Woodbridge remained in support of the established government. The revolutionary assembly proceeded to elect Capt. James Carteret, the younger son of the proprietor, as "President of the Province." The rallying around Carteret as the revolutionary leader was, of course, a master-stroke; his family connection was calculated to throw doubt and confusion into anyone loyal to the proprietary. On May 28, the governor and the Council issued an edict ordering the illegal deputies to submit to the governor's authority in ten days or face arrest as mutineers. To insure the split of Middletown and Shrewsbury from the revolutionary towns, the governor confirmed their old rights and privileges, including full power to dispose of their granted lands, freedom from taxation to support any minister that might be established in the towns, and the privilege to try their own minor cases. But the governor could not end the rebellion, and the revolutionary leader, James Carteret, arrested several of the governor's key aides. Finally, in July the governor fled to New England to seek support against the rebellion.

By the end of 1672 the tide had turned. Arriving from the Duke of York and from King Charles himself were stern and unmistakable orders that commanded the New Jersey rebels to submit. The proprietors completely disowned the old Nicolls land grants, restored the property taken from their aides, ordered the collection of quitrent arrears (for four years), and restored full governmental authority. Woodbridge was rewarded for its support, part of its quitrents were canceled. And finally, in December, the proprietors reinterpreted the Concessions so as to restrict many of the homerule rights of the colonists. The powers of the governor and Council were greatly increased at the expense of the Assembly and the towns.

The New Jersey rebellion was over. By June 1673 James Carteret, in disgrace, had sailed away. The restored government ordered all the rebels to offer their submissions personally, and confined voting in any elections strictly to those holding qualified land titles from the proprietors.

Neither was the west bank of the Delaware untroubled, although the little settlements were not as persistently rebellious as New Jersey. The majority of the residents of the New Castle district were Swedes, and in 1669 many of them rose in rebellion against oppressive English rule. The revolt was led by Henry Coleman and especially by Marcus Jacobsen, the "Long Finn" who, in the words of the governor's indictment, went "up and down from one place to another, frequently raising speeches, very seditious and false, tending to the disturbance of His Majesty's peace." But the uprising proved abortive against overwhelming New York power. Jacobsen was taken to New York in irons, convicted, severely whipped, branded with an *R* for rebel, and sold into slavery in Barbados. All the other rebels were forced to surrender to the Crown one-half of their funds, and they suffered numerous other fines and levies. To prevent any repetition of this uprising, Governor Lovelace decided to impose very heavy taxes on the hapless people of New Castle, so as not to "give them liberty to entertain any other thoughts than how to discharge them." In 1672 the governor took the precaution of building a fort at New Castle, to guard against any further rebellion by the citizenry or possible incursions from Maryland.

In the summer of 1673 the former provinces of New Netherland were unexpectedly reunited—and under their old auspices. The previous year the third Anglo-Dutch War had been launched with an attack on the Dutch by Charles II. The chief impact of the war on America was the almost bloodless conquest of New York—indeed of the whole former New Netherland—by the powerful Dutch fleet in August 1673. The conquest was made easy and virtually bloodless by the enthusiasm of the Dutch inhabitants of New York City for the return of their countrymen. The joyous citizens welcomed the Dutch ships, and the merchants welcomed trade with Holland once again.

Immediately, the Middle Colonies were again renamed: New York, New Jersey, and New Castle reverted to New Netherland; New York City was changed to New Orange; Kingston to Swanenburg; Albany to Willemstadt; and New Jersey became Achter Kull. The Dutch officers appointed Capt. Anthony Colve as governor of the reconstructed New Netherland. Colve also appointed Peter Alrichs to be the commander at New Castle. All English and French property in New Orange was confiscated, especially the speculative land properties of the former governor, Francis Lovelace.

Almost all the inhabitants submitted readily and gratefully to the new rule. The Dutch towns of Breukelen and Flatbush yielded with special enthusiasm, and even the English towns of western Long Island were docile. The major resistance came from the stubborn New England towns of the East Riding, on Long Island: Southhampton, East Hampton, Brookhaven, Southold, and Huntington. The eastern Long Island towns consistently repeated their basic demands: a popular assembly (and the corollary, no taxation without representation), freedom of trade, and confirmation of their land titles. Governor Colve was willing to grant such other demands as religious freedom and equal rights—rights that belonged also to the Dutch citizens—but concerning their three basic demands, the towns received no more satisfaction than under Lovelace.

Southhampton therefore sent a ringing declaration throughout New England that it was not going to submit voluntarily "to this foreign government." Appealed to by the eastern towns, Governor Winthrop of Connecticut decided to guarantee their independence and sent troops into Long Island, even though Massachusetts refused to support him. Battles between Connecticut and Dutch shipping now ensued, and Governor Colve was warned by Connecticut in October 1673 to keep away from these towns. The reactivated New England Confederation also threatened attacks on New Netherland; less menacing, the colonies of Massachusetts, Plymouth, and Connecticut pledged a mutual-defense alliance. The eastern Long Islanders also asked that Governor John Winthrop, Jr.'s son, Fitz, be named their commander.

With the help of Connecticut, the eastern Long Island towns were able to preserve their virtual independence, and join once again their Connecticut homeland. From October 1673 to April 1674 there was a series of battles between Connecticut and the towns on the one side and the Dutch on the other. At the turn of the year, the Dutch raided English shipping and threatened to plunder the Connecticut coastal towns. In retaliation, the eastern Long Islanders attacked the west end of the island, forcing the Dutch farmers again into Fort Amsterdam. Dutch ships were also driven off by Long Island and Connecticut resistance.

In the New Jersey towns, rule under the Dutch was exercised by the popular, or old revolutionary party. Two of its chief officials were John Ogden, chief *Schout* of the district of Kull, and Samuel Hopkins, its secretary. The former ruling oligarchy under Governor Carteret completely lost favor under the Dutch.

The new Dutch rule did not last long enough to have much direct impact. With the Treaty of Westminster, February 1674, the last of the Anglo-Dutch wars came to a close, and New Netherland was returned to England. From then on, Dutch rule was purely interim, until the new English governor, Major Edmund Andros, could arrive in November to resume English proprietary rule.

There were, however, important indirect consequences of the final war with Holland. The Crown lawyers decided that the old grant of the New Netherland area to the Duke of York was now invalid. Although King Charles regranted his brother the area in July, the confusion was enough to induce Lord Berkeley, who had little interest in New Jersey at best, to sell his half of the proprietorship in March 1674. Berkeley sold his interest for 1,000 pounds to two English Quakers, Major John Fenwick and Edward Byllinge. This was a landmark in the history of America. From a universally persecuted sect, the Quakers now became a free, sometimes even a dominant, group. For a while it seemed that Berkeley's sale was prudent indeed. For the new tables meant new conditions. In August the Duke of York regranted New

Jersey but not as a whole. He now gave northern New Jersey, north of a line due west of Barnegat Bay, to Sir George Carteret; while granting him the ownership, the new patent did not grant him the sovereign power. The sale of Berkeley's share was still unrecognized, but the new buyers now laid claim to the southern portion of New Jersey.

Southern New Jersey was now in limbo. Edward Byllinge soon went into bankruptcy and his interest was taken over by three trustees, all Quakers, one of whom was William Penn. The trustees also persuaded the equally bankrupt Fenwick to sell them ninety percent of his share for 900 pounds.

The ambitious Fenwick promptly organized an expedition and founded a settlement of his own in southern New Jersey, at Salem, in late 1675. At this time, there were only a handful of people in southern New Jersey and virtually no Englishmen. Having organized the first English settlement, Fenwick forthwith proclaimed himself governor and sole landowner of the area. He then brazenly announced his terms for "selling" the land to settlers—one pound per one thousand acres. Those who bought more than one thousand acres were to be freeholders, with the right to vote for a council of twelve to help Fenwick rule. For having one's passage paid by Fenwick, a person was to be an indentured servant for four years, and receive 100 acres at the end of the term. Every freeholder was to pay Fenwick an annual feudal quitrent of one penny per acre. All this was to be Fenwick's as his supposed "tenth" share of the southern New Jersey proprietorship. In short order, Fenwick sold 148,000 acres to fifty purchasers, most of them Quakers.

Unsurprisingly, Fenwick came quickly into conflict with the handful of Dutch settlers in the area. Led by the Reverend Mr. Fabricius, these settlers refused to serve in the *corvée*—the compulsory labor force to work on the roads, a common practice in the colonies. To break this mass refusal, several arrests were made and Reverend Mr. Fabricius was forcibly suspended from his duties.

The trustees naturally denounced Fenwick's assumption of power as illegal, and in July 1676 they were able to persuade Sir George Carteret to sign the *Quintipartite Deed* granting the trustees all the lands of New Jersey south and west of a new partition line, which ran from Barnegat Bay northwest to the Delaware River. For one thing, William Penn was a close friend of the Duke of York, and Carteret wished to cement his rather shaky title by coming to an agreement with Penn. The trustees now had a clear, official title to a larger (though uninhabited) area, called West New Jersey, while Carteret's area was called East New Jersey. As part of the imminent crackdown on Fenwick, his ten percent was granted in the deed not to Fenwick himself, but to his mortgagors, John Eldridge and Edward Warner, who had financed his expedition. Fenwick was arrested in late 1676 for assuming governmental functions as "lord proprietor" and especially for divesting existing settlers of "his" lands in order to sell them for his own gain. Fenwick was convicted by the Court of Assizes in New York, but released on parole after paying a modest fine.

44

The Beginning of Andros' Rule in New York

Sir Edmund Andros arrived in November 1674. Almost immediately he renamed New York and its towns, reappointed the old English magistrates, confirmed previous land grants, and again proclaimed the Duke's Laws throughout the province. Andros also confronted a problem: the revolutionary towns on eastern Long Island. Having been liberated by Connecticut troops, these long-time rebellious towns—expecially Southold, East Hampton, and Southampton—now proclaimed themselves to be part of Connecticut. Andros threatened to deal with these towns as if they were in outright rebellion. He successfully insisted that Winthrop give up any claim to the Long Island towns and managed to intimidate the protesters. One Long Island critic was sentenced to a severe whipping for writing "seditious letters." Confronted by *force majeure* as well as the royal charter, the Long Island towns reluctantly succumbed.

In that era, a change of regime often meant imposition of a loyalty oath, and Andros decided the following spring (1675) to impose on all an oath of allegiance, similar to the one imposed by Nicolls a decade earlier. But the Dutch burghers of New York City remembered that Nicolls had promised them religious liberty and other rights against oppression, and that Nicolls had readily agreed to a proviso that his forced loyalty oath would not impinge on these rights protected by the articles of capitulation. The leading Dutch burghers of Manhattan, headed by the original leader of a decade before, Cornelius Steenwyck, now urged the same proviso upon Andros. But the Dutch burghers soon found that Andros was no Nicolls. Andros promptly charged them with inciting a rebellion. The stunned burghers—including such leaders as DePeyster, Kip, Bayard, and Beekman—asked for permission to sell their estates and leave New York. Andros' answer was to send eight of them to jail for "mutinous" and inflammatory behavior. When their case came to trial in October 1675, Andros shrewdly reduced the charge to trading without having taken the oath of allegiance. Facing confiscation of their goods, the burghers scrambled to take the oath and secure remission of the penalty, and the other rebellious citizens of Manhattan followed their example.

The Long Island towns, in the meanwhile, found none of their long-standing grievances abated. Indeed, their troubles were greater now under the tyrannical Andros. Andros insisted on payment of fees to confirm land titles and subsequent payment of the hated annual quitrent. The Long Island towns, led by Southampton and Southold, insisted, as they had before, that the freemen were entitled to their lands, by Indian purchase and subsequent settlement and use. But Andros refused to be lenient and in fact threatened to confiscate all the lands and throw them open to all would-be occupiers. It was only then, in 1676, that the towns reluctantly complied. But even then the quitrents that Andros levied on these towns as a penalty for their resistance could only be collected by force.

One significant development of this era was the widening of libertarian discontent over the oppressive policies of the central government, from the Long Island towns to other parts of New York. Such Dutch towns as Kingston speedily grew delinquent in payment of the newly imposed quitrents. The Long Island towns again led in vigorous opposition to taxes imposed by the Andros administration. Once again they dragged their heels in contributing toward the upkeep of Fort James, this time in 1674. Further, they resisted paying for the construction of a fort in their own Oyster Bay. During King Philip's War of 1675–76, Andros did not dare impose higher taxes on Long Island, but asked instead for voluntary contributions. And as early as 1676 Huntington was already over a year behind in payment of its property tax to the province, and various towns continued to refuse to pay excise taxes on liquor. Eastern Long Island also continued to press for a popular assembly, but here again, the significant new factor was the spread of the desire for an assembly to the rest of the colony. The merchants of all the towns began to see an assembly as their only hope of reducing the burden of new and higher customs duties, and of gaining the rights and liberties of their colonial neighbors. The Duke of York, however, flatly rejected the idea as "of dangerous consequence, nothing being more known than the aptness of such bodies to assume to themselves many privileges which prove destructive to, or very oft disturb, the peace of the government. . . ." And so New York continued to be the only English colony without a representative assembly.

The same English ship that brought Major Andros to America also brought Philip Carteret, returning as governor of New Jersey, at least of its northeastern—and overwhelmingly the most populous—half. The governor, under instructions from Sir George Carteret, reconfirmed the interpretation of the original Concessions, issued in 1672, therewith expanding the powers of governor and Council at the expense of the Assembly. Land grants made by Carteret were confirmed, and those by Nicolls disavowed. All were required to obtain their land titles from the governor and pay the imposed quitrents. Nicolls' patentees were to receive 500 acres of land each. The old magistracy was returned to power. However, an act of amnesty, or "oblivion," was adopted in the first Assembly of 1675, pardoning all rebellious and treasonable offenses made during the time of troubles, from 1670 to 1673.

From the very first meeting of the New Jersey Assembly in 1675, however, the deputies resumed their objections, and demanded joint sessions of the governor's Council and the Assembly. And yet, the same Assembly imposed penalties up to and including banishment for such "crimes" as speaking contemptuously of officials. The original law forcing every male to equip himself with arms and ammunition, and to undergo military training for four days a year, was reconfirmed. Every town was commanded to maintain a fort. There were no exceptions for Quakers, who were virtually nonexistent in Eastern New Jersey.

Until 1675 there had been no levy in New Jersey to pay a salary to the governor, but now, along with the general increase of taxes, special appropriations for this expense were voted by the Assembly. In addition, a voluntary subscription was authorized for the salary in arrears. When subscriptions lagged, the Assembly directed each town to appoint a committee to raise the amount, and a lag in response was to be met by a compulsory levy on the town. The subscription was now clearly less "voluntary" than before. Even so, the Assembly voted, in the fall of 1676, a tax for the governor's salary, payable in wheat, peas, and tobacco. Taxes in general were payable in wheat, tobacco, and other agricultural staples.

Although no jurisdictional clashes occurred in these years between New York and New Jersey, troubles were in store. For instance, the Duke of York, at the very time he regranted northern New Jersey to Sir George Carteret, also appointed Andros as governor of all the land from the Connecticut to the Delaware rivers! This manifest contradiction could not hope to remain dormant and unresolved forever.

We have already touched on the remarkable change in the political fortunes of the Quakers. A similar shift occurred in New York itself. The Duke of York appointed, along with Andros, William Dyer, a Quaker and son of William and Mary Dyer of Rhode Island, as collector of the port of New York. Further, Andros, an Anglican, had a lieutenant governor who was a Catholic, Anthony Brockholls. These appointments reflected what has been called a "peculiar" alliance among Quakers, Catholics, and high Anglicans during the Restoration era. The alliance was not so peculiar, however, if we remember that these three groups had been persecuted in England, and in English and Dutch America, by a common enemy—Calvinism.

45

Further Decline of the Massachusetts Theocracy

The late 1660s and early 1670s saw an intensification of the trends that had arisen in Massachusetts Bay: a continuing decline in the power and vitality of the Puritan theocracy, and a rise in the influence of the nonzealot and even non-Puritan merchants in Boston and the other large towns.

The rise of the merchants, and the relative affluence and cosmopolitanism accompanying that rise, brought a growing awareness of doom to the older Puritan generation. The growing wealth and sophistication greatly weakened Puritan zeal among the younger generation. Mobility, enterprise, and consumer enjoyments more and more replaced the old fanatical asceticism. Many of the leading merchants were Anglicans who could not, with the advent of Restoration, be any longer persecuted, and even the Puritan merchants grew less and less interested in becoming church members.

The old-guard Puritans ranted and raved, of course, against the rising new order as they saw their power and ideals slipping from view. Frantically the theocrats denounced avarice, gain, pride, the spirit of trade, "idolatry," and the pursuit of wealth and the good things of life. The Reverend John Higginson, whose own sons were to be merchants, thundered in 1663 that "this is never to be forgotten: that New England was originally a plantation of Religion, not a plantation of Trade." At every hand came a lament for the good old days. The Reverend Urian Oakes declared sadly in 1673: "He that remembers the good old spirit of those who followed God into this wilderness . . . cannot but easily discern a sad alteration." The following year Rev. Samuel Torrey bemoaned the new "spirit of profaneness, a spirit of pride, a spirit of worldliness, a spirit of libertinism, a spirit of carnality. . . . Truly, the very heart of New England is changed and exceedingly corrupted with the sins of the times."

341

A few years later Rev. Increase Mather, emerging as the spiritual leader of the colony, again recalled that "religion and not the world was what our fathers came hither for." He railed against the new luxurious fashions being increasingly adopted, against those "monstrous and horrid periwigs," the new wigs for women, and "such like whorish fashions, whereby the anger of the Lord is kindled against the sinful land!" The colony was also increasingly "infected" with such sinful pastimes as mixed dancing.

The New England Synod of 1679 also complained of the growing inattention to the Lord's Day: many people were insisting on walking and traveling, talking in a worldly manner, and working on the Sabbath. Here again we see that rigorous persecution had proved to be a failure. Profanity was on the increase too, and the Synod worried that the "glorious name of God" was being commonly profaned. Long hair among men, long denounced by Puritans, was deplored by the General Court in 1675 as "a sign of evil pride." But here the long-haired had ample Puritan precedent, including Oliver Cromwell and such magistrates as John Winthrop, John Endecott, and Simon Bradstreet.

We have seen that even the good old Massachusetts tradition of religious persecution was fading away during this period. In the latter 1670s the persecution of Quakers and Baptists ceased and a Quaker meetinghouse and Baptist church were allowed, at last, to continue unmolested.

As the theocracy dwindled in importance, the merchants arose. For private merchants, trade connections often depended on family connections, and intermarriage among merchants began to breed new names of stature in the colony: the Tyngs and Bradstreets; the Whartons and Dudleys, Breedons and Hutchinsons; in the New Hampshire towns, the Vaughans, Waldrons, and Cutts were becoming prominent; and in the Maine towns, the Frosts and Pepperrells.

The Navigation Acts, as we have noted, had so far not been a hindrance to New England trade; they had not yet been enforced, and they remained unenforced after Massachusetts sent the royal commission packing. But in 1673 Parliament passed another Navigation Act that was to have a fateful impact on the American colonies. In the Navigation Act of 1660, important "enumerated articles" of colonial produce, such as tobacco, could be shipped only to England or its colonies. The New England merchants evaded this act by the tortuous interpretation that if Boston ships carrying tobacco from Virginia and North Carolina stopped first in Boston, then Boston was free to re-export the tobacco to France and other European countries. Seeing their expected monopoly dissolved by this practice, the London merchants clamored for, and obtained, the Navigation Act of 1673, which cracked down on this newly emergent trade. According to this act, (1) a heavy tax on the enumerated products was levied at the port of clearance (for example Boston), a tax that was equal to the import tax on those goods in England; (2) shipmasters had to be bonded in order to ensure that their exported goods arrived in England or an English colony; and, perhaps most important, (3) English customs commissioners were to appoint agents *in the colonies* to enforce these and other regulations. These provisions not only outlawed the export of sugar and tobacco to any country but England; they also meant a double tax on such goods if exported to England in New England ships, which had to pay a double tax by stopping in Boston, whereas English ships, importing directly to England, paid only one tax.

We have observed the terrible impact of the 1673 act on the North Carolina economy—and, for that matter, of the whole structure of the Acts on the Virginia economy and on the price of tobacco. And we have remarked the impossibility of the enforcement of this act on the thinly populated North Carolina coast; the Culpeper rebellion of 1677 was occasioned by the enforcement of the act, and was supported by the New England merchants.

The London merchants also wanted enforcement of all the Navigation Acts because their New England rivals had been extensively smuggling cheap imports from European countries. The Massachusetts government strongly protested the Navigation Act of 1673, but to no avail. In fact, by the mid-1670s England, the Dutch wars over, was prepared to strike the decisive blow against Massachusetts' independence, self-government, and free and flourishing trade. England's resumption of its previously abortive policy of cracking down on Massachusetts stemmed largely from the breaking up of the Cabal government, and the fall from power of the Earl of Shaftesbury in 1673. Before that fall, Shaftesbury's powerful Plantation Council had urged the king to send over to New England a new, far more moderate commission, one "not too much contrary to the present humor of the people."

46

King Philip's War

Since the massacre of the Pequots in 1637, there had been no open warfare between whites and Indians in New England. The expansion of the white settlers encroached seriously on ancient Indian lands, hunting grounds, and fisheries. Generally, the land was sold voluntarily by the Indians, but, as previously noted, the Indians had no firm concept of private property in land, as landed property was held communally and inalienably by the tribe. The Indians therefore regarded the purchases as a form of lease and thus could not help being hostile to the whites' clearing the forests for agricultural purposes. *More* justifiable was the Indian resentment at the white government's arrogant insistence on imposing white colonial laws and sovereignty over the Indians. Indians were hauled into white courts to settle disputes (even all-Indian disputes), and for failing to pay tribute and to obey such rigorous white laws—obviously incomprehensible to the Indians—as observing the Sabbath, and not blaspheming. Blasphemy, in fact, was punishable by death. And particularly significant was the New Englanders' penchant for confiscating Indian land as punishment for Indian infractions. Furthermore, the Narragansett Indians, who had been induced by Roger Williams to remain friendly during the Pequot War, were continually threatened by the Atherton Company's pressure for their lands. The murder of the Narragansett chief Miantonomo had, moreover, gone unavenged, because the Mohegan chief Uncas, who had done the deed with the connivance of Massachusetts Bay, remained under white protection. In addition, the Mohegans, Shawutucks, and Cowesits, Indians in alliance with the whites, were protected by the white governments though they repeatedly pillaged and murdered the Narragansett and Nipmuc Indians of southern New England.

In 1660 the venerable Indian chief Massasoit died. As chief of the Wampanoags of western Plymouth, on the eastern shores of Narragansett Bay, Massasoit had saved the original Pilgrims from starvation, and had sheltered Roger Williams in his lonely trek to Narragansett Bay. He was now succeeded by his elder son, Wamsutta, or Alexander. At this point, Plymouth began a series of outrageous harassments of the Wampanoags, who had by this time been driven into the Mt. Hope Peninsula, on Narragansett Bay, now the site of Bristol, Rhode Island. On mere rumor, and with no real evidence, Plymouth ordered Alexander into the General Court in 1662 to defend himself against the absurdly vague charge of plotting mischief. Having successfully defended himself against this accusation, Alexander unfortunately died, giving rise to suspicion among some Indians that he had been poisoned by the whites. Shortly afterward, Alexander's successor, his brother Metacom (or Philip), was similarly hauled into court to defend himself against similar rumor-based charges. He too was found innocent.

In 1671 vague rumors about Philip's unfriendliness toward the whites were again heard, and at this time the Plymouth magistrates wanted to adopt the hard-line policy of striking hard and destroying the Wampanoags. The other colonies held Plymouth back, however, and persuaded the colony to agree to a meeting in April of Philip and several leading Massachusetts citizens, as well as Plymouth officials, at Taunton. Philip, incidentally, insisted that Roger Williams be present as guarantee of fair treatment, and this request was granted.

At Taunton the Plymouth authorities made the arrogant demand that the Wampanoags render themselves defenseless by surrendering all their arms to Plymouth—and this despite the fact that no evidence against Philip was ever revealed. Seventy guns were surrendered. In addition to this humiliation, Philip and several sachems were again forced to appear in September, and gratuitously subjected to the insulting warning that he must "amend his ways if he expected peace; and that, if he went on in his refractory way, he must expect to smart for it." The Indians again submitted and consented to pay a yearly tribute of five wolves' heads to the colony.

Three years later, the harassment by Plymouth of the Wampanoags came to a climax. Causamon, a Christian or "praying" Indian, who had once been employed by Philip as a private secretary, now informed Plymouth of suspicious goings-on and possible conspiracies of some kind at Mt. Hope. Once again, Plymouth proposed to haul Philip into General Court to answer privately disclosed rumors against him. This time Philip heard of the proceedings, and in March 1675 came of his own accord to the court to defend himself. The authorities admitted they had no evidence of Philip's guilt, but were displeased that not all the Wampanoags' arms had been surrendered. They again harried Philip with the warning that if they heard any further rumors (even unproven ones), they would insist on confiscating all of the Wampanoags' arms. Shortly after Philip left Plymouth, the informer Causamon was found murdered. Before a jury composed of whites and Indians, three Wampanoags were tried, convicted, and executed for the murder, albeit on the flimsy evidence of only one Indian eyewitness. The execution was carried out despite Roger Williams' warning of the untrustworthiness of such Indian testimony. Here was the final straw in the accumulation of humiliations and provocations heaped upon Philip, capped by a further warning from Plymouth that Philip send away many Indians of other tribes who had now come to Mt. Hope.

The provocations had gone far enough. But five eminent Quakers, leaders of Rhode Island, headed by the deputy governor John Easton, now tried to persuade Philip, in a final peace conference, to agree to impartial arbitration. Philip was willing to arbitrate, but was also convinced that the other colonies would never agree. A few days later, on June 20, the Wampanoags retaliated for the execution with a raid on the neighboring town of Swansea, burning a couple of houses. In a few days, the raids on Swansea escalated into a few killings. King Philip's War had now begun. A joint force from Plymouth and Boston now captured Mt. Hope, but the Indians managed to escape from the peninsula.

Philip proceeded to burn and ravage several Plymouth towns: Dartmouth, Middleborough, and Taunton. In the middle of July the war took a more ominous turn. The Nipmuc Indians in Massachusetts entered the war and ravaged the Massachusetts towns of Menlen and Brookfield; they successfully ambushed an armed troop sent for a peace parley. All-out war now commenced. Town after town was devastated. The northern Connecticut Valley towns of Northfield and Deerfield in Massachusetts had to be abandoned. The temporarily reactivated New England Confederation met on September 9 and decided on a united and intense war effort. The three colonies agreed to contribute 1,000 armed men to the united force, and a quota was assigned to each colony: Massachusetts would supply 527 men; Connecticut, 315; and Plymouth, which had started it all, 158. Military conscription reached every male between sixteen and sixty. Massachusetts decreed death for any refusal to serve, and Connecticut prohibited the emigration of any eligible person. The following spring Massachusetts also forced its citizens into a farm-labor draft; officials were authorized "to impress men for the . . . carrying on of the husbandry of such persons as were called off from the same into the service, who had not sufficient help of their own left at home to manage the same." Any labor conscript who failed to report was fined, and if this failure was "accompanied with refractoriness . . . or contempt upon authority," then the malefactor was liable to the death penalty. All men driven from their homes by the Indians were to be conscripted automatically for military duty in the places of their refuge. All trade with the Indians, not on government account, was forbidden on penalty of confiscation of all the trader's property. And, finally, no person in Massachusetts was to leave the town of his residence without getting the permission of the local military committee. It would not be surprising if some of the more reflective citizens of Massachusetts began to wonder *who* their enemy was, the Indians or their own government.

The New England Confederation, in the summer of 1675, faced the question: Should it limit the war to its existing confines, or should it use the war as a *point d'appui* for the virtual extermination of the Indians of New England? Bearing in mind the usual white attitude toward the Indians, we are not surprised that New England chose the latter alternative. The particular problem was the land-rich Narragansetts, by far the most powerful of the New England Indians. Despite harassment, the traditionally friendly Narragansetts showed no sign of joining Philip's antiwhite crusade. And even the almost fanatically pro-Puritan historian of New England, John Palfrey, admits that the confederation found not one scintilla of evidence of any sort of conspiracy between Philip and the other warring Indian tribes, let alone the peaceful Narragansetts.

Provocation against the Narragansetts had been particularly virulent in early 1675. The son of Uncas, the white-protected Mohegan chieftain, murdered a relative of the Narragansett chief Canonchet. Yet the whites refused to take any action to punish the murderers. They refused, as well, to take the case to an impartial justice, and to permit any armed action against Uncas—thereby closing every door of redress to the Narragansetts. In July 1675, soon after Philip launched his attack, the confederation commissioners of Massachusetts and Connecticut sent a strong military force to negotiate a new treaty of friendship with the Narragansetts. By mid-July the Narragansetts had signed a treaty, agreeing not to permit Wampanoag invasion of their land, and to turn over to the whites any Wampanoag refugees. By October it was learned that the Narragansetts had, instead, harbored some Indian refugees. Though a breach of the treaty, the Narragansett decision to give haven to refugees of war was hardly a *casus belli:* indeed, offering asylum to refugees from war is a simple humanitarian act. But the commissioners of the New England Confederation did not react this way. Instead, they delivered to the Narragansetts an ultimatum that if the refugees were not delivered up, the uttermost severities of war would be visited upon them. The confederation promptly raised another 1,000 men under the command of Plymouth's Governor Winslow and marched in a war of aggression against the Narragansetts.

This action triggered a war hysteria that swept Boston and the rest of New England. Even some harmless "praying Indians" living near Boston were set upon and murdered by white mobs. The highly respected Daniel Gookin, who was friend and superintendent of the Christian Indians, was told that it would not be safe for him to appear on the streets of Boston. In a final flurry, Massachusetts again persecuted the Quakers. Some Puritans disseminated the notion that the Indian war was God's punishment of New England for relaxing its persecution of the "idolatrous Quakers." Other Puritans, characteristically, theorized that God was punishing New England for the new fashions in wigs and fancy hairdos.

Winslow's march into the Narrangansett Country was made without the consent, and against the will, of the government of Rhode Island. Hence the invasion was a flagrant violation of the Rhode Island charter. But the confederation was heedless of this fact, and heedless also of the devastation that this extension of the war to the Narragansetts would wreak on the Rhode Island settlements. In fact, the Rhode Island government proposed to take the whole dispute to arbitration, and the Narragansetts approved. Implacably hard-line Plymouth refused. The Winslow forces invaded Rhode Island and, by the typically white tactic against the Indians of surprise attack, on December 19 captured the main Narragansett fort at the later site of South Kingstown, Rhode Island. In this terrible "Swamp Fight," about one thousand Indians were slaughtered, including some three hundred women and children. This was the turning point of the war, as it broke the great Narragansett power.

How had Rhode Island arrived at its peace policy? During the late 1650s and 1660s, the Quakers had made enormous strides in converting a colony already individualistic and libertarian in spirit. In particular, the Quakers were dominant in Newport. In 1672 the increasingly irascible Roger Williams had once more called his old enemy the litigious William Harris, into court. This time the charge was disloyalty and high treason for favoring Connecticut's claims to the Narragansett lands. At the same time the administration of Governor Benedict Arnold, in league with Williams, passed rigorous measures to suppress agitation against high taxes, largely by the Quakers, and to confiscate the property of disloyal "plotters" against the state. It was clear that Roger Williams had been outstripped as a champion of liberty and freedom of advocacy. The result of Arnold's despotic act was an alliance between two opposition groups, the Quakers and the Harris forces, which jointly came to power in the Rhode Island elections of May 1672.

The world's first Quaker government, with Nicholas Easton, now a Quaker, as governor, now embarked on a highly liberal course. Harris was immediately released from prison, and made an assistant of the province. The laws suppressing anti-tax agitators were quickly repealed as an invasion of the "liberties of the people." And, in an act of August 13, 1673, conscientious objectors were now exempted completely from military service for the first time in America.

The act declared that since Rhode Island already refused to force Quakers or other conscientious objectors to take an oath, "how much more ought such men forbear to compel their equal neighbors, against their consciences, to train to fight and to kill!" In detail this historic act provided: "That no person . . . that is, or hereafter shall be persuaded in his conscience that he cannot or ought not to train, to learn to fight, nor to war, nor to kill any person or persons, shall at any time be compelled against his judgment and conscience to train, arm, or fight, to kill any person or persons by reason of, or at the command of, any officer of this colony, civil nor military, nor by reason of any by-laws here passed or formerly enacted . . . ."

During the Anglo-Dutch War, however, the Easton administration seriously compromised pacifist Quaker principles, by instructing the magistrates and town military officers to build the colony's defenses. And after the Dutch recaptured New York, the Quaker-dominated assembly gave authority to the governor to appoint military commanders, and to provide military training for the citizens.

In the polarization of ideology that took place, Roger Williams was pushed even further in a statist direction. He had already shown himself many times to be willing to abandon the principle of freedom of speech and advocacy of political ideas. He now showed himself ready to abandon his most cherished principle: religious liberty. In the summer of 1672 the great founder of the Quakers, George Fox, visited Rhode Island. In August, following the visit, Roger Williams engaged in a four-days long Great Debate first in Newport, and then in Providence, with three of Fox's leading disciples. The public debate attracted large crowds, and Williams rowed all the way from Providence to Newport to participate. That Williams was bitterly opposed to the Quaker creed was, of course, his privilege, and to be expected. But he also went so far as to call for "moderate" legal penalties against Quaker "uncivilities," which should be "restrained and punished." These incivilities, let us note, expressly included such harmless Quaker practices as refusing to take off their hats, and using the forms "thee" and "thou." All these were examples to Williams of "irreverence to superiors" in office, as was the Quaker refusal "to bend the knee or bow the head" to civil authority out of "pretense . . . that Christ's amity, even in civil things, respecteth no man's person." Moreover, the Quakers refused to "perform the ordinary civil duties" to the state. Williams also denounced the freedom of trade practiced by Quaker merchants in bootlegging liquor to the Indians. Here Williams betrayed jealousy of his Quaker competitors in trading with the Indians, for he denounced Quakers for selling ammunition and liquor to the Indians more cheaply than their competitors.

All this was far from being a mere exaggeration uttered in the heat of debate, for it was repeated in Williams' ensuing anti-Quaker pamphlet, *George Fox Digged out of His Burrowes*. Here Williams again called for moderate legal punishment of these crimes of disrespect to "superiors," and echoed the very argument of Rev. John Cotton against himself three decades before, that such punishment would be "as far from persecution (properly so called) as that is a duty and command of God unto all mankind." It is no wonder that one of the debaters, William Edmundson, was moved to transgress the bounds of polite debate and rudely cry at Williams, "Old man! Old man!" (for which, by the way, he was reprimanded by Coddington and other leading Quakers present). Perhaps Williams was angered far more by the apt reproof of William Harris, who reminded Williams of "his former large profession of liberty of conscience. . . ." At any rate Williams' abandonment of religious liberty had little impact on the citizens of Rhode Island, who were more true to his original principles than was Williams himself. In fact, Quaker conversions in the colony proceeded all the more rapidly after the debate. William Harris was soon converted, and even some of the venerable Samuell Gorton's followers were converted to the Quaker faith.

And so Rhode Island came to have a Quaker government at the start of King Philip's War, with the now Quaker William Coddington governor since 1674. It was a government that maintained Rhode Island's position against Connecticut land claims, but strongly insisted on a policy of neutrality and peace. It was also convinced that King Philip's War was an unnecessary conflict, caused by the unfair treatment and persecution of the Indians by the other New England colonies.

Now despite the destruction of the great Swamp Fight, Canonchet had managed to escape with 700 of his warriors, and they proceeded to retaliate against Rhode Island, burning and devastating Warwick, Pawtuxet, and Providence. The Coddington administration now risked its own popularity by sticking to Quaker and libertarian principle and refusing to levy taxes on everyone to engage in a costly defense of the mainland towns. The Assembly decided that each town should provide for its own military security, and in March 1676 urged the mainland citizens to take refuge on Aquidneck Island, even promising the settlers land for each new family on the island. The Quakers also refused to repeal the exemption of conscientious objectors from the draft. The Rhode Island Assembly also provided that no Indian in the colony could be made a slave.

Most of the mainlanders took advantage of the proposed refuge, and were joined by many people from Plymouth. A group of purist Quakers refused to nurse wounded confederation soldiers who had been shipped to the island on the grounds that this would be taking part in an unjust war. Governor Coddington, in a most un-Quakerlike reaction, forced them to do so. In a letter to the Massachusetts governor, Coddington noted wryly that Quakers were nursing wounded Massachusetts soldiers at the very same time that Massachusetts was castigating itself for laxity in persecuting the Quakers and was passing new laws of persecution. "We have prepared a hospital for yours," wrote Coddington, "while you prepare a house of correction for us."

Roger Williams remained as a captain and as part of a defensive garrison, but Canonchet, though bitter at almost all whites, told Williams that "you have been kind to us for many years. Not a hair of your head shall be touched." And this in the midst of a desperate, inevitably hopeless war against overwhelming odds!

In June Canonchet, son of Miantonomo, met the same fate as his father. Captured by the white forces, he was turned over to his old Indian enemies and was promptly butchered. For the Narragansetts, the rest was mopping up. By the end of the year, almost all the women, children, and aged had been slaughtered by the troops; the remaining warriors were fleeing north to Nipmuc territory.

Just as the war was ending, Rhode Island was succumbing to war hysteria. Under pressure, the Quakers began to compromise their principles once again. Governor Coddington, who had already forced purist Quakers to tend wounded confederation soldiers, agreed in April to provide a military garrison at Providence. And Quaker assemblymen led in setting up this garrison. In May Walter Clarke, a compromising Quaker, was elected governor and stepped up military preparations. Roger Williams now provided for the coerced sale into servitude of the Indian prisoners and did the same to the hapless Indian refugees who had found their way to Providence, formerly a town of refuge. Captain Roger Williams, among the handful of others who had remained in devastated Providence during the war, reaped the gains of the sales of the Indians into servitude. Was it for *this* that Canonchet had spared the head of Roger Williams? It should be noted, however, that Williams refused to allow the Indians to be sold into permanent slavery; apparently nine years of involuntary servitude were not so long a term as to offend his libertarian instincts. Finally, Williams and a few other magistrates held a military court-martial in August and executed several of the Indian prisoners. To the last Indian, Roger Williams warmly participated in the populace's demands for execution, and in the "clearing" of the town of "all the Indians, to the great peace and content of all—the "all" presumably not including the Indians who had been sold into servitude.

The elections of May 1677 demonstrated the political futility of compromise; the war party led by Benedict Arnold swept the Quakers out of office. One of the first acts of the new Assembly was to repeal the exemption of conscientious objectors from military service. While inconsistently protesting devotion to religious liberty, the new act thundered that "some under pretense of conscience" had taken the liberty to void the power of the military, and therefore of the civil power itself. As as result, Rhode Island was now destitute of required military forces—though who the new "enemy" was supposed to be, was not explained.

To return to King Philip's War, with the destruction of Canonchet and the Narragansetts only fighting to the north remained. There the Wampanoags and their allies fought valiantly on, through the winter and spring of 1676, holding their own in raids and sorties against far superior military odds. But the Indian guerrilla warfare was defeated, in the long run, by the Indians' shortage of food. They did not have the food supplies to permit them to fight en masse. Throughout the entire war, the Indians could find food only by pillaging settlements, and that source inevitably dried up after a few months. The Indians could not take the route of successful guerrilla fighting by living off a much larger group of peasant supporters.

By April and May the Nipmucs had been largely annihilated, and by the end of June the remainder of the Narragansetts had gone the way of the fallen Canonchet. The war now began to accelerate toward its end. Only King Philip and his Wampanoags remained and he was deserted by informers and defecting tribesmen. Driven into his old lair at Mt. Hope, Philip was betrayed by an informer. In a white sneak attack on August 12, King Philip was shot. His skull was publicly exhibited on a pole at Plymouth for the next quarter of a century.

King Philip's War was thus over by the end of August 1676 and New England faced the question of what to do about those scattered Indians who had not been exterminated. Faced with the problem of Indian prisoners, New England did not hesitate: mass deportation into slavery. Most of the Indian captives were shipped to the West Indies to be sold into slavery. But Indians, in contrast to African Negroes, were notoriously unsuited for slave labor and died quickly in slavery. Those slaves for whom the confederation could not find purchasers were set ashore on deserted coasts and abandoned to their fate. There were several objectors to this barbarity, including one of the heroes of the war, Capt. Benjamin Church, and the saintly John Eliot, long-time friend and missionary to the Indians. Eliot warned the confederation commissioners that "to sell souls for money seemeth to me dangerous merchandise." But more typical was the sentiment of the colony's leaders concerning what to do with the little nine-year-old son of Philip, now a prisoner of war. The child was finally sold into slavery in the West Indies, but some ministers urged a more severe penalty. One minister insisted that the Bible *did* permit murder of innocent children for the sins of their parents. The eminent Rev. Increase Mather opined that "though David had spared the infant Hadad, yet it might have been better for his people if he had been less merciful."

Although the little heir to Philip was not killed outright, over a dozen leading Indian sachem prisoners were executed. And the mostly friendly "praying" Indians were, during the war, herded into concentration camps, from which they could not go further than a mile unless accompanied by a white man. Violation meant imprisonment or death. Many of these were later conscripted into military service for the whites. And even after the war, the praying Indians, as well as other remaining Indians, were either herded into prescribed and supervised villages and deprived of their arms, or ordered to remain as indentured servants in white families, there to be "taught and inducted in the Christian religion." Now virtually wards of the white government, the Indians were prevented from assembling. One Indian in each group of ten was appointed by the government to be held "responsible" for all the deeds of the others in his cell.

The hard-line policy of total victory, or the virtual extermination of the Indians of New England, had in little more than a year succeeded in its highly dubious objective. But at what cost? Fully six percent of the men of military age in New England, or about a thousand men, had been killed.

Twenty towns in New England had been totally destroyed. Of the ninety towns in Massachusetts and Plymouth, twelve had been destroyed. And fully half of the towns in New England had been severely damaged. The monetary cost was fearful; a total of 90,000 pounds had been spent by the government to prosecute the war. The war debt of Plymouth alone has been calculated at greater than the total valuation of personal property of the colony at that time.

A direct sequel to King Philip's War took place in the far north, as soon as the main war had ended. In the fall of 1675 the Tarratine Indians of Maine had ravaged Falmouth and other towns of the Maine coast. With food scarce, the Tarratines concluded a treaty with the whites in December and promised to remain peaceful from then on. The Indians complained, however, of ill treatment at the hands of the whites, and particularly chafed at being prohibited from purchasing ammunition, so necessary for hunting game. The fall of Philip the next August stimulated the Tarratines to go on the warpath again, and the English had to abandon every settlement between Casco Bay and the Penobscot (that is, east of the densest concentration of settlements north of the Piscataqua). Massachusetts organized a military force in the area, headed by Major Richard Waldron, the eminent merchant of Dover. At this point, on September 15, four hundred Indians came peacefully into the white camp to parley for peace, and Major Waldron employed a typical white stratagem to seize them. Convivially, Waldron proposed a mock battle between the two forces. The Indians shot their muskets into the air as part of the war game, but the whites held their fire, surrounded the Indians, and disarmed them. One-half of the Indians, supposedly identified either as "murderers of white colonists or as violators of the old treaty," were sent as prisoners to Boston. Naturally, the rest of the tribe promptly resumed its attacks, and other Maine settlements were devastated or abandoned. The war continued during all of 1677, with little success for the whites. Finally, the colonial government decided that a peace policy might be wiser after all. In August 1677 the Indians concluded peace with Edmund Andros' representative in the province of Cornwall, and the following April Massachusetts concluded a treaty of peace with the Indians. This was not unconditional surrender on either side; the Indians agreed to surrender all prisoners without a ransom, and to refrain from molesting the settlers. In return, the white governments were to pay the Indians an annual tribute of a peck of corn for each family settled in Maine.

When King Philip's War began, Sir Edmund Andros decided to take advantage of New England's distraction by seizing Connecticut in behalf of New York—or at least the great bulk of Connecticut west of the Connecticut River. Since the Duke of York's charter was now brand new, cogent legal argument held that the Nicolls treaty of 1664, granting the territory west of the river to Connecticut, was now invalid. In this aggressive design, Andros was encouraged by the Duke of York. In May 1675

Andros informed the Connecticut Assembly of his intention of assuming jurisdiction. To Connecticut's reminder of the favorable award of the royal commission, Andros again replied that the duke's charter superseded the commission. Connecticut again refused, and suggested a friendly conference.

Governor Andros, however, was not the man for friendly conferences when violence could be employed. He denounced Connecticut's stubbornness as virtual rebellion. With King Philip's War now breaking out in June, Andros informed the Connecticut Council on July 7 that he was dispatching posthaste his troops to the Connecticut River. Professor Dunn aptly summarizes the Connecticut reaction: "Whether Andros' soldiers were to be used against the Indians or against the Connecticut government was unclear, but the Council members could guess. They sent a company of militia commanded by Capt. Thomas Bull to Saybrook with the instructions to protect the seacoast from 'the approach of an enemy'— either redskinned or redcoated."* Andros managed to reach Fort Saybrook first, but there he was confronted with armed and glowering local militiamen. Andros had expected to find the militia away fighting Indians and to seize the undefended fort. Instead, the militiamen were preparing their cannons. In this crisis the Connecticut General Assembly stood fast. It directed Captain Bull to tell Andros to go to Mt. Hope if he really wanted to fight Indians, but to resist if he tried to land his troops. Andros, his bluff called, contented himself with reading aloud a proclamation of the duke's charter. The Connecticut force countered with a proclamation of its own, protesting Andros' illegal actions, and calling Andros a disturber of the public peace. Feebly protesting this as slander, Andros sailed back home. Connecticut had successfully resisted the loss of its self-government by the imperialist seizure of Andros and New York. Interestingly enough, the Hartford government's reaction was to commend Bull and the other officers, but to complain that they acted too mildly. Andros' reading of the duke's charter, they said, should have been drowned out by the drums of Connecticut troops.

*Richard S. Dunn, *Puritans and Yankees* (Princeton, N. J.: Princeton University Press, 1962), p. 183.

47

The Crown Begins the Takeover
of New England, 1676-1679

It was 1675. The last Dutch war was well over and King Charles II was free to turn his attention to longer-run concerns. Furthermore, the relatively liberal Cabal administration, which had succeeded Clarendon in the mid-1660s, had now fallen, to be replaced by the absolutist Earl of Danby. With the accession of Danby, Charles determined to scrap his relatively tolerant administration at home, his flirting with liberty for Catholics and Dissenters, and to embark instead on an absolutist course: royalist and theocratic-Anglican. In colonial affairs, with the relatively liberal Shaftesbury now in opposition instead of in power, Charles determined that absolutism would hold sway there as well. As he looked overseas, it became obvious what was the stumbling block to absolute royal power: New England; New England that had the temerity to govern itself, without so much as a royal governor, and to trade freely with blithe disregard for the ever-tightening English imperial Navigation Acts. And at the heart and head of New England, Massachusetts Bay, overwhelmingly the most populous and most prosperous colony, the successful defier of the king's royal commission a decade before. Massachusetts—the seat of the prosperous rising merchant groups, who were the primary scoffers at restrictive trade laws and the main thorns in the side of those London merchants that had pushed through the Navigation Act of 1673, the purpose of which was to enforce the navigation laws. It was high time, on many counts, to impose the imperial power on New England.

The first preliminary step in the drive to centralize royal power over the colonies came in 1675, when the king transferred the handling of colonial affairs to a new committee of the Privy Council, the Lords of Trade and

Plantations, with more power than previous committees in the imperial bureaucracy. The lords realized that the main function of the goal of absolute power was to regulate, monopolize, and extract revenue from colonial trade.

The first direct step in King Charles' campaign to seize New England began in 1676, when the Lords of Trade appointed Edward Randolph to go to New England and check on its situation and on enforcement of the Navigation Acts. Randolph also carried a letter from the king to Massachusetts, ordering the colony once again to send agents to answer the various charges against her, including the Gorges and Mason claims to the Maine and New Hampshire towns. The June morning in 1676 when Randolph arrived in Massachusetts marked the beginning of the end of the autonomy and virtual independence, and many of the liberties, of the New England colonies.

Edward Randolph was the perfect choice for heading an expanded imperial bureaucracy. He was the very model of the royal bureaucrat and placeman, dedicated to maximizing the power and plunder of the Crown—for the benefit of king and self. He was an arch-royalist and high Anglican. He was grasping and arrogant before his inferiors, while obsequious before his betters. Randolph was by marriage a cousin to Robert T. Mason, the son of John Mason, who was pressing for his old claim over the New Hampshire towns and who was largely responsible for Randolph's appointment. Thus, Randolph had a special, personal interest in the assertion of royal authority over the New Hampshire towns, and their separation from Massachusetts rule.

Edward Randolph was also a model of the new breed of imperial bureaucrat for another critical reason: he was a leading official emerging not from the great aristocratic families, but from the ranks of the burgeoning royal bureaucracy itself. Like such contemporaries as Sir Robert Southwell and William Blathwayt, Randolph was a creature of the new imperial civil service. And this common experience forged in this new breed a common class or "caste" interest, an interest that joined the power and fortunes of the king to their own.*

Massachusetts, used to its independence, treated Randolph's message from the king with its accustomed short shrift. Governor John Leverett at first refused to take off his hat for the reading of the king's letter. When Randolph complained of the extensive violations of the navigation laws, of the foreign ships and the cargo of Spanish wines he had seen in the harbor, Leverett staunchly replied that English laws were only applicable in "what consists with the interest of New England."

*As Professor Hall expresses it: "Early in the decade of the 1670s . . . the great families were being replaced in high government office by men of more humble origins. The permanent Civil Service was being born. . . . These men owed their position not to family or wealth, but to the crown. To the crown they returned a heightened loyalty, and they would expect the same from others" (Michael Garibaldi Hall, *Edward Randolph and the American Colonies, 1676-1703* [Chapel Hill: University of North Carolina Press, 1960], p. 18).

It took Randolph only a week to decide on what should be done with Massachusetts: smash it. It was a course he would urge for years. King Philip's War was not quite over, and so now—*now* was the time to act. He warned: "Three frigates of forty guns with three ketches well manned lying a league or two below Boston with his Majesty's express orders to seize all shipping and perform other acts of hostility against these revolters would . . . do more in one week's time than all the orders of King and Council to them in seven years." To make Massachusetts look even blacker, Randolph grandiloquently claimed that the other New England colonies would like nothing better than a royal governor general to rule over them. The plan was a little too abrupt for the Lords of Trade, but it echoed a considerable amount of influential opinion in England.

Before leaving for England, Randolph traveled through New England trying to round up allies for his campaign to take over the colonial governments in behalf of the Crown. The motley group of allies that Randolph was able to accumulate has generally been called the "moderate party"—a curious concept, since they were neither moderate nor a party. It is difficult to see why these satellites of the Crown should be called moderate. And they were by no means a homogeneous party, but a varied group of individuals, collected from different circumstances and occupations. Neither is it true that these "moderates" were "the merchants." It is true that the ruling oligarchy of magistrate gentry and Puritan ministers in Massachusetts generally excluded the merchants, and that the ranks of Randolph's favorites were drawn from the opponents to the existing regime. But merchants never form any sort of homogeneous "class," and they differed on this issue too. Furthermore, those seeking government privileges, or lucrative posts in the bureaucracy, perform an economic role entirely different from that of people genuinely engaged in trade; those so engaged oppose interference with their trade. It is highly misleading to lump the two together into the term "merchants."*

In each case, Randolph tried to find the factor that would turn the person against the Massachusetts government. As in the case of the royal commissioners a decade earlier, Randolph found his first allies outside Massachusetts: Anglicans, especially in the Maine and New Hampshire towns; and Governor Josiah Winslow of Plymouth, who made Randolph a freeman of the colony. Winslow was motivated by understandable fear of Massachusetts aggression, a fear heightened by the unfortunate precedent set by Connecticut's swallowing up of New Haven. Plymouth was still in limbo without a charter and Winslow was anxious to curry favor with the Crown to obtain such a charter.

---

*"Certainly a sizable number of colonists cooperated, or appeared to cooperate with Randolph. . . . But they were too multifarious to form a party. . . . Some wanted closer ties with England, some wanted religious toleration, some wanted aristocratic government, some . . . simply wanted political power" (Dunn, *Puritans and Yankees,* p. 218).

Returning to England, Randolph wrote two lengthy reports in the fall of 1676. In these he denounced Massachusetts in detail and erroneously asserted that the bulk of the people would welcome the capture of the government by the Crown and the consequent overthrow of the existing oligarchy. But with the theocracy already decidedly on the wane, many Massachusetts citizens undoubtedly felt that its elimination by such a route would be much too high a price to pay.

Randolph tried to turn every contingency to his anti-Massachusetts designs. Thus, in late 1676 he wrote a series of papers in which he tried to tie in the measures under way against Bacon's Rebellion in Virginia. One paper suggested that the anti-Bacon fleet in Virginia proceed to Boston to help settle matters there.

This time in peril, Massachusetts sent two agents to England to argue against Randolph's designs. In response, Randolph launched another series of detailed attacks on the colony. In the summer of 1677 the Committee of Chief Justices of the Lords of Trade issued their report on New England. The committee recommended for Massachusetts a supplementary charter, which Boston hailed as a great victory over Randolph's proposals. The Massachusetts General Court, cockily triumphant, ignored almost all of the other recommendations of the committee, brushing aside its demands that Massachusetts allow appeals or reviews of its laws to the Crown. Massachusetts even ignored a royal request of great symbolic, but only symbolic, importance: taking an oath of allegiance to the Crown. Instead, Massachusetts repeated its own independent Oath of Fidelity. Massachusetts' only concession was to agree to enforce the Navigation Acts in the colony—a very sore point with the Crown. But here, Massachusetts staunchly insisted on its view of its own absolute right to make laws for itself, and not have English laws apply overseas. Therefore, the Bay Colony proclaimed the Navigation Acts to be its own voluntary statute; it thereby evaded submitting to the authority of Crown or Parliament.

The Committee of Chief Justices also decided to reject the Mason claim to New Hampshire; it also rejected the right of Massachusetts to rule there. This left New Hampshire explicitly in limbo, but with the implicit threat of being converted into a royal colony. Massachusetts expected, however, that the end of the Mason threat would soon result in the acknowledgment of its own jurisdiction over New Hampshire. For the Maine towns, however, the committee decided to acknowledge the Gorges claim. At this point, the King received shocking news. King Charles had hoped to buy the Maine charter back from Gorges, and then grant the area as a proprietary gift to his natural son, the Duke of Monmouth. But Massachusetts now executed a brilliant maneuver, purchasing all of Gorges' rights to Maine for £1,250 cash. Massachusetts now had an excellent royal title to the Maine towns and it later proceeded to enforce that title by trying to collect quitrents from the Maine settlers.

At the turn of 1678 a clamor grew on all sides for the reopening of the

Massachusetts case. Overconfident, Massachusetts itself wished to push on to final victory: the official incorporation of New Hampshire. And Randolph wished to bombard the Lords of Trade with anti-Massachusetts arguments, to reverse the decisions of the previous year. Finally, the report of Massachusetts' maneuver in Maine angered the committee and moved it to a general reevaluation of New England affairs.

At the reopened proceedings of the committee, Randolph maneuvered masterfully. He first attacked the personal acts of the Massachusetts agents and heaped discredit on the agents, then turned to the Bay Colony itself. Here he stressed the colony's insistence that only Puritan church members could vote, and especially its lofty rejection, the previous fall, of the committee's proposals—a point well calculated to inflame the committee against Massachusetts Bay. Randolph also warned that Massachusetts' imposition of an Oath of Fidelity was a direct threat to his own informers in the colony.

By May 1678 Randolph's victory over Massachusetts was complete. The King insisted on the oath of allegiance in the colony, which Massachusetts finally accepted in October. But most important, the attorney general's advice was accepted: Massachusetts' crimes and violations were sufficient to void its charter, and the Crown prepared to sue to nullify the charter in the courts. To complete the rout, Randolph was himself appointed, over Massachusetts' bitter protests, to be the collector of customs for New England—the first salaried bureaucrat to be stationed by the Crown in that region. Randolph's task was primarily to enforce the collection of duties from the Navigation Acts. The decisions in the spring of 1678 spelled the beginning of the end of independence in Massachusetts and New England.

At this point, with the jubilant Randolph prepared to distribute patronage to his friends, events in England forced another turn: a postponement of the destruction of the Massachusetts charter. In 1678 Titus Oates and his friends touched off a mighty wave of anti-Catholic hysteria, with his elaborate hoax of a "Popish Plot" to assassinate the king and impose Roman Catholicism upon England. This hysteria was manipulated by a relatively liberal Country party, headed by Lord Shaftesbury, to ride briefly back into power. The Earl of Danby was impeached and sent to the Tower, and Shaftesbury became president of the Privy Council in early 1679 and a member of the Lords of Trade. In view of this, the committee of the Lords of Trade realized that it had to postpone indefinitely its plans for crushing Massachusetts. The lords contented themselves with urging the colony to adopt liberty of conscience—especially of Anglican conscience—to repeal the religious restrictions on voting, and to impose the oath of allegiance. They also decided to move quickly on New Hampshire. The Lords of Trade made New Hampshire a new royal colony, with a president appointed by the king, an Assembly, and a Council of nine, of whom six were to be appointed by the Crown and the three others to be selected by those six. Robert Mason was persuaded to acknowledge the land titles of existing settlers, in return for a yearly feudal quitrent of not more than six pence on the pound. And the vital timberlands were to be reserved to the ownership of Mason.

Edward Randolph finally returned to New England, after a delay of more than a year, to take up his post and to put the royal government of New Hampshire into effect. Randolph was instructed to administer an oath to uphold the Navigation Acts to each of the four colonial governors of New England.

48

The Crown Takes over
New Hampshire, 1680-1685

Edward Randolph arrived in America in December 1679. His first task was to set up the royal government in New Hampshire. At Portsmouth in mid-January, Randolph invested John Cutt, a leading Portsmouth merchant, with the office of President. Randolph's problem in New Hampshire was to rule the four towns that were led by a small group of wealthy Puritan and Massachusetts merchants: the Vaughans, the Waldrons, the Cutts. As elsewhere, his policy was to divide and conquer. He achieved this aim by finding an ally in John Cutt. Next, Randolph appointed to the posts of councillor the other key merchant leaders; these included: Richard Waldron, Richard Martin, and William Vaughan. But five of the six councillors at first refused to serve, and it was the influence of John Cutt that finally persuaded them to end their civil disobedience and to assume their posts. Waldron became vice president of the colony.

The new General Court of New Hampshire, consisting of Council and elected Assembly, met in March and bravely passed a kind of declaration of rights, asserting that "no act, imposition, law, or ordinance be made or imposed upon us, but such as shall be made by the Assembly, and approved by the President and Council. . . ." Brave words, but they ran straight against the intentions of the royal power.

Leaving New Hampshire, Randolph left behind him another pliable ally, Walter Barefoot, his deputy collector of customs. Barefoot was to enforce the Navigation Acts strictly and collect the corollary revenue. Another ally was the Englishman Richard Chamberlain, a friend of Mason's who was appointed secretary of the New Hampshire Council.

However, Randolph lost his number-one ally, Cutt, who died in early 1681. Succeeding him in the post was the tough-minded merchant Richard Waldron. The new spirit was evident when Barefoot decreed that all ships entering and leaving Portsmouth must do so only under his authority. Waldron and his colleagues immediately displayed the old Massachusetts spirit of independence, promptly arresting Barefoot and trying him before the president and Council as the supreme court of the colony. Barefoot was charged with "having in a high and presumptuous manner set up His Majesty's office of customs without leave from the president and Council . . . for disturbing and obstructing the subjects in passing from harbor to harbor and from town to town. . . ." Barefoot was found guilty and fined the considerable sum of ten pounds.

New Hampshire was now in virtual revolt against the Crown's rule. King Charles quickly disallowed the colony's declaration of rights, and Robert Mason came to New Hampshire in late 1681 with the king's order requiring Mason to be admitted as a member of the Council. Mason's agents then began to demand his current and back quitrents from the settlers on pain of eviction, and to forbid the settlers to cut timber on "his lands." Acting on numerous aggrieved petitions, the Council commanded Mason and his agents to cease and desist from these harassments. There followed a test of strength: Mason summoned the Council to appear before the king, the Council issued a warrant for Mason's arrest as an usurper. Upon losing the test, Mason escaped arrest and fled back to England.

But New Hampshire had also to face the royal might of England. Mason having told his tale, and Richard Chamberlain, Francis Champernowne, and Walter Barefoot having complained, the king decided to remodel the administration of New Hampshire and bring the rebellious colony to heel. Instead of a president, New Hampshire was now to have a royally appointed governor with greatly expanded powers. The governor could convoke or dissolve the General Court, veto its laws, remove councillors, constitute courts, and appoint officers. Selected to be the first royal governor was the court favorite, Edward Cranfield, who was promised a handsome salary and one-fifth of all the quitrents received.

Cranfield arrived in New Hampshire in October 1682. Virtually his first act was to remove the independent-minded Waldron and Martin from office. He called an Assembly, which promulgated a new code of laws, this time omitting the declaration of rights.

By December Cranfield had discovered that Mason, in persuading him to take the office, had misrepresented the little colony by stating that it was far wealthier and more populated than it was. For a short while, Cranfield, disappointed at the poor pickings, turned against Mason and Randolph, and restored Waldron and Martin to office.

In a few more weeks, however, Cranfield remembered what he was there for, and settled down to his job of plundering as best he could. As Cranfield was reported to have said, he had come to New Hampshire for money and money he would have. Cementing his alliance with Randolph, he put Randolph on the New Hampshire Council, and also appointed him attorney general of the colony. Toward the end of December, Cranfield seized and dragged into court George Jaffrey, a Puritan merchant of Portsmouth, for shipping goods deemed contraband under the navigation laws. At the trial, the jury, following the great English tradition of deciding on the justice of the *law* as well as the facts of the specific case, decided against the law and brought a verdict with court costs against the Crown. Cranfield reacted by removing Elias Stileman from his offices of councilman and commander of the fort. Stileman had disobeyed an order to fire on Jaffrey's ship and was replaced as commander by the always pliable Capt. Walter Barefoot. The most high-handed reaction of Cranfield was to direct Randolph to prosecute the jury and all others involved in the criminal conspiracy. Cranfield would have liked to proceed against the main leader of the resistance, Rev. Joshua Moody, a Puritan minister who was also a merchant.

Cranfield now found the popularly elected Assembly refusing to pass his demands for higher taxes. The governor decided to institute a complete executive despotism and subdue the recalcitrant colonists. Cranfield dissolved the Assembly and made himself and the Council the supreme legislative and judicial power. He changed the juries from being elective to agencies appointed by the governor.

Virtually the entire populace of the colony, led by the merchants, freeholders, and Puritans, bitterly opposed the despotic regime that Cranfield had managed to impose in three short months in office. The people of New Hampshire were not the sort to take this treatment passively. Many people in Exeter resisted payment of the tax levy, but Edward Gove, a deputy from Hampton, decided on more active resistance: rebellion. Gove, aided by Nathaniel Ladd, of a prominent New Hampshire family, rode to and fro between Hampton and Exeter on January 27 trying to raise a rebellion and claiming that Cranfield's commission was invalid. Gove raised the cry of "liberty and reformation," but the other leaders of the colony decided that rebellion was imprudent, and the tiny band of eleven men was quickly arrested by the soldiery. There is reason to believe that the Gove rising was premature, and that the leaders of the popular opposition were themselves preparing to revolt three days later.

The Gove rebels were tried for high treason on February 2—ironically, the chief judge was Richard Waldron, a man whose views and sentiments were all with Gove. Waldron knew that Gove was right, and that he, Waldron, should have been standing in the dock instead of judging the man now there. But as often happens when men confront the embodiment of their conscience, Waldron was especially severe. For daring to speak in his own defense, Gove was denounced by Waldron for "insolence" and then sentenced to be tortured and executed. Gove's property was duly confiscated, and part of the spoils, as was the rule, was pocketed personally by Governor Cranfield. But Cranfield feared the rising revolutionary situation and was worried that Gove might escape, so he decided to follow the royal rule for rebels and ship Gove to England. Gove's colleagues, though also convicted of treason, were released. In England Gove was imprisoned in the Tower of London, where there may have been an attempt to poison him.

Cranfield and his little clique now imposed a grinding despotism upon the colony. Cranfield speedily removed Waldron and Martin from the Council once again, and appointed Barefoot his deputy governor and Mason the chancellor. With the magistrates and juries all appointed by the governor, Mason began mass prosecution for failure to pay quitrents. Cranfield was supplied with a special incentive to enforce Mason's claims: one-fifth of the quitrents extracted from the people was to go to Cranfield himself. Mason won thirty or forty suits before packed juries, and had the satisfaction of winning the first suit against none other than Waldron; the jury consisted of tenants of Robert Mason. But when executions were levied, no one would buy the confiscated lands or take possession of them. They remained in the hands of the property owners.

Cranfield now tried to meet this nonviolent resistance and extract Mason's rents by force, but the people, emboldened by news of Gove's life being spared, rose up and met force with force, led by Waldron, Vaughan, and Reverend Mr. Moody. Cranfield promptly retaliated by clamping the colony's leaders—including Waldron, Moody, Vaughan, and Stileman—into jail. But this also failed, for the people managed to release many of them from prison and the rest were bailed out.

Cranfield, undaunted, pressed on in his despotic course. The ships of Massachusetts (thought to be anti-Cranfield) were excluded from New Hampshire, because of Massachusetts' persistent violations of the navigation laws. He altered town boundaries, and forbade the collection of town and parish taxes until taxes to the province were paid.

Executive despots have traditionally had one Achilles' heel: taxes. Cranfield found himself forced in January 1684 to recall the Assembly to try to raise more tax revenues. Cranfield used the old device of despots: trying to frighten the Assembly with dark forebodings of a foreign and an Indian threat. He had secret intelligence, said Cranfield, that New Hampshire was in danger of foreign invasion; he therefore demanded the doubling of tax rates for various increased expenses of government, including the repair of the Portsmouth fort. But the Assembly staunchly refused to be intimidated by war scares and refused to pass the revenue bill.

Governor Cranfield now dissolved the Assembly again, and proceeded to the ultimate length of levying taxes himself, without consent of the

Assembly. He also angered the colonists deeply by deciding to suppress completely the colony's largest church, the Puritan church, and to impose Anglicanism on New Hampshire by force. Cranfield's goal was to suppress the Puritan ministers and force them to administer the sacraments according to the Anglican rite. He also called for an Anglican test for holding any public office. Concretely, he proceeded with enthusiasm against one of the leading opponents of his despotic regime, Portsmouth's Puritan minister, Rev. Joshua Moody. Cranfield, backed by Mason and Councillor John Hinckes, ordered Moody to administer to them the sacrament of the Lord's Supper after the Anglican order. When Moody refused, he was arrested. Cranfield put considerable pressure on the judges and Moody was condemned and sentenced to six months' imprisonment. After his release, Moody was prohibited from preaching, which forced him to move to Boston.

But the tide now began to turn against the governor. The sober, moderate Nathaniel Weare, justice of the peace and leading citizen of Hampton, was sent secretly out of the colony. Financed by the leading planters and merchants, he sailed to London. Weare came armed with an extensive petition to the king against the tyranny of Cranfield. Even Edward Randolph, apprised of the Weare petition, turned against the extremes of Cranfield. Cranfield's own response to the Weare petition, incidentally, was characteristic of the man: he would get the names of all the signers "and it would be the best hand he ever had, for it would be worth £100 a man." For helping Weare with the petition, the prominent merchant and landowner William Vaughan was imprisoned for nine months by Cranfield. However, the cause of New England in general, and New Hampshire specifically, was now being argued by the liberal George Savile, Marquis of Halifax, and president of the Privy Council. Halifax argued frankly, according to the report of a French envoy, "that the same laws in force in England ought to be established in a country inhabited by Englishmen; that an absolute government was neither so happy nor so safe as one that is tempered by laws; and that he could not make his mind easy to live in a country where the King should have the power to take the money he had in his pocket, whenever His Majesty saw fit."

The first sign of the Crown's displeasure with Cranfield came in April 1684, when the Lords of Trade rebuked him for deciding the Mason claims himself, instead of sending them to England to be adjudicated, as per his instructions. But Cranfield's internal troubles were even greater. The attempt to enforce payment of the new taxes led to general civil disobedience in the colony. All refused to pay taxes to the constables. And when the property of the resistors was finally seized, no one would buy. In December the resistance began to move into the stage of outright revolution. At Exeter, cudgels and boiling water were used to drive off the marshal, the hated Thomas Thurston. In Hampton, Thurston was disarmed and beaten, and from there was escorted to the village of Salisbury with a rope around his neck. When the Magistrate Robie ordered seizure of some of the mob, he was assaulted instead. The governor ordered a troop of cavalry, commanded by Robert Mason, into the field to put down the rebellion. But so widespread was the revolutionary movement that at the appointed time and place, Mason found himself alone on his horse. During the height of the turmoil, in June 1685, Cranfield took the precaution of taking extended leave of absence in the West Indies, for his "health"; he left Barefoot to face the music.

Meanwhile, England was rapidly turning against its agent. King Charles II died in February 1685 and was succeeded by his brother, the Duke of York, James II. In April, Halifax again censured Cranfield for not sending the Massachusetts disputes to England. Edward Randolph now began to denounce his former creature openly and bitterly: "Cranfield in New Hampshire by his arbitrary proceedings has so harassed that poor people that they. . . wish again to be under the Bostoners. For Mr. Cranfield has quite ruined that place. . . . And should a Governor go over who will tread in Mr. Cranfield's steps or do worse things (if possible), it will cool the inclinations of good men, and make them take the first occasion to free themselves."

With the accession of King James, Edward Gove was freed from the Tower, pardoned, and returned home in the autumn of 1685. Walter Barefoot was now in precarious charge of the province, but he and Mason lay discreetly low. The symbolic end to the Cranfield reign of terror came in December when the once mighty Barefoot and Mason were severely beaten up in the former's home by two leading citizens of the colony. A former despotism had become *opera bouffe*. And Cranfield? Cranfield found it best—for his health—to make his leave permanent. He remained in the West Indies as collector on Barbados.

49

Edward Randolph Versus Massachusetts, 1680-1684

After Randolph established the royal government in New Hampshire, he repaired to Boston, where he took up his duties as collector of customs at the end of January 1680. At Boston, Randolph was treated by the bulk of the populace of Massachusetts as their determined enemy. Complained Randolph: "I am received at Boston more like a spy, than one of His Majesty's servants . . . all persons taking liberty to abuse me in their discourses." His servant was beaten. Efforts were made to prevent the hated official from finding lodgings, but now Massachusetts' past persecutions came home to roost. Randolph found lodgings—and allies—among the Quakers.

The key to Randolph's appointed task of enforcing the Navigation Acts was the process of seizure and trial. Any vessel under suspicion of violating the law could be seized by a royal officer, and the owner could not touch the ship or the cargo until the case came to trial. During this period, the owner was, in effect, treated as guilty before so proven. Court action was initiated by filing a formal charge by the informer, the man who detected the alleged violation. Any person could perform the job of informing. If the owner was found guilty, the vessel was ordered sold and the proceeds to be divided among the king, the colonial government, and the informer. In practice, however, violators were allowed to settle for much smaller payments. In Massachusetts Randolph himself was the sole officer and the only one empowered to search shipping.

In May 1680 Randolph seized his first vessel, the *Expectation*. During the next three years, Randolph seized thirty-six ships charged with violating the navigation laws. All but two of the shipowners were acquitted. No case tried by a jury won a conviction. And as for the Massachusetts magistrates, they tried in every way to obstruct Randolph's path. They either refused to recognize Randolph's commission from the Crown or interpreted it very narrowly. They charged to Randolph the costs of special sessions of the courts and payable in advance. In a brilliant counterstroke, the Massachusetts magistrates encouraged the merchants to bring damage suits against Randolph as soon as they won their almost inevitable acquittal in the courts. All the deputies and employees hired by Randolph were systematically harassed, and often boldly imprisoned for trespassing private property.

Randolph, moreover, was none too scrupulous in his choice of vessels to seize. Much of Randolph's personal income was to come from the revenues collected, as well as from fees of fifty percent of the value of confiscated goods for being his own informer. So Randolph had a direct personal interest in maximizing the severity of enforcement of the Navigation Acts.

There are always people eager to crook the knee to power, and here and there Randolph found his allies. His main confederate was Governor Simon Bradstreet. Along with Bradstreet came several of the magistrates, including Bradstreet's brother-in-law, Joseph Dudley. But Bradstreet could not intimidate the popular juries. In one case, Bradstreet himself angrily sent the jury out three times in a vain attempt to reverse its verdict of acquittal. At the head of the popular opposition, on the other hand, was the deputy governor Thomas Danforth. It was Danforth who incurred the brunt of Randolph's frustrated ire. Yet, the opposition was unwilling to push its resistance to the point of directly opposing the incursions of royal power. Thus, in the case of Capt. Peter Lawrence, who forcibly resisted royal seizure and drove Randolph off, the Court of Assistants arrested him summarily. In another case, the jury quickly acquitted the shipmaster for breaking the Navigation Acts, but did fine him for obstructing Randolph in the course of his duty.

By the turn of 1681, the turmoil of the "Popish Plot" and the temporary ascendancy of Shaftesbury and the liberals were over. Tory reaction was again in firm control of the English government. The Crown was once again ready to resume its campaign against Massachusetts, and, of course, it was continually excited to do so by Randolph, Mason, and others. And once again the king, in a message delivered by Robert Mason, ordered Massachusetts to send agents to England. Everyone now knew that drastic modification of the Massachusetts charter would shortly ensue. The smell of doom for Massachusetts was in the air.

At the crossroads, Massachusetts now, in January 1681, began to crumble. Resistance ebbed. Perhaps the Puritans and magistrates had lost much of their spirit of sturdy independence as well as their zeal for persecution. Thomas Danforth argued at length the vital importance of Massachusetts' taking its stand right here and refusing to send the agents. He warned of the end of "the country's liberties." But the bulk of the leadership was caving in. The Puritan church elders; a committee of six leading Puritan ministers headed by the Reverend Increase Mather; and such leading merchants as the magistrate Joseph Dudley and William Stoughton—all argued for submission and for sending the agents. But Danforth perceived that here would be the critical turn, that submission here would mean betrayal of the entire cause. Almost single-handed and alone, Danforth charged the ministers with treason and betrayal of their liberty. He was scoffed at for his supposed extremism. Stoughton and Bradstreet denounced him for going too far. Randolph sneered at him as "the bellows of the Court of Deputies."

Massachusetts voted to send agents, and Randolph took the opportunity of traveling to England to wage his campaign against Massachusetts in person. After arriving in England in spring, Randolph asked the king for a *quo warranto* to invalidate the Massachusetts charter. He proposed that he be allowed to nominate a president and council of the colony to be a transitional substitute, and then he suggested that the king appoint a governor general for all New England. After considerable difficulties, Randolph did secure a new and rather more extensive commission, explicitly authorizing him to enforce all the Navigation Acts and to collect miscellaneous Crown revenues. As a result, when Randolph returned to New England in late 1681, he was greeted with even more hatred than before. One local versifier put Boston's sentiments as follows:

> Welcome, Sir, welcome from the eastern shore,
> With a commission stronger than before,
> To Play the horse-leech; rob us of our fleeces,
> To rend our land, and tear it all to pieces . . .
> Boston, make room, Randolph's returned, that hector,
> Confirmed at home to be the sharp Collector . . .
> So royal Charles is now about to prove,
> Our Loyalty, Allegiance and our Love,
> In giving license to a publican
> To pinch the purse . . . to hurt the man.

Now Massachusetts, having already tried to gain some favor from the king by repealing the fanatical Puritan laws against keeping Christmas and punishing Quakers returning from banishment with death, attempted a shrewd maneuver: it would pass a Naval Office Law enacting the Navigation Acts of 1660 and 1663, thereby making them Massachusetts' own. This would enable Massachusetts itself to appoint the naval officer to enforce the acts, and to undercut and bypass Randolph completely. The Navigation Act of 1673 was ignored, because it was the only statute that gave Randolph his legal foothold in America. The General Court itself would appoint the naval officer; the hard-core opposition did not want appointive power to rest in the hands of Randolph's ally, the opportunist Governor Bradstreet. Furthermore, the informer was at last made fully liable for any damages resulting from false seizure.

This Naval Office Law was pushed through the General Court in early 1682 at the insistence of the House of Deputies, which was under the firm control of the popular opposition, and over the stubborn resistance of the more timorous and opportunistic upper house, the Council of Magistrates. The magistrates were almost evenly split between the opportunists and the popular opposition.*

It did not take long for Edward Randolph to make a severe protest against the Naval Office Law. He reiterated the full force of his royal commission as well as the invalidity of the Massachusetts law. The opposition party now took measures to proceed against Randolph, who expected imprisonment at the very least, knowing that as a rider to the Naval Office Law there had been reenacted the death penalty against subversion—a clear warning to the likes of Randolph.

But once again timorousness won out over bold action for independence and against royal tyranny. Growing stronger, the opportunists were able to squash the proceedings against Randolph, and were also able to reelect their leader Bradstreet over Thomas Danforth the following May. Bradstreet had never administered the Naval Office Law, and now, emboldened by his victory, he counterattacked and maintained that the Naval Office Law somehow did not affect Randolph's powers.

But now, in June 1682, Randolph grew overconfident, and tried to press his advantage by putting the General Court of Massachusetts to the test. He propounded a series of blunt questions that would force the court to state directly its views as to which laws, English or American, ruled the colony. But the House of Deputies simply refused to answer, and the Council thought Randolph had gone too far and reprimanded him for abusing the laws and government of Massachusetts. The battle of Randolph vs. Massachusetts was still stalemated.

In the meanwhile, Massachusetts' two agents, the opportunist Joseph Dudley and the oppositionist Capt. John Richards, had arrived in England and Danforth's gloomy prophecy was beginning to come true. In England Tory reaction had set in with a vengeance. Charles II ruled without Parliament, and the religious Dissenters were vigorously persecuted. The Lords of Trade now wasted little time; at the end of 1682 the fatal question was put to Massachusetts: Would Massachusetts empower its agents to make revisions of the charter, or, failing that, would the charter be dissolved altogether?

Massachusetts now tried desperately to placate the Crown. It repealed the Naval Office Law in early 1683, and conceded Randolph's explicit authority to search and seize vessels. Massachusetts, nobly, would not yield on the crucial issue; even if it had to die, it would not commit suicide. It would not allow its agents to revise its precious charter. As

*Roughly, the general lineup of the Council of Magistrates was as follows: for the Naval Office Law were Thomas Danforth, Daniel Gookin, Humphrey Davy, John Richards, Samuel Nowell, James Russell, Bartholomew Gedney, Samuel Appleton, and Peter Tilton.

Against the law, Governor Simon Bradstreet (who refused even to participate in swearing in the naval officer), Daniel Denison, William Stoughton, Joseph Dudley, Peter Bulkeley, John Hull, John Pynchon, William Brown, and Thomas Savage. There were two Saltonstalls on the Council, Richard Jr., in the popular opposition party, and Nathaniel in the opportunist party.

the oppositionist magistrate Samuel Nowell explained to John Richards, "If we do give you the power required, (and) you do make use of the power to answer demands, we do then pull down the house ourselves, which is worse than to be passive only."

Once again, Randolph rushed back to England to administer the *coup de grace* to the independence of Massachusetts. The Lords of Trade decided in June to recommend a *quo warranto* against the Massachusetts charter; the writ would be drawn up by Randolph and the attorney general. The writ would mean that Massachusetts would be forced to appear in court to defend its behavior, and the verdict of such a trial would, almost certainly, go against the colony. On Randolph's suggestion the king offered Massachusetts one last chance—if it would now submit to revision, the *quo warranto* would not be executed and the king would "regulate" the charter for everyone's benefit. Randolph hurried back to Massachusetts to present the royal offer.

What should Massachusetts do? Once again a great debate broke out between the opportunists and the oppositionists. The opportunists took the age-old line of a spurious "realism" to scoff at devotion to principle. Thus, Peter Bulkeley expressed his puzzlement at such consistency and purist extremism: "By such [apelike] overfondness, we are hugging our privileges and franchises to death and prefer the dissolution of our body politic, rather than to suffer amputation in any of its limbs." To Bulkeley the opposition appeared ignorant and simplistic: "Many of these men, being very ignorant in such affairs, do not well understand the matter . . . nor have a clear prospect of the effect and issue of not resigning ourselves to the King, and so are rather to be pitied than marked out."

But, as Professor Hall aptly points out, "In truth, these ignorant fellows, the freemen and their deputies, understood well enough. They could hardly have failed to foresee the consequences of submission, especially since Cranfield was playing the royal leech in New Hampshire."*

And not only were Cranfield and Mason plundering and persecuting Puritan ministers in New Hampshire, but already Capt. William Phips, master of the *Rose*, on which Randolph had returned to Boston, was giving orders to all the merchant ships in the harbor. The consequences of English rule were foreseeable enough. The opposition argued against voting for the colony's own suicide; true Englishmen "who are under a limited monarchy" should never consent to be "in misery and slavery."

By December Massachusetts had made its fateful decision. The magistrates voted for submission by a small majority. But virtually the entire House of Deputies voted repeatedly against submission, and now, in a turnabout, they were backed by a substantial majority of Puritan clergymen. Even Increase Mather, who had been denounced for preaching submission the year before, now joined the independence cause and became one of the prime leaders of the opposition party.

*Michael Garibaldi Hall, *Edward Randolph and the American Colonies, 1676-1703*, p. 80.

Randolph again sailed for England with the news, and now the Crown executed a piece of legal trickery to avoid giving Massachusetts even the right to appear in court in its own defense. By changing the writ,* the Crown was able to declare the Massachusetts charter annulled, and did so on October 23, 1684. The boom had finally been lowered on Massachusetts; the Crown had at last dissolved the Bay Colony's charter.

Edward Randolph's war against Massachusetts now entered an entirely new phase. His first objective—to smash the independent government of Massachusetts—had been achieved. But now there remained his next and final objective: to take control of Massachusetts and, indeed, of all New England, and to rule the land for the profit of himself and the Crown. Energetic as always, Randolph lost no time in putting the next phase of his grand design into effect. He found a perfect ally in the opportunist leader Joseph Dudley, who had gone to England to represent the interest of Massachusetts and had stayed to represent his own. In fact, Randolph and Dudley had worked out a plan for Massachusetts and New England as early as the summer of 1683. The plan proposed a governor general and a Council for all New England, and all were to be appointed by the king. The Council was to be selected, however, from the elected magistrates of the various New England colonies. There was to be no New England Assembly. The Massachusetts government would continue to be elected by the freemen, but the franchise was to be narrowed to those owning over four hundred pounds in assets. The governor general would have the power to veto the seating of any elected official. The governor general would also have the ultimate appellate judicial power. The militia would be ruled by royal officers. All landowners would pay a yearly quitrent to the king. This Dudley-Randolph plan in effect provided for an absolute royal despotism (ruling along with handpicked colonial satellites) over all of New England, but with a thin and hollow façade of democracy and home rule.

Such leading merchants as Richard Wharton and William Stoughton now lined up with Dudley, ready and eager to enjoy the privileges won by political favor. Richard Wharton was typical of this group. Formerly opposed to Randolph's enforcement of the navigation laws, Wharton now saw where the power lay and determined to gain himself some of its perquisites. Massachusetts, however, was increasingly balking at the promised new dispensation. Although Bradstreet was reelected in the May 1684 elections, it was only by a hairbreadth over Danforth; and Dudley, the main leader of the opportunists, lost his post as assistant—Stoughton resigned his place in sympathy. Nonetheless, Randolph and his cohorts spent the summer and early fall happily working out their plans for the takeover of New England.

*The Crown got a writ of *scire facias et alias,* which it could use to speed a judgment in the Court of Chancery without giving Massachusetts any time to prepare a defense.

50

The Re-Opening of the
Narragansett Claims, 1679-1683

During his first four years in high office in New England, Edward Randolph exerted a most powerful influence on the Narragansett Country. We have seen that the settlement by the royal commission in 1665 granted the Narragansett Country "as King's Province" to Rhode Island, but continued the arbitrary Atherton Company land claims in force. Before 1676 the land dispute had been more or less academic, but the eradication of the Narragansett Indians in King Philip's War now opened the entire country to land settlement. Aware that the Narragansett lands were now a glowing prize, the Atherton Company claimed that Rhode Island had forfeited jurisdiction by failing to do its part in New England's extermination of the Narragansett Indians.

In early 1679 the king wrote to the colonies, ordering the status quo to remain in the Narragansett lands, and suggesting that all interested parties submit their claims to England. In reply the commissioners of the New England Confederation got together and strongly backed the claim of Connecticut to the territory. They asserted bitterly that the citizens of Rhode Island "were an ungoverned people, utterly incapable to advance His Majesty's interest, or the peace and happiness of their neighbors." In the same year, the Atherton Company expanded its membership, with Richard Wharton soon becoming a leading partner. The company petitioned Connecticut to assume jurisdiction, but to no avail. Randolph now agreed to plead the Atherton Company's case and in 1680 backed up the New Atherton plan for an independent charter for King's Province. The company also managed to win the support of Governor Andros of New York for its claims. But its most important friend at court was Lord Culpeper, the royal governor of Virginia, whose support was purchased by Wharton in exchange for a partnership in the Atherton Company.

Lord Culpeper urged the Lords of Trade to appoint a new set of commissioners to decide the Narragansett problem, for which he suggested a list of "substantial, able and . . . uninterested persons." The list included such an "uninterested" group as Fitz-John Winthrop, son of the late John Winthrop, Jr., and a partner in the Atherton Company; Winthrop's brother-in-law Edward Palmes; Edward Randolph; and William Stoughton and Joseph Dudley, of the pro-Crown opportunists group of Massachusetts merchants.

The Lords of Trade accepted Culpeper's suggestion, their agreement being facilitated by Wharton's discreet offer—sent via Randolph—to the secretary of the lords, William Blathwayt, of payment for services rendered. In April 1683 the lords appointed a new royal commission to investigate the Narragansett claims. They accepted Culpeper's eight-man list, adding to it only Governor Cranfield of New Hampshire as chairman. The commission, reeking with built-in bias, gathered at the house of one of the Atherton proprietors, and surrounded itself with several of the other partners. The Rhode Island government vigorously protested these proceedings and ordered the commission out of its jurisdiction. The commission sent in its report, in October 1683, finding for Connecticut and the Atherton Company, and invalidating the previous royal commission and the jurisdiction of Rhode Island. Typical of the commission's almost egregious cynicism was Chairman Cranfield's message to Blathwayt, accompanying the report. The message informed the latter that the Atherton proprietors "do all intend to compliment you with a parcel of land within their claim." So it was that the Cranfield commission paved the path for the land-grab of the Narragansett Country by the Atherton Company.

51

The Rule of Joseph Dudley and the Council of New England

During the year 1684, while Randolph, Dudley, and their allies were happily spinning plans for the government of New England after the abolition of the Massachusetts charter, the Lords of Trade made their own modifications of the Randolph-Dudley plan of the year before. Their proposal, though very similar, provided that royal despotism be stripped of even the thin façade of home rule allowed by Randolph and Dudley. In the lords' plan the governor general and the Council for New England would all be *appointed*—the latter to be appointed, of course, by the governor—and unchecked by any representative assembly. Governor and Council would have full power to legislate, adjudicate, tax, regulate trade, foster the Church of England, and impose a system of quitrents. In short, it was a fully centralized royal despotism over all of New England. The characteristic Tory regime of this era, imposing throne, altar, mercantilism, big government, and feudalism, was to be imposed upon the one area in America that had been self-governing and blissfully free of most of these elements. Since the Rhode Island and Connecticut charters were still in operation, the lords' initial plan was to begin with one royal government for Massachusetts (including Maine), New Hampshire, and, after study of the Cranfield report, the Narragansett Country. The Narragansett lands were to be detached from Rhode Island and joined to the expanded Massachusetts; the governor general would confirm all land titles upon payment of quitrent. The Lords of Trade then decided to add Plymouth to the expanded Massachusetts and looked forward to adding Rhode Island and Connecticut should their charters be abrogated.

No sooner had the Massachusetts charter been dissolved at the end of

October, however, than a grave blow fell on the carefully constructed plan. The king suddenly decided to appoint as royal governor of Massachusetts the notoriously brutal Col. Percy Kirke.

At this juncture, with all plans in limbo, Charles II died in early February 1685 and was succeeded by his brother, James II, a Roman Catholic and high Tory. James, in a frenzy to eliminate all independent and proprietary colonies, and to change them to outright royal colonies, began *quo warranto* proceedings against several colonial charters, with Randolph enthusiastically drawing up the charges against Connecticut and Rhode Island. The plans for a new, expanded Massachusetts government were temporarily postponed in order to settle the problems of a new reign. But finally, in September 1685, James II decreed the governmental form that the new royal colony of Massachusetts would take.

The new royal colony was to be the Dominion of New England, a colony made up of the former colonies of Massachusetts and New Hampshire, and the Narragansett Country. Ruling over the Dominion was to be a Grand Council, appointed by the Crown and drawn from residents of all the previous colonies. Secretary and registrar of the Dominion was Edward Randolph, whose suggestions for the Council had all been accepted by King James. Chosen as president of the Council was Joseph Dudley. The appointment of Colonel Kirke had fallen through, and the Randolph-Dudley clique was now in complete control. With the exception of Connecticut and Rhode Island, takeover of the colonies was now complete. There would now be no representative assembly to block the clique's path to power and plunder. The triumphant Randolph was now reconfirmed in his old commission of collector of customs, his royal salary and fees were considerably increased, and he also acquired the royal offices of auditor for New England, deputy postmaster general, and surveyor of the New England woods.

The Dudley-Randolph government took office in Boston, after Randolph arrived at the end of May 1686. The Dudley Council was to rule until the king could send over a governor general to take charge. The new governing Council of the Dominion of New England was an instructive collection of all the leading pro-English opportunists in Massachusetts and New Hampshire: Joseph Dudley, president; William Stoughton, deputy president; Edward Randolph, secretary; John Usher, treasurer; plus Robert Mason, Fitz-John Winthrop, John Pynchon, Peter Bulkeley, Wait Winthrop, Richard Wharton, Nathaniel Saltonstall, Simon Bradstreet, Dudley Bradstreet, Bartholomew Gedney, John Hinckes, Francis Champernowne, Edward Tyng, and Jonathan Tyng. Of these councillors, all resided in Massachusetts proper except Mason and Hinckes who resided in New Hampshire; Champernowne and Edward Tyng, who came from the Maine towns; and Fitz-John Winthrop, of King's Province. Of these, however, Saltonstall, Champernowne, and the Bradstreets refused to serve, the latter two because the office was "a thing contrived to abridge them of their liberty and, indeed, against the Magna Carta."

Meanwhile, how did once proud Massachusetts react to the stunning news of its demise? The popular opposition party remained in power as the blow fell, and stubbornly refused to make a formal submission. It even proceeded to indict a man for saying that the Massachusetts government no longer existed, but Randolph's arrival in May put a stop to these proceedings. The General Court had decided on nonviolent civil disobedience: not revolting, but refusing to consent to the new arrangement. Understandably, the court was particularly exercised over the elimination of a representative assembly, and of its sole right to levy taxes. But this did not faze Randolph and Dudley, who successfully proceeded to ignore the General Court and to assume the reins of government.

On May 25 the Dudley Council assumed office over Massachusetts and New Hampshire, and quickly began to make its impact upon New England. The Dudley regime has been accurately termed a "feast of political privilege" for the members of the new ruling clique. Dudley and his relatives took care to grant themselves large tracts of vacant land, and to assign to themselves and their friends all the government offices having any degree of patronage or influence. In this spirit, they determined legal fees, imports, and duties, selected ports of entry, exempted themselves from town taxation, and had themselves paid handsomely for these services to themselves. The ruling clique was composed mostly of merchants who by intermarriage formed a tangled web of family connections. John Usher, treasurer of the Dominion, was the brother-in-law of Dudley's brother-in-law. Richard Wharton, councillor, had married the first cousin of Dudley's wife, and had later married Martha Winthrop, sister of Fitz-John and Wait Winthrop. Edward Palmes, made a justice of the peace, had married another Winthrop sister, Lucy. Edward and Jonathan Tyng were the brothers of Dudley's wife, Rebecca.

The Dudley clique happily engaged in their feast of privilege. Dudley, Wharton, the Winthrops, and others banded together to secure themselves a grant to the vast "Million Acre Purchase" of the Merrimack River, a territory that included consolidation of previous arbitrary land claims and dubious Indian purchases. To facilitate the granting of governmental powers over the area, the Council formed the Merrimack land into a new Merrimack County, and these grants were secured by giving both William Blathwayt and Edward Randolph shares in the new company.

But it took only a few weeks in office for Edward Randolph to become disenchanted with the Dudley regime. For he saw, to his horror, that the opportunist clique was interested far more in using power to gain privileges for itself, than in regulating and taxing its fellow citizens to benefit the English Crown. In general, this was an easygoing regime. In his inaugural address, Dudley had promised a transition as "plain and easy as possible." Indeed, many of the old officeholders were reappointed by the Council; only a few men were hauled before the Council for contempt, and only one was imprisoned for voicing sedition. Some of the Puritans were scandalized at the appearance of Anglican services and the use of the Anglican Prayer Book and by the "high-handed wickedness" of non-Puritans in Boston, drinking, and talking "profanely and bawdily to the great disturbance of the town, and grief of good people." But the Council, to Randolph's chagrin, did not foster the Church of England actively. Randolph also grumbled about the paucity of Anglicans in high office in the Dominion. On the Council only he and Mason were Anglicans, and only a handful of the more than sixty officers of the militia were not Puritan church members. Randolph also found himself losing out in the division of the patronage spoils to the numerous relatives of the Dudley-Wharton clique.

Randolph's chagrin was also directed to the alleged failure of this merchant ruling group to enforce the Navigation Acts with the enthusiasm that he felt was required. Dudley, however, had really proceeded auspiciously from the Randolph point of view—quickly launching the radical innovation of trying Navigation Act violations in newly constituted admiralty courts. These were royal prerogative courts that decided cases outside the safeguards of jury trial and of the features of the common law. In this way, the government could bypass the checks of jury trial. Dudley worked out the stratagem with Samuel Pepys, secretary of the Navy Board in England, and in only two weeks had condemned three ships. But the implacable Randolph was not satisfied. Writing home, he denounced Dudley as "a man of base, servile and anti-monarchial principle," and portrayed Wharton as a smuggler and a seditionary who had criticized his, Randolph's, appointment to the secretariat as "intended to enthrall this people in vassalage." Actually, the root of Randolph's carping was the fact that Dudley allowed the naval commander, as well as Randolph, to initiate actions enforcing the navigation laws, thus depriving Randolph of the financial rewards for the commander's successful suits.

Above all, Randolph chafed at the failure of the Council to adopt his cherished goal of imposing a drastic program of despotism and plunder, run by himself, on the Dominion. Randolph wanted to replace the county officers registering land titles with one central office—his own—where everyone, for a handsome fee, would be forced to register his land title. When the Council refused this attempted grab, Randolph cried out in righteous indignation to his friends in England: "The beneficial perquisites of my office are alienated!" Randolph went on to propose a grand compulsory registry of all persons over sixteen; the forced licensing of all ministers; and the requirement that all ministers must have the approval of the governor to assume their posts—in short, a virtual Anglican establishment, and restriction of non-Anglican services in the Dominion. These proposals too were rebuffed. To Randolph this was base ingratitude by his own creatures whom he had elevated to state power. Randolph now found that his erstwhile allies were individuals who "agree in nothing but sharing the country amongst themselves and laying out long tracts of lands," and who believe that "this change was intended only to advantage them"—rather than Randolph or the Crown. Of all the councillors, only Usher and Stoughton now met with his approval.

One saving grace of the Dudley administration, a grace that worked to keep its power relatively weak, was scarcity of funds. Virtually its only meager sources of supply were the excise on liquors, and fees. It did not dare levy any direct taxes without having the approval of an assembly.

As partners in the Atherton Company, councillors Fitz-John and Wait Winthrop were largely interested in finally seizing control of the Narragansett Country, now incorporated into the Dominion of New England. The Council, which included several other partners of the Atherton Company, promptly moved to implement the Cranfield report of three years earlier. At the end of June, Dudley, Fitz-John Winthrop, Randolph, and Wharton traveled to Kingston in King's Province and reorganized the whole government of the Narragansett Country. They proclaimed that absolute ownership of the land belonged to the Atherton proprietors, and announced that anyone settling on these lands without the permission of these arbitrarily decreed proprietors would have to purchase or rent the land. Rhode Island dared not contest this naked seizure of its territory, its life being under the continuing threat of *quo warranto* action. The proprietors quickly began to exploit this windfall by selling a tract of land to a group of French Huguenot refugees at twenty pounds for 100 acres.

Finally, in December 1686 the complexion of New England and the northern colonies underwent another change. Sir Edmund Andros arrived in Boston to assume the rule of an expanded, far more centralized and Crown-oriented Dominion of New England. The history of the northern colonies was entering a new and fateful phase.

52

New York, 1676-1686

Having failed to seize Connecticut in the midst of King Philip's War, Governor Edmund Andros cemented an agreement with the Iroquois, to continue the old arrangement they had with the Dutch for the fur trade. He did this particularly because French Jesuit missionaries from Canada were beginning to dissolve some of the traditional enmity of the Iroquois toward the French. The furthest white outpost of New York was now Schenectady, a Dutch hamlet founded over a decade earlier by an agent of Rensselaerswyck, the only continuing patroonship which extended over several counties' worth of area around Albany. To regularize Iroquois relations, Andros created a Board of Commissioners of Indian Affairs, stationed at Albany. Appointed secretary was a young Scotsman, Robert Livingston, son of an eminent Presbyterian minister and secretary of the manor of Rensselaerswyck, as well as of the town of Albany.

Albany's vital importance for the fur trade stemmed from its locus at the junction of the Hudson and the Mohawk rivers. The Mohawk provided the opening to the west, along which the Iroquois could serve as middlemen by purchasing the furs of the Indian tribes of the middle west, and reselling them to the Dutch or English, who would transport them down the Hudson overseas. The most important citizens of Albany, even after the English reconquest, continued to be the Dutch *Handlaers*, the merchants engaged in fur trading.

The fur trade was crucial to the economy of the northern colonies in this era, and fur traders were always attempting to opt out of the shifting winds of free competition by obtaining exclusive monopoly privileges for themselves from the government. Governor Andros proved amenable to granting monopolies. In the summer of 1678 he granted a monopoly of the fur trade to the resident merchants of Albany, reserving the monopoly of the overseas trade for the merchants of New York City. The privileged monopolists (or oligopolists) of Albany, were, of course, not happy about having to sell their furs to a similarly privileged set of oligopolists (here defined as several receivers of common grants of exclusive privilege). The twenty-odd Albany *Handlaers*, however, did manage to get rid of Timothy Cooper, an Albany agent for the manorial ruler of Springfield, Massachusetts, John Pynchon. Cooper's private mail was purloined by the Albany magistrates, and on the strength of critical statements about the *Handlaers*, Cooper was officially expelled from Albany by the governor and the Council.

In the same year, Andros took the highly significant step of establishing a monopoly of the important export commodity, flour. By 1680 all bolting and packaging of flour was reserved exclusively to resident merchants of New York City, who also had to be freemen of that city. This flour monopoly brought in much revenue to the Crown; the monopolists payed for the privilege in the form of inspection fees, taxes, etc. But it rightly embittered the merchants outside the city, who were grievously injured, and the wheat farmers of New York, who saw their prices fall sharply as their market was greatly narrowed to a few privileged New York City merchants. The result was the crushing of the successful flour mills already established at such spots as Rensselaerswyck, Albany, and Kingston, the last town barely escaping fines to punish the vigor of its protests.

The wheat and other grain farmers were further mulcted by an absolute prohibition on the export of grain in force since 1673. This ban greatly depressed the price of wheat earned by the farmer, while privileging the New York merchants with an artificially cheap cost for the grain purchased. Grain prices were further lowered artificially by prohibiting the distilling of liquor in New York, thus shutting off an important market for local grain. This prohibition privileged the New York City merchants again by lowering the cost of grain and by choking off the effective competition of local whiskey with West India rum, which constituted one of the merchants' major imports.

Furthermore, the Duke of York ordered Andros to set up a port monopoly for New York City. All ships bound for any port within the original territory of New Netherland were now compelled to enter their goods at the New York Customs House. This provided the Crown with assured customs revenue at a port it could easily watch, and furnished much extra income for the privileged merchants, but again at the expense of greatly crippling trade at such places as Long Island. The settlers of Suffolk County on eastern Long Island, long accustomed to exchanging their whale oil for the manufactured goods of New England, were now forced into the extra costs of transporting these goods via the long detour of New York City and of paying there the customs duties that they could have avoided at Long Island. With all these monopolistic privileges granted to the New York City merchants by the government, it is not surprising that their profits often ranged from one hundred to several hundred percent.

The network of monopoly privilege also tightened in all the several towns of New York Province. Each town and village government laid down severe restrictions against competition from outside its locale or from non-resident visitors. Only qualified freemen of each town enjoyed the "freedom" of the town, including the right to carry on a trade or craft without hindrance or harassment. Thus the bakers of Albany pushed through an ordinance forbidding any transients to bake in the city, and a special tax was levied on seasonal visitors. And even the relatively liberal town of Huntington forbade "any person . . . of any other town upon this island" to whale or fish within its jurisdiction.

A particularly important urban monopoly had been granted, in the days of New Netherland, to the carters of New York City. Historians have erroneously termed the carters "workers," in the sense of modern employees, but they were not at all proletarians. They were, rather, self-employed artisans, who sold their wares to the public; therefore, monopoly privileges made them in effect virtually medieval and mercantilistic guilds. The very creation of the monopoly introduced a conflict of interest between the privileged carters and the rest of the colony: the carters exploited their monopoly fully by working less and charging more; whereas the colony balked at the obvious shortage of carting service created by the privilege. During the Dutch reoccupation, the carters complained that non-licensed men and boys were engaging in trucking—that is, taking advantage of the attractive monopoly-won conditions, as well as of the shortage, to enter the field. The court obligingly ordered these boys not to "ride cart any more." Negroes, free or slave, had long been prohibited from becoming carters. But in 1674 Governor Andros suspended the right to cart for one carter who refused to haul cobblestones for the governor. Two years later the city decreed minimum loads that the licensed carters would be forced to carry. In 1677 twelve New York City carters were expelled from their occupation and heavily fined, whereupon the carters submitted and promised not to disobey again. The carters thus found that a monopoly privilege could cut both ways.

In addition to imposing monopoly privileges and crippling Long Island trade, Andros also offended the Dutch citizens by partiality to Anglican practice. In 1676 Rev. Nicholas Van Rensselaer, a protégé of King Charles and the Duke of York, came to New York to take up his holdings at Rensselaerswyck, the only Dutch patroonship that had withstood the rigors of the years. Although Van Rensselaer had been ordained by an Anglican bishop and not by the ruling Classis of Amsterdam of the Dutch Reformed Church, Governor Andros still had the effrontery to appoint Van Rensselaer to the pastoral ministry of the Dutch Reformed Church at Albany. The Reverend Mr. Van Nieuwenhuysen of New York City protested vigorously and was joined by the young Dutch Reformed merchant who had emigrated from Germany, Jacob Leisler, whose wife was related to the leading Dutch families of the colony. Leisler accused Van Rensselaer of "false preaching" but the court found for the patroon, and Leisler was forced to pay court costs and imprisoned for a time.

Soon Andros moved in to compel the virtual separation of the Dutch Reformed Church in New York from its connection with the Classis of Amsterdam. In 1678 the Dutch church in New Castle on the Delaware appointed a young minister and asked for his ordination without having to send him to Amsterdam. At this point, Andros saw his opportunity, and ordered Van Nieuwenhuysen and the other Dutch ministers to form themselves into their own classis, and then to ordain the minister if qualified. The Dutch minister complied because "it would not be safe to disobey" Andros. The Amsterdam classis approved this *fait accompli*.

A corollary to the economic tyranny imposed by the Andros regime was the placing of political power into the hands of a tight-knit oligarchy, which filled all the public offices and used them for its own benefit. Public office generally provides a twofold economic privilege for its holder: the salary directly attendant on the job, and the additional economic benefits from wielding the powers of office. Generally both sets of powers are used to the full by the rulers. From 1664 to 1689, for example, only twenty-one men held office in the appointed governor's Council. Of these, ten were wealthy merchants of New York City basking in the monopoly privileges they helped to award themselves, two were wealthy lawyers of the city connected with the merchants, and four were high English officials in the bureaucracy.

A major economic grievance was Andros' imposition of a mass of higher taxes, shortly after assuming power in New York. This included not only the quitrents, property, and excise taxes mentioned above, but also: a two percent import duty on English goods; a ten percent import duty on non-English goods; a three percent duty on salt; specific import duties on fur, tobacco, and liquor; and an added three percent duty on goods traveling up the Hudson River. Added to the New York port monopoly, this was a formidable grievance indeed. The reimposition in 1679 of the excise tax on liquor (which was canceled in 1676) also added to opposition to the tax levies.

The economic, political, and religious grievances all intensified the New Yorkers' long-standing demand for a representative assembly. And New Yorkers were painfully conscious of the fact that theirs was the only English colony in America lacking such an assembly. Now the demand had spread from Long Island to the rest of the colony.

In 1681 the grievances against the Andros administration came to a head. Numerous charges had piled up against the governor. Twice Andros had been brought into court for appropriating confiscated goods for his own personal use—the court freed him only for lack of jurisdiction. In January, therefore, Andros was recalled to England to answer the charges, which included: favoritism in enforcing the Navigation Acts, fraud, private speculation, taxing the people without their consent and sometimes without the consent of his own Council, and denial of the right to jury trial. There were also charges of favoritism to leading Dutch merchants, particularly the two richest men in the colony: Frederick Philipse and O. S. Van Cortlandt. The duke's agent sent to investigate the charges found them true, but Andros still managed to convince the Duke of York of his innocence.

In the meanwhile, however, Andros committed a very costly oversight. The hated customs duties imposed by Andros had expired in November 1680. The governor, in the press of preparing for his voyage home, neglected to order them renewed. This was the only opening that the embittered merchants needed. As soon as Andros left, with deputy governor Anthony Brockholls remaining in charge, one merchant after another refused to pay the duties, claiming rather speciously that Brockholls had no power to continue them in force. Brockholls himself was inclined to yield the point, even though Andros had told him to continue everything as before. Brockholls' point was reinforced by the Council's agreeing with the merchants that it had no authority to continue the taxes.

William Dyer, the duke's collector of customs at New York, determined to collect the duties nevertheless. After confiscating goods for nonpayment, Dyer was sued by a merchant he had victimized, and a grand jury indicted Dyer for high treason because he assumed "regal power and authority" by imposing taxes illegally. Even before Andros' departure, the mayor's court simply and illegally refused to try a smuggler, and Andros had disciplined that body. When Dyer challenged the jurisdiction of the Court of Assizes, the court shipped him to England to stand trial for treason, where he was, of course, promptly freed.

Dyer might be freed, but he was at least temporarily out of the country and the citizens of New York for a while had successfully revolted against payment of the oppressive duties. The revolutionary impetus now pressed on to a clamor for a representative assembly. The old principle of no taxation without representation was put forward again. A mass petition was sent to the Duke of York, declaring the lack of an assembly an intolerable grievance.

All this pressure, loss of revenue, turmoil, and virtual rebellion now had its impact: it began to weary the duke. Advised by his Quaker friend William Penn to grant New York an assembly—"just give it self-government and there will be no more trouble"—the duke at last agreed. The duke retired Governor Andros, and replaced him with Col. Thomas Dongan, an Irish Catholic, with instructions to institute an assembly.

Dongan promptly convened the first representative assembly in New York history in October 1683 to the jubilation of the New Yorkers. The Assembly had the power to levy taxes, though not to appropriate them, and its legislative acts were subject to the veto of the governor, Council, and the ultimate veto of the proprietor. Moreover, the power to convoke and dissolve the Assembly was strictly in the hands of the governor. The Assembly consisted of deputies from New York City, Long Island (King's, Queen's, and Suffolk counties), Kingston (Esopus County), Albany, Schenectady, Staten Island (Richmond County), Martha's Vineyard and Nantucket (Duke's County), and Cornwall (the Maine towns). The Assembly drew up a charter, which it eagerly sent to the Duke of York for approval, and which provided for regular meetings of the Assembly, trial by jury, due process of law, and the right of habeas corpus, restriction of martial law, and religious toleration of all Christians. But the New Yorkers were to find, once again, that the parable of being chastized with whips and then with scorpions could apply particularly well to them. For one thing, the Assembly met only once more, the following fall—with the exception of a brief session in the fall of 1685. And the charter didn't last long, for in February 1685 King Charles II died and was replaced by the Duke of York, James II.

The accession of James II greatly changed New York's status. In the first place, with New York's proprietor now the king, it automatically was transformed from a proprietary into a royal colony. And second, the interest of James in the colony was now revived with a vengeance. As king he moved steadily toward imposing a highly centralized royal despotism on all the northern colonies. The separate charter for New York was now revoked, and Dongan ordered it voided in 1686. Furthermore, Dongan decreed that the taxing power was from then on to be lodged in the governor and Council. The most precious power of any assembly, taxing power, was now taken away. In January 1687 Dongan offically dissolved the Assembly, which had not met in over a year. In protest against this crushing of the stillborn Assembly, the militia of Richmond revolted, and rioting occurred in Jamaica. Both protests were quickly suppressed.

Apart from the plans of James II and the abortiveness of the Assembly, the Dongan administration proved no great improvement over that of Andros. In the first place, the various oppressive tendencies of the Andros' regime were continued in force. Dongan continued the embargoes on the export of grain and the various monopolies, and tightened the Albany monopoly of the fur trade. Dongan severely tightened the New York City flour monopoly as well. When flourmakers sprang up outside New York City and evaded the legal prohibition, Dongan in 1683 instructed the sheriffs to seize and confiscate all flour bolted or packed outside the city. In addition, Dongan added to the exploitation of other groups for the benefit of the city merchants by prohibiting tanneries in New York. This forced the cattle farmers to sell hides to the merchants for export to tanneries. This created extra business for the merchants at the expense of both the farmers, who suffered from the restriction of their market, and the shoemakers, who now had to pay a higher price for imported leather.

The result of the continuing governmental oppression of the grain farmers was a one-third fall in the price of wheat. Priced at four shillings, sixpence per bushel in 1673, wheat by 1688 had fallen to three shillings a bushel. This caused a corollary fall in land values in New York; total value of property fell from 101,000 pounds in 1673 to 78,000 pounds in 1688.

The struggle with the carting monopoly continued. Dongan forced the carters to carry over a hundred loads annually to the fort without compensation. When the carters refused to work under Dongan's regulations in 1684, the authorities decided to allow anyone to enter the trade *except* the disobeying carters. This double-barreled blow quickly forced the carters to obey the government decrees.

For a short while, Governor Dongan did lessen the New York City port monopoly a trifle. The Long Island towns were granted port privileges, but only with those ships posting a 100-pound bond against engaging in smuggling, and with revenue officials stationed on Long Island to enforce the various trade and customs regulations. The Long Islanders complained, however, of the revenue officers and the high duties, while Dongan chafed at continued smuggling in violation of the Navigation Acts. By 1688 Dongan had again closed the Long Island ports.

One monopoly was relaxed, however, with the accession of Dongan: New York *merchants* (in contrast to the New York *port*) lost their monopoly of the overseas trade. In addition, New York was still prohibited from trading with Holland.

Dutch discontent continued. The Albany Dutch Reformed church became the center of complaint against government interference. In 1684 this church petitioned for permission to select a few of its minor officials rather than have the civil government making the appointments. The request was refused. The following year, the Dutch minister of the Albany church refused to be ousted from his post by a civil court on the grounds that this decision could only be made by the Amsterdam classis.

But Governor Dongan did not simply follow in his predecessor's footsteps. He added more oppressions and grievances of his own. Most important was his determined drive for the imposition of quitrents. As soon as he arrived, Dongan decreed the compulsory reconfirmation of all land titles, including all confirmed previously by Andros, and the use of these land rolls to exact higher quitrents, out of which Dongan himself received a commission. Meeting with considerable resistance, Dongan threatened to "buy" from the Indians all land within existing townships not yet so purchased, and to resell the lands to strangers. The towns surrendered to this threat but only with bitterness. Kingston and the Hudson River towns suffered from the decree, but the most aggrieved were, again, the Long Island towns. In East Hampton, a Puritan minister was moved to curse anyone, even the governor, who dared to injure settlers by removing their landmarkers. Dongan promptly arrested the minister and several of his congregation, and only a humble apology won their liberty. Huntington felt it necessary to assure renewal of its patents, so made Dongan a gift of land, which the governor cheerfully accepted. Dongan generally insisted on personal fees for the regranting of land titles and town patents. For granting a town charter, the governor exacted 300 pounds from New York City and also mulcted Albany for a similar service. But even while granting a modicum of self-rule to New York City, Dongan's charter provided for a veto of municipal actions by the governor and the Council, and for the appointment of the mayor by the governor. Dongan was also accused, with some justification, of aiding his friends in evading the Navigation Acts, of forcing merchants into giving him a share of their enterprises, and of selling land to his friends.

Dongan not only raised quitrents, but added further injury to a declining economy by increasing taxation, even though he himself recognized taxation as one of the reasons for New York's economic decline: "When I come to New York to impose another tax on the people, I am afraid they will desert the province."

Dongan embarked on a program of tampering with the land that had a long-run impact far more severe than any of his other policies. The Dutch attempt to engross the land of New York under a feudal landholding aristocracy had failed; of all the patroonships, only the vast Rensselaerswyck had survived. Now Governor Dongan revived the policy of feudal handouts of unused land to privileged grantees. Dongan literally *created* a privileged class of large quasi-feudal landholders by erecting numerous manors and by other large land grants. Here was the origin of the long alliance in New York between two privileged ruling castes: the royal bureaucracy, and the great landholding oligarchy, which came to include such old merchant families as Philipse, Bayard, and Van Cortlandt. And here was the beginning of a policy that fastened feudal landholding onto New York, for a far longer period than transpired in the other colonies, where after a short time feudalistic landholding tended to dissolve into the hands of actual settlers.

The million-acre Rensselaerswyck, surrounding Albany, was reconfirmed as a manor by Dongan in 1685, with the "Lord of the Manor" obtaining virtually the full feudal powers of the Durham Palatinate type. The manor lord could appoint manorial courts and impose military burdens. This grant could be made because the Duke of York decided not to apply the English antifeudal statutes of 1660 to his province.

The largest new manor created was Livingston Manor, given to the ambitious young Scot, Robert Livingston, who had managed to marry into the leading Schuyler–Van Rensselaer and Van Cortlandt families. Livingston based his claim upon a fraudulent Indian purchase. After the manner of the day, the location of the "purchased" land was kept deliberately vague in the contract, enabling the owner, aided by a friendly governor, to stretch his land enormously by suitably elastic interpretation of the land area. In this way, Livingston was able to inflate his manor from 26,000 acres to 160,000 acres, constituting the southern third of what is now Columbia County. Van Rensselaer was also able to add nearly 300,000 acres to his manor by similar fraudulent extension of an Indian purchase, aided and abetted by the governor.

Another new element of friction largely introduced by the Dongan administration was the Roman Catholic issue. James II was a Catholic king and this in itself was sufficient to raise the hackles of the ardent English and Dutch Calvinists of New York. At the same time, Roman Catholic influence was growing in the colony. The acting governor, Anthony Brockholls, was a Catholic, as was Dongan, who brought with him several English Jesuits. The Jesuit order, the great order of the Catholic Counter-Reformation, had always been held in something akin to superstitious fear, but this was now enhanced in the minds of the colonists by mounting hysteria over the French Jesuit missionaries to the Iroquois. The emerging anti-Catholic hysteria over the proximity of French Canada, it should be noted, had also a hard economic basis: the danger of the Iroquois' selling their precious furs to the French instead of to New Yorkers. There was also much carping over the new Jesuit Latin School in New York, which proved so efficient that a great many children of influential New Yorkers were sent there. Here too a Catholic "plot" could be sensed—and rather easily, in the era of the Titus Oates hoax and the resumption of French Catholic persecution of the Huguenots.

And yet so far was Dongan from being involved in a vast Catholic plot that he took it upon himself to launch aggressive moves against the French in Iroquois country. Dongan did his best to save the fur-trade monopoly, and to gain new Crown territory by whipping up Indian hatred of far less populous New France to the north. Neither did the considerable relative weakness of New France prevent a spread of anti-Catholicism, vague but intense fears of a French fifth column, of subversive French agents, etc.

Dongan's tactic in pursuing his designs against the French was to look on benignly while the Iroquois plundered and ravaged French settlements, and then warn that the Iroquois were "British subjects" and their land in New York territory under British protection. So far did Dongan's Catholicism not influence his behavior toward the French that he tried to send English and Irish priests to the Iroquois to counter the missionary efforts of French Jesuits. But to no avail, for the English and Irish priests refused to go into the wilderness to live with the Indians.

In November 1686 France and England signed a treaty of neutrality in London. The treaty provided for peace in America, and each signatory agreed that neither country would violate the territories of the other, even if war should break out between them in Europe. Doubtless the French thought that this would put a stop to Dongan's antics in Iroquois country, and New France proceeded to send an expedition against the Iroquois. But Dongan, careless of the treaty, countered this by supplying arms and ammunition to the Iroquois, and stimulating them to attack the French. The Indians responded by ravaging and destroying French settlements in Canada. Louis XIV naturally complained to King James and asked him to stop Dongan's aggressions. James, however, was influenced by Dongan's pointed reference to the value of the Iroquois beaver trade and also claimed the Iroquois as English subjects.

53

Turmoil in East New Jersey, 1678-1686

When Governor Edmund Andros returned in 1678 from his trip to England, he had decided that he had a mandate for sovereignty under the Duke of York over East New Jersey and West New Jersey. The latent explosiveness of two contradictory charters for New Jersey had now erupted. In March 1680 Andros seized ships going to Elizabeth that had not paid customs fees in New York. He ordered Governor Philip Carteret of East New Jersey to cease exercising jurisdiction, and all the inhabitants to bow to his own authority as governor. Andros' action was clearly stimulated by Carteret's permitting all ships to trade freely in East New Jersey, without paying customs duties in New York. In short, Andros' aggressive actions were partly motivated by an attempt to secure a monopoly of trade for the New York port.

Carteret replied forthrightly that East New Jersey was subject to the proprietorship of Sir George Carteret, and that East New Jersey would defend itself as best it could against any force by Andros. When the New York Council ordered the New Jersey towns to send representatives to a meeting at Woodbridge on April 7, the alarmed Carteret countermanded the order and warned that he would arrest any emissaries of Andros as subversive "spies and disturbers of the public peace." Carteret insisted on his province's independence: "It was by His Majesty's command that this government was established, and without the same command we shall never be resigned, but with our lives and fortunes, the people resolving to live and die with the name of true subjects and not traitors."

In May Andros issued a warrant for the arrest of Philip Carteret and a few of his leading councillors "for having presumed to assume and exercise authority and jurisdiction over the King's subjects." Carteret was seized, beaten, and tried before the New York Court of Assizes. He defended himself vigorously and protested a court where the accuser, jailor, and judge were one. The jury, however, upset Andros' imperialist plans by acquitting Carteret, a verdict they thrice persisted in, even under severe pressure from Andros. The court, however, ordered Carteret to cease jurisdiction, and Andros and his Council went to Elizabethtown to meet the deputies from Jersey.

Edmund Andros had now assumed the governorship of East New Jersey. Addressing the meeting of the deputies in June 1680, he told them he forgave their trespasses against authority, and suggested that they put the Duke's Laws into effect and name Isaac Whitehead as clerk. The Assembly demanded that it be called annually, but Andros and his Council retorted that an Assembly would be called whenever Andros deemed it necessary. The Assembly also asked Andros to confirm the privileges granted it in the Concessions and Agreements, but the governor dismissed this as irrelevant and unnecessary. When the Assembly kept pressing its requests for confirmation of New Jersey liberties and provisions for regular meetings, Andros and his Council peremptorily dissolved the New Jersey representative body.

Philip Carteret, not able to muster force against his powerful neighbor, was now in a doubly weak position: Sir George Carteret had died, and his grandson and heir, Sir George, did not have the old proprietor's influence at court. But resistance appeared among the people of New Jersey. In the July meeting at Woodbridge, the freeholders refused to obey Andros' order to nominate local magistrates for his approval. They insisted, instead, that their charter gave them the right to choose their own magistrates. A month later Samuel Moore signed a further refusal by Woodbridge to obey the order and Samuel Dennis refused Andros' appointment as court clerk. Moore was arrested and tried before Andros and the New York court. Upon recanting this error and promising good behavior, Moore was released.

Two Jerseyites were also arrested for speaking words tending to disturb the peace. A transient surveyor, William Taylor, denounced Andros and the Council as rogues and traitors and said that he would not be governed by such men. Taylor was arrested and after recanting, dismissed on good behavior by Andros and his Council. A laborer, John Curtis, arrested for similar seditious remarks, broke bail and disappeared.

By late 1680, however, the Duke of York's political position in England had deteriorated, and he was anxious to avoid making further enemies at home. In November the duke informed Andros that the Jerseys were to be governed by their proprietors. Andros was shortly recalled as governor and returned to England.

The Andros menace removed, Philip Carteret, in early 1681, jubilantly countermanded Andros' usurpations and ordered the citizens of New Jersey to ignore the courts that New York had intended to operate there. But in his joy, Carteret grew cocky and began to assert his authority aggressively, internally and externally. Externally, Carteret suddenly laid claim to Staten Island, and ordered its citizens to obey him rather than New York. This question remained in the hands of the Duke of York. Meanwhile, Carteret faced far greater troubles at home.

The Assembly (with the former anti-Andros seditionist John Curtis a member) met in October and took the opportunity to have a new regime to urge reaffirmation of the original Concessions of 1665 without the oppressive amendments of the declarations of 1672 and 1674. These amendments had shifted many powers from the Assembly to the appointed executive, and had deprived the people of many of their liberties. Carteret's old troubles with the people now resumed. Carteret and his Council bitterly attacked the Assembly for its presumption. Once again, the lower house threw down the gauntlet, declaring that the inhabitants of New Jersey "were not obliged to conform" to these later declarations and instructions. The New Jersey rebellion was now in full bloom against Carteret.

The Council now insisted that the deputies pay the governor's salary and also the past and current quitrents to the proprietor, a request met with only scorn by the Assembly. After several furious interchanges, the governor and Council dissolved the Assembly at the suggestion of Councillor Robert Vicars. To protest this dissolution, Edward Slater, deputy from Piscataway, called a protest meeting that was invaded by two Council members, Henry Greenland and Robert Vicars. The councillors accused Slater of sedition and of rendering Carteret and his government "odious in the eyes and hearts of the people." They also accused Slater of trying to stir up mutiny, insurrection, and open rebellion. Greenland and Vicars promptly had Slater arrested. They then tried Slater in their capacity as justices of the peace, and convicted him on their own testimony! This court was conducted on no legal grounds; yet the two judges sentenced Slater to a six-month term in prison.

Vicars now urged Carteret to take full control of the colony by ignoring the requirement that the Assembly establish the courts and by creating his own prerogative courts instead. New Jersey was now back to the appointed courts and the despotism of the 1666–73 era. Meanwhile, however, a great change in the government of East New Jersey was under way. The estate of Sir George Carteret sold the proprietorship of East New Jersey at auction in February 1682 to a group of twelve men (eleven of them Quakers) headed by the eminent William Penn, for 3,400 pounds. In August the twelve expanded the partnership to twenty-four, including ten more Quakers, and this patent was reconfirmed by the Duke of York the following March. Thus, by the end of 1682, Quakers, though still periodically persecuted in England, owned the colonies of East New Jersey, West New Jersey, and the extensive new territory on the west bank of the upper Delaware known as Pennsylvania, granted by King Charles II to William Penn in March 1681.

However, with Quakers already settled in West New Jersey and prepared to pour into Pennsylvania, East New Jersey was not a likely field for Quaker settlement. There were Quaker groups at Shrewsbury and Middletown, but most other Jersey towns were ardently Puritan. With the English Quakers immigrating to Pennsylvania and West New Jersey, the leading role in East New Jersey was taken by the Scots among the proprietors, particularly by young Robert Barclay and his prominent non-Quaker relatives, the arch-royalists James Drummond, Earl of Percy, and his brother John Drummond, the Viscount Melfort. An eminent Quaker, Barclay was a close friend of the Duke of York and was appointed governor of East New Jersey in the fall of 1682. Barclay immediately began to organize Scottish settlements in East New Jersey and to remodel the government of the colony. Many leading Scots were induced to buy fractional proprietorships in the colony; eventually, Scots formed a majority of the proprietary ownership.

The proprietors appointed the prominent English Quaker lawyer Thomas Rudyard, one of the proprietors and a close friend of Penn, to be resident deputy governor of East New Jersey. Rudyard arrived in Jersey to take office in November 1682. The proprietors instructed Rudyard to convey to the Jersey citizens the welcome news of the confirming of their rights granted to them by the Concessions of 1665. The proprietors adopted the Fundamental Constitutions, a highly complex and overblown constitution for the colony, which would have granted great power to themselves—voting by proxy in the East New Jersey Council. But the Fundamental Constitutions was never put into effect, not only because it was rejected by the Assembly, but also because it was even turned down by the deputy governor and his Council.

The Assembly, called into being again, met frequently during Governor Rudyard's rule in 1683. All sides were determined to be conciliatory and to undo the influence of the despotic Carteret clique. As a result, the court proceedings since late 1681 were voided and the leaders of the Carteret clique— Robert Vicars, who had been secretary of the colony, Henry Greenland, Samuel Edsall, and Robert Vauquellin, former surveyor general—were debarred from all public office. Edward Slater now took the opportunity to sue Vicars for trespass, false arrest, and imprisonment; he collected forty-five pounds in damages. Vicars was also convicted of keeping fraudulent records and was fined and imprisoned until payment of the fine.

But despite the harmony of Council and Assembly in ridding the colony of the influence of the Carteret clique, divisions between deputies and ruling Council again emerged and deepened during 1683. The deputies urged the right of each town to adopt local ordinances without being subject to veto by the governor and Council, and the similar right to impose local taxes. Furthermore, Middletown and Shrewsbury again raised the question of the old Nicolls patents and claimed that by these they were exempt from paying quitrents to the new proprietors. Rudyard and the Council rejected these claims, and considerable friction developed over them. The towns and the deputies also vainly objected to the continuation of the compulsory militia, a provision of the declaration of 1672. In each case, as before, the deputies assumed the role of libertarian opposition to the existing regime. However, the Assembly did create a regular judicial system; the law code continued the Puritan outlawing of such "deviations" as stage plays, games, dances, drunkenness, and profaning the Sabbath. Here, the Anglican Council played a more liberal role than did the Puritan deputies; the Council reduced the penalty for not attending church services. The Council also declared itself for liberty of conscience and against compulsory worship.

By the end of 1683 Governor Rudyard had incurred the displeasure of the proprietors, largely because Rudyard and the Council, eager to attract settlers to East New Jersey, failed to adhere to the clause in the Concessions reserving one-seventh of the lands to the proprietors. Samuel Groom, one of the Quaker proprietors, had been sent out with Rudyard to serve under him as surveyor general of the colony. Groom now insisted on the land reservation and was quickly dismissed by Rudyard. Rudyard's firing of Groom led to his own dismissal and replacement, toward the end of 1683, by the Quaker Gawen Larie, lately become one of the proprietors.

By the end of 1684, enough of the proprietors, particularly the Scots, had immigrated to East New Jersey that the governing proprietors' interest in the colony, especially in land matters, was transferred to the fourteen *resident* proprietors, forming the Board of Proprietors of East New Jersey. The board was empowered to deal with all matters concerning proprietary land, land claims, collecting quitrents, boundaries, etc. The resident proprietors ratified the laws of the Rudyard Assembly, but added what the Assembly had refused to pass: exemption of the pacifist Quakers from military service.

The biggest problem of the Larie administration was an attempt to collect feudal quitrents from the settlers in behalf of the proprietors. Larie was originally instructed by the impatient proprietors to collect the quitrents. In late 1684 the proprietors instructed Larie and the resident proprietors to make an end of all controversies over land titles and quitrents. Specifically, they arrogantly declared their absolute refusal to recognize any of the old Nicolls patents or to commute any of their quitrents, even including the arrears. Wrangling between the Larie administration and the various towns lasted a year and a half, so that no further Assembly was convened until the spring of 1686.

In 1684 all East New Jersey towns except Bergen were still claiming exemption from all quitrents on the ground that their old Nicolls land patents, or Indian purchases, were superior to the proprietary claim. Moreover, many settlers avoided payment of quitrents by not officially patenting their lands. The old Navesink towns of Middletown and Shrewsbury also claimed the full right to make their own laws and elect their officers under the Nicolls patents and the Nicolls-promulgated Duke's Laws (but now forgotten by the East New Jersey governors). Over against this permanent state of quasirebellion, Larie was supposed to persuade the six towns of the colony that the Nicolls patents—or Indian lands or governmental patents—were invalid, and that all landowners must pay the quitrents due since their inception in 1670.

The new proprietary program of strict enforcement of quitrents was bound to create fierce opposition in the colony. The first crackdown was imposed in late 1684 on John Berry of Bergen, who was a revered old settler, an agent of William Penn in East Jersey, a councillor, and a former deputy governor. Berry was opposed to enforcing quitrents and had never paid any due on his own extensive lands. He countered by dramatically challenging the validity of the Court of Common Right—the new supreme court of the colony, founded during the Rudyard regime. The court fined Berry for contempt, and Berry's refusal to pay finally caused his imprisonment in early 1685. By now Berry had become the leader of the colony's resistance to quitrents, and the outcome of the Berry case would greatly influence the path of opposition. The Board of Proprietors, in one of its first acts, backed up Larie, determined on no abatement of quitrents, and took up the prosecution of Berry. Berry finally yielded, however, when the board commuted his back quitrents of over 116 pounds to 70 pounds.

During this time, negotiations began with the Navesink towns of Middletown and Shrewsbury. The men of these towns, headed by the Quaker Richard Hartshorne, steadfastly refused to pay quitrents and Larie and the Board of Proprietors began to seize the property of the resisters. This forced the Navesink towns to yield by mid-1685. No agreement, however, was concluded with Piscataway, Newark, or Elizabethtown, although some individual owners in the last town took out their patents to land titles, thus following the lead of Navesink. On the other hand, Woodbridge surrendered to the proprietary in the spring, following the lead of former provincial treasurer Samuel Moore, who capitulated after having vowed to pay no quitrents whatever.

Larie and the Council finally, in April 1686, called the Assembly into session to demand an increase in taxes, largely for the expenses of the secretary and the Council. The deputies incisively replied that they saw no reason why the people should be forced to pay for the expenses of officers whom they had no power to select.

In the fall of 1686 Governor Larie was removed, the proprietors being disgruntled with what they believed to be Larie's (as well as Rudyard's before him) lack of zeal in reserving land to the proprietors. Larie had also shown a lack of interest in obtaining a high price in the sale of land to the settlers. The proprietors censured Larie's granting himself a large tract of unused land at a cheap price, and his failure to push for approval of the Fundamental Constitutions.

Larie was succeeded as governor by the Scot Neil Campbell. In the fall meeting of the Assembly, Lord Campbell tried once again to insist that it increase taxes. Speaker Richard Hartshorne defiantly spoke for the deputies when he bluntly declared that the people "were not willing to maintain a government against themselves." Hence no revenue act was passed. At the end of the year, Campbell returned to Scotland. He nominated the Scottish merchant and proprietor Andrew Hamilton as deputy governor.

The failure of New York's attempt to assume power over East Jersey created a gaping hole in New York's attempted port monopoly. Smuggling was also rampant in East Jersey, and New Yorkers kept agitating for forcible annexation of that colony; the merchants desired to secure their monopoly, and the New York farmers and rural elements were envious of Jersey's freedom of trade. These grievances culminated in 1678, when a royal order made Perth Amboy, the newly built capital of East Jersey, an approved port of entry, an act which accelerated the migration of merchants and other citizens from New York to New Jersey.

54

The Development of
West New Jersey

Despite the Quaker control of East New Jersey from 1682 on, and the eager plans of Robert Barclay, that colony was never in any sense a Quaker settlement. The preponderance of Scots that immigrated there in the 1680s were Presbyterians fleeing from persecution, rather than Quakers. The same was not true, however, of West New Jersey.

West New Jersey was far more sparsely populated in the 1670s than its sister colony. There were no previously existing Puritan settlements as in East New Jersey. We have seen that John Fenwick, a part proprietor of West New Jersey, founded the settlement of Salem and began to act as the virtual dictator and feudal owner of the colony. Fenwick was arrested in late 1676 for usurping the government of the colony and was convicted and fined in New York. At this time the joint proprietors of West New Jersey—all Quakers—were Edward Byllinge, William Penn, Gawen Larie, and Nicholas Lucas, and Fenwick's small share was transferred to two of his creditors.

In March 1677 the proprietors issued the Concessions and Agreements, a document written largely by Edward Byllinge, who was assisted by William Penn. It was signed by all the proprietors and freeholders of the colony. The Concessions and Agreements established a frame of government for West New Jersey. This was a highly liberal document—especially for a proprietary decree—that guaranteed no taxation save by consent of the people ("we put the power in the people"), a representative assembly, trial by jury, full religious liberty ("no person to be called into question or molested for conscience under any pretext whatever"), and no imprisonment for debt. Penn, in 1675, had urged the liberal program of civil freedom, liberty of conscience, and trial by jury, but the veteran libertarian here was Edward Byllinge. In 1659 Byllinge, in *A Mite of Affection,* had called for, among other liberal demands, freedom for all Christians, no coercion in religious matters, no imprisonment for debt or execution for theft. Byllinge's views were in turn deeply influenced by the libertarian Leveller movement, which had earlier been prominent during England's civil war.*

Another remarkable feature of the Concessions and Agreements was that, in keeping with the Levellers'—and Byllinge's—hostility to feudalism, it reserved virtually no governmental powers to the proprietors. This was a refreshing contrast to the usual practice of grabbing as much power as was feasible.

The West New Jersey Assembly was to be elected by all freeholders, by the unusual institution of secret ballot, and was to be empowered to create courts and levy taxes. All legislation required a two-thirds vote of the Assembly, thus assuring a greater consensus for legislation than under mere majority rule. Furthermore, the colony was to be fully self-governing, with all executive power in the hands of ten commissioners appointed by the Assembly. Judges and constables were to be elected by popular vote rather than appointed. There were other unusually libertarian features of this constitution. Except for treason, felony, and murder, the plaintiff had full power to forgive, pardon, or remit punishment, thus placing the decision to prosecute and punish for a crime in the hands of the original victim rather than the remotely concerned government. Punishment for theft did not consist in paying a supposed debt to a mythical "society" by languishing unproductively in prison at taxpayers' expense; instead, it consisted in making restitution to the *victim* for the crime, and in working off this "debt" to the specific injured party. Furthermore, the beginnings of excellent long-standing white-Indian relations in the colony were assured by the provision that any Indian claim of injury would go to a jury of six whites and six Indians.

In keeping with the old Leveller opposition to feudalism, there was no provision for reserving land to proprietors; the shares of the proprietary were widened to a hundred, and the lands offered for sale. A headright system for wide distribution of land was instituted to induce settlement, with seventy acres granted to the first settler, plus an extra fifty to seventy acres for each servant brought over. Later settlers were to receive forty acres and twenty to thirty for each servant. Fortunately, there were few indentured servants in the colony, and therefore the land distribution was closer than usual to libertarian "homestead" allocation of new lands to first settlers. The unit farm was generally of medium size. The lands divided among the proprietors, however, were sold to speculators and therefore remained in large units until sold by them to the actual settlers. This transfer of land to the settlers was fortunately rapid, however, as the proprietors and speculators, eager for quick returns, subdivided the land into small

*See H. N. Brailsford, *The Levellers in the English Revolution* (Stanford, Calif.: Stanford University Press, 1961), pp. 639–41.

one-hundred-to-two-hundred-acre plots to ensure rapid sale. Another concession to feudalism and land monopoly was the requirement of a quitrent, ranging from a halfpenny to one penny per acre.

The proprietors quickly organized a Quaker settlement in 1677 at Burlington in West New Jersey. However, self-government under the Concessions and Agreements was not to be established readily. Governor Andros of New York, who had arrested Fenwick for assuming governmental powers in West New Jersey, now asserted his right to govern the territory from his New Castle bailiwick, and to subject it to New Castle constables and courts. Furthermore, Andros insisted that all ships trading with West New Jersey had to pay the New York customs levy at New Castle. West New Jersey's protests against this levy were to no avail. Andros did benefit the West New Jersey citizens, however, by remitting quitrents for three years to encourage settlement.

But even as Governor Andros was imposing his rule over West New Jersey, John Fenwick, in 1678, began to make trouble again. For his own purposes he protested Andros' rule and grandiosely threatened to dispossess any West New Jerseyan paying a tax to New Castle and Andros. By 1683 the rather remote Fenwick threat to the colony was ended, as his proprietary shares were deeded to William Penn.

As noted, in late 1680 the Duke of York, beset by political troubles at home, ended the Andros threat to the Jerseys by recalling the New York governor and positively reaffirming the proprietary rule of the East and West Jerseys. For West Jersey this confirmation, of course, included the right to trade without paying the hated customs duties to New Castle. The duke also was influenced in his decision by the desire at this time to placate powerful friends like William Penn.

Despite Andros' rule, the West Jersey Quakers had already been able to rule themselves in remarkably libertarian ways. For example, the settlers found that they had little need for courts. The Quakers settled their disputes out of court, voluntarily through informal mediators. This simple, direct, peaceful, rapid, highly efficient, and purely voluntary method of settling disputes was embodied in the phrase "Jersey justice," which stemmed from Thomas Olive's practice of mediating disputes while plowing in the fields. Thus, in the entire year of 1680, there were only two or three court actions in the whole colony.

The people of West New Jersey were not, however, destined to enjoy the rights and liberties of the Concessions and Agreements unmolested or undiluted. For in confirming the proprietary rule of West New Jersey, the Duke of York took it in his head to grant the sole right of government in the colony to Edward Byllinge, who thus became by far the most important proprietor.

Alas! The behavior of Edward Byllinge is yet another illustration of the heady wine of power corrupting the principles of liberty. For no sooner did Byllinge obtain the sole right to govern than he brazenly proclaimed himself governor of West New Jersey, thus repudiating the essence of his own libertarian Concessions. Byllinge appointed Samuel Jennings as deputy governor; Jennings would be his resident agent.

Thus, when the democratic General Assembly of West New Jersey first met in late 1681, a cloud hung over it; the promise of self-government was now much diluted by a proprietary governor. Elected Speaker of the Assembly was the highly popular Thomas Olive. Girded for action, the Assembly induced Jennings to agree to ten fundamental propositions, which in essence reconfirmed the rights and liberties of the beloved Concessions and Agreements. The propositions included these guarantees: yearly assemblies; no laws instituted by the deputy governor alone; no dissolution of the assembly by the governor; the sole right of the Assembly to raise taxes and armies and to declare war; election of *all* public officers by the Assembly for one year, rather than appointment by the governor; all taxes to last for only one year; and religious freedom for all. Even those principles of criminal law emphasizing restitution to the victim of theft were reinstituted. And indicative of the liberalism of Jennings and Byllinge, Jennings agreed to these provisions without consulting the governor.

With Jennings and the Assembly working harmoniously, no feudal manors were erected in West New Jersey. A 500-acre maximum of land grants discouraged the arbitrary accumulation of large estates, and the competition for settlers led the government to make the quitrents negligible. The consequence of West New Jersey land policy then was an approach toward the libertarian homesteading principle, with land being sold at the reltively cheap rate of five to ten pounds per hundred acres.

A struggle now ensued between the angered Edward Byllinge, who refused to recognize the agreement, and the people of West New Jersey, led now by Samuel Jennings, who was in thorough accord with the liberties granted in the original Concessions. Finally, in 1683, on hearing rumors that Byllinge was coming to Jersey to take the reigns of command personally, West New Jersey revolted; the Assembly elected Jennings as governor and elected a Council to help him. The colony was now totally self-governing. The Assembly then reproclaimed the original Concessions as the colony's fundamental law, with this addition: it provided for amendments to the Concessions by a six-sevenths vote of the Assembly. *No* amendment was to be permitted to weaken liberty of conscience, procedural protections such as the laws of evidence in trials, or guarantees of trial by jury.

Byllinge's reaction was to have his sole right to govern immediately reconfirmed by the Crown, and then to submit the dispute to a Quaker arbitration board of fourteen, who decided for Byllinge on the peculiar ground that it was impossible to divide the right to govern into many parties. Byllinge then appointed John Skene as deputy governor. In late 1685 Skene formally took over the government and fired most of the magistrates. The Assembly, however, overwhelmingly rejected a new charter proposed by Byllinge.

By now, Edward Byllinge was not only the sole governor, but also the largest proprietor of West New Jersey, holding twenty shares of the more than one hundred. During 1687 the resident proprietors of the colony, like their counterparts in East New Jersey, established a Council of Proprietors of West New Jersey to decide on use and disposal of proprietary lands. Before his death at the turn of 1687, Byllinge sold all of his rights to Dr. Daniel Coxe, the English court physician and non-Quaker, who announced his repudiation of the Concessions.

55

"The Holy Experiment": The Founding of Pennsylvania, 1681-1690

The example of West Jersey taught William Penn two lessons: it was possible, given sufficient territory, to found a large Quaker settlement in America; and it was best to secure a charter for such a colony directly from the king. In the vast stretches of America, Penn envisaged a truly Quaker colony, "a Holy experiment . . . that an example may be set up to the nations."

In his quest for such a charter, Penn was aided by the fact that the Crown had owed his father, Admiral Sir William Penn, the huge sum of 16,000 pounds for loans and back salary. In March 1681 the king agreed to grant young William, the admiral's heir, proprietary ownership of the lands west of the Delaware River and north of the Maryland border in exchange for canceling the old debt. The land was to be called Pennsylvania. Penn was greatly aided in securing the charter by his friendship with the king and other high officials of the court.

The proprietary charter was not quite as absolute as the colonial charters granted earlier in the century. The proprietor could rule only with the advice and consent of an assembly of freemen—a provision quite satisfactory to Penn. The Privy Council could veto Pennsylvania's actions, and the Crown, of course, could hear appeals from litigation in the colony. The Navigation Acts had to be enforced, and there was an ambiguous provision implying that England could impose taxes in Pennsylvania.

As soon as Penn heard news of the charter, he dispatched his cousin William Markham to be deputy governor of Pennsylvania. The latter informed the five hundred or so Swedish and Dutch residents on the west bank of the Delaware of the new charter. In the fall Markham was succeeded by four commissioners, and they were succeeded by Thomas Holme as deputy governor in early 1682.

In May William Penn made the Frame of Government the constitution for the colony. The Frame was amended and streamlined, and became the Second Frame of 1683, also called the Charter of Liberties. The Frame provided, first, for full religious freedom for all theists. No compulsory religion was to be enforced. The Quaker ideal of religious liberty was put into practice. Only Christians, however, were to be eligible for public office; later, at the insistence of the Crown, Catholics were barred from official posts in the colony.

The government, as instituted by the Frame, comprised a governor, the proprietor; an elected Council, which performed executive and supreme judicial functions; and an Assembly, elected by the freeholders. Justices of lower courts were appointed by the governor. But while the Assembly, like those in other colonies, had the only power to levy taxes, its powers were more restricted than those of assemblies elsewhere. Only the Council could initiate laws, and the Assembly was confined to ratifying or vetoing the Council's proposals.

William Penn himself arrived in America in the fall of 1682 to institute the new colony. He announced that the Duke's Laws would be temporarily in force and then called an Assembly for December. The Assembly included representatives not only of three counties of Pennsylvania, but also of the three lower counties of Delaware. For Delaware—or New Castle and the lower counties on the west bank of Delaware Bay—had been secured from the Duke of York in August. While Penn's legal title to exercising governmental functions over Delaware was dubious, he pursued it boldly. William Penn now owned the entire west bank of the Delaware River.

The Assembly confirmed the amended Frame of Government, including the declaration of religious liberty, and this code of laws constituted the "Great Law of Pennsylvania." The three lower Delaware counties were placed under one administration, separate from Pennsylvania proper.

Penn was anxious to promote settlement as rapidly as possible, both for religious (a haven to Quakers) and for economic (income for himself) reasons. Penn advertised the virtues of the new colony far and wide throughout Europe. Although he tried to impose quitrents and extracted selling prices for land, he disposed of the land at easy terms. The prices of land were cheap. Fifty acres were granted to each servant at the end of his term of service. Fifty acres also were given for each servant brought into the colony. Land sales were mainly in moderate-sized parcels. Penn soon found that at the rate of one shilling per hundred acres, quitrents were extremely difficult to collect from the settlers.

Induced by religious liberty and relatively cheap land, settlers poured into Pennsylvania at a remarkably rapid rate, beginning in 1682. Most of the immigrants were Quakers; in addition to English Quakers came Welsh, Irish, and German Quakers. Penn laid out the capital, destined to become the great city of Philadelphia, and changed the name of the old Swedish settlement of Upland to Chester. The German Quakers, led by Francis Daniel Pastorius, founded Germantown. In addition to Quakers, there came other groups attracted by the promise of full religious liberty: German Lutherans, Catholics, Mennonites, and Huguenots. The growth of Pennsylvania was rapid: 3,000 immigrants arrived during this first year; by 1684 the population of Philadelphia was 2,500, and of Pennsylvania, 8,000. There were over 350 dwellings in Philadelphia by the end of 1683. By 1689 there were over 12,000 people in Pennsylvania.

One of William Penn's most notable achievements was to set a remarkable pattern of peace and justice with the Indians. In November 1682 Penn concluded the first of several treaties of peace and friendship with the Delaware Indians at Shackamaxon, near Philadelphia. The Quaker achievement of maintaining peace with the Indians for well over half a century has been disparaged; some have held that it applied to only the mild Delaware Indians, who were perpetually cowed by the fierce but pro-English Iroquois. But this surely accounts for only part of the story. For the Quakers not only insisted on voluntary purchase of land from the Indians; they also treated the Indians as human beings, as deserving of respect and dignity as anyone else. Hence they deserved to be treated with honesty, friendliness, and evenhanded justice. As a consequence, the Quakers were treated precisely the same way in return. No drop of Quaker blood was ever shed by the Indians. So strong was the mutual trust between the races that Quaker farmers unhesitatingly left their children in the care of the Indians. Originally, too, the law provided that whenever an Indian was involved in a trial, six whites and six Indians would constitute the jury.

Voltaire, rapturous over the Quaker achievement, wittily and perceptively wrote that the Shackamaxon treaty was "the only treaty between Indians and Christians that was never sworn to and that was never broken." Voltaire went on to say that for the Indians "it was truly a new sight to see a sovereign [William Penn] to whom everyone said 'thou' and to whom one spoke with one's hat on one's head; a government without priests, a people without arms, citizens as equal as the magistrate, and neighbors without jealousy." Other features of the Assembly's early laws were Puritanical acts barring dramas, drunkenness, etc. More liberally, oaths were not required and the death penalty applied only to the crime of murder. Punishment was considered for purposes of reform. Feudal primogeniture was abolished. To make justice more efficient and informal, the government undertook to appoint three arbitrators in every precinct, to hand down decisions in disputes. The Quakers, however, unsatisfactorily evaded the problem of what to do about a military force. So as not to violate Quaker principle against bearing arms, the Friends refused to serve in the militia, but they still maintained a militia in the province, and non-Quaker officials were appointed in command. But surely if armies are evil, then voting for taxes and for laws in support of the evil is serving that evil and therefore not to be condoned.

On the question of free speech for criticizing government, laws were, unfortunately, passed prohibiting the writing or uttering of anything malicious, of anything stirring up dislike of the governor, or of anything tending to subvert the government.

The tax burden was extremely light in Pennsylvania. The only tax laws were enacted in 1683; these placed a small duty on liquor and cider, a general duty on goods, and an export duty on hides and furs. But Governor Penn promptly set aside all taxes for a year to encourage settlers. In 1684, however, another bill to raise import and other duties for William Penn's personal use was tabled; instead, a group of leaders of Pennsylvania pointed out that the colony would progress much faster if there were no taxes to cripple trade. These men heroically promised to raise 500 pounds for Penn as a gift, if the tax bill were dropped. The tax bill was dropped, but not all the money raised.

As might have been predicted, the first political conflict in Pennsylvania came as a protest against the curious provisions of the Frame restricting the Assembly to ratifying bills initiated by the Council. In the spring of 1683, several assemblymen urged that the Assembly be granted the power to initiate legislation. Several of Penn's devotees attacked the request as that which seemed "to render him ingratitude for his goodness towards the people." The Assembly balked too at granting the governor veto power over itself. There are indications that the non-Quaker elements in the Assembly were particularly active in criticizing the great powers assumed by the governor and the Council. One of the leaders of the incipient opposition to Penn was the non-Quaker Nicholas More, Speaker of the Assembly in 1684. And Anthony Weston, apparently a non-Quaker, was publicly whipped on three successive days for his "presumption and contempt of this government and authority."

Having founded the new colony and its government, and hearing of renewed persecution of Quakers at home, William Penn returned to England in the fall of 1684. He soon found his expectations of large proprietary profits from the vast royal grant to be in vain. For the people of the struggling young colony of Pennsylvania extended the principles of liberty far beyond what Penn was willing to allow. The free people of Pennsylvania would not vote for taxes, and simply would not pay the quitrents to Penn as feudal overlord. As a result, Penn's deficits in ruling Pennsylvania were large and his fortune dwindled steadily. In late 1685 Penn ordered the officials to use force to protect the monopoly of lime production that he had granted himself, in order to prevent others from opening lime quarries.

As to quitrents, Penn, to encourage settlement, had granted a moratorium until 1685. The people insisted that payment be postponed another year, and Penn's threatened legal proceedings were without success. Penn was especially aggrieved that his agents in Pennsylvania failed to press his levies upon the people with sufficient zeal. Presumably, the free tax-less air of Pennsylvania had contaminated them. As Penn complained in the fall of 1686: "The great fault is, that those who are there lose their authority one way or another in the spirits of the people and then they can do little with their outward powers."

After Penn returned to England in 1684, the Council virtually succeeded him in governing the colony. The Council assumed full executive powers, and, since it was elected rather than appointed, this left Pennsylvania as a virtually self-governing colony. Though Thomas Lloyd, a Welsh Quaker, had by Penn been appointed as president of the Council, the president had virtually no power and could make no decisions on his own. Because the Council met very infrequently, and because no officials had any power to act in the interim, during these intervals Pennsylvania had almost no government at all—and seemed not to suffer from the experience. During the period from late 1684 to late 1688, there were no meetings of the Council from the end of October 1684 to the end of March 1685; none from November 1686 to March 1687; and virtually none from May 1687 to late 1688. The councillors, for one thing, had little to do. And being private citizens rather than bureaucrats, and being unpaid as councillors, they had their own struggling businesses to attend to. There was no inclination under these conditions to dabble in political affairs. The laws had called for a small payment to the councillors, but, typically, it was found to be almost impossible to extract these funds from the populace.

If for most of 1684-88 there was no colonywide government in existence, what of the local officials? Were they not around to provide that evidence of the state's continued existence, which so many people through the ages have deemed vital to man's very survival? The answer is no. The lower courts met only a few days a year, and the county officials were, again, private citizens who devoted very little time to upholding the law. No, the reality must be faced that the new, but rather large, colony of Pennsylvania lived for the greater part of four years in a *de facto* condition of individual anarchism, and seemed none the worse for the experience. Furthermore, the Assembly passed no laws after 1686, as it was involved in a continual wrangle over attempts to increase its powers and to amend, rather than just reject, legislation.

A bit of government came in 1685, in the person of William Dyer as collector of the king's customs. But despite the frantic urgings of William Penn for cooperation with Dyer, Pennsylvanians persisted in their *de facto* anarchism by blithely and regularly evading the royal navigation laws.

William Penn had the strong and distinct impression that his "holy experiment" had slipped away from him, had taken a new and bewildering turn. Penn had launched a colony that he thought would be quietly subject to his dictates and yield him a handsome profit. By providing a prosperous haven of refuge for Quakers, he had expected in turn the rewards of wealth and power. Instead, he found himself without either. Unable to collect revenue from the free and independent-minded Pennsylvanians, he saw the colony slipping gracefully into outright anarchism—into a growing and flourishing land of no taxes and virtually no state. Penn frantically determined to force Pennsylvania back into the familiar mold of the old order. Accordingly, he appointed vice commissioners of state in February 1687 "to act in the execution of laws, as if I myself were there present, reserving myself the confirming of what is done, and my peculiar royalties and advantages." Another purpose of the appointments, he added, was "that there may be a more constant residence of the honorary and governing part of the government for the keeping all things in good order." Penn appointed the five commissioners from the colony's leading citizens, Quakers and non-Quakers, and ordered them to enforce the laws.

The colonists were evidently content in their anarchism, and shrewdly engaged in nonviolent resistance against the commission. In fact, they scarcely paid any attention to the commission. A year passed before the commission was even mentioned in the minutes of the Council. News about the commission was delayed until the summer of 1687 and protests against the plan poured in to Penn. The commissioners, and the protesters too, pretended that they had taken up their posts as a continuing executive. Finally, however, Penn grew suspicious and asked why he had received no communication from the supposedly governing body.

Unable to delay matters any longer, the reluctant commissioners of state took office in February 1688, a year after their appointment. Three and one-half years of substantive anarchism were over. The state was back in its heaven; once more all was right with the world. Typically, Penn urged the commissioners to conceal any differences they might have among themselves, so as to deceive and overawe the public: "Show your virtues but conceal your infirmities; this will make you awful and revered with ye people." He further urged them to enforce the king's duties and to levy taxes to support the government.

The commissioners confined themselves to calling the Assembly into session in the spring of 1688, and this time the Assembly did pass some laws, for the first time in three years. The two crucial bills presented by the commissioners and the Council regulated the export of deerskins and once again, levied customs duties on imports so as to obtain funds to finance the government—in short, imposed taxes on a taxless colony. After almost passing the tax bill, the Assembly heroically defied the government once again and rejected the two bills.

The state had reappeared in a flurry of activity in early 1688, but was found wanting, and the colony, still taxless, quickly lapsed back into a state of anarchism. The commissioners somehow failed to meet and the Council met only only once between the spring meeting and December. Pennsylvania was once again content with a supposedly dreadful and impossible state of affairs. And when this idyll came to an end in December 1688 with the arrival of a new deputy governor, appointed by Penn, the deputy governor "had difficulty finding the officers of the government. . . . [He] found the Council room deserted and covered with dust and scattered papers. The wheels of government had nearly stopped turning."*

William Penn, seeing that the Pennsylvanians had happily lapsed into an anarchism that precluded taxes, quitrents, and political power for himself, decided to appoint a deputy governor. But the people of Pennsylvania, having tasted the sweets of pure liberty, were almost unanimously reluctant to relinquish that liberty. We have observed that the commissioners of state had failed to assume their posts and had virtually failed to function after it was presumed they accepted. No one wanted to rule others. For this reason, Thomas Lloyd, the president of the Council, refused appointment as deputy governor. At this point, Penn concluded that he could not induce the Quakers of Pennsylvania to institute a state, and so he turned to a tough non-Quaker, an old Puritan soldier and a non-Pennsylvanian, John Blackwell.

Once a state has completely withered away, it is an extremely difficult task to re-create it, as Blackwell quickly discovered. If Blackwell had been under any illusions that the Quakers were a meek and passive people, he was in for a rude surprise. He was to find very quickly that devotion to peace, to liberty, and to individualism in no sense implies passive resignation to tyranny. Quite the contrary.

In announcing Blackwell's appointment in September 1688, Penn made it clear that his primary task was to collect Penn's quitrents and secondarily to reestablish a government. As Penn instructed Blackwell: "Rule the meek meekly, and those that will not be ruled, rule with authority."

John Blackwell's initial reception as deputy governor was an omen of things to come. Sending word ahead for someone to meet him upon his arrival in New York, he landed there only to find no one to receive him. After waiting in vain for three days, Blackwell went alone to New Jersey. When he arrived at Philadelphia on December 17, he found no escort, no parade, no reception committee. We have mentioned that Blackwell couldn't find the Council or any other government officials—and this was after he had ordered the Council to meet upon his arrival. One surly escort appeared and he refused to speak to the new governor. And when Blackwell arrived at the empty Council room, a group of boys from the neighborhood gathered around to hoot and jeer.

The Quakers, led by Thomas Lloyd, now embarked on a shrewd and determined campaign of resistance to the imposition of a state. Thomas Lloyd, as keeper of the great seal, insisted that none of Blackwell's orders or commissions was valid unless stamped with the great seal. Lloyd, the

*Edwin B. Bronner, *William Penn's "Holy Experiment"* (New York; Temple University Publications, 1962), p. 108. To Professor Bronner belongs the credit for discovering this era of anarchism in Pennsylvania.

keeper, refused to do the stamping. It is amusing to find Edward Channing and other thorough but not overly imaginative historians deeply puzzled by this resistance: "This portion of Pennsylvania history is unusually difficult to understand. We find, for instance, so strong and intelligent a man as Thomas Lloyd declining to obey what appeared to be reasonable and legal direction on the part of the proprietor. As keeper of the great seal of the province, Lloyd refused point blank to affix that emblem of authenticity to commissions which Blackwell presented to him."* What Channing failed to understand was that Pennsylvanians were engaged in a true revolutionary situation, that they were all fiercely determined to thwart the reimposition of a burdensome state upon their flourishing stateless society. That is why even the most "reasonable and legal" orders were disobeyed, for Pennsylvanians had for some years been living in a world where *no one* was giving orders to anyone else.

Lloyd persistently refused to hand over the great seal or to stamp any of Blackwell's documents or appointments with it. Furthermore, David Lloyd, clerk of the court and a distant relative of Thomas, refused absolutely to turn over the documents of cases to Blackwell even if the judges so ordered. For this act of defiance, Blackwell declared David Lloyd unfit to serve as court clerk and dismissed him, but Thomas Lloyd promptly reappointed David by virtue of his alleged power as keeper of the great seal.

As a revolutionary situation grows and intensifies, unanimity can never prevail; the timid and the shortsighted begin to betray the cause. Thus the Council, frightened at the Lloyds' direct acts of rebellion, now sided with Blackwell. The pro-Blackwell clique was headed by Griffith Jones, who had consented to let Blackwell live at his home in Philadelphia. Jones warned that "it is the King's authority that is opposed and looks to me as if it were raising a force to rebel." Of the members of the Council, only Arthur Cook remained loyal to the Lloyds and to the resistance movement. Of a dozen justices of the peace named by Blackwell, four bluntly refused to serve.

When Blackwell found out the true state of affairs in Pennsylvania, his state-bound soul was understandably appalled. Here was a thriving trade based on continuing violations of the navigation laws. Here, above all, were no taxes, hence no funds to set up a government. As Bronner puts it: "He [Blackwell] deplored the lack of public funds in the colony which made it impossible to hire a messenger to call the Council, a doorkeeper, and someone to search ships to enforce the laws of England. He believed that some means should be found to collect taxes for the operation of the government."** His general view, as he wrote to

---

*Edward Channing, *A History of the United States*, 6 Vols. (New York: Macmillan, 1905-25) 2:125.

**Bronner, *"Holy Experiment,"* p. 119.

Penn, was the familiar statist cry that the colonists were suffering from excessive liberty: they had eaten more of the "honey of your concessions . . . than their stomachs can bear."

Blackwell managed to force the Council to meet every week during the first months of 1689, but his suggestion that every county be forced to maintain a permanent councillor in Philadelphia was protested by the Council. Arthur Cook led the successful resistance, maintaining that the "people were not able to bear the charge of constant attendance."

As Blackwell continued to denounce the Council and Pennsylvania as a whole before his accession, Pennsylvanian opposition to his call for statism was further intensified. On the Council, Arthur Cook was joined in the intransigent camp by Samuel Richardson, who launched the cry that Penn had no power to name a deputy governor. For this open defiance, Richardson was ejected from the Council.

The conflict of views continued to polarize Blackwell and the Pennsylvanians. Finally, the climax came on April 2, 1689, when Blackwell introduced proceedings for the impeachment of Thomas Lloyd, charging him with eleven high crimes and misdemeanors. (Blackwell had also refused to seat Lloyd when the latter was elected councillor from Bucks County.) In his impeachment speech, Blackwell trumpeted to his stunned listeners that Penn's and therefore his own powers over the colony were absolute. Penn was a feudal lord who could create manorial courts; furthermore, Penn could not transfer his royally delegated powers to the people, but only to a deputy such as himself. The Council, according to Blackwell's theory, existed in no sense to represent the people, but to be an instrument for William Penn's will. Blackwell concluded this harangue by threatening to unsheathe and wield his sword against his insolent and unruly opponents.

Blackwell's proclamation of absolute rule now truly polarized the conflict. The choice was now narrowed: the old anarchism or the absolute rule by Blackwell. Given this confrontation, those wavering had little choice but to give Thomas Lloyd their full support.

Blackwell now summarily dismissed from the Council Thomas Lloyd, Samuel Richardson, and John Eckly. On April 9, while the Council—the supreme judicial arm of the colony—was debating the charge against Lloyd, Blackwell threatened to remove Joseph Growdon. At this point, the Council rebelled and demanded the right to approve its own members. Refusing to meet further without its duly elected members, the Council was then dissolved by Blackwell.

With the Council homeward bound, the disheartened Blackwell sent his resignation to Penn, while seven councillors bitterly protested to Penn against his deputy's attempt to deprive them of their liberties. As for Blackwell, he believed the Quakers to be those agents of the devil foretold in the New Testament, who "despise dominion and speak evil of dignities."

From this point on, the decision was in the hands of Governor Penn, and Penn decided in favor of the Quakers and against Blackwell. For the rest of the year, Blackwell continued formally in office, but lost all concern for making changes or exerting his rule. From April 1689 until early 1690 he was waiting out his term. Blackwell wrote to Penn that "I now only wait for the hour of my deliverance." He summed up his grievance against the Quakers: "These people have not the principles of government amongst them, nor will be informed. . . ."

Meanwhile, the Assembly, headed by Arthur Cook, met in May and fell apart on the issue of protesting the arrest of one of its members. Between May and the end of the year, the Council met only twice. Pennsylvania was rapidly slipping back toward its previous state of anarchism. William Penn enlivened this trend by deciding to reestablish the old system with the Council as a whole his deputy governor. Writing to the leading Quakers of Pennsylvania, Penn apologized for his mistake in appointing Blackwell but wistfully reminded them that he had done so because "no Friend would undertake the Governor's place." Now he told them: "I have thought fit . . . to throw all into your hands, that you may all see the confidence I have in you." With Blackwell out of office, the Council, back in control, resumed its somnolent ways. Again headed by Thomas Lloyd, it met rarely, did virtually nothing, and told William Penn even less. Anarchism had returned in triumph to Pennsylvania. And when Secretary William Markham, who had been one of the hated Blackwell clique, submitted a petition for levying taxes to provide some financial help for William Penn, the Council completely ignored the request.

56

The Dominion of New England

When Sir Edmund Andros arrived at Boston at the end of December 1686 to take up his post as governor general of the Dominion of New England, the history of all the northern colonies entered a new and significant phase. James II could not have picked a better instrument for the fulfillment of his grand design to smash all self-government, all local government, in the northern colonies, and to inflict on them an absolute centralized despotism under the English Crown. So congenial was this task to him that in America the name "Andros" was for generations afterward synonymous with tyranny.

Andros lost no time in forcefully impressing upon the people of Massachusetts that the old easy days of the Dudley feast of privilege were over. Arriving with two companies of English soldiers to intimidate the colony, one of Andros' first acts was to force South Church, one of the Puritan churches of Boston, to permit Anglicans to hold services there. Furthermore, Andros' frankly proclaimed goal was to force the Puritan community of the colony to pay for the establishment of an Anglican church.

Andros speedily imposed despotic rule upon Dominion territory. He ran roughshod over the Council, consulting only a few of his favorites and accumulating full power in his own hands. Edward Randolph stayed on as faithful servitor and collector of customs, but he had no share in Andros' decisions. He was, in fact, persuaded to rent the office of secretary to a friend of Andros', John West, who proceeded to mulct the public by greatly increasing his fees to the citizenry. Moreover, all documents, deeds, wills, mortgages, etc., now had to be registered centrally with

West, and for heavy fees. All government officials, furthermore, were now to hold their appointments solely from the Crown.

Andros' tyrannical reign placed the Massachusetts economy in a crippling vise. For one thing, Andros grievously crippled the economy by strictly enforcing the Navigation Acts. Two years after Andros' arrival, Randolph admitted, "This country is poor, the exact execution of the acts of trade hath much impoverished them [the colonists]." The economic depression was aggravated by heavy new duties imposed by James II on tobacco and sugar; these injured New England's trade with the West Indies and the Southern colonies. Depression of trade under the Dominion was so severe that one of New England's leading merchants, Richard Wharton, left such a debt-burdened estate when he died in early 1689 that his daughters had to open a shop to make a living.

But just when Andros' crackdown greatly crippled the Massachusetts economy, his steeply increased expenditures burdened it even further and aggravated the depression. In short, just at the time when the ability to pay taxes in Massachusetts was sharply lowered, more taxes were imposed upon it. Ironically, part of the increased burden of government was to pay for enforcement of the very laws that were crippling the economy.

One of the biggest factors in the increased governmental burden was Andros' own salary of 1,200 pounds, an item larger than the entire appropriation for the Dudley government during 1686. In addition, Andros built expensive and useless forts at the seaports. The largest single financial drain was the maintenance of a standard army of two companies of infantry.

The funds of the Dudley government were limited by its unwillingness to impose further taxes without an Assembly, but Andros had no such scruples. Andros decreed raises in taxes, including a doubled excise on liquor, increased import duties, and a direct tax on land. Total estimated revenue in the Dominion rose over fifty percent, from 2,500 to 3,800 pounds per annum. Furthermore, Andros barred the towns from levying their own taxes, thus reducing them to subservient instruments of the central government.

To the citizens of Massachusetts, one of Andros' most frightening and threatening actions was ordering the reconfirmation of all private land titles, for high fees for this coerced "service." The reconfirmation meant going on the land rolls for payment of a high quitrent of two shillings, sixpence per hundred acres on all the lands. Furthermore, most land titles had been obtained from town proprietors, and the New Englanders feared that Andros would not recognize town titles as legal, since the General Courts had not been authorized in their charters to incorporate towns. Horror at the Andros land policy united diverse groups in opposition to his regime. Only about two hundred persons in the Dominion actually applied for land titles during Andros' administration, and these were largely government favorites or Crown officers. The general indignation at the quitrents was voiced by Rev. Increase Mather, who charged that the Massachusetts settlements were "houses which their own hands have built, and the lands which at vast charges in subduing a wilderness they have for many years had as rightful possession of, as ever any people in the world have or can have." Another Massachusetts citizen denounced the "parcel of strangers" who proposed to come in and seize what the people and "their fathers before them had labored for."

In the course of opposing the new aggressive theory of the Crown, the Massachusetts Puritans developed a radically libertarian theory of land titles. In a public confrontation with Governor Andros, Rev. John Higginson of Salem declared that the right to soil came not from the Crown, but from God, and God gave the land to the people who actually occupied it and brought it into use—that is, either the Indians, from whom lands could be bought by voluntary purchase, or the settlers. The Crown, in truth, had no right to ownership of the new lands. The idea that Christians had an automatic right to the land of heathens, added Higginson, was a "popish" principle and hence abhorrent. Governor Andros' reply was characteristic: "Either you are subjects, or you are rebels!"

In mid-1688 Andros moved to force land applications by proceeding with a test case of eviction against the eminent old Puritan Samuel Sewall, who joined in Wharton's protest and sailed to England to complain to the Crown. He also proceeded against Samuel Shrimpton, an Anglican merchant who also decided to appeal to the king. Symbolic of the drawing together of diverse groups against the Andros tyranny was the uniting of Sewall, Shrimpton, and Rev. Cotton Mather to plan strategy against the regime.

In addition, Andros engaged in enough land-grabbing for his favorites to anger the people even more. He seized 150 acres of common pasture land in Charlestown, owned jointly by James Russell and others, and gave the land to a favorite, Col. Charles Lidgett, a merchant who supplied masts to the royal navy. Russell, vehemently protesting this legalized theft, was punished by a writ of intrusion to eject him from his own farm. When the outraged citizens of Charlestown pulled up Lidgett's stakes on the pasture land, they were imprisoned and fined. Common pasture land of several other towns, including Lynn and Cambridge, was forcibly enclosed by Andros' edict and given to several of his friends.

Edward Randolph, characteristically, attempted to join in the plunder and to grab several tracts of land. One such tract was 500 acres of common pasture at Lynn, Massachusetts. But after vigorous protest by the citizens of Lynn, a happy solution was found: the common land was divided among several inhabitants of Lynn on a quitrent basis. Randolph also tried to seize land tracts near Cambridge and Watertown and in

Rhode Island. Other Council members able to grab land for themselves were Jonathan Tyng and John Usher, who obtained an island in Casco Bay.

In Maine, disputes over land claims and titles were referred to Edward Tyng and Silvanus Davis for settlement, both of whom were personally interested in land claims there. In New Hampshire there arose bitter resistance against Andros' enforcement of court judgments to eject settlers from their lands in order to satisfy the property claims of Robert Mason. The citizens of New Hampshire petitioned Andros to stop these confiscations, for they were "likely to be sore oppressed if not wholly ruined." Happily, however, the king ended the grievance by purchasing Mason's proprietary and quitrent claims in exchange for an annual pension. Moreover, the king instructed Andros to reconfirm all existing land titles in New Hampshire. The Mason threat to the people of New Hampshire was again ended.

Andros' regime speedily alienated not only the Puritans but also the merchants, including the former opportunist supporters of Dudley. On the one hand, Andros frightened the landowners by ordering reconfirmation of all land titles and the imposition of quitrents; on the other, the merchants were alienated by strict enforcement of the Navigation Acts. The pet schemes for privileges of Dudley and the other councillors were discarded, and even the bureaucratic plums went, not to the Massachusetts opportunists, but to such old New York cronies of Andros as John West and John Palmer. Andros not only was making himself the most hated man in years, but was cutting himself off from bases of support in the colony. Of course, the naked force of the Crown and its bayonets remained to him, as did the costly English troops—whom the Massachusetts citizens were forced to support for their own suppression. In addition, he angered the people by centralizing the town militia under his direct command.

One of Andros' better acts served especially to alienate the opportunist clique. As governor of the Dominion, Andros began as ruler of the Maine towns, New Hampshire, Massachusetts, and King's Province (the Narragansett Country). Surveying the situation, Andros decided that the powerful Atherton Company's claim to the Narragansett lands was arbitrary and unjust. He realized that the claim was gravely restricting settlement in these fertile lands, and recommended to the Lords of Trade that all the claims of unimproved—unsettled—land be vacated. This excellent recommendation frantically drove one of the proprietors, Richard Wharton, to London to press his claim.

The sturdily independent citizens of Massachusetts did not let these hammer blows to liberty go by without vigorous protest. When Andros imposed his new taxes, he required all the towns to levy a compulsory assessment upon themselves for the required amount. Each town was

415

ordered to choose a commissioner to assess and collect these taxes. Many towns steadfastly refused to make such appointments; among the towns were those of Essex County (north of Boston) except Salem, Newbury, and Marblehead.

Essex County resistance centered in the town of Ipswich. When Ipswich in August 1687 received the government order to choose a commissioner to assess the taxes, the leaders of the town, headed by its young liberal Puritan minister, Rev. John Wise, and the town clerk, former deputy John Appleton, met and decided that it was "not the town's duty any way to assist that ill way of raising money without a General Assembly." The government order was condemned as abridging their "liberty as Englishmen." The next day the Ipswich town meeting approved this view; it refused to elect a commissioner and forbade the selectmen from imposing any taxes. The bold example set by Ipswich was followed by other Essex towns: Rowley, Haverhill, and Salisbury refused to elect commissioners, and the commissioners of Bradford and Andover refused to perform their functions.

For this resistance, Wise, Appleton, and four other leaders were imprisoned and tried, before a judicial system thoroughly reconstituted by the Andros regime. The selectmen and commissioners of the other resisting towns were also arrested; in all, twenty-eight leaders of Essex were indicted for "refusing to pay their rates . . . and making and publishing factious and seditious votes and writings against the same." The mass indictment cowed most of the prisoners into submission, and most of them made humble apology and were released on large bond to insure good behavior.

The six Ipswich leaders, however, remained adamant—the Reverend Mr. Wise "asserting the privilege of Englishmen according to Magna Carta"—and were subject to special trial. Instead of a trial before a jury at the place of the crime, the prisoners were dragged to Boston and the jurors deliberately selected from among foreigners and nonfreeholders of the colony. Constituting the special court were four leading officials in the Andros administration: Edward Randolph and three of the opportunists—Joseph Dudley, William Stoughton, and John Usher, treasurer. Dudley had typically landed on his feet and had found himself appointed to the congenial new post of censor of the press. Nothing in the colony was publishable without his permission.

The four judges gloried in their power at the trial. Dudley lorded it over Reverend Mr. Wise: "Mr. Wise, you have no more privileges left you than not to be sold for slaves." To Wise's pleas for English liberties, Dudley sharply replied that the laws of England could not follow them to the ends of the earth. A contemporary wag aptly remarked that if the *privileges* of English law did not follow them to the colonies, apparently its *penalties* did. The convicted prisoners were imprisoned for almost a month and then heavily fined. Wise and Appleton were fined fifty pounds and placed under the enormous bond of 1,000 pounds for a year's "good behavior." Under the lash of the staggering sentences, the remaining resistance to the new taxes in the colony collapsed. The following year, Andros crippled local powers of resistance even further by prohibiting more than one town meeting a year.

As the Andros tyranny continued, we have noted that various protesters sailed to England to seek redress, including Samuel Sewall and Richard Wharton. But the most powerful protester and agent of the Massachusetts people was the leading Puritan divine in the colony, the Reverend Increase Mather. Mather had been earlier denounced by Thomas Danforth in General Court as a traitor to Massachusetts for his willingness to compromise with the Crown. But Mather had now had enough and was ardently in favor of independence. In October 1687 Mather won the support of his church to go to England to plead New England's cause against Andros.

Edward Randolph now moved quickly to prevent Mather from going to England, suing him on a trumped-up charge of defamation to keep him in the colony. Mather was acquitted at the trial, but Randolph soon fabricated another charge. Mather, however, hid from the subpoena server, was spirited out of Boston in disguise, and lay in a small boat to board a ship for London. Andros sent out two boats to stop Mather's escape but the chase failed.

The meaning of the Dominion of New England must not be confined to the internal despotism imposed on Massachusetts Bay, for the main point of the Dominion was to impose the same central and absolute rule over *all* the northern colonies; under Andros, law was to be administered to the colonies as one unit. The colonies were to be centralized under one yoke—that of the Crown.

The Maine towns were already a part of Massachusetts, and the Andros tax, fee, and land policies were pursued with even more vigor in Maine, where resistance was so much weaker. New Hampshire had already been part of the Dominion during the Dudley regime, and after the Cranfield troubles, potential resistance to the Andros policy was exhausted. King's Province had also been part of the Dudley domain, but, as noted, Andros ruled against the Atherton Company's claim to that territory.

As soon as Andros arrived in Boston, he moved to seize Plymouth, Rhode Island, Cornwall (all of Maine east of the Kennebec), and Connecticut, and to place them alongside the other colonies under his Dominion rule. Rhode Island succumbed quickly and with surprising ease, and made no protest against the Andros rule. What had happened to Rhode Island individualism and its spirit of independence? Two major reasons can be pleaded for this change in Rhode Island's spirit.

First, all the old greats of the colony, the founding fathers of the first generation—Williams, Gorton, Coddington, Easton et al.—had recently died, and inferior men had replaced them. Second, the colony was charmed by Andros' siding with them and against the Atherton Company over the issue of the Narragansett lands.

Plymouth surrendered equally quickly, but with much greater opposition in the colony. The Judas who delivered Plymouth was Nathaniel Clarke, secretary of the colony. For his treachery he received an appointment on the Council of the Dominion, and from Andros a gift of the valuable Clarke's Island in Plymouth harbor. Rich in salt, pasturage, and timber, the island had been set aside by the Plymouth town government for support of its minister and the poor. The Reverend Ichabod Wiswall of Duxbury and Deacon John Founce, town clerk of Plymouth, were so incensed at this gift that they began to raise funds to carry the matter into the courts. Andros immediately had them arrested on the charge of "levying taxes" without his consent, and forced them to stand trial in Boston. The sickly Wiswall almost died during the ordeal.

There was also considerable opposition in Plymouth to the arbitary increase in taxes by Andros. The town of Taunton refused to elect a commissioner, declaring that it "did not feel free to raise money for the inhabitants without their own assent by an assembly." For daring to transmit this defiant resolution, the Taunton town clerk, Shadrach Wilbur, was imprisoned for three months by Andros and punished with a heavy fine. The town constables of Taunton were also arrested for neglect of duty, and one of the local justices was suspended for not arguing against the protest at the town meeting.

Also annexed to the new Dominion in early 1687 was eastern Maine, or Cornwall, transferred from New York. While under New York, Thomas Dongan had sent two commissioners, John West and John Palmer, to manage its affairs. West and Palmer there pioneered in the Andros technique of forcing the inhabitants to buy new confirmations for their land titles at exorbitant fees. Now Andros declared that the old Dongan-West-Palmer confirmations were invalid and that the matter must begin anew.

Connecticut, however, proved a far more difficult nut to crack. For one thing, Connecticut had bitter memories of Andros' attempted aggression against it during King Philip's War a dozen years before. It procrastinated for months. Its leaders, such as secretary John Allyn and Fitz-John Winthrop, were eager to sell out to Andros. Winthrop even praised the Dominion as containing "all things that will really conduce to the growth and prosperity of the people." But the General Court stood firm, and refused to surrender to Dominion rule. Finally, at the end of October 1687, after nearly a year had elapsed, Andros went to Hartford and simply seized the government. Fitz-John Winthrop was well rewarded by being made major general—the highest military office in New England—in charge of the militia of Connecticut, Rhode Island, and King's Province. In return Winthrop played the sycophant to the uttermost, expressing his admiration for Andros' loving care over New England and for "those designs your excellency lays to settle a lasting happiness to the prosperity of this country." Andros also made certain to appoint new courts, militia, and customs officers in Connecticut.

It should not be thought that his expansion of the area of Dominion brought the incidental but important advantages of a unified trade area for New England. On the contrary, Andros soon outlawed all traveling merchants and peddlers, thus narrowly confining trade to each local town and area.

In the area of religion, however, the creation of the Dominion had, willy-nilly, a libertarian impact. The Crown could not move toward the establishment of Anglicanism without disestablishing the Puritan church and providing religious liberty for non-Puritans. This problem was acute in Massachusetts, Plymouth, and Connecticut. Despite the great decline in Puritan fervor over the years, the theocracy still held sway. Especially was this true in Massachusetts, though even here it was now favored by only a minority of population of the colony, and was increasingly challenged by merchants who were not church members.

The Council of the Dominion, making laws for all New England, now had to decide whether to extend the Puritan establishment to the rest of New England (Rhode Island and Cornwall) or to end it everywhere. The Council's committee on codification urged the former course, but the Anglicans and Quakers on the Council fought this bitterly. Walter Clarke, a Quaker and former governor of Rhode Island, pointed out that since the Puritan ministers were just as much Dissenters from the Church of England as the Quakers or any other sect, they should therefore depend on voluntary contributions in the same way as all the others. Those citizens who would not voluntarily support a Puritan minister, said Clarke, should not be forced to pay against their will. The Council defeated the Puritan attempts at expansion, the Puritan establishment lapsed, and religious liberty and separation of church and state won the day. This result was aided by news of King James' Declaration of Indulgence of April 4, 1687, which granted liberty of conscience to all Englishmen, including Dissenters. The Quakers of Scituate (in Plymouth) promptly tested the law by refusing to pay taxes for the Puritan ministry, standing on the Declaration of Indulgence. Andros and the Council granted the Quakers' request for return of their property seized by the constables for nonpayment. Thus the Declaration of Indulgence and the refusal of Council to continue coerced support for the Puritans jointly brought disestablishment to New England.

Since the network of government schools in Massachusetts was Puritan, the Council's decision not to continue the Puritan establishment had the corollary libertarian effect of dissolving the government schools. Thrown back on voluntary or market support, many of the schools that had been artificially extended by relying on compulsion now had to close. Randolph would have liked to replace them with Anglican public schools, but was thwarted by lack of funds.

The crippling blow to the Puritan theocracy intensified the decline of Puritan zeal among the populace, and such ungodly customs as maypole dancing, stage plays, Sabbath breaking, and the drinking of alcohol spread more widely.

By the end of 1687 Sir Edmund Andros, as head of the Dominion of New England, was the sole and absolute ruler of all of New England from the towns of Maine to western Connecticut. But this was only the beginning of the expansion of the Dominion and of Andros' power. In the spring of 1688 Andros received instructions from King James II to incorporate the colonies of New York and the two New Jerseys into the Dominion. The king named Andros governor of the enlarged Dominion, with his headquarters still at Boston. He was, in addition, to appoint a deputy governor at New York to administer that colony and the Jerseys. The Dominion institutions, including the new taxes, quitrents, and press and book censorship, were now to be imposed on the expanded territory.

During August Andros traveled throughout New York and the Jerseys incorporating these colonies into the giant Dominion of New England. Captain Francis Nicholson, of Andros' footguard, was named deputy governor for New York and the Jerseys.

Governor Dongan of New York was, of course, unhappy at being replaced. For the citizens of that colony, the sudden loss of their home rule and their annexation by the Dominion of New England were additional important straws to add to their accumulating list of grievances. At first, some New Yorkers were mollified, as the Long Island towns were at long last reunited with New England, and the anti-Catholics were happy to see the departure of Dongan. But Andros' tyrannical policy soon changed their attitudes, especially his action in seizing the bulk of New York's public records and carrying them off to Boston. Francis Nicholson protested this seizure, and later was to note "how fatal it hath been to this city and the province of New York for to be annexed to that of Boston, which, if it had continued would have occasioned the total ruin of the inhabitants. . . ." Furthermore, the Dutch in New York were unhappy at being joined to their old enemy, New England. Nicholson too aroused the suspicions of the frenetic and was believed by many New Yorkers to be a crypto-Catholic.

East Jersey and West Jersey were incorporated into the Dominion without much difficulty, although there was considerable protest in West New Jersey at Andros' practice of reappointing existing public officials if they paid him a substantial fee. Some officials refused to pay for reappointment and launched public protests.

Governor Andros' foreign policy for the expanded Dominion continued the Dongan course of aggressive pressure on New France. Andros repeated a Dongan ultimatum that the French withdraw from a fort in Seneca country. The French quickly complied. English-oriented historians like to speak of a "French menace" to the American colonies, in justifying the aggressive actions of England and the English colonies against New France. And yet, New England *alone* had a population in 1688 of over 100,000, as compared with 12,000 in all of New France. Furthermore, the English were firmly allied against the French with the most powerful, bloodthirsty, and aggressive of the Indian tribes—the Iroquois. The real menace was to the thinly populated French; the record of Anglo-American aggression against New France in the colonial era is ample witness to that fact.

As soon as he took over the government of New York and the Jerseys, Andros held a conference at Albany with the Iroquois, reminiscent of a similar conference a decade and a half earlier. There he cemented the long-standing Iroquois-English alliance. In eastern Maine Andros issued an order forbidding anyone to trade or settle in the territory without a license from his government. Andros then proceeded to break into the Penobscot River trading post of a French resident, the Baron de St. Castine, and to confiscate his arms, furniture, and other supplies.

While Andros was away from Boston, some Indian depredations occurred at Saco. Immediately, Captain Blackman seized twenty suspect Indians and shipped them to Boston. Their alarmed tribesmen seized a few whites at Casco Bay to hold for a prisoner exchange. The prisoner exchange was agreed upon, but, typically, the white captain refused to admit an Indian peace party and several whites were killed in the skirmish that followed. The embittered Indians now joined forces with the equally embittered Castine, who promised them aid for raids against the English. Andros quieted the situation down by sternly rebuking Colonel Tyng of Casco Bay for exceeding his instructions by making war on the Indians: "By your seizing and disturbing the Indians you have alarmed all your parts and put them in a posture of war." Andros wisely ordered the release of all the Indians except the actual criminals. But the leaders on the spot, such as Tyng, John Hinckes, and William Stoughton, whipped up hysteria in Boston against the Indians and asked for supplies and troops. A draft of manpower ensued, and troops were sent north. The absurd hysteria over the Indians is seen in this account: "Upon receipt of news that two or three Indians had been seen skulking about along the frontier, orders were dispatched to the outlying towns . . . to send eight or ten armed horsemen every day to scout in search of Indians and kill any who refused to submit themselves."

The military commander of Cornwall went to the length of implicitly accusing Andros of excessive leniency to the Indians. As if to disprove the charge of softness in the face of the (nonexistent) threat, Andros sent two companies and several ships to the frontier and ordered the Indians to release all Englishmen and surrender all murderers of Englishmen. When the Indians retaliated by burning two towns, Andros mobilized a force of several hundred and garrisoned eleven forts along the frontier. Then, before any warfare occurred, Andros, in the venerable white tradition, launched a sneak attack on the Indians, destroying their homes, canoes, and supplies. In the traditional rationale of preventive war, this was done before the "least harm of mischief was done" by the Indians.

By the end of 1688 Sir Edmund Andros stood master of all he surveyed. Virtually the absolute ruler of all English America from the Delaware River to the St. Croix River in eastern Maine, the governor of the expanded Dominion of New England stood at the pinnacle of power. Indeed, with *quo warranto* action brewing against the remaining proprietary colonies, new peaks of power and expansion were on the horizon. But, as often happens, pride went before the fall; Andros was only a few more months at the pinnacle before he was tumbled, unceremoniously, into the trough.

57

The Glorious Revolution in the Northern Colonies, 1689-1690

The fall of Sir Edmund Andros, crucial as it was, was a reflection of the fall of his far mightier sovereign, James II, who was deposed in the virtually bloodless Glorious Revolution of November–December 1688 and replaced by William and Mary of Orange. William and Mary (the Protestant daughter of the Catholic James) were crowned the sovereigns of England in February 1689. This moderate shift from James II's despotism, as well as from his attempt to grant religious liberty to his fellow Catholics, brought an end to the seventeenth-century era of conflict and rebellion in England, Indeed, there has been nothing like a revolutionary upheaval in England since.

The news of the Glorious Revolution brought the thrill and joy of expected liberation to the northern colonies, all of which, save Pennsylvania, were groaning under the tyranny of Andros and the Dominion of New England. The example of the Glorious Revolution was all that was needed to fire the spark of revolt in the northern colonies. If the English tyrant could be overthrown, why not his American henchman?

Indeed all that was needed to spark a revolution was the news that the Glorious Revolution had begun. The news of William's November landing in England first reached Boston on April 5, and the successful outcome was not yet known in America. Andros, who had privately heard the truth in eastern Maine many weeks before, tried to keep the news from the people by arresting the hapless young man who brought the news. When he refused to remain silent, Andros sent him to prison without bail "for bringing traitorous and treasonable libels and papers of news." But news of this sort could not now be kept secret and preparation for a coup against Andros got quietly under way.

Wild rumors spread about the colony that Andros was a secret "papist," that he was conspiring with the French and the Indians to take over the colony, etc. It became evident to the leaders of the colony that a popular revolution against Andros was inevitable. So the leaders determined to take charge of the revolution to keep it in channels that would be safe for themselves and "to prevent what ill-effects an unformed tumult might produce." Not only did John Usher shift to insurrection, but even that old rogue William Stoughton managed to preserve his record of being on the winning side by joining the leaders of the impending rebellion.

The revolution was precipitated by Andros' panicky attempt to suppress the growing opposition to his rule; specifically, an attempt at a special meeting of the Council to try Rev. Cotton Mather, eminent son of Rev. Increase Mather, for preaching sedition. The revolution broke out on the morning set for the trial, April 28. The speedy and virtually bloodless revolt was launched that morning when bands of boys and youths ran through Boston shouting falsely that the popular revolution had already begun in the other parts of town. Captain George of the naval frigate *Rose* was seized. Two hundred armed rebels of the militia gathered under the command of Capt. John Nelson. The English soldiers at the fort showed reluctance to fire on the people of Boston. Edmund Andros surrendered, and was kept in prison for a year by the revolutionaries, as were the other hated leaders of the Andros regime, including Edward Randolph, Joseph Dudley, John West, John Palmer, and Charles Lidgett. Of the twenty-four men imprisoned with Andros, twenty were English bureaucrats, military and civilian, and only four were from New England.

To justify this revolution, the leaders issued on April 18 a Declaration of the Gentlemen, Merchants and Inhabitants and the County Adjacent, drawn up by Cotton Mather. The Declaration set forth the rebel case, including the numerous oppressions the citizenry had suffered, and praised the Glorious Revolution in England.

The revolutionaries were now faced with the inevitable problem of what to do next. The radicals urged the frank reproclamation of the old Massachusetts Bay charter that had been vacated five years before. But the leadership was not prepared to take so drastic a step. Instead, the leaders quickly established on April 20 a thirty-seven-man revolutionary Council for the Safety of the People and Conservation of the Peace. This council was heavily weighted with Boston merchants, and included old magistrates, councillors of the Dominion, and former private citizens. This self-constituted council now named the cautious and venerable ex-governor Simon Bradstreet as president and Wait Winthrop as commander of the militia. The Council for Safety then summoned a popular convention to meet on May 9. To unite the people of Massachusetts, the council took the highly significant step of suggesting that the towns extend the right to vote from Puritan church members to all freeholders. Most of the Massachusetts towns quickly complied. Delegates were selected at meetings of the "freemen and inhabitants" of the towns (an "inhabitant" being someone over the age of twenty-four, with an estate of eighty pounds or more). At the convention that met on May 9 were sixty-six delegates from forty-four towns of the colony.

The relatively radical convention wanted the old charter reproclaimed and it appealed to the old pre-Dudley Council of Magistrates—the last under the old charter—to resume its functions and to reconstitute a General Court with the convention delegates as the House of Deputies. The more conservative magistrates, however, refused, and the Council for Safety continued to exercise rule until the next enlarged convention met on May 22.

The second convention represented fifty-four towns, of which forty-two had instructed their delegates to insist on resumption of the old charter. Once again, the majority of the more timid and conservative magistrates opposed the plan. Finally, however, the popular will prevailed with forty-four towns voting for restoration of the charter government, and nine for continuing temporary rule by the Council for Safety while awaiting the final royal decision.

The last charter governor, Simon Bradstreet, as well as the charter magistrates, now jointly agreed to reconstitute the old General Court and to resume the charter government. The convention further overruled the governor and magistrates by insisting that the Council for Safety *not* continue as ruling magistrate body of the colony. With good reason, the delegates distrusted the revolutionary fervor of such council members as Wait Winthrop and the notorious William Stoughton. This action of the convention removed them from their posts of power. However, within a week the convention decided to compromise slightly by naming Winthrop, Samuel Shrimpton, and three other opportunists to vacancies in the old Council of Magistrates. By the end of May this arrangement had been completed, and the general joy was at this moment redoubled by news of the coronation of William and Mary. A great celebration ensued in Boston, with pomp and banquets, and wine literally flowing in the streets.

But celebration was not enough to secure the fruits of victory. Caution was the watchword of the new monarch, and one of his first actions in January was to order all previous arrangements continued in force until further notice; specifically, Sir Edmund Andros was to continue his rule over New England. Fortunately, however, Rev. Increase Mather, who had fled to England to plead Massachusetts case against Andros, was able to block transmission of the king's order to New England. Indeed, Mather went further and, with his old friend and parishioner Sir William Phips—a native of eastern Maine—petitioned the king to restore all the New England charters. The cautious Crown would not go that far, but it did agree to remove Andros immediately and to call him "unto an account for his maladministration." The king also agreed to draft for Massachusetts a new charter that was to grant at least some of the colony's demands. Mather even succeeded in introducing into Parliament a bill to restore the Massachusetts charter. The bill passed the House of Commons, but was blocked by the House of Lords. The old guard of the royal bureaucracy politicked for this roadblock. Sir Robert Southwell of the Plantation Office warned a colleague that the bill would "so confound the present settlement in those parts and their dependence on England, that, 'tis hard to say where the mischief will stop or how far the Act of Navigation will be overthrown thereby."

While Mather's valiant efforts failed to win resumption of the old charter, he did succeed in winning temporary royal recognition of the revolutionary government. This news too was received with great joy, as if the old charter was as good as renewed; for on June 5 the old political institutions of Massachusetts had been reconstituted, including a General Court and a newly elected House of Deputies.

Along with the temporary recognition of the Massachusetts regime, the king ordered Andros and the other prisoners sent back to England. Many radicals wanted to ignore the order and keep the hated oppressors in jail. But after many weeks of delay, the prisoners were shipped back to England in February 1690.

The citizens of Massachusetts realized that the first order of the day was to convince the Crown of the justice of the grievances against Andros and the need to restore the old charter. Right after the two-day revolution, local committees busily gathered evidence of grievance against the Andros regime. By the end of 1689 a central committee was organized in Boston to collect the testimony. Numerous pamphlets on the Andros regime were published in Massachusetts to try to win the minds of the Crown. And on May 20, 1689, as soon as Massachusetts heard the news of the proclamation of William and Mary, the colony explained to the sovereign that the people had risen "as one man" in emulation of the "late glorious enterprise" and were able to accomplish the victory "without the least bloodshed or plunder."

In England during 1690, Massachusetts and the Andros-Randolph party argued their respective cases, their charges and countercharges, before the Committee for Trade and Plantations. Massachusetts sent over two agents, Thomas Oates and Elisha Cooke, to aid Mather. The committee, headed by the former Earl of Danby—now the Marquis of Carmarthen—showed obvious partiality to the Andros side in the hearings. Quickly the committee cleared Andros and Randolph of charges against them; Carmarthen did not even give Massachusetts the chance to present its case. Also powerful on the pro-Andros side were the two prominent royal bureaucrats, Robert Southwell and William Blathwayt. Edward Randolph helped turn the hearings into an attack on Massachusetts by open testimony and by publishing anonymous tracts against the colony, concentrating on its failure to enforce the navigation laws. In the meanwhile, Parliament tried to pass a bill prohibiting the voiding of any corporate charters. This would have restored the old Massachusetts charter; but the bill took too much power away from the Crown for William III's comfort, and King William defeated the bill by dissolving Parliament in February 1690. It was becoming clear that Massachusetts would have to settle for a new charter granting far less independence than the old.

At home, the Massachusetts regime made halting last-minute attempts to gain support among non-Puritan church members. By the end of May 1689 the towns had pledged "enlargement of the freemen," but nothing had been done for a year. After a petition for enlargement was sent to the General Court in 1690, the court finally repealed the restrictive clauses, and voted to admit to freemanship anyone able to pay four shillings and the poll tax, or whose income from land was six pounds. In the spring of 1690 seven hundred new freemen were admitted, of whom nearly two-thirds were nonchurch members. But Puritans were still favored in the new regulations, for church members were specially exempt from the property qualifications.

As might be expected, the electrifying news of the overthrow and arrest of Andros in Boston galvanized the other colonies under Andros' sway. In Plymouth the people seized Andros' main henchman, the councillor Nathaniel Clarke, and reestablished the old Plymouth government under former governor Thomas Hinckley. Clarke was sent to England along with Andros and the others, hopefully to answer for his "high crimes and misdemeanors."

Plymouth, always charterless, and anxious to obtain a proper charter, naively thanked Increase Mather for supposedly presenting Plymouth's case at court. But on arriving in England, Plymouth's agent, Rev. Ichabod Wiswall, soon discovered that Massachusetts was trying to absorb Plymouth in its *own* charter—in short, to play the same game by which Connecticut had seized New Haven three decades before. Mather, indeed, had already managed to incorporate Plymouth when Wiswall arrived and was able to strike out the clause, an act for which Mather dubbed Wiswall "the weasel."

But Mather had an enormous advantage for winning his way: money. Mather was supplied with the very large sum of 1,700 pounds, which he was able to use for the purpose intended: to spread about in the right places. Plymouth, on the other hand, was a poor colony and had little money to supply; Wiswall had virtually nothing to bestow for favors. When in February 1691 the Plymouth General Court in desperation asked the towns to subscribe 500 pounds "to keep their independence," the sum could not be raised. Plymouth's future was fading fast.

When New Hampshire heard the glorious news of Andros' arrest, it did not, like the other New England colonies, have a recent self-governing past to look back upon. Instead, it had been strictly a royally controlled colony, and before that, for decades part of Massachusetts.

The four New Hampshire towns first attempted to draw up a self-governing constitution to frame a government. The constitutional convention met at Portsmouth on January 24, 1690, and included twenty-two of the leading men of the colony. It included also the rehabilitated revolutionary hero, Edward Gove of Hampton, as well as Major William Vaughan and Major Richard Waldron from Portsmouth. The convention agreed to a brief constitution providing for election of a president, to be head of the province's militia, and a Council of Ten representing the people of the four towns. The president and Council were also to call an assembly of representatives from each town.

This was the first constitution in American history to be drawn up by popular convention and then submitted to the people for ratification. But the town of Hampton, worried about too much power accruing to Portsmouth under this arrangement, refused to elect representatives, and so the constitution fell through.

The immediate reaction was a petition signed by hundreds of the leading men of New Hampshire, urging Massachusetts to resume, at least temporarily, government of the colony. The revolutionary Massachusetts government promptly granted the request at the end of February, and in England Mather did his best to absorb New Hampshire as well as Plymouth in his forthcoming new charter. But Massachusetts' plans were foiled from two sides. In the first place, the independent and unbridled town of Hampton, led by Nathaniel Weare, balked at a permanent surrender to Massachusetts. And Weare was known in England as the man who had gone there from New Hampshire to lay low the hated Governor Cranfield five years before. Perhaps more important was the partial reactivation of the old Mason menace to the liberty and property of the residents of New Hampshire. Mason, who had been on the Council for New England, had sold his proprietary claim to New Hampshire to Samuel Allen, and Allen was able to persuade the king to nominate himself to be governor of the new royal colony of New Hampshire. Allen named his son-in-law, the former Dominion treasurer John Usher, to be lieutenant governor and operating head of the colony. Usher assumed his post in August 1692. New Hampshire had lost its struggle for self-government.

Usher was not only a son-in-law of the new proprietary pretender, but had himself bought a great amount of New Hampshire land from Mason, and therefore depended on the latter's rather dubious title. Usher's return brought the Mason (now Allen) claims once again into the forefront of New Hampshire politics. The leading enemies of the Mason claims—Vaughan, Waldron, Weare—now banded together to oppose the Usher regime.

Connecticut too received the news of the Boston revolution with jubilation. Facing the question of what to do next, the colony confronted three alternatives: to resume the old charter government, which, unlike Massachusetts, had not been formally voided; to continue the Dominion government, which had virtually dissolved; or to follow Massachusetts' path and establish a provincial Committee for Safety. Leading the fight for the first alternative was James Fitch, who also wanted to exclude such top Andros supporters as Fitz-John Winthrop and John Allyn from public office. Counterpressure for continuing the defunct Dominion came from Rev. Gershom Bulkeley, of Wethersfield, and Edward Palmes, both of whom had been made judges by Andros.

Connecticut had an election on May 9, 1689, and the delegates decided to reestablish the former governor Robert Treat and the General Court. One of the court's first acts was to resume the old laws and institutions of the colony. But while the bulk of the freemen agreed with Fitch that the old Andros henchmen must be excluded, the more conservative delegates decided to reappoint the old Council of Magistrates. As a further blow to the revolutionary forces, they appointed such old Andros supporters as Fitz-John Winthrop and Samuel Willys members of the Council. The old opportunist clique, anxious to head off Fitch's likely drive for democratic reform of the charter, had managed to outmaneuver the popular party. The decisions of the convention were submitted to the body of freemen for approval, but the freemen could only vote for or against the entire panel of officials selected by the delegates. They did not have the option of voting down such individual nominees as Allyn or Winthrop. Still battling the new dispensation, however, were such ultrareactionaries as Gershom Bulkeley and Edward Palmes, who pleaded with England to restore the old Dominion rule.

In a sense, Bulkeley was more prophetic than his more moderate colleagues. For James Fitch, councillor and the great leader of the Connecticut revolution, soon came to dominate the Council and the Connecticut government; the newly elected councillors were followers of Fitch. Fitch, an open admirer of Jacob Leisler's revolutionary government in New York, was able by 1692 to widen the Connecticut franchise. The only requirement for freemanship was now possession of a forty-shilling freehold. Moreover, a highly democratic election system was installed: each freeman could write out a list of twenty nominees for the fourteen posts of governor, deputy governor, and magistrates.

The officials were to be elected from the top twenty names submitted by the freemen, in a second series of town meetings.

Connecticut had decided for self-government and for resuming its old charter, but the Crown had not yet spoken. Despite a lack of able agents in England, Connecticut won from the king's lawyers in August 1690 a decision that its old charter was still valid. Connecticut was not yet wholly out of the woods, though its self-governing charter had been reconfirmed.

Rhode Island did not receive the news of Andros' arrest with the same enthusiasm as its sister colonies. For one thing, it shared Andros' deep antipathy to Massachusetts. For another, it was grateful for Andros' support in the old Narragansett controversy with Connecticut. Indeed, Andros had been preparing to flee to Rhode Island before his capture. Rhode Island now determined to return to its old self-governing charter. The timorous former governor Walter Clarke, however, refused to reassume his office; it was temporarily occupied at the end of February by John Coggeshall, the previous deputy governor. At the end of April, Newport issued a summons to the other towns of Rhode Island to meet there on May 1 to plot the colony's future course. There the delegates decided to resume operations under the old and never officially vacated charter. But once more the timid Walter Clarke refused to reassume his post, and the permanent post of governor was granted to the Quaker Henry Bull.

Thus, on the advent of the Glorious Revolution in England, the New England colonies took the welcome opportunity to overthrow the Dominion regime. Upon the imprisonment of Andros and his henchmen, Massachusetts returned, at least temporarily, to self-government according to its old charter and institutions, and was followed by Plymouth, Connecticut, Rhode Island, and New Hampshire—the last temporarily placing itself under Massachusetts sovereignty.

We remember, however, that the Dominion of New England had expanded to New York and to the banks of the Delaware. These lower colonies had been left in charge of Lt. Gov. Francis Nicholson. Nicholson also learned of the Glorious Revolution in early February but kept it from the public. Finally, news of the overthrow of Andros reached New York at approximately the end of April.

Already the Dominion was in a far stronger position in New York than in New England, for when Andros and his colleagues were arrested there were no other Dominion officials in New England to continue the old regime in power. Furthermore, there were previous charters to which the colonies could conveniently return. But New York and the lower Dominion areas were still controlled by Nicholson and his subordinate officials; and there were no charters to fall back upon.

Governor Nicholson, the representative of the king's authority in New

York and the Jerseys, was now faced with the problem of what to do at this point. His first step was to call the New York members of the Council of the Dominion together, but, prudently, they failed to appear. Nicholson was left with the appointed civil and military officials who constituted the *de facto* government under him. At the end of April, twenty-six such officials began to meet as a ruling convention or council.

The first rebellion against the Dominion in New York broke out, as might be expected, in the always turbulent Suffolk County on eastern Long Island. Led by Southold, the freeholders of Suffolk met at Southhampton on May 3, ousted all the local appointed civil and military officials, and elected their own. They also demanded the return of the tax monies that had been "extorted" from them. The Suffolk towns were soon followed by the towns of Westchester and Queens, each of which established home rule. The grievances of Queens (on western Long Island) were aggravated by the fact that drafted militiamen from that county had not been paid for their part in a military expedition Dongan had sent against French Canada. Now Nicholson decided to pay these ex-soldiers, but determined to raise the funds by ordering the collection of Queens County's arrears for back taxes. The money was never collected from the rebellious people of Queens, and this protest of militiamen's pay was promptly joined by Kings and Suffolk counties. On May 9 the protesting ex-soldiers gathered, *armed,* at Jamaica to demand their promised pay. Nicholson and his Council agreed. This was followed on the same day by demonstrations for back pay by the New York City militia, with similar results.

We have seen that the Catholicism of several high officials in New York had intensified the anti-Catholic hysteria in New York attendant on troubles with the French. New York was the colony closest to French Canada and the Iroquois, and conflicts with the Catholic French had grown in recent years.

By May 6 discontent had spread to New York City itself. After a vote to apply customs revenue to strengthen the fortification of New York, the charge was made that the collector of customs, Matthew Plowman, was a Catholic. So hypersensitive were New Yorkers becoming on this issue that a government official at Setauket (Brookhaven), Long Island, refused to serve as a messenger to Andros, fearing that the people, "taking him to be a papist . . . would raise and plunder his house, if not offer violence to his family." Using the accusation against Plowman as a convenient excuse, the merchants of New York City now refused to pay the customs duties, asserting that they were illegal decrees of the executive.

In short, the atmosphere in New York by the end of the first week in May was becoming increasingly revolutionary. Anti-Catholic prejudice quickly spurred a tax rebellion and an implicit call for a representative assembly with sole power to levy taxes. And meanwhile, Dominion government was caught in an increasingly aggravated "inner contradiction": The clamor for promised back pay by the armed militia grew at the same time that refusal to pay taxes increased in scope and depth. How then could the Nicholson regime impose more taxes to pay the promised back salaries?

Nicholson's promises were not enough to satisfy the increasingly revolutionary militia. On May 10 the militia captains of the Long Island towns of Southampton, East Hampton, and Huntington demanded that the Manhattan fort "be delivered into the hands of such persons as the country shall choose"—that is, clearly *out* of existing hands. The ruling convention of New York City officials denounced the militia action as mutinous, but the Long Island towns, joined by Hempstead, refused to send delegates to any expanded convention called by Nicholson. On May 22 the Nicholson convention ordered the signers of the various petitions to appear before it. They flatly refused.

The developing revolutionary temper of the militia was further aggravated by Nicholson's failure to proclaim William and Mary as his sovereign. This prompted further suspicions of his allegiance to the Catholic and absolutist James II. Matters finally came to a head on May 30. Lieutenant Hendrick Cuyler of the militia directed a corporal to place a militiaman at a certain sensitive post at the fort. When the regular English soldier refused to give way to a New Yorker at the post, Cuyler took the dispute to Nicholson. Not only did the governor side with the soldier and order the militia corporal from his room at gunpoint, but he told Lieutenant Cuyler that he feared for his life and would "set the town in fire" rather than see the situation continue.

Word of Nicholson's threats spread through New York City like wildfire, and caused an immediate revolt by the militia. The New York militia decided to ignore all commands from either Nicholson or his appointed militia commander, Col. Nicholas Bayard. Further, the militia proceeded to take over and hold the fort. The day after this revolt, the militia issued A Declaration of the Inhabitant Soldiers. The Declaration, signed by some four hundred men, avowed militia support for the new Protestant monarch, and explained the militia's seizure of the fort by Nicholson's threat to burn the city, and by his alleged aid to a Catholic plot to slaughter New Yorkers.

There was now no definite government in New York. The revolutionary militiamen held the fort themselves, but had not yet openly repudiated Nicholson as governor. The governor now foolishly precipitated his own ouster by ordering Colonel Bayard to take command of the militia. When Bayard ordered the militia companies to leave the neighborhood of the fort, most of them refused; they joined the company that happened to be taking its turn occupying the fort that day, a company headed by a leading Dutch Calvinist merchant of German origin, Capt. Jacob Leisler. The militiamen had now openly repudiated the orders and the rule of the governor.

There were now two parallel governments in New York: the militia, and Governor Nicholson and his convention officials. On June 3 and 4, four of the five captains of the militia—the leading officers subordinate to the repudiated Bayard—signed a Humble Address of the militia and people of the city. This document recognized and hailed King William as liberator from "tyranny, popery and slavery," and as the protector of "the true Protestant religion, liberty and property." The militia also proceeded to call for a new, revolutionary governmental form: a Committee of Safety. The committee consisted of two delegates from each county and was to meet on June 26.

The Nicholson government had precipitated this revolutionary step by ordering all the New York funds, now kept at the fort, transferred to the home of Councillor Frederick Philipse, and by commanding the militia captains to appear before the convention. Both demands were refused by four of the five militia captains, with Leisler the most outspoken. With the Council denouncing the rebels, Nicholson sailed on June 24 to England for help. Before going, he angered New Yorkers still further by ordering the Catholic customs collector, Matthew Plowman, to enforce the payment of duties.

The Nicholson Council now decided, way too late, to remove Plowman and to fill his post with four collectors, including the hated Nicholas Bayard. The militiamen, however, were by now in far too rebellious a mood to accept this arrangement. They evicted the four men from the customhouse and substituted their own appointee, Peter Delanoy, a former treasurer and collector of New York City. Some of the militiamen tried to assault Bayard, but were stopped by Captain Leisler.

On June 26, the revolutionary Committee of Safety met in Queens. Most of the counties of New York accepted the invitation to send delegates, and prominent citizens attended from New York City, Kings, Queens, Westchester, and Richmond (Staten Island) counties, as well as one each from the towns of Tappan, Hackensack, and Elizabethtown in New Jersey. The county delegates were in turn elected at county meetings of delegates elected by the towns. Refusing to send delegates was Suffolk County, where the towns—especially Southold and Setauket —once again hoped to join Connecticut. Albany, Kingston, and most of New Jersey also failed to send representatives. It seems clear that the town elections were highly democratic, with almost all of the adult males of the participating towns voting in the elections for delegates.

The Suffolk towns were not, incidentally, the only ones that wanted to merge with Connecticut. Jacob Leisler was particularly active in working for such a merger, and Connecticut did agree to send two delegates to the meeting of the Committee of Safety along with ten friendly soldiers.

The delegates to the committee, to repeat, were not unknown members of a mob, but prominent citizens of the community. The revolutionary committee, for example, included in its ranks Dr. Gerardus Beekman of Kings, a future acting governor of the colony; William Lawrence of Hackensack, a future councillor; and Samuel Edsall, father-in-law of both Lawrence and Delanoy, and a prominent trader who had held political office in New Jersey. The Committee of Safety officially dissolved the authority of the royal Council and its customs commissioners, appointed Peter Delanoy as moderator of the committee, and confirmed his appointment as collector. It also named Jacob Leisler as permanent captain of the fort.

The old municipal court now ceased to meet; Leisler refused to guarantee the safety of its members. The reactionary pro-Andros mayor of New York City, Stephanus Van Cortlandt, and his fellow councillors made themselves scarce. The revolutionary government was now the sole government in New York City and vicinity.

Now that the revolution had been accomplished and the old order completely overthrown, we may pause to ask about the meaning of this revolution. For it is important, when weighing the reasons for the outbreak of a revolution, to separate this stage from the later history of the revolutionary government *after* it has taken power. Many writers have judged the rebellion to be a class struggle, a pure outbreak of religious hatred, or an ethnic war of Dutch against English rule. Yet it should be clear that all these explanations are either fallacious or—in the case of the religious explanation—partial and misleading. The revolution was *not* a class struggle of the poor against the rich, or of the laborer against other occupations. It was the culmination of many years of political and economic grievances suffered by every great economic class in the colony, by every section, by English and Dutch alike. The aggressively English towns of Suffolk were and had always been even more revolutionary than the Dutch of New York. And the Dutch members of the ruling oligarchy—the Bayards, the Van Cortlandts, and the leading Dutch ministers—were just as fiercely opposed to the revolution as were the English members. Economically, the leaders of the revolutionary movement ranged from the prominent merchants, and other citizens named above, to such men as Joost Stol, a carter and an ensign in Leisler's militia company. Stol was probably the single person most responsible for the fateful decision of the militia to seize the fort on May 30. In short, this was truly a liberal *people's* revolution, a revolution of all classes and ethnic strains in New York against the common oppressors: the oligarchical ruling clique and its favorites, receivers of patronage, privilege, and monopolistic land grants from the royal government. Indeed, the counterrevolutionaries—the opponents of this popular rebellion—were almost invariably the ruling clique: the royal bureaucracy and the recipients of monopolistic land grants. In this group were Bayard, Van Cortlandt, Philipse, William Nicolls, and Peter Schuyler and his brother-in-law, Robert Livingston.* As in the other colonies under Dominion rule, though with greater difficulty because of the Nicholsonian bureaucracy, the people took heart from the overthrow of Andros in Boston to end the hated rule of the Dominion in New York as well. Even the anti-Catholicism is largely explainable by the Catholicism of James II and many of his ruling henchmen in New York. And, finally, the revolution in New York cannot correctly be termed "Leisler's Rebellion." The fact that Jacob Leisler acquired control of the revolutionary government after it had assumed power should not be allowed to obscure the fact that Leisler was only one of the many leaders of the actual revolution, and that this was a spontaneous uprising of the mass of the people.

Any libertarian revolution that *takes power* immediately confronts a grave inner contradiction: in the last analysis, liberty and power are incompatible. Thus, Peter Delanoy was now supposed to collect the colony's taxes. But a tax paid to a Delanoy was no less oppressive or tyrannical than the same tax paid to a Nicholson. And so the merchants still refused to pay the duties, again using the argument that they had not been levied by a representative assembly. Six weeks later, the revolution took a decisive step from liberty to power. On August 16 the Committee of Safety, in its second meeting, created an executive of almost unlimited authority—by naming Jacob Leisler commander in chief of New York Province.

As soon as Leisler assumed supreme power, he, naturally, began to use it. The first step was to arrest whoever dared to criticize the new regime. Arrests included merchants and laborers, Dutchmen such as the Schuylers and Philipses, and Anglicans such as Thomas Clark. Many were arrested on suspicion of disloyalty. It is true, however, that the prisoners were treated with relative moderation and many were freed on taking a loyalty oath to William and Mary. Leisler also used his power to conscript youths and even children into labor gangs to repair Manhattan's Fort James.

*A leading historian of the rebellion has written: "A fair characterization of all [the opponents of the revolution] . . . would be that they were officials and landed, or would-be landed, aristocrats. There are, however, no grounds for terming the 'rebellion' a 'class struggle' in the Marxist sense. Capitalists were found in both camps" (Jerome Reich, *Leisler's Rebellion* [Chicago: University of Chicago Press, 1953], p. 73). The reason for the last statement might be added: "capitalists" are never a homogeneous entity, as is true of all Marxian classes that are not, as we have noted above, "estates" or "castes." The capitalists who gained their money from government privilege were against the revolution; the capitalists who earned their money in free market activity joined all the other producers in the colony to favor it.

The revolutionary Committee of Safety, before adjourning, decided to press ahead with the annual September elections that had been held in pre-Dominion years; also, to expand democracy and check oligarchy by subjecting justices of the peace and militia captains to the decisions of the voters. In an action reflecting the bitter anti-Catholicism of the people, all Protestant freeholders were made eligible to vote. In New York City the people elected aldermen and common councillors according to the old charter. In addition, Leisler made elective the three top posts in the city—mayor, sheriff, and town clerk—which had always been appointive. The free elections removed the counterrevolutionaries from office, and Stephanus Van Cortlandt was replaced as mayor by Peter Delanoy (who was to be the last popularly elected mayor of New York until the nineteenth century).

Although Leisler and the committee controlled the bulk of New York, they did not command the allegiance of Albany. Albany, tightly run by the privileged monopolists of the Iroquois fur trade, was devoted to the Dominion. Its top officials were leaders of the Andros oligarchy: for example, Mayor Peter Schuyler and his assistant and brother-in-law, Robert Livingston. In the fall elections, Albany simply reelected its old officials.

The shift from liberty to power was now proceeding apace. Leisler and the committee became filled with imperialistic zeal to impose their unwanted rule on Albany. An expedition of three ships was sent by Leisler, under his future son-in-law, the merchant Jacob Milborne, to seize Albany. Albany, to cover itself, forced every townsman to take an oath of allegiance to William and Mary. The Albany convention then refused to permit Milborne to enter the fort. Milborne now tried to appeal to the people of Albany over the heads of their rulers; he urged them to overthrow all government derived from James II and promised free elections and other liberties. Milborne's stirring words had some effect, and a hundred citizens of Albany elected Jochim Staats as captain of Milborne's troops in Albany.

But the support of Staats and the Albany opposition for Milborne was not enough. The convention oligarchy and the fort determined to resist and they threw into the breach the powerful support of the Iroquois, fur-trading allies of the Albany oligarchs. The Iroquois threatened to attack Milborne should he persist, and Milborne finally left ignominiously for home. Moreover, to complete the fiasco, Captain Staats and his Milborne militia were now obliged to take orders from the convention. Albany was the more strengthened by Connecticut's recognition of its convention government.

At this point, Leisler's fortunes took a swift turn upward. A letter arrived in mid-December from King William, legitimizing the rule of either Nicholson or "such as for the time being take care for preserving the peace and administering the laws," and naming said person lieutenant governor.

Thus, by the end of 1689 the revolutionary government in New York, as in Massachusetts, had been at least temporarily legitimized by the Crown, while the other New England colonies resumed their old ways of self-government. As with the other colonies, the key to their fate rested on the decisions of the new monarch.

The August session of the Committee of Safety had decided to send an agent to England to plead its case. Chosen was the revolutionary cartman, Joost Stol, whose lower-class ways were not, alas! calculated to endear him to the aristocratic officials of the Crown. Stol presented seven bold demands to the Privy Council, including royal and parliamentary approval of the actions of the revolution, a new self-governing charter for New York, and encouragement for a united colonial effort to conquer French Canada. But unlike the cause of Massachusetts at court, Leisler's regime was doomed from the start. For even as Leisler was being temporarily confirmed in his post, the king prepared to end his rule and all self-government in New York. Heavily influenced by the reports of the old oligarchs, Bayard and Van Cortlandt, the Lords of Trade recommended that a royal governor, with two companies of troops, be sent to rule New York. Colonel Henry Sloughter was promptly chosen as governor. Only a war in France held up Sloughter's actual arrival in New York and permitted Leisler to continue his interim rule.

In contrast to conditions in other colonies under Dominion rule, everything was quiet during the Glorious Revolution in the colonies of East Jersey and West Jersey. While the New England colonies aimed to resume self-government and while New York tried to move from royal colony to self-government, the Jerseys had been proprietary colonies before the Dominion. With Nicholson and his royal officials gone, the proprietors, who had been facing *quo warranto* action against their territories, trod warily indeed, and did nothing during the years of turmoil after 1689. Central government in the Jerseys disappeared with the end of the Dominion and the colonies were left with existing local governments only. In this state of purely minimal government, the people of the Jerseys were happy. The royal officials were gone. Their ancient proprietary enemies were cautious and inactive. Indeed, there was virtually nothing against which to revolt.

58

The Glorious Revolution in the Northern Colonies, 1690-1692

While the northern colonies were routing the hated Dominion and at least temporarily restoring self-government, King William was inaugurating his reign by taking England into a general European alliance (the League of Augsburg) against France. William had already been at war with France as stadtholder of Holland, and he was now eager to continue in that tradition. The war with France, beginning in 1689, had important repercussions in the New World.

Historians of each nation, when treating their country's foreign affairs and conflicts, almost always make it appear that *their* side was the righteous one and *their* state beset and threatened by lowering enemies. Any objective historian of New France and the English colonies, however, should certainly conclude that the menace was *to* New France, and not *from* New France. New France had a population of 12,000 compared with that of 100,000 in New England alone. Second, the English were solidly allied with the most feared, most aggressive, and most imperialistic Indians in the northeast—the Iroquois.

The basic struggle between the French on the one hand and the Iroquois, Dutch, and English on the other was economic—the beaver trade. In the seventeenth century the French had settled in Quebec and along the St. Lawrence and had developed a thriving fur trade with the Indian tribes farther west. But this trade interfered with the Iroquois, who tried by coercion to obtain a monopoly of the intermediate fur trade. The French in Canada could deal directly with the western tribes, but the Dutch and English in Albany could not. In Albany the Iroquois could find a market for resale of the furs purchased from the Indians farther west. In short, both the Iroquois and the English had a vested interest in aggressions against the French: the Iroquois to eliminate competition for the purchase of furs from the western Indians, and to obtain a monopoly of the middleman fur trade; the English to oust the French from the fur trade, and to grab French land for the glory and benefit of the Crown.

The Iroquois had plagued and ravaged the French settlers, as well as the more peaceful Indians in the northeast, for decades. During the 1640s the Iroquois plundered the French and drove out friendly tribes, but in the course of another war, were able to reestablish their position. We have observed that Governor Dongan urged the Iroquois to attack the French during the 1680's. The Iroquois went unerringly to the heart of the matter: the fur trade. After the Iroquois had driven the peaceful fur-trading Hurons from the St. Lawrence, the latter settled in the Great Lakes areas as far west as Wisconsin, and a direct fur trade with the French was established from there. Now, in the mid-1680s, the Iroquois invaded Huron country and by 1686 were able by force of arms to break the vital chain between the Great Lakes fur trade and the French. After the French made a feeble attempt to oust the Iroquois and restore the fur trade, the Iroquois began mercilessly to ravage the French settlements on the St. Lawrence, even to the environs of Montreal itself. The raids reached a peak in the summer of 1689. When the venerable Comte de Frontenac resumed his old post as governor of New France that fall, his obvious task was to try to preserve the colony from the Iroquois menace.

Now that England had declared war on France, Frontenac did not have to respect the status of privileged sanctuary with which the English had cloaked the Iroquois. Seeing English military strength weakened by the overthrow of the Dominion, the French and allied Indians executed a daring raid on February 9, 1690, upon the upstate New York trading post of Schenectady. The raiders burned the town, massacred a large portion of the inhabitants, and captured the rest. Two other daring and successful raids with similar results were engineered by Frontenac against Salmon Falls, New Hampshire, and Falmouth, Maine, on Casco Bay.

Ever since the previous December (1689), Jacob Leisler had been in control as the temporarily recognized ruler of the New York colony. But Albany still proved recalcitrant. Now, with Albany frightened by the raid on Schenectady, Leisler made a determined move to assume control.

Leisler had lost no time in transforming the revolution in New York into a virtual duplication of the old power. The old Committee of Safety was now made Leisler's Council. It quickly decreed the Revenue Act of 1683 to be still in force, and went so far as to order Delanoy to collect back taxes as well. Seeing the liberalism of the revolution vanish, a group of angry merchants issued a Declaration of the Freeholders of New York in protest. Leisler's order was torn down and the declaration substituted.

Leisler by decree prohibited defacing his orders. He also established a new Court of the Exchequer to try to collect revenue. Still, Leisler had enormous difficulty in collecting taxes. Like many another tyrant, Leisler then decided that this was the result of a subversive "hellish conspiracy" and he ordered a summary search of all suspect houses and the arrest of his opponents. By February there were numerous arrests of people caught speaking contemptuously of his government, and also of suspected "papists."

Leisler's imposition of a despotism in order to levy taxes was a fateful step. Before then the Leisler movement had been truly a people's revolution; its only opponents had been members of the discredited ruling oligarchy. But now the liberals, who had been his staunchest supporters, began to leave the Leisler cause in droves. In mid-May 1690, merchants and other leading citizens of New York drew up a Humble Address to the King protesting Leisler's "slavery," "arbitrary power," and "ruling us by the sword." The authors included such prominent merchants and great leaders of the revolution as Leisler's former fellow militia captains: DePeyster, Lodwyck, and Stuyvesant. The petition also complained of Leisler's confiscation of goods—even as far as Elizabethtown, New Jersey—plundering of homes, and searching of mails.

Jacob Leisler's frenzy to collect taxes was largely because of his determination to seize Albany and then to mount a giant intercolonial invasion to conquer New France. He had always been a hard-liner on "papist" New France, and now the war and the massacre at Schenectady gave him his long-awaited opportunity. The higher taxes and the rigorous enforcement were to pay for Leisler's cherished invasion plans.

By the end of February, Leisler decided to call a representative assembly in New York to make the raising of taxes more palatable to the increasingly restive populace. The Assembly finally met at the end of April. Suffolk County (except for Hempstead) refused to send any delegates. Suffolk still hoped to join Connecticut and also balked at the high-tax program. Leisler barred from voting all those who had not taken what was, in effect, an oath of allegiance to himself. Therefore, the election, especially in the upstate anti-Leisler county of Ulster, was not truly free. The Assembly dutifully imposed a new property tax of three pence per pound, but tried to win the support of the farmers and the New York masses by ending the hated New York City flour monopoly, the New York port monopoly, and the Albany fur monopoly. Abolition of the three hated monopolies was highly welcome to the people. Leisler, though, was angered by the growing popular movement for release of his political prisoners. He brusquely dissolved the Assembly for even daring to *receive* the petitions of the people urging him to free the prisoners.

The popularity that Leisler could have earned by ending the monopolies never materialized because of his taxes and confiscations to finance his unrealistic dream of the conquest of French Canada. To confiscate supplies for an expedition against the French, Leisler imposed on grain exports an embargo, which allowed him to seize the grain for military purposes. Ending the flour monopoly did little good when farmers and merchants could not export the grain at all. Moreover, by decree Leisler embargoed all exports of pork and confiscated all private stores of pork meat. He also searched all suspected places without bothering about a warrant. Stocks of cloth in the city were also confiscated.

Other foci of resistance to Leisler were New Rochelle, where the newly settled Huguenots objected to a tax burden for his needless expedition, and traditionally antitax Suffolk County, which Leisler had to force to "submit to him." An East Hampton meeting in May, for example, was evenly split between accepting Leisler's authority on condition of some redress of grievances, or not submitting at all without further word from England. *No one* at the meeting advocated unconditional submission to Leisler's authority.

Despite an increasingly restless home base behind him, Leisler proceeded on his course of seizing Albany and then mounting an invasion of Canada. As soon as Leisler acquired legitimacy in December, he ordered Albany to submit and to hold new municipal elections. But the Albany convention refused, and was backed by the Connecticut militia, sent there to aid against the French. The Schenectady massacre, however, changed the situation. Leisler was now able to blame Albany's recalcitrance for the poor preparation against the attack. Furthermore, the Albany oligarchy was now beginning to face numerous internal and external troubles. First, Leisler conscripted a militia and ordered it to seize Albany and Ulster counties. Second, the people of Albany, fearful of a French attack, began to ship their goods downriver to New York City; the Albany convention ordered all such shipments stopped. And finally, Connecticut withdrew its troops and advised Albany to submit to Leisler, while Massachusetts, as fellow revolutionaries against the Dominion, inclined toward Leisler and joined in this plea.

Connecticut and Massachusetts were entreated by Albany and Ulster to support them and to send more troops. Leisler demanded that Connecticut put its troops under his command. Albany's chief agent to Connecticut and Massachusetts in the spring of 1690 was Robert Livingston, perhaps Leisler's most determined enemy among the Albany oligarchy. Leisler sent agents to urge Connecticut to arrest "this rebel Livingston." Connecticut did finally decide to remove its troops from Albany, but refused to arrest Livingston. New York's comrade in revolution, Massachusetts, almost did arrest Livingston, but he was able to save himself by citing the friendship of the Iroquois to the Albany oligarchs.

Under pressure from all sides, Albany could only give in; it submitted to Leisler on March 20. Leisler appointed three commissioners to govern Albany, including Jacob Milborne. Esopus (Kingston) also submitted, and

Milborne imposed Leisler's authority there. As opponents of Leisler began to flee Albany, the commissioners issued an order prohibiting any male from leaving the city. They also forced into submission several burghers who had previously refused to obey the militia. Generally, though, Leisler conciliated the oligarchy by reappointing existing officials. The exception was Livingston, who was still in Connecticut and whom Leisler attempted to try for "treason."

With Albany secured, Jacob Leisler proceeded to the second stage of his grand design: the united colonial conquest of Canada. Leisler called a great intercolonial conference at Albany for May 1, 1690. He assured the various governments that New York would contribute 400 men to such an expedition (260 of whom were already in arms) and the Iroquois had promised 1,000. Virginia refused the invitation and Quaker Pennsylvania, again in a state of anarchism, simply ignored it. The Jerseys, unfriendly to New York anyway, and a haven for many of Leisler's enemies, also ignored the invitation. Maryland was sympathetic but was now in the midst of Coode's rebellion, and had little time or men to spare. This left the New England colonies, which appeared at the conference and pledged a total of 355 men for the expedition, to be conducted under a supreme commander named by Leisler. Sixty men were pledged by Plymouth, Massachusetts promised 160, and Connecticut 135. Rhode Island sent no delegates and would conscript no men, but it agreed to contribute 300 pounds to help finance the campaign. Massachusetts had itself proposed an intercolonial conference concerning an invasion of Canada, and had in fact scheduled a New England conference at Newport before the New York meeting was called.

It was the attempt to finance and supply this mammoth campaign that led to the despotic exactions and confiscations, and to the rising opposition to Leisler in New York. The raising of the militia aggravated resentments still further. One Westchester realist pointed out that "they was fools if any of them did go and said who would give them a leg or arm if they lost them." Kings and Queens counties were restive and desertions from the conscript militia began to mount.

In accordance with the decision of the Albany conference, Leisler named his righthand man Jacob Milborne to be supreme commander. It was decided that a naval attack on Quebec would be coordinated with a land assault on Montreal. But the other colonies had never really been enthusiastic about the Leisler expedition and had only joined under pressure of popular enthusiasm in New England for Leisler's promised conquest of New France. Plymouth now withdrew its commitment, pleading poverty and lack of resources. And Massachusetts threw its resources instead into the naval expedition headed by Sir William Phips to capture Quebec. Moreover, Massachusetts found that its citizens refused en masse to be drafted into the militia, much less to volunteer. Only Connecticut now remained a direct ally of Leisler; and Connecticut

—guided by such enemies of Leisler as Secretary John Allyn (whom Leisler had wanted arrested as a Jacobite) and Robert Livingston—took advantage of the situation to take over the expedition. Connecticut now insisted that Milborne be replaced as supreme commander by Fitz-John Winthrop of Connecticut, a close friend of Livingston's. Finally, at the end of June, Leisler was forced to yield, and appointed Winthrop head of the expedition.

While Leisler's military plans were beginning to crumble, the mounting opposition to his rule at home culminated in an armed revolt on June 6. Sparked by an attempt of the relatives of Nicholas Bayard to release him from a Leisler jail, the rebels assaulted Leisler. But the governor was saved by the people and thirteen of the rebels were arrested. When the tumult died down the prisoners were released upon paying a fine.

Although his support was crumbling on all sides, Leisler stubbornly determined to press on with the invasion. The expedition, begun on August 1, was a study in absurdity. The enmity between Winthrop and Livingston on the one hand and Leisler on the other could not have been more intense. To cap the picture, of 1,000 warriors promised by the Iroquois, only seventy Indians appeared, and they accomplished virtually nothing. And yet, despite the evident folly of the attempt, Winthrop set forth with 500 men—less than half the number (1,200) Frontenac rapidly raised to defend Montreal. After wandering around in the woods of New York for two weeks, short of canoes and supplies, Winthrop ignominiously returned home. Phips' naval attack on Quebec in October was bungled so disastrously that he did well to get most of his men back to Boston. The grandiose attempt to conquer French Canada had proved a fiasco. Massachusetts characteristically met its failure by clamping a tight censorship on any criticism of the regime.

Phips had succeeded, however, in capturing Port Royal in Acadia (Nova Scotia) on an expedition the previous spring. The motivations for Phips' expedition were incisively set forth in a diary of the conquest: "May 11—the fort surrendered; May 12—went ashore to search for hidden goods. We cut down the cross, rifled the church, pulled down the high altar, and broke their images. May 13—kept gathering plunder all day; May 14—the inhabitants swore allegiance to King William and Queen Mary."

Having pursued his goal of invasion with single-minded fanaticism, Leisler now looked around paranoiacally for a scapegoat for the debacle. He fastened, naturally enough, upon Fitz-John Winthrop. Leisler promptly put Winthrop and some of Winthrop's officers under arrest, along with the leading burghers of Albany. Leisler intended to court-martial Winthrop for failure—or rather, for plotting to ruin the invasion. Finally, Leisler was forced to release Winthrop under pressure of Connecticut and especially of the Iroquois. But he continued to snarl to the last, accusing Allyn of being part of the so-called sabotage plot and charging Winthrop with being a "tool" of Livingston. Connecticut's refusal to grant further military aid was greeted by the irascible Leisler with the charge that the men of Connecticut were responsible for the failure of the invasion, and he termed them "fiends" and "hypocrites."

Leisler's dream of conquering Canada was a shambles; following the classic course of tyrants, the now desperate Leisler redoubled his tyranny to maintain himself in power. The New York Assembly met again in September 1690 and levied a tax of three pence per pound sterling on all property for military purposes. It also demanded the return, in three weeks, of all who had fled the colony—on the rather absurd enticement of a promised fair trial. A seventy-five-pound penalty was placed on anyone refusing a military or civilian appointment by Leisler. A 100-pound penalty was levied on everyone leaving Albany or Ulster without Leisler's consent, and all emigres were ordered to return.

Again, resistance arose in New York to Leisler's depradations. The town of New Rochelle continued evading Leisler's order to all towns to name justices of the peace and tax collectors. In Queens County an armed revolt flared in October. The courts were suspended and Leisler directed the prohibition of anyone aiding or encouraging the rebels. Thomas Willett, who had participated in the previous personal assault on Leisler, now gathered 150 men for a march on New York. But Milborne's armed group of 300 easily routed the rebel forces. The Kings County militia also showed signs of rebellion, but Milborne's ample use of court-martials soon quelled that disturbance. Finally, Leisler tried desperately to collect the property tax, but the towns failed to name assessors and tax collectors and few of them paid. Petitions against Leisler were sent to London, old women taunted him on the street, and crowds stoned him, denouncing his tyranny and calling him such names as "dog driver," "deacon jailer," and "little Cromwell."

Cracking in all directions, Jacob Leisler's reign in New York was swiftly coming to an end in more ways than one. On March 19, 1691, Governor Henry Sloughter, appointed by the king almost two years before, finally made his long-delayed arrival in New York. Sloughter was thoroughly opposed to Leisler and his supposed "rabble" and thoroughly partial to the old oligarchy, as seen by his defense before the Lords of Trade of the alleged necessity of New York City's port monopoly.

But before Sloughter could arrive, Leisler had more troubles. At the beginning of 1691, Major Richard Ingoldesby arrived at New York with a troop of English regulars. Ingoldesby demanded that Leisler surrender the fort, but Leisler stubbornly maintained that Ingoldesby had no written authority from Sloughter or the king. Both sides now began to recruit forces. Large numbers of militiamen joined Leisler in response to the menace of the royal troop. Meanwhile, Thomas Clark, veteran opponent of Leisler, was raising troops for Ingoldesby on Long Island and arresting some Leislerians. Flatbush and Kings County were also centers of recruitment by Ingoldesby, and Westchester arrested several

Leislerians. Civil war was now in the offing, although an uneasy truce permitted Ingoldesby to quarter his troops at the city hall. Both sides continued to threaten and to raise forces; Leisler darkly warned that all this was a papist plot against William and Mary and himself.

Most eager for war against Leisler were Ingoldesby's theoreticians—the men appointed to Sloughter's Council. This group, largely representing the old oligarchy, consisted of the still imprisoned Nicholas Bayard, Stephanus Van Cortlandt, Frederick Philipse, William Nicolls (who had been imprisoned along with Bayard), Gabriel Minvielle (the lone militia captain who had always been against the revolution), William Smith (an anti-Leislerian), Thomas Willett (who had led Long Island revolts against Leisler and had plotted the June 6 assault upon him), William Pinhorne (an English merchant who had fled Leisler tyranny to East New Jersey), Chidley Brooke (a relative of Sloughter), and the notorious Joseph Dudley (governor of the Dominion of New England before Andros). This group of advisers called on Ingoldesby to overthrow the Leisler rule.

On March 16 Leisler issued a proclamation ordering Ingoldesby to cease his preparations for war and demanded an answer in two hours. Civil war then ensued within the city with Ingoldesby capturing a blockhouse. Several hundred men on each side now skirmished with each other.

When Governor Sloughter finally arrived on the 19th, he stepped into a developing civil war. Leisler continued to delay surrendering the fort, but finally did so. It is possible that pressure by Leisler's own men helped end his purposeless stubbornness. Since Leisler never proposed to mount a direct revolt against King William's authority, his continued balkiness made little sense.

The old oligarchy now moved back in, thirsting for vengeance. Leisler and all his leading supporters were arrested and imprisoned. On the advice of his Council, Sloughter quickly created a special court with ten supposedly "unconcerned" judges: four bitter anti-Leislerians and six veteran royal officials and partisans of Andros and Sloughter. Three of Leisler's most implacable enemies were assigned to prepare the evidence against the Leislerians, and the three prosecuting attorneys were also bitter enemies of the prisoners.

Charges against Leisler and his nine fellow-defendants were the maximum: treason and murder, including "traitorously levying war" upon the king. Instead of following the usual practice of sending the defendants to England for a sober trial, the enemies of Leisler determined on speedy "justice." To say that the charges, let alone the procedure, were excessively harsh would be an understatement; after all, Leisler, as lieutenant governor and commander in chief, had been acting upon a plausible commission from the king. The conflict with

Ingoldesby, on which the charges rested, was a jurisdictional dispute, with legal lines hardly clear-cut.

Yet, by March 31 the ten defendants had been indicted for treason and murder by a grand jury. The trial proceeded rapidly. Finally, Leisler, Milborne, and six others (Gerardus Beekman, Abraham Gouverneur, Johannes Vermilge, Thomas Williams, Myndert Coerteus, and Abraham Brasher) were convicted and sentenced to death, and their property was confiscated by a bill of attainder. Numerous other Leislerians, such as Joost Stol, were indicted for riot. The Leisler jury, incidentally, was as packed as the special court of ten judges: three of them had been leaders in the attempted June 6 assassination of Leisler! Two of the defendants, however—Peter Delanoy and Samuel Edsall—were acquitted by the jury; this shocked people like Bayard, and later historians have hinted at bribery.

Governor Sloughter, at this point, began to lose his nerve about carrying out these mass executions on his own responsibility. He therefore reprieved the six lesser Leislerians and even asked for a royal pardon for them. The question now was what to do with Leisler and Milborne. Sloughter's close friend, Nicholas Bayard, now led the pack calling for Leisler's blood, as a warning against all future rebellion against the royal government. Three Dutch ministers close to the old oligarchy, led by Reverend Mr. Selyus, also called for death. The only minister pleading for reprieve was the Reverend Peter Daille, a Huguenot, who was fined by the new anti-Leisler Assembly for these activities. Opposing the oligarchs was the voice of the people, who once again rallied around their former champion. Petitions, with over 1,800 signatures, were circulated calling for Leisler's reprieve. The sheriffs of Staten Island and other counties were ordered to arrest anyone circulating petitions for reprieve.

Sloughter's Council, led by Bayard, was bent on death, and overrode the opposition of the relatively disinterested Dudley. The Assembly agreed, and Leisler and Milborne were executed on May 16, 1691. Sloughter was perhaps helped to decide for execution by a special gift of money from the anti-Leislerian Assembly. One interesting story about the hanging is that no carpenter could be found to supply a ladder, which had to be provided by the Reverend Mr. Selyus. If not strictly accurate, the story is indicative of the depth of popular feeling against the killing of Leisler. The revolutionary government in Massachusetts was, of course, none too pleased at this potential precedent; Rev. Increase Mather declared that the two men were "barbarously murdered." But Massachusetts did not, like New York, have to face a strong and vindictive royal oligarchy.

The upshot of the Glorious Revolution for New York was that, by the spring of 1691, the self-governing regime of Leisler was ended and New York was again a royal colony, headed by a royal governor, with the old oligarchy back in power. But the retrogression was only partial;

Sloughter came bearing instructions for New York to have a regularly elected Assembly, an institution which that colony had never really had before. To this extent, considerable progress had been made since Dongan's pre-Dominion government.

The first regular Assembly met at the end of March 1691. While it was anti-Leislerian, its actions of most lasting significance were those repealing the Carting Act—the provision for permanent financial support of the government—and the other acts of Dongan's short-lived Assembly of 1683. The Assembly thus placed the governor on notice that though he could call and dissolve it at will, he was continually dependent on the Assembly for the raising of revenue. The new Assembly also greatly extended the definitions of rebellion and treason to include such vague offenses as disturbing "the peace . . . and quiet" of the government. All land grants were reconfirmed. The New York City Council passed tighter regulations for carters and made requirements for freemanship more restrictive.

The oligarchy was in power, but the Leislerians remained active and embittered. The quarrel was intensified by the numerous damage suits put through by the oligarchy against the former Leislerian leaders. And Delanoy, freed on the treason charge, was imprisoned by Sloughter for being Leisler's collector of customs.

Governor Sloughter died in the summer of 1691 but his policy of vengeance was continued in full force by his acting successor, Major Ingoldesby, who was selected by the Council. The new governor, arriving in late summer 1692, was Benjamin Fletcher. Fletcher, who ruled during the 1690s, sided with the oligarchy but was not the zealot that Ingoldesby was. He finally agreed to release the six Leislerian prisoners as well as the minor convicts, and to restore their confiscated estates. But first he forced the Leislerians to admit their guilt, and he arbitrarily voided the election of several of them to the Assembly. Fletcher, moreover, continued to mutter threats of execution against them until they finally secured a full pardon from the Crown in 1694. Finally, Leisler was fully though posthumously vindicated when Parliament, in 1695, retroactively absolved Leisler and Milborne of guilt and annulled their convictions.

The end of turmoil in New York in 1691 still left the status of post-Glorious Revolution Massachusetts unresolved. By the spring of 1690, the Crown had dismissed the Massachusetts charges against Andros and his aides, but argument over the permanent settlement continued to rage. Finally, in October 1691, after almost two years of struggle over the type of new charter to be issued, the Crown promulgated the new Massachusetts charter.

The new charter, which fixed the course of Massachusetts government for three-quarters of a century, was part-way between the old charter and the royal absolutism of the Dominion. On the one hand. the self-government of the old charter was completely buried; Massachusetts was now a *royal* colony, with a governor and lieutenant governor appointed by the Crown rather than elected by the people. Furthermore, the governor was the dominant ruler of the colony; all military and judicial officers were to be appointed by him, with one exception—admiralty courts, which enforced customs duties, would still depend on the Crown for their makeup. Moreover, the governor could veto any legislation. In addition, the General Court was to be called into being and dissolved at the governor's command. On the other hand, in contrast to the totally dictatorial Dominion, there *was* an elected assembly—the House of Representatives, which was to levy taxes and pay the salary of the government officials, including the governor. This power over government salaries was a mighty weapon for the House to wield. The Council—the upper house of the General Court—was to be elected indirectly by the whole General Court rather than by the people (old charter) or royally appointed (the Dominion). Its membership, however, was subject to the governor's veto, giving him substantial control over its affairs. Furthermore, the new Council was not nearly as powerful as the old Council of Assistants; the latter's judicial powers were transferred to a new, appointed Supreme Court and its executive powers shifted to the new governor. Royal control was further provided by giving the king a veto of legislation and the power of appeal of major judicial decisions in the colony. In short, as a royal colony, Massachusetts' formal political structure was quite close to that of Virginia or even of New York—especially after its newly formed Assembly exerted itself against the executive.

One of the most momentous features of the Massachusetts charter of 1691 was its change in the requirement for voting; its sole test was now either a modest freehold property yielding forty shillings in annual rent, or *any* property, personal or landed, with a total value of forty pounds sterling. No longer did Puritan church members have exclusive or even discriminatory rights to vote. Now everyone could vote who met the property qualifications, pitched so low as to make suffrage almost universal in the colony.* A lethal blow had at long last been delivered to the Puritan theocracy.

*Professor Robert E. Brown investigated the effect of the property qualification on voting eligibility. He found that in the eighteenth century, with over ninety percent of the people of Massachusetts being farmers and artisans owning their own farms, and with the average farm ranging from eighty to 180 acres, even an unusually tiny farm of twelve acres was worth over twice the minimum needed for voting. Even the two percent of the farmers who were tenants were generally worth considerably more than the requirement. And the great bulk of the small number of town laborers were, even in the late eighteenth century, let alone the late seventeenth, artisan-entrepreneurs rather than wage workers in the modern sense. Generally, the estates of even the humblest artisans were far above the voting minimum. Robert E. Brown, *Middle-Class Democracy and the Revolution in Massachusetts, 1691–1780* (Ithaca, N.Y.: Cornell University Press, 1955), pp. 21–31 and passim.

Liberty of conscience was granted by the charter to all Christians except Catholics. The vital land question was amicably settled by automatically reconfirming New England land titles, and by not requiring quitrents on any land to be granted in the future. All mineral rights were, happily, granted to the colony, but the king reserved to himself all trees with a diameter larger than two feet, for the use of the Royal Navy.

As a sweetener to Massachusetts for the deprivation of its old self-government, the new charter granted to Massachusetts the Maine towns, Pemaquid (eastern Maine, transferred from New York), Nova Scotia (newly captured from the French), and Plymouth. The Mason claims, as we have seen, kept New Hampshire as an independent royal colony, with the people struggling against the gubernatorial rule of the proprietary claimant.

Long without an agent in England to defend its interests, Plymouth— the old mother colony—met its demise, suffering the same fate at the hands of Massachusetts as New Haven had at the hands of Connecticut three decades before. Plymouth's General Court met for the last time in July 1692. Before dissolving, it set aside a day "to be kept as a day of solemn fasting and humiliation."

Apart from Massachusetts' territorial expansion, the only remaining remnant of the Dominion concept was the charter's grant to Massachusetts of command over the militia of all the New England colonies. But this attempt at centralized command proved to be ineffective, as the colonists refused to serve outside their own colonies.

Elisha Cooke and Thomas Oates, Massachusetts' agents in England, were too embittered to agree to the new charter, but Rev. Increase Mather decided to swallow his chagrin (particularly at granting the vote to non-Puritans) and to lead the colony to acceptance of the new dispensation. He and his friends of the ruling clique could at least look forward to sharing power with the Crown.

Increase Mather was also able to take comfort in the fact that he was allowed by the Crown to name the first governor, lieutenant governor, and councillors (who, in contrast to all the succeeding concillors, were appointive). At Mather's guidance, the lusty Sir William Phips, an old friend of Mather's and the hero of Port Royal, was appointed governor. William Stoughton, always emerging on top, was selected as lieutenant governor. Committed to the new dispensation, Mather brought back into the Council Wait Winthrop and others of the old merchant opportunists and excluded several of the most hard-line advocates of the old charter. These included such determined men of principle as Cooke, Oates, and their leader, Thomas Danforth. Finally, Phips, with Mather, arrived in Boston to take charge in May 1692.

During its first session in that year, the new General Court completed the framework that was to rule Massachusetts until the end of the eighteenth century. One law chartered town corporations, another established the framework of representation in elections for the new General Court.

A common myth about this framework, much propagated by later writers, asserts that the seaboard towns were overrepresented in the General Court and that this malapportionment was perpetuated during the following century, giving ever-greater overrepresentation to the "merchant aristocracy" of the seaboard towns, as against the newer and smaller agricultural towns. In the first place, we have noted that the forty-shilling or forty-pound property qualification was—again contrary to later myths—low enough to allow almost everyone to vote. Therefore, if the seaboard did dominate, it was a domination based upon the votes of the seaboard's average man. But, second, this plausible contention—plausible because population in fact moved westward from the seaboard, and a democracy will almost inevitably overrepresent older sections—turns out to be the reverse of the truth. For the 1692 apportionment law laid down the following rules: A town with less than forty eligible voters *could* send one representative to the House if it desired, but this was not compulsory. A town of more than forty qualified voters was *compelled* to send a representative. A town of over one hundred twenty eligible voters could send two delegates, but was forced to send at least one. Furthermore, no town, regardless of size, could send more than two delegates except Boston, which could send four. Note that this basic law of 1692, which remained essentially in effect until 1775, far from privileging the large old towns, did precisely the *opposite. Any* new town was entitled to a representative, but *no* town could have more than two. This ensured substantial overrepresentation of the smaller agricultural towns as against the larger seaboard areas. And it also ensured that as new small towns were added over the years, this agricultural, small-town overrepresentation would be intensified.

It is intriguing that, far from complaining about discrimination, the larger towns were quite satisfied with this arrangement; whereas it was the *smaller* towns that were constantly trying to reduce their own representation, to evade the necessity of sending delegates. It must be concluded that in those days of small pay for legislators, the cost of sending a delegate to Boston was greater than the benefits resulting—a startling testimony to the low degree of state intervention in Massachusetts society during the eighteenth century. For the absence of privileges and benefits from sharing in state power indicates that the overall impact of that power on society and the economy must have been low indeed.

Another basic law passed in 1692 established the new framework for town government in Massachusetts. As developed in this and later acts, the town meeting had many highly democratic and liberal features: notably, annual elections to insure very frequent popular checks on municipal officials; also the provision that any ten persons could place an item on the town-meeting agenda. By this period, the town proprietors had little political say-so, rule being exercised by the freemen of the town. It is, again, another heralded myth that town voting was more democratic than voting for representatives. Quite the contrary. Although relative quantities fluctuated because of changes in money value, in the basic law the property qualifications for town voting, while still low, averaged about twenty-five percent higher than for provincial voting. As a result, the best estimate is that under this basic law, the town franchise comprised seventy-five to eighty percent of the males as compared to well over ninety percent for provincial elections.*

The brutal domination of the Puritan theocracy, having faded under compelling pressures during three decades, had now been eliminated. No longer could the Puritan theocrats hang Quakers or persecute heretics; no longer could they compel people to attend the Puritan church; no more could they preclude non-Puritans from voting in town or provincial elections. The watchful eye of the royal governor and the rising influence of the far more worldly, though nominally, Puritan merchants would be there to prevent a resurrection. What was the reaction of the Puritans to this new charter?

The basic reaction of the Puritans to their bitter defeat was to fall back on a second line of defense. If they could no longer persecute Anglicans or Quakers, they could at least *establish* the Puritan church and have the satisfaction of forcing the unbelievers to pay for Puritan church support. The Puritans lost no time in so doing. A law of 1692 forced each town to pay for or maintain one or more Puritan ministers. All taxpayers were forced to pay for their support. The first year, all the taxpayers of each town, being forced to finance their local Puritan ministers, were entitled to choose their own. But the following year, 1693, the choice of its minister was placed on each congregation, to be ratified by town taxpayers and attendees of the church. In 1694 the Puritan establishment tightened further; a group of ministers protested that non-Puritans were blocking ratification of ministers. The General Court obligingly provided that a council of local Puritan elders could keep a minister in office regardless of the vote of the town freemen. As a corollary to the establishment of the Puritan church, a law of 1692 also forced every town to hire a schoolmaster; here was an attempt to erect a network of public education in the colony.

If the Puritans could no longer force everyone to attend their churches, they could at least impose Sunday blue laws on all. A law of 1692 prohibited all work, games, travel, and entertainment on the Sabbath. Violations were punishable by fine, stocks, whipping, or jail. But enforcement of these edicts became an increasingly aggravating problem.

*On the problems of geographical representation and of town *vis-a-vis* provincial voting, see Robert E. Brown, *Middle-Class Democracy,* chaps. 4, 5.

59

Aftermath in the 1690s:
The Salem Witch-Hunt and
Stoughton's Rise to Power

The Glorious Revolution imposed the last great settlement on the northern colonies. After the smoke of the tumult was over, Massachusetts, New York, and New Hampshire were royal colonies similarly structured; the main forces of conflict were, as they had long been in Virginia, the royal governor and his oligarchic council on the one hand, and the more democratic assembly, representing the people of the colony, on the other. In New York, the royal and landed oligarchy had been particularly strong and rapacious for many years, and the institution of a representative assembly was just beginning. In Massachusetts, as we have seen, the electoral base made the always more democratic assembly an especially democratic and relatively liberal voice of the people; whereas the new royal post of governor bid fair to preserve the rewards of oligarchic and royal rule.

When Massachusetts heard the news of the new charter at the turn of 1692, a power vacuum opened in the colony. The new institution of royal governor offered a tempting prospect for oligarchic power and plunder—despite the prospect of conflict with the popular House of Representatives. But it was still not clear which group would take control. The old Puritan theocracy was in rather frantic retreat from external and internal blows, but still remained strong in the colony. The new coalition of Governor Phips and Increase Mather was an alliance of moderates. Mather rather halfheartedly was trying to lead the more fanatical Puritans to the new realities of a more pluralistic and liberal society. Phips, highly liberal for a royal official and as Massachusetts' governor, was strongly sympathetic to the colony's desires for freedom from the exactions and regulations of the Crown.

If the Mather-Phips coalition had been allowed to continue in control, Massachusetts might have found a tolerable and even welcome path into the eighteenth century: the steady easing of Puritan restrictions combined with a decided drift back to effective Massachusetts independence from royal depredations. In short, Massachusetts might have been able to advance toward a synthesis of the best of the two contending sides of the recent past: the self-government and freedom of trade of the Puritans (without the theocratic persecutions), and the religious freedom and mercantile cosmopolitanism of the pro-royal opportunists (without the royal despotism). But such a synthesis for liberal independence was not to be. For at the heart of the new regime was a sinister canker: Lieutenant Governor William Stoughton. Stoughton was determined to overthrow this moderate liberalism in order that he and his friends—including the formerly discredited Joseph Dudley—might return to power, and that he might renew his plundering of Massachusetts.

Stoughton and Dudley were determined to regain power and to reimpose a royal absolutism that they would lead, at the head of a newly plundering oligarchy. To do this they would have to discredit and eliminate Governor Phips. With great luck, William Stoughton found his opportunity at hand; opportunity to split the ordinarily antiroyalist masses and to rally the body of Puritan theocrats behind him. In short, Stoughton found a way to rally the two extremes, to swing the Puritan masses behind his Tory opportunists in order to crush the moderate center. This opportunity was the notorious Salem witch-hunt of 1692.

Witchcraft had always been a capital crime in New England, but it had also been almost entirely a dead letter. The problem, after all, was obtaining evidence of guilt, and until now the sober judges and leaders of the community had not been willing to credit "spectral evidence"—the unsupported testimony of an hysterical "victim" of witchcraft that somebody's spectral witch-shape had appeared to attack him. But now, Puritan zeal was in retreat on many fronts; notably was it retreating from the burgeoning rationalistic and skeptical temper. Perhaps, the Puritan leaders felt, a reemphasis on spectral evidence and the powers of witchcraft could vindicate the true faith and roll back the tide of rationalism and secularism. As early as 1681 a group of leading Puritan divines had decided to combat rationalism by gathering supposed evidence of the supernatural in earthly affairs. Among these "evidences" was witchcraft. One of the leaders of this project was Rev. Increase Mather. In 1684 he compiled a galaxy of superstitions, *An Essay for the Recording of Illustrious Providences,* which is a record of the deeds of magicians and gremlins and which had considerable impact on the public temper. Careful attention was paid by the Puritan ministers to any cases of hysterical children that they could find; the ministers would quickly see in them evidences of witchcraft and demon possession. With the most eminent divines of the colony paying eager and almost loving attention to any signs of juvenile hysteria, these signs were accordingly encouraged and nurtured by the eager solemnity with which they were greeted. The Reverend Cotton Mather took one of these young girls into his home, the better to record the *Memorable Providences* (1689). The time was now ripe for the Puritan divines to lead a frenzied mob in a determined rearguard attempt to reinstall Puritan fanaticism in its old home; an attempt that would be abetted and used by Stoughton and the Tory opportunists.

In February 1692, at the town of Salem Village (now Danvers), these reactionary forces found their chance. The stage had been set by the solemn findings of the Mathers. Now a group of young girls of Salem Village became "bewitched" and began the delightful game of accusing other people—at first mostly personal enemies—of witchcraft. The leaders of the bewitched girls were the two daughters of the Puritan divine, Rev. Samuel Parris, and so their accusations were taken all the more seriously. At first, neighbors who had annoyed the girls were accused of being witch-tormentors. But like an infection, the accusations spread with great speed throughout the colony. Legal proceedings commenced. Since spectral evidence was now accepted by the courts, the supposed witches were quickly condemned, imprisoned, and hanged. After the classic pattern of intimidation and informing, reprieve came only if the witch would confess his or her guilt; and the confession was deemed sincere only if *other* people—accomplices—were named. Many of these confessions were extracted under torture. The circle of accusations thus became ever wider. The first hanging was that of a neighbor of the Parris family, Sarah Good, whose five-year-old daughter was even imprisoned as a witch.

Beginning with helpless old women, the circle of victims of the witch-hunt soon expanded. The Reverend George Burroughs, a retired Puritan minister himself, had the bad fortune of incurring the dislike of the Parrises. Burroughs was duly accused of being a leading witch (witches are male as well as female), of "confederacy with the Devil," etc. Reverend Mr. Burroughs was accused by several of the girls of witchcraft. The unfortunate minister became the most prominent victim of the witch-hunt. Although the more moderate Increase Mather was dubious of the spectral evidence, his son Cotton had no such doubts, and eagerly whipped up the witch-hunt generally, and specifically against Burroughs. Plagued by dishonest or deluded witnesses and biased judges, Burroughs was sentenced to be hanged.

It was no wonder that Burroughs, a good Puritan, was led by these proceedings to disbelieve in witchcraft altogether—a dose of rationalism imbibed by many who were falsely accused in their turn. On the day of Burroughs' execution, he made a brief and moving statement of his innocence, concluding with the Lord's Prayer. The crowd, convinced of his innocence, began to move to free the unfortunate Burroughs, but Cotton Mather—playing a role reminiscent of Reverend Mr. Wilson's at the hanging of Mary Dyer a generation before—stepped to the fore and explained to the crowd that it was easy for an agent of the Devil to simulate innocence. Thanks to Cotton Mather, the hanging of the venerable wizard proceeded according to schedule.

The witch-hunt flourished. One unfortunate woman, Martha Carrier, denounced by Cotton Mather as a "rampant hag," found that her four children had been induced to testify against her. In a Boston court, even a "bewitched" dog was solemnly tried, convicted, and executed.

When Sir William Phips arrived in Boston he found the colony under a full head of witch-hunt steam. He found over one hundred accused witches in prison and awaiting trial. In over his depth, he turned unfortunately to the Mathers for advice. The Mathers and the rest of the clergy called for continual efforts to detect and root out witchcraft in the colony. The crime must meet "speedy and vigorous prosecution." The Mathers did warn that more than spectral evidence should be required for conviction, but this was a mere *pro forma* note of caution, unheeded by them or by the judges. Phips then centralized the witch trials. On advice of the Council, he turned over all witch trials to a special court of seven councillors. Naively, Phips wrote William Blathwayt that the seven judges were "persons of the best prudence." Chief judge and strongman of the new court was Lieutenant Governor Stoughton. The other councillors constituted, in the words of Professor Dunn, a "perfect microcosm of the Massachusetts ruling coalition"—Puritans and Tory opportunists. Trustingly believing that all was safe and in sober hands, Phips left for Maine to fight Indians; Stoughton was left in charge of the court, which opened in Salem in early June.

Too many writers have treated the Salem witch-hunt in psychological terms: childish neuroses and mob hysteria. The vital point is not the hysteria of children, but the *use* made of it by the adult society. Neither can the witch-hunt be treated as a case study in mob psychology; for the witch-hunt was not a lynching bee, but a program carried out by the elite of the colony and directed by the lieutenant governor himself, the man whose major aim had long been the exercise of power.

During the summer, the witch-hunt centering in Salem spread through the colony. Other young girls joined in the business of being bewitched and of leveling accusations, until their number rose to fifty. Favorite targets of accusations were any who dared to raise their voice to criticize the witch-hunt, or even to assert that witches didn't exist at all. Concentration on these targets served to intimidate critics of the veritable reign of terror. This same cause was served by executing, as evident proof of diabolism, any conscience-stricken informer who dared to recant his implication of other persons.

To make sure of verdicts against the accused, Lieutenant Governor Stoughton decided, remarkably, to operate under the old charter rules. As a result, the jurors were chosen only from the ranks of Puritan church members, and the hapless defendants were allowed no rights of counsel. And, crucially, the special high court decided to admit all spectral evidence, under the rather dubious assumption that the devil could not assume the spectral shape of nonwitches. All of the witch executions, including Burroughs', were the handiwork of the Stoughton court. By the end of September, the high court had condemned twenty-seven for witchcraft and had executed twenty. Fifty witches had escaped punishment by confession, an additional hundred were in prison awaiting trial, and some two hundred more were accused but not yet imprisoned. This amounted to almost one percent of Massachusetts' population being accused of witchcraft during a period of only a few months.

Here and there brave men literally took their lives in their hands by coming out openly against the monstrous proceedings. Young Joseph Putnam, a relative of one of the bewitched girls, offered his home as refuge to any accused witch, and announced with loaded guns that anyone who should come to arrest him for witchcraft would come at his own peril. More silently, Councillor Nathaniel Saltonstall, one of the judges on the special court, withdrew in disgust from the proceedings. The eminent young liberal Puritan of Ipswich, Rev. John Wise, who had led Massachusetts' opposition to the Andros regime, now spoke up in defense of two accused parishioners, as did twenty neighbors of the accused couple. And the prominent liberal merchant of Boston, Thomas Brattle, widely distributed an open letter, "A Full and Candid Account of the Delusion Called Witchcraft Which Prevailed in New England." Brattle denounced the "new Salem philosophy," and attacked the suppression of personal liberty upon spectral evidence. Prophetically, Brattle warned: "What will be the issue of these troubles, God only knows. I am afraid that ages will not wear off that reproach and those stains which these things will leave behind them upon our land."

As the bewitched girls and their adult supporters felt their newfound power, the social level of their accusations continued to rise. Beginning with poor crones, the accusers now began to strike at some of the most eminent men of the colony. The renowned Puritan minister of Boston, Rev. Samuel Willard, was accused of witchcraft (though this was understandable in view of Willard's criticism of the witch trials). But soon the girls moved to strike at some of the leaders of the witch-hunt itself: the wife of Rev. John Hale of Beverly, one of the most ardent of the witchhunters, was accused of being a witch; so too the mother-in-law of one of the most zealous of the judges in prosecuting the witches. It is not surprising that Hale soon came to see that the witch-hunt was a double-edged sword, and he joined the outspoken critics of the witch trials. Perhaps the most interesting, and tactically the most mistaken, of the accusations was the one leveled against none other than Lady Phips, wife of the governor. The Phipses were liberally inclined, and during her husband's absence,

Lady Phips angered the hard-line witch-hunters by ordering that one of the accused witches be freed. And so, in the full heady exercise of its terrorizing power, the witch-hunt reached too far. It moved against the Phipses themselves; against, in short, the major obstacle to Stoughton's assumption of power in Massachusetts.

The witch-hunters had made their fatal mistake. Phips, never enthusiastic about the witch-hunt, now turned flatly against it. At the end of September he suspended the special court and all its proceedings for a three-month period. As Phips explained to the Crown, "Some were accused of whose innocency I was well assured and many considerable persons of unblamable life and conversations were cried out upon as witches and wizards. . . ." Increase Mather concurred in suspending the infamous court, but his son Cotton tried his best to have the witch trials continued. In fact, the witch-hunt was not yet over. Phips again journeyed to Maine, and a large number of colonists—including ministers and judges—seized this opportunity to press for a continuation of the trials, even though in defiance of Phips' order. The Reverend Samuel Torrey was particularly eager to get on with the prosecutions.

The matter now came before the General Court and debate was intense. The hard-liners were determined to continue the trials as before; the moderates called instead for a convocation of ministers to advise the government, with the trials to be suspended meanwhile. The resolution for a convocation passed the General Court by a very close 33-29 vote. The margin of victory included those who either had been themselves accused of witchcraft or had had relatives so accused. If not for their votes, the General Court would have continued the witch-hunt. When Phips returned, such councillors as the old Puritan Samuel Sewall and James Russell tried desperately to persuade him to change his mind and continue the prosecutions, but to no avail.

When the convocation of Puritan ministers assembled, the hard-line old guard, sensing its defeat, remained away, and so the proceedings were dominated by such relative liberals as William Hubbard, Samuel Willard, and John Wise. The ministers put the question to Increase Mather, who gave the expected moderate advice. The devil, Mather maintained, is capable of taking the shape of innocent persons. This could be seen, he shrewdly noted, by the fact that many ardent believers in the guilt of the witches were themselves soon accused or found a close relative in that position. And with the devil that able, spectral evidence was clearly worth little or nothing.

Using the moderate Mather formula, Phips ended the old special court, and after the General Court incorporated the Massachusetts judicial system into the charter, Phips created in January 1693 a new Superior Court, which heard the witch cases. The court, under Phips' orders to prohibit the use of spectral evidence, found it difficult to indict or convict witches. Of over fifty suspect witches, twenty-six were tried and only three convicted and sentenced to death. William Stoughton, chief justice of the old court, now assumed that office in the new. A hard-liner to the end, he happily prepared to execute the three convicted women, along with five who had been condemned by the old court. But despite Stoughton's indecent haste, the eight executions were barred at the end of January by a last-minute reprieve from Governor Phips. The reprieve was cheered by thousands in the colony, but it infuriated Stoughton. Rising in "passionate anger," Stoughton thundered that the court, if left unhampered, would have cleared Massachusetts at last of witches. But now, justice was obstructed and the task unfulfilled, thus advancing the kingdom of Satan. Stoughton left the implied question unstated: Was Phips *consciously* doing the devil's work?

With this diatribe, Stoughton tempestuously quit the court. The court proceedings dragged on for several months, but the heart was now out of it. The juries began to acquit everyone despite the anger of the judges. Finally, in April, a servant girl, May Watkins, was indicted for witchcraft and acquitted by the jury. The court forced the jury to reconsider, but the panel was adamant. About this time, the remaining prisoners were released. The Salem reign of terror was over.

The side of the coin opposite that of the myth of mob hysteria should be noted. For one thing, the witch-hunt was led and directed by the elite of the colony, the magistrates and the ministers. In addition, by no means were all the masses caught up in the witch frenzy. On the contrary, it was the revulsion of the people—as shown at the Burroughs execution and particularly by the jury acquittals—that was instrumental in bringing the witch trials to an end. In addition, popular petitions had flowed into the government, denouncing the informers and defending the accused.

The end of the witch-hunt left Phips in a very weak political position in the colony. Hated by the hard-liners for stopping the witch trials, Phips had equally disenchanted his natural supporters—the liberals—by condoning the trials in the first place. The whole prosecution, after all, had been conducted by officials of his administration and so Phips bore ultimate responsibility.

The fanatical Puritan old guard, meanwhile, was not so constituted as to give up without a fight. The people of Massachusetts had almost been won back to the old faith and zeal by the frenzy of the witch-hunt. Perhaps they could yet be won back with a further campaign against witchcraft. The indefatigable Cotton Mather now dug up the case of Margaret Rule, a bewitched girl of seventeen. Mather found the case, asked the girl numerous leading questions, gave her great publicity, tried in vain to get some accusations, and then wrote up the case in the monograph "Another Brand Plucked out of the Burning." Mather distributed the essay widely as an open letter (Phips had banned any publication on witchcraft).

Mather might have been successful in reviving the witch-hunting spirit had it not been for a courageous Boston cloth merchant, Robert Calef, who stopped him in his tracks. Bitter at the clergy's whipping up of the Salem witch-hunt, Calef attended Margaret's public examination by Mather and refuted it in 1694 in an open letter of his own. Infuriated, Mather denounced Calef as "one of the worst of liars" and had him arrested for slander. But Mather prudently decided not to press charges, and Calef kept peppering Mather with letters pointing to the unreliability of the evidence and the absurdity of the accusation of witchcraft. Ministers and magistrates joined in reviling Calef as an atheist, but he stood his ground. President Increase Mather and the fellows of Harvard College, all but one of them Puritan ministers, joined the fray in March 1694, trumpeting the "remarkables" of supernatural intervention in the natural world, and asking people to send to the Harvard fellows more such evidences. Calef, with cutting sarcasm, sent in his own list of "remarkables": the deaths of one of the witch-hunting judges, of two sons of another judge, etc. Finally, in 1700 the intrepid Calef gathered the whole inflammable discussion into one book, *More Wonders of the Invisible World,* published in London, as no Boston printer would dare to publish it. Increase Mather had the book publicly burned in Harvard Yard, but this only served to spread the book more widely. Calef's *More Wonders,* indeed, had served to crystallize the popular revulsion against the whole witch-hunt episode and its leadership. The instigator of the witch-hunt, Rev. Samuel Parris, was now driven out of his Salem parish by the aroused congregation, and one of the main "bewitched" girls of Salem confessed her dishonesty and begged forgiveness. The Massachusetts General Court itself admitted in 1696 that it had committed wrongs by participating in the witch-hunt. And in the same year, Councillor Samuel Sewall, one of the witch-hunt judges, confessed his errors publicly, and had the liberal Rev. Samuel Willard read the confession aloud in church. Willard read the noble words: "Samuel Sewall . . . being made sensible that as to the guilt . . . at Salem, he is . . . more concerned than any that he knows of, desires to take the blame and shame of it, asking of men and especially desiring prayers that God . . . would pardon that sin." Perhaps the supreme irony of the entire affair was that Margaret Rule (who, like so many of the other "afflicted," turned to promiscuity in later life), after prodding by Cotton Mather to tell the name of the witch who was afflicting her, named Mather *himself* as the guilty wizard. Unsurprisingly, Cotton Mather's interest in witchcraft dwindled markedly after that.

But through it all remained Lieutenant Governor William Stoughton; as always, unrepentant; as always, ready to come out on top. Phips had lost prestige from the witch frenzy; the old Puritan theocrats had been thoroughly discredited; rationalism was now stronger than ever—but political events were bringing Stoughton to the brink of power.

Governor Phips now lost the confidence of the Crown for taking a vigorous part in defending Massachusetts liberties against the depredations of royal officials, and for his conflicts with other governors. In the summer of 1692 a Captain Short tried to impress Bostonians into the English navy. When two members of the Massachusetts General Court opposed these despotic acts, Short invaded their homes and assaulted them. Short then failed to obey orders by Phips to follow him eastward to Maine. Infuriated at these peccadilloes, Phips, on his return to Boston in early 1693, fought with Captain Short on the street, knocked him down, and beat his cane over Short's head. Phips then imprisoned Short and had him shipped to England for trial. In connection with Short's arrest, the Governor also got into a row with Short's successor and with the government of New Hampshire. In addition, Phips, in his capacity as commander in chief of the king's armed forces in the Northeast, came into conflict with Lieutenant Governor Usher of New Hampshire, who repulsed Phips' attempt to inspect the fort at Portsmouth as well as his demand to search the New Hampshire towns for deserters from an English ship.

Governor Phips also defended Massachusetts' liberties in opposing the depredations of Jahleel Brenton, whom Edward Randolph had contrived to have appointed as royal collector of customs for New England. Brenton, son of Rhode Island merchant William Brenton, enforced the duties rigorously, but Phips joined the Massachusetts merchants in arguing that jurisdiction over customs collecting belonged to his own, more pliable, naval officers. When Brenton, toward the end of 1693, seized a ship arriving in Boston from the West Indies, the irascible Phips threatened to break every bone in Brenton's body and to cut off the ears of Brenton's witnesses, if he did not release the vessel. Phips punctuated the threat by beating Brenton with his cane and fists. Even Edward Randolph, though surveyor general of the king's customs in America, was flatly refused an accounting of the customs books by Governor Phips.

Moreover, Phips sponsored a proposal to exempt Massachusetts from the exactions and requirements of the Navigation Acts. And when the Speaker of the Massachusetts House, Nathaniel Byfield, had the temerity to call for greater royal control over Massachusetts, with the notorious Joseph Dudley as governor, Phips had him expelled from the House.

In addition, Phips, a man of decided pro-Leislerian sympathies, came into sharp conflict with Governor Benjamin Fletcher of New York, a partisan of the royalist oligarchy of that colony. Both men claimed jurisdiction over the Connecticut militia, and Fletcher threatened to take under New York jurisdiction the island of Martha's Vineyard, by this time a part of Massachusetts. Fletcher also demanded the surrender of young Abraham Gouverneur, one of the convicted (but released) Leislerians, who had moved to Boston. Gouverneur had written a letter, seized by Fletcher, highly critical of the New York chief executive. Phips angrily refused Fletcher's importunate demand, and also informed Fletcher's agent that New York's former governor Henry Sloughter should have been brought to trial because of his murder of Leisler and Milborne.

With the accumulation of cases concerning Phips' opposition to royal power over Massachusetts, the king finally yielded to the charges (especially Brenton's) and to the anti-Phips machinations of men like Joseph Dudley, and recalled Phips to England in February 1694 to answer charges of misconduct. Fighting for his political life, Phips tried to obtain a vote of support for his continuance by the General Court. Bolstered by the support of Increase Mather, Phips won a bare majority of the democratic House of Representatives but the relatively oligarchic Council, headed by the implacable Stoughton, was determined to dispose of Phips. Phips finally sailed for England at the end of 1694 and died soon after arriving in England.

Phips' recall and death left the executive power in the hands of none other than Lieutenant-Governor Stoughton, who now achieved his long-term objective of assuming power in Massachusetts. Stoughton was to remain as acting governor for the remainder of the decade.

With Phips gone, the days of a liberal governor were over. No more any quixotic defense of Massachusetts liberties. Instead, Stoughton swiftly molded a proroyalist ruling clique of spoilsmen and plunderers in the best Dudley tradition. Stoughton's major allies were the selfsame Dudley, still trying to win the permanent spot of governor, and Speaker Byfield, whose daughter was married to Stoughton's nephew. Opposition to Stoughton centered in the more democratic lower house. Thus, in 1696 the House of Representatives voted to send an agent to England to work for restoration of the old Massachusetts charter, but the Council oligarchy naturally vetoed the plan.

With the Glorious Revolution over, a royal government fixed on Massachusetts, and the inconclusive war with France dragging to a close (and in 1697 with the *status quo ante* restored in the colonies), King William now had time to turn his attention to enforcing the imperial system upon America. The great trading center of Massachusetts especially needed attention, for there the navigation laws were still virtually unenforced. The London merchants, in particular, were pressing the Crown more than ever to crack down on their colonial rivals.

As a result, three significant steps were taken to tighten imperial control of the colonies and to compel enforcement of the navigation laws. For one thing, Parliament in 1696 passed another Navigation Act, which (1) confined all colonial trade to English-built ships; (2) required all colonial governors—including the elected governors of Connecticut and Rhode Island—to take an oath to enforce the navigation laws; (3) gave the royal customs official in the colonies the right of forcible search and seizure; (4) stipulated that colonial governors appointed by proprietors must be approved by the king; (5) forced merchants reexporting enumerated articles bought from another colony (for example, tobacco from the South) to post a bond to insure that the goods not be sold to another European country; and (6) authorized the Crown to establish special vice admiralty courts to enforce the navigation laws.

Second, also in 1696, the administration of colonial affairs was taken from the Lords of Trade, a committee of the Privy Council dominated by the court aristocracy, and shifted to a new and independent Board of Trade. Although the new board contained seven privy councillors, the active working members were eight paid officials generally representing the London merchants. Among its many functions, the board was empowered to recommend the disallowing of laws conflicting with English law or policy.

The third step, the following year, was the creation by the Privy Council of the network of vice admiralty courts for the colonies, authorized in the Navigation Act. These courts were specially created for the trial and punishment of violators of the Navigation Acts. Prior to 1697, accused violators were tried at the regular common-law colonial courts. This meant that the judges were colonists who probably disapproved of the restrictive laws, and that the trials were by juries almost invariably sympathetic to the violators. To surmount this problem, the Privy Council now commissioned the royal colonial governors as vice admirals, each empowered to create a vice admiralty court under his jurisdiction. The vice admiralty court could now convict violators without the inconvenience of putting the case to a jury of the defendant's peers, for here trial was conducted by the judge only. The judges, of course, were to be royal officials, in effect appointed by the governors, as were all of the vice admiralty court officials. In practice, the judges had the full management of the vice admiralty courts; and to ensure diligence in convicting offenders, the judges were paid a percentage of the value of the violator's goods that they condemned. Enhancing the power of each judge was the fact that each court had one judge only, although in some cases the judge appointed a deputy to try cases; for instance, the judge of the Massachusetts court, the jurisdiction of which covered New Hampshire, appointed a deputy for the latter colony.

Since the vice admiralty posts were only assigned to royal governors, the Massachusetts court was assigned jurisdiction over Rhode Island, and the New York court over Connecticut and the Jerseys.

In 1699 the English also moved against the growth of manufacturing in America. The colonists were accustomed to rural household manufacture of textiles for their own use, but now New England and Long Island were beginning to manufacture woolens for commercial markets and beginning to outcompete the powerful English woolen industry. Not only were the English manufacturers alarmed, but so also were the English merchants, who stood to lose control of the trade of the Southern colonies should the latter purchase their manufactured goods from Boston instead of from England. Therefore, Parliament passed the Woolen Act of 1699, prohibiting the export of wool or woolens from any American colony, even to another colony.

Instrumental in drafting and implementing these measures was none other than the old enemy of the American colonies, Edward Randolph. Randolph had had a great deal of experience with recalcitrant juries in the early 1680s and renewed that experience when surveyor general of the customs in America in the early 1690s. His later enforcement difficulties occurred particularly in Maryland and by the spring of 1694 Randolph was reporting to England on trade-act enforcement: "I find that by the partiality of juries and others, that I can obtain no cause for His Majesty upon the most apparent evidences."

Returning home in the fall of 1695, Randolph submitted a lengthy memorandum on his findings. Randolph was now brought in to advise on the new Navigation Act, and he was one of the two coauthors of the original draft of the act. Randolph then went to work for the new Board of Trade, of which his old friend the Earl of Bridgewater was president. And when the officers of the vice admiralty courts were selected, Randolph's suggestions were adopted, as were, roughly, the boundaries of the court districts.

One of the major disputes in framing the Navigation Act stemmed from Randolph's attempt to impose a royally appointed attorney general in every colony. To transfer full power over their trade from the colonies to the Crown, it was necessary for the prosecuting attorneys to be under Crown control. Randolph wanted the Crown to appoint all the attorneys general of the colonies directly. But the colonies themselves and their proprietors bitterly protested such a change and the Crown finally decided to appoint "advocates general" to prosecute admiralty cases, but to allow the colonies to continue to choose their own attorneys general. This meant that Crown agents would be limited to admiralty cases and, further, that jurisdictional disputes over the courts of trial might loom large in the future. The upshot was a diversity of pattern in the several colonies. But, generally, the colonial attorneys general were used also as Crown advocates general; only in Massachusetts and Virginia was a separate Crown official appointed. Because of Randolph's good offices, Nathaniel Byfield was selected as the judge of the Massachusetts and New Hampshire Admiralty Court. But Wait Winthrop, the old weak-willed moderate and member of the Council, could not possibly accept this crowning of the nefarious Stoughton-Byfield alliance. These were the men whom Winthrop privately referred to as the Jacobite clique (the high Tory followers of the pretender James II), "who have in a little time got more by the government than all that have been before . . . [who] eat up the poor as bread and squeeze them to death by virtue of an office. . . ." With the Massachusetts Council overriding Stoughton and refusing to assent to Byfield's appointment, Winthrop, pulling strings in England, was able to get himself appointed as judge instead. Randolph bitterly concluded that the Massachusetts smugglers had "turned out Mr. Byfield, a man zealous for having the Acts of Trade duly executed."

60

The Liberalism of Lord Bellomont
in the Royal Colonies

The settlement after the Glorious Revolution had made New Hampshire a royal colony; Samuel Allen, claimant to the proprietorship, was named royal governor. Allen's son-in-law, the wealthy John Usher, served as lieutenant governor and resident executive of the colony. Usher struggled with the Assembly throughout the 1690s; he continually asked it for tax money, which the assemblymen claimed the colony was too poor to afford, and tried to conscript troops, which they failed to supply. The Assembly was thus the spokesman for the liberties of the people against the exactions of the royal and proprietary executive. Usher's attempts to collect quitrents were largely futile, as no quitrents could be collected from a New Hampshire jury. When Usher urged the Assembly to raise more taxes, it replied that it would do so only if Usher would join them in petitioning for a return of the province to Massachusetts.

Finally, mass pressure from the citizens of New Hampshire persuaded Allen to discharge his generally hated son-in-law and to fill his post, in 1697, with the treasurer of New Hampshire, William Partridge. Partridge, powerful at court as a heavy supplier of masts and timber to the Royal Navy, now fought it out with Usher before the legislature for the office of lieutenant governor. The Council and Assembly insisted on Partridge in what the rattled Usher described as the "Piscataqua Rebellion"; the Assembly sent its profound thanks to the king for the new appointment. In regard to the tyrannical Usher, the Assembly assured the Crown that "there had been no disturbances but what he himself had made."

We already noted that Benjamin Fletcher became royal governor of New York in 1692, and that though the convicted Leislerians were allowed their rehabilitation, Fletcher was a staunch partisan of the old oligarchy. After the Leislerians received full royal pardon, Fletcher had to let Delanoy and others take their seats as assemblymen; he later blamed their obstructions for the allegedly inadequate defenses of the colony. In addition, Fletcher kept the conflicts alive by threatening to shoot anyone who in the May 1695 election would dare to vote for Delanoy. In the New York City elections that year, the despotic Fletcher sent roving bands of soldiers and sailors through the streets threatening to draft anyone who happened to vote "incorrectly." These troops were also made freemen of the city arbitrarily in order to gain their votes against the popular Leislerian party. Such methods of intimidation were successful in confining public offices to the hands of the minority oligarchy.

Economically, Fletcher feathered his own nest and those of the oligarchy in many ways. For one thing, in return for lavish bribes, Fletcher granted the protection of New York to pirates, who abounded in that era. As a result, many prominent New Yorkers accumulated fortunes from piracy. In addition, huge arbitrary land grants were handed out to favorites of Fletcher, thus sewing the seeds of trouble for over a century to come. These vast privileges to the landed oligarchy widened the gulf between the New York oligarchy and the rest of the people. In 1697 alone, Adolph Philipse received the Highland Patent of 205,000 acres (a large chunk of Putnam County), Stephanus Van Cortlandt received 86,000 acres of choice land in Westchester, and Robert Livingston received 160,000 acres in Dutchess County. During the Fletcher years, Philipse also received many thousands of acres in Westchester, and other large grants were handed out in a rush to Beekman, Schuyler, Rhinebeck, Heathcote, Van Rensselaer, and others. William Smith, ally of the oligarchy on Long Island, received a grant of no less than fifty square miles in Nassau County. Fletcher specialized in buying the allegiance of members of his Council; thus one councillor, Capt. John Evans, received an enormous tract of 800 square miles in 1694. And Fletcher made a grant of almost 540,000 acres in the Mohawk River Valley to a Dutch minister, the Reverend Mr. Dellius, and a group of other members of the oligarchy.

In return for these services, the grantees paid Fletcher large amounts in bribes, an "intolerable corrupt selling away," as Fletcher's successor described it. Fletcher received a total of approximately 4,000 pounds sterling in bribes.

Concerning the grants of monopoly privilege that required Assembly approval, Fletcher had a more difficult time. This new democratic institution naturally represented the farmers, the bulk of the New York populace. The farmers bitterly opposed attempts by the old New York City monopolists to regain their old flour-bolting and -packing monopoly. So determined was the Assembly to secure free trade in flour that it insisted on refusing to pass any other measure whatever until Fletcher agreed to this bill. Finally, under this pressure and after the Assembly had bribed

Fletcher with 400 pounds, free trade in flour became law in 1695. New York City made repeated frantic attempts to regain the flour-milling monopoly. In 1700 it adopted an ordinance placing heavy duties on all flour and biscuits imported into the city from the outlying farms, but again the Assembly refused to pass any appropriation or tax bill until this ordinance was repealed. Finally, after an unsuccessful attempt to pack the Assembly with city representatives, the New York City merchants had to reconcile themselves to the loss of their monopoly privileges in the flour industry.

Governor Fletcher was also eager to establish the Anglican church in New York. He also wanted the Assembly to vote taxes for government for the duration of the life of the current king. The Assembly, of course, adamantly refused to do either one.

Fletcher also had no success in exerting his will over the Connecticut militia, to the rule of which he had a royal claim. Ordered in 1693 to place its forces at his disposal, Connecticut absolutely refused. The embittered Fletcher announced to England that "the laws of England have no force in this colony. . . . They set up for a free state." Instead of chastising Connecticut, the Crown, in effect, removed Fletcher's authority.

By the mid-1690s, the three royal colonies of the North—Massachusetts, New Hampshire, and New York—were all suffering under Tory oligarchs (Stoughton, Allen and Usher, Fletcher), and conflicts raged between them and the liberal Assemblies. In the meanwhile, the Tories were rapidly losing favor in the home country. The Tories were being replaced in political favor by the more liberal Whigs. The naming of the Whig William Popple as secretary of the new Board of Trade signified a decline in the influence of the powerful Tory bureaucrat William Blathwayt. By 1695 the king had decided to bring unity to his strife-torn royal colonies by appointing a common governor over all of them—the highly influential liberal Whig Robert Coote, Earl of Bellomont, friend of the great liberal philosopher John Locke. News of the appointment of Bellomont was greeted with joy by the liberal forces in these colonies—and with heart-rending anguish by Dudley and Stoughton in Massachusetts, by Fletcher and the New York oligarchy, and by Allen and Usher in New Hampshire. William Penn, Peter Delanoy of New York, and the Winthrop brothers, Fitz-John and Wait, were also jubilant. Bellomont was known to have been bitterly anti-Dudley and anti-Andros, and a staunch defender of the Leislerian revolution. In fact, he had charged that Leisler and Milborne had been "barbarously murdered."

After two years of delay, Lord Bellomont's appointment as royal governor of the three colonies was announced in 1697, and Bellomont arrived in New York to take up his post in April 1698. It took a year for Bellomont to assume his post in the New England colonies; he arrived to take over as governor in Massachusetts in May 1699 and in New Hampshire in July of the same year. This common appointment, incidentally, did not mean that the colonies of Massachusetts, New Hampshire, and New York were amalgamated as under the Dominion; instead, each kept its separate political institutions, but simply had a common governor.

Lord Bellomont lost no time in aligning himself with the popular liberal forces in all three of these colonies. From Massachusetts, Wait Winthrop traveled to New York with two other delegates of the General Court to greet the new governor. He later wrote to a friend of Bellomont's "noble character." In his inaugural speech in the Bay Colony, Bellomont boldly attacked Charles II and James II as "aliens," and hailed William III. Bellomont associated with such liberal leaders as Winthrop and Elisha Cooke. He deplored with equal fervor the Puritan fanatics and the Tory oligarchs. The grateful General Court voted Bellomont a very large salary of 1,500 pounds, the largest sum that Massachusetts ever voted for a colonial governor before or since. Unfortunately, Bellomont did not have enough time to exert any real impact on Massachusetts. He left the colony after little more than a year, in the summer of 1700, and he met his untimely death the following spring.

Bellomont's impact on New Hampshire was considerably greater, despite the short span. For Bellomont decisively confirmed the relatively liberal William Partridge as lieutenant governor in place of the Tory John Usher. Bellomont was totally disgusted with the proprietary party, and with Allen's persistent attempts to grant him huge bribes and to "divide the province" with him. Bellomont curtly told Allen, "I would not sell justice, if I might have the world"; and he denounced Blathwayt for being on Allen's payroll. Under Bellomont's aegis, the courts of New Hampshire gave short shrift to Allen's proprietary presumptions, and Partridge and the Assembly reconfirmed all the land titles that Allen had tried to dislodge. Allen took his case to the king, and the proprietary claims were to drag on for an additional half-century, but never again was proprietary feudalism to come close to imposing itself on the settlers and landowners of New Hampshire. Bellomont had, in effect, delivered a decisive blow to proprietary predation in New Hampshire.

Lord Bellomont spent most of his all-too-brief tenure in New York and there had the greatest impact. In the first place, Bellomont launched a determined and uncompromising attack on the land grants to the oligarchy. In the short time that proved to be available to him, he accomplished a remarkable amount. He publicly deplored the fact that three-quarters of the land of New York had been placed in the hands of less than a dozen men, because of the large land grants. Fletcher's corruption and arbitrary subsidies were denounced, and Bellomont managed in 1699, after a bitter struggle, to drive through the Council the invalidation of many of the Fletcher grants. The Mohawk grant to Dellius and company, and the land gifts to Bayard, Evans, and others were invalidated. The

Dellius grant was considered particularly unfortunate, for dispossessed Indians were forced to leave, and began trading with the French. The grant, therefore, had aroused the hostility of the Albany fur traders as well as the Leislerians. Lord Bellomont had to overcome the implacable opposition of three Council members, themselves the recipients of huge land grants from Fletcher: Stephanus Van Cortlandt, Robert Livingston, and William Smith. Because of this opposition, Bellomont was unable to get many other Fletcher, as well as previous, grants annulled. He was, however, able to get the Crown to impose a 1,000-acre limit on future grants, to annul extravagant grants, and to require forfeiture of lands that had not been settled and improved within three years.

Much of Bellomont's short term was concerned with cracking down on piracy, and on the connivance of the New York oligarchy in that organized theft. Such leading oligarchs and anti-Leislerians as Frederick Philipse, Thomas Willett, Thomas Clark, and William Smith were all denounced for piracy, and six oligarch councillors (including William Nicolls, Nicholas Bayard, and Capt. Gabriel Minvielle) were suspended by Bellomont for the same reason.

Bellomont began more as a determined opponent of the oligarchy than as an ardent Leislerian, but his furious struggle with the oligarchy inevitably made him leader of the Leislerian party in the colony. Bellomont also endeared himself to the Leislerians in 1698 by rescuing Leisler and Milborne from their graves near the scaffold and reburying their bodies with pomp and ceremony near a Dutch Reformed church.

When Bellomont arrived in New York, he found the Assembly dominated by the oligarchy. Even though the Assembly was a relatively democratic organ, much of the rural electorate represented the feudal manors rather than the tenants living on them. To carry through his land reform program, Bellomont needed a liberal Assembly, and he obtained the defeat of the "Jacobite party" in the 1699 election. He did this partly by holding all voting on the same day, thus preventing the customary practice of a man's voting in every county in which he owned property. In fact, Bellomont issued a proclamation for a truly free election, and charged that "the people have been heretofore interrupted in their freedom of elections." After Bellomont removed the councillors implicated in piracy, it was this Assembly that drove through the Bellomont land reforms. The Assembly also compensated some former Leislerians for expenses, pardoned the remaining Leislerians under sentence, and arrested several of the tax-farming oligarchy for misappropriation of funds. The grateful Assembly also voted the large sum of 1,500 pounds as salary to Bellomont. It was the Leislerian Assembly, incidentally, along with Bellomont, that put the severe and successful pressure on New York City to end its tax on rural flour. The Assembly, however, did belie its general antimonopoly record by prohibiting the importing of empty casks into the city of New

York—thus, in effect, granting a monopoly of caskmaking to the coopers of New York City.

It should be noted that, after the death of Leisler, the Leislerian party did not have to suffer any of the embarrassing contradictions of Leisler's own dictatorial and warmongering program. The movement now blossomed forth as a truly liberal one, with the major emphasis on freedom as over against monopoly privilege, whether in flour or in land. Indeed, Bellomont's goal in land reform envisioned not only invalidating all the land grants, but also cutting the public domain into small plots and granting them free and clear to individual settlers—thereby anticipating the libertarian "homestead" program. Bellomont recognized that the repressive landed monopoly in New York would drive away potential settlers in droves to neighboring colonies, where land was free, abundant, and unengrossed by privilege.

The landed oligarchs of New York were so worried by Bellomont's thoroughgoing plans for land reform that they hired a lawyer, John Montague, to plead their cause in England. Montague continued the feudal landowners' traditional policy of confusing their arbitrary property claims, granted by government privilege, with the rights of private property itself. He did not point out that arbitrary land grants sharply conflicted with the genuine property rights of past and future settlers.

In one important respect only did Bellomont betray the liberal cause, and thereby undercut his own liberal support. This was his emphatic determination to enforce the Navigation Acts. This, of course, was in keeping with the new tightening of imperial mercantilism, put through, in the last analysis, by the Whiggish merchants of England, eager to gain monopolistic privileges for themselves. Here Bellomont made common cause with the Tory Edward Randolph, who as surveyor general of the customs praised Bellomont's rigor in enforcement and denounced Fletcher's laxity. Using his office for plunder, Fletcher had not been particularly interested in enforcing regulations.

This attempt to enforce the hated navigation laws alienated the merchants of New York from Bellomont, and split the liberal movement in the colony. The merchants and the Assembly threatened to vote no more taxes and to tear down the customs house; many actually fled the colony and moved to the East New Jersey port of Perth Amboy. Large-scale petitions of merchants and others asked for Bellomont's dismissal.

Other opponents of Bellomont were part-and-parcel of the oligarchy. His annulment of a land grant that had been leased to the Anglican church led to a typically Tory outcry that "the church was in danger," and to pressure upon the bishop to ask for Bellomont's recall. The Anglican minister, Rev. William Vesey, led in this hypocritical attack, and Vesey was to remain the leader of the high-church party in New York for many years thereafter. In a counterattack, Bellomont unsuccessfully tried to have Vesey removed from the post on the ground of Jacobite sympathies. When the Reverend Mr. Dellius, who had lost his huge land grant, was suspended by the Assembly from his church post, the wrath of the Dutch church fell on Bellomont's head. Petitions poured in in behalf of Dellius; they came from the elders, deacons, and members of his Albany church, as well as from many others, including Fletcher in England, diligently trying to blacken his successor's reputation.

61

The Aftermath of Bellomont

The sudden death of Lord Bellomont in March 1701 ended the liberal interlude in the Northern royal colonies just as it was getting under way. A power vacuum immediately followed in each of the colonies, and competing groups rushed in to try to fill it. In Massachusetts Lieutenant Governor Stoughton happily prepared to reassume power. By this time, ordinary conditions were reversed in the colony: the Council was liberal while the House of Representatives had a majority for the royal oligarchy. Stoughton tried to dissolve the General Court and rule alone, but the Council was able to force him to call a special session quickly. In that session the Stoughton-dominated lower house voted to ask the king to promote Stoughton to governor, but the Council angrily defeated the plan.

By late spring 1701, the succession crisis was becoming ever more acute, for the venerable Stoughton was dying. Councillor Wait Winthrop, assuming leadership of the liberal camp, was appointed chairman of a joint committee of the General Court. Making a last try for resumption of self-government unencumbered by the Crown and its oligarchy, Winthrop's committee recommended to the king a petition for restoration of an elected governor and other elected executive officials to the colony. The Council warmly approved, but again the House of Representatives rejected the plan.

When Stoughton died in July, Winthrop, as the senior councillor, functioned as the chief executive of the colony. The Council, moreover, elected him to succeed Stoughton as chief justice of the Superior Court. In the Council, Elisha Cooke was Winthrop's chief supporter, while former Speaker Nathaniel Byfield led the opposition. Massachusetts then decided to send Winthrop as its agent to England, but when he prepared to ask bluntly for resumption of the old Massachusetts charter, the House of Representatives again vetoed the plan.

Wait Winthrop's little moment of glory disappeared all too quickly. A furious struggle raged in England. Massachusetts' agent and friend of Winthrop, the liberal Sir Henry Ashurst, was trying desperately to block Joseph Dudley's appointment as governor. Ashurst, who had helped Increase Mather try to restore the old charter a decade before, suggested that Winthrop be appointed to succeed Stoughton. Ashurst, however, was undercut by the unseemly haste of the General Court in dumping him as its agent and naming one of the Jacobite clique to succeed him. It is true that the court did this after hearing in September of Dudley's appointment. Ashurst, though, would have had a good chance of having the appointment canceled. Furthermore, Winthrop ruined his chance for a royal appointment by repeating his old call for resumption of the old charter; even his friend Ashurst, a moderate liberal after all, would not go that far. As it was, Dudley, backed by the Board of Trade and letters from his Massachusetts supporters, including the Mathers—now apparently willing to bow to whoever was successfully in power—finally received the appointment as governor of Massachusetts and New Hampshire in December 1701.

The collapse of the liberal opposition, particularly in the democratically elected House of Representatives, and the supine acceptance of the same Dudley whom the colony had happily imprisoned a dozen years before, were signs of the new spirit that had come to rule over Massachusetts. It was a spirit of resignation to the royal oligarchy and placemen, and a shift from opposition to those attempting to get on the gravy train. No better sign of this shift was the action of Wait Winthrop. A would-be liberal crusader in 1701, the aging Winthrop was happy to become Dudley's pliant henchman in 1708. But while Dudley was to rule Massachusetts—and New Hampshire—for over a decade, he did succeed at least in reinvigorating a liberal opposition in its traditional home, the lower house. The ever-despotic Dudley moved determinedly to crush the will of the Council and mold it as his creature. For example, the secret ballot was now prohibited in Council meetings. Dudley also tried to dictate to and bully the House, but the representatives, holding the purse, fought back; for example, they kept Dudley on an annual salary of less than 300 pounds. There was thus formed a liberal opposition to the depredations of the royal governor and his allied oligarchy. The pattern of eighteenth-century politics in the royal colonies in America had been woven in Massachusetts.

In New Hampshire the hated John Usher was appointed lieutenant governor under Dudley. The Assembly expressed its opposition to

Usher by failing to vote him a salary. The Allen proprietary claims were pushed in the courts by Usher. But not only did the juries rule against them; even Dudley threw his weight against the feudal proprietary. Dudley thought it better to throw in his lot with the leading merchant oligarchs of the province—with the Waldrons and the Hinckes. The proprietary claims were to be lost in the courts and the people of New Hampshire were finally able to get rid of Usher when he was removed as lieutenant governor in 1715.

The death of Lord Bellomont threw the colony of New York into a turmoil. His lieutenant governor was John Nanfan, a cousin of Bellomont's wife, who would be expected to carry on the old governor's policies. But Nanfan happened to be in Barbados at the time. The Council was now in charge and the Council had a Leislerian majority. But the senior councillor and therefore its president was William Smith, one of the most implacable of the anti-Leislerian oligarchy. Smith now claimed that all the governor's powers devolved on him alone rather than on the Council as a body. But the Leislerian Council quickly overruled Smith and the latter had to bow to its decision, a decision that was later to be vindicated by the Crown.

Their first attempt to take power having failed, the counterrevolutionaries saw that their only hope for power lay in England. And so they began to pepper the Crown with requests and advice. The highly reactionary Nicholas Bayard tried to whip up nationalistic prejudices by complaining that Bellomont had favored the Dutch element. Livingston, Smith, and Schuyler wrote lengthy letters complaining of the regime.

When Lieutenant Governor Nanfan returned to New York in May, he effectively placed his prestige on the Leislerian side. The heated spring elections of 1701 strengthened Leislerian control of the Assembly, which was enhanced by the overthrow by the people of Albany of its local oligarchy. The Leislerians now passed a bill to compensate Jacob Leisler's son, and moved against the landed monopolists by ordering the payment of taxes and quitrents on all unimproved (arbitrarily granted) land. However, the Leislerians alienated the merchants still further by financing compensations through raising duties on imports. Some Leislerian leaders also succumbed to the temptations of power by violating their own principles, and granted themselves substantial tracts of land; among such were DePeyster, Staats, and Delanoy. The degree of land plunder was, however, very small compared with that of previous grants. The Assembly also proceeded to confiscate the property of Livingston and part of the estate of Van Cortlandt for misappropriation of public funds while in power.

Nanfan cheered the Leislerian reformers on, and Chief Justice William Atwood, newly arrived from England, set himself squarely on the Leislerian side. But this idyll of liberal reform was not to last. By the end of 1701 the New Yorkers heard with dismay of the appointment of Lord Cornbury as new governor. He was known to be partial to the Tory oligarchy, and was coming over with the hated Richard Ingoldesby and with the former private secretary of Benjamin Fletcher. Rumor had it that the newly appointed councillors were all to be hard-line anti-Leislerians.

The Tory reaction involved in the choices of Dudley, Usher, and Cornbury to succeed the liberal Bellomont was no coincidence. For in England, Toryism was again dominant by 1701 and the Tories were able to strengthen their dominance with the accession to the throne of Queen Anne, in 1702. As an English friend wrote jubilantly to Livingston toward the end of 1701: "Most or all of the knot of Lords whereof the Lord of Bellomont was one are removed and dead."

But the Leislerians were determined that if they must go out, they would do so with a bang, not a whimper. They determined to leave in a blaze of revenge. The arch-reactionary Nicholas Bayard, on hearing of Cornbury's appointment, was impudent enough not to conceal his jubilation; he promptly sent Cornbury a congratulatory address signed by eight hundred New Yorkers. Bayard's address contained bitter indictments of the existing government, including charges of corruption, injustice, and, most serious of all, the willingness to grant the vote to nonfreeholders and to "attack the foundations of property" by annulling the privileged land grants.

Now the Leislerians had the chance to pay back Bayard with some of his own favorite coin. Noting that many soldiers had been induced to sign the petition, the Council indicted Bayard and his aid William Hutchins, New York city alderman and tavernkeeper, for treason and "conspiring to raise sedition and mutiny." The indictment came under the very law of treason of 1691 that Bayard had helped frame and used so devastatingly against the Leislerians. It soon became known, by the way, that the soldiers knew little of the contents of the petition, but were attracted by free beer or promises provided by Alderman Hutchins.

The trial was arranged quickly, with Atwood as judge and the Leislerian leader, Councillor Thomas Weaver, as prosecutor. In imitation of the trial of Jacob Leisler, the jury was packed—this time against Bayard. The foreman, for example, was a brother of Abraham De-Peyster, a leading Leislerian. Bayard (a Dutchman himself) also protested because the jurors were Dutch and relatively poor. Judge Atwood concluded the trial by virtually demanding a verdict of guilty, which was duly obtained. Convicted of treason, Bayard was sentenced in March 1702 to death; his property was to be confiscated.

John Nanfan, however, did not wish to go too far. Having made his point forcefully, he reprieved Bayard in exchange for the prisoner's expressing sorrow for the crime for which he was convicted—a round-about confession of guilt. Expecting Cornbury to arrive at any time, Bayard refused to make a direct confession. Hutchins was also tried and convicted for treason, and won his reprieve in the same way. Other leading anti-Leislerians, in a panic, fled the colony vowing vengeance against Atwood. Two of the emigres, Thomas Wenham and Philip French, had been indicted for complicity in treason and were now outlawed. They were joined in flight by the Reverend Mr. Vesey, who had propagandized widely against the regime, even though amnesty had been promised to all but one of the exiles. And even Bayard and Hutchins received the benefit of a letter to the Crown from Nanfan, asking for a royal pardon. The prosecutions were never to go beyond giving Bayard and the oligarchs a sampling of their own medicine.

The last great gesture of the Bellomont-Nanfan regime was Nanfan's ouster of Robert Livingston from the Council at the end of April—the very least punishment, remarked Atwood, that Livingston deserved. But the shades of night were approaching fast. Cornbury was to arrive in early May. And the temper of the oligarchy was revealed in such signs as "God save the king and hang John Nanfan," and a poem that warned the Leislerians to "wait the approaching change and then lament their fate."

Lord Cornbury did not disappoint the expectations of either side. Indeed, historians most partial to the oligarchy blanch at Cornbury's record. Even the arch-Tory historian William Smith, son of the anti-Leislerian leader, admitted, "We never had a governor so universally detested, nor one who so richly deserved the public abhorrence." His guiding purpose was personal plunder, and "it was natural for him, just as it had previously been for Fletcher, to align himself with that party which needed the most favors and was in a position to pay the most for them."*

Soon after assuming office, Cornbury ousted the Leislerians from the Council and filled Atwood's chief justice post with William Smith. He attacked the Leislerians as "troublesome spirits," and freed Bayard and Hutchins, who were cleared by the Privy Council. After packing the Council, Cornbury dissolved the Assembly, made many English soldiers freemen of New York City, and removed all Leislerian sheriffs from office. Having secured a pliant Assembly, Cornbury proceeded to persecute the Leislerians further. John Nanfan was clapped into jail for years under charge of false imprisonment and misuse of public funds, and was kept there despite repeated orders from England to release him. Nanfan finally escaped, but his property had all been confiscated. Lady Bellomont's estate was confiscated for Cornbury's

*Jerome R. Reich, *Leisler's Rebellion* (Chicago: University of Chicago Press, 1953), p. 160.

personal use. One mercy, though: Bayard was not allowed to wreak full revenge; his suits against leading Leislerians and his jurors for damages were disallowed by the Crown and his bill to prohibit any of his judges from holding any government office was too much even for Cornbury and the Assembly.

The new Cornbury-dominated Assembly promptly repealed all the acts of the Nanfan Assembly, and also repealed the Bellomont-secured annulment of the enormous land grants of the Fletcher administration. And while Queen Anne refused to allow this repeal to stand, Cornbury himself returned to the Fletcher policy of huge land grants to favorite oligarchs. Large tracts were granted to Rhinebeck, Livingston, Philipse, Schuyler, Smith, Van Rensselaer, and Heathcote, and the boundaries of the grants were defined so vaguely as to permit the grantees to stretch the tracts a hundredfold. The old feudal grant of Rensselaerswyck was reconfirmed by Cornbury, and a large tract was granted to Cornbury's relative, George Clarke, the new secretary of the colony. Cornbury was more than able to compensate the landed oligarchy for the setback it had received under Bellomont.

Cornbury also tried to restore the flour monopoly to New York City merchants, and to overload the city's representation in the Assembly. He also wanted restored the old power to prohibit the export of wheat (thus oppressing the farmers for the benefit of the flourmakers) by executive order.

By this time, however, Leislerians were able to bounce back in the new Assembly; the Assembly was in any case disgusted with Cornbury's flagrant appropriation of tax funds for his personal use. By 1704 it was refusing to vote any more money unless it was allowed to appoint a treasurer in charge of the public funds. The Assembly was able to win its case in England for "extraordinary" expenses; naturally, it then tended to make all grants of money "extraordinary" ones. The Assembly also denounced Cornbury's practice of charging ruinous fees to defendants being prosecuted at court.

Lord Cornbury was finally removed from office in late 1708. Characteristically, he then had to flee New York to escape creditors to whom he owed several thousand pounds. After very brief terms by Lord Lovelace and Richard Ingoldesby, Robert Hunter became governor in 1710. By now, twenty years had elapsed since the Leisler rebellion, and under the lengthy and soothing rule of Hunter, the Leislerian passions died down and faded away. In one of his first addresses, Hunter warned that no faction would receive any encouragement from him. His appointments to the Council and other offices were consciously designed to be impartial and to allay tempers on both sides. Furthermore, both factions had already begun to cooperate in asserting the power of the Assembly as a check against the excesses of Cornbury. Thus Hunter fought the Assembly for years, and dissolved session after session, but each time "all the same members . . . [returned] with greater fury." Finally, by 1713, Hunter was forced to accept from the Assembly skimpy revenue bills of a purposely short one-year duration. Clearly, New York was beginning to settle down into the governor-versus-Assembly structure that was becoming characteristic of the royal colonies.

But even though the Leislerian movement had faded away, that which had provoked its rise—the quasi-feudal oligarchy—had, unfortunately, not faded too. Although the Leislerian revolution had succeeded in bringing an Assembly to New York, which would become the focus of popular opposition to government, it did not succeed in destroying the feudal oligarchy. Indeed, land monopoly was now aggravated by the grants of Fletcher and Cornbury. Governor Hunter saw the danger, and prophetically warned the Crown that the owners of the vast estates in New York would cripple the growth of population in the colony by insisting on renting out, instead of dividing and selling, their lands. Retaining the land and renting it out, as under feudalism, will not succeed in America, Hunter warned, where full ownership of cheap and fertile land can be obtained in all the other colonies. But Hunter, alas, was not a crusader. So while basically opposed to landed monopoly, his policy of balance and moderation only left the problem of land monopoly and quasi-feudalism a festering sore that would linger in the New York social and political structure for over a century. Hunter did not add to the arbitrary land grants in New York, but, by pursuing moderation instead of principled reform, he made no move to remedy the problem. In fact, Hunter even appeased the landlords by recommending a waiver of the requirement that a certain proportion of each landed estate be settled within three years of the grant. Hunter's only long-run achievement was to eliminate the one social movement dedicated to the removal of the feudal land monopoly.

62

Rhode Island and Connecticut After the Glorious Revolution

We have seen what happened in the Northern royal colonies after the Glorious Revolution. Connecticut and Rhode Island, alone of all the colonies, continued on their old self-governing path. Connecticut's charter was reconfirmed, as we have seen, in 1690; Rhode Island's in late 1693.

Rhode Island was probably the only colony that did not greet the overthrow of Andros with great joy. Not only did Andros and Rhode Island have in common a profound hatred of Massachusetts, but the little colony was thoroughly grateful for Andros' decision to stand with it on the Narragansett Country question and against the aggressive claims of Connecticut and the Atherton Company.

Upon the overthrow of the Dominion, Rhode Island assumed possession of King's Province, never to relinquish it again, even though the territorial dispute dragged on for years. In 1703 commissioners from Rhode Island and Connecticut finally settled the dispute. In a compromise, the territory of the Narragansett Country was conceded to Rhode Island; but Rhode Island agreed to ratify all existing land claims to the area, thereby granting victory to the huge, arbitrary Atherton Company land claims. In effect, the decision foisted on the future of the Narragansett Country a large-plantation way of life.

Rhode Island remained one of the most libertarian of the colonies. The Quaker governor John Easton found it impossible, for example, to raise troops in 1691 to join in the war to conquer Canada. The basic cause was inability to impose enough taxation on the colony. The libertarian bent of the colony continued when the non-Quaker Samuel Cranston was elected governor in 1698. A nephew of the former Quaker governor Walter Clarke,

Cranston essentially continued Quaker policy. Thus, tax laws were scarcely enforced, and laws in general almost totally ignored in the colony. In 1698 Edward Randolph ranted that "neither judges, juries, nor witnesses were under any obligation." His explanation for this unusual breadth of liberty and minimization of government in the colony was that "the management of the government (such as it is) was in the hands of Quakers and Anabaptists" who, for one thing, would take no oath. This included a refusal of the Quaker governor, in 1698, to take the required oath to enforce the navigation laws. Neither did Rhode Island impose any government schooling on its citizens. The elected governors of Rhode Island assumed admiralty powers; hence the Quaker governor Walter Clarke refused to permit the English admiralty judge to function in the province.

Since the Crown could not control Rhode Island by appointing a governor, it tried to bring the colony's militia under neighboring royal governors. Governor Phips of Massachusetts tried to send agents to take over the Rhode Island militia in 1692, but the Assembly and government fought back, ordered their own officers to retain command, and asked the king for redress. Rhode Island also pointed out that several Massachusetts councillors had a vested interest in the Narragansett Country, and thus in bringing Rhode Island to heel. The Crown replied against Rhode Island, but shifted the militia power to New York. It did concede Rhode Island's control of its own militia in peacetime.

Ironically, Rhode Island's gravest conflict with the governors of New York came under the relatively liberal Bellomont administration. One of Bellomont's nonliberal traits was an excessive zeal in hunting down pirates, a practice which absorbed a good deal of his energies during his brief term. Unquestionably, Rhode Island governors had aided and abetted piracy during the war with France in the 1690s by commissioning "privateers," whose only difference from pirates was an official license to plunder. Bellomont, investigating conditions in Rhode Island during 1699, was already prejudiced against Rhode Island, and denounced its leaders as poor, lower-class, and generally "Quakers and sectaries." He was particularly bitter at the absence of religious orthodoxy among them and the lack of governmental schools. Bellomont's liberalism, so refreshingly intense in benighted New York, virtually disappeared in the highly individualistic colony of Rhode Island.

So far, no outside governor had successfully made good his claim to command of Rhode Island's militia. But the tyrannical Joseph Dudley, who had lobbied in England for abolition of the Rhode Island charter, dearly tried. On assuming the governorship of Massachusetts in 1702, Dudley attempted to assume command of the colony's militia as well as impose an admiralty judge on Rhode Island. Going to Rhode Island, he pressed his militia claim, but the Rhode Island governor and Council refused, and asserted their own authority. Dudley ordered the militia major to serve under him, but the major stood with Rhode Island. In more turbulent King's Province,

Dudley was more successful and the militia joined his command. But the Rhode Island officials soon went to the Narragansett Country and won the militia back again.

Dudley's exercise of admiralty jurisdiction also greatly angered the colony. Dudley, as had Bellomont, objected to Rhode Island commissions to privateer-pirates, and when his admiralty judge, Nathaniel Byfield, released a French prize captured by a Rhode Island privateer, he was hooted down the street by an angry Newport mob.

Once again, Rhode Island's disdain for war and the state, its quite obvious lack of patriotic exultation in killing officially declared enemies, brought down upon its head numerous denunciations for being a "rogue's land." Dudley complained to the Crown that the colony was "a perfect receptacle of rogues and pirates." He was particularly bitter that the Quaker-run colony would contribute neither men nor money to the great war to conquer French Canada, which had been resumed in 1701. In fact, the Rhode Islanders went so far as to shelter deserters from the army. In this, of course, Rhode Island was following in its great tradition of being the haven for refugees from all types of state persecution. Dudley was also bitter at Rhode Island's low taxes; while Massachusetts strained and groaned under a tax burden of 2,200 pounds per month to pay for war against France, Dudley noted that Rhode Island relaxed happily with taxes of less than one penny on the pound.

Dudley kept up his harangue and charges against Rhode Island, and by late 1705 they were endorsed by the Board of Trade. Beginning in 1701 the board had tried several times, but failed, to induce Parliament to liquidate the self-governing and proprietary colonies, that is, those not under direct control of the Crown. The proposal had largely been engineered by Randolph and Dudley, the old enemies of the American colonies. Now, in 1704–05, the board took its case to a more sympathetic Crown, and urged that the queen appoint royal governors for Rhode Island and Connecticut. The leader in the drive to smash Connecticut's and Rhode Island's independence was again Joseph Dudley, but the tide was stemmed by Sir Henry Ashurst, the indefatigable English liberal and now an agent of Connecticut, who was aided by Robert Livingston and William Penn.

The Board of Trade made its last attempt to cripple the Rhode Island and Connecticut charters in a parliamentary bill of 1706. Ashurst was again easily able to defeat the bill. Moreover, the Board of Trade was by now losing its power and its Tory drive; the war against France was going well; Edward Randolph, the board's great champion of aggressive imperialism, had died in 1703; and Blathwayt and the other high Tory members of the board were to be dismissed in 1707 and succeeded by far more moderate and liberal members.

As the war with France dragged on, however, Rhode Island began to drift from pacifist and libertarian principles and to tax its resources heavily by contributing men and material. As we shall see in a later volume,

Rhode Island, following the lead of Massachusetts, financed the ruinous expeditions against the French by turning to a dangerous and mischievous instrument completely new to the Western world: the creation of paper money. And with the Quakers losing control of the provincial government, the non-Quaker Assembly decided to shift control of the militia to the central government from the towns, where Quaker influence was still strong.

Connecticut, of course, in these years followed much the same path as her sister colony, Rhode Island. It similarly rebuffed attempts by Massachusetts and New York to assume command over its militia, and led in repelling attempts by Dudley, Randolph, and the Board of Trade to liquidate its independence. Connecticut too hung back at first in the resumed war against France, but at the end of the first decade of the eighteenth century was zealously participating in attempts to invade Canada. Connecticut, however, continued to handle her own meager maritime cases, even though she was technically under New York's jurisdiction.

When Connecticut effected its revolution against the Dominion in 1689, the true leadership of its government rested in the hands of the main architect of the revolution, the pro-Leislerian James Fitch. As leader of the popular liberal party, Fitch, though only a councillor, dominated the government. Fitch drove through a democratic extension of the franchise to freeholders of forty shillings, as well as a uniquely democratic method of selecting public officials. Taking his stand squarely for the old charter, Fitch threatened reprisals against the partisans of the royal oligarchy. The arch-reactionary party continued, well after 1690, its desperate attempts to restore royal government in Connecticut. Thus Gershom Bulkeley, Edward Palmes, and William Rosewell, aided by the Tory governor Fletcher of New York, petitioned the king in 1690 to restore royal government. Bulkeley expanded his diatribe against the charter government into a book, *Will and Doom* (1692), which remained unpublished, but which furnished ammunition for all the Board of Trade attempts of the following decade to liquidate independent Connecticut.

Governor Fletcher, after command of the militia was transferred from Massachusetts in 1693, tried to assume control of the militia in Connecticut. The Connecticut government resisted Fletcher's demands, and the threat of bloodshed forced Fletcher to return to New York. Fletcher finally obtained the limited power to requisition a quota of troops in the colony, but Connecticut managed to resist this as well.

The liberal revolutionaries headed by Fitch were, however, destined to go down to defeat—not at the hands of Tory opponents of Connecticut independence, such as Bulkeley and Palmes, but at the hands of more subtle middle-of-the-roaders headed by Fitz-John Winthrop. Having headed off various assaults on Connecticut's charter during his stay in England, Winthrop returned to Connecticut a popular hero in 1698. He won election as governor that year, and Fitch was ousted from his Council post. Winthrop's method was deadly to the liberal cause: while disarming the liberals by successfully defending Connecticut's charter against Tory assault, Winthrop reimposed government power and oligarchic rule at home. Winthrop moved quickly to enlarge the powers of the governor, only nominal during the liberal days of Fitch. The Assembly granted Winthrop more power to act between legislative sessions, to appoint government officials, and to manage military affairs. Furthermore, in 1699 Connecticut, like Rhode Island three years earlier, split its legislature into two chambers. This bicameral split was a maneuver to increase executive and oligarchic power, for now the governor and his upper House of Assistants were able to veto the popularly elected deputies. Furthermore, the judicial system was converted into an independent oligarchic power; whereas before 1698, judges were elected annually in each county, now county judges remained independently in office on good behavior. In this way, the judges were freed of the checks put on their power by popular elections, and were transformed into a quasi-permanent oligarchic bureaucracy. Or as the reactionary Samuel Willys put it, they were freed from "the arbitrary humors of the people."

Finally, to complete the litany of counterrevolutionary statism imposed by the Winthrop regime, a law of 1699 established the Puritan or Congregational church in each town. Every taxpayer was now forced to pay for its maintenance, and new churches could be formed only on permission of the General Court. New public schools were also forced upon the colony.*

With support increasing for Fitch, and with Winthrop kept busy for the next decade in defending Connecticut's charter, there was no time for further changes of this type in Connecticut. But the damage had been done. Furthermore, the main result of the Board of Trade's assault on Connecticut was to force the colony to agree to the right of appeal, in judicial decisions, to the Crown.

Moreover, the statist Winthrop program was not yet ended. For when Winthrop died in 1707, he was succeeded by his chief adviser, Rev. Gurdon Saltonstall, who proceeded, in the Saybrook Platform of 1708, to organize the Puritan churches into a tight Presbyterian system. If a community is to have a state-run church, it is far easier for the state to control a centrally governed church than one of independent congregations. So Connecticut transformed its Puritan churches, halfway between truly Congregational and Presbyterian forms, into a fully Presbyterian structure. The legislature convoked a synod of ministers and elders at Saybrook, which adopted the new regime. The General Court then imposed the system, taking care to allow religious liberty to Dissenters provided their churches were licensed

*Professor Dunn's comments on Winthrop's reactionary "reforms" are more favorable, but provide correct insight into the facts; for example: "By curbing the colonists' undisciplined, anarchic [that is, individualistic] behavior, he [Winthrop] could meet charges from the Board of Trade that Connecticut's government was inadequate and irregular. The reforms were particularly designed to break James Fitch's democratic faction" (Dunn, *Puritans and Yankees*, p. 323).

by the state. From then on, only a minister legally recognized by the General Court could receive state support.

It was also in Saltonstall's regime that Connecticut threw itself into expensive attempts to carry the war to Canada. During the long tenure of Rev. Mr. Saltonstall the oligarchic faction became cemented in the colony; here was the beginning of Connecticut's later reputation as a "land of steady habits."

63

The Unification of the Jerseys

During the crisis years of the Glorious Revolution, both Jerseys at last rested peaceful and content. The Dominion bureaucracy had gone, and the respective sets of proprietors did not dare to stir lest their grants be revoked by the Crown. They therefore decided not to impose any rule until the smoke had cleared. Government, in both colonies, was local and purely minimal.

Dr. Daniel Coxe, court physician and non-Quaker, had, before the onset of the Dominion, bought from Edward Byllinge the sole right to govern West New Jersey as well as the largest proprietary share in that colony. He also held a much smaller share of the East New Jersey proprietorship. Coxe fought hard and successfully to prevent the Lords of Trade from annulling the charters of the two Jerseys or from amalgamating them into New York and thereby converting them into royal colonies. In the spring of 1692 Coxe sold all his rights and titles in the Jerseys to a group of non-Quaker businessmen, the West New Jersey Society, for 9,800 pounds. The society was owned by holders of 1,600 shares of stock issued at ten pounds each. Originally, the society had forty-eight stockholders, the most prominent being Sir Thomas Lane, who was to serve also as lord mayor of London.

We have already noted that the proprietors of East New Jersey had chosen the Scot Andrew Hamilton to be deputy governor in 1687. After the Dominion was imposed in 1688, Hamilton returned to England, and both the Jerseys remained without a central government until 1692. In that year, however, with the proprietorships at least temporarily saved, *both* of the Jerseys appointed Hamilton to be governor. The first step toward unity of the two Jerseys had begun. Hamilton took up his post in the far wealthier and more populous East New Jersey, of which Perth Amboy was the capital, and appointed Edward Hunloke to be his deputy in West New Jersey.

With the return of central and proprietary government came the return of turmoil and conflict in the Jerseys. Hamilton's guiding instruction was to begin, once again, to enforce collections of the hated feudal quitrent.

Fearful of attempts to submerge the Jerseys into New York, East Jersey now made particular efforts to aid New York in attempting to prosecute the war against New France, and New York's Governor Fletcher expressed his gratitude to Hamilton for the 400 pounds and the sixty-five men supplied.

Despite the fact that the proprietors of both colonies had been Quakers, the ethnic composition of the two Jerseys differed greatly. East New Jersey was heterogeneous, comprising Dutch, Puritans from New England, and Scotsmen. The Scots were mostly Presbyterians, not Quakers, despite the fact of Quaker proprietorship during the years of their migration. West New Jersey, on the other hand, was a poor, sparsely inhabited, predominantly Quaker colony.

Despite the differences, Governor Hamilton had no difficulty in persuading the supposedly pacifist Quaker Assembly of West New Jersey to join that of the East in voting ample funds to help New York in the French war. As early as the year before, the West Jersey Assembly had resolved that, while the people of the colony could not bear arms or participate in war, they *could* help "defend" the province, and in 1693 they voted 300 pounds for the war effort.

Paradoxically, Hamilton met the only resistance to his war plans in non-Quaker East New Jersey. Hamilton wanted the colony to supply thirty soldiers for the war, but Speaker William Lawrence of the East Jersey Assembly forced him to cut the supply to twenty. However, 430 pounds were raised for the war effort, more than matching the contribution of the year before. Even so, Hamilton wrote apologetically to Fletcher that volunteers could not be raised and that he could only raise troops to send to New York in case of invasion, and then only on condition that they would return as soon as the campaign was over.

Under Hamilton's aegis, the powers of the local governments over the people were greatly strengthened. The counties were now authorized to levy taxes, to repay debts, and to maintain jails; the levies and appropriations were to be raised by the county judges, meeting with representatives of each town in the county. The townships were also authorized to impose the maintenance of government schools on all taxpayers of the town, even on those opposing the idea. Also, the term of conscripted militiamen was lengthened.

Hamilton ran into trouble in 1694 trying to persuade the Assembly to increase taxes in order to pay salaries to himself and other government officials. On the other hand, the Council vetoed the bill passed by the deputies raising their own salaries, the Council pointing out that *its* members remained unpaid.

The quitrent problem came to a head in 1695. Speaker Richard Hartshorne was the leader of the popular opposition to Hamilton and his Council. Conflicts continued in succeeding years over Hamilton's demands for regular levying of revenue for the government as well as enforcement of the quitrent. Once again, Elizabethtown, joined by Newtown and Shrewsbury, was in the forefront of the opposition.

The landlords took the quitrent cases to the courts, and after the juries (in the words of the proprietors), "being all planters, gave a general verdict against their proprietors," the judges arrogantly reversed the juries' decisions. On appeal of the cases to England, the claims of the proprietors were years later rejected by the Crown. The proprietary claim to quitrents had been finally rejected.

As soon as the first of these cases had been so decided by the Crown in 1697, sixty-five citizens of Elizabethtown immediately petitioned the king for an end to the tyrannical proprietary government that persisted in exacting tribute for lands rightfully theirs.

At about this time, however, a grave new threat arose to plague the owners of landed property in East Jersey. An English court decided, on a technicality, that the land titles confirmed by former Governor Carteret had only been valid for life rather than in fee simple, for perpetuity. Hamilton now offered to reconfirm the absolute land titles, but only at the price of paying the large backlog of arrears in quitrents.

In 1697 Andrew Hamilton was removed as governor in both Jerseys. Under the general interpretation of the Navigation Act of 1696, all Scotsmen were removed from positions of public trust in the colonies. Hamilton was, therefore, replaced as governor of both Jerseys by the former Baptist minister Jeremiah Basse, who assumed his new post in early 1698.

Basse, even before his appointment, had come to be thoroughly hated in West New Jersey and the other colonies. He had earned this ire as a former agent of Dr. Coxe and the West New Jersey Society, and as an opponent of the colony's violations of the navigation laws.

The arch-Tory and inveterate enemy of the colonies, Edward Randolph, had come to the conclusion that Scotsmen were particularly active as "smugglers" and merchants. He therefore inserted a clause into the Navigation Act of 1696 to keep them out of public office in the colonies. Basse was known as one of Randolph's clique of "prerogative men," and he schemed at London to use the clause to oust Hamilton and obtain the post for himself.

At first, conflict between Basse and the people of East New Jersey was not widespread or intense. The people and the proprietary were jointly engaged in another chapter of continual struggle with New York: winning for Perth Amboy the right to be a free port, unhindered by New York regulations. Using the external dispute as a method of mobilizing support, Basse managed to induce the Assembly in the spring of 1699 to increase taxes sharply, with new taxes being levied on a wide variety of property.

The new tax burdens stirred up widespread opposition in East New Jersey. A Newark town meeting denounced the tax and warned that there was no guarantee that the money would be used for the announced purposes. Anyway, there was clearly no danger of invasion from New York. The Newark meeting resolved unanimously not to pay the new tax and to resist its collection. Led by young Lewis Morris II, a councillor and merchant (later chief justice of New York and governor of New Jersey), the towns of Newark, Elizabethtown, Perth Amboy, and Freehold joined to protest to the proprietors against the rule of Basse. They also specifically attacked a resolution of the lower house of the Assembly praising the Basse administration.

Morris, indeed, had challenged Basse's rule from the beginning, denying the authority of the Basse-appointed court. Fined for contempt, Morris managed to escape from prison. He continued relentlessly to challenge the basis of proprietary rule; such rule, he asserted, was by persons "who really have not the right to govern." He also denounced the quitrent as an unjust tax "upon us and our heirs forever."

Morris was now, in April 1699, charged by the Council with seditious assembly, with intent to subvert the laws, and with "malicious and reproachful words" against Governor Basse. In May a grand jury indicted Morris, along with Surveyor General George Willocks, and Secretary Thomas Gordon, for stirring up opposition in the towns to the taxes levied in March. The next day a large group from Elizabethtown attacked the jail holding Morris et al. and freed the eminent prisoners. Among the leaders of this revolutionary attack were such well-known citizens as Justice Benjamin Price, Isaac Whitehead, and Jonathan Ogden, Jr.

By this time, Basse had left for England to discuss the dispute with New York. Andrew Bowne now ruled as deputy governor. Shortly after their coerced release from prison, Morris and Willocks called on the Council to yield, and sent an armed sloop against Perth Amboy "firing guns by way of defiance to the government." Bowne and the Assembly decided to order the suppression of the insurrection in the province. But the Assembly realized that virtually the whole province opposed the new taxes, and the bulk of its members walked out in protest against them. Only placid Bergen County was not in a state of rebellion.

With this kind of opposition in the Assembly, reinforced by the proprietors' decision to appoint the revolutionary Thomas Gordon as attorney general of the colony, Bowne did nothing to enforce the tax act or to suppress the insurrection.

Morris' rebellion had succeeded, for soon after Basse returned from England in the summer of 1699, Andrew Hamilton was reappointed governor of the Jerseys. Scotsmen, it was now ruled, were able to hold office in the colonies, and the proprietors seized the opportunity to reappoint Hamilton and end the calamitous regime of Basse.

If Governor Basse precipitated conflict and oppression in East New Jersey, his rule over the Quaker colony of West New Jersey was a veritable reign of terror. Hamilton had left West New Jersey alone. As a result, the Quakers' largely libertarian society was not confronted, as in previous years, with the threat of proprietary despotism. As soon as Basse took power, however, he imposed a program of reactionary change upon the colony. Virtually his first act was to oust the previous Council and the judges, and to fill their posts with his friends and favorites, almost all non-Quakers.

The Quaker lower house tried to oppose Basse's accession to power, whereupon he promptly began to throw them into prison. Peter Fretwell, former treasurer of the colony, was jailed by Basse for "not acknowledging the government." Furthermore, the great leader of the liberal forces in West New Jersey, Speaker of the House Samuel Jennings, was arrested in the spring of 1699 for saying that Basse's commission as governor was illegal, and for slandering one of Basse's appointed councillors as "a papist."

Three of the new councillors, indeed, published a book denouncing Jennings as the key to the seditious opposition. They wrote: "Samuel Jennings being the leading man of that party . . . now sings his old song over again, and affirms the Government to be in the people thereby encouraging and exciting the people to rebellion against the present Governor, and other their lawful rulers, to the great obstruction of the peace and property of the Province." Fretwell and Thomas Gardiner, furthermore, were indicted "for setting the province in a flame," but they refused to appear for their trial.

Rebellion did, indeed, burst forth in Salem, where the government was resisted and the Basse-appointed magistrates expelled from the town. But the governor sent in fifty soldiers and was able to suppress the rebellion. Basse found, however, that he could not suppress the voices of his opposition. Samuel Jennings, undaunted, not only organized a giant anti-Basse petition, but also broadened his attack to include the whole proprietary regime, particularly for violating the rights of liberty and self-government that had been granted to the people in the old Concessions.

Andrew Hamilton returned as governor in December 1699 only to find both colonies in a state of outright rebellion. In West New Jersey the Basse-puppet council was unceremoniously removed, and the revolutionary leaders returned to their posts: Jennings to Speaker of the House, Fretwell to treasurer; Gardiner became king's attorney.

But both Jerseys were now in the midst of a revolutionary situation, and a mere change of governors was no longer enough to appease the popular opposition. The spark for the rebellion in both colonies was the increase in taxes, and a mere change of personnel would not be enough to relieve the situation.

To Lewis Morris and the people of East New Jersey, only the liquidation of the proprietorship would suffice to end the rebellion. The proprietors were, indeed, negotiating with the Crown for surrender of their right to govern, though not of their land claims. However, proprietary government continued in the meanwhile, until the Crown's decision should be made. But the revolution roared on. In March 1700, justices of the Middlesex County Court—all councillors—were barred from the courtroom by a rebellious crowd led by Edward Slater, one of the main leaders of the rebellion against Carteret nearly twenty years before. A week later, Samuel Carter, leading an angry crowd, denounced the proceedings of the Essex County Court, and the court ordered Carter arrested for contempt, "which may, if not timely prevented, turn to a convulsion in government to the ruin of the colony." It may be noted that the crowd supporting Carter included such prominent citizens as Justice Benjamin Price, a former councillor.

By July, however, Lewis Morris had betrayed the revolution he had led, and now shifted vigorously to the other side. Returning to the Council as Hamilton's appointee for president, Morris warned everyone to submit to the governor. Soon Morris had an opportunity to betray his own neighbors in Monmouth County. The newly appointed sheriff, the Scotsman John Stewart, was on a rampage in the county, jailing rebels. Friends of those about to be arrested thereupon attacked Stewart and forced him to flee. Learning of a plan to free one of the captured men, Morris informed Hamilton, who appeared with an armed troop and then demanded the surrender of two of the opposition leaders, Richard Salter and John Bray. But the free men of Monmouth County by now numbered six-to-one against Hamilton and Morris. Aroused, a hundred citizens of Middletown, armed with clubs, marched to confront the governor's force. A compromise averted an armed clash when the prisoners agreed to put up bail as security for good behavior.

The renegade Morris had been given the task of suppressing the rebellion, and his unpopularity was assured when he threatened to drench the colony in the blood of the rebels who did not yield. With Morris ordered to seize Salter and Bray, Monmouth, Middlesex, and Essex counties conferred to decide their next move. They decided to resist Morris' power and to seize, arrest, and incarcerate Hamilton, Morris, and Councillor Samuel Leonard until the Crown made up its mind on the future of the colony. Town after town rose in revolt against arbitrary arrests.

A grand jury of Monmouth County soon indicted sixteen men, including Salter and Bray, for riotous assembly and assault of Sheriff Stewart. But the rebels remained undaunted. In September the Essex County Court at Newark had its proceedings interrupted by Samuel Carter, who challenged the authority of the court. The constable ordered to seize the prisoner was himself assaulted by the rebels. The rebels also assaulted Councillor William Sandford, the president of the court. The rebels were led by Carter and Thomas Johnson, a long-time high official in the colony and a leader of the rebellion under Carteret. Two days later a large group of horsemen arrived from Elizabethtown to demand of the Essex County judges the freeing of one of the prisoners, Joseph Parmeter. Led by Samuel Carter and Samuel Whitehead, the rebels, on being refused, seized the sheriff and forced him to free Parmeter. Soon afterward, in retaliation, two grand juries indicted eighty-five Elizabethtown men for joining in the insurrectionary action.

The revolutionaries countered by signing an Elizabethtown petition to the king against the proprietors. In it they attacked the quitrent, which was being exacted even after the royal courts had disallowed it, and they asked the Crown to replace the proprietary with a royal governor. Leading the opposition to the proprietary in the Assembly, which convened in May 1700, was Councillor John Royce. The councillor held an old Nicolls patent for his lands; this fact jeopardized the lands and subjected it to quitrent exactions so long as the proprietary continued.

Hamilton convened the Assembly, but only to try to get a tax bill passed. He soon saw that there was no chance of success. Moreover, he saw the danger of the Assembly approving the antiproprietary petition. Therefore, Hamilton made haste to dissolve the Assembly. But the East New Jersey petition helped galvanize the Board of Trade to annul the Jersey proprietary. The East New Jersey proprietary tried to stem the tide by its "Answer" to the petition, sent to the Crown in December. The "Answer" trenchantly attacked the colonial resistance to payment of quitrents as a logical prelude to denial of the royal power itself. It concluded that the settlers viewed themselves as the absolute owners of the soil, and hence entitled to an independent government of their own. The proprietors darkly charged that the rebels were merely "a few factious and mutinous people impatient of any government."

The following March (1701), the pattern of revolt against the proprietary courts continued. As the Monmouth court, headed by Governor Hamilton, was examining an accused smuggler named Moses Butterworth, Samuel Willet, an innkeeper, challenged the authority of the court. Willet charged into the court with a company of fifty militiamen. A battle ensued between the police on one side, and the militiamen and the crowd, led by Benjamin Price and Richard Borden, on the other. The rebels proceeded to free Butterworth and to seize the justices, the attorney general, and the other officers of the court. The next day the court, with Samuel Leonard presiding, was able to reassert its authority despite a challenge by Eleazer Catterall, who refused to serve on the compulsory jury, and the refusal of the former court clerk James Bollen to surrender the court records. The court quickly seized, convicted, and fined all those denying its authority and refusing to serve on the grand jury.

After the disastrous Assembly session, Hamilton had decided not to convene it again and to rule only with the help of the Council. In May 1701 Hamilton and the Council petitioned the king to order the people of East New Jersey to obey the proprietary government. Hamilton complained that since he had not received official approbation of the Crown, "the licentious past" of the people, "who look on all government to be a yoke," had repudiated his authority and all of his actions. As a result, he pointed out, the "reins of government" are "cut in pieces" and the people run into "anarchy and confusion."

But Hamilton was soon to find that the Council was hardly more tractable than the House of Deputies. First, in late 1700 George Willocks, deputy for the proprietors, led a revolt against the leading proprietor, William Dockwra, the proprietors' executive secretary. The Council stalled hearings on Willocks' charges of corruption and injustice against Dockwra, but it finally consented to a hearing the following August. Willocks charged Dockwra with usurpation of governmental rule, levying arbitrary fines on local landowners, voiding good land titles, and demanding bribes for settling land claims. Backed by the deputy secretary and six resident proprietors, the Council turned against Dockwra and the Board of Resident Proprietors finally removed him from his post.

But the Dockwra problem was purely internal to the ruling oligarchy of proprietors and their favorites. Also internal, but far more challenging to the existing regime, was a sudden move by former governor Andrew Bowne at the Council meeting in June 1701 to claim the post of governor. Bowne declared that the proprietors had appointed him, but he was challenged by the resident proprietors, headed by David Lyell, who pronounced Bowne's claim defective and who charged that the whole thing was an anti-Hamilton maneuver invented by Richard Salter. Bowne's claim was also backed by William Dockwra, who was evidently taking the opportunity to try to oust a regime that had already turned against him.

Lewis Morris, now agent of the resident proprietors, decided that the best course would be to abolish the weak and confused proprietary rule, and to replace it with a royal government headed by Hamilton. In that way, Hamilton and the ruling oligarchy in East New Jersey could end the permanent rebellion and entrench themselves in power, backed by the might and prestige of the royal government.

As rebellion settled into a permanent state, the Tory advisers of the colonies began to offer their solutions. Edward Randolph, in February 1701, advocated not only the end of proprietary government (though not of its land claims) but also the annihilation of the Jerseys. Randolph urged that East New Jersey be annexed to New York and West New Jersey to Pennsylvania; in the meanwhile, all is "in confusion for want of government."

Andrew Bowne also moved in again, hoping to have his post restored. He called for drastic enforcement of the generally violated Navigation Acts. Bowne suggested amalgamating the Jerseys with Delaware, as part of Pennsylvania.

The proprietors themselves, indeed, were rapidly becoming reconciled to the end of their rule, and they submitted a memorial to the Crown outlining the conditions for voluntary surrender of their governmental rights. The petition, incidentally, was jointly submitted by the proprietors of East New Jersey and West New Jersey. The final surrender by the proprietors and the acceptance by the Crown were accomplished in mid-April 1702. The Crown decided to grant some, but not all, of the proprietors' original conditions. Proprietary rights to the soil were reconfirmed, along with the quitrents due. All land titles issued by the proprietors were confirmed. The governor was instructed to forbid any tax on unimproved (that is, arbitrarily granted) lands, thus greatly aiding the land engrossing pursued by the proprietors. Another important privilege granted to the proprietors was a monopoly of all purchase of land from the Indians; this gratuity in effect made vague and arbitrary land grants to the existing landed proprietors.

After April 1702, then, the proprietary government was no more; both Jerseys were now united into one New Jersey, a royal colony.

Andrew Hamilton had had no easier time in West New Jersey. The revolutionary state had continued in that colony as well. To a greater extent than in the East, the focal point of resistance was taxation. The unique element in West New Jersey was that a high tax program had been instituted by an alliance of Hamilton with the Quaker-dominated House. By 1701 a general refusal to pay taxes pervaded the colony, a refusal which included the threat of violence against the hated tax collectors. As in East New Jersey, the rebels refused to pay the courts security for good behavior. In March nearly eighty people rioted in Burlington, broke into prison, and released two men who had refused to put up security for failing to pay taxes.

Furthermore, Quaker imposition of high taxes seemed inconsistent with Quaker principles to a group of dissident Quakers, who had seceded from the fold. It was these dissident Quakers who formed the bulk of the revolutionaries in West New Jersey. At regular Quaker meetings they were denounced as "seditious."

The proprietors were anxious to have Andrew Hamilton appointed royal governor of the united New Jersey, but this was one privilege they were not to receive. The Crown's appointed Council for the new colony included six officials from each Jersey, largely taken from the oligarchical leadership of the two former colonies. Councillor Lewis Morris was designated acting governor by the Crown in June 1702, pending a final appointment. Finally, toward the end of the year, the Crown made New York's governor,

Lord Cornbury, governor of New Jersey as well. Cornbury assumed his post in July of the following year.

The Crown decided to alternate meetings of the unified General Assembly between the respective capitals of Perth Amboy and Burlington. The House of Representatives was to consist of twelve representatives from each of the two former divisions, two apiece to be sent by the two capital cities.

Thus, the structure of New Jersey was now similar to that of the other royal colonies: an appointed governor and Council, an elected lower house. Appeals could be made to the king in major judicial cases. The Crown accepted the proprietors' request for high minimum voting requirements: voters had to own at least one hundred acres and representatives one thousand acres. Lewis Morris had warned that without the latter requirement "those persons of best estate . . . and the proprietors' interest . . . would be at the disposal of the tag, rag, and rascality." In short, the property qualification was a method of attempting to secure control of even the Assembly by the proprietors. In addition, the people lost the right to have a regular annual Assembly. The rights to call and dissolve the legislature, and to appoint judges and courts, were lodged in the royal governors. But the crucial rights, those of levying taxes for support of the government, remained with the Assembly.

Also granted were more worthwhile requests of the proprietors: for example, permitting Quakers to avoid taking an oath of office. Religious liberty was also granted to everyone but Roman Catholics, continuing the East New Jersey policy passed under the Law of Rights and Privileges of 1698. But this provision was a mixed blessing. From the time of the original Concessions, at the outset of the colonies, both Jerseys had enjoyed extensive religious liberty. By its discrimination, the new proviso was a setback for the Catholics. On the other hand, there was an advance in another direction. The law of 1698 had eliminated the power of the Assembly to establish ministers; but now separation of church and state, without which there can be no full religious liberty, was decreed for the colony as a whole. The important exception was a proprietary grant to each township of two hundred acres of government land for support of a minister; this feature enabled some of the Puritan towns in New Jersey to keep an established church.

As to the proprietors' request to make Perth Amboy and Burlington free ports, without harassment from New York, the Crown suggested that this would be granted only if the New Jersey Assembly raised its customs duties and regulations to equal New York's—thus ending embarrassing free competition with the highly taxed and regulated port of New York, and increasing the royal revenue extracted from the colonies.

Lewis Morris tried to use the new accession of royal power, as well as his leading role in the colony, to establish the Anglican church. As early as

1697 he tried to pass such a bill, but it was defeated by the combined efforts of Richard Hartshorne, Quaker, and Andrew Bowne, Baptist. One of Morris' main reasons for wanting the proprietors ousted was to further the project of an Anglican establishment. But the royal government would not establish a religion that was very weak in the colony—indeed, weak everywhere north of Maryland. The lack of a bishop resident in the colonies also handicapped the growth of Anglicanism. For example, it was difficult for one aspiring to the Anglican ministry to be ordained; either a bishop had to come from England to perform the ceremony (and few chose to come) or the would-be priest had to travel to England.

What happened, incidentally, to the ultra-Puritan settlement at Newark that was founded by the former New Haven minister Abraham Pierson in 1667? Newark continued at first as a rigorously Puritan township, but Pierson died in 1678 and was succeeded by his son, Rev. Abraham Pierson, Jr. Typical of the Puritan ministry throughout New England, New York, and New Jersey, the younger Pierson was drifting strongly toward Presbyterianism. As a result, Newark ended its established church in 1687 and threw Pierson's salary open to voluntary subscription. Pierson was thereby obliged to move elsewhere. The ultratheocratic experiment at Newark had collapsed.

Thus New Jersey took its place after 1702 as a Northern royal colony, with appointed governor and Council, and a popularly elected Assembly. Proprietary tyranny and attempts to impose taxes, quitrents, and arbitrary land allocations ceased, but royal government, in alliance with the land claims of the proprietary, continued the power of the old oligarchy. Also ended, forcibly, were the several years of successful rebellion in New Jersey. The colony continued to be relatively individualistic, however, and to enjoy religious liberty and diversity.

64

Government Returns to Pennsylvania

Let us now return to the situation of Pennsylvania in 1690. We have seen that by almost unanimous resistance of the Quaker colony, Governor Blackwell's harsh attempt to reimpose a state on an essentially anarchist Pennsylvania had failed ignominiously. Blackwell was forced to return to England. We have also seen that the Assembly, in the spring of 1690, refused to vote funds to aid Governor Penn; it also ignored a request from Jacob Leisler to help fight the French in King William's War. When a former Blackwellite, Secretary William Markham, asked for a governmental organization of the colony to provide for military defense against a supposed French and Indian threat (which never materialized), the Council preserved the anarchist status of the colony by replying that any people interested might provide for their own defense *at their own expense.* And even so, any militia had to be obedient to civil authority. This effectively killed the idea of a militia in the colony; the militiamongers were reluctant to pay for the services that they professed to desire so ardently.

Furthermore, the Assembly and Council continued their pre-1688 practice of rarely meeting, of doing little even then, and therefore of rarely governing.

But William Penn, the absent proprietor, was not disposed to let Pennsylvania continue in this anarchistic idyll. In March 1691 the colony received a message from Penn announcing his aim of appointing a deputy governor and of giving Pennsylvania the option of naming its ruler. Penn expressed a preference for a five-man commission of state to serve as deputy governor, but the Pennsylvania Council overruled him and chose

Thomas Lloyd, the great leader of the anti-Blackwell resistance. Lloyd assumed his new post in April. With the accession of a continuous government official, government, unfortunately, was back in Pennsylvania, but its power remained at an absolute minimum. The Assembly and Council still met infrequently and there was still no taxation in the colony.

In the meanwhile, the leading political dispute centered on the three lower counties of (non-Quaker) Delaware. Delaware, eager for self-government of its own, objected to all of its judges being named by the central government in Philadelphia. This dispute, becoming prominent in late 1690, reached its high point when Pennsylvania was forced to reassume government. Now a single governor would appoint Delaware's officials. Bitter at this turn of affairs and at the idea of a tax to support a Pennsylvania governor, the Delaware counties immediately decided to secede and to found their own self-governing colony. The reimposition of government had directly provoked secession by Delaware.

Governor Lloyd did his best to induce the seceding counties to return, promising, in fact, that they would never be forced by the central government to pay any of his salary and that they would be allowed full local self-government without central interference. Delaware preferred, however, to assure itself of noninterference by remaining independent.

Finally a compromise was reached in the winter of 1691–92. William Penn agreed to appoint two deputy governors: Lloyd in Pennsylvania, Markham in Delaware. These executives would control their respective appointments of officials as well as local matters, while both areas agreed to elect representatives to a joint Council and a General Assembly. Pennsylvania-Delaware now had two sets of executive officials and a common legislature.

Although a permanent government now existed and had nominal power, Pennsylvania society was still quasi-anarchic, since no taxes were yet being levied by the government. The government was still being wholly supported by voluntary subsidization from the proprietor. But in April 1692 the Council had passed a new bill for the reestablishment of taxation. Making this a particularly bitter blow was Governor Lloyd's concurrence in the bill. The specific tax proposal was one penny per pound of property, or less than .25 percent, with a minimum payment of two shillings.

Would the May Assembly, always the great stronghold of libertarianism, ratify this drastic and far-reaching proposal to reintroduce taxation? The freemen of Philadelphia and Chester sent the Assembly petitions strongly protesting the proposed tax. The petitioners urged the assemblymen to keep "their country free from bondage and slavery, and avoiding such ill methods, as may render themselves and posterity liable thereto." Heeding these protests, the Assembly proved itself still a stronghold of liberty and ended its session without passing any tax law.

Unable to collect quitrents or impose taxes, William Penn, rapidly losing money in his support of the Pennsylvania government, cried poverty and begged the Quakers of Pennsylvania, in early 1693, to lend him ten thousand pounds. But the practical Quakers saw no sense in making such an enormous loan at heavy risk, heavy not only because of Penn's financial straits, but also because of his shaky position at court owing to his friendship with the deposed James II. The loan request failed.

With the government treasury literally empty, Lloyd had to refuse the requests of New York for funds to prosecute the war against New France. In 1691 and again in 1693, Lloyd replied that there was no public treasury and that he himself was in great financial difficulty from lack of tax support.

At about this time George Keith began to exert a great impact on Pennsylvania and on the neighboring Quaker colony of West New Jersey. A scholarly Scottish Quaker, Keith had as surveyor general immigrated to East New Jersey in the mid-1680s. He soon established himself as the outstanding Quaker minister of the Middle Colonies, but strong differences with the regular Quakers soon became evident. Religiously far more conservative, Keith leaned toward Presbyterianism—toward formal articles of creed, institutions of elders and deacons, and emphasis on Scripture rather than on inner light. Politically, Keith also was different from the regular Quakers; he was considerably more individualistic. Having moved to Philadelphia in 1689 and become the Quaker schoolmaster there, Keith was stimulated by the anarchistic condition of the colony. He concluded logically that *all* participation in government was counter to Quaker principles. Keith's fervor was particularly stimulated by Pennsylvania's return to government in the spring of 1691. And even before 1691, Quakers served, at least intermittently, as government councillors in the colony. How, asked Keith, could a Quaker minister like Thomas Lloyd or Samuel Jennings (during these years living in Pennsylvania), professing belief in nonviolence, serve as a magistrate at all? Keith, in short, wished to press on from Quaker nonviolence to pure individualistic anarchism, of the nonviolent variety.

With the religious, and especially the political, disagreements between the two groups of Quakers ever intensifying, the split finally became open in the spring of 1692. The Keithians, now calling themselves Christian Quakers, left the standard body of Quakers. As they struggled for influence over the body of the faithful, feeling ran high between the two Quaker factions. In September the Keithian Quakers were expelled and formed their own organization.

After being persecuted so widely for religious differences, how did the Quakers react to a split in their *own* ranks? Unfortunately, not very differently from other groups. The Keithians had drawn up a statement of their political and religious position, and William Bradford, the only printer in Philadelphia and a Keithian, printed the document. In reply the Quaker officials arrested Bradford and the distributor of the pamphlet, John McComb, on the charge of printing unlicensed books without including the name of the printer. The Quaker magistrates confiscated the press and type of Bradford and withdrew McComb's license as a retailer. The Quaker government might not yet be able to levy taxes, but it was now indeed a government with a vengeance. And from being the persecuted, the Quakers had now become the persecutors. Keith was naturally bitter; he protested the cruel treatment meted out to the two men, and denounced Governor Lloyd, Samuel Jennings, and the other magistrates on the Council. Although Keith tried to mitigate his offense in the eyes of the government by calling the quarrel strictly a religious one, the government issued a proclamation against Keith at the end of August. The magistrates demanded that Keith stop making speeches and publishing pamphlets that "have a tendency to sedition, and disturbance of the peace, as also to the subversion of the present government."

When the Keithians persisted in their protest, the grand jury in October 1692 indicted three Keithian leaders, including Keith, for writing a book denouncing Jennings and other magistrates. The jury, incidentally, was packed with friends of Jennings, and Keith fittingly accused his enemies of constituting the judge and jury as well as the prosecution. Keith also pointed out that Quakers never should go to court, and thus resort to the use of violence, but should always settle their disputes peacefully and voluntarily. The three men, however, were convicted and fined (though the fines were never paid); and they were denied the right to appeal to the Council or to the provincial court. Keith's charges—that ministers were being judges and were using governmental authority to suppress religious liberty—must have seemed all too familiar to the colonists in America.

While the dispute over the Keithians was raging in the colonies, William Penn was, as a close friend of the deposed James II, in deep political trouble in England. King William was also peeved at the anarchistic conditions in the colony and angered—as rulers always are—at the Quaker principles of pacifism. Moreover, the king was anxious to weld the Northern colonies into a fighting force for attacking the French; a pacifistic, virtually unarmed colony hardly suited his purpose. Consequently, when Benjamin Fletcher was named governor of New York in late 1692, he was *also* named governor of Pennsylvania and Delaware. Pennsylvania was now a royal colony.

William Penn courageously tried to raise a resistance in Pennsylvania against this invasion by royal officials. The colonists, however, cared little about the proprietary, and became critical of Fletcher only when he tried to reimpose taxation on the colony.

Fletcher formally assumed the reins of government in Pennsylvania in April 1693. As in the other royal colonies, the Council was now appointed by the governor, instead of being elected by the people, and laws could now be vetoed by the Crown. Fletcher's appointments took the Council out of Quaker control; of the nine new councillors, only four were Quakers, and two of these were Keithians. One immediately beneficial result of the new regime was the freeing of Keith and his friends, and the restoration to Bradford of his confiscated press. Keith and Bradford both left the inhospitable colony, however, Bradford for New York and Keith for England.

With Keith's return to England, the Keithian movement, deprived of its founder, began to disintegrate. Some Keithians drifted into Pietism, others became Baptists or Anglicans. By the late 1690s, the only Keithian remnants were in Burlington, capital of West New Jersey; in addition, there were some "Baptist Quakers" in Pennsylvania. In 1700 Keith himself delivered the lethal blow to the movement by converting to Anglicanism; shortly thereafter, he became an ardent Anglican minister, and a missionary to America. It is ironic that in these later years, their individualistic anarchism forgotten, George Keith and William Bradford, now ardent Anglicans, helped to impose a year's imprisonment on Rev. Samuel Bownes of Long Island—on grounds of sedition against the established Anglican church of New York..

Fletcher appointed William Markham as his lieutenant governor. Now the *de facto* operating head of the colony, Markham was the leader of the old Blackwell clique. At this time the Quakers were taken up with the Keithian schism and could not form a fully unified or consistently libertarian opposition to royal or Markhamite rule.

Fletcher did not succeed in imposing a militia on Pennsylvania, although there were some formations in the Delaware counties. He believed that his main mission there was imposing taxation on Pennsylvania in order to raise funds for the New York war against New France. Fletcher convened the Assembly in May and speciously argued that any taxes it might provide him for war would go for nonbelligerent uses "and shall not be dipped in blood." The argument was deceptive because military funds must always be divided between strictly belligerent and supportive "nonbelligerent" uses, and any aid to the latter frees additional funds for the former. Fletcher was able to drive through a tax bill, but not by this reasoning; he succeeded because he and the Council had the power to reconfirm or not reconfirm all the existing laws of Pennsylvania. To save the colony's legal structure, as well as ward off a threatened annexation by New York, the Assembly finally and reluctantly passed a tax bill. Taxes had arrived at last in Pennsylvania and the unique glory of that colony was now no more. Pennsylvanians, like everyone else, now suffered the burdens of taxation.

As might be expected, taxation was still very low; a tax of one penny per pound had been levied on all real and personal property, and a six-shilling tax on those without assessed property. Fletcher, interested less in the principles involved in taxation versus no taxation than in raising money for the war with Canada, was highly disappointed with this "trifling" amount of money. He believed it a petty "introduction of future supply." Of the tax raised, half went to Fletcher and the other half to the Crown. Furthermore, the Assembly refused to agree to vote funds for salaries for the upper house. Writing home, Fletcher denounced the pacifism of the unarmed Quakers, as well as their resistance to any militia.

The Assembly gained in power during the Fletcher regime, because the new rules gave it the authority to initiate legislation. On the other hand, the Council, so powerful a body before, now became a virtual puppet of the governor, functioning, as it did, on his appointment and renewal.

Between the spring of 1693, when taxes were first imposed, and the Assembly session the following spring, the government collected a little over half of its tax quota. Of the three Delaware counties, Kent paid more than three-quarters of its assessment and Sussex about one-half; northernmost New Castle County paid nothing. Of the three counties of Pennsylvania proper, Philadelphia paid over three-quarters of its assessment, Chester paid ninety percent, and Bucks County paid nothing. In May 1694 Fletcher urged the Assembly to increase its tax revenue for war purposes. But not only did the Assembly continue the tax at the same rate; it also decided to allocate almost half of the revenue for the personal use of Lloyd and Markham for past services as deputy governors. This infuriated Fletcher, because it promised to deprive him and the Crown of the whole revenue. When Fletcher denied that the Assembly could raise taxes except for giving to the Crown, the Assembly retorted that it could appropriate money as it saw fit. Fletcher berated the Assembly for neglecting the Crown's request to "defend" the province, and angrily dissolved the Assembly. Taxation had again gone from Pennsylvania.

Even though Fletcher had managed to enforce a monopoly of ferry service on the Schuylkill (a monopoly which had been granted by Pennsylvania) and to suppress two competing ferries, the dissolution of the Assembly now made him lose interest in Pennsylvania. If he could not raise money there, he saw no point in worrying about the affairs of the province. The colony returned to its former quasi-anarchist state, with no taxes and a Council that did little and met infrequently.

Meanwhile, William Penn was campaigning energetically for return of the province to his ownership. He abjectly promised the Crown that Pennsylvania would be good; that it would levy taxes for war, raise a militia, and obey royal orders like the other dutiful colonies. He also promised that he would continue Fletcher's laws and keep Markham, well-liked by the Crown, as his deputy governor. As a result of this cajolery, the Crown restored Pennsylvania to William Penn in the summer of 1694.

William Penn was as good as his word. By the spring of 1695 William Markham was installed as deputy governor under the restored proprietary.

The people of Pennsylvania had long been independent in spirit from the proprietary; Penn's surrender of all Quaker principles in order to resume his proprietorship, as well as to extract quitrents, was hardly calculated to endear him further to the colony.

Reverting back to its previous governmental form, the Council was now elected by the people. At its first meeting in the spring of 1695, Markham revealed that his major aim was the old one of Fletcher's—imposing taxation on the colony for prosecuting the war against New France. The Council proved, however, that the spirit of liberty and independence in Pennsylvania had not slackened; it refused to consider any tax or militia bill and Markham could only end the session.

The first Assembly of the restored regime met in September. The Assembly first indicated that it would levy money for nonbelligerent military needs, but not for a militia; but it coupled debate on a tax bill with revision of the Pennsylvania constitution. It was particularly interested in safeguarding the recently acquired right of the Assembly to initiate laws. Again Markham was forced to dissolve the Assembly. Pennsylvania, remarkably, retained that unique splendor of being a taxless and armsless land. Markham could do little, and the situation of minimal government continued in this fashion for another year. In the summer of 1696, the Crown again directed Markham to build up military fortifications in the colony. Again the Council refused.

Finally, in the fall of 1696, Markham decided to usurp the powers of government. He decreed a new constitution of his own, since the colonists were not willing to return simply to the constitution of 1683. The most flagrant of Markham's usurpations of power was his decision to return to the royal practice of appointing the Council members. The elected Council was replaced by his own appointees, chosen frankly from among the large landowners. It was by this naked usurpation and by the promulgation of his own "Markham's Frame" as the new constitution that the governor was able to push a tax bill through the Assembly. He was able also to appropriate revenue for the New York war effort as well as an equal sum for his personal benefit. Under Markham's Frame, the Assembly kept its right to initiate laws, and the property requirements were lowered in the rural areas and raised in the towns.

And so the Quakers, who led the Assembly, and who had been able to repulse and rout the attempts of such despotic governors as Blackwell and Fletcher to impose burdensome taxation on Pennsylvania, now succumbed to the usurper Markham. It is clear that a deal had been made; Markham obtained the tax bill, and the Assembly was assured of the power to initiate legislation. Furthermore, the Quakers, who dominated the Assembly, also won the concession of raising the property requirement in the towns, thus excluding the largely non-Quaker urban poor from the vote. As the persecution of the Keithians first indicated, the Quakers were beginning to abandon the consistent principles of individual liberty for the alluring perquisites of political power.

A minority group of leaders formed a coalition to oppose the new dispensation. Making up the coalition were dissidents ranging from Keithians like Robert Turner to old Blackwell henchmen like Griffith Jones. Significantly, its main leader was Arthur Cook, an assistant to Markham. Cook had, along with the now deceased Lloyd, led the libertarian opposition to Governor Blackwell. The opposition gathered a petition in March 1697, signed by over a hundred, and sent to the proprietor letters attacking the major features of Markham's Frame. The opposition particularly denounced the raising of urban suffrage requirements and the institution of taxation.

The libertarian opposition now contested Markham's Frame; a separate set of elections were held in 1697 in Philadelphia County, under the old charter of 1683. When the elected councillors and assemblymen presented themselves and were duly rejected, Robert Turner protested the threat to "our ancient rights, liberties, and freedom," as well as Quaker domination of the colony's political affairs. Turner also denounced the tax bill of 1696, and urged that the money seized from its rightful owners "by that unwarrantable, illegal and arbitrary act, be forthwith restored." He noted that people were coerced into paying the tax by threats and trickery.

Popular resistance to the reimposition of taxation in 1696 is indicated by the fact that little more than half of the taxes levied were collected. So many citizens refused to pay the tax that an additional law was passed to enforce collection.

Meanwhile, the atmosphere of accelerating statism was reflected in William Penn's messages to Pennsylvania, in which he ordered the suppression of all trade that violated the navigation laws, and of such immoral businesses as taverns, which were proliferating in Philadelphia. And the structure and mores of Pennsylvania affairs were beginning to take on an uncomfortable resemblance to all the other English colonies in America. The "holy experiment" was beginning to fade. Pennsylvania, until now the envy—thus the occasion of hatred—of the other colonies and their royal officials because of its magnetic attractions of individual liberty, peace, and absence of taxation, was now falling into step with its neighbors.

In 1696—the year of the punitive Navigation Act and the creation of the Board of Trade—new trouble came to Pennsylvania, this time in the form of royal officialdom. Edward Randolph was particularly incensed at the individualism rampant in Pennsylvania, so he and Col. Robert Quary, appointed judge of the vice admiralty Court in Pennsylvania, launched a determined assault on the colony's freedoms. The Tory views of Randolph and Quary recognized no subtle distinctions between the quasi-statism of Pennsylvania and the Markham Frame on the one hand, and the libertarian opposition on the other. To these royal officials, all Pennsylvania was a pesthole and Markham the leader of the lawlessness. When in 1698 a justice of the peace issued a writ against Quary's marshal, forcing him to return gold confiscated from a merchant engaged in illegal trade, Quary wrote to the Board of Trade of Pennsylvania's "beloved profitable darling, illegal trade." Quary went on to denounce the Pennsylvanians as a "perverse, obstinate and turbulent people, that will not submit to any power or laws but their own. . . . they have so long encouraged and carried on a most pernicious illegal trade. . .which hath been so advantageous to them, that no ordinary means can make them part with it."

The new threat from the royal officials and courts easily superseded that posed by the Markham Frame to the liberties of Pennsylvania, and tended to bring new factions to the fore. So it was in the case of Quary's marshal; David Lloyd led the prosecution and became a popular hero by denouncing admiralty courts as being "greater enemies to the rights and liberties of the people" than ship taxes in the days of Charles I. Lloyd was censured by the Council for his remarks.

In the same year, 1698, the Pennsylvania Assembly courageously passed a law granting accused violators of the Navigation Acts the common-law privileges of trial by jury, thus going counter to imperial decisions. William Penn, anxious to continue toadying to the Crown in order to keep his proprietary, hastened to veto the law, but in 1699 Quary reported that he was forced for reasons of safety to hold admiralty court sessions forty miles from Philadelphia. Furthermore, Quary complained, no one in Pennsylvania deigned to pay any attention to the decisions and orders of the admiralty court.

Finally, though, the Randolph-Quary campaign of vilification of Pennsylvania took effect. William Penn was ordered by the Board of Trade to return to Pennsylvania to take charge of the colony, enforce the navigation laws, cooperate with the admiralty courts, remove Markham from the post of lieutenant governor and David Lloyd from the office of attorney general, and establish a militia in the colony. Penn agreed to return, and arrived in December 1699.

From the time of his return, Penn tried his best to placate the Tories. Quary was made attorney general of Pennsylvania, and the marshal of the admiralty court was appointed undersheriff of the colony. But Quary, Randolph, and their allies on the Board of Trade were implacable, and attempted to eliminate all the proprietary and self-governing colonies in America. Penn would finally be forced to return to England in late 1701 to fight this enormous extension of imperial control, and he was the main force behind the bill's defeat.

Penn carried to Pennsylvania Crown orders to impose on Pennsylvania a tyranny, that would be subservient to the Crown. Obediently, Penn vetoed the act for jury trial for Navigation Act violations, and summarily removed from office Markham, David Lloyd, and other leaders of the popular resistance against the Navigation Acts. Not only was Lloyd ousted as attorney general and court clerk; he was also prevented from assuming his elective seat on the Council. An act against illegal trade was also passed. Concessions, already mentioned, were made to Quary and the admiralty courts. Penn moved close to the conditions of the other colonies by levying duties on imports. He did not dare attempt to create a militia, but he did maintain a military watch at the mouth of the Delaware Bay.

Penn's actions soon engendered strong opposition in the colony. The Quakers resented Penn's treatment of Lloyd and the other popular leaders, and the Assembly only reluctantly granted tax monies for payment of a salary to Penn. The people of Delaware also resented the act to repress the illegal trade.

With the former constitution of the colony in abeyance, Penn quickened his reactionary course by deciding to appoint his Council rather than have it elected. In protest, several members of the Council refused the appointment and were instead elected in the fall of 1700 to the Assembly. Heading this move was Joseph Growdon, who was elected as Speaker of the Assembly.

At the summer 1701 meeting of the Assembly, Penn commended the king's request for 350 pounds for military fortifications of New York, but the Assembly resumed its old role as champion of the colony's liberties by rejecting the request. The Delaware counties protested sending any tax money for armed forces in New York; rather, any such funds should be kept for their own defense.

Penn's return also meant a renewed assault upon the liberties of the colonists from yet another quarter: the imposition of feudal quitrents by the proprietary. Though the Assembly voted Penn a huge grant of two thousand pounds in 1700, to be collected from property taxes, the colonists were always reluctant to pay quitrents. Penn appointed his aide James Logan as receiver general and secretary of the colony, and Logan was to enforce payment of the quitrents. Moreover, the duties on imports levied in 1700 also went to Penn's private purse, as did another tax on the retailing of alcoholic beverages.

The last General Assembly to meet under Penn's personal rule convened in the fall of 1701. It was during this Assembly that the representatives of the Delaware counties walked out. Delaware secession had long been brewing. The differences between Delaware and Pennsylvania were striking. Pennsylvania was predominantly Quaker, growing rapidly, and flourishing economically. Delaware was largely Dutch Calvinist, Swedish Lutheran, and Anglican, and was comparatively stagnant. Delaware, having none of the pacifist ideals of Pennsylvania, desired a militia. As soon as Penn arrived, New Castle County in Delaware refused to send representatives to the Pennsylvania Assembly. Now with the Delaware representatives walking out, and Penn proposing to defend his proprietary against royal assault, William Penn decided to grant Delaware its secession from Pennsylvania. Delaware took the step in 1704 and from then on the two colonies were completely separate, except for a common governor appointed by the proprietary.

The Assembly continued to be the focal point of resistance to Penn and his exactions. It passed a bill to give freemen the right to bring court action against Penn and other government officials, but Penn's appointed Council buried the measure. The Assembly also favored a bill to repeal the liquor tax, but Penn insisted that the revenue must then be raised by some other form of taxation.

Penn still had the task of resolving the constitutional quarrels of the colony. A new constitution, the Charter of Privileges, was finally approved by Assembly and Council and signed by Penn at the end of October 1701. This charter replaced both the old charter of 1683 and the Markham Frame, and was to govern Pennsylvania for the remainder of the colony's existence. The Assembly kept its cherished power to initiate legislation, but, significantly, the Council was now to be appointed by the proprietary governor, and was thus taken permanently out of popular control. The Council was now, as in most other royal colonies, a puppet agency of the governor, instead of a formidable elective body capable of checking the chief executive. Furthermore, the governor retained the power to veto all legislation. The Assembly was still elected according to limited suffrage, with modest property restrictions. The new charter also included guarantees of liberty of conscience as well as procedural guarantees for property against arbitrary attack by the governor.

Pennsylvania now truly resembled its fellows, especially the royal colonies. It now joined them in possessing a (proprietary) governor outside the colonists' control and a Council appointed by the governor, and suffered the agonies of a network of taxes, duties, and quitrents. It too faced the threats of royal bureaucracy and enforcement of the crippling navigation laws. Apart from a continued reluctance to arm, a peaceful policy toward the Indians, and the limiting of capital punishment strictly to murderers, there were few traces of the unique "holy experiment" that had been established in Pennsylvania.*

The enormously greater freedom that had prevailed so much longer in Pennsylvania than in the other colonies had given, however, the colony a tremendous push toward growth and prosperity. Farmers and merchants had prospered. Philadelphia, with a population of 5,000 in 1700, had begun

---

*Even the rational limitation of capital punishment to proportionate retribution against the crime of murder was destined to disappear in 1718, when Pennsylvania adopted the English criminal code, which provided for a much broader application of capital punishment. However, Pennsylvania continued to be unique in its widespread opposition to Negro slavery. As early as 1688, German Quakers, headed by Francis Pastorius, had attacked slavery, and a yearly meeting of Quakers in 1696 at least urged discouragement of further importation of Negro slaves. The Keithians had gone much further, declaring in 1693 that slavery was theft and opposed to the Golden Rule, and warning that it was only moral to buy Negroes for the purpose of freeing them.

the remarkable rise that was to make it one of America's foremost cities. That city had already become the commercial port for the farmers not only of Pennsylvania, but of West New Jersey as well. In 1690 Governor Fletcher of New York admitted that "the town of Philadelphia in fourteen years' time has become nearly equal to the city of New York in trade and riches"—an unwitting tribute to the propulsive powers of individual freedom, unencumbered by taxes and restrictions, as over against the crippling effects of monopoly and high taxation on the older colony.

It was not long before the unique Pennsylvania attribute of pacifism was also to wither away. After Penn's return to England, James Logan remained as builder of the proprietary party, which favored taxation and quitrents, and was willing to abandon the Quaker resistance to war and to an armed militia. The leader of the popular libertarian party, dominant in the Assembly, was the Welsh Quaker David Lloyd. The Assembly consistently resisted proprietary demands for a militia; it did allow a voluntary one, which could not sustain itself. Finally, William Penn brought an end to the opposition by (1) removing from the governor's chair the hated John Evans, who had tried to raise a war panic by false scares of French and Indian invasion, and who had illegally imposed a tax by Delaware on Philadelphia shipping ("powder money"); and (2) threatening the colonists that he would sell his proprietary rights to the Crown. Under this blackmail threat, the election of 1710 brought complete victory to the Logan-Penn forces. Under Logan's aegis, Penn quickly voted the Crown the large sum of 2,000 pounds, which was expected to be used for military purposes against New France.

65

The Colonies in the First Decade
of the Eighteenth Century

We have seen that the colonies in the first decade of the eighteenth century were again embroiled in projects for invasions of New France. Indeed, England had only four years of respite from war with France after the Treaty of Ryswick in 1697. In 1701 England and the other powers of Europe became involved in the War of the Spanish Succession, largely against the ambitions of Louis XIV. The war was marked by a series of expensive but futile attempts to invade Canada. Early expeditions failed to conquer Acadia, but a large expedition in 1709, having failed to mount an attack on Quebec, consoled itself by seizing Port Royal and the rest of Acadia. Another huge expedition was mounted against Quebec in 1711, but the invasion was so badly bungled that some ships were wrecked in a storm, and the rest hastily returned.

Peace between England and France came in 1713 with the Peace of Utrecht. Essentially beaten in the European war, France agreed to turn over Acadia (now Nova Scotia), Newfoundland, and Hudson's Bay permanently to the English, and to recognize the Iroquois (among whom French Jesuits had made considerable headway) as being under English jurisdiction.

By the first decade of the eighteenth century, the previously highly disparate colonies had become far more uniform. The political structures of the colonies, in particular, were now more alike. By 1710 the great liberal revolutions of the 1670s and 80s had made their attempt and failed, but their failure at least succeeded in gaining a few crucial concessions from the ruling power. In each of the colonies, by 1710, a royal or proprietary governor ruled the territory. He appointed the Council and the lesser administrative and judicial bureaucracies, and ruled in alliance with a colonial oligarchy largely created by English rule, as well as with a bureaucracy of royal officialdom. The oligarchy received all manner of subsidies and privileges by virtue of its share in the control of the state apparatus; conspicuous among these privileges were arbitrary large land grants to favored individuals and groups. In each of the colonies an elected Assembly had emerged as the representative of the popular liberal forces, in continuing battle against the power of the royal officials and their appointed upper house.

Most of the provinces were now royal colonies, and even the proprietors were not the proud independent rulers of yore. Once feisty and independent Massachusetts had now been brought under the royal heel. New York, formerly a proprietary colony lacking any elected Assembly, was now a royal colony similar to the others, with an elected Assembly possessing the taxing power partially offsetting the royal appointees. The proprietary New Jerseys were now a single royal colony. New Hampshire too was finally established as a royal colony. Of the five proprietary colonies remaining in the first decade of the eighteenth century, two (the Carolinas) were soon to be forcibly transformed into royal provinces. Furthermore, the previously remarkable religious freedom and separation of church and state in the Carolinas was now replaced by an Anglican establishment serving a small minority, particularly in North Carolina. In Maryland, Lord Baltimore had been deprived of his proprietary, and though it was soon to be returned to the Baltimore family, it was returned as an Anglican colony. Gone was Maryland as a haven for Catholics from religious persecution. In short, the former uniqueness of the various proprietary, and self-governing, colonies had now disappeared, and there was little to distinguish the royal from the remaining proprietary colonies. The same was true for originally pacifist and anarchistic Pennsylvania; Pennsylvania and its sister proprietary Delaware had been made royal colonies; William Penn received them back only on the condition that he would mold his colonies into what had become the standard North American pattern. Of the original self-governing colonies of New England, only Connecticut and Rhode Island remained as anomalies, still in the seventeenth-century framework.

A proprietary always meant that there would be annoying attempts to collect feudal quitrents from the landowners. The Crown too tried to impose quitrents, but they proved, despite continuing efforts by the governors, to be virtually impossible to collect. The dissolution of the quitrent threat meant that true feudal tenure could not take hold in America, since the proprietary could not enforce its claims to feudal tribute. Even less could such plans as Maryland's consciously created feudal hierachy of land claims persist under American conditions of abundant cheap land and individual independence. Of course, such feudalistic institutions as servitude and Negro slavery greatly increased the privileged ownership of large tracts of land. Fortunately, although the tobacco country of the Southern colonies and isolated areas such as the Naragansett Country and West New Jersey had large plantations, no permanent landlord-tenancy relations prevailed—even where arbitrary and privileged land grants had been extensive. For speculative land monopolists, perhaps wanting nothing better than to be feudal lords over a host of servants and subtenants, invariably decided to take their wealth quickly and reap speculative gains without suffering the risks of land ownership. The one crucial exception was New York, where receivers of huge land grants—the *manors,* following after the patroonships of the Dutch—decided to continue as landlords exacting rents from their tenants. Deciding to rent out and not to sell, the New York landlords thereby made the fateful decision to freeze land monopoly in existing huge tracts. Except for the master-slave relation, all major aspects of feudalism in the colonies disappeared rather quickly upon their introduction—New York, of course, excepted; here essentially feudal landholding continued for at least a century. As a result, New York's growth, compared with that of the other colonies, was retarded.

Negro slaves were becoming an increasingly large part of the coerced labor force. They were used everywhere in the colonies, but especially and increasingly on the large plantations of the South.

The following tabulation is the estimated population of the American colonies in 1710 and 1680, the figures in parenthesis being the estimated number of Negroes (overwhelmingly slave).

AMERICAN POPULATION, 1710 AND 1680 *(in thousands)*

Colony	1710	1680
New Hampshire	6 (0)	2
Massachusetts (including Plymouth and Maine)	62 (1)	46
Connecticut	39 (1)	17
Rhode Island	8 (0)	3
New York	22 (3)	10
New Jersey	20 (1)	3
Pennsylvania	24 (2)	1
Delaware	4 (0.5)	1
Maryland	43 (8)	18
Virginia	78 (23)	44
North Carolina	15 (1)	5
South Carolina	11 (4)	1
Total	332 (44.5)	151

The table reveals the comparatively slow growth of New York, the phenomenal growth of Pennsylvania, and the high proportion of Negro slaves in Virginia and South Carolina.

The religious structure of the colonies was also becoming uniform, in a sense, by 1710. Whereas in the seventeenth century religious persecution in behalf of the dominant sect had been the norm, except in such maverick colonies as Rhode Island and North Carolina, by the eighteenth century religious freedom generally prevailed. But only partially, since many colonies had their established church: for example, the Puritan in Massachusetts, the Presbyterian in Connecticut, and the Anglican in the Southern colonies.

The noted historian Carl Becker once raised the question about the extent to which the American Revolution was a battle for "home rule" of the colonies *vis-à-vis* England, as opposed to a battle about "who should rule at home," within the colonies. In short, to what degree was the Revolution "internal," and to what degree "external?" We are now able to frame a judgment about this issue for the earlier revolutions of the late seventeenth century and for their aftermath. We have seen how revolution, in the 1670s and especially after 1688, swept almost every colony in America: from Bacon's Rebellion in Virginia to Leisler's in New York to the continuing state of revolution in the two New Jerseys. All of these revolutions may be classified as "liberal" and popular; in short, as essentially mass movements in behalf of libertarian objectives and in opposition to the tyranny, high taxes, monopolies, and restrictions imposed by the various governments. Separating the strands of "home rule" and "rule at home" is an artificial and misleading way of treating the problem. For the revolutionaries were battling against the oppressions of the state apparatus. This apparatus was certainly dominated by the "external" element, that is, the colonial governors appointed by the royal or proprietary rulers. But these governors created and then allied themselves with a "domestic" oligarchy. Through subsidies, taxes, privileges, monopolies, land grants, etc., the royal or proprietary governor and his Council *formed* an allied oligarchy, against which the people and their representatives in the lower house rebelled. The colonies, especially in New England, had been almost totally independent during most of the seventeenth century and deeply resented later English interference. But when these colonies rebelled, they did so not against England *per se,* but against the oppressions of the state, dominated by the English government. And the fact that the sudden weakening of English authority during the Glorious Revolution touched off these revolts in no sense negates this conclusion.

The liberal revolutions of the 1680s and 90s failed largely because the domestic oligarchs were propped up and reimposed by the English power. The Berkeleys and their successors, the Dudleys, the Androses, and the Hamiltons remained. But the revolutions were not a complete failure by any means. The populace was left with lower houses, Assemblies, willing

510

to fight continually against oligarchic oppression, and they had a great tradition of revolution to look back upon and from which to gain inspiration. By the turn of the eighteenth century the English state had come to play a much greater and more direct role in the overall sum of governmental burdens on the American colonists. For by 1696 the structure of the Navigation Acts restricting colonial trade was complete, and a royal bureaucracy, replete with customs collectors and vice admiralty courts, began to impose itself on the colonies. The increasing weight of English imperial rule began to draw the brunt of popular liberal opposition.

Hence, by the turn of the eighteenth century, the revolutions of the late seventeenth century behind, the increasingly uniform American colonies had settled down to a period of uneasy balance. It was a balance filled with inner tension and conflict, but for most of the coming century, this conflict would no longer erupt into open confrontation or result in radical change. But when the eruption eventually occurred, it was to be an explosion that would change the face of the globe.

Bibliographical Essay

In recommending books and references, the historian is in a happier position than his colleagues in political philosophy or the social sciences. In contrast to these other disciplines, a work of history does not lose the bulk of its value because of errors in ideology or points of view. An historical work can be extremely valuable despite great differences in basic political or even historical points of view, provided that it focuses on the right questions and that its scholarship is sound. For one thing, such a book can supply the factual data which are the vital stuff of history. The following references, then, are not in the least to be construed as endorsements of the basic points of view of the authors.

It is the increasing loss of the stuff of history, in fact, that provided much of the inspiration for the present volume. It is rare these days to find a general work on American history that retains the richness of narrative and the vital factual record. Instead, while historians have written excellent monographs on specific areas, the more comprehensive works have either been brief essays presenting the author's point of view, or textbooks remarkable for the increasing skimpiness of their material. Perhaps college students these days are expected to know less and less actual history in their courses. The result is a series of unproven, *ad hoc* dicta by the historian; such a product fails to present the student or the reader with the factual data that support the historian's conclusions or that allow the reader to make up his own mind about the material.

As a result of these trends, the reader interested in American history is no longer in a position to find those multivolume works so plentiful in the past, works which not only presented the author's point of view and conclusions, but also brought to the reader the narrative events, the stuff of history itself, that enabled the reader to find a comprehensive viewpoint backed by the data, and to make up his own mind about the American past. The present volume undertakes to begin to fill this gap.

No one can write an overall history of America in a single lifetime out of primary sources; but fortunately there are generally sufficient secondary works available in which the reader can find further references to the primary sources. The unfortunate fact remains that, despite the thousands of academic American historians in this country, there are still great gaps in historical research. When we consider, for example, that there is no modern history of such a vitally important organization as the Sons of Liberty or of the Committees of Correspondence in the American Revolution, we see how much work remains to be done.

The most useful and thorough text on colonial America is David Hawke, *The Colonial Experience* (1966). Still useful is Oliver P. Chitwood, *A History of Colonial America* (1st ed., 1931; 3rd ed., 1961). On the explorations and the European background to the American settlements, there is vitally important new material on the influence of the Spanish Empire on England and of the English attitude and policy toward the Irish on their attitudes towards the Indians, to be found in Charles Verlinden, *The Beginning of Modern Colonization* (trans. from the French, 1970), and in the work of David Beers Quinn, including *The Elizabethans and the Irish* (1966) and such journal articles as: "Henry VIII and Ireland, 1509-34," *Irish Historical Studies* (1961); "Sir Thomas Smith (1513–1577) and the Beginnings of English Colonial Theory," *Proceedings of the American Philosophical Society* (1945); R. Dudley Edwards and Quinn, "Sixteenth Century Ireland," *Irish Historical Studies* (1968); Quinn, "Ireland and Sixteenth Century European Expansion," *Historical Studies* (1958); see also Quinn, *Raleigh and the British Empire* (1949). Similar material is presented in the brilliant work of cultural history of colonial America by Howard Mumford Jones, *O Strange New World* (1964); see also Jones, *Ideas in America* (1944), and "Origins of the Colonial Idea in England," *Proceedings of the American Philosophical Society* (1945). Also suggestive is Peter N. Carroll, *Puritanism and the Wilderness: The Intellectual Significance of the New England Frontier, 1629-1700* (1969). This material, as well as studies of early slavery and racism, has been synthesized in a notable unpublished paper by Leonard P. Liggio, "English Origins of Early American Racism," delivered at a conference on the origins of racism at the Tuskegee Institute (1973).

Philip W. Powell, *Tree of Hate* (1971), has exploded the myth ("the Black Legend") of the unique evil of the Spanish as compared to other European empires, a myth propagated by the English and by emigrés from Spain. Colonialism and slavery in the West Indies are explored by Carl and Roberta Bridenbaugh, *No Peace Beyond the Line: The English in the Caribbean, 1624-1690* (1972); and by Richard S. Dunn, *Sugar and Slaves* (1972).

Winthrop D. Jordan's prize-winning *White Over Black: American Attitudes Toward the Negro, 1550-1812* (1968) is the major history of American racism, although in the light of the above material on the Irish, it is clear that Jordan overemphasizes the importance of skin color in the development of racism. Almon W. Lauber, *Indian Slavery in Colonial Times Within the Present Limits of the United States* (1913), is still the best book on the subject. Abbot Emerson Smith's *Colonists in Bondage: White Servitude and Convict Labor in America, 1607-1776* (1947) is the major work on indentured servitude in America.

Still useful on the European background is Edward P. Cheyney, *European Background of American History, 1300-1600* (1904), as are J. H. Parry, *The Age of Reconnaissance* (1963), and Wallace Notestein, *England on the Eve of Colonization, 1603-1630* (1951). Also see the newer work by Carl Bridenbaugh, *Vexed and Troubled Englishmen, 1500-1642* (1968). The literature on English Puritanism and the Civil War is enormous; perhaps the most useful for insights into the New England scene are the pro-Puritan *The Century of Revolution, 1603-1714* (1961) by Christopher Hill, and Hill's *God's Englishman: Oliver Cromwell and the English Revolution* (1970); and the pro-Leveller book by H. N. Brailsford, *The Levellers and the English Revolution* (1961). Critical of Puritan migration to New England is James Truslow Adams, *Founding of New England* (1921). A neglected part of the story is told in William L. Sachse, "The Migration of New Englanders to England, 1640-1660," *American Historical Review* (1948). An overall history of the migration is presented in Marcus L. Hansen, *The Atlantic Migration, 1607-1860* (1940).

On the American colonies themselves, overall surveys can be found in two volumes in the always useful New American Nation Series of Harper and Row: John E. Pomfret, *Founding the American Colonies, 1583-1660* (1970), and Wesley Frank Craven, *The Colonies in Transition, 1660-1713* (1968).

On economic affairs, Richard B. Morris's *Government and Labor in Early America* (1946) is a thorough and magisterial work. Also useful is Marcus Jernegan, *The Laboring and Dependent Classes in Colonial America (1931)*. The classic work on the vital topic of land tenure is Marshall D. Harris, *Origin of the Land Tenure System in the United States* (1953). Aaron M. Sakolski's *The Great American Land Bubble* (1932) is lively, but needs to be used with caution; it also suffers from a Henry Georgist bias. Beverly W. Bond's *The Quitrent System in the American Colonies* (1919) is still the definitive book on the quitrent problem.

The classic works on agriculture in the colonies are P. W. Bidwell and J. I. Falconer, *History of Agriculture in Northern United States, 1620-1860* (1925); and Lewis C. Grey, *History of Agriculture in the Southern United States* (1933), vol 1. Manufactures are covered in Victor S. Clark, *History of Manufactures in the United States* (1929), vol. 1, and Rolla M. Tryon, *Household Manufactures in the United States, 1640-1860* (1917). Carl Bridenbaugh's *Cities in the Wilderness* (1938) and *The Colonial Craftsman* (1950) deal with special aspects of seventeenth-century society and economy. Joseph Dorfman's *Economic Mind in American Civilization, 1606–1865* (1946), vol. 1, is indispensable for economic opinion in the colonial period. It should be supplemented by Harry E. Miller, *Banking Theories in the United States Before 1860* (1927).

The most thorough work on colonial culture is Louis B. Wright, *The Cultural Life of the American Colonies, 1607–1763* (1957), in the New American Nation Series. Bernard Bailyn's *Education in the Forming of American Society* (1960) is already a little classic on colonial education. William W. Sweet's *Religion in Colonial America* (1942) is a thorough survey. Rufus M. Jones's *The Quakers in the American Colonies* (1911) is a definitive study; it should be supplemented by Sydney V. James, *A People Among Peoples* (1963).

On the earliest colonial settlements, the older multivolume histories are still useful; in particular: Charles M. Andrews, *The Colonial Period of American History* (4 vols., 1934–38), and Herbert L. Osgood, *The American Colonies in the Seventeenth Century* (3 vols., 1904–07). Style and narrative power are distinctive in the various works of John Fiske; in particular: *The Discovery of America* (2 vols., 1892); *The Beginnings of New England* (1889); *The Dutch and Quaker Colonies in America* (2 vols., 1899); *New France and New England* (1902); and *Old Virginia and Her Neighbors* (2 vols., 1897).

On New England, Roy H. Akagi, *The Town Proprietors of the New England Colonies* (1924), is a classic on town government that has not been superseded. Bernard Bailyn's *New England Merchants in the Seventeenth Century* (1955) is indispensable for the economic history of the period. Douglas E. Leach's *Flintlock and Tomahawk* (1958) is the story of King Philip's War. The classic work on the Dominion of New England is Viola F. Barnes, *The Dominion of New England* (1928), which may be supplemented by the broader work of Harry M. Ward, *The United Colonies of New England: 1643–1690* (1961). An excellent study on the American career of Edward Randolph is Michael Garibaldi Hall, *Edward Randolph and the American Colonies, 1676–1703* (1960). Richard S. Dunn, *Puritans and Yankees: The Winthrop Dynasty of New England, 1630–1717* (1962), masterfully interweaves the life and times of three generations of Winthrops. George L. Kittredge's *Witchcraft in Old and New England* (1929) is the best background work on the subject.

The best account of communism in Plymouth Colony is in the memoir by William Bradford, *Of Plymouth Plantation* (Morison ed., 1952). George F. Willison, *Saints and Strangers* (1945), is a history of the Plymouth Colony. More scholarly and up to date is George D. Langdon, Jr.'s *Pilgrim Colony: A History of New Plymouth, 1620–1691* (1966). Harry M. Ward's *Statism in Plymouth Colony* (1973) is a recent attempt to cast the political history of the colony in a rosy glow.

The literature on Massachusetts Bay is legion. Brilliant and deeply critical is Thomas Jefferson Wertenbaker, *The Puritan Oligarchy* (1947), which can be supplemented by James Truslow Adams's *The Founding of New England* (1921). Darrett B. Rutman ʾhas a realistic view of Massachusetts; see his *Winthrop's Boston: Portrait of a Puritan Town, 1630-1649* (1965), and his "The Mirror of Puritan Authority," in G. A. Billias, ed., *Law and Authority in Colonial America* (1965). Apologias for Massachusetts Bay Puritanism are legion; probably the best are such works of Edmund S. Morgan as *Visible Saints* (1963) and *The Puritan Dilemma* (1958). Marion L. Starkey, *The Devil in Massachusetts* (1949), is the best account of the Salem witch-hunt, but it considerably overemphasizes psychological factors.

Roger Williams has given rise to many biographies, none of which is outstanding. The best is Ola Elizabeth Winslow, *Master Roger Williams* (1957). Also worth looking at are Perry Miller, *Roger Williams* (1963); Edmund S. Morgan's *Roger Williams* (1967); and James E. Ernst, *The Political Thought of Roger Williams* (1929). Samuel H. Brockunier's *The Irrepressible Democrat: Roger Williams* (1952) is far overdrawn in trying to make of Williams a twentieth-century democrat.

There is no satisfactory biography of Anne Hutchinson or history of the Hutchinsonian movement. Best are Winifred K. Rugg, *Unafraid: A Life of Anne Hutchinson* (1930), and Edith Curtis, *Anne Hutchinson* (1930). Emery Battis's *Saints and Sectaries: Anne Hutchinson and the Antinomian Controversy in the Massachusetts Bay Colony* (1962) is a totally reprehensible work that tries to smear Mrs. Hutchinson and antinomianism by reducing them to personal neuroses and by implying she had menopausal difficulties. The best account of Samuell Gorton is Kenneth W. Porter, "Samuell Gorton, " *New England Quarterly* (1934).

The best work on the history of early Rhode Island is still Irving B. Richman, *Rhode Island: Its Making and Its Meaning* (2 vols., 1902). See also Edward Field, ed., *The State of Rhode Island and Providence Plantations* (3 vols., 1902). The Narragansett country is discussed in Edward Channing, *The Narragansett Planters* (1886), and more recently in William D. Miller, "The Narragansett Planters," American Antiquarian Society *Proceedings* (1953).

There is no satisfactory comprehensive study of New Netherland or New York during the seventeenth centruy. Dixon Ryan Fox, *Yankees and Yorkers* (1940), is well written; Samuel G. Nissenson, *The Patroon's Domain* (1937), is the best work on Dutch patroonship. The best single work on New York politics in the seventeenth century is Lawrence H. Leder, *Robert Livingston, 1654-1728, and the Politics of Colonial New York* (1961). Jerome R. Reich, *Leisler's Rebellion: A Study of Democracy in New York, 1664-1720* (1953), is the only full-scale account of that rebellion, but it suffers from trying to place Leisler's rebellion in the "democratic," class-struggle mold of poor vs. rich. David S. Lovejoy in his recent *The Glorious*

Revolution in America (1972) tries to tie together Leisler's rebellion with all the other colonial responses to the Glorious Revolution against James II.

Those interested in the New Jerseys are fortunate to have two comprehensive works by John E. Pomfret, *The Province of West New Jersey, 1609-1702* (1954), and *The Province of East New Jersey, 1609-1702* (1962). New Sweden is covered in Amandus Johnson, *The Swedish Settlements on the Delaware* (2 vols., 1911); Christopher Ward, *The Dutch and Swedes on the Delaware, 1609-1664* (1930); and John H. Wuorinen, *The Finns on the Delaware 1638-1655* (1938).

Wesley Frank Craven's *The Southern Colonies in the Seventeenth Century, 1607-1689* (1949) is a thorough account, and part of the distinguished series, *A History of the South*. Verner W. Crane's *The Southern Frontier, 1670-1732* (1928) is outstanding on the Southern frontier and relations with the Indians during this period.

The best history of old Virginia is Richard L. Morton, *Colonial Virginia* (2 vols., 1960), vol 1., *The Tidewater Period, 1607-1710*. Morton is the most judicious on Bacon's Rebellion. The classic account of that rebellion is Thomas Jefferson Wertenbaker, *Torchbearer of the Revolution* (1940), which overdraws Bacon as democratic hero and precursor of the American Revolution; but Wilcomb E. Washburn's revisionist *The Governor and the Rebel* (1957) errs far more in the opposite direction by dismissing the libertarian and democratic elements in Bacon's Rebellion and in trying to make Governor Berkeley the hero of the story. See also the always trenchant Bernard Bailyn's discussion of Bacon's Rebellion and its aftermath in "Politics and Social Structure in Virginia," in James M. Smith, ed., *Seventeenth-Century America* (1959). A cultural study of the Virginia aristocracy is Louis B. Wright's *The First Gentlemen of Virginia* (1940).

Recent literature on Maryland is sparse. But Matthew P. Andrews, *The Founding of Maryland* (1933), and the first volume of James T. Scharf, *History of Maryland* (3 vols., 1879), are useful. Michael G. Kammen, "The Causes of the Maryland Revolution of 1689," *Maryland Historical Magazine* (1960), deals with Coode's Rebellion.

The major history of North Carolina for many years was R. D. W. Connor, *History of North Carolina* (4 vols., 1919), of which volume one is on the colonial period. A later overall history is Hugh T. Lefler and Albert R. Newsome, *The History of a Southern State: North Carolina* (1954). Also of use is Samuel A. Ashe, *The History of North Carolina* (2 vols., 1908). The classic history of South Carolina is still Edward McCrady's *The History of South Carolina Under the Proprietary Government, 1670-1719* (1897). This should be supplemented by the broader *History of South Carolina* (4 vols., 1934) by David D. Wallace, which is summarized in Wallace's *South Carolina: A Short History, 1520-1948* (1951). A more recent history of the early colony is M. Eugene Sirmans, *Colonial South Carolina: A Political History, 1663-1763* (1966).

Edwin B. Bronner, *William Penn's "Holy Experiment": The Founding of Pennsylvania, 1681–1701* (1962), is a superb work on the early days of the last colony to be founded in the seventeenth century. The early chapters of Frederick B. Tolles, *Meeting House and Counting House: The Quaker Merchants of Colonial Philadelphia, 1682–1763* (1960), are important on the Quaker merchants of early Pennsylvania. On culture in Pennsylvania, also see Tolles, *James Logan and the Culture of Provincial America* (1957). Rufus Jones, *The Quakers in the American Colonies* (1911), is the classic study on the Quakers. The best biography of William Penn is Catherine O. Peare, *William Penn: A Biography* (1957). Roy Lokken, *David Lloyd, Colonial Lawmaker* (1959), is a study of one of the major opposition leaders of the early colony.

The tightening of the English imperial system by the end of the century is covered in such classic works as Leonard W. Labaree, *Royal Government in America: A Study of the British Colonial System Before 1783* (1930); Lawrence A. Harper's *The English Navigation Laws* (1939); and Oliver M. Dickerson's work on the Board of Trade, *American Colonial Government, 1696–1765—A Study of the Board of Trade . . .* (1912). The best work on the new vice admiralty court system is Carl Ubbelohde, *The Vice-Admiralty Courts and the American Revolution* (1960). The growing influence of the British Treasury in American colonial affairs is studied in Dora M. Clark, *The Rise of the British Treasury* (1960). The new breed of Tory royal bureaucrat is brilliantly studied in Michael Garibaldi Hall, *Edward Randolph and the American Colonies, 1676–1703* (1960); see also Gertrude A. Jacobsen, *William Blathwayt: A Late Seventeenth-Century English Administrator* (1932).

Index

Littleworth, Capt., 174
Livingston, Robert, 380, 387, 388, 435, 436, 441, 442, 443, 465, 468, 473, 474, 475, 476, 480
Lloyd, David, 409, 503, 504, 506
Lloyd, Thomas, 406, 408, 409, 410, 411, 496, 497, 498, 500, 502
Locke, John, 123, 138, 466
Logan, James, 504, 506
London Company, 42, 43, 44, 159
Lothrop, Rev. John, 274
Louis XIII, King, 234
Louis XIV, King, 389, 507
Lovelace, Francis, 332, 335
Lovelace, Lord, 476
Lucas, Nicholas, 397
Ludlow, Roger, 219, 230
Ludwell, Philip, 113, 135, 136, 138, 147, 149, 151
Lyell, David, 491
Lyford, Rev. John, 162, 163

Mack, George, 121
Madison, Isaac, 96
Magellan, Ferdinand, 27
Maine: founding, 224-26
Maltraven, Henry Lord, 122
Markham, William, 402, 411, 495, 496, 499, 500, 501, 502, 503
Marston, Edward, 140
Martin, Richard, 361, 362, 364
Mary, Queen, 157
Maryland, 114-20, 126-27, 131-35
Mason, George, 100
Mason, John, 224, 225, 229, 356, 358
Mason, Robert T., 285, 356, 360, 361, 362, 364, 365, 366, 368, 371, 376, 415, 428, 449
Massachusetts: founding, 165-73; theocracy, 174-81; suppressing heresy, 182-96, 237-50; economics dissolves theocracy, 251-59, 263-66; half-way covenant, 271-72; decline of

theocracy, 341-43; takeover by Crown, 355-60, 367-72; Salem witch hunt, 452-60
Massasoit, 345
Mather, Rev. Cotton, 414, 424, 454, 455, 458, 459, 472
Mather, Rev. Increase, 342, 368, 371, 413, 417, 424, 425, 427, 428, 429, 446, 449, 452, 453, 454, 455, 457, 459, 461, 472
Mathew, Thomas, 100
Mathews, Samuel, 81, 82, 85, 98
Maurice (Prince of Orange), 296
Maverick, Samuel, 237, 283
May, Cornelis, 298
McComb, John, 498
Megapolensis, Rev. Mr., 318, 320, 324
Melyn, Cornelis, 308, 309, 310, 313
Menefie, George, 82
Merchant Adventurers, 34, 35, 165
Merchants of the Staple, 19-20, 30
Miantonomo, 201, 344, 350
Michel, Robert, 334
Milborne, Jacob, 436, 441, 442, 444, 446, 447, 461, 466, 468
Miller, Thomas, 128, 129
Milton, John, 210, 211
Mingoe, 152
Minuit, Peter, 223, 298, 299, 301, 304, 311
Minvielle, Gabriel, 445, 468
Mises, Ludwig von, 261n
Mitchell, Rev. Jonathan, 249
Montague, John, 469
Montesquieu, 75
Moody, Lady Deborah, 306, 319, 320
Moody, Rev. Joshua, 286, 363, 364, 365
Moore, Samuel, 391, 395
More, Nicholas, 405
Morris Lewis, II, 487, 489, 491, 492, 493, 494
Morris, Richard, 210